JACK YEATS

Jack Yeats

Bruce Arnold

1998
Yale University Press
New Haven & London

Half-title: Self portrait drawn for *T.P.'s Weekly*, July 1914.

Frontispiece: Jack Yeats in his twenties.

Set in Garamond by Best-set Typesetter Ltd., Hong Kong
Printed and bound by C.S. Graphics, Singapore

Library of Congress Cataloging-in-Publication Data
Arnold, Bruce.
    Jack Yeats: a biography / Bruce Arnold.
       p.   cm.
    Includes bibliographical references and index.
    ISBN 0-300-07549-9 (alk. paper)
    1. Yeats, Jack Butler, 1871–1957.   2. Artists – Ireland – Biography.
I. Title.
N6797.Y4A76   1998
759.2'915 – dc21
    [B]   98–19116
                                                                           CIP

CONTENTS

Acknowledgements		*vii*
Prologue		*ix*

CHAPTER ONE	Origins	1
CHAPTER TWO	Early Life in Sligo	17
CHAPTER THREE	Art School in London 1887–1889	29
CHAPTER FOUR	Bedford Park – the 1890s	45
CHAPTER FIVE	Work and Marriage 1891–1897	57
CHAPTER SIX	Devon and the First London Shows 1897–1899	68
CHAPTER SEVEN	Miniature Theatre 1900–1901	81
CHAPTER EIGHT	The *Broadsheets* and John Masefield 1901–1903	100
CHAPTER NINE	Ireland and the United States 1904–1905	116
CHAPTER TEN	John M. Synge 1905–1909	132
CHAPTER ELEVEN	Last Days in England 1909–1910	152
CHAPTER TWELVE	The *Broadsides* 1910–1915	166
CHAPTER THIRTEEN	Nervous Breakdown 1915–1918	185
CHAPTER FOURTEEN	A Dublin Man 1919–1922	202
CHAPTER FIFTEEN	Modernism and the Issue of Style 1923–1930	217
CHAPTER SIXTEEN	Career as a Writer 1931–1935	238
CHAPTER SEVENTEEN	'Lives' 1936–1938	258
CHAPTER EIGHTEEN	Death of William Butler Yeats 1939	272
CHAPTER NINETEEN	The Outbreak of War 1940–1942	293
CHAPTER TWENTY	Painter Triumphant 1943–1945	307
CHAPTER TWENTY-ONE	Death for Only One 1945–1947	322
CHAPTER TWENTY-TWO	Last Years 1948–1957	337

Colour Plates	*357*
Epilogue	*375*
Abbreviations	*378*
Notes	*379*
Note on Illustrations and Photographic Credits	*403*
Index	*405*

ACKNOWLEDGEMENTS

WE ARE PRIVILEGED that an enormous amount of material about Jack Yeats has been preserved, in family records, letters, diaries, sketch-books, and a range of personal documents. In the following pages, I have tried where possible to let the contemporary record tell the story.

None of this work would have been possible without the commitment of Michael Yeats and Anne Yeats, the artist's nephew and niece. Above all else was the enormous generosity of Anne; she made available her house, her friendship, her patient interest in what I discovered, and the huge Jack Yeats archive which she kept so carefully. She looked after it from her uncle's death until it was deposited in the National Gallery of Ireland early in 1997. Spending time in her company was always rewarding, and her concern that a full life of her uncle would be written was coupled with complete freedom as to how the story would be told. Michael fully supported her in this.

I have many others to thank: Ivan Allen, Ian Baird, Jocelyn Barker, Wendy Board, F.W. Blackwell for information on Snails Castle, Pamela Blunden, Alan Browne, son of Perceval Browne, Jack's solicitor, who also knew the artist when a student in Trinity, and entertained him at Boat Club events; Mary Brennan-Holohan who carried out early research work for me, R.J. Britcher, Declan Budd, Una Budd, Finbar Callanan and John Callanan, of the Institute of Engineers, Mark Crilly, Canon Charles Carter for details of Jack's funeral service, Christopher Casson, Frank Coffey; I owe a particlar debt to Maurice Craig, for a helpful and constructive reading of the book; John Carolan, Francis Carnwath and Caroline Cuthbert of the Tate Gallery, and Sir Andrew Carnwath; Leonora Dand, Norris Davidson.

To Alan Denson I am indebted for a detailed recollection of meetings with Jack, and to Ione Dobbin, Arnold Harvey's daughter, for information about her father's long friendship with Jack; Stephen Dixon, Gerry Dukes, Revd Canon Adrian Empey, Patrick Fallon, Harold Fish and the British Council, Roy Foster, Eddie Fraser, Father Cathal Geraghty for information on the work at Loughrea, John Gallagher, Aideen Gore-Booth, Robert Greacen, Declan Grehan, Bryan and Elizabeth Guinness, Aidan Grennell, Carolyn Hammond of the Hounslow Library, Sally K. Hine of the BBC sound archives, David Hone, Robert Hogan for information from the Holloway Journals, the late Robert Jacob, Finola Kennedy, Raymond Keaveney, director of the National Gallery of Ireland, and other members of the gallery staff, the staff of the

Hugh Lane Municipal Gallery of Modern Art, John Keohane, the late Mary Lappin, Therese Law, for help with the Berg Collection in the New York Public Library, Hector Legge, James Leonard, Geraldine Lloyd, Teresa Lunn for information on Olympia.

I owe a special debt to Gifford Lewis, both for her work on Jack's two sisters, but also for her knowledge of Pollexfen antecedents; Ciaran Mac Gonigal, the Revd S.I. McGee of St John's Cathedral, Sligo, Jim McGarry, Cyril McKeown, Harry McCarthy, Dr Garret May; John McTernan, librarian in Sligo, for help with the Yeats works there; Bernard McDonagh, Cróine Magan, Manchán Magan, Kenneth Malcolm, Bobbie Mitchell, Liam Miller; Catherine Munro helped me with early researches for the book; William M. Murphy was a source of early encouragement; David Marcus, Val Mulkerns, Aidan H. O'Flanagan, Daire O'Connell, the late Alpho O'Reilly, Rose Mary O'Brien, George O'Brien, Frank O'Reilly of Whitney, Moore & Keller, who found fresh Yeats material.

Brian O'Doherty provided most valuable first-hand recollections of Jack at the end of his life, including the drawing which is reproduced in the book; Cormac O'Malley helped with his father's recollections, sketchbooks and paintings owned by the family; John Purser was patient and helpful about Jack's writing, and gave me valuable advice more generally about the book; I am grateful, too, to Donald Pratt, Maureen Potter, Jean Parnell, William Roth; I am indebted to Elizabeth Solterer for her recollections of Jack at the time of the 1945 exhibition; Douglas Sealy read a version of the book and helped me with detail and critical assessments; Seán Sweeney, Ralph Sutton, S.C., Ann Saddlemyer, Colin Smythe, Michael Solomons, Father Sean Swayne, Leslie Scott, Robin Tamplin, Sarah Tooley all assisted me and Tim Vignoles offered inspiring encouragement throughout; I am greatly in Leslie Waddington's debt for his recollections, and throughout my work Theo Waddington was a tower of strength; the late Mervyn Wall, James White, Bernard Williams of Christie's, Susan Wigham and her husband with further information on Arnold Harvey letters, Pat Woods, Eva Yalland, F.G. Yoakley.

Hilary Pyle occupies a unique place in Yeats scholarship, and without her work no one can venture into study of Yeats, still less into writing about him. My decision to undertake a fresh biography of the painter had her support, for which I am grateful.

During the greater part of writing the book Helen Moss was my research assistant, and her diligence and care, her cool assessment of character and action in the story, and her painstaking capacity for checking and rechecking detail, was of the utmost value. I was greatly assisted by a number of friends. My agent, Giles Gordon, was of very particular help; his prudence and wit sustained me through difficulties and I owe him a unique debt of gratitude. My family, and particularly my wife, Mavis, gave me great support during difficult times in the writing of this book. It has been a rewarding book, however, whose subject was a perpetual source of inspiration. I hope I have done him justice.

OF THE MAJOR Irish artists born in the second half of the nineteenth century, or living and working through the first half of the twentieth, Jack Yeats stands out for his dedication to a nationalist ideal. Yet his was a subtle and elusive form of nationalism. It was never overtly political, but always attached to the human side of events. He painted Ireland into an existence which it did not previously enjoy. Before Jack Yeats, no artist had set out to rescue the national character from nineteenth-century caricature and give it an embodiment which was serious, and which lasted. It is within the purpose and the act of doing this that a substantial part of his greatness lies.

He made a single, profound and irreversible decision about his life: to dedicate it to Ireland. Like many Irish men and women of his generation and later, he had the choice, at least between two countries, maybe more. Unlike so many of his contemporaries, perhaps even including his brother, he made an artistic, emotional and physical commitment to Ireland, and he held to it until his death. It grew in depth and magnitude, and came to govern every aspect of his life as an artist, his paintings, his plays, his novels. He resolved the most stressful and complicated conundrum: that of the relationship between Ireland and England. Out of it he evoked through his work the nature of Irishness, and out of that a more comprehensive definition of Ireland. This became the main theme in all his art. Only infrequently did he paint his own class. His attention, like J.M. Synge's, was on the peasants, the workers, the tinkers, the clowns. He gave them vitality, he imagined and then realised their richness of character.

Jack Yeats stands as an isolated, giant figure in Irish twentieth-century art. He dominated solely through the talent, magic and inventiveness of his painting. He was a man of calm, self-effacing disposition, witty, elusive, kind, generous, enigmatic. He had an innate originality. His urge was to tell stories. His early drawings were anecdotal. His early paintings were the same. He observed events, read into them the motives and aspirations of the protagonists, and delivered memorable versions of them throughout his life. In later years the 'stories' became symbolic; men and their affairs went through an apotheosis into Man and his place in the Universe. His development was towards greater economy, sharper visual shorthand, but never away from the inspiration of some kind of happening which gave to each work its life and internal rhythm. He eschewed all movements, took no pupils, taught only by example. He was modest, restrained, undemonstrative. He conforms to no labelling as a painter.

The west of Ireland was always part of him. His childhood in Sligo cradled his early experience, formed his imagination. From Malin Head to Mizen Head there is no sweep of mountain as fine and dramatic as the majestic curving cliff that stretches from Ben Bulbin north towards Grange and Cliffoney or back along the high wall of its southern slopes above Lough Gill. The wind from the Atlantic, blowing in over Sligo Bay and Rosses Point, and across those craggy slopes, ruffled for ever his hair and left perpetual salt spray on his lips. He wrote 'Every painting I have made has somewhere in it a thought of Sligo'.

'I have always watched things happening', he once said, acknowledging a passive disposition redeemed by curiosity. He loved the sea, sport, music hall entertainment, prize-fighting, the race course, children, good conversation, practical jokes. Yet he never went to sea, participated in no sport, rode a pony only as a child, disclaimed any singing or entertaining ability, was a listener rather than a talker, and never had children. Only through his eyes, and his restless hand recording everything in his sketchbook, was he eternally active.

CHAPTER ONE

Origins

Not first love or love at all . . .

JACK YEATS'S PLACE of birth was of no particular significance to him. The country which eventually he was to call his own only obtained its formal existence when he was fifty years old. He did not grow up with his family, but with his grandparents. He saw his mother infrequently, and learned from an early age to distrust his father. He had the unsettling experience of being treated in totally different ways by his two sisters and his elder brother; the girls were loving and indulgent, Willie was lofty and distant. These youthful experiences gave him a deep commitment to the things of which he had been deprived; he was a family man, proud of his Yeats and Pollexfen origins, kind to his sisters, adoring of his mother, gracious towards his brother, and, when not enraged, guardedly tolerant of his eccentric and unreliable father.

Jack experienced Irish politics in all its manifestations, from staunch unionism to romantic – even violent – nationalism. He learned the turbulent history of Ireland by observing political meetings, rallies, demonstrations, violent acts and their aftermath, and political treachery which he came to abhor. He was passionately committed, both culturally and politically, to Ireland, to the country and to its people. And once he had chosen his way, he never faltered. He is the most purposeful artist Ireland has ever known, and he prided himself on this, just as Ireland was to pride itself in him.

His political experience began early. During his formative years, growing up in Sligo, in the west of Ireland, the dominant Irish political figure was Charles Stewart Parnell and the dominant issue land and the fortunes of the landed classes. Post-Famine expressions of Irish nationalism involved the Roman Catholic Church under the subtle and intelligent leadership of Cardinal Cullen. With educational progress, and perhaps above all with the increased political unity within Irish politics at Westminster, Parnell's leadership had been firmly established. At the time of Jack's birth in 1871 he had placed the subject of Ireland – perhaps 'problem' is a better word – high on the political agenda of William Ewart Gladstone, who led the Liberal Government at this time.

With some truth, the propensity for an acute and intense interest in politics is seen as peculiarly Irish. This interest has its roots in disaffection; but it was sustained and given life by the constant change and evolution in the political arena, and this was particularly powerful when Jack was young. Land issues, trade, social disparity, poverty, emigration, are never so well

1. John Butler Yeats on a visit to Sligo in September 1863, at the time of his engagement.

understood as they are in a small-town environment. And living with a prosperous Protestant merchant at the centre of Sligo's trade and commerce gave him an instinctive knowledge and understanding quite different from the theoretical and voluble politics rehearsed in the various London homes occupied by the rest of the Yeats family, and dominated by their father's opinionated views. From the beginning, Jack saw a different Ireland, more immediate, more peasant, more human; and it stamped and shaped him, as we shall see.

He was born on 29 August 1871 at 23 Fitzroy Road, in London, just north of Regent's Park, the fifth child of John Butler Yeats and Susan Pollexfen (figs 1–2).[1] He was christened John Butler, and for some time during his infancy he was called Johnnie.

His parents' life together had begun on what seemed a happy and optimistic note. When they met, in the late summer of 1862, Susan was twenty-one. She was good-looking, with fair skin and distinguished by one unusual feature: her large, deep-set eyes were of different colours, one blue, one brown, and had rather heavy lids. She has been described as 'extraordinarily pretty'[2] although this is not fully borne out by family photographs of her at the time, nor by John Butler Yeats's early drawings of her (see fig. 3). But she was apparently much sought after, and was described to her son, Willie, as 'the most beautiful woman in Sligo'.[3] Before his return to Dublin, John Butler Yeats proposed to Susan Pollexfen while exploring caves at Bundoran. She accepted him, and thus began 'one of the most frustrating and fruitful marriages in the history of Ireland'.[4]

The union was, at the very least, unhappy; more truthfully, it was disastrous, disintegrating slowly over a number of years, and with few redeeming moments. Yet out of the difficulties and the poverty into which John Butler Yeats, like some woeful, errant knight, valiantly led his growing family, there emerged brilliance and gifted, rich talent. These qualities were to dominate Ireland's culture in poetry and painting more permanently than those of any other family in the country's history. The Yeats's stamp on Irish life, and on art and letters, thought and self-awareness, has a dynastic quality which is unique. Sad, then, to present an early domestic scene which was never right. At the heart of the trouble was the question mark over the very sincerity of John Butler Yeats's love for his wife, creating a central defect in the marriage. Many years later he wrote to Rosa Butt: 'I became engaged on two or three days acquaintance, and it was not first love or love at all (this really entre nous – I have never confessed to anyone) but just destiny'.[5]

John Butler Yeats described the Pollexfen family, 'gathered in force and [seated] together mostly in one room, and all disliking each other, at any rate alien mutually, in gloomy silence broken only by the sound of your grandmother turning over the leaf of a book, or by the creaking of some one's brace, or by a sigh from George Pollexfen.'[6] His disdainful tone is significant; the young John Butler Yeats was a man of distinguished stock, a landowner, well educated, qualified to practice at the Bar, and well connected with other distinguished Dublin families. Socially, the Yeatses were well above the Pollexfens, who were merchants. In the marriage settlement Susan was promised a widow's jointure of £150 a year, with John Butler Yeats's property at Thomastown secured for this purpose. Both from Susan's point of view and that of her parents it was a good match. But their marriage on 10 September 1863 started badly. They went to Galway on their honeymoon and stayed

2. Susan Pollexfen in 1863 aged 22, before her marriage to John Butler Yeats.

there in the Railway Hotel. She had never been to a hotel before. John Butler Yeats became quite ill, with diphtheria, and Susan tried to light a fire in one of the two rooms they had, but failed.

> . . . and then she went out for help . . . and heard some children on the top floor saying their prayers and she felt homesick. She sat alone for dinner and they brought her a shoulder of mutton. . . . she had not the courage to cut off even one slice, and so took just the vegetables. Next day Papa sent for his mother, who came and took him to Dublin in an invalid carriage.[7]

It would be cruel, and indeed difficult, to suggest that this set the tone for the marriage, yet within it are several critical ingredients which continued throughout their life together including her inability to please him and his innate distrust of her, a distrust of her aptitude, judgment and abilities. Eight years later, at the time of Jack's birth, virtually all the promises of that first encounter, the marriage, honeymoon, and early married life, lay in tatters. And John Butler Yeats had managed to make a mess of everything, his birthright, his career, his domestic arrangements in London, and his relations with his in-laws. Every promise had come to nothing. John Butler Yeats had presented himself as strong-minded, determined, articulate.

> At Sligo, I was the social man where it was the individual man that counted. It is a curious fact that entering this sombre house of stern preoccupation with business I for the first time in my life felt myself to be a free man, and that I was invited by the example of everyone around me to be my very self, thereby receiving the most important lesson in my life.[8]

But he did not learn it. He was never really free, unless running away makes one free. He was not strong-minded. He was not determined. And such little freedoms as he did enjoy, or imagined that he enjoyed, were dearly-bought, and spent with a prodigality that was extravagant and irresponsible and largely at the expense of his family.

As a landowner he had proved unequal to the task of administration, and had undermined his most important source of income. When his father died he inherited the Thomastown estate and a house in Dorset Street, Dublin, but promptly passed over their management to his uncle, Robert Corbet. Together, the properties were worth £10,000, and yielded an income of £380 a year, which, with further earnings, would have sustained the family, and allowed for the development of his career as an artist. But John Butler Yeats ruined their chance of financial security. At the time of the inheritance, there were mortgages against the property of £2,200. The new owner then increased the indebtedness in 1867 to over £3,000, imposing on himself twice-yearly interest payments. What was more serious, however, was the fact that Susan's prior right to a widow's jointure had to be waived. Worse was to follow. Corbet himself fell on hard times, gave up his home Sandymount Castle, dismissed his staff, and moved into lodgings in Mount Street. He subsequently committed suicide by jumping off the Dublin-Holyhead mailboat. The duties of managing the Thomastown property passed to Thomas Yeats, another uncle who enjoyed the distinct disadvantage – for land management purposes – of being a brilliant mathematician. Shortly afterwards, the duties passed to another relation Matthew Yeats, who was a land agent. The estate, small by Irish standards, was complicated by the fact that no less than seventeen tenants held separate leases to the 345 acres, some

3. *Susan Yeats*, in 1867, two years after the birth of William Butler Yeats. Pencil drawing by her husband.

of them prompt about paying their dues, others more dilatory. There were, in addition, disputes, one of which, in 1869, led to the shooting and serious wounding of the family bailiff, John Doran. Yeats the free-thinker, the Irish nationalist and friend of Isaac Butt, and a man who was later to become the friend of William Morris, a founder of British socialism, not only had the embarrassment of being an Irish absentee landlord, but of being an unsuccessful one as well.

The family's circumstances had steadily worsened over the eight years before Jack was born. During the time in which Susan had borne her five children, she had set up home in both Dublin and London, making intermittent trips back to her parents in Sligo, not for holidays, but out of need. The first home had been in Sandymount, Dublin. It was there that their eldest child, William Butler, was born in the summer of 1865. At that stage, John Butler Yeats was trying to pursue a career in the city as a lawyer. Their second child, Lily, was born in Sligo. Shortly after this, at the beginning of 1867, their father decided to change to the life of a painter, and moved to London, and to art school there. Lolly, Robert, Jack and Grace were all born in London. Like so many of the decisions in his life, John Butler Yeats acted precipitately in giving up the law. He continued to act in a haphazard way, governed by his emotions, and now, as he was to do many times afterwards when under pressure, he took the easy way out, and deposited his wife and children with her parents in Sligo.

Susan loved Sligo intensely, and hated London. She felt morose and dispirited there. By the time Jack was born, his mother had witnessed her husband's uncertain pursuit of two prospective careers, neither of which had been realised. After four years at art school, John Butler Yeats's crucial decision in favour of art had a distinctly unfulfilled look to it. He undoubtedly regarded painting as a way of life; though not as a career or a profession. Though talented as a draughtsman, and competent in the use of paint, he seemed perversely disinterested in applying himself to his immediate responsibilities of providing for his young family and wife, whose health was already in decline. Without a permanent job, even his few and intermittent commissions were treated in an illogical and self-indulgent way. Having signally failed to make a career for himself, either as a lawyer or as an artist, he was faced with five children under seven, no regular source of income, and the self-imposed need to keep up appearances among fellow-artists. They probably mattered more to him at the time than anyone else.

He was asking for, and accepting, money from Susan's father; the circumstances were humiliating. In February 1871, for example, while Susan was pregnant with Jack, William Pollexfen wrote:

> Your note of the 3 to hand Enclosed you have a check for twenty pounds which will be as good as cash to your Butcher if you give it to him. Glad to learn your picture is well hung, this time, that it's thought a good deal of . . . The weather has quite changed here, from the Eastward, now from the Westward and quite warm. Family quite well at Merville, give my love to all yours. Remaining yours William Pollexfen.[9]

Jack's birth, six months later, coincided with this low point in the Yeats family fortunes. His mother left London when he was a month old and returned to Sligo with her young family, giving Jack his first experience of the sea. It was a long journey, involving a train to Liverpool and a sea voyage

4. *Susan Yeats and Lily*, 13 February 1870. Susan was pregnant with her fourth child, Robert Corbet Yeats, who died young. Unlike the earlier drawing, her husband has clearly shown the eye defect.

5. No 23, Fitzroy Road, the house where Jack was born.

around the northern coast of Ireland to Sligo. That she made it so soon after he was born suggests a serious deterioration in her relationship with her husband. The departure presaged a virtual breach between them, a physical separation which lasted, on and off, for five years; more seriously, the emotional separation was effectively permanent.

The extent to which Susan had been made to suffer by him during her first eight years of marriage can be gauged, immediately and dramatically, from an examination of John Butler Yeats drawings of his wife (figs 3–4). There is something impressively striking, even luscious, in the young wife of 1867, mother of two children, alert and confident, her carriage upright, her large brave eyes open in optimism upon the world which seemed then to lie invitingly at the feet of the young family. If we turn then to the drawing John Butler Yeats did of her on 13 February 1870, just six weeks before the birth of her fourth child, Robert Corbet Yeats, and a year and a half before Jack's birth, we see an unhappy transformation. In the intervening period she had suffered much, including damage to her eyesight. Her blue eye had developed a cataract when Willie was still only a few months old. She was seen by the famous oculist of the day and a friend of the Yeats family, Sir William Wilde. He believed the cataract was too delicate to operate on. He told her: 'You are married so just leave it alone.' Then he added as an afterthought: 'And ask your husband when Thomas Yeats is going to send me that fishing rod he promised me.'[10] The 1870 drawing, clearly shows the damaged eye. But it shows much more besides. The expression is withdrawn and the eyes look inward. A handkerchief is held over the mouth, and the chubby-cheeked Lily, in the foreground, appears to have drained from her mother all her vitality and energy. This sad transformation must have weighed heavily on her family as they witnessed it during each successive visit to the family home in Sligo.

After one such visit, in the late summer of 1871, Susan and the family returned to the Fitzroy Road house (fig. 5). It was the beginning of probably the worst year in her life. She was deeply affected, both mentally and physically, by the stress of poverty. She was also worn down by childbearing. She was unable to deal with her husband. She could not persuade him of the seriousness of his responsibilities. She could not cope with the burdens which fell upon her. She could not please him. The self-styled rational man did not act according to reason; and his wife could not reason. In a penetrating phrase, her eldest son describes 'my Sligo-born mother whose actions were unreasoning and habitual like the seasons'.[11]

It is not clear how practical she was, though it is certain she did not deserve quite such a poor opinion from her husband, who claimed: 'Susan could not have boiled an egg', and that he never left the house – which he did all the time, with scant regard for the consequences – without 'wondering what would happen in his absence'.[12] In all those years nothing untoward did happen. Her upbringing had not given her any domestic training or talents to suit her to an impoverished life. She had been conditioned to the smooth management of a large house in Sligo. She was also imaginative, if at the same time melancholy.

The relationship contained many explosive ingredients, among them John Butler Yeats's distrust of his wife's capacities in the home. But the growing disaffection was rooted in more fundamental differences. These went far beyond his failures to make money. The spiritual dimension of their lives caused problems too. Religion played an important part in Susan's life, and

5

she wanted her children brought up in the Protestant faith. John Butler Yeats, despite being the son and grandson of clergymen, and knowing how much it would mean to his wife, refused to allow this. For him the Christian faith was no more than myth and fable, and he imposed this 'free-thinking' in a doctrinaire way on his wife and children.

On the three key issues of faith, art and politics, John and Susan Yeats were at odds. She did not understand his art nor his artistic friends. He could not accept her faith, and sought to deprive his children of it. Politically, John Butler Yeats was a free-thinker; he espoused a demonstrative form of nationalism, derived from his friend, Isaac Butt, and augmented intellectually by his own vigorous faculty for reasoning and arguing. Susan, on the other hand, was conservative; she came from a more cautious and conventional background in which mercantile objectives went hand-in-hand with support for the political establishment.

So Susan returned to London with a sinking heart, and settled to face the daunting task of bringing up her five children, while her husband tried to roar on down the road of art. Combined with his studies, he embarked uncertainly on a painter's career. Given that he was thirty-two years old at the time of Jack's birth, and had four other children, it was late enough to be approaching so momentous a decision without greater conviction. He relied on his own good intentions and, as we have mentioned, they were largely unsupported either by concrete achievement or adequate financial resources. Gifted, fluent, clear in expressing his liberal, nationalist opinions, he used none of his talents effectively. The best that can be asserted is that his nationalism, his instinctive talent for art, and his good manners, were all inherited by his son, Jack. But too much talk and argument, too much speculation and philosophising, far too much dithering over commissions and an unrealistic fastidiousness about taking work as an illustrator, meant that he earned no money.

Established Irish artists working in London, among them John Henry Foley, the sculptor, and Richard Doyle, the fantasy artist, gave him help, encouragement and advice.[13] Among fellow-students John Trivett Nettleship and Edwin J. Ellis were close friends, and to a slightly lesser extent George Wilson, a Scot. None of them achieved any great success. Willie claimed that Ellis had a natural gift for poetry, which he found 'moving'; and he was astonished at the painter's ability to 'cast something just said into a dozen lines of musical verse, without apparently ceasing to talk'. But he was not interested in him as a painter; too late for Pre-Raphaelitism, too early for the French painters, he 'showed no influence but that of Leighton'.[14] Together, the four artists constituted 'The Brotherhood', and their passionate devotion to ideas, and the belief that all the arts were interdependent, gave them inexhaustible material for endless and high-flown debate.

6. Edward J. Ellis, fellow student.

Ellis was the closest friend of all (fig. 6), but uncongenial to Susan, who really hated him. As a fellow-artist he declared art was a common bond: 'It is our wife,' he told John Butler Yeats in a letter; 'Were we to lose it, nothing would make up for the loss'.[15] This veneration of art implicitly strengthened the friendship between the two men, further excluding Susan. And it was a telling metaphor, insulting to the threadbare domesticity into which he so rudely and so regularly intruded. John Butler Yeats, however, accepted this view and leaned more heavily on Ellis as his friend. According to a letter from John Todhunter to Edward Dowden, Yeats, 'told me that marriage was a fatal

7. The mature student. A puzzled and uncertain John Butler Yeats in 1875.

mistake and that I should spend it hereafter in sackcloth & ashes Friendship is only thing worth living for'.[16] Ellis visited the house often, was rude to Susan, often ignoring her completely, or using terms about art and literature which were obscure, pompous and almost explicitly disdainful of her more ordinary interests and knowledge. In another letter, Todhunter wrote: 'His [Ellis's] manners are to me disgusting, although Yeats insists on it that he is a perfect gentleman. I don't wonder at all at poor little Mrs Yeats's hatred of him – he has not only estranged her husband from her, but he quietly . . . ignores her existence'. The children were the silent and largely uncomprehending witnesses to the frequent distress.[17]

It was a time of 'wearing anxiety', John Butler Yeats told Susan, 'injuring our characters as well as our physical strength'.[18] And their unhappiness no doubt had a subconscious impact on the children. Worse was to follow: by the time Jack was approaching his first birthday a decision had been made, in principle, that Susan, with all the children, would go home to Sligo, and that no plans would be made for the usual autumn return to London. John Butler Yeats would remain alone, to grapple with his art and philosophise with his friends.

Thus it was, with Jack not yet a year old, that the five children and their mother again left London, on 23 July 1872, and took the train for Liverpool. Charles Pollexfen, the eldest son, was in charge of the Liverpool offices of their father's steamship service, the Sligo Steamship Navigation Company. He welcomed Susan and her family who were given special treatment on the voyage round the north-west coast of Ulster and into the Atlantic. Everyone, the shipping staff at the quayside, the crew on board, and the familiar faces when they docked in Sligo, indulged them and the journey was like a welcome home. The children were William Pollexfen's first grandchildren, and William Butler Yeats recalls the special pleasures of that summer voyage:

> When I arrived at the Clarence Basin, Liverpool,[19] on my way to Sligo for my holidays I was among Sligo people . . . I came and went once or twice in every year . . . I waited for this voyage always with excitement and boasted to other boys about it . . . while I remember stories . . . and the look of the great cliffs of Donegal and Tory Island men coming alongside with lobsters, talking Irish and, if it was night, blowing on a burning sod to draw our attention.[20]

It is perhaps not surprising that the seamen, when once they saw Willie's father travelling with his family, would say, 'There is John Yeats and we shall have a storm.' He was considered unlucky, though whether by instinct or reputation is not known. Two photographs show that he too bore the marks of an unhappy marriage. The first is of him in 1863, with dundreary whiskers but no beard, solid, self-confident, good-looking and certainly determined in his expression. The second, from about 1875, shows him bearded, with the hairline just beginning to recede, and with a sad and pensive look in his face; the brow is beginning to be furrowed with doubt, and the eyes are sad and without sparkle (fig. 7).

Even more compelling evidence is a letter he wrote to Susan from Fitzroy Street not long after her departure with the children in July 1872. He was a prince among letter-writers as we shall see, sending a fluid, magical flow of literally hundreds of thousands of words to friends and children through a long life. This letter, however, is quite the opposite: a halting and

8. Sligo Street Scene, *c*. 1910.

9. View of Sligo, looking north, Ben Bulbin in the distance, *c*. 1900.

10. Pollexfen Mills at Ballisodare, *c*. 1900.

embarrassed mixture of homily and news, uncertain and self-doubting, with just occasional touches of his wise concern.

> I hope you continue reading to the children; working and caring for children makes one anxious and careful of them, but amusing them makes one fond of them. Tell me constantly of the children. Ellis and Nettleship had their pictures rejected by the New British Ex, in Bond St. to which they sent them after they had been refused by the Dudley. I hope you let Isabella know these little bits of artistic gossip and such-like. Ask her to write to me. Your affectionate husband – J.B. Yeats.
> P.S. I am glad you are doing nothing. If you could be got to do this oftener – particularly when you have a cold beginning you would now be a strong woman . . .[21]

Closer to that Christmas, John Butler Yeats wrote an even more poignant letter to his wife.

> I do not at all wonder at your mother thinking I have no common sense – I fancy she cant understand my reading so much or occupying myself with ideas – she of course cannot know that these are the materials with which I work. I know that years back I have night and day thought of nothing else except how and when I can get a competency – time only can tell whether I am on the right track – I cannot say when I shall (have) enough for you to come to London . . . I shall be more worth your liking when we next live together –[22]

On this second trip, for Jack, to the west of Ireland, the family stayed for a period of two years and four months. Those early years instilled in him a powerful debt to a part of Ireland 'at its Westernmost and finest . . . in a deep broad country, with a magnificent sea-coast, and Mountains stooping to the beaches, and lakes and bogs and Inland Towns; and a fine sea port.'[23]

In the case of Sligo, the remarkable beauty of the place was reinforced by the comfort, welcome and affection within the Pollexfen home. Merville 'was a pleasant house to come to, up under haunted trees . . . an old house in that old town. And every night the dining-room, and the passages near it, are suffused with a sweet and comforting smell which permeates no passages now. It is the smell of Whiskey Punch.'[24]

All the children loved Sligo. Willie in his fifties, passing by the drinking fountain in Holland Park, had a moment of Proustian recall when he remembered himself and Lily standing in the same place and speaking together of their longing for Sligo and their hatred of London.

> I know we were both very close to tears and remember with wonder, for I had never known any one that cared for such mementoes, that I longed for a sod of earth from some field I knew, something of Sligo to hold in my hand. It was some old race instinct like that of a savage, for we had been brought up to laugh at all display of emotion.[25]

There are other memories, comic or fearful by turn, but rich and abiding, told and retold by his sister and his brother, clearly recounted first by his mother, or by one or other of the many family members who surrounded the children during the Sligo visits. Over all these people looms the figure of Jack's grandfather, the man who dominated his life then and for years to come, William Pollexfen.

11. William Pollexfen, Sligo ship-owner and merchant, c. 1865.

Each of the children had a different view of this man. Willie was fearful, Lily respectful, Lolly amused. But Jack regarded him, from the start, with an instinctive and fearless understanding. He was too young to be intimidated by the myths; from the outset, he treated his grandfather as a companion. Of all the children he was the only one to talk with his grandfather, to go about with him, and, in a childlike way, to direct and control him. Pollexfen became Jack's replacement father for the crucial early years of his life. The association was powerful and pervasive.

William Pollexfen was a powerfully built man (fig. 11). Though neither stout, nor particularly tall, at 5′ 9″, he was physically formidable, and widely respected and feared for his physical courage and intrepid spirit. His complexion was fresh, his eyes very blue, and, when the Yeats children knew him, his hair and beard were white. 'He held himself very upright and walked stiffly, creaking a little as he went; he always looked the sea captain.'[26] His clothes, according to Lily, were generally grey. He wore shoes made to his own design by a Sligo shoemaker called Andie May; they were pumps with no laces or buttons, but with 'a little gusset of elastic'. May used to visit the house and make William Pollexfen stand on a sheet of white paper, 'nervously' drawing round his foot with a pencil. In summer his granddaughter remembers that he liked to wear a buff linen waistcoat. She writes that 'he never went to a shop. The tailors came in the same way, and measured him up for his clothes.'[27]

He was indisputably the head of the house, although he was neither oppressive nor unfair. Lily, who endeavoured to present an objective portrait of her grandparents in her memoir, writes 'Grandpapa Pollexfen was liked, admired and avoided, he never talked to anyone, he grumbled, complained and ejaculated all day long, the past and the future had no interest for him at all, he was in such a state of irritation with the present moment that he could think of nothing else.'

He was a successful merchant surrounded by a grown family, and reliant on his wife for the smooth running of their large house which was central to Sligo's mercantile society. To the breakfast table came the patriarch, dressed for the day's many challenges. He struck off the top of his egg as though it were the head of a prisoner being executed, and it flew away across the room. 'Where the top of the egg went to was not his business. It might hit a grandchild or the ceiling. He never looked.'[28] The children tried to seat themselves on the same side of the table as their grandfather in order not to be noticed, since he noticed everything, yet there is no evidence of any retribution. William Pollexfen was a rational individual, a practical man, and intensely hard-working.

Until he was over eighty he remained very vigorous, happiest when out on the quayside, in his ships, or with his men. His wife still did the housekeeping, and attended to all his wants herself, preparing his linen, ensuring that his cufflinks and collar studs were in the right place (see fig. 12). Lily was later called on to write letters on their behalf, and did so from her grandmother's dictation. But her grandfather, sitting on the sofa, would interrupt, saying crossly, 'That will do now, you have said enough'. Sometimes, when his irritability was excessive, or when he overstepped some unwritten, unspoken mark of tolerance, his wife Elizabeth would look nervous and blink her eyes. Then he would look at her, give a short laugh, and be quiet. She seems to have had a tranquillising effect on him. He would sit with her while she read to him, often from the Bible, which was constantly beside her, with a marker in the page on which the 109th Psalm appeared, as a warning against ever reading it,[29] 'until tired out he went to bed. Coming over to Grandmama he took off a little silk skull cap he wore – kissed her like a good child, and went to his own room. And a great peace fell on us all.'[30]

William Pollexfen was brave and successful, even in ways heroic. He had lived a life of adventure at sea before settling in Sligo. He had a great scar round one thumb which, it was claimed, had come from a 'flensing' hook, used to cut open a whale's body and take off skin. It was assumed that there must have been a fight, but no one dared ask him. On his right hand he wore a large ring containing a red cartouche. One day on the quays in Sligo he lost his temper, and struck out at a man who fell. The ring cut the man, and he was brought up to the house and compensated in some way, though he kept repeating, 'The Master never meant it at all, it was his big ring.' This of course invested the ring with compelling properties for the grandchildren, and Lily recounts staring at it in church. William Pollexfen and his wife were devout members of the Church of Ireland. He was also a Freemason.[31] He took pride in what was then St John's Church, and is now the cathedral. And he was a vestryman. Lily recalls once in church, during very disturbed times, 'a revolver just showing out of his side pocket'.

Willie also had many recollections:

> the jar of water from the Jordan for the baptising of his children and Chinese pictures upon rice-paper and ivory walking-stick from India that came to me after his death. He had great physical strength and had the reputation of never ordering a man to do anything he would not do himself . . . He had a violent temper and kept a hatchet at his bedside for burglars and would knock a man down instead of going to law, and I once saw him hunt a group of men with a horsewhip. He had no relation for he was an only child and, being solitary and silent, he had few friends. He corresponded with Campbell of Islay who had befriended him and his crew after a shipwreck, and Captain Webb, the first man who had swum the Channel and who was drowned swimming the Niagara Rapids, had been a mate in his employ and a close friend . . . Yet for all my admiration and alarm, neither I nor any one else thought it wrong to outwit his violence or his rigour; and his lack of suspicion and a certain helplessness made that easy while it stirred our affection.[32]

William Pollexfen was born in March 1811 at Berry Head, in Devon. He ran away to sea in 1823, at the age of twelve. 'I went to sea through the hawse hole' was how he expressed it, and he seems to have voyaged widely for a period of ten years before moving to Sligo. He was the only child of Anthony Pollexfen and Mary Stephens.[33] In the mid-eighteenth century the family, which had a tradition of antagonism to Court and Crown, became non-conformist. 'Charles Pollexfen (Anthony Pollexfen's cousin) was an evangelising Wesleyan minister, and happened to be stationed on circuit in the Channel Islands, when his fifteen-year-old daughter in 1813 accepted the hand of the Sligo merchant William Middleton.'[34] In any history involving the Yeatses, the Middleton name, famous in Sligo over the last two centuries, is of great importance, and for Jack in particular. They were *his* family. Both his Pollexfen and Middleton ancestors brought with them an association with the sea, piracy and nautical adventure. This was to play a large part in his imagination, inspiring innumerable early drawings, watercolours, and his plays for children. Though not as dominant in the family story as the Pollexfens, William Middleton, his great-grandfather on his grandmother's side, and his family are responsible for the founding of the family fortune and for the connection which led to Pollexfen's initial and momentous arrival in Sligo. For William Pollexfen's arrival in Sligo, in 1832, was no accident. He came to the town because of his kinsfolk there, the Middletons.

Elizabeth Pollexfen, Susan's grandmother was no more than a 'child wife',[35] when she married William Middleton and she brought her five-year old brother with her to the far Atlantic coast of Ireland. This strange act, blessed it seems by her parents, had tragic consequences, for the boy died not long after. Lily reports that her great-grandmother 'had not the courage to break it to her people, history says, for years, but I hardly think that can be true'.[36]

In Sligo William Middleton became prominent not only in commercial affairs, but also in charitable works. He played a brave part in the cholera epidemic which more than decimated the town population, in the great European epidemic of the disease in 1832. This work, to which he dedicated all his efforts, had tragic conclusions. Coming home one evening he found a victim dying by the roadside, and carried the person home. He contracted the disease himself, and died, leaving his young wife of only thirty seven years, and her young children.

When he heard of William Middleton's death, William Pollexfen went to Sligo, in his own ship, called The Dasher, to see if he could help his cousin. She accepted the offer of help, and he remained for the rest of his life in Sligo. Five years later he married his cousin's eldest daughter, also Elizabeth, and he and his brother-in-law, who was then a boy, ran the business.

William and Elizabeth Pollexfen had a family of twelve children. Jack's mother, Susan, was the third child, and the eldest daughter. She was born in 1841. Her two elder brothers, Charles and George, were at school with John Butler Yeats. It was this association which led to their meeting, and then to marriage. There were nine other Pollexfen children, one of whom, William, died at the age of two, in 1846, his name then being used for the next child, born the following year.[37]

Lily, in her charming memoir of her maternal grandparents, and of other Middleton and Pollexfen connections, writes of the transfer of power which took place in the early years of the nineteenth century, and of the fruits of this which played so great a part on their childhood days in Sligo, and on later memories. 'The great magnates who controlled the milling industry, the late Abram Martin, Culbertson and Madden, passed out one by one.'[38] William Middleton became a central figure amongst the tightly managed business community, and himself 'emerged into the limelight', side-by-side with his brother-in-law, William Pollexfen.

There was a dark side to Sligo port business during the Famine, when ships left with human cargo. Among these vessels were the infamous 'coffin ships', chartered as part of the process of land clearance. These were often inadequate hulks, unsuited to the ocean journeys they had to make, and catering badly for the destitute people on board them. Some were doomed, and known to be so by their masters, who took the passage money, and then, when the ships met bad weather, abandoned them and their living cargo, often battened below decks, taking to sea in a cutter which held only the crew. William Butler Yeats recalls an old naval officer singing a ballad about a coffin ship leaving Sligo after the famine. 'When she was moved from the berth she had lain in, an unknown dead man's body had floated up, a very evil omen; and my grandfather, who was Lloyd's agent, had condemned her, but she slipped out in the night.'[39] Jack remembered the story also, but recorded it in a different way, years later, when he made the fate of emigrants aboard a 'coffin-ship' the main theme in his play for miniature theatre, *The Treasure of the Garden*.[40]

And Willie tells another, quite different story, instructive of Pollexfen's character and his courage:

> Once too I was driving with my grandmother a little after dark close to the Channel that runs for some five miles from Sligo to the sea, and my grandmother showed me the red light of an outward-bound steamer and told me that my grandfather was on board, and that night in my sleep I screamed out and described the steamer's wreck. The next morning my grandfather arrived on a blind horse found for him by grateful passengers. He had, as I remember the story, been asleep when the captain aroused him to say they were going on the rocks. He said, 'Have you tried sail on her?' and judging from some answer that the captain was demoralised took over the command and, when the ship could not be saved, got the crew and passenger into the boats. His own boat was upset and he saved himself and some others by swimming; some women had drifted ashore, buoyed up by their crinolines. 'I was not so much afraid of the sea as of that terrible man with his oar,' was the comment of a schoolmaster who was among the survivors. Eight men were, however, drowned and my grandfather suffered from that memory at intervals all his life, and if asked to read family prayers never read anything but the shipwreck of St Paul.[41]

When William Pollexfen returned for dinner at the old-fashioned hour of four o'clock each afternoon, he brought with him his partner and brother-in-law, William Middleton. Middleton was a bachelor and spent the early evening with his sister's family before going out to Rosses Point. He was a sympathetic man, and had inherited some of his father's boundless compassion. By mid-century Sligo was set fair on the road to becoming Ireland's busiest west coast trading port, which Thomas Carlyle described as the Liverpool of the west of Ireland. The Middleton-Pollexfen partnership had recognised the importance of shipping.

William Middleton had standing in the town of Sligo; but rapidly enough William Pollexfen's drive and ambition, backed by great physical strength and powerful courage, made him the dominant partner. It was he who ran the enterprise, day-to-day, and planned its development. When he joined both the family and the firm, they were running a fleet of fast sailing vessels between Sligo, Portugal and Spain. The cargoes were mixed. Grain was brought in for the mills in Sligo. Salt was brought from Portugal. Sheep, cattle, wool were exported. William's eldest son, George, used to name the vessels for Lily, and would recall for her his one adventure, a voyage to Portugal aboard the Bacalieu. As the sailing vessels were replaced by steam they were turned into lighters. The ocean-going steamers were too large to negotiate the five-mile channel into Sligo port from Rosses Point, and lay out in the deep-water anchorages in Sligo Bay while their cargoes of wheat were unloaded onto the old sailing ships. 'In our day these gay little ships' lives were over, and they, as old black hulls . . . clustered round the great corn steamers from America and the Black Sea, the yellow corn being poured into them with a delightful rushing sound.'[42]

As well as managing the family fleet, William Pollexfen was also responsible for buying the Ballysodare and Sligo Mills. By the time the Yeats children were born, the firm was big, its owners rich and proud men. Without question, the presiding genius was William Pollexfen himself. Murphy says of him: 'His lack of interest in education was matched only by his desire to accumulate worldly goods and to raise his family in station.' Where the alleged lack of interest in education came from, in a man who sent two sons to the same Atholl Academy on the Isle of Man to which John Butler Yeats was sent, it is difficult to say. As to the desire to raise his family in social standing, William Pollexfen would have pleaded guilty, and the court of Victorian virtue would have exonerated him from all blame. That court would also have admired — and perhaps envied — the fine house with sixty acres, the large, well-dressed and well-cared for family, the extensive business, the servants, horses, carriages, and many other 'worldly goods'.

The huge figure of William Pollexfen was to occupy a central position in Jack's life from his infancy until he went to art school, in 1887, at the age of sixteen. His wife Elizabeth played an equally important role (fig. 12). When William Pollexfen first met her, in 1832, she was the eldest of the Middleton children. She was born in Wine Street in a comfortable house which afterwards became the offices for the firm. She went to school in Sligo, but studied music and painting at the convent. She lived through the cholera epidemic in 1832, and hers is the moving account of her father at that time, who said that enough people were caring for the souls of the sick and dying, he would attend to their bodies and worldly affairs. He nursed them, made their wills, put up a notice in the town urging people not to be afraid, but to have courage. And it was when the epidemic was almost over that he succumbed to the disease. At the time of his death a little daughter, Mary, who was four years old, also died. 'There is a story that he and she were seen after death walking hand in hand in the garden and that a pet dog saw them also and ran to meet them.'[43]

12. Elizabeth, William Pollexfen's wife, shortly after the birth of her grandson, Jack.

Elizabeth Middleton had a sister, Agnes, and two brothers, William and John. There were several other children, but they died young. Great aunt Agnes, and the two great uncles, were all part of Jack's childhood. His grandmother was a small, handsome woman, only 5' 4" in height, and while still young he towered over her — and his grandfather.

She dressed very daintily. She wore black silk dresses generally, a cap, collar and cuffs of real lace, a quilted black satin petticoat, cream coloured stockings and thin black shoes. Out of doors she wore a long black silk jacket and a wide bonnet. She loved the garden, and spent much time there. She would put on a sunbonnet of flowered silk over her cap, and would make little plantations of carnation cuttings by dividing the violet sections and rooting them herself. 'She also grew a strange plant with big shiny leaves out of which she had big brews of ointment made which she gave away to all who came for it. People came miles for it. The plant had been sent to her from America. It was just called "the healing plant".'[44]

Elizabeth Pollexfen had a great impact on Lily. She recalls:

I can remember her so well, see her so clearly, running her big house with dignity. She had many maids and no servant trouble, she was calm and

13

13. Merville at the time it was owned by William Pollexfen.

14. William Butler Yeats as a young boy, Sligo, c. 1873.

even-tempered and was always their friend and as I look back I think she must have had real talent as an organiser. Grandmama Pollexfen had a strong character, not forceful, but strong. She was most unselfish, even-tempered, intuitive, observant, progressive and, I am sure, ambitious.[45]

In the 1860s the grandparents moved to Merville with their children. It was a fine stone-built house of considerable elegance, and probably dating from the end of the eighteenth century.[46] Though a two-storey house, it was entered upstairs; at either end of the two main rooms the walls, which contained fine windows, were semi-circular. It was a big house, with an extension at the back and about sixty acres around it. It had a long avenue and a splendid view of Ben Bulben.

However, not all the Yeats children were happy at Merville, least of all Willie, just seven at the beginning of that 1872 extended visit. He was at a difficult age, and in any case awkward and ill at ease. In the conventional sense, he was poorly educated. He still did not know the letters of the alphabet. His father, predictably enough, had absorbed imperfectly a theory derived from Herbert Spencer, to the effect that educating children too early might impede their intellectual progress.[47] It was a theory which found little favour with the family at Merville, and Willie, as the eldest son and heir of an unsuccessful but still propertied brother-in-law, became the prime object of concern among his aunts, a concern which amounted almost to ill-treatment. From Fitzroy Road his father wrote of the bad effect the 'dictatorial aunts' were having on Willie, and how he had 'disimproved' during his stay at Merville. 'Tell Willie not to forget me,' he added at the end of one letter.

With Lily and Lolly the problems were different. Lily had trouble with her breathing; even at that early age, Lolly was subject to long fits of gloom. Robert Corbet, who was then just over two, was robust and hardy, according to his mother, and able to take the rough and tumble of life in a large and busy household. As for Jack, he was either 'too young to be affected'[48] or just the right age to benefit in a natural and wholesome way from the overall stability of that impressive household.

Jack lived within a Sligo galaxy of energetic figures moving around the central patriarch and his careful, commanding and able wife, weaving her seamless robe of comfort and care for them all. Though we have Jack's fictional recollection, his theatre and the subject matter of his paintings, we have little factual evidence on the deeper aspects of his early life and experiences there. Willie tells us what he felt about his grandfather; Jack does not. Everything points to a happy and untroubled infancy and childhood in Sligo, in marked contrast with his eldest brother who was afraid of his grandfather. As we have mentioned, Jack never was. And William Pollexfen's attitude to the two boys was coloured by this; he took to Jack from the start, and Jack to him, while with Willie there was conflict. Willie gives us an ambiguous picture of his grandfather. 'There was no reason for my unhappiness. Nobody was unkind, and my grandmother has still after so many years my gratitude and my reverence.'[49] What made him fearful of William Pollexfen remains a mystery. 'He was never unkind, and I cannot remember that he ever spoke harshly to me, but it was the custom to fear and admire him.'[50] William Pollexfen was not the only figure to be considered, though as we have seen it was he who attained mythic attributes, and was revered; there was also his brother-in-law as part of the household, for at least one important visit each

15. Lily and Lolly Yeats, in *c*. 1875.

16. Jack as a young child.

day. Willie records that William Middleton, 'a cleverer man than my grandfather', came and went without notice, whereas 'I confused my grandfather with God, for I remember in one of my attacks of melancholy praying that he might punish me for my sins'.[51] Murphy tells us that when Willie in later years read *King Lear*, 'the image of his grandfather filled his mind's eye'.[52] But he does not complete the recollection, which was more than that; not only was the image of Grandfather Pollexfen before the poet and playwright, but the idea possessed him that his 'own delight in passionate men' as expressed both in his plays and his poetry derived from memory of his grandfather.[53] William Pollexfen's past adventures and achievements went largely unnoticed by his family. It was Jack who learned later of these exploits, and used them as inspiration. There is a hint of the man's simplicity in his passion for *Treasure Island*, which he read 'upon his death-bed with infinite satisfaction.'[54] Willie claimed that it was 'well nigh the only book I ever heard of him reading', and spoke admiringly of that quality in Stevenson's writing 'which while delighting studious & cloistered spirits, can yet hush into admiration such as he'.

Their extended stay of 1872 included Christmas. John Butler Yeats was in Ireland, to carry out portrait commissions for the Herbert family in Muckross House, Killarney, and came for the festival, staying on into the New Year. In March he was again recalled to Sligo, this time in tragic circumstances caused by the death of his son, Robert, who caught a cold and then developed croup. When the death was reported formally to the local authorities, the father was tellingly described by his brother-in-law, William, as 'barrister'.

One measure of Pollexfen's standing in Sligo may be gained from the fact that bonfires were lit along the railway line into Sligo to herald his return from Bath for his daughter Elizabeth's wedding to a clergyman, Alexander Barrington Orr. John Butler Yeats returned also for the event. Jack then aged two, wore a white dress which was the fashion for small boys at the time, and a red sash. His two sisters were in white with blue sashes, and Willie wore a blue knickerbocker sailing suit. In July of 1873, the lease on the Fitzroy Road house ended, and Susan went to England to help John Butler Yeats clear out their property. They had nowhere to put it, and for the next year or so Merville was the family home.

What of the Yeats family, and Jack's ancestry on that side? The Yeatses were of a different class altogether, with a background in the Church of Ireland, Trinity College, the Law; and in normal circumstances the paths of the Yeatses and Pollexfens would not readily have crossed, still less would there have been the union which produced so distinguished a progeny. But the Pollexfens were on an upward path toward great wealth and status, while the Yeatses were in a slow, genteel decline which John Butler Yeats was accelerating.

John Butler Yeats came from the same merchant stock in the seventeenth century as the Pollexfens and Middletons did in the nineteenth. The Yeats family traced its origins back to a linen merchant, Jervis Yeats, working in Dublin at the end of the seventeenth century. The family is thought to have originated in Yorkshire. He left a son, Benjamin, who was also a Dublin merchant, and in the linen trade, in William Street. He married well, his wife inheriting the property of 625 acres at Thomastown in County Kildare. Their eldest son, John, born on 13 November 1774, and the artist's great-grandfather, became Rector of Drumcliffe, where he died in 1846. William

15

Butler Yeats was the eldest son, the artist's grandfather, and the first to bear the mother's maiden name, Butler. It remained a family name thereafter.[55]

William Butler Yeats the elder proved himself an able horseman, and had the reputation of being the best jockey of his day, a skill he indulged after taking holy orders, causing his first rector to complain that he did not want a jockey but a curate. He was a friend of Isaac Butt, like his son, and edited with him the *Dublin University Magazine*.[56] In November 1835, he married Jane Grace Corbet, the daughter of a solicitor. She seems to have had a sporting disposition not unlike her husband's, and bribed the postillion of their coach, after the wedding, to race against another bridal couple who were going down the same road. This delighted her husband.[57] He later became curate of Moira, in County Down, and was then given the living at Tullylish, near Portadown, County Armagh, where, on 16 March 1839, John Butler Yeats was born.

He was the eldest surviving child of a family of nine, at least two of whom died in infancy from scarlet fever. He enjoyed a happy, privileged, even indulged childhood. There was a warmth and softness about it, with his father 'always on the lookout for the beautiful and the pleasing. It was this made him the most agreeable of companions and the finest of gentlemen. With a wave of his hand he made all difficulties disappear as if by magic.'[58]

John Butler Yeats was awakened rudely from this by his first school, in Seaforth, outside Liverpool, and even more so by his second. He and the second eldest son, William, carried the name Butler; the third son was Robert Corbet, and the fourth was named after William Butler Yeats's friend and hero, Isaac Butt Yeats. The first three boys went to school at the Atholl Academy, on the Isle of Man, and it was there, as mentioned, that John Butler Yeats met the two Pollexfen brothers, whose friendship led him to invite himself to visit the family in Sligo. This was some years later, after his studies at Trinity, where he enrolled in December 1857. He lived, before and during his time as a student, at Sandymount Castle, where his uncle, Robert Corbet, lived. His father, after retirement, had settled in a smaller house immediately beside the castle.

To the dismay of his uncle, who wanted him to enter the church, John Butler Yeats first questioned and then abandoned his father's faith, convinced that Christianity was '. . . mainly a myth of the frightened imagination'.[59] He studied law; he lived on at Sandymount, not liking student life greatly, perhaps because of the rich intellectual stimulation which was readily available at home; and he qualified in law with an unclassified degree in the spring of 1862. He enrolled to his father's delight, and his uncles's grudging acceptance, at the King's Inns, then went on to be the only competitor and therefore the winner of a £10 prize for political economy; his first earnings. They were to be his only earnings for a decade, and, in keeping with his imprudent nature, he spent them on a visit to his schoolfriend, George Pollexfen, in Sligo. The visit took place in early September of that year. The Pollexfens were staying out at Elsinore, the house at Rosses Point owned by their Uncle William Middleton. John Butler Yeats was once again captivated by his old school friend, George, who on that first evening was 'so companionable'.[60] Even more attractive was George's younger sister. Jack's father had met his mother. The inherited chemistries of his life and his art were at work.

17. *Jack*, pencil drawing by John Butler
Yeats, 1875.

18. *Willie*, pencil drawing by John Butler
Yeats, *c.* 1876.

CHAPTER TWO

Early Life in Sligo

In every painting . . . a thought of Sligo

JOHN BUTLER YEATS considered his apprenticeship as an artist to be over
with the Muckross and Stradbally commissions of 1873–4. They were
meant to be the beginning of a new profession, and for a man of thirty-
five it was none too soon. He brought his family back to London with him,
in the autumn of 1874, and they moved into a house in Edith Villas, in Earls
Court. Much smaller than the Fitzroy Road house, it stood in a small terrace
of houses off North End Road. It was inadequate for the family's needs, and
uncongenial after the spacious comfort of Merville. It was to be the scene of
further disillusionment. John Butler Yeats continued his relentless pursuit –
or 'lust', as Nettleship called it – for perfection, which meant, among other
things, that he found it difficult to finish anything. He could not leave well
alone. He painted slowly and carefully, even at times brilliantly. But he also
persisted in revising, and frequently spoiling, the earlier freshness and appeal
of what he had done. He argued strenuously, and at length, with his own
unique fluency, in favour of doing things his own way. It infuriated his
friends, depressed his wife, and may well have inspired in Jack a lifelong
antagonism to long drawn-out performance at the easel. It may also have
inspired in him a deep and lasting distrust of portraiture; apart from sketchbook drawings and very rare painted likenesses, he did not follow his father
in the many sittings and revisions which certainly attended each of his
commissions. Yet Jack never once considered a career other than that of artist.
He was bred to it, and remained faithful to it throughout his life.[1]

Not unreasonably, Grandfather Pollexfen wanted to know why John Butler
Yeats was not selling pictures. His philosophy was simple: work had to
support the family, which meant paying the rent and feeding them. Susan
had probably given up asking about his capacity to keep them all or any other
questions about her husband's career. But his friends were still, to their
credit, encouraging and supportive, though they too were increasingly frustrated. Their kindness, particularly that of Edward Dowden, is astonishing.
Dowden commissioned a work.

Yeats declared he would probably not ask more than fifty pounds and
certainly not more than a hundred, as it probably wouldn't be much good
anyhow. Dowden promptly agreed to pay one hundred pounds, but then
gently but wisely spread seeds of counsel on stony ground: 'I must object
to the ignorance both you and I display of the true relations of buyer and

19. The Bedford Park house occupied by the Yeats family.

20. *Jack by Lolly*, painting from the family album, *c.* 1880.

seller. Let me tell you that the seller always looks for a high price, and the highest he can get; and the buyer, then, tries to cut him down to the lowest possible. You and I seem likely to take just the opposite view.'[2]

Yeats family life remained fairly unhappy through the 1870s. Money was always short. The mismanagement of the properties in Ireland was wasteful, the yields unreliable, and then misspent. Willie was increasingly difficult; he suffered from the instability of their life, both in his work at school, and in his melancholy view of the world; this increased his shyness. Lolly was also moody. Such records of Jack as have survived show him as cheerful and amusing, a good mimic, and self-reliant. On his fourth birthday, 29 August 1875, his sister, Jane Grace was born. Her brief life ended in early summer of the following year. Jack and his two sisters, with their mother, went to stay with their married aunt, Elizabeth Orr, and her clergyman husband, in the north of England.

In the spring of 1879 the family took a house in Bedford Park, Chiswick, at 8 Woodstock Road (fig. 19). Bedford Park was an integrated housing scheme, the first 'Garden Suburb' in England, and designed for writers and artists.[3] Jack's stay there was brief. He had time enough, during that first spring, to plant seeds in the garden, mixing all of his together – a characteristic flourish in the face of rational order – before scattering them in the ground. In the summer the family went to Branscombe, in Devon, on the coast looking south into Lyme Bay.

At this stage, at eight years old, Jack's 'Farm' was already an established part of the household. It consisted of a collection of dolls and a house in which they were kept. There were elaborate relationships between the toys, with frequent birthday celebrations, and they later developed directly into Jack's miniature theatre. The 'Farm' had to travel with Jack, and his father recalled that 'it was sometimes a nuisance . . . when we left London and journeyed down to the seaside, luggage was troublesome to transport, but Jack's Farm had to come; without it, as it seemed to us, Jack would have lost his happiness.'[4]

Holiday drawings by the children demonstrate Willie's artistic ability, Lily's imitation of her elder brother, whom she greatly admired, and Lolly's sense of form and composition (fig. 20), all in a sense prophetic. Most prophetic of all, however, is the charming drawing by Jack of himself standing in a field on the farm where they stayed, and dressed in boots, sou'wester and oilskin (figs 21–4). His hands are held up in the air, in one of them a pencil, in the other a drawing pad. He also drew a scene of drama, as the coast-guards pull away from the shore in their boat, the last of them leaping in. Together with his sisters, he decorated stones with faces and they pretended they were dolls. When they washed the dolls, 'off came the faces and Jack put them on again.'[5] There was a large stone which kept open the door to the dairy; on it Jack painted horses and huntsmen.

There had been no Sligo holiday the previous year. Nor did the family go the following year, with the exception of Jack. It seems that the family could no longer afford a governess for the children. Martha Jowitt, who was twenty-two and came from Yorkshire, had been in charge of them for three years, and had been a great success, teaching them to read, and prevailing on them to be tidy. When she left Jack went to Sligo, followed by Lolly for a while, and then Lily, who had been at the Notting Hill Gate High School, but had become ill and had been sent off to spend the winter in the west of Ireland,

21 to 24. Family sketches in an album made by the children when at Branscombe, Devon in the summer of 1879.

a farm by Jack

22. *A Farm by Jack.*

23. *Lily and Lolly by Jack.*

24. *Boat by Jack.*

Lilly & Lolly by Jack

21. *Jack by Jack* (his first self-portrait).

Jack by Jack

Boat

By Jack

just Jack and I and our grandparents in the big house all our aunts and uncles were married and away. I rode every day on the red pony with the coachman coming behind me on a big horse – lovely warm days I remember in the soft air riding round Knocknarea – through Hazelwood or to Ballysodare – Grandmama looked quietly after my health and I was better.[6]

The red pony was a favourite in the family; Jack used his watercolour of it as the frontispiece to *Life in the West of Ireland*. Quite how long Jack stayed, to begin with, is uncertain, but his visit obviously proved successful enough for it to be decided that he would live with his grandparents for the foreseeable future. And when the family went to Sligo, in the late summer of 1880, Jack made Merville his home. At this time he had a soft mop of straight blond hair, a direct and serious gaze, full lips. He was the Cupid of his father's description, happy and indulged. But there is apparent, in the portrait photograph done in 1880, a definite strength of will. He would need it.

He parted from the family, and from all the domestic uncertainties which had been constant since his birth. Lily noted later: 'We really did not grow up with him.' And it was her view that in Sligo Jack 'gathered much that has made him.' She presumably placed their grandfather in the forefront of the influences. She said in her diary that Jack was 'the only one who ever had talk with Grandpapa.'[7] The rest of the family left London for Dublin, first, briefly, to a cottage on the cliffs at Howth, then to one overlooking the harbour, and then to a house in Terenure. John's studio was in York Street, off St Stephen's Green; and he later moved to one at 7 St Stephen's Green.[8]

Jack's life in Sligo focused upon his grandparents. John Butler Yeats, in his unpublished autobiography, says of them: 'I think they are still, both of them, and she especially, the strongest influence in his life. He has a good memory. We are all at the mercy of our mental qualities, and a tenacious memory makes for loyalty and a constant affection. As long as my son lives these old people are alive also.' William Pollexfen's impact is the more powerful, and there is an abiding image of him and Jack sitting side-by-side in the pony phaeton. Perhaps the most memorable occasion, when all Sligo must have witnessed or heard about the pair of them together, was at the funeral of a well-known Scottish mill-owner outside Sligo. He was a man of questionable morals, who had a reputation for womanising, and a man whom Pollexfen had regarded with great contempt all his life. Finding himself on the day of the funeral going slowly and respectfully behind such a man suddenly enraged Jack's grandfather, who decided he could stand it no longer. He drove swiftly down a side road, coming out in front of the hearse and, in a remarkable breach of decorum, took up his position at the head of the funeral column on its way to the graveyard.

Jack's schooling from the age of eight until he went to art school, on his return to London in 1887, was in Sligo. His father claimed that there was only one thing to be said about it:

During all his time as a schoolboy he was never known to leave the lowest place in his class. There he stayed and there he was contented to stay. Lucky Jack! Well constellated Jack! Had he lived with me I should have seen that he learned his lessons . . . but if he neglected his lessons he kept to his own ideas, his own plans, his life plan as it turned out to be, that is he diligently observed and diligently drew what he observed.[9]

Jack gives us only hints about those schooldays. He went to the grammar school in Sligo. Irked because he thought that people later believed it was Willie who had gone there, he told the Irish actor, Jack MacGowran: 'You know, I was the boy who walked the road to Grammar School in Sligo – but – when one removes one's personage from a place, one remembers only the name. Now they think that the Yeats that is buried there is me.'[10] Before grammar school he went to a private establishment run by the three Blythe sisters, where one of his contemporaries was the youngest sister of the writer, Susan Mitchell.[11] He thought the level of teaching rather poor. Then, as was the form a century later in many schools, history for young people pinned its drama on such 'silly old wives tales' as Alfred the Great and the burning of the cakes.

> Whenever I passed the school I wish I had the heart to do as a bookmaker's clerk I know of in London, who, whenever he passes his boyhood's 'College for the sons of gentlemen' stoops clothed as he is in gorgeous raiment and gathers up the mud of the street in his hands and spatters all the windows and he doesn't care that the place has long ceased to be a school.[12]

Jack wrote a number of letters to members of his family from Merville during his schooldays in Sligo. Contrary to his father's appraisal they show him to have been competitive in his attitude, and good at school. Far from being at the bottom of the class, he was often at the top, and he consistently recorded, in letters from 1883 to 1886, his high marks in examinations and the possibility of getting prizes. In a letter to Lolly he wrote: 'I was first in the Exam 66 the next to me was Vernon fifty two . . .' The following year he wrote: 'I am second in my class, I was 68 per cent last time. I dont think I will be as good this week Wood is third.' And in a later letter, also to Lolly: 'I am second of my class now There is to be another Exam on the 22nd for Scripture for the bishops medal and some books in our class friends are invited to come.' And at the end of one summer term, he wrote:

> We get our holidays tomorrow I think, I suppose we will get six weeks, we had an examination today I was pretty good in some things but I think I will not get a prize because Eads and Woods were better than me and Middleton was about the same as Eads but we will have French, Latin, Scripture and Recitation tomorrow and besides the weekly marks will be counted and so I might have a chance of a second prize there will be a separate prize for scripture.[13]

He was also competitive at sport. Lawn tennis was then very popular, and there was a club in Sligo of which Uncles Arthur and Robert, and Aunts Agnes and Alice, were all members. Jack records playing with his Uncle Arthur, and with Lucy Middleton. His game improved sufficiently for him to be able to claim 'I can beat Uncle Arthur very nearly'.[14] He wrote at this time with equal enthusiasm and fluency to both his sisters, charming letters full of chat and humour.

> I will tell you a nice little story 'In a certain school there was one boy who one Saturday had for punishment to say double repetition and when he was saying it he used to make fearful face – and the master to whom he had to say it was very cross so the other boys used to quote Shakespeare in a kind of way and say 'the young man seeking repetition e'en at the cannon's

mouth' Why don't you write to me It is a fearfully wet day I have not much news.[15]

He could also be obscurely witty: one of his earliest surviving letters, from the Sligo days, was written to Lily, and described a new suit made for him, with silk collar and cuffs. It contained an illustration of the head of a cow and an obscure play on words: 'There is no good sending any primroses as you are slow at cow slips.'[16]

He followed the comic papers, the family subscribing to *Punch*, and often sent details of humorous cartoons and stories to one or other of his sisters; it seemed Lolly was the more receptive of the two, responding well to his quaint sense of humour. He wrote affectionately at Christmas, thanking other members of the family for presents and cards, but there is no evidence of him missing them.

As well as making much of Jack's lowly place in the classroom, John Butler Yeats also proudly quotes his own and Jack's friend, York Powell, who was regius professor of modern history at Oxford and a man much interested in education, who later considered Jack Yeats 'the best-educated man he had ever met'.[17]

The richness of his life in Sligo, the colour and the excitement which John Butler Yeats tells us his son observed and then drew, was underpinned by the solid middle-class virtues of his grandparents, who had a clear view based on personal experience of the needs of a young boy growing from childhood into adolescence. Perhaps, in the light of the realities of the relationship between John Butler Yeats and his parents-in-law, his mildly ironic recollection of their place in his son's education will be taken with the pinch of salt it merits: 'Although they did not concern themselves about his education, they were themselves the very best education to a susceptible and affectionate boy like my son, better than any school or than any university. Their influence will last all his life long, and strengthen with every year that passes.'[18]

The rare occasions when John Butler Yeats had first-hand experience of Jack's life in Sligo were either in summer time, during holidays from school when all children roamed the countryside, or at Christmas. John Butler Yeats has Jack seeing and representing

> the dramatic skies, all cloud and storm and sunshine and all the life of that little town and its people, with so many 'characters', and humorists, half-tragic, half-comic. His knowledge of the west of Ireland is amazing; not a detail is missing from his most retentive memory . . . There is a river meandering through the town of Sligo spanned by two bridges. Beneath one of these bridges is a deep pool always full of trout. Jack told me that he has spent many hours leaning over that bridge looking into that pool and he regrets that he did not spend many more hours in that apparently unprofitable pastime.[19]

In reality, Jack's childhood and early adolescence were spent quite conventionally.

Jack modelled his way of walking on his grandfather, an easy, swaying, seaman's lope which he retained all his life. As an old man Jack claimed that he would like to have been able to say he was a sailor, 'because I'd like to be a retired sailor'. But he was neither, although rumours about his sea-going exploits persisted throughout his life.[20] He reinforced the plots of his earliest

25. Jack's letter with a drawing of William Pollexfen, *c.* 1881.

26. The Quays, Sligo.

plays for the miniature theatre from his recollections of the stories told him in childhood by Grandfather Pollexfen, and he created in drawings a world peopled by pirates, their victims, their vessels and their sweethearts.

William Middleton occupied Elsinore, at Rosses Point, all summer, but moved to Ballysodare, from where the Middletons originated, in the winter. Elsinore, which Jack knew well, was said to have underground passages leading to caves overlooking Bowmore Strand, the great sweep of golden sand used for horse- and pony-racing which stretches in a gentle curve north towards Drumcliff Bay, at the north-east corner of Sligo Bay. Elsinore was a house of strange noises, tappings on the windows, footsteps in the night, where door handles turned but where no one came in. It was originally built by a smuggler named Black, whose ghost was supposed to walk on the verandah. Lily stayed there, and one summer's evening she heard voices, and a drunken Italian sailor was brought before William Middleton, who was seated on the verandah. The man, who had been disorderly in some way, was supported by two policemen and declared he had only drunk a glass of milk. 'Lock him up till he's sober' was Middleton's extempore sentence on the malefactor.

Much of the time at Merville Jack was the only guest present, but sometimes visiting sea captains would be invited to dine. If their wives were on board with them, Jack's grandmother would send the car for them, and have them out for lunch. They would be taken for country drives, and sent back to the ship laden with flowers, eggs and cream. Sometimes this would lead to treats for Jack. In 1886 he wrote to Lily:

There is a big steamer here now of which the Captain was here to tea on Monday evening with his wife who is rather nice looking. Willy and I went and had tea with him on Tuesday evening and he gave us each our choice of a walking stick, Willy chose a palm stick and I chose a coffey stick. The captain showed us some card tricks and tricks with money and told us stories.[21]

23

In January 1882 William Middleton died at Merville. He had moved there to be with his sister in his last illness. The successful and profitable partnership which had begun with William Pollexfen's arrival in Sligo half a century earlier was brought to an end and his death marked the beginning of the decline in the business. During the 1880s a number of the company's vessels were sold off.

Amongst the characteristics Jack learned from his grandfather was reserve. In his parents he had witnessed the profound contrast between his father's inexhaustible flow of words, his persistent and often faulty reasoning, and his mother's increasingly pained taciturnity. To some extent, at least, the one must have seemed the cause of the other. In his grandparents he saw greater harmony, and a better balance of strengths. Jack modelled himself on his grandfather's characteristics of reticence about himself, his feelings, his desires and intentions; also privacy about family affairs, personal experiences, and judgments about others. Words were a substitute for deeds, an excuse for action; a burden for those who had to hear them, and then discover that they were hollow. This sad or purposeful lesson, taught from one point of view by his parents, was then taught from an entirely different standpoint by his grandparents. Jack absorbed all this. It gave him subtlety, strength, staying power; and his grandfather's example made him fearless. Jack lived his whole life without ever being afraid of any person or conceding any authority other than through contracts or agreements freely given or made. Within the distinctive commonwealth of the Yeats family, then and later, he was the most calmly independent of them all.

He continued to learn from his grandmother, a calm and even-tempered woman. Some of the servants made a huge impact on Jack, and on the other Yeats children. Kate McDermott used to come down the corridor on all fours at Christmas, and go in behind the screen in the dining room, with lighted tapers or candles in her hair. She made sure she was seen only by the children, and not by older members of the family. 'It was a thrilling moment and required great self-control on all our parts. Kate backed out unseen by the elders and we never told . . . There was another former maid called Bella. She had seen better days. Her parents kept a shop. She used to come to sew and to pack when the aunts were going away.'[22]

Bella was always in demand on the days when the family went to the races at Hazelwood. On these occasions George Pollexfen would drive up from Ballina, with postillions, and his own racehorses. Both he and his younger brother, Frederick Pollexfen, would race, using their own colours, George's were primrose and violet, Frederick's primrose and blue.

> I can see Bella mounted on a chair, being held round the waist by the groom from Ballina, while she squealed with genteel fear as she plaited the horses' manes with ribbons. A great day for Bella and for all of us, driving in state to the races with the outriders, all of us wearing primroses and violets or primroses and forget-me-nots.[23]

Jack's first taste of racing, before experiencing the races he later knew which took place on Bowmore Strand, would have been those at the beautiful course at Hazelwood, where Lolly once ran out at the water jump and was snatched back by her father, from the galloping horses, roaring with rage and fear. Lily remembered the crunch of the hoofs, the smell of bruised grass, the thud of the horses over the jumps.

Bella eventually went to America and married an elderly Frenchman. The servant girls were always going to America. It was as if they came to Merville for domestic training, and then went off to the New World, where real life began, usually in service, either privately or in hotels. 'Often and often were we in the nursery wakened in chilly dawns, to be kissed and cried over by sad emigrants, grandmama tearful and silent standing behind the girl, dressed as if it was 4 o'clock in the afternoon and not 4 o'clock in the morning.'[24] As well as the live-in maids, Mrs Pollexfen kept a supply of what were known to Lily as 'wild colts of girls', who came to work during the day but lived in their own homes. When a live-in maid left, it was from this supply of trainees that she was replaced. Contact was always maintained with those who crossed the Atlantic to work. They were given outfits, and Mrs Pollexfen knew where they lived and when they moved. She wrote and received letters for years. And she kept a special album for photographs which they sent home to her, of themselves, their husbands and their children.

'The servants at Merville played a big part in our lives,' Lily wrote. 'They were so friendly and wise and knew so intimately angels, saints, banshees and fairies. Our English nurses and English servant in London knew none of these, but knew a great deal too much of murders and suicides.'[25] One of them, called Ellie Connolly, loved Willie. She never minded about his clumsiness, or his forgetfulness. He would upset his water jug, or let the fire go out, and she never scolded him. And when the family came home from Liverpool on the boat, there would be a voice from behind a group of quayside labourers, 'The Lord love you, Master Willie.'[26]

The nursery where the children slept, and which Jack used when he lived there on his own, was a long room with four windows which looked out in two directions. Two windows were above the stable yard, two gave a view of the rising fields to the south. The view of country landscape was not much favoured by the children, not even by Jack; he was much more interested in events below, in the stable yard, where Scanlon, the coachman, presided over the busy outdoor life of a large and active household. Waking in the night, they would hear the comforting rattle of the manger chains as the horses moved below, in the stables. Scanlon, according to Lily, used to shave there, using little bits of mirror, propped up in the wall. When washing he would drive the children out, telling them – no doubt intending it to sound like a threat – 'Now, children, I am going to strip.' It was he, according to Lily, who 'settled who was to sit by him on the box and kept us strictly to our turn'. Scanlon spoke in Irish all the time to himself about horses and oats, and the more subtle demands of farriery. His wife, an untidy woman, took snuff and kept the snuffbox 'hidden deep in her bosom among the folds of many little shawls'.[27]

John Butler Yeats wrote of Jack:

> As soon as he left his nurse's arms he began to draw and he has continued to draw ever since . . . About his baby drawings two things were to be noticed. He never showed them to anyone. Also . . . his drawings were never of one object, one person or one animal, but of groups engaged in some kind of drama.[28]

At the time of the drawing 'Jack's education had not got beyond learning his letters'. He recalls Jack bending his head over the table and weeping when one of his aunts failed completely to draw a horse. Jack was then in 'his tender

27. *F.S. Walker*, crayon drawing said by Lily to be Jack's earliest.

infancy . . . very chubby and rosy, with large blue eyes and fair hair, a perfect Cupid, and the darling of kind ladies.' He was also, at that stage and later, not entirely in command of the difficult business of correctly drawing a horse. Even much later many of the ubiquitous representations of horses by the artist demonstrate often lunatic contortions on the long and difficult road towards absolute mastery, which came only in the 1890s.

Among the works that we have which date from the period before he left Sligo, in 1887, should be mentioned one early drawing (fig. 27), a portrait sketch, his first picture of the Metal Man at Rosses Point, and the two small story books about the 'Pasha'.[29] Lily came across the drawing among Lolly's things, when she was sorting them after her death, and inscribed on the back:

> I enclose Jack's first known drawing. I came on it among Lolys (sic) things. It is a portrait of F.S. Walker the artist and very like. Jack was so young he didnt know his name and called him the Irishman he had one of those unfortunate swellings on one side of his face that was always there. Jack has given him it.[30]

It is not known what brought him into contact with the Yeats family, though John Butler Yeats's various attempts at getting work as an illustrator may have brought them together.

The picture of the Metal Man, in mixed media on a stiff card, is something of a curiosity. Jack has fixed in place at the point where the statue meets the stone base, a small glass phial of phosphorus, which no doubt once glowed. The drawing is forceful, the man seen from below, as if drawn from a boat, out in the sound across from Rosses Point.[31]

The two small picture-books tell us much about the young artist. They date from the summer of 1885. The first, 'The Beauty and the Beast', was given to Lolly; the second, called simply 'The Pasha' (fig. 28), to Lily.[32] 'The Beauty and the Beast' combines that legend with bits out of Cinderella, and is given a setting somewhere within the Middle Eastern minarets of *A Thousand and One Nights*. These are all watercolour, pencil, pen and ink, and are lively drawings, with pretty washes and sustained likenesses, but with no special merit. That is preserved for the second part. Jack does not show the Beast's transformation, but presents us with him as the Prince, a less hand-some figure altogether, wearing a multi-coloured football jersey and a pair of gauntlets, and apparently puny and rather worried. Beauty is unimpressed. The Pasha is shown 'in the days of prosperity'. This is the best drawing in the book, full of life and movement. Like John Butler Yeats, the Pasha has acquired, with the turning of one page, a long flowing beard, and is stepping along, dressed in colourful blue and grey pantaloons, white socks , pink shoes, and with a pink turban on his head.

On the cover of the second story-book is a watercolour drawing of a more aged version of the Pasha. He holds his scimitar behind his back. Another scimitar is suspended in the air underneath the title. The story begins dramatically enough with a title in Jack's youthful and uncertain hand, 'he discharges a servant'. This familiar household event, motivated more by shortage of pay on the employer's side than misdemeanour on that of the employed, is followed by 'The servant pleads', which shows the Pasha clutch-ing the wretched man by the neck, holding the scimitar in his other hand. With continued drama we switch to another domestic scene — 'he dont like it' — in which the Pasha stands in front of a portrait of himself, on an easel.

28. *The Pasha in the days of prosperity*, mixed media on paper, from 'The Beauty and the Beast', ms. National Library of Ireland.

the Pasha in the days of
prosperity

He is cutting the portrait down the centre with his scimitar. A servant, to the right, is running out of the picture, and out of the studio. What more telling justification than this never ending event in the career of the father, his perpetual dissatisfaction with portraits? The final page has simply a wash drawing of the overall symbol of the Pasha's authority: the scimitar, hanging, disembodied, on the back cover of the little book which must have been read and admired by Lily during that 1885 summer respite in Sligo, when the continued vicissitudes of the family would have been debated in a mood of resignation or blame.

It gave Jack pleasure and delight to give pleasure and delight with his drawings. It is something which he enjoyed giving at all times, particularly to those he loved, and among these the two grandparents stood very high. They had given him so much of the security, comfort and richness in his childhood which in different ways had been denied his brother and sister. It is certainly the truth that his early life, after the painful and difficult years in which the whole Yeats family shared in the prolonged struggles of John Butler Yeats, moved into clear, calm waters during the Sligo years, and gave Jack an advantage which would benefit him throughout his life.

Jack's grandmother was herself an amateur artist, who painted capable watercolours when she had time, and sent one of her children to art school. It tells us something of her wisdom and judgment when art had been the source of so much misery in her daughter's life, that she should have encouraged Jack to follow the same profession. 'When urged by his unselfish and noble-minded grandmother . . . he set his face towards London and came to me and entered an art school.'[33] It is not known what her husband thought about Jack and art; not only had he no artistic talent that we know of, but had learnt, with steadily increasing pain on his eldest daughter's behalf, and from a more rigorous business standpoint, just how perilous the career of art could be to a man and to any family which depended on the profession. And here was his best-loved grandson showing an unswerving talent for drawing and painting, and making the ominous decision to undertake a training in art when the time came. It must have been endorsed, however.

Jack's departure, at the end of the time spent with his grandparents, marked the end of an era. He left to go to art school in 1887. The Pollexfen house, Merville, was sold the year before, and his grandparents, with all their children either married or gone, including poor William in his lunatic asylum in Northampton – the greatest sorrow in his grandmother's life – moved to Rathedmond, a less imposing, less gracious, but still quite large house on the Strandhill road. Management of the business was now in the hands of George Pollexfen, a solemn, serious-faced autocrat who loved hunting and believed – wrongly, as it turned out – that the business would thrive in its old ways, without any innovative skills. He lived across the road from the new house. William Pollexfen became concerned now with the final settling of his affairs, and walked often to the Church of St John's where he was supervising his own and his wife's tomb, and the memorial which would be placed on the walls in the chancel. The days of the pony phaeton were over. Jack had learnt much from his grandmother, but infinitely more from his grandfather, probably understanding this difficult but rewarding individual better than anyone else.[34]

29. William Pollexfen in old age, c. 1890.

CHAPTER THREE

Art School in London 1887–1889

It is jolly having Jack back

JOHN BUTLER YEATS'S first full portrait in oils of Jack is among the finest he painted (fig. 30).[1] In the first of two youthful diaries of this time, Jack records sittings with his father from the very beginning of 1888.[2] These diary entries suggest that the portrait is already well started and so may well have been commenced in Dublin, late in 1886, or immediately after the family's return to London to the Eardley Crescent house. His youthful features are in marked contrast with the worldly wisdom of his eyes. They are filled with sadness, and look upon his father in unspoken judgment. The subject of this haunting work is at the end of his childhood, though still to all appearances a child. Realities, harsh ones, have touched him. The happy years in the west of Ireland are, for the present, over. The struggle for existence, the struggle to make his own way in London, now faces him. The innate wisdom of his genius gazes calmly, almost pityingly out. With a rare mixture of economy and perception, John Butler Yeats portrays the emotions carefully balanced, the passions burning beneath the surface in this brilliant study of his youngest surviving child.

Jack was sixteen years old. Physically, as other portraits and photographs show us, Jack was a slow developer. In the later John Butler Yeats portrait, from about 1894, he is still raw-boned and youthful, and has not yet the mature appearance which is to be seen in the 1899 drawing.[3] In contrast to the later works, where it is interesting to see the degree to which Jack has withdrawn into himself, here, in *Jack Yeats as a Boy*, we have eye-contact of a depth and feeling that is remarkably revealing.

The painter of this work had been trying to establish himself in Dublin and make a practice there of professional portraiture. The experiment had failed. By 1886 John Butler Yeats was on the move once again. Jack had been drawn back directly into the family life so affected by this man's ineptitude, and perhaps his eyes register the fact. Back now in London Jack was self-contained and relaxed. From his diary it is clear that he dealt with his new life in a sensible and balanced way. He went to art school, did everything required of him, and enjoyed it. He had fun with his sisters and brother. They went out together, to the theatre, skating, and to see friends. He drew constantly, and often very wittily. He undertook commissions for cartoons and illustrations, and he read widely. Unlike the other three children, he had known of the family vicissitudes mostly from a distance, and possibly distilled by his grandparents. Rejoining them he had come armed with stability and

confidence; at the same time, as the youngest, he was entitled to a measure of special indulgence from the others.

Jack's stability and independence were strengthened now by the maturing of his own character. He had maintained his Christian faith, which continued to survive in the face of his father's egocentric agnosticism. In marked contrast with the pursuit by his brother of eccentric beliefs and dogmas, and to his sisters' admiration, Jack remained a lifelong church-goer. In this he was fulfilling his mother's wishes for all of them, as well as conforming to the staunch, Church of Ireland faith of his grandparents.[4] But he was not merely conforming. His faith was genuine and lasting. It inspired much of his art, both his painting and writing, and there are many biblical echoes in the events in his novels, and the subject-matter of his pictures. The detail is elusive. From an early age Jack had defined permanently what God to follow and which sacraments mattered. From his early monumental religious banners, to a late canvas like *The Basin in Which Pilate Washed his Hands*, there is evidence of a rock-like steadiness of belief.

Politics also mattered. In a letter early in 1888 Willie writes to his friend, the poet and novelist Katherine Tynan, 'Jack has gone to the meeting in Hyde Park for the reception of the Irish Members'. This meeting, attended by 50,000 people, and organised by Liberal Party and Home Rule associations, was to welcome T.D. Sullivan and other members at Westminster of the Irish Parliamentary Party who had been imprisoned under the Conservatives' Crimes Act. Jack alone in the family actually went to the meeting. Was it a commitment, or merely curiosity? He had come from a settled and staunchly Unionist household. Attitudes there had been benignly pragmatic towards agrarian unrest, poverty and emigration. William Pollexfen, as part of the town's merchant class, itself associated with Protestantism and Freemasonry, was a firm opponent of political violence and unrest, and like so many of his class tended towards silence on the larger political issues.

It was a significant time in Irish history. Parnell was supreme within the Irish Parliamentary Party, and had made Home Rule central to the Liberal Party agenda. He had benefited from Fenian extremism, while at the same time controlling it and making it marginal to the strategy of a genuinely powerful, even formidable Irish presence at Westminster. The occasion on that cold Monday in February at Hyde Park was to be a demonstration of power and of intent, complicated by the fact that the Liberals had lost power precisely because of Gladstone's espousal of Home Rule.

If not as the returned prodigal son, Jack asserted himself as a new focus of firmness and determination within a family struggling and demoralised under the poverty-stricken ministrations of the father. Others perceived the situation differently. Willie, writing of John Butler Yeats during this period, 'saw his mind in fragments',[5] but he added that the fragmentary material always had 'hidden connections I only now begin to discover'. Jack was never of the same opinion. His view of his father was generally cool and critical, if at times coloured by concern for his mother and her suffering and worry.

It was a family driven by mutual criticism and well-developed outspokeness, and ironically, for a man unable to earn the necessary funds for family prosperity, the strongest propensity to criticise and deliver judgments came from the father. In one letter John Butler Yeats had the temerity to advise Sarah Purser: 'As to your work, I have here also only one fault to find – *you are too anxious to arrive*.'[6] His own problem continued to be the opposite;

31

31. Olympia, on its completion, and as Jack would have known it at the time of the earliest Buffalo Bill shows.

33. (opposite page) *Cowboy on Rearing Horse,* early sketch, *c.* 1889.

32. Buffalo Bill Cody

his life as portrait-painter, and then as landscape artist having failed, he now painted the occasional, and often very beautiful genre-works and portraits – mainly of friends and family, because the tricky business of getting a proper fee, and abiding by an agreed timetable, could be obviated. There was no professional practice. Luckily, an alternative temporary salvation offered itself.

By 1885, brief rescue for the fallen family fortunes had come in the form of the Ashbourne Act. This piece of legislation might have been designed for the likes of John Butler Yeats. It allowed tenants to buy out their holdings from their landlords, if the landlords were willing, and it subsidised the deal from government funds in order to encourage a genuine shift in land owner-ship. If we combine John Butler Yeats's political unease about the ownership of land in Ireland, his shortcomings in the management of his own estate, his disappointment over the attempts to create a portrait painter's practice in Dublin, we have the explanation for the disposal of his property in Ireland and the family's return to London at the end of 1886. There were then successive difficulties, and one disaster. The family arrived back in England piecemeal, and stayed with relations while the new home, at 58 Eardley Crescent, was prepared for them. It was a horrible house. Susan suffered a stroke there, which was to be followed by another, later in the year. She was effectively an invalid for the remaining twelve years of her life.

Before beginning the serious business of his art school studies, Jack enjoyed the sudden and all-embracing delights of Olympia, and its Buffalo Bill Cody spectacular, during the summer of 1887. It seemed tailor-made for the young man, familiar with west of Ireland circuses, fairs and race meetings. The Grand Hall at Olympia stood conveniently close to Eardley Crescent, just a three-minute walk along Warwick Road. It was an indoor stadium, first opened in 1886. As well as providing space for lavish military tournaments and reviews, spectaculars which became a mainstay of its entertainment for the next hundred years, the hall was also a place for circuses and other entertainments, 'rational healthy amusement for the people; to reinvigorate by brilliant demonstrations the natural love of athletic exercises and con-tests of skill; to raise the tone of popular taste by entertainments and displays . . . of the purest and highest character; to educate . . . by exhibitions of art . . .'[7] These expressions represent all the things that Jack Yeats loved at that time. More seriously, they also embrace the subject-matter of his early work as a professional artist.

Olympia was huge. Designed by the architect, Henry E. Coe, on a truly grand scale, its greatest feature was the roof, built of glass, zinc and iron, and spanning 170 feet to a height of over 100 feet (fig. 31). It covered three and a half acres. And the lighting was electric. It opened in 1886 with the Paris Hippodrome Circus. Queen Victoria visited, beginning a royal family involvement with Olympia lasting for a century. And she came back for more of the same light-hearted stuff when Buffalo Bill arrived for the first time in the summer of 1887.

The Buffalo Bill Cody show attracted enormous attention, and continued in performance at Olympia for almost twenty years (fig. 32). The first appear-ance of Cody was treated with the utmost seriousness. The Indian Wars were not yet over. In the United States the West was still Wild. And the impact of Cody's whole career was carefully manipulated to the fullest advantage by himself and those running the show. Cody's 1887 European tour was a huge

34 and 35. Drawings from Jack's diary for 1888.

success. Queen Victoria not only visited it, but met Cody. He was also introduced to the prince and princess of Wales. When the first London show closed *The Times* gave it credit for initiating a debate about the establishment of 'a Court of Arbitration for the settlement of disputes between this country and the United States. . . Nothing that is American comes altogether amiss to an Englishman'.[8] With his buckskin clothes fringed with tasselled leather, his hair flowing over his shoulders, his 'imperial' – that tufted beard on the chin called after the type of face hair worn by the Emperor Napoleon III – and his entourage of Indian chiefs wearing full ceremonial costume and head-dresses, he found time to go everywhere, see everything, and to be seen by all the world, capturing the imagination of young and old alike.

His importance for Jack Yeats was practical; he saw horses in action, in the most exciting tableaux possible, and he drew them. Not only did he draw them and the cowboys and indians riding them, but he went on drawing them through the whole of the following year. In his 1888 diary, Jack drew more horses and Wild-West scenes than anything else (figs 34–5). They are galloping, rearing, bucking, or reined back on their haunches. They are seen from every angle, with riders and without. And their appearance is punctuated by realistic little sketches of bar-room confrontations, discussions, fist-fights and pow-wows. John Butler Yeats, more than once, suggested that Jack's first drawings of horses were 'The ramping roaring rearing horse which was his infant's delight'.[9] His boyish horse drawings were realistic, and the sense of movement which he achieved as a result of seeing them, day after day, galloping round the Olympia arena, is convincing and skilful (fig. 33). These are among the liveliest of his diary sketches.[10] One example is his pen and watercolour study of a lynching (fig. 36). The hard-bitten cowboys, toting their guns, and crowding around the scaffold, witness a tough-faced leader, with classic gnarled features and frowning eyes, standing in final judgment over the supposed horse-rustler, as he pleads for his life, the noose around his neck and slung over the branch of the tree. But then Jack throws in the lifebelt of inevitable, added humour, by making the victim a trembling and callow youth, as incapable of horse thieving as he would be of stealing rabbits or apples. 'All I ask now gentlemen is do I look like a horse thief,' appeals the condemned man to the indifferent sporting gentlemen – characters whom we are going to meet later among the crowds discovered by Jack around the boxing rings in the East End of London, witnesses to the same kind of prospective slaughter. He used cowboy subjects in paintings as late as the 1940s, and was quite happy to absorb the unflattering later revelations about aspects of Cody's career which are less honourable than his first great impact on London suggests.[11]

Olympia, as an apology for the disturbance, issued free season tickets to local households. No one in the Yeats family was interested except Jack. He went at every opportunity, and came to know each detail of the show from the crashes and roars which echoed from the hall. He could explain each event and predict the next explosion of simulated warfare, to the delight of the rest of the family.

Jack's infatuation with Bill Cody also offered a welcome escape from the house in Eardley Crescent. Lily wrote, 'at the back was what the landlord may have called a garden, it was to us a bit of cat-haunted, sooty gravel, & as the house was the last in the crescent, it was the shape of a piece of cheese.'[12] Lily and Lolly came to the house after the others, and Jack made them close their

36. *The Hanging*, early drawing, mixed media, *c.* 1889.

eyes and led them to the back window, overlooking the garden. 'Now he said Look & as Americans say to those seeing Niagara for the first time how do you feel. And so the back garden became to us a joke.'[13] It was the year of Queen Victoria's Jubilee, and Lily particularly remembered the airless heat of the city, made more oppressive by the 'horrible house'.

But Jack needed to learn his trade. He had already developed his own style, and was ambivalent about what art school might add to this. He was, in fact, a reluctant student, and his art education was far from perfect or comprehensive. He was interested in too much else. Nevertheless, he went to several art schools, beginning with South Kensington in the autumn of 1887, where he studied with Professor Frederick Brown.[14] He moved the following year to the Chiswick School of Art, at Bedford Park, where he studied from 1888. He recorded being at the West London School of Art from 1890 to 1893, and at the Westminster from 1890 to 1894, and he saw nothing strange in recording the overlap between these two institutions which were several miles apart.[15]

He seems to have applied himself reluctantly but obediently to classical drawing – from the antique, from the life, or related to design and decoration – then a central part of art school training. But nothing has survived of what he did at art school. Also, there is nothing in his early work, and very little later, to indicate that any of the main strands in teaching practice at the time had even a superficial impact on his technique or his imagination, save possibly an emphasis on design which came out later in his *Broadsheets* and *A Broadside*. He *tried* to be conscientious. We know from the 1888 diary that he regularly attended classes in classical drawing from the antique plaster models, and life classes; and he records 'horse anatomy' and muscle drawing both in words and pictures, as well as 'shaded hand', and 'shaded foot'. He told Lady Gregory, when her son Robert started his life class studies, 'In South Kensington for two months I drew eyes and noses with a thick and thin pencil line until the paper was grey with the marks of my grubby paws.'[16]

His apparent dislike for art school teaching, and his dismissal of its importance, may be a later invention. In those early art school days, he did what was necessary, stuck at it, and at the same time got on with other, more exciting activities, including commercial work inspired by an urge to get out and earn money with his artistic skills. This attitude was not uncommon among art students at the time. Art schools generally were the subject of criticism, and during these years were under scrutiny which eventually led to reform. Harry Furniss, for whom Jack later worked, and who studied art in Dublin, wrote: 'as years went on I made a really serious effort to study at an art school under the Kensington system, which I must confess I believe to be positively prejudicial to a young artist possessing imagination and originality'.[17] These sentiments were widely echoed.

Jack was rescued from the indifferent resources of the art education system when the family returned to Bedford Park, in Chiswick, in the spring of 1888. At least, what was left of the Yeats household went back. At the time of the move this consisted of their father, Willie, Jack, and Lolly. Their previous residence there, which had begun in 1879 at 8 Woodstock Road, had been one of the happier periods for the whole family. For Jack it had been brief, since it coincided with the decision to send him to Sligo, and he had stayed only for the first few months. This time, however, it would be his home for an important period in his life – the completion of his education, the beginning of his professional career and its expansion into a busy life as a journalist, as well as his decision to get married.

The second Bedford Park house, at 3 Blenheim Road, was not as attractive as the first, less spacious, with smaller rooms, and a much smaller garden. But it was cheap, with an annual rent of £45, convenient for Turnham Green railway station, on the District Line, and it was in congenial surroundings. The close proximity of the railway station mattered for the other members of the family. At this stage the principal breadwinner was Willie, then making a living from journalism. He wanted to write about literature, and to engage in literary criticism, but his father disapproved:

> He wants me to write stories. I am working at one, as you know. It is almost done now. There is some good character-drawing, I think, but the construction is patchy and incoherent. I have not much hope of it. It will join, I fear, my ever-multiplying boxes of unsaleable MSS work too strange one moment and too incoherent the next for any first-class magazine, and too ambitious for local papers. Yet I don't know that it is ambition, for I have no wish but to write a saleable story.[18]

While Willie was having difficulties selling his writing, John Butler Yeats was having no success at all selling his art. He was trying to sell illustrations to publications based in central London, and also trying to write. His efforts were rather sad. He seems at sea, unable to decide on a direction, thinking up new and doomed schemes. He deployed Lolly to help him. For two months she took daily dictation of a ghost story which was rejected by *Harper's*, never subsequently published, and has since vanished; the drawings remain in the possession of the family. Referring to Lolly's diary covering this period, Murphy says of the more than fifty entries about John Butler Yeats, 'there is no mention of JBY's making any money whatever'.[19]

37. Sarah Purser, who encouraged and supported both Jack and his father in their careers.

Jack made his own contribution, helped by Sarah Purser, who commissioned designs for menus, visiting cards and Christmas cards. She asked friends, including Lady Cloncurry and a Mrs Farrar, and a certain baron, possibly the Comte de Basterot, as well as George du Maurier, to support Jack.[20] Some of her efforts resulted in commissions which he worked at during the summer of 1888. At the end of July, missing his old 'home', he went back to Sligo for a holiday, and it was from there he wrote:

> I will send the menus immediately. I think Du Mauriers letter was very nice indeed but I didn't think to keep a copy; I sent the menus to Mrs Farrar, but I didn't hear anything about them except that she had got them. I have nearly finished the baron's I have some Name cards to do yet for him and then I will have 3 Doz of each. Will you tell me his address when you write . . . Did Lady Cloncurry like her cards.[21]

The 1888 diary demonstrates clearly the beneficial effects of his Sligo holiday (figs 38–9). 'Arrived this morning in the land of the free,' he recorded, for 2 August, and the pages, from then until the end of September, are crammed with an account of all the things he did: riding his pony, Lucy, out at Rosses Point, travelling around with his grandfather, going to the Club with Uncle George, and going up Lough Gill with Uncle Arthur, who worked in Liverpool, and was home on holiday. He went to the 'Back Strand Races' on

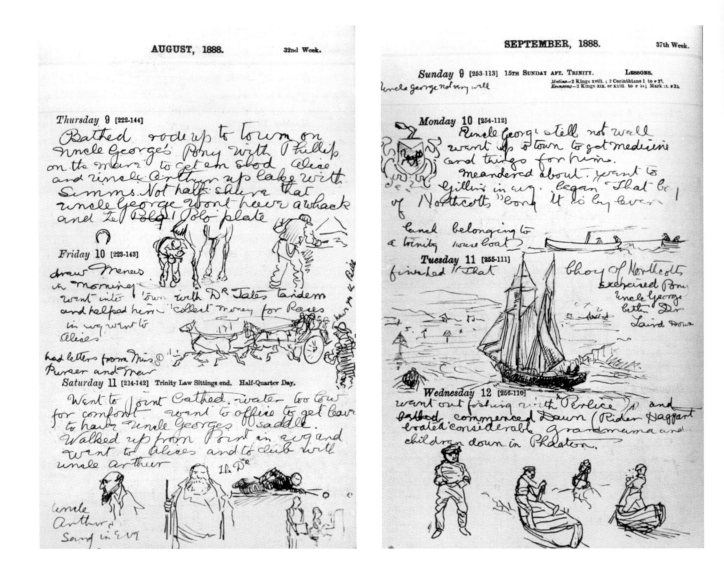

38 and 39. Drawings from Jack's diary for August and September 1888, depicting his time in Sligo.

Bowmore Strand, describing it as 'Bully', and he recorded there his first image of Muldoon, the well-known west coast jockey, who was the subject of a ballad, and later inspired Jack's view of how Synge's Christy Mahon would appear after the race in *The Playboy of the Western World*. There were parties in the evening at aunts' houses; Uncle Arthur, who was musical, sang, and Jack drew him. He went out in Pollexfen steamers, he boated, wrote his name on the Metal Man, swam from sailing dinghies. And he travelled to Lissadell for a cricket match between Lissadell and Bundoran. 'After every race the people want to fight. There is going to be a cattle show round here soon . . . I was down at Lissadell at a cricket match. They were all there.'[22] There is a drawing of Muldoon shaping up for a fight in his diary, as well as in his letter to Sarah Purser. And when recording the cricket match he adds a telling phrase not used in his letter: 'Spent the day all among the nobs oh!' He was always irreverent towards 'nobs', and had a lifelong distaste for pomp and ceremony. He reported that everyone was well at home.

But he had only limited time to think of London. His diary for the whole of August is packed with detail. He was made to have his hair cut, and did a tiny drawing of the ordeal. He read voraciously, devouring *Huckleberry Finn* – which remained a favourite book all his life – as well as stories by Bret Harte, who was probably his favourite author of all. He read Hardy's *The Trumpet Major*, and novels by Charles Lever and Rider Haggard. He does not identify the author of *Flag of Distress*, but describes it as a 'good old fashioned plug ugly sort of book'. Towards the end of September he sailed back to Liverpool and recorded in his diary, 'hadn't strength enough to kick a blind cat suffering from a severe attack of the jim jams'.[23] He stayed there with Uncle Arthur for a few days, read *Tom Sawyer*, another book for which he had a lifelong affection, and bought a present of slippers for his mother.

Lolly gives a charming picture of Jack at this time. 'We expect the Baby home this week,' she wrote in her diary. (It was a neighbour, Miss Cole, who named him 'the Baby' 'because he has such nice sleepy blue eyes'.) Lolly records, on Tuesday 2 October: 'Another horrid day – letter from Jack he arrived Blundell Sands 9.30 Sunday night is going to stay a few days, just as well maybe as there is no money and none too much food here.'[24] On Saturday 6 October, Lolly wrote:

> Cold and dreary no letter from Jack but at about 8 o'clock in the evening we heard a loud rat tatting at the letter box which if you please was Master Jack we were glad to see him, he looks well we got him tea and cold beef & he said he had some shrimps himself in his portmanteau which he forthwith began rummaging for in the search he came upon and brought out a large bag of damsons & box of kippered herrings & finally the shrimps which turned out not to be loose as we supposed but in a broken cup made their appearance out of the pocket of his best coat – later on in the evening Lily while rummaging in his pocket came on an old piece of rope at which he called out put that back that has hair he is a comical boy & I cant convey the serious way in which he delivers these remarks, we finished up the evening by having kippered herrings 'from stornaway' for supper. It is jolly having Jack back.[25]

He arrived in London to find orders for sketches. He wrote, 'The air is stiff with women'. He had sold his first drawing for publication in April 1888.[26] In a letter to Katherine Tynan, on 11 April 1888, Willie writes: 'Jack had his first printed drawing the other day in the "Vegetarian" a drawing of Fairies. There will be another this week. I will try and get you a copy'[27] (fig. 40). A sketch of a man and a boy feeding birds appeared in *The Vegetarian* on 14 April.[28] Willie later reported in June: 'He has another batch of drawings in the Vegetarian and is going next Saturday to a picnic given by the Vegetarian Society, I think, to make sketches for the paper.'[29] Jack was already, in effect, a professional illustrator. *The Vegetarian* was his first sustained source of income, and the association was to last until 1895. Willie had difficulty getting a copy of *The Vegetarian* for Katherine Tynan, but told her on 20 April that although Jack 'has had a great many [drawings] taken, only three have yet come out'.[30]

Though the paper was humorous – at least in those early years – its purpose was serious. Vegetarianism – the word itself only came into use in 1847 – had grown into an international movement, with many different societies around the world and widespread propaganda, including magazines promoting the

40. Jack's first drawing for *The Vegetarian*, 1888.

different advantages of a diet which excluded 'flesh and fowl' and frequently fish as well. In addition to the justification on grounds of health – animals being thought of as disease-carriers, and responsible for gout, cancer, and other illnesses – cogent and valid arguments on economic, social, racial and character grounds were put forward. One argument was that vegetarianism benefited sportsmen – later successes in track and field events were recorded by vegetarian competitors – and this appealed to Jack, whose drawings included several of sporting subjects.[31]

Jack had been introduced to the society and to vegetarianism the previous year. Among those who were engaged in planning the publication of the weekly humorous paper was Harry Hall, who may himself have been a member of the Vegetarian Society.[32] He was to become a good friend of Jack. Both he and his father knew the Yeats family, Sydney Prior Hall, who lived in Swiss Cottage, having been an art student with John Butler Yeats. Harry Hall's generally boisterous and at times mischievous sense of humour appealed to all the Yeatses. On one visit he exploded gunpowder to amuse Jack and his two sisters, who were on a joint visit to the Halls and the Walkers.[33] Though Harry Hall's behaviour was sometimes alarming, his father clearly had charm: 'Miss Jowitt nearly lost her heart to Mr Hall he is a awefully nice man'.[34] On another occasion, when visiting the Yeatses, Harry Hall took an interest in their cat, Dan, and contrived to write on the cat's collar 'Daniel O'Connell Esqre 3 Blenheim Road, Bedford Park.' Poor Dan the cat subsequently died, and was buried in the garden by Harry Hall and Jack.

Jack told Sarah Purser in September: 'I have sent some hunting sketches to the Graphic; but have'nt heard yet, but if they return them I will try them for the Pictorial.' These sketches were precise, linear drawings, carefully coloured, and in the manner of Randolph Caldecott.[35] One of them is on the verso of his Wild West drawing of the lynching of a horse thief, a group of huntsmen mill about in a composition which lacks focus, and which Jack clearly rejected, scribbling over it in pencil. But two other small pen and ink drawings, coloured in wash, demonstrate an accomplished feeling for line and movement, and a sense of humour well suited to the market he was aiming at.[36]

Bedford Park was a modern housing development, which was appropriate in its character to the needs of the Yeats family and offered Jack an art school within walking distance of home. But it also gave them a coherently planned, community framework for their somewhat fractured lives. Bedford Park remains to this day certainly one of the most successful of the many garden suburbs developed in England.[37] It was a way of life, and was so intended, making it the butt of jokes. Largely designed for artists, its most famous residents included Lucien Pissarro, who lived at 62 Bath Road between 1897 and 1902, and T.M. Rooke, who lived at 7 Queen Anne's Gardens. Pissarro's father, Camille, did paintings of Bedford Park; and the Yeatses – Willie, Jack, Lily and Lolly – all took dancing lessons in Rooke's house. Lolly, and then Lily, attended the art school, and they all became involved in other artistic activities including the summer sketching club. There were sports and entertainments. Jack recorded playing badminton – 'with the accent on the Bad' – in his 1889 diary. It was clearly a craze of the time.

The Chiswick School of Art opened in the autumn of 1881, just five years after the overall scheme at Bedford Park had started (fig. 41).[38] It was therefore in place at the time of the Yeats family's first period in Bedford

Park, though not, of course, while Jack was with them. One of those promoting the scheme was the younger brother of the man responsible for the overall development of Bedford Park. Joseph Comyns Carr was the friend of Edward Burne Jones, William Morris and Dante Gabriel Rossetti. He was an art critic, and editor of *The English Illustrated Magazine*; he was also associated with Sir Coutts Lindsay in the founding of the Grosvenor Gallery, so that the weight he threw behind the art school was significant. Its first directors brought together two traditions. E.S. Burchett came from the Science and Art Department at South Kensington; F. Hamilton Jackson came from the Slade School of Art and was a first class medallist of the Royal Academy.

It is perhaps appropriate that when it opened, in 1881, a *conversazione* was held in the presence of Thomas Armstrong, the Art Director of the Science and Art Department at South Kensington, and a distinguished figure in late nineteenth-century art and art politics. George Augustus Sala gave an address. What could have suited John Butler Yeats more than a community in which conversation was one of the admired arts?[39]

The Chiswick school had modest beginnings. Most students – seventy-one at the outset – came in the evening, with only thirteen full-time, or day students. But it developed rapidly, and by the time Jack enrolled there, in the autumn of 1888, there were 273 students. Three years earlier it had become the Chiswick School of Art and Science, but art students outnumbered those taking science or technical studies by four to one.

41. Chiswick School of Art at Bedford Park where Jack was a pupil, from *The Building News*, 25 November 1881.

The year of Jack's entry was the school's high point. Numbers declined thereafter, and there is some evidence that the administration came adrift. In any case, local government reforms shifted control of the school to Middlesex, inevitably diluting the special Bedford Park atmosphere. This process of change began during Jack's student days, but was mainly advanced after he had left. It was funded, in part, by 'whiskey money', revenues transferred under the 1890 Customs and Excise Act.

Jack tells us little of his own experiences at the Chiswick School of Art. There was a design club at the school, and he told Sarah Purser in December 1888 'I send things but the master generally says "The artist evidently is not serious" or something to that effect.'[40] He also commented: 'The Director of the Art School is a desperate man for telling yarns. He told us that his father (they're all about near relatives) once painted a monochrome of a band and it was so like that the porter dusted it for ten years under the idea that it was a cast.'[41] But his letters to her are far more concerned with the work he was doing for her and her friends, and his early efforts to sell drawings commercially. In December he reported on his illustrations for one of his brother's poems.

In one of his characteristic illustrations in the letter he depicts the whole Yeats family at a public gallery viewing the portrait of a judge. He was good at injecting humour into these swiftly drawn sketches, and shared with William Orpen a capacity to make fun of himself more than any of the other figures in whatever event is being described, thus adding strength to the wit. Here he shows himself half the size of everyone else, and eyeing the catalogue with demonic urgency, while his father, the great procrastinator, has his head thrown back in solemn assessment of style, or the professional application he was finding so difficult to sell. Willie appears to be writing a note.

Jack's menus were strange affairs. One that has survived shows two curious beasts with backs like dragons, sitting down to a meal in a cauldron. He also

42. Design for a doyley.

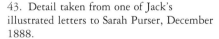
43. Detail taken from one of Jack's
illustrated letters to Sarah Purser, December
1888.

did designs for 'doyleys' (fig. 42). He clearly got on extremely well with Sarah Purser, not the easiest of achievements, and they remained lifelong friends. His letters are peppered with witty drawings, one of which depicts a friend of Willie's whom the family nicknamed 'the beautiful Theodore' because he said of Jack's brother 'we think him very beautiful'. A drawing of him sitting on a chair is beside a rather sad profile of John Butler Yeats looking old and battered (fig. 43).

Jack kept at his studies, even while he was making every effort to earn money. He was selling pictures the following summer through a shop in Piccadilly run by a man called Young. Some of Jack's sketches were in the window, and he received a commission to do a drawing of a crowd for a member of parliament called Brooke Robinson. By 1889, however, Jack was launched as an illustrator, and clearly found the work both congenial and profitable. The commissions grew steadily in number, as did the outlets, and the range of subject-matter covered sport, entertainment, comedy, including domestic events and mishaps in the street. Jack's commissions, together with the work of everyone else, produced a humming domestic industry in the house. Of course it was not non-stop work. The sisters, together with some friends, anticipating their lifelong interest in book-production and craft, produced a magazine in manuscript called 'The Pleiades', the first issue of which was made for Christmas 1887. There were seven women involved, hence the name, and they met together to read their own work to each other, and criticise it. Though it was a society of 'females', Jack was content to become an 'honorary member'. John Butler Yeats described them as 'a mutual improvement society'.[42] The first number, was an ambitious venture, running to more than 100 pages of manuscript. Jack contributed to it with 'The Diary of Sir Long Lean Claterly Bones', an illustrated narrative of his own devising, though the story may owe something to Mark Twain's 'The Canterville Ghost'.[43] What Jack excelled in was humour, and it is amply demonstrated in his drawings for his sisters' magazine. He contributed 'The Letters of Denis O'Grady', ostensibly sent to London from 'Our West of Ireland Correspondent', who lived in Tullynagracken, Sligo. They depict hunting and sporting scenes, but also included a faint echo of the parish life of St John's Church in Sligo, in a humorous drawing of a window to St Valentine, in 'Tullynagracken Cathedral', showing the saint steaming open a love letter.

It has been traditional to claim no artistic influences on Jack Yeats. In his slightly ponderous introduction to *Jack B. Yeats*, Thomas MacGreevy dismisses virtually all influences, and suggests that Yeats 'obviously found his own way to artistic maturity . . . There is no trace of even approximate imitation of other painters in his work.'[44] And this line is followed by other commentators. Hilary Pyle says 'He worked alone. His model was mankind: his studio the world of his experience.' And she emphasises, not infrequently in her book, his solitary disposition in everything. 'Jack Yeats's basic influences were his personality and his family background.'[45] These of course played a part.

But there was more to it than the solitary development of genius. A particular world of illustration and caricature, powerful throughout the British Isles in the nineteenth century, was the biggest influence on Jack Yeats. This, and its practitioners, created him. This world of humorous graphic art did so as the result of need. It gave him employment. It liberated him from his family. It made him independent, resourceful, inventive. It gave him a profession, which he followed diligently for many years, and never really relinquished until long after the need had vanished. It was responsible almost entirely for the development of his early work, and created the inner convictions about the motive and function of art which were to remain with him throughout his life.

He chose the path of the humorous cartoonist and caricaturist. It was precise, and relatively narrow. It only broadened later. He never sustained any lasting interest in landscape, subject-painting, narrative painting, genre painting, or portraiture. He avoided decorative art, which was also a strong product of the system then prevailing in art schools, and in the workplaces to which a certain number of trained men and women moved for employment after completing the courses at places just like the Chiswick School of Art. And he never engaged in the then popular and widely followed profession of the graphic artist, working in copper, wood or on stone. He may have said that he followed the profession of his father, as if this answered questions. It does not.

Three or four names are important. Jack Yeats's very earliest drawings intended for publication are directly imitative of Randolph Caldecott, with his precise and comprehensive representation. Another powerful early influence was Phil May. Thirdly, there was the distinctive, robust appeal of the earlier artist, Thomas Hood. As he developed, Yeats continued to reflect interest in and admiration for a number of artists, his later style owing something, too, to William Nicholson, ten years younger than himself. And there are others.

In addition to the practitioners, there was the practice. Illustrating as a means of reporting on events imposed strains and stresses of performance, of travel, and of the vicissitudes of climate and circumstance. The demands of this world of capturing event in drawings actually dictated Yeats's life completely for a number of years. It ordered his daily travel, where he went, what he saw and drew, what he earned, how much he did, how quickly, and of course how well. It was a keenly competitive profession, and it required atmosphere, life, a sense of event, truthfulness, and humour. In almost everything he did, then and throughout his later life as a painter, there is movement. And this derived directly from the demands of the editors of the sporting and humorous magazines for which he worked. Line illustration, in its day, was a central part of most branches of journalism. The written word, whether it dealt with humour, sport, social life or history, was permanently underpinned by drawings transferred onto copper, steel, zinc, wood and stone, by a variety of methods, all of which demanded from the artist speed, fluency, accuracy, vigour and – more often than not – humour. The publications in which these drawings appeared were legion, and at the same time ephemeral.[46]

The influence of Randolph Caldecott was considerable.[47] Caldecott, after working for local publications in the north of England, began drawing for *London Society* in 1871, and went on to become a contributor to several other periodicals, including *The Graphic* and *Pictorial World*. From the first parcel of his work 'drawings of matchless freedom spilled out . . . pen and ink sketches full of humour, presenting a world as seen by a jovial overgrown schoolboy'.[48] By the time Jack was growing up in Sligo, virtually all of Caldecott's wonderful illustrated books for children had appeared, and these, together with many other volumes in the same genre, large in scale, and with brilliant illustrations, formed part of Jack's library.[49] Though he was dead before Jack returned to London late in 1886, it was to his nostalgic manner he turned in the earliest drawings he did for sale. Part of the nostalgia was for the eighteenth century, and this dominated a whole period of illustration, attracting numerous exponents of whom Caldecott and Hugh Thomson were the leading artists.[50] The world they depicted was genteel, well-mannered, artificial. The past it recreated was sanitised, with all its robust vulgarity drained away in scrupulous fashion and archaic manner. Apart from its sporting content, it related poorly, both to the life Yeats had known in Sligo, and his new life in London. But it did suit the early transition, while he was coming to terms with the kind of Londoner he wished to be. He saw himself increasingly as a cockney, an 'arf-a-mo' coster-boy, and he developed quite consciously a taste for the low-life which was very clearly at odds with his brother's pursuit of a career as a poet, and his father's self-conscious life as a painter. This was decidedly not for Jack, and it quite soon shifted the focus of his art away from the slightly artificial, early drawings in the Caldecott manner with its tight form of representation to an approach more immediate and spontaneous, to a looser, more flexible Londoner's voice which derived at least some of its characteristics from Phil May, and arguably from the earlier artist, Thomas Hood, and, to a lesser extent, Thomas Hood the Younger. Hood's drawings are frequently based on a single device, often a pun. But it is not the conventional use, where the double meaning of words or phrases is an end in itself; Hood takes the words, and creates the pun in the drawing. There is a crude strength to his work; it is somewhat static; and there are elements of eighteenth-century callousness to the humour. But it did appeal to Jack.

The most important influence, however, was Phil May.[51] Jack Yeats followed May in several of the publications to which he sold drawings. He shared with him a love of the theatre and of sport, of children, of drinking scenes and street life. Yeats too sided with the underdog, and had sympathy with the eccentric. He drew children sympathetically and well. Technically, May developed great economy of line. He used to do drawings in sketchbooks of thin, partly transparent paper, repeating the same subject again and again, but eliminating, as he progressed with a story, many of the lines in order to produce a tightly argued expression of the visual idea.

Jack did not immediately conquer the world of the illustrated paper. His early efforts show a degree of uncertainty, and there was often a hard, slogging side to the work. He was sent off to cover sporting events, he travelled widely, he was sent stories to illustrate. He did small vignettes and decorations. And though we can trace in his printed work during the period 1889–1906 many hallmarks of his later style, it was essentially a period during which he was responsive to the demands made on him by editors who worked in a profession which devoured material, verbal and visual, and in the process came near to consuming the practitioners. May was consumed; succumbing to all the temptations of the bohemian artist's life, he died of phthisis and cirrhosis of the liver at thirty-nine. Jack was more careful. Being an illustrator was a way of earning a living, not a life. It would allow him to escape from his family life, get married, and become an artist in a more lasting and serious fashion. He got better and better at what he did. But even his most brilliant work, from well into the 1890s, belongs essentially to the life of the journalist illustrator.

Chapter Four
Bedford Park – the 1890s

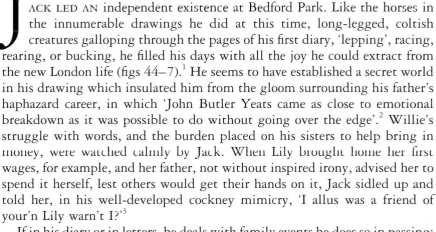

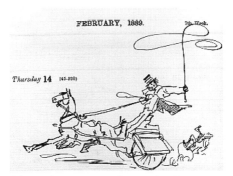

44 and 45. Drawings from Jack's diary, February 1889.

No brain only a nerve centre

JACK LED AN independent existence at Bedford Park. Like the horses in the innumerable drawings he did at this time, long-legged, coltish creatures galloping through the pages of his first diary, 'lepping', racing, rearing, or bucking, he filled his days with all the joy he could extract from the new London life (figs 44–7).[1] He seems to have established a secret world in his drawing which insulated him from the gloom surrounding his father's haphazard career, in which 'John Butler Yeats came as close to emotional breakdown as it was possible to do without going over the edge'.[2] Willie's struggle with words, and the burden placed on his sisters to help bring in money, were watched calmly by Jack. When Lily brought home her first wages, for example, and her father, not without inspired irony, advised her to spend it herself, lest others would get their hands on it, Jack sidled up and told her, in his well-developed cockney mimicry, 'I allus was a friend of your'n Lily warn't I?'[3]

If in his diary or in letters, he deals with family events he does so in passing; the touch is light and affectionate. He ran errands for his brother, going to Kegan Paul, the publishers, for copies of *The Wanderings of Oisin*.[4] The following day, writing to Katherine Tynan, Willie offers to send her a copy from this supply. Later in the spring the two brothers painted a design on the ceiling in Willie's study, and Jack did a drawing. He got on well with Lolly. They went skating together; when she went to Dublin, Jack saw her off. She was the keeper of the family accounts; she was more disposed than her elder sister or Willie to join with Jack in outings and escapades. Close familiarity with the permanently perilous financial situation may well have made her carefree in the face of disaster. Lily was more severe towards Jack. There is only one reference to her at this time: 'Was insulted – Lilly said I had no brain only a nerve centre.'[5] It seems that with his father Jack could be severe enough to intimidate. Willie records a quarrel with John Butler Yeats who followed him up to the bedroom he shared with Jack and tried to pick a fight:

He squared up at me, and wanted to box, and when I said I could not fight my own father replied, 'I don't see why you should not'. My brother, who had been in bed for some time, started up in a violent passion because we had awaked him. My father fled without speaking, and my brother turned to me with, 'Mind, not a word till he apologises'. Though my father and I are very talkative, a couple of days passed before I spoke or he apologised.[6]

45

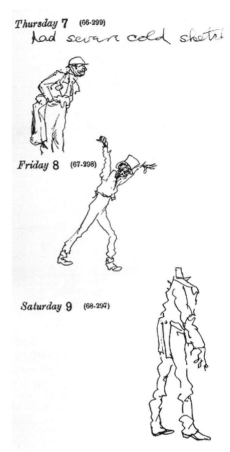

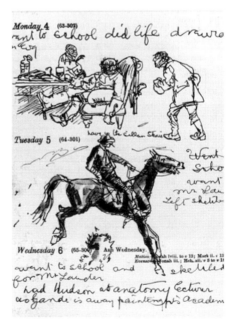

46 and 47. Drawings from Jack's diary, February 1889.

Jack continued his art school studies, including life drawing, recording on one occasion that they had a 'first class modle [sic]', on another that the model was 'middling' but shortly to be replaced by a 'Black man'. It seems that by the autumn he had transferred to evening class. He records numerous occasions when he drew for *The Vegetarian* in the mornings, a principal source of income.

Jack discussed his career with the much older artist, Francis Walker, who was a family friend. Walker was then actively engaged in mezzotint work.[7] He was also an experienced illustrator. On a visit to the Walkers in September, Jack met Joseph Pennell, the American illustrator, and Sir James Drogmole Linton, president of the Royal Institute of Painters in Watercolours.[8] These artists straddled the difficult divide between complicated graphic processes, including the then fashionable soft and hard-ground etching, lithography and mezzotint – on most of which Pennell was a published authority – and the much more mechanical transfer of black and white drawings into engraved steel for the purpose of illustration. On a subsequent visit, in early December, while Lily and Lolly spent their time talking with Mrs Walker, who was 'ill and has to lie on the sofa', Jack and her husband were in serious conversation about 'etchings, the process etc'.[9] Despite his interest, he never took up any graphic skills. Jack seems to have kept a sharp eye on Lolly's diary-keeping: 'Jack says that I put too much about the weather in my diary . . . and I say I dont feel inclined to fill it full of myself entirely whereat he replied "That is because you dont bear reproduction".'

As we know, Jack's love of sport ranged from the genteel badminton played with art school friends or Bedford Park neighbours, to the low-life of the racecourse. He took his friend Griffin to the mid-March meeting at Kempton Park, recording cryptically 'were cleared out and had to walk back'. And he did a drawing in his diary of 'the chap that tried to rook us'.[10] Undeterred, they returned in April, and another drawing of a racecourse tout was accompanied by a note of some despair: 'Well after a rooking day at Kempton to be beat at seven-up by a thing like that is the last straw. Its time we turned it up.'[11] Two days later Jack attended the funeral of the Duchess of Cambridge, whose husband was Queen Victoria's uncle, and commander-in-chief of the British Army. She was a very popular woman; Jack described the event as 'more like a race meeting than a funeral'. Street touts sold 'memorium cards of the dear old Dutchie', and charged fourpence for standing room at the kerbside. Griffin was with Jack.[12]

He had more than a passing interest in this favourite British pastime of pageantry with displays of military splendour. Early in 1889 he became a 'Volunteer', first sending in his 'measurements', then joining up and going to his first drill session. He was with 'the Artists Corps', and his sergeant was a forbidding figure with large black moustache and severe expression.[13] Despite this, Jack found it all 'very jolly', and took up enthusiastically the whole business of drill and training. 'The call to be a man at arms and able' was noted down in his entry for 5 February, when the Volunteers were drilling in rehearsal for a 'comic history' parade, based possibly on Gilbert A. Beckett's *Comic History of England*, and referred to in his diary by Jack as 'Comic History Tabloos [sic]'. Later that month he did a drawing, *The Volunteer Officer on Wildesden Heights* and later still recorded being 'passed by the adjutant'. There was an Easter camp of the Volunteers at Shorncliffe, on the south coast, from 18 to 23 April 1889, for which he was issued with a rifle. And he was still actively involved in December of that year.

Early after his return to London Jack extended his love of entertainment to the theatre. He delighted in its comic side, whether on-stage or off. He went to the Henry Irving production of *Macbeth*, in the long series of Shakespeare productions at the Lyceum Theatre which lasted from the late 1870s to the end of the century. Ellen Terry was playing Lady Macbeth, a part she created in 1888.[14] What amused Jack was 'the way the curtain used to go down on some terribly exciting scene and immediately it was down the man in the galleries used to roar out "Lemonade and bitter, all empty glarses this way" '.[15] Ellen Terry's acting he found 'awfully good some of the scenery was jolly'. He went with a friend called Nash to see Herbert Beerbohm Tree playing Falstaff in *The Merry Wives of Windsor*, and described him as 'bully in the basket'.[16] 'Bully' is a term of great approval. He saw other Irving plays. On 30 October Lolly records: 'Got four orders for Lyceum. Willie Jack Lily and I went . . . the seats were the back row of the stalls the play Prince Karl by the author of Mr Barnes of New York splendid so witty and bright every small dialogue amusing the Boston girl so bright and pretty with vivid red flowers on her dress. I dont think I ever enjoyed anything so much.'

Since 1878 Bram Stoker had been Henry Irving's manager at the Lyceum. It may well have been that the complimentary tickets – the 'orders for the Lyceum' – came from this Dublin writer whose background was not greatly different from the Yeatses, and who knew them, and corresponded with John Butler Yeats. Jack did a drawing of Mansfield as Prince Karl.[17] His enthusiasm for the stage was lifelong. It provided him with material for drawings, later for paintings, and led him into writing plays, firstly for the miniature theatre, then the professional stage.

At this time Louis Purser (Lolly spells his name 'Lewis' which is how it was pronounced), who was a kindly man concerned about the family's poverty, invited them out to dinner and the theatre. He sent Lolly a postcard on Wednesday 12 September: 'saying he had got four excellent tickets for the Lyceum for Friday Papa Lily and me we are to dine with Mr Purser first. I am half sorry it will be Dr Jekyll and Mr Hyde as I suppose it will be rather horrible.' The visit, however, was a success.[18] A month later, on Saturday 13 October, Jack and Willie went to see the play. It encouraged in Willie his lifelong passion for detective fiction. He devoured it endlessly, boasting about his comprehensive reading in the genre. It had a rather different impact on Jack, who spent the Sunday after the performance 'going about the house saying, Dear, dear, dear, dear, in exactly the same tone as the detective in the play last night did'.[19] Jack recorded two visits to *Dr Jeckle* [sic] *and Mr Hyde*. On one of these, when a character called out in the play: 'I like-e-e-e you!' A voice came from the pit: 'Oh eavens'. He probably shared with Lolly her interest in racier fare. A fortnight later they went to see a play called *Still Alarm*, which she described as a 'fine rousing play plenty of killing, villains, etc.'.[20] This would have been to Jack's taste entirely.

Jack's tendency to mimicry also manifested itself in private entertainment for his sisters. Lolly gives a telling example. They had gone to dinner with neighbours, the Veseys (this may have been the family from Dublin whose son, Cyril, was at school with Willie). On the way home Jack did imitations of British soldiers, '*bustle* & all, then horse soldiers swaggering along *of course* he did them drunk as well as sober, & this is the boy who at the Veaseys sat silent looking as shy as possible'. The picture emphasises the difference between the brothers, Willie liberal with his views in public, serious and

48. Maud Gonne.

49. William Butler Yeats in 1894.

fulsome about literature, prone to lecture and pontificate 'upon the supreme theme of art and song', while Jack kept his council in front of all but those most intimately associated with him, for whom he provided precisely the kind of entertainment for which Willie was temperamentally unsuited.[21] Lolly records intermittently who went to church, and on one occasion claims 'Jack bullied Lily into going to Church with him'. Jack and his sisters were not greatly enamoured of High Church ritual: 'Its altogether too playacting especially when the officiating priest is as fat & comfortable looking as Mr Wilson'.[22]

In keeping with the culture of Bedford Park there was a faintly commune-like atmosphere. The formidable Maud Gonne called, in January 1889 (fig. 48). Already firmly committed to the movement for Irish independence from Britain, she had taken on the role of an Irish Joan of Arc and by the autumn of 1888 her outspoken flamboyance and extremism were something of an embarrassment to the Irish Party. She impressed John O'Leary, though he never took her nationalism too seriously, and he became what she called 'her Irish philosopher and friend'.[23] He introduced her to the Yeatses. Her first visit was to John Butler Yeats. But O'Leary was at least as interested in Willie as he was in the father, and had briefed 'the Dublin beauty who is marching on to glory over the hearts of the Dublin youths' about the eldest Yeats son.[24] Willie succumbed. He later wrote: 'She had heard of me from O'Leary; he had praised me, and it was natural that she should give and take without stint.' He was referring to the initial affinity between them: how they dined together every evening of her nine-day visit; how they talked of theatre, she to tell him of her wish for a play she could act in Dublin, he to offer to write one; how he wished to become an Irish Victor Hugo; and how she gave her time to him 'in overflowing abundance', and with 'something so exuberant in her ways', that it all seemed so natural. Yet it was not; nor did it become happy, nor fulfilled. 'I was twenty-three years old when the troubling of my life began,' he later wrote, and added the clue to why this was so: 'for her beauty as I saw it in those days seemed incompatible with private, intimate life'. In any case, Willie fell for her, and commenced an unrequited and often painful love affair which lasted for the best part of thirty years.

Lily's delight at her first wage packet for her embroidery job was short-lived. She was employed by William Morris's daughter, May. To begin with, Lily worked at William Morris's own home, Kelmscott House, in the Mall at Hammersmith, and while there she was happy: 'Morris nearly always in good heart and full of talk at lunch,' she wrote, and listed the many famous visitors who came to see him, including George Bernard Shaw and R.B. Cunninghame Graham.[25] Willie wrote of this in a letter of 4 December 1888 and said how much his sister enjoyed the making of cushion and mantel-piece covers. 'She dines at the Morrises every day. Morris is greatly disturbed by little boys who insist in playing under his study windows.'[26] The milkboy also used to run his empty can along the railings, probably because Morris had specifically instructed him not to. May Morris moved the operation to 'three rooms over a vegetable shop in a slummy street off Hammersmith High Street'. This was Hammersmith Terrace, on the other side of Hammersmith High Street from Bedford Park, a curving row of houses, now gone, but which then backed onto the River Thames: 'Most of all I hated the muddy Thames flowing at the end of the little garden'. In the early days the work excited her, and the embroidery itself she continued to enjoy. It brought in regular money, indeed the only regular wage packet of any of them, and the initial ten shillings a week increased to thirty shillings by the time she and May Morris parted company. But increasingly she found it a form of drudgery, and, apart from that first wage packet, the money went towards satisfying family needs. The unfortunate truth is that Lily, vibrant and clear-headed spirit that she was, for the period from 1888 until her health broke down and she left May Morris's employment, in very bitter and unpleasant circumstances six years later, slowly became another of the family's casualties.

'Baby' was growing up in the hard school of life. He was surrounded by family members all, with the possible exception of Lolly, troubled or distressed. After her return from Huddersfield, their mother:

> Got slowly worse – and finally was all the time in her room – she would never allow it to be said that she was an invalid – She was grim and austere – suffered all in silence – she asked no sympathy and gave none. I don't think she was unhappy during all those long years – she had no worry – and worry she was never able for – she read a good deal – and latterly she slept a good deal. Rose and Maria cared for her with kindness and patience. Maria slept in her room.[27]

Susan Yeats listened attentively when others in the family read, but usually with her eyes closed, giving the appearance of being asleep. 'Called on suddenly to tell the subject, she invariably repeated the last sentence, with a quaint little smile.'[28] According to Lolly, however, her mother was generally bad-tempered, unkempt, and difficult to manage. Willie found her impossible, and would confine her to an armchair.[29]

Lily refers to Rose in her scrapbook as 'our kind friend and confident servant all those years'. Katherine Tynan described her as 'for years the presiding domestic genius, the homely guardian angel of a family too endowed with the gifts of the spirit to be very efficient in mundane affairs. . . . "Rose is never afraid of us," said Mr Yeats once, "but we are very often afraid of her." We used to say that his extravagantly good opinion of servants as a class was because he saw them through Rose-coloured spectacles.'[30]

Jack coped well with his dysfunctional family, being more detached, particularly so at crucial periods in his young life. He did not often argue with his father, since he was not by nature argumentative; he ignored him. It would appear that while he was more indulgent than his brother, he was less affectionate. John Butler Yeats felt that his relationship with Willie was a difficult one, and often said so. But he also said the same about Jack, and it would be a mistake to assume that affection between himself and his youngest child was uncomplicated and satisfactory merely because there is less evidence to the contrary. Like all those who fail in their ambitions and in self-fulfilment, John Butler Yeats craved constant affection. To a certain extent he was denied it. Willie refused on one occasion to allow his father to meet with George Pollexfen, then on a visit to London, and John Butler Yeats wrote tellingly to his elder daughter: 'I wish Willie had Jack's tender gracious manner, and did not sometimes treat me as if I was a black beetle.'[31] Padraic Colum recalls an occasion when the father told him: 'Willie is like his mother. She seldom if ever showed any signs of affection. I could be six months in Africa, and when I came back all she would say would be "Did you have your dinner?"' However, his father also acknowledged his Yeats side –

'He is expansive and he loves discourse.'[32] John Butler Yeats gives an account of his preference for Willie:

> It is curious, but I find Willie with all his faults more lovable than Jack. The latter was too long in Sligo and so is full of ill will towards all his fellow creatures and suspicion and contempt. It is the way with commercial people. Willie thinks well of his fellow creatures except when he is fighting them, at any rate has a high opinion of human nature and believes it has a noble destiny. Jack of course sticks manfully to duty which makes him an admirable fellow citizen, but then it makes him a little cold and self complacent.[33]

In a letter a month later John Butler Yeats refers to Jack's seriousness and how it made him a great success with Americans; even Jack's jokes 'are always serious'.

With Willie head of the family and shouldering responsibility, and with Jack still the 'Baby' – at least in the minds of his sisters – Jack showed a deference towards his brother which was sensible and well-judged. But he seems, then and later, to have relied upon his two sisters (fig. 50). In John Butler Yeats's view Jack was closest of all to Lily:

> All my family are strangely different from each other, but Jack and Lily are closest to each other. That's why they have always been such good friends. In London when Jack arrived late at night, in his polite way he would stop a while with me and talk and then ask if I thought Lily was awake. And long after when I climbed up to bed, as I passed her room I could hear laughter and talking. It was Jack and Lily.[34]

Despite his father's remarks, however, much family comment points towards Jack's rippling, bubbling sense of humour. Willie's letters, numerous for this period, and dominated by those he wrote to Katherine Tynan, who knew Jack, refer to him infrequently; but when they do, laughter is never far away: 'We have a little cousin staying with us Gereldine by name she & Jack keep up a continual joking together. At dinner they have to be kept quiet almost by force.'[35] Geraldine was the eldest daughter of Susan's younger sister, Elizabeth, 'somewhat vague, light-headed and easy-going',[36] who married Alexander Barrington Orr, a clergyman, in 1873, and went to live near Huddersfield. The two sisters remained close, and when Geraldine visited Bedford Park she would have been renewing a much closer childhood friendship with Jack than she had with the other cousins on account of him always being in Sligo when her own family stayed at Merville. Jack had a hammock at the bottom of the garden, between a chestnut and a beech tree. On his return from a summer holiday in Sligo, Willie wrote to tell Katherine Tynan: 'With us there is nothing to tell other than that Jack has come home with a number of sketches of Sligo. I have got one framed for my room. He keeps shouting mostly, Sligo nonsense [sic] rhymes (he always comes home full of them) such as

> You take the needle & I'll take the thread
> And we'll sow the dog's tail to the Orange man's head.'[37]

Lolly tells us more of the relationship between the two boys in her diary. Writing on 10 October 1889, she tell us: 'Jack drew silk doyleys all evening keeping up a running fire of sarcastic jokes and riddles with Willie'.

50. Lily and Lolly in the early 1890s.

Jack enjoyed parties, and was determined to learn dancing. At the family Halloween party in 1888 he ate quantities of cake in order to be sure to get the gold ring baked within it. Lolly wrote: 'he managed to stow away most cake so perhaps he deserved it.' A month later he commenced dancing lessons; Jack, she said, 'is very persevering'. Perhaps he had Cottie in mind. The following April in a dance programme which she preserved Jack is down for all the waltzes, as well as for the 'extras' listed on the back cover. But the more immediate target was a 20 December dance organised by the Bedford Park Badminton Club to which Jack went with his two sisters, having borrowed his brother's dress clothes. It is probable that May Morris, with her fiancé, Herbert Halliday Sparling, were also there. They were keen members, and often coerced Jack and Lily into badminton sessions. 'Mr Sparling says J & L are such fun together, the way they tease one another.'[38] The dance was a grand affair, though Jack was suffering from toothache. There were more than a 100 guests, more men than girls, and the hall was decorated with coloured lanterns, bows and ribbons. Dressed up in his brother's white tie and tails Jack 'looked very well and I enjoyed it awfully we danced from 8.30 till 4.30 we were dead tired yesterday.' The dancing craze took hold of them. On Christmas Eve Jack and Lily, according to Lolly, were still at it: 'Lily & Jack are dancing on one another on the hearth rug all because she said supper was coming in and it isn't it is a very friendly encounter.'

On Christmas Eve 1888 two geese arrived for the family from Sligo, one sent by their grandmother, a second from Uncle George. There was also a hamper from Dr Fitzgerald.[39] Best of all, William Pollexfen sent his daughter £25. 'Papa got some new clothes not before he wanted them an umbrella and we paid Rose £6 and Mrs Watson £7. Jack & I went off in all the pouring rain to give it to her & she brought us into her little parlour and talked to us about her washing, her sons, her rent etc. I think she was very glad of the money but would not pretend to be eager for it, as she sat and chatted to us with her hard worked hands folded on her white apron . . .'[40]

Jack's succeeded in establishing himself very firmly with *The Vegetarian* during 1888 and 1889, even getting commissions for other members of the family. This seems to have led to the publication of 'A Legend', by his brother. Lolly, in her diary, recorded that she 'went to town with Jack to Vegetarian Cassells & tract Society Vegetarian took Willie's poem about buried city under Lough Gill & Jack's illustrations, it is to appear in Christmas Number.' And she added, a little sadly, 'I wish the old Vegetable man would take my story then I might too be the owner of 10/-.' Jack himself wrote to Sarah Purser: 'My illustrating a poem of Willy's is funny but when you know its all about "The Maker of the stars and World" it makes it funnier.' Purser was interested in his progress. Jack attempted to sell work to an American publication, but the drawings were sent back. Lolly reported: 'they only take those done by Americans.' He did some work for the *Daily Graphic* in 1890, but with only one set of drawings, of a '£4 19s' race meeting on Bowmore Strand, and in 1891 was to begin to work for *Ariel, or the London Puck*, as well as for *Paddock Life*, and also *Lock to Lock Times*.[41]

Two publications for which he worked over a lengthy period – *The Vegetarian*, and *Ariel, or the London Puck* – placed considerable emphasis on humour. He used the *double-entendre* device beloved of Thomas Hood. *Hugging the Rails* shows a drunk holding onto rails, but falling down; *A Small Punter* is a drawing of a small man in a punt approaching a lock; *A Waiting Race* depicts two waiters running, with filled trays and articles on their heads; *A Racing Fixture* is of a fat man stuck in turnstiles holding up the increasingly angry crowd behind him. Some drawings are of domestic scenes: *Tommy's Opportune Moment* shows a small boy holding a large jar on a string with water in it. A frog is seated in the jar. He stands beside his father, who is shaving, his head lifted up towards the ceiling, and a cut-throat razor laid across his jugular. The boy is about to place a live frog in his father's hand; the caption: 'In giving presents the great point is to choose an opportune moment.'[42] In another he depicts a cab horse which has fallen outside a public house and is sprawled between the shafts, its legs outstretched, its eye looking over its shoulder. A small Boy is saying to the Cabby, who is peering out of the pub door, 'Mister! I soy! Yer 'orse's been and fell.' The cabby: 'Garn! You must a' shoved 'im down.' A man and woman are at the Crystal Palace Dog Show, looking at a dachshund. 'I say, Charlie, what sort o' dog is that?' 'Oh, that's a bungalow-dawg, don't cher know – built all on one storey.' He did a large, well-finished drawing of a black maria, with a well-dressed gent at the grill, saying to the police officer, 'Don't forget to set me down at Chancery lane, Conductor.' Another is of a hunting scene with a man lying on the ground attended by countrymen while a youth holds his horse. Well-dressed onlooker asks solicitously: 'Have you had an accident, Sir?' Cross old huntsman replies: 'Accident? No, sir! I did it on purpose.'

Horses predominate in Jack's drawings. When, many years later, MacGreevy asked him what change there had been in his own lifetime, between the London of his youth and the London he visited after the Second World War, he said without hesitation it had been the passing of the horse. He gave numerous examples, of climbing aboard the old London 'knife-board' buses, and joining the coachman, who would share his great leather apron; of the great horse-drawn market carts, with three horses knowing their way and the driver fast asleep. Jack himself travelled once on such a cart, he said, 'for experience – the only experience was stiffness – very stiff and cold'.[43] Jack kept a large album of printed ephemera during the 1930s and 1940s. In it he pasted from the *Irish Independent* for 26 October 1939 a photo entitled 'London Fifty Years Ago'; it showed Piccadilly, with horse-drawn vehicles; the caption read: 'When the horse moved the whole city'. Jack's own cryptic annotation reads: 'Say 1889'.[44] The horse was then his stock-in-trade and even assumed nightmare proportions. In one published drawing, entitled *Our Artist's Nightmare*, Jack has a horse, with flashing eyes and steaming nostrils, standing on the chest of the artist, who is lying in bed trying to sketch (fig. 51). The artist depicted is a not unreasonable self-portrait, with hair brushed wet to one side, a smile on the face, and the unmistakable lantern jaw. There is a jacket on the chair beside the bed, and a fob-watch hanging up on the bedhead.[45] Time and the horse wait for no man.

William Frederick Cody returned to Olympia after a five-year absence. In that time the Indian Wars had ceased, the material for the Wild West Show was becoming the stuff of history. Unfortunately, the period had also produced scepticism about the exploits of Buffalo Bill. Had he really done all the things he claimed? Had he done *any* of them? Or was he a charlatan and a mountebank? Had he actually served as a Pony Express Rider, part of that famous mail service? When he came back to London, in 1892, the programme for the Earls Court show contained a spirited defence of the veracity of Cody's claims about his career. The success of his first Wild West Show was

51. *Our Artist's Nightmare*, pen and ink, illustration from *Paddock Life*, April 1892.

52 to 55. Drawings inspired by the Wild West show. Jack, clearly captivated by the huge growth in interest in the Wild West which the series of Buffalo Bill shows provoked, created his own cowboy stories.

a story of show-business promotion. By 1892 Cody was on the defensive, not just of his reputation, but of the Wild West Show itself.

Jack viewed it as good theatre, made better by controversy. The possibility that this ageing charlatan had never ridden, armed, between Cheyenne and Deadwood, turned everything into a wonderful fiction, with a panoply of cowboys, stagecoaches, Indian braves and maidens. Jack's wiser, calmer, professional eye watched as the great entertainer galloped his horse around the arena, shooting down glass balls which were thrown into the air for him. Jack inspected, as a shrewd visual reporter, the tribe of Sioux Indians, with their tepees and war dances. He looked at the uncomfortable interior of 'the original Deadwood Stagecoach', as it too was trundled around the arena, and then exhibited as part of a display of Wild West novelties. And he drew magically from all that he saw. He no longer did so for magazine illustrations; Cody's visits are not recorded at all extensively in the many drawings done for professional purposes. But in *Mexican Joe* and *Crystal Palace* we see the artist glorying in the magic of the horse, the breathless compulsion of performance, and the profound appeal of human skill (figs 56–7).

Jack was better organised professionally than his brother. He built up outlets for his drawings, and was faithful and consistent in honouring the obligations which these jobs created. Unlike Willie and John Butler Yeats, who were both freelancing, Jack worked steadily for *The Vegetarian*, and then, one by one, he added other publications in a way that was not unlike the

53

54

Pollexfen mercantile expansion. He was essentially prudent and far-sighted. He recognised, from family experience, that a great deal of money coming in was needed if plans were to be made into the future, and this was so even when the bulk of that money went towards the family.

Lolly, who briefly kept family accounts for the period, records interesting detail regarding their various contributions. Willie's earnings in 1889–90, for example, based on articles done for the *Manchester Courier*, *The Boston Pilot*, *The Scots Observer* and *The Weekly Review*, came to a total of £28 18s 8d. Jack, in the same period, earned £18 11s 8d. He was just a year into his studies at the Chiswick Art School, and only eighteen years old at the outset; as an illustrator he was working exclusively for *The Vegetarian*, but as well was doing his menu designs and decorated doyleys. Lolly only partially recorded the earnings for the following year, but by the end of April Jack had earned £10, and his brother £25. With Lolly earning between £10 and £12 a term for her teaching, Lily getting ten shillings a week from May Morris, and John Butler Yeats getting virtually nothing at all, the contribution 'the Baby' made was not inconsiderable.

There was a lighter side to their lives. Jack's diary entry for one Sunday reads simply: 'freezing you like anything – spent the day teasing my sisters'.[46] But the following morning – it was still vacation time – Jack and Lolly, together with friends, the Goddards, the Dervins and a boy called Thomas, went out ice-skating from 11.30 in the morning until four. When the weather warmed up, they switched from ice skating to roller-skating.

At the end of the 1880s, from diary entries it is clear that he still regarded Sligo as home. The exuberance and delight he felt for the place are palpable; on holiday he gets back to familiar places and much-loved faces, plays billiards with Uncle George, goes boating and swimming beneath the shadow of the Metal Man, rides the pony at Rosses Point and on Bowmore Strand: 'Went for ride on pony to drumcliffe and ever since have been possessed with a natural aversion to sitting down.' He sketched all the time, his pencil moving across the pages of his diary and sketchbooks with growing facility and accelerating speed. Summer regattas were attended with much excitement, and considerable drinking and fighting took place, recorded in little cameos in line which were later developed into archetypal drawings and watercolours.

But though Sligo still filled his heart, he had adjusted to London. He had developed a sense of his future. The comic drawing was not an end in itself, but a means; perhaps as yet unfocused and ill-defined. Like every late teenager his ambition was thick-sighted, his character not fully defined, his way of life still uncertain. He was still boyish in habit and behaviour. But he was well-adjusted, he was earning money, and he was contributing to the needs of a hungry household.

From this obligation there emerged a more serious set of concerns. The comparison between Sligo and London was in part a comparison between the uncomplicated happiness, affection and comfort of his childhood, and the irreducible complexities of parental disaffection, unremitting poverty and uncertain shadows over the futures of all the Yeatses. They were struggling in a sea of difficulty, faced with the challenge of their own independence set against their collective duty towards their parents. John Butler Yeats must have seemed a lost cause by the end of the 1880s; so, in a different way, must their mother, whose life had become a bruised and visible expression of inner

58. *Jack B. Yeats* by John Butler Yeats, oil on canvas, 24 × 20. National Gallery of Ireland, *c.* 1892.

mental tensions and unhappiness. Serious ill-health faced her, affecting them all, and little or nothing could be done about it. Murphy writes:

> JBY, at the lowest depth of his always low financial resources, could not afford a doctor or nurses. Lily, reflecting on her mother's troubles years later, thought that in a later time her blood pressure could have been treated with medication, but at the time 'nothing could be done.' Nevertheless, Jack, the youngest in the family, with 'his first earnings' hired a specialist to visit his mother . . . It is possible to read into his actions a silent rebuke of his hapless father, who stood by and did nothing. They also suggest that Jack, alone in the family, felt a special affection for his mother. Yet he revealed no more of those feelings in words than he did about other personal matters.[47]

Jack was ready to fly the nest (fig. 58). Though the youngest in the family, Sligo had made him independent and free. He had probably judged correctly that his father would never change, that his mother had already been damaged beyond recovery, and that the lives of his two sisters and his brother were separate from his own – neither his concern, nor legitimate reason to hold him back from making his way in the world. It would need further time and thought, but looking forward into the last decade of the nineteenth century, and assessing all his experiences to date, Jack had a life and a career broadly mapped out, and his childhood and youth, were now behind him.

CHAPTER FIVE

Work and Marriage 1891–1897

Cottie, not Dottie, please, Father

DURING THE FIRST half of the 1890s important changes took place in the Yeats family. The two brothers left home, Willie to struggle on his own, and Jack, with much more financial security, to marry. Lily tendered her resignation to May Morris, who replied rudely that she should have dismissed Lily long before. Prompted by her father, who set aside his habitual long-windedness, Lily put her name to these words: 'Dear May, I have received your malicious and impudent letter and will leave at once. Lily Yeats.'[1] She suffered a breakdown in her health, and possibly a nervous breakdown of some kind as well. Meanwhile Susan Yeats was a permanent invalid, and even John Butler Yeats seems to have succumbed to illnesses at this time. It was accepted that the boys had 'to make their way in the world', while the girls were obliged to stay and care for their parents. In her diary Lily made a point of referring to her elder brother as 'the poet', sometimes within inverted commas, sometimes not; and throughout her comments about him there is a faintly wry tone. 'The poet has not a halfpenny so he has been hard at work all day at a story so as to make enough to pay his railway fares.'[2] Two days later 'Willie reduced to borrowing 2d from me – so as to call on Miss Vynne'. She paints an amusing picture of her brother's use of a typist, Miss Allport, whose whole family needed to be in attendance as the poet's work was deciphered, 'what with the writing & unknown Irish names'. A week later Lily ' painted in the morning & gave Mr O'Leary & the 'poet' their breakfast'. Willie went into a fine frenzy when he was being 'the poet', reciting the words to himself over and over. 'W.B. writing a poem the last couple of days to judge by the groan, coming from his room – must be a painful performance.' Then her brother departed. At the time of his departure Lily was in Sligo, and she heard in a letter from Lolly. 'Fine sunny day big white clouds & racing shadows over the country – heard from Lolly – W.B. has taken a room says he can live on 10/– a week, let him try –'[3]

Willie was caught in the familiar trap of gaining reputation without money. Being a published author, and a poet as well, was impressive, even if *The Wanderings of Oisin* had been published on a subscription basis. It made him lofty and distant – perhaps already an acknowledged inclination – setting him apart. This was reinforced by the shyness Willie felt in company and his awkwardness with people. Not only do Lily and Lolly indicate this; it comes to us also from his cousins, the daughters of two Pollexfen aunts.[4] One

59 and 60. Illustrations to Ernest Rhys's book, *The Great Cockney Tragedy*. Jack did eight in all, and they depict a Dickensian London of poverty, intimidation and despair. Willie felt they had 'a very genuine tragic intensity'.

of these, Ida, found Willie affected in his manner, his voice loud and "unnatural". He greeted her with, 'Oh, ah, so this is Ida,' pronouncing the name as though savouring each syllable in turn. Jack, in contrast, was 'very sweet and gentle, not noisy like the Yeatses but quiet like the other side of the family'. There is, however, no evidence for the view that Willie was derisive, either towards or about his sisters or his brother, nor that he was 'less than brotherly' towards Jack.[5] In his letters he recorded some of the details of Jack's life; and on occasion they are the only references we have. In the main, however, the interest is a passing one. The two brothers had shared a bedroom, but not much in the way of thoughts and idea.

Willie was a poet and writer moving among his peers, noted widely by critics, and increasingly a significant voice in literary circles. While Jack's work amused, it had limited critical impact. This was to remain the case for many years to come. Jack worked in silence, and in some secrecy. Willie records his brother's early successes, such as the drawing he did of Drumcliffe Races for the *Daily Graphic*,[6] and his first book commission – to illustrate *The Great Cockney Tragedy*, by Ernest Rhys, to whom he introduced Jack (figs 59– 60).[7] *The Great Cockney Tragedy* tells of the birth, fortunes and death of a Cockney Jew, in a sequence of sonnets. The events are wretched and lamentable; the treatment neither heroic nor pessimistic. A surviving review of the book says of Rhys that he had produced 'a praiseworthy poem upon modern London life'. It then went on:

> To the public, which is always longing for novelties, the work of Mr Yeats may be more attractive than that of Mr Rhys, who is already well known and recognised. These seven sketches, notwithstanding an obvious exaggeration of manner, are exceedingly remarkable: it will serve partly to describe them if we say that they suggest the work of Cruickshank and of Mr Strang. In their tragic energy and life, their fearless and true realism, they are admirable. Experience will supply the rest: and meanwhile, Mr Yeats' work shows an experienced mind, which is better than the dexterous hand of a mindless man.[8]

Jack and Rhys remained in touch, and were to work together again on *A Broadsheet*. Rhys, in his own words, was 'an undecided visionary, trying to adapt myself to the fashions and imitate the men of the moment'.[9]

There were plans for Jack to collaborate with Willie in his collection of essays and articles which eventually appeared as *The Celtic Twilight*. 'Jack is to make twenty illustrations.' In the event the book was delayed, the publisher changed, and instead of Jack it was their father who supplied a frontispiece, his portrait drawing of the poet. But Jack did provide illustrations for *Irish Fairy Tales* (fig. 61).[10]

Jack's silence and reserve were never so marked as they were in the matter of his marriage. He met his future wife, Mary Cottenham White, at a dance given by her mother, on 11 April 1889. He records the presence there of his art school friends, among them a student called Allingham. In July, they went on an outing and he records in his diary: 'Went up river with Allingham, Miss White, Miss Aegeon and Lolly. Bully.' We know from his father that three years before the marriage, in the autumn of 1891, he indicated his intentions, and dedicated himself to the business of saving money.

61. An illustration for *Irish Fairy Tales*.

One morning, before he was fully grown up, he gave me what I confess was a surprise, by announcing that he was engaged to be married to a young lady, a very talented art student; and then he showed his moral fibre. It was winter time and every morning from 6 o'clock till late at night he worked in a fireless room producing black and white drawings for comic journals, etc. At the end of three years he had made enough money to marry the young lady and have a comfortable house very beautifully situated on the banks of the Thames, some miles from London.[11]

The decision separated Jack from the others. He was absolved from responsibility for family finances. There was never any reproach about this, though there is a hint that Willie became more financially concerned for their father, and at a difficult time. There is virtually no contemporary reference to Jack marrying, or to his fiancé, Mary Cottenham White, until after the event itself. Apart from references in Jack's diary, and the survival of one or two documents, we have nothing to go on in piecing together a prolonged courtship.

Jack's desire to be married, and his recognition of the need for practical action to make this both possible and comfortably assured, dates from May and June of 1891. At this time his career took off in the notoriously difficult field of mainly freelance journalism. His editor on *Ariel* was the youthful Israel Zangwill, a fierce Zionist, who gave up his religion but clung passionately to his race, writing notable Jewish novels.[12] Zangwill may have been attracted to Jack by the artist's sympathetic treatment of the struggles and death of the Jew in the drawings for *The Great Cockney Tragedy*. In May Jack had nine drawings in *Ariel*; in June ten and thirteen in *Paddock Life*, his first appearance in that paper. This was to sustain his career for the next two and a half years. Month after month, through that summer, autumn and winter, he worked extremely hard for these two publications, adding a brief spell of work during the season of the Thames regattas in July and August, for *Lock to Lock Times*, a newspaper which dealt with the then highly popular range of sports which focused on the river, best reflected by *Three Men in a Boat*, Jerome K. Jerome's extraordinarily popular and successful account of a humorous river holiday.[13]

There was a marked shift in emphasis in the work he did during that summer of 1891. The drawings for the *Vegetarian* were principally light-hearted in their tone, and mixed humorous imaginary subject-matter with occasional jobs of on-the-spot reporting. *My Pet Cat* and *A Whip or a Word* were early drawings of the first kind; his covering of events included the Drury Lane Pantomime of 1891, which was *Beauty and the Beast*, and the Oxford and Cambridge boat race.[14] He also did advertisement drawings, and sketches and decorations for general use in the pages of the magazine.

His work for *Ariel* began in much the same way, but by Whit Monday he was drawing the event – in his *Whit Monday – and Wisdom Tuesday* – and in June he started, significantly enough, what would be the equivalent for a writer of a regular column — a series of drawings which ran through the summer months at roughly fortnightly intervals under the title 'Round the Town'. It was short-lived, coming to an end at the end of August; but it punctuated his busy schedule, and it inspired some important drawings.

Paddock Life had much the same mixture of humour and sporting life in its

62. 'The Typical Horse Jobber' detail from sketches for *The Illustrated London News*, September 1892.

63. 'If yer carn't drive it, take it 'ome', detail from sketches for *The Illustrated London News*, September 1892.

64. An illustration from a Nora Borthwick primer.

pages, but demanded much more of Jack. After a brief apprenticeship using his imagination to depict jokes – 'Directions: You wind up the Clerk, and the Bookie "goes"!' – they began sending him to cover events in different parts of the British Isles. He covered trotting races at Alexandra Park and at Aintree, the Baddeley Lawn Tennis Championship, cricket in Bedfordshire, long-distance foot-racing, and the Henley Regatta. In August 1891 he went to Dublin to do drawings of the Horse Show and of the Second Summer Race Meeting at Leopardstown, and these appeared in the magazine for 1 September. Willie refers to Jack's Dublin visit in a postscript to a letter to Katherine Tynan, but was too immersed in his unrequited passion for Maud Gonne, his literary work and discussions with Katherine Tynan – who lived at Clondalkin – to pay much attention to the quite different sporting life which his brother followed.

He covered all sports: the autumn brought the cubbing season, followed by hunting, and he even went out as a foot-follower of hunts, trudging through misty days in Kent, and coming home wet and worn, without having seen much of the action. The football season opened, and Jack was at the Arsenal versus Sheffield United Match; and he covered rugby matches between London and Scottish, at Blackheath, and London versus the Counties at Richmond. He was paid expenses for travel, and the experience of dealing with the editorial staff on this score was of great value later, when he and John Synge worked together for the *Manchester Guardian*.[15]

Even if we reckon between ten shillings and a pound for each drawing, based on the supposition that *Ariel* and *Paddock Life*, particularly the latter, paid better than the *Vegetarian*, then his monthly earnings in 1891, from June to December, could have run at about £15. In July and August there was additional income from *Lock to Lock Times*. In 1891, his total earnings, taking into account the possibility of occasional sales of drawings which had been going on since 1889, as well as commissioned design work for menus and other ephemera, could hardly have been less than £150. For a man in his twentieth year, and still studying art, this represented a serious professional career.

Throughout 1892 Jack worked on similar assignments. In February *Ariel* folded, abruptly terminating his first staff job. His *Paddock Life* commissions read like a sporting almanac, and the editor kept him busy throughout that year and the next. In the late summer and autumn he did his first drawings for *Judy*, a sporting and humorous paper, and he appeared in a single issue of *The Illustrated London News* with a group of sketches of the Metropolitan Cattle Market in Caledonian Road, Holloway (figs 62–3).[16]

In 1892 he worked on theatre posters for seven months, and did a group of Irish drawings of children in west of Ireland settings which much later were used to illustrate Nora Borthwick's Gaelic primers (fig. 64). The stint on theatre posters was with the firm of David Allen, then as now involved in promotion and publicity, and it took him to Manchester. 'Manchester is the only city in the world which has so pleased itself as to pay me a salary. And that was a long while ago. And the salary was not so enormous as for any part of it to remain with me yet.'

He stayed in Manchester at weekends, since he records friends who were kind to him, and to whom he went on Sundays. The most important of these was the English literary scholar, Oliver Elton, introduced to Jack and the Yeatses by York Powell, a friend from Bedford Park.[17] The renewal of friendship in Manchester, where Oliver Elton had been lecturing in English literature since 1890, was helpful to Jack, who otherwise seems to have been disparaging about his working colleagues. In a remark to his father, made on one of his visits home, he referred to the other artists in the office as the 'lees', meaning dregs, or leftovers, and they were clearly not congenial company. But the job was satisfactory; Jack went so far as to say that good salaries were paid, 'once they find you are indispensable to them'.[18] Jack's father, as one might expect, expressed his usual enthusiastic pleasure at Jack's visits back to London from Manchester: 'We were all you may suppose glad to see Jack, who was quite pleasant and talkative. He *evidently likes his work*. He looks better and is far more cheerful and he went away in very good spirits.'[19] In a movingly prophetic picture, revealing of their father's genuine, frustrated concern for them all, John Butler Yeats wrote:

> Some day Jack will be a substantial man with a cheerful kind hearted spouse and an open-handed way of welcoming friends, something on the Merville pattern though on a smaller scale of course and Willie will be famous and shed a bright light on us all, and sometimes have a little money, and sometimes not. Lolly will have a good prosperous school and as I before remarked give away as prizes her eminent brother's volumes of poetry.[20]

Writing in September 1892 he says: 'Jack was here the other day. He left us in the middle of the night in the rain and WALKED all the way to St Pancras terminus to get a five o'clock morning train for Manchester so as to be at his office in good time. It seemed to me madness.'[21] Clearly, Jack worked hard in Manchester. He later regretted what he saw as a waste of his energy and talent. 'I overworked conscientiously. I thought then that I was investing in something which would pay me hereafter . . .'[22] Jack omits to tell us, of course, in that *Manchester Guardian* essay, that he was working in order to earn the money to get married. It is hardly surprising that he adopted a light-hearted attitude to his art school training, provoking his father's speculation: 'What he did at the art school I could never find out. I fancy he was the wag and the wit and the storyteller, welcome with everybody . . . [he] must have been eager for companions.'[23]

Jack never tackled the serious side of his studies as an art student. He did not grapple with painting in oil, or with work on canvas; he engaged briefly in the rigour of life drawing, though without leaving any evidence; and his command of compositional skills derived more from his attendance at sporting events and the demands of his editors than it did from classroom teaching. All the available evidence is that he remained a comic draughtsman, an illustrator, a sketchbook artist working in soft pencil and washes, a painter in watercolours, and a brilliant black-and-white artist.

During these years Jack dressed the part of the sporting artist. He wore a long and capacious coat, literally down to his ankles, with several pockets, and skirted with good lining to provide warmth when sitting out of doors. His hat was a low-crowned bowler, or 'Derby', and he wore ankle-length boots. He was no less elegant than his brother, who dressed the part of the bohemian and poet. Jack dressed for the job and the status of artist working among sportsmen (fig. 65). Though the status was to change somewhat, the dress sense did not vary greatly from then on. Jack managed throughout his life to combine elegance with a certain robust practicality. He wore good long

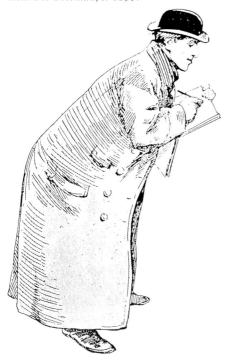

65. Cartoon of Jack in a long sporting coat, from *The Bohemian*, c. 1895.

warm overcoats all his life, the cut of them waisted to allow the extra warmth from the skirts when he was sitting down out of doors. He always wore a hat, though the hard sporting hat of his youthful days gave way to the softer, wide-brimmed fedora or trilby of later years, and on certain occasions he wore a stetson. In his brother's case, the faintly foppish necktie – affected by artists because it concealed the absence of fresh linen or clean collars for their shirts – may well have served this purpose. But Jack was not quite so impoverished, and he wore then and later a collared shirt with tie. In his Dublin days he bought his clothes from the best outfitters, and his suits were tailor-made.

He used a large sketchbook, and drew in pencil, taking back numerous drawings from which he worked up his black and white illustrations in 'a fireless room' in Bedford Park. John Butler Yeats refers to him doing this in winter time, indicating the very real pressure which the various editors put him under. The page waits for no one; these were drawings which recorded sporting events, and readers were impatient for them. But the immediacy of the experience, on race-course or running track, had to be translated into a careful and balanced drawing using only pen and ink, everything conveyed by sharp line, painstaking hatching, and a strong compositional focus. He felt that 'of all places for sketching "character" he likes a country race meeting best, and if he may make a choice he would have a Western meeting he wots of where the track is so hilly that it has been likened unto a "switchback" railway. There is a precipice twenty yards from the rails, thimble-riggers, three-card men, and "trig-o'-the loup" operators abound, and as for the non-conformist conscience – well, it has never been heard of.'[24]

It seems Jack told the rest of his family in the summer of 1891 that he intended to marry Cottie. He had known her since April of 1889. That summer, Jack and Cottie went on Thames boating trips together. The transition from first affection to engagement was a lengthy one, realised only in stages. 'Lily Yeats once told me how Jack, while still working in the art school, had found himself sitting next a fellow-student, pleasing to the eye and of sympathetic outlook. He used to return home to receive his father's periodic inquiry "And how is Dottie?" "*Cottie*, not Dottie, please, Father." It was a long time before his parent could get it right.'[25] John Butler Yeats reported in a letter to Lily, who was away on holiday in Sligo, that Jack had found a house for himself and Cottie, '35 minutes from Waterloo', and quite substantial. It had '3 sitting rooms, 5 bedrooms, large garden full of roses – £45 a year . . .'[26]

Jack was in command of his own affairs, setting up himself and his wife-to-be in a suitable house, properly furnished, making provision for an income on which they could survive. The impending marriage weighed on Cottie. John Butler Yeats was doing a portrait of her at the time, and in another letter to Lily said that she had been looking 'quite ill and thin for some weeks. She tells me it is the worry . . . She has been most kind and friendly in her talk about everything, and very honest and simple.'[27]

Towards the end of July 1894 wedding invitations were sent out. Mary Cottenham White's mother, Georgina, was a widow, her husband having died some years before. The Whites were a distinguished family, tracing their forebears back, in one branch, to the famous Isle of Man family of Kelly. The marriage took place at Emmanuel Church in Wellesley Road, Gunnersbury, on the afternoon of Thursday, 23 August 1894 at 2.30. It rained all day long, heavy downpours. Lily described Jack, 'about seven feet tall, his grey frock coat was so long'. Cottie did everything right; a carriage came to Blenheim Road to bring the male members of the party to the church, and to drop off Lily at the White's home, where she and Polly, who was Cottie's sister, were bridesmaids. They then went ahead of the bride and waited in the porch, and waited and waited, Cottie was so late. She was given away, rather unusually, by her solicitor; but he had known her all her life, and was responsible for the trust fund set up by her dead father. 'We spread out her train + walked up behind her – the whole thing took about twenty minutes – + the important pair were not at all nervous + both looked well.'[28] There seem to have been no photographs, either at the church or later, but Cottie was dressed in silk, with a diamond pin in her hair, and a veil of tulle. There was music, and palms lining the steps to the chancel.

> Our dresses looked very well + were I am told most becoming – we had beautiful bouquets of carnations tied with pink ribbons 'en suite' as the Sligo papers say – Cottie did it handsome + gave me bronze shoes + pink silk stockings – the hats were made of brown chiffon with pink carnations 'en suite' Cottie looked very well going away in hat & all 'en suite'.

The reception was held in the Whites' home at 7 Brandenburg Road. The couple then went to Dawlish, on the east Devon coast, for their honeymoon. Jack took good care to shake out all the rice, for fear it would be noticed. But it was noticed anyway, by the guard on the train, and he treated them with due respect. In later years Jack made reference to Dawlish; in an Easter card to Cottie, in 1946, he referred to the fact that 'ginger-bread cakes are smallish at Dawlish, Keats said,' and that scent-bottles were the same:

> The Scent Shop man said
> 'The scent is very strong, and Lasting'
> And I say 'And so is the memory
> -of Dawlish'[29]

66. Jack with his cat outside the house in Chertsey, *c.* 1895.

Cottie was a slim brunette. An accomplished artist, the style of her work, then and later, was art nouveau. She painted in watercolour and gouache, never, as far as we know, in oils. As a pupil of the Chiswick School of Art, one who had been there much longer than Jack, she was a well-trained product of the art teaching at Chiswick, which leaned heavily towards decorative techniques, and design, and this was later to make her a confident and proficient contributor to the Cuala Press series of prints, and to other design work. She had money. Her father had made independent financial provision for her in the form of a trust, thus protecting her in the event of her mother's remarriage, and this assured the couple a degree of financial security and independence; Cottie herself retained, for the rest of her life, independent investments which she was able to enlarge with purchases of shares after the couple's move to Dublin. Whether or not the income was 'substantial' is hard to establish, but no serious evidence has survived to indicate such large investment. On Cottie's death, since she had no children, the trust reverted.

The couple lived their lives frugally. The Chestnuts in Chertsey was comfortable, and more than adequately furnished (fig. 66). They bought furnishings for the house from Maples, in Tottenham Court Road, then a huge firm of cabinet makers, upholsterers, carpet and bedding manufacturers, with several branches in London and Paris, and one in Smyrna, in Turkey. The main account has survived, and lists chairs, settees, wardrobes, bedsteads, and washstands, together with linen and curtaining for the house. Much of it was still in Jack's flat at the time of his death, and identifiable items are in the inventory. They kept one servant, and from early in their marriage – certainly by January of the following year – they had acquired the dog, Hooligan, who became part of their lives. In fact he was originally named Hooley, and later nicknamed Hooligan. Jack chose the name after a famous, even notorious financier of the times, Ernest Terah Hooley.[30] Hooley the man had many characteristics which would have appealed to Jack; he was warm-hearted, musically-gifted, playing both the piano and organ, and with a contagious sense of humour. But his financial dealings ran him into no less than four bankruptcies, the most sensational of which coincided with the decline in the craze for cycling. Though this occurred after the acquisition of the dog, something of the speculator's doings provoked from Jack a comment in a letter to his friend, J.C. Miles: 'the dog Hooley is well – how the man Hooley has been going it of late deters him from buying the British Empire and floating it out to sea to be used as a winter garden and jumping off place.'[31]

A month after the wedding ceremony, on 20 September, they held an 'At Home', sending out to their friends small portions of wedding cake with tiny, deckle-edged compliment cards printed in silver. In the months immediately preceding the wedding, Jack's workload had been much reduced; the magazines which had employed him during the previous four or five years had either ceased publication, or he had parted company with them – with the exception of *Chums*, and he was only doing two or three drawings a month for this magazine. He was also working, from May 1894, for *Sporting Sketches*.[32]

Despite the fall in work, Jack was getting on as an illustrator. That summer, in a celebrated row with *Punch*, Harry Furniss walked out and founded his own comic paper, *Lika Joko*, asking Jack to join it, which he did. Furniss was a brilliant black-and-white artist, and one of the quickest workers with pen and ink, though, like Jack, he worked up his finished drawings from pencil. Perhaps he lacked the consistency to be a great illustrator which one finds with Phil May; his notorious egotism and taste for argument made him a less than ideal candidate for successful editing. Though there is no record of any row with Jack, their association lasted only seven months. A paragraph appeared in the gossip column of an unidentified publication under the heading, 'HE LIKESA JOKO', which referred to Jack as belonging to

> the new school of youthful black-and-white men who can draw really funny pictures. He is still considerably on the sunny side of 25, and has already earned the warmest praises of many good judges of this sort of work. One of this artist's brothers is Mr W.B. Yeats, the well-known Irish poet. His father is the well-known artist of that name. Mr Yeats is married and lives in a pretty Middlesex village to which the 'madding crowd' has not yet penetrated.[33]

The family kept in close touch. There was a good train service from Richmond to Shepperton or Chertsey, and not only the Yeatses, but also their servant, Rose, went to visit the young couple. In summer weather Jack would take them all on the river, picnicking. Lily wrote of a visit where, 'after lunch went on the river & made tea on the banks after surmounting the difficulties brought about by Cottie forgetting the water & the servant the matches'.[34]

67. 'Low Life' sketch.

68. 'Low Life' sketch.

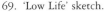
69. 'Low Life' sketch.

They passed another camping party, with several tents, and a piano. From its distant sound, Lily surmised that it must have been out in the last thunderstorm. On that occasion Jack rowed Lily and her friend Maud on to Shepperton, from where they caught an evening train back to Richmond. When their servant, Rose, went down for the day, later that same week, she also had a wonderful time with Jack and Cottie. John Butler Yeats was unwell, and the threat made by Jack to come up and take his father to the doctor forced the old man to go of his own accord for treatment.

Jack and Cottie were frequent visitors to Bedford Park. Late in August 1895 their visit coincided with one from Louise Imogen Guiney, the American poet, who, in Lily's words, 'made a dreadful mistake & asked poor Cottie how the baby was – Cottie was so confused & looked wildly round to see who was listening'. Cottie was to have no children. They came up in October, when Lily was about to go to France to take up new employment as a governess, and Cottie paid her £2 10s for work, while Jack bought from her one of her sketches done in Sligo, a small but pleasing watercolour of a roadway at Drumcliffe, with Ben Bulben in the background. An undertaking had been given, on Jack's behalf – presumably by Cottie – to pay for Lily's French lessons, once she arrived in Hyères. 'He is not aware of the honour yet,' she wrote.[35]

Jack had a reputation and a following. But his letters and his diary tell us virtually nothing about his art, and record almost no detail of his working life. He let the drawings speak (figs 67–9). They have much to say, and are filled with life, energy, force, purpose. But they are circumscribed artistically; and as a genre were being superseded anyway by more naturalistic methods of reproduction requiring a less comical, less cartoon-like approach. The advent of photography in popular journalism was not far off, and Jack was turning his back on his own early professional life to concentrate on becoming an artist. His rise had been rapid and self-assured. From the earliest drawings there is a sense of movement, and a feeling for character. He is at this stage gradually putting behind him the long-legged, spavined horses, set between the shafts of hansom cabs, or out on the roadway or hunting field. He is abandoning, in favour of more complex human types, the awkward, youthful misfits, criminal caricatures, gormless policemen, and East End figures from 'Low Life' occupations. Even at their best it must be said, they do not have the accuracy, economy and excellence of Phil May. Jack was never in the first rank as a comic draughtsman.[36]

Within a year of their marriage, Jack and Cottie had decided to move to the west of England. Jack's Pollexfen ancestors came from Devon, and the family had visited over the years, from the Branscombe childhood holiday to the Dawlish honeymoon. In the autumn of 1895 the couple bought land on the north bank of the Gara River, which runs into the sea at Strete, four miles south of Dartmouth. It is still remote countryside, the narrow roads wide enough only for a single vehicle, the hedges high up on banks, the gentle rolling hills tilled to show the rich red earth, the fields under grass full of fat cattle. A century ago it was even more isolated. The land was farmed, the orchards yielded their working crops of cider apples, and many of the farms still had cider presses. Travel to London and elsewhere was by rail only, and the local Strete carrier, with his horse-drawn omnibus, brought visitors to and from Kingsbridge, which was then the main railhead.

It took almost two years to organise their move from Chertsey to Devon. They called the ruined cottage Snail's Castle, and the original house, consisting of four rooms, had been built in 1704. When Jack and Cottie bought the property, from a farmer called Foal, and rebuilt it, it was also known as 'Rogue's Roost'. It was entirely roofed in traditional Devon thatching, and snails would collect there, hence the name.[37] Jack gave the house an Irish version of the name, Cashlauna Shelmiddy, which he used on writing paper, some of which he printed himself from stencils. During the winter of 1895–6 Jack and Cottie came to an agreement with a builder for the reconstruction of the cottage on what Jack called his 'estate'. They added the small wing on the northern side of the house. They then acquired further land, nearly two acres, stretching as far as the Gara River, and on the bank, close to the water, Jack reconstructed his studio from an old barn.[38] He wrote to Lily in March 1896 to tell her of a visit they made.

> Our estate you know is a small garden in Devonshire on which a local builder (who when he writes to me dots his (is) but he dots them all first person singular & is building us a very small cottage that we may run down there occasionally to recover from the excitement of life in Chertsey. It (the estate) is about four miles from Dartmouth to the westard. if you have a good map and look youll see something like this. [There is the drawing of a map of the coast south of Dartmouth] Of course we dont know what the cottage will look like when built. It may be a perfect horriblyness. In front of us a steep wooded valley going down to the (river) stream Gara. There isnt much more to tell about the estate but when the cottage is built Ill send you a sketch thereof.[39]

The excitement of life in Chertsey seems to have included a visit to the town by the English comedian, Chevalier, for whom Jack had a high regard. John Butler Yeats also came down to see them, and, unlike his busy daughters, stayed a night or two with the young couple, and did a drawing of Cottie.

The couple visited Ireland in the late summer, and stayed in Sligo. Willie was there, with Arthur Symons.[40] Lolly was also there, on her summer holidays, and it was she who wrote, giving 'a most rosy account of the Sligo doings' to her father, who swiftly passed on to Lily, in France, details of a holiday which he clearly enjoyed vicariously.

> Cottie and Arthur Symons, the two Saxons, had a *very pleasant* time, and saw everything to the best advantage. The two poets were much liked. All the natives, men and women, fell in love with Arthur Symons – he is so quiet and unassuming. Lucy came down every day. She said, when Willie and Symons were gone – 'the house is melancholy without the two poets.' Evidently Willie and Arthur Symons coalesced nicely with everybody, though of course they were nowhere when Jack came. Cottie would ask Jack in the evening, 'Where were you all those hours?' 'In a hayloft,' he would answer. Then details would come out, the fishermen and pilots he was with and the stories he told and they told.[41]

Jack is of course on home ground, but was only gently introducing his wife, who was not. She succumbed completely to the captivating magic of Sligo, and saw a quite different side to her husband's family. The Pollexfen connection was also the Devon connection, and George Pollexfen, now head of the firm and of the family, represented an impressive new dimension to her husband and all his relations. Here were solid values, mercantile security, love of sport, of swimming, the sea, and a refreshing absence of the cares which weighed heavily enough back in Bedford Park.

In addition to Jack providing the heart and soul of entertainment, outclassing his brother and Symons in his command of witty stories, he was also now the most independent member of the family, in marked contrast with the others. At the time, Willie was so hard up that he was seeking advice from Rose, their maid, about selling his microscope to Lolly. Whereas Jack, at the time, was trying to buy from other members of the family all the shares he could get in the family firm, the Sligo Steam Navigation Company 'as they pay good interest'.[42] John Butler Yeats was predictably excited at the prospect of selling his own share – it seems to have been just one – 'but George Pollexfen says at present it is impossible'.[43]

Jack's agreement with the builder produced a pretty cottage set into the steep hillside and looking down through woods to the river. His other agreement at that time was with the Clifford Gallery, in the Haymarket, for an exhibition in the late autumn of 1897. It took until then for the cottage to be completed to their satisfaction, and instead of using it as an occasional retreat from their home in Surrey, they moved themselves there completely. Jack and Cottie set off in April to their 'Castle' to work for the autumn show.[44] He was to transform all that he had learnt and expressed in the turmoil of deadline publishing into the more permanent creativity of works of art. He had already gathered together a substantial body of watercolours and drawings, including several which derived from his work as a poster artist, and an even larger number of 'Wild West' watercolours and other Earls Court paintings. But in keeping with his delight in the principle of immediacy, what he actually aimed at was a complete exhibition covering 'Life in the West Country'. He was setting out for Devon in the spring, with a gallery booking in the autumn in London, and the express purpose was to recreate Devonshire life in all its variety in one sustained output of watercolours and drawings.

CHAPTER SIX

Devon and the First London Shows
1897–1899

A knack of catching attitudes

'**R**ARELY HAVE I come across the work of a man with such a refreshing sense of humour, and such a marvellous gift for expressing violent and rapid movement with brush and pencil.' This eulogy, one of many greeting Jack's first solo exhibition in London at the Clifford Gallery in 1897, set the tone for its reception, secured the artist's youthful reputation, and confirmed his decision to abandon the life of an illustrator and take up art in the purer form of imaginative drawings and watercolours. Jack had departed to the west of England in order to paint, and the catalogue for this first show lists forty-three works depicting 'fairs, country race meetings, sales, market days, horse shows, and other times and places where farmers, graziers and drivers foregather. The artist, Mr Jack B. Yeats, evidently knows the terrain.' In reality, he had had just six months experience of Devonshire life. Yet he had indeed mastered the territory. The long warm summer of 1897 with visits to country events produced a small group of early masterpieces distinguished by their Devonshire settings and the grandeur of his watercolour conception.

A few examples: *The Cattle Drover, Cider, They'll Take a Lot of Catching!*, *A Cigar for a Kick*, and supreme among them all, *Waiting*, with its wonderful tension between shadow and sunlight, the mounted and the unmounted riders, and the heavy, brooding presence of the middle-aged man of the course (figs 70–2).

In the reviews, Jack's ability to read and present character, his command of colour and his representation of the horse in movement are all praised. The first review, quoted above, appeared in *Table Talk*, and is signed P.G.K. It continues:

The majority of these very rough water-colour sketches represent sporting subjects, such as prize-fights and racing scenes . . . They are all more or less slightly caricatured, so much so that I was in doubt at first whether the ludicrously bad drawing of some of the horses is due to intention or to lack of skill . . . But quite apart from the exquisite humour of these sketches, there is another reason which makes them quite remarkable and worthy of attention. They show an astounding capacity for grasping and retaining the impression of certain short moments, which but few of us possess. A glance at 'A Tussle with a Moor Pony,' 'Jumping at the Horse Show,' or 'Totnes Races' will speak more eloquently than any words could do. 'The

70 to 72. Watercolours of scenes in Devon *c.* 1897.

70. (top left) *Talk of the Fair*, watercolour and pencil, 18 × 13.

71. (top right) *Local and Travelling Champions*, watercolour and pencil, 14 × 10.

72. *Waiting*, watercolour and pencil, 9 × 12.

Man on the Merry-go-round,' with its vivid suggestion of a rapid whirl —
so vivid that it almost makes you giddy to look at — is quite the best thing
in an exhibition which is well worth a visit.

P.G.K. were the initials of the art critic, Paul George Konody, who was later
to be Orpen's first biographer. None of the other reviews are signed; but
there were plenty of them. No less than thirty-nine individual publications
reviewed the show, the overwhelming majority favourably, emphatically
encouraging him in the direction his career had now taken. 'He showed
distinct promise; he can characterise. His figures have movement.'[1] 'Mr Yeats
has a keen eye for character, though he seems able to express it only by
caricature.'[2] 'An admirable collection of water-colours by Mr Jack B. Yeats, a
young Irish artist . . . The sketches show a great deal of feeling and some very
fine colour effects, especially by so young an artist.'[3] '. . . Though slight in
execution they evince grasp of character, as well as power of
draughtsmanship . . . The artist has manifestly a feeling for colour. "The New
Purchase" is a horse which, harnessed to a gig, has mounted a hilly road at
high speed. The vehicle, with its passengers, is boldly relieved against a sky
flushed with sunset hues. "The Cattle-Drover" is a lean little man who sits on
a broad window-sill with a glass by his side, which, being empty, may
perhaps account for his air of rueful meditation. A character-sketch equally
good is that of an ancient rustic servitor, who goes up the stairs at an inn,
carrying a tray well filled with rummers of spirits "For the Farmers".'[4]
'. . . very talented water-colour sketches of life in the west country, by Mr
JBY, a young artist of considerable promise . . . drawn with much rapidity of
execution, but with great skill, and, in many instances, much delicacy of
colouring.'[5] 'He has a knack of catching attitudes and expressions, and he can
draw horses in motion.'[6] '. . . on account not only of their cleverness of
observation, but also of their charm of colour and treatment, they deserve a
degree of praise much higher than it is usually possible to bestow on art of
this class. They are really in many instances quite excellent.'[7]

There was acclaim for *The Man on the Merry-go-round*. There were also
references to Jack as 'brother of Mr W.B. Yeats, one of the most distinctive
of the younger poets — the one certainly who has most magic and glamour'.[8]
Elsewhere he was referred to as the '. . . clever brother of a clever brother'.[9]
They foreshadowed what was to become a regular and uncongenial comparison. There were some unfavourable comments, but the show, by any standards, was a resounding critical success. Few young artists starting out could
have anticipated such coverage. It was doubtless helped by the fact that Jack
had already earned a reputation among journalists as a lively illustrator. But
in this 1897 exhibition of Devon watercolours, Jack had achieved two important changes in his art, one technical, the other psychological. He shifted
from drawings to watercolours. He still used a pencil; he was essentially a
draughtsman. But the large-scale works already mentioned combined softer
line, freer shading, with the subtle use of washes, and a broader palette than
he had previously deployed. These are large-scale paintings, freer, more open,
more composed. Psychologically, Jack had made the transition into a new
and quite different world, predominantly that of the farmer in the west of
England, and he had absorbed a whole range of activities and situations which
clearly demanded, and got, the benefit of his probing and receptive capacities
as an artist. Not only the individuals, drawn from different generations, but

their relationships with each other, are carefully and sensitively explored. This had been achieved, more or less from scratch, in the space of about a year from the time he and Cottie moved from Surrey to Devon. Whatever previous knowledge either had of this part of the world, the complete command with which Jack presents it, in the dozen or so great watercolours from this exhibition, is profoundly impressive.

One exception should be mentioned, and it is significant for his work in the future. As one reviewer pointed out, '... the scenes are almost entirely masculine. The one thing wanting is the feminine charm, to soften the virile strength of strapping countrymen who are depicted. Even the waiters who are serving beer to the farmers at an agricultural show are men. A rosy West Country lass might have been happily introduced behind the extemporised bar in this picture . . .'[10] Jack had moved on from the immediacy of the sports illustrator to a particular locality where family life was part of the hidden picture. But he seems to avoid it. His interest in these drawings remains an interest in the masculine world of the racecourse, the tavern, the hunting field and the fairground. He was quite conventional, and of his time, in viewing the world as male-dominated. Where women appear in his illustrations, from 1891, they fall into very limited categories; the 'Gibson Girl' type, clean-jawed, handsome, with large bonnet and piled-up hair, the East End 'Character', or the frail, winsome creature, whose eyes are cast down in embarrassment or shyness. When he moved to Devon, and turned his hand to larger, more subtle work, he still seems to have avoided scenes or subjects which included women. They were later to feature, particularly as his young female emigrants, the grieving mothers, and the aged women of Ireland; but here again Jack reverts to conventions, and presents his women more or less as 'types', not as characters, not really understood or explored in artistic terms.

Just over a quarter of the works at the exhibition were sold, grossing 67 guineas. The principal purchaser was Mrs Corscadden, for whom Jack had designed and decorated doyleys; she bought three watercolours, including *The Glow Worm*. Elkin Mathews, later to become the artist's first publisher, for his early plays and other books, bought *The Light on the Foam*.

Behind this exhibition lay a vast collection of detailed work which is revealed in Jack's main sketchbook for 1897, which again is one of a small, rare group of larger format sketchbooks, assembled at home, and mainly used there. Into it he pasted numerous watercolour and pencil sketches from elsewhere. He was later to confine himself, almost exclusively, to five-by-three sketchbooks, the smallest on the market, and all of them hinged with two metal split rings, allowing individual drawings to be extracted and returned. What was seen in the exhibition was his public work, perceptive, varied, but also entirely objective. In the sketchbooks we go behind the scenes, as with a diary, and discover his private and intimate life (see figs 73–5; plates III and IV).

A favoured subject was Hooligan. No man loved his dog more than Jack loved Hooligan. Only he was allowed to watch Jack at his labours. Hooligan was a mongrel, yellow ochre in colour, as intelligent as Socrates, as beautiful as Helen of Troy. Hooligan went with his master down the steep slope through the valley wood to the studio beside the river each morning, and sat, sometimes at the open door, sometimes in the window, while Jack painted. He was a prince among pets, free to move anywhere. He is depicted lying on

73. *Hooley with Cat*, sketchbook drawing with watercolour, 1897.

or beside Jack's desk, surrounded by pen, pipe, water, boxes, alarm clock, paintbox, paper and portfolios. One drawing is inscribed: 'Hooligan looking down the lane for happenings' (fig. 74), and another: 'hearing things behind his back – the mighty hunter'. Jack caught him in all his moods, the black smudge of his muzzle in marked contrast with his yellow coat.

Jack and Cottie had their own hens. These were models for watercolours. He painted the sheep and cattle, the lapwings which he first saw at East Allington, and thought them blackbacked gulls. He drew the carthorses, the dead moles, grasshoppers, ducks, rabbits, a bull irritated by flies burying its head in a bank and goring the earth. He captures the arched wingspread of a heron rising from marshy ground, and the plodding labour of two great carthorses. He did three drawings of insects, in pencil and watercolour, inscribing one of them *The Whackinist Grasshopper*.

The people in his sketchbooks are mainly local farmers, children, the west country gipsies camped on the edge of Slapton Lea. He watched and recorded harvesting, there are five numbered drawings of the gathering of corn near Slapton, and a watercolour of Wallace, the man who helped the Yeatses in their garden, working in the local allotments.

Jack was fond of children, and his tiny sketches of the Strete children for whom he was to construct his miniature theatre, write his plays, and design all his characters, are brilliantly observed in village occupations. A small boy drives calves home; Jack captures in a few simple lines the wayward cattle and the turned sole of the child's boot lined with studs. There is also a study of the young Gillards drinking – two tiny children bent over a square stone trough.

He revisited Branscombe, where the whole family had spent a summer holiday in 1879. This inspired one of relatively few straightforward watercolour landscapes. In general such studies did not contain the life and action which seemed so essential to him. Nevertheless, he did a certain number of rich, lush studies of the valley and the woods below their house.

Snail's Castle itself, the laneway beside it, the garden with its flowers and vegetables, are extensively drawn in the early sketchbooks. It was as if Jack, transported from sport and action to the remote bucolic life of the country-side, redirected his restless eyes to everything around him, recording the latch on a gate, a truss of wood, a brilliant interior, in watercolour over pencil, which very delicately conveys the comfort and the security of his new life. He shows us the plants in the garden, the view through a window at night, towards the steep hillside, with the outline at the top etched in evening indigo through the trees. In the autumn he drew the interior at Snail's Castle, the fireplace, with fire burning, the apples on the shelf, beans drying on the window sill, a vase of flowers, a mouse caught in a trap, the breakfast table, with french windows and garden beyond. And there is another interior of Snail's Castle showing a boxroom with empty luggage piled up, among it Jack's portmanteau from his journeys as an illustrator (plate II).

They loved the house. It was small, comfortable, remote, secure. It nestled into the hillside, facing towards the south, with woods below through which he walked – one has to scramble today through undergrowth; the path down to the studio has vanished, and the studio itself is a ruin. Then, his vital energies were exercised in silence and stillness, with only the sound of the river running outside and the distant cry of sea birds rising above Slapton Lea. In his garden he erected strange figures, one of a Red Indian, a memento of the Wild West Show. The Brownie Camera was in vogue, and he and Cottie

75. *Morning, Snail's Castle, August,* sketchbook drawing with watercolour, 1897.

76. Jack and Cottie, with Hooley, outside the studio at Snail's Castle, *c.* 1897.

77. Jack on the shingle at Strete, *c.* 1897.

78. *Lady Gregory*, pencil drawing by John Butler Yeats, *c.* 1900.

used it to record their life together, and their first guests. Jack installed a window on which had been inscribed the message, 'To Cottie from Jack', with a sketch cut in the glass of a small ship.[11]

One of the visitors to the Clifford Gallery exhibition was Lady Gregory, who liked Jack's work and was to become a practical supporter, acquiring works from subsequent shows, and greatly encouraging him (fig. 78).[12] Willie wrote to her: 'I am glad you like my brother's drawings. If his exhibition does well or fairly well he intends to go to the West of Ireland next year.' The brief comment, from one of the principal architects of Ireland's artistic renaissance, possibly implies a remark made to Willie which went beyond the mere announcement of future travel plans. But Jack was in no hurry to join any movement, or become part of a concerted programme of artistic or cultural action on behalf of the Irish people. He had determined on a course of action, in moving from Chertsey to Strete, and it had paid off.

Though he laid plans for a visit to Ireland in 1898, the first thing he and Cottie did was to set out on a celebratory trip to Italy in the spring of that year. They crossed the channel and took a train to Venice, where they spent a few days, with Jack painting gondoliers, and views across the lagoon. Then they went on to Milan before travelling up to Lake Como. They stayed in a rather grand, corner room on the first floor of the exceptionally smart Grand Hotel Villa d'Este et Reine d'Angleterre, in Cernobbio, on the lake shore, ten minutes from Como. Their booking confirmation – for Room 100 – is pasted in to Jack's sketchbook of the holiday. Jack had come a long way from Bedford Park, where John Butler Yeats was struggling to get the house redecorated, and meeting with obstruction from the landlord, to whom he owed £13 arrears in rent.

Jack sketched constantly. His sketchbooks are filled, as always, with character studies of men and women seen in the streets, minor officials in uniform, who always had a particular appeal for him, in part because of their colourful appearance, in part their propensity for striking attitudes which had an innate appeal to Jack's sense of humour. At this time he was doing a light yellow ochre wash across the paper, giving a dusky richness to the subsequent blues and greens. When they went out on a lake steamer, Jack drew the passengers, and the bill of fare pasted up on a bulkhead offering, in English, '2 mutton chops'. They travelled on to Lucerne. Then they came home.

No work was developed out of this European trip, or indeed out of subsequent Continental visits. Only his visit to New York, in 1904, had any direct impact on his more substantial work. It was not part of the artist's design. He was neither a landscape artist depicting distant places, like Edward Lear, nor a genre painter or painter of street scenes, wishing to produce work and build towards an exhibition which would, in part, be a record of personal experience. On the other hand he could not be other than working, wherever he was, so his 'visual' diary depicts his trip across Europe and back.

The couple returned to a summer of shows and events in Devon which included the Brent Races, the Bampton Druids' pageant, and the Blackwater Show. Jack inscribed his sketchbook with the cryptic title: 'BEGUN IN MAY ENDED IN JUNE – LIKE THE PROMISE', and he packed it with all the rural excitement of South Brent steeplechasing, under the auspices of the Devon and Cornwall Hunt. He had an indexing method; he would write a heading to sections in each sketchbook, and then conclude them with 'END OF

75

79. *Over the Fence*, pencil and watercolour, *c.* 1897.

80 to 83. Line drawings of Devon racing life, *c.* 1895.

BRENT', so that the record is clear and chronological, even if the material is a tumbling mixture of odd and delightful characters picked out from the passing scene, a bearded fiddler, children watching the water-jump from a vantage point up a tree, or a solemn-faced Devon countryman dressed up in Druid costume carrying a banner on the May Bank Holiday festival. More or less unobtrusively, he was able to record people enjoying themselves; in this he often records the self-parody and self-exaggeration, which are so often a part of such holiday occasions.

The day's events consisted mainly of races: the mile, the hundred yards, the 120 yards hurdles, the pole jump, 'Boys' Race', Horse potato race, and a half-mile flat race 'for Druids over thirty years, and for juvenile Druids – a handicap.' Sports were to commence 'at 3 o'clock p.m.; 'all disputes to be settled by the Judge, whose decision shall be final'. There was 'A Grand Procession – with 'Two Bands'. It was so grand that it promised a 'total eclipse of all previous attempts – Great Tableau of Ancient Kings and Queens in Original costumes, drawn by 4 grey horses, with Maids of Honour and Body-Guard in uniform . . . The first Tiverton Company of the Boys' Brigade and Brass Band in full uniform are expected under the command of Captain Davey, and will join in the Procession, and go through various drills in the field.' Jack witnessed and drew the details. He was soon drawn more closely into other activities as well, and recorded in a later letter to Lily how he went out to the sportsfield in Strete to assist in laying it out for sportsday.

The glorious June of 1898 was followed by fine weather in July and August, with the visit of Lord John Sanger's Circus to Dartmouth the high-point of mid-July, recorded extensively in a single sketchbook into which Jack pasted a brilliantly colourful poster of the event. He loved printed ephemera. He kept many scrapbooks of the oddest items assembled together, tram tickets, the colourful printed tissues with which Spanish oranges were wrapped, cigar papers, embossed letterheads, advertisements and member-ship cards.

Later in the summer, Jack and Cottie set out for Ireland. He was commit-ted to two exhibitions the following year, one in February at Walker's Gallery in London, the second in May in Dublin at the Leinster Hall in Molesworth Street. His decision to paint Ireland was a bold step. If life in the west of England could have the undoubted appeal which his Clifford Gallery exhibi-tion had enjoyed, then life in the west of Ireland might do the same, and would fulfil much deeper yearnings within his soul. What he had done in Devon was to paint the people around him. And this was a development of what he had been doing as an artist since he started out earning his living as a teenager. Bent on this course of action, Jack declined an invitation from Lady Gregory to bring Cottie to stay with her at Coole. John Butler Yeats had fostered the notion, thinking that it would be valuable for Jack. 'I was very sorry Jack and his wife could not accept your kind invitation. Jack does not know his Ireland outside Sligo. A hurried rush through the country is bad for work, and especially in the case of Jack who is contemplative and sensitive and finds all his ideas in that direction.'[13]

John Butler Yeats went on promoting the idea of a visit to Coole. Murphy suggests that Jack was reticent about visiting Coole because of Lady Gregory's disdain for Cottie, and there is limited evidence for this, though the relationship developed and flourished later. It is more likely that Jack was developing his wider knowledge of Ireland in his own fashion, and had no wish to have this confused by the literary activities at Coole which were directed towards the creation of a national drama.[14] He was also working for the two exhibitions, in London and in Dublin, and they represented a major undertaking. So it was a working trip without social dimensions.

They spent several weeks in Ireland that summer, starting in Galway and Connemara, moving up the west coast to Sligo, on to Donegal, then travelling south to Limerick, and finally to Cork. To say that Jack soaked himself in the life of the west is an understatement. He lived, breathed, smelled and tasted nothing but Ireland, its life and its people. He missed nothing. His sketch-books are filled with every possible event. The Galway races, the dry stone walls, the market women selling gooseberries, the hurling and football championships of Munster, boats, ships and the sea, all are tumbled together in a multitude of tiny watercolours, drawings and sketches which fill sketchbook after sketchbook, and have a quest-like pattern to them.

His love of racing took him, inevitably, to rather different kinds of meeting from those he knew in Sligo or London. The Galway races are a west of Ireland institution, a great social event. Everything stops dead, shops close, serious drinking is undertaken, and a medley of people arrive in the city for the week. It was no different in Jack's day, and he covered the event, painting the race course across two pages, in pencil and watercolour – the touches of wash are delicate. He stuck into his sketchbook a Galway racecard for Wednesday 3 August 1898. There are drawings of details, slight sketches of a child, barefoot, with hurling stick; a youth, similarly attired; an adjacent sports ground, with fence made of sacking; a scene in pencil, of a man sliding down the corrugated roof of a barn, having negotiated barbed wire at the top, and then sitting with his feet overhanging a counter. The man behind the counter is saying, 'Yer bloody big eejit!'

He went from Galway into Mayo, recording countryside, farm animals, mauve cows in green grass; studies of boats, seashore, sky; boatmen, clothing on a wall; the rocky seashore; a headland, with everywhere the deep mauve colours of heather. This was classic Irish landscape.

In mid-August, Jack and Cottie headed north into County Sligo, staying until the second week in September. The children were returning to school, recorded by Jack, who must have been reminded of days idly spent contemplating the brown waters of the Garavogue from the bridge in the middle of the town, when he was returning to school. They were in time for the Rosses Annual Regatta; yet events of this kind seemed less compelling than the task of remembering and recovering the artist's own past experience. He spent a good deal of time doing this on the quayside in Sligo, where he wandered among the sheds and warehouses after the arrival of a Pollexfen boat, the S.S. Killowen, in order to draw in pencil and watercolour the ropes and skillets tied with red tape, the butter in buckets, and a girl holding a baby sitting in the stern of a boat.

IRELAND MUST BE FREE! said the banner, invoking the centenary spirit of 1798, then being celebrated in every town and village in the country. Jack's imagination was caught by it all. Every little shop had in its window cheap prints of Robert Emmet, and others of 'The Illustrious Sons of Ireland' – Thomas Moore, Oliver Goldsmith, Patrick Sarsfield, dressed in his armour, and Brian Boru. Jack did two drawings of Robert Emmet, based on the famous prints, and showing the patriot in green coat, his hand outflung clasping his hat, or alternatively standing, with arms folded.

But the great event for nationalist Sligo was the laying of the foundation stone for the Bartholomew Teeling statue on the road between Ballysodare and Collooney. It was here that the Franco-Irish Army under General Humbert was confronted by the heavily armed English force. An English cannon mounted on rising ground was wreaking havoc in the French-Irish ranks. Teeling, a native of County Antrim, rode through the enemy lines, charged up the hill and shot the gunner dead. This turned the tide in the engagement, and the English were routed. The French and the Irish were later defeated at Ballinamuck, in County Longford, and after the battle, though the French were granted prisoner-of-war status, over 500 Irish soldiers were slaughtered. Teeling, despite being a French officer, was later hanged in Dublin. *The Sligo Champion* devoted a two-page spread on Saturday 10 September 1898, describing it as a 'Magnificent Demonstration'. The crowd, Jack among them, was addressed by local politicians, and by Father Brady. Jack's drawings of them, and of the tents and booths which turned the event into a pageant of patriotism, filled a sketchbook. The leader of the Tubbercurry Band, which played for the afternoon, was dressed up in Emmet Green, wore a tricorne hat, and carried a sword.[15] Jack recalled his visit in a letter to Ernie O'Malley,[16] who bought *Death for Only One* in 1939, and who visited Sligo at that time. Jack wrote: 'Those were good conversations you gathered under the shadow of Benbulbin and Teeling. I was at the Carrignagat meeting in 1898 when the statue was unveiled. There was an orator there clothed in his special suit for oratory, not cloth of gold, but cloth of billiard table.'[17]

Before they left Sligo Jack and Cottie weighed themselves on a public weighing machine which delivered up its verdict on small printed cards; Cottie was seven stone three pounds, Jack twelve stone. They travelled north on a train for Donegal pulled by The Connaught, sketched rapidly by the artist before their departure, and they ended their trek through the two counties in a circuit which included Dungloe, Burton Port, Ballybofey, Stranorlar, the Barnsmore Gap, and the Diamond in Donegal Town, all of which are recorded.

He loved the odd and the unusual. He did a tiny sketch of a gate made from two wheels locked together, and wrote at the bottom, 'at least I don't think it moved'. He stopped at sunset to sketch Aran More from the road coming back from Dungloe, a rich and atmospheric watercolour, with vivid orange and mauve in the sky. There were donkeys on the sandhills on Sundays, musicians playing brass instruments, the interior of a shop with a man behind the counter checking letters and the people crowding in 'waiting to hear of letters'. The mail came in a mail basket slung below the postman's cart. Donkeys rolled on the roadway, and he did a wonderful drawing of a cart moving away in the distance, being watched by villagers outside each house, with the mournful caption, which he was later to develop in further watercolours: 'TO AMERICA' The low-life was ever-present: two men carrying a third, slumped between them: 'trying to get him by braces but the buttons burst'; a second drawing of man lying flat on his back, with the two men crouched on either side.

84. *'Let Me See Wan Fight!'*, watercolour and pencil, 16 × 11, 1905.

The conscientious labour bore fruit. For the London exhibition at the Walker Gallery Jack showed forty-four works. They were of racing scenes, political events, sport and of course people. Muldoon, the famous Sligo jockey, well-known to Jack, is exhibited for the first time. There is a celebrated fight on the race-course in *Let me See Wan Fight*, a watercolour from a drawing done at the Galway races, and depicting a farmer trying to stop his son from becoming embroiled in a race-course scrap (fig. 84). Others include *Looking Back*, *The Three Card Man Meets his Match*, *Donkey Races*, *Inside the Whiskey Tent*, *St Stephens*, and *Going to the Races*. *The Rolling Donkey* was much commented on in reviews. Several works in the show reflected the impact made on Jack by the Carricknagat celebration. One, called *Political*, depicts Father Brady, in top hat, on a rearing horse. Then there is *Robert Emmet*. But in this group also must be placed his commentaries on social life, *The Cow Doctor*, *The Dispensary Doctor*, *The Emigrant*, *The Returned American*.

There are human interest subjects, such as *Johnny Patterson Singing 'Brigid Donoghue'*, *It's the largest fi-irm in Ireland*, *The Yankee Table Cloth*, *The German who played 'O'Donnell Aboo' in the Rosses*, *A Long Team*. And finally there are his sporting subjects, a grim-face boxer – *Not Pretty but Useful*, and a West of Ireland rowing race crew, *The Losing Crew Going Home*.

In critical terms, though not in sales, Jack's first Irish exhibition was a success. 'Mr Yeats, in a word, gives us, with wonderful go, not indeed without some elements of caricature, a very personal view of Irish scenes and Irish life.'[18] Jack marked important passages in his reviews with a cross but wrote no comments. One review, by Lady Gregory, was particularly apt, and invoked the Gaelic wisdom of Douglas Hyde: 'Yet the Exhibition, as a whole, emphasises the words of 'An Chraoibhin' – "Not careless and light-hearted alone is the Gaelic nature; there is also beneath the loudest mirth a melancholy spirit, and if they let on to be without heed for anything but sport and revelry, there is nothing in it but letting on." '[19] And the reviewer goes on to deliver more detailed comment about individual drawings, emphasising the inherent melancholy of the Irish situation, the sadness of the departing emigrant, the awkwardness of the one who has returned, prosperous, smart, well-dressed and well-to-do, 'but out of tune now with his old home and his old life, and with more than American restlessness in his heart.' The review was signed with the letter 'G'.

Praise was not universal. Jack also had his first really bad notice, in *The New Age*:

It has often been a matter of surprise that so few artists select Ireland as a painting-ground. A visit to an exhibition of 'Sketches in the West of Ireland' by Mr Jack B Yeats may explain the reason. If nature, animate and inanimate, is in reality so repellent as he portrays it, the mystery is solved. We fear, however, that the fault lies with the artist . . . weak and faulty draughtsmanship . . . crude and dirty colour . . . subjects utterly hideous . . . the liquid and transparent qualities of water beyond Mr Yeats's grasp . . . well advised to have kept these 'sketches' in the privacy of his portfolio . . . he seems to have devoted more care to his catalogue titles than to his drawings . . .

CHAPTER SEVEN

Miniature Theatre 1900–1901

Have I done anything or nothing?

85. *The Merry-go-Round Man's Horse*, watercolour and pencil, $19\frac{1}{2} \times 11$, *c.* 1900.

IN LONDON, JACK had a considerable professional reputation as a success ful illustrator, and was enjoying his first recognition as creative artist. Holding his second solo exhibition, in February of 1899, this time at the Walker Art Gallery, he certainly had a London following. Dublin was quite different; he was a newcomer, and an outsider. There were no professionally-run galleries; instead, artists took halls and organised their own showings, and this was to be Jack's method, in Dublin, throughout much of his career. This casualness reflected Dublin's, indeed Ireland's, attitude to the visual arts. His impact could not be measured in the same terms as his brother's, which spanned poetry, drama and politics, three pursuits innately expressive of the Irish character. Moreover, what he was doing, as a painter, came at a time of literary and political ferment in which the visual arts could play only a relatively marginal role. In thanking Lady Gregory for her helpful notice of the earlier London exhibition, he mentioned that it seemed to be doing better than the Devon watercolours, 'which is encouraging'.[1] But he says no more of the reception his work received in Ireland.

He was detached from so much of what was going on in Ireland. His brother and father had spent time in the late 1880s and the 1890s in contact with enthusiastic nationalists. Jack had made no significant contribution to the events which drove his brother with such determination onto the barricades of Irish nationalism in the period following Parnell's downfall and death in 1891. Nor were those 'barricades' at all suited to Jack's temperament. Politics took a turn from parliamentary activity to cultural enthusiasm, but it was the culture of the word rather than of the visual image. Though it is simplistic to suggest a total switch, it is undeniably true that Irish nationalism was reforged and made infinitely more sophisticated and powerful by the creation or rediscovery of an Irish literature, part-Gaelic, wholly of the countryside, of the people, and of the myths and legends of the past. While Jack's brother was at the centre, with his retelling of Irish folk and fairy tales, and his drama, there was no equivalent expression of nationalism in the visual arts. Even ten years later, following the Irish Art exhibition at the Guildhall, in London, in 1904, the response to an Irish visual tradition remained slow and uncertain.

Jack's detachment lasted till as late as 1898. Temperamentally unsuited to the high seriousness of revolutionary politics, he was more interested in sport than Hyde's objective of 'De-Anglicising the Irish People'. He was immune

86. *Talk*, watercolour and pencil on board,
10 × 14, *c.* 1905.

to the emotional manipulation of a Maud Gonne, and content to pursue his
talent in isolation from events in Ireland. He would eventually come to it in
his own way. But his work was not part of any 'movement'. He wanted
freedom and independence for himself, from his troublesome family, in order
to get on with being an artist, and he had no wish to investigate or bring
about the freedom and independence of the Irish people. There is a cool and
laconic quality to his query in a letter to Lily: 'What's Willy full of these
times – He must feel mild minded after the theatre and all is over.'[2]

Jack and Willie had grown from different psychological and emotional
roots, had been conditioned by contrasting political debate during their early
years, had operated at different cultural and creative levels of inspiration and
performance, and had gone their separate ways. Willie's early books, both
prose and poetry, had fulfilled many of the preliminary demands for self-
definition which laid the foundations for the 'Movement' or 'Revival', and he
had inevitably been drawn into politics. Willie had been present at the
meeting in London, in January 1892, when the formal decision was made to
establish an Irish literary society there. He followed this, in the spring, when
he went to Dublin and joined forces with Douglas Hyde to promote the
National Literary Society at a public meeting later in 1893. In December
1896 another meeting of enormous significance for Willie and for Ireland
occurred in Paris, when he and Synge debated the rival merits of different
European literatures, with Synge being persuaded by the older man to turn
his back on France and Germany, and travel to the west of Ireland in order to
discover the rich language of his own people.

In the later 1890s the pace of development gradually quickened. A cast of
characters had been recruited; lines were written, scenes set, stage designs and
properties acquired; and a vast drama, which was to change Ireland for ever,
was about to have its première. Lady Gregory joined forces with Edward
Martyn and Douglas Hyde.[3] Coole became the Green Room. In July 1897,

during an extended two month visit by Willie to Coole, the possibility of 'a Celtic Theatre' was extensively debated. Standish O'Grady, Sir Horace Plunkett, George Russell, were there, in addition to Lady Gregory, Hyde and Willie.[4] And this debate about the literary ideas which should guide Ireland into the new century was extended in the months which followed. An added political tension was given by the centenary of the 1798 Rising.

Was Jack's absence from all this intentional? He had expressed his interest in Ireland to Willie. He had done Irish illustrations for his brother's books, and he had determined on visits to Dublin and the west which had a specific artistic purpose, to record life in the west of Ireland (see fig. 85). But it was done from the remote home which he and Cottie had established for themselves in Devon. And it was done cautiously, even shyly. Jack, by nature self-effacing, was ill-suited to polemic and agitation. His art, in the end, could only express the people, the landscape, the life of Ireland as he found it during the extended summer visit. He was by nature and training an observer, a reporter. There was no way in which he could adapt his work to the representation of Celtic myth and legend, just as it was quite impossible to isolate, in his work, the 'Irish' content-matter, from more universal visual imagery. What he did is clearly defined in the title he gave to his shows: 'Sketches of the West of Ireland.' But they included the Anglo-Irish gentry, and members of the Royal Irish Constabulary. In all the literature of the Irish Cultural Revival – wrongly called the Irish *Literary* Revival, since it was much more than that – Jack remained a shadowy figure. Contemporary newspaper records give him fair coverage, and describe him accurately as part of the revolution. Literary historians have relegated him to the sidelines.[5]

His future hung in the balance. Had his decision to provide images of 'Life in the West of Ireland' been the right one? It seems so.

'This is regular Yeats week in Dublin,' wrote a commentator in the *Irish Independent*.

> The sombre Yeats has his poem-play enacted in the Antient Concert Rooms, and the sunny Yeats has his pictures on exhibition at the Leinster Lecture Hall. No two brothers were ever so different and yet so alike. The Celtic characteristics are alive in both . . . The painter boy has the advantage in many ways, and he laughs so pleasantly. He tells the stories of his pictures with a charm that has a fascination all its own.[6]

The newspaper included this as social comment, and the writer interviewed the artist. Jack talked about his work and the experience which lay behind it:

> 'You see that Emigrant?' Well, I passed that car in County Sligo, and give you only what I saw. There is not a single detail there that did not impress me as I moved by. That is why I got the effect. It strikes me now as it struck me then. It was very pitiful. Oh, yes; that sketch taken at a political meeting. It was there I heard a funny old man keep interjecting the word 'undoubtedly' as a running approbation to one of the speakers. 'I feel I'm out of place, coming, as I do, after the gifted orators who have gone before me.' 'Undoubtedly,' nodded the old man in the audience, with genial consent. 'Nothing that I could say would make ye do more for the cause.' 'Undoubtedly,' again from the man below the platform. 'I can't say much – ' 'Undoubtedly' smiled the punctuator. Then the row began.

84

87. *The Squireen*, watercolour and pencil, 14 × 20, *c.* 1899.

These contributions appeared in addition to a lengthy review of the show. The newspaper also carried a line illustration of the first rough sketch for *The Emigrant*. The review was written by Mick Manning, a journalist on the paper who was known to Jack Yeats. He saw the point of what Jack was trying to do in the emotive context of this particular work: 'The story is heart-breaking in its terrible simplicity.' And he goes on to set down the sad outline, the driver of the jaunting car, listless and dejected, and no doubt related to his passengers; the old woman, crying her heart out; and the girl, her daughter, off to employment in New York. It is, as the writer admits, a common enough scene that many visitors to the exhibition could shrug off easily enough. Yet the heart-break is in the simplicity of it all, 'the young girl, attractive beyond measure in the ugliness of dry-eyed misery, looking back upon the barren lonely tract of mountain side that was, until now, her world . . .'

George Russell (fig. 89),[7] wrote an important review in the Dublin *Express*:

These sketches of the West of Ireland reveal a quite extraordinary ability in depicting character and movement . . . the old rollicking, sporting, drinking, unthinking aspect of Irish life, familiar enough in literature, but never hitherto adequately represented in art. There is a weird power in these sketches which gives them a distinct place of their own in art. It is not due to caricature but to an almost poetical excess of energy in the conception. Scenes and characters such as we meet with every day have been stored up in the artist's memory, and then have been re-created by a vivid imagination . . . It is not an ideal Ireland that has been reflected in Mr Yeats' mind, but it is in a certain measure true, and the intense vigour, originality, and grim power of these sketches ought to attract many visitors to the exhibition.

89. *George Russell*, by John Butler Yeats, oil on canvas, National Gallery of Ireland, 1903.

Lady Gregory wanted Jack as part of her 'Revival' team. There is a diary entry at the time where she says: 'He is too good an artist to leave to Devonshire, I want to keep him to Irish things –'[8]

Jack was far from being nervous about his first Dublin show. The London exhibition in February had done so well that he was short of work, and wrote to Edward Martyn to borrow back an earlier picture:

Dear Mr Martin (sic), I am going to have a show in Dublin of the remains of my sketches that were in London as there are not very many I am borrowing back some of the ones that were sold – Can I have yours – If yes then will you if the picture is in London fill in the address at which it is on the enclosed postcard and please post it. If it is in Galway then we can call for it and take it up to Dublin with us. The show is going to be the same week as the plays.[9]

His brother's play, *The Countess Cathleen*, with Maud Gonne in the title role, was the first production of the Irish Literary Theatre, together with *The Heather Field*, by Edward Martyn. It seems that John Synge attended the opening night of the two plays and the opening of the exhibition. He then went to Wicklow and was there in the early summer before his own second visit to Aran, in September.

Lady Gregory attended the exhibition. Jack's father was delighted. She bought *The Strolling Donkey*. There had been some possibility of Clare Marsh's aunt buying the same work, but her uncle blocked this. And in writing to

88. *Galloping Horses*, watercolour, *c.* 1899.

90. *Portrait of Jack*, by John Butler Yeats, 1903.

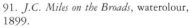

91. *J.C. Miles on the Broads*, waterolour, 1899.

commiserate, John Butler Yeats, with a rare display of commercial acumen, commented on Jack's art: 'Jack is a Pioneer. His style is quite new. Therefore all his pictures are sure to rise in price. As it is he has raised his prices greatly over what he got a year ago.'[10]

Lady Gregory liked Jack, and said so in a letter to his father which brought a rapid and fulsome response:

I am so glad you like Jack and I am so glad you asked him and his better half to come and stay with you. I hope we shall shortly have them here. I expect to see them greatly improved and *expanded* by the liberating influence of your house and presence. I notice a *subtle* alteration in Jack's letters, as if his horizon had widened. When Jack's exhibition was in London, I saw two students with their faces close up to the pictures together trying to guess what his method was, i.e. how he mixed his colours. I thought to myself 'This is the sign that Jack is an initiator.' Jack is getting his happiness early.[11]

John Butler Yeats was later to refer to Lady Gregory's 'courageous eyes', which his brother, Isaac Yeats, who met her at the exhibition opening, thought irresistible. In a typically gushing letter, John Butler Yeats wrote of Cottie's 'wifely glee' at the fact that Jack did everything which Lady Gregory advised him to do.[12]

Lady Gregory was impressed by the whole family. A year before she had expressed admiration for a portrait of Jack by John Butler Yeats, who did several at this time, and a week after the references to Jack being 'expanded' by the contact, his father wrote to her again, telling of yet another sketch of his son, and alluding to a physical aspect which is interesting:

I have done a sketch of Jack, which in point of skill is the best I have yet done. The mouth, however, is not quite right. There is an ill-favoured want of proportion about the upper lip, to which I have not yet done full justice . . . I think you have done a great deal with Jack. I don't allude to the sixty pounds – but he has ideas, ambitions, hopes, that he never had before. I have had very little talk with him, but I gather this from his wife as well as himself. Jack having this very short upper lip is not quick at explaining himself.[13]

Jack and Cottie went off to Paris in June of 1899. Continental travel was a reward for critical success. The sketchbook of the trip is an inconsequential delight, full of tiny observations about the people. Later that year he and Cottie were invited for a holiday on the Norfolk Broads by a friend, J.C. Miles, and his wife (fig. 91). They also visited Yarmouth, and he did sketchbook drawings, which include a group in a large-paper sketchbook. These capture vividly the open atmosphere of Norfolk, and the gentle, safe tug of the sails and lapping of the water across the great open reaches with their flat, reed-lined shores. Miles and his wife remained good friends for a number of years, and Jack invited them to visit his London exhibitions. Miles was a subscriber to *A Broadsheet*, and expressed admiration for Jack's art. He owned a fine drawing done on the Norfolk Broads. On the occasion of one of his London shows Jack hoped they would be able to meet, 'and we might go and see some bloodshed or something'.[14]

Later that summer Jack and Cottie returned to Coole, and he filled several sketchbooks with sketches of their more relaxed and extended visit. It

92. *Robert Gregory on Sarsfield*, sketchbook
ink and watercolour, 1906.

93. *Tea at Coole*, sketchbook watercolour,
1906.

included a trip to the Aran Islands, Jack's first. At the time Lady Gregory had employed Arnold Harvey, a Divinity student at Dublin University, to tutor her son, Robert, who was then eighteen years old. Harvey and Jack became friends. Jack preferred the company of the younger people at Coole, particularly Harvey. They played 'Up Jenkins!' and other country house games.

As autumn approached he and Cottie went home to their castle. They were deeply attached, and liked entertaining their friends there. One of the first to stay was Harry Hall, who came several times. Arnold Harvey also took up an offer to visit when Jack met him at Coole. Hall was then engaged in archaeological work in Egypt, and wrote out 'Snail's Castle' and 'Ello, Yeats' in Egyptian hieroglyphics. 'It is very funny with him because anything of the last couple of centuries is horribly modern and up to date to him – dealing as he does always with only the earliest of Egyptians. We find a vase we have is I dont know how many years before Christ.'[15]

Susan Yeats died on 4 January 1900. There had been a long period of illness with increasing failure of her mental faculties. Her death was misdiagnosed by the family doctor. She had really succumbed to a series of strokes, and this had led to mental breakdown during the last six years of her life. Willie, in a letter to Lady Gregory, on the day of his mother's death, said that it had been inevitable 'for a long time', and added, 'it is long since my mother has been able to recognize any of us'. It was 'a great blow to Jack & there was no softening of the news, for it came too suddenly; and he was devoted to his mother'.[16] He recognised in her many qualities which become evident in him. His mother, like his grandmother, had an easy way with people, and John Butler Yeats described her as sharing with Lily and Jack the 'facility for understanding and being interested in poor people, and this not out of benevolence, but a sheer liking'.[17] In fact, Jack, unlike the others, ignored his mother's declining mental faculties, and right to the end wrote her entertaining and loving letters, and went on sending her money for medical treatment long after it was useless. In one such letter he wrote:

> My dear Mama – The weather has turned cold lately. perhaps we will have a hard winter it is about due they have been so mild for some time now – We have made our cider and it is now working rumbling in a hogshed. I went to see it pressed – which is quite a romantic process – a great wooden press – in a dark shed – a horse to turn the mill – and a farmer's boy and man in leggings to do the laying out of the apples under the press – and to force the long iron lever round – and little fat children peek in at the door and – are given a drink of the new sweet juice – then the carter brings the juice home to you and slops it from his little barrels into yours – and you walk in zider for a week for the barrel overflows but there are worse things in store. I believe if the weather turns stormy you have to sit up all night with the zider – Your affectionate son – Jack B Yeats.[18]

He included in the letter a drawing of a man holding a candle sitting beside a leaking barrel. In another letter, dated 30 December, he wrote:

> I hope this finds you all well. People ought to be after Christmas – I remember years ago how amused Willy was one Christmas at Merville when I was feeling very poo poo on St. Stephens day – it seemed to him

that I upheld in my person all the traditions of little boys and Christmas – it was as though he'd woken in the night-time and seen Father Christmas looking for his stockings. The Valley children have not yet seen the theatre – Some other children of whom Lilly will wot – the little girls and boy at the Fosses – were to come first but the weather has been very bad – Fairly mild but raining like Billyo – We will like to have Willy come down very much and hope the weather will be better. I have had a cold in my nose but am better now. Theres no news Cottie got a good many letters and cards at Christmas more *letters* I am glad to say than cards. With wishing you all a happy new Year – Your loving son – Jack B. Yeats – I send cheque.[19]

Hilary Pyle points out that Jack's sketchbooks cease for a period of six months, and he would undoubtedly have felt grief. But he was extremely busy at this time with several projects, including his exhibition in Dublin. This was in February 1900, and was his second in the city. It did not go as well as the previous show, despite, in Lady Gregory's view, 'a great improvement in colour from last year, & as full of energy and imagination'.[20] The attendance was extremely good. She listed Provost Mahaffy, Lord Powerscourt, Lady Arnott, Lady Fingall, Douglas Hyde, Miss Stokes, and Sir George and Lady Morris. 'The pictures much appreciated & admired, but alas, no sales – it was dark & the gas turned on, & some people said they would come & see them by daylight – but anyhow buying wasn't in the air – Poor Jack ill after a working night – I went out for bovril & champagne for him & he cheered up.'[21]

He was also busy producing a prototype broadsheet, using handwriting and stencilled illustrations. It was primitive compared with what was going to appear in January 1902, but Jack was quite proud of it, and wrote to tell Lily how glad he was that she liked the broadsheet, 'but weep that you do not understand – I sent one to Low he didn't understand either and was seriously annoyed with me I believe –.'[22] He was also attempting to produce a book on the pastimes of Londoners.

At the beginning of March Lady Gregory sent Jack a telegram, asking him if he would like to meet the American writer, Mark Twain. Jack, who was staying with Uncle Isaac at 52 Morehampton Road, wrote back that he 'would like *very much* to meet the man who wrote "Huckleberry Finn"'. Lady Gregory wrote in her diary: 'Jack came out, & told anecdotes & did a sketch of George Moore from memory which delighted them – & Willie read Mary Hynes, & some of the Rafterys – & they wanted to hear one of his own poems, & he couldn't remember one, & I wrote out 'Angus' for him to read.'[23] It was a great success and Jack amused people by telling them Mark Twain's 'second advent story'.[24]

The death of their mother brought the family together. Jack arranged a memorial plaque in St John's Church in Sligo. He contacted the vestry for approval, and then wrote to Lily and asked her to confirm the wording with Willie, and to choose the design and style. He later wrote to say that everything could be done by letter, 'perhaps without bothering him as there is nothing to say but "erected in loving memory &c"'.[25] Lolly was on a visit and was also consulted. It was to be coppered brass, with red and black lettering. John Butler Yeats was not consulted, and there is a note of relief in a letter from Jack to Lily that their father went off suddenly to Paris at the time. 'Now when Papa is away is the time to arrange everything.'[26] The brass tablet, to the left of the pulpit as one faces the altar, has the inscription: 'To the Memory of Susan Mary, wife of John Butler Yeats and eldest daughter of the late William and Elizabeth Pollexfen, of this Town. Born July 13, 1841, Died in London January 3rd 1900. Erected by her Four Children.' The exclusive 'Four children' is significant.

Jack is otherwise quite well disposed towards his father at this time, makes jokes about him being 'the Paris boyo', and 'the Parisien' (sic), and looks forward to a visit after his return from France. John Butler Yeats visited later that summer. In the meantime Jack was anxious to help in arranging an exhibition of his father's pencil sketches, but felt that they would have to wait until the war in South Africa was over. 'I am sure it would be a good thing if the expenses were kept very low – frames cheap though chosen with care and only one week at Walkers costing a fiver. And sending out a lot of invitations stating that Papa was open to do similar portraits of people perhaps mentioning that price £5.5 a piece.'[27]

Following his father's trip to Paris, York Powell suggested to Jack 'a picture show in Paris – perhaps papa could mention vaguely the idea to Mr. Ellis, about where – galleries and costs – also what about duty? Perhaps an empty studio?'[28]

Lolly's stay with Jack and Cottie at this time was happy, and coincided with a great deal of activity in the house and garden. It was a warm spring. 'You would like the wind here it comes right out of the west and hits you very hard but it has boxing gloves on.' Jack and Cottie went fishing in Slapton Ley. They were hoping to catch perch, 'that we may cook them according to Isaac Walton's receipt. And who knows they may have the effect of making poetry roll off our tongues.'[29]

'When you come down', he wrote to Lily, 'we will hope to have some fruit to give you – currants and goosegogs look well, but the birds will come later on and bring up their young entirely on a fruit diet.'[30] Jack spent one day tarring parts of the roof of Snail's Castle, while Lolly went off to sketch in the orchard, their cat perched on her shoulder. She had been unwell, but recovered greatly during her stay, 'doing herself well,' Jack wrote, 'eats breakfast!' Lolly was contemplating getting a bicycle. Jack thought it would do them all good, and cautioned Lily: 'Only whisper this to the bicycle *not* to Lolly – *It is Difficult to Talk on a Bicycle.*'

Jack and Cottie were much involved in local life. Children picked Easter lilies in the garden to decorate the church, and they were terribly proud to have marsh mallow growing, the leaves of which were needed 'for the trapper's knee'. Jack urged the bucolic life on the Londoners, suggesting that their father should take to bicycling as well, and go out by train to 'West Drayton or one of those places about a sixpenny fare – after which there would be real *Hedgerows* to ride through anyway – with inns – bread and cheese or a cup of tea would make a turning point . . . You yourself should ride a bicycle with a southerly aspect.'

In June John Butler Yeats and Lily had a holiday in the Gara river valley, both of them painting, Lily painted a fine water-colour of Jack's studio on the edge of the wood below the house, looking across the meadow towards the river bank (fig. 94). When John and Lily came to stay they were put up in the farmhouse beside Snail's Castle. Whatever rules Jack later made, at that stage he was happy to share his studio with his father, and the two men worked side by side, John doing a portrait of Lily, and writing to tell Clare Marsh how

94. *Studio at Snail's Castle*, by Lily Yeats, watercolour, 1902.

happy he was that it rained every day, since it meant that both he and his sitter were confined to the studio. 'I had three weeks in Devonshire; Lily and myself were at a farmhouse only a few minutes from Jack, so that we enjoyed ourselves very much and did not trouble about the rain.' He wrote to Willie, who had been ill,

> It is beautiful here. I wish it were possible for you to come and occupy Jack's spare room. He was speaking about it yesterday. His house is extraordinarily nice and comfortable – Chippendale furniture etc. with pictures and art in a small thatched house among thick woods seems as if it were something quite new. I think you would like the place greatly. Cottie is as hospitable as possible and both have the gift of making life peaceable.[31]

He added 'I worked all day in Jack's studio, he also being busy there, and Lilly was sitting to me, so that the rain did not matter. In fact I think I liked the rain, my daughter being better satisfied to remain indoors with me.'[32] On one occasion the rain brought thunderstorms; John wrote in a letter to Willie: 'I suppose you heard that Jack and Lily were as near as possible being killed by a flash of lightning. Both were knocked down.'[33]

All that spring Jack worked on his 'Pastimes of the Londoners' (figs 95–7). 'My big London sport book grows & is pleasant work to do', he wrote in one letter to Lily, and then later reported: 'Well tis nearly done . . . Willy said the 'Dome' people called about it – I must go see Willy or write to him about it as I don't know whether the 'Dome' people have money or not. It is a very fine book but I don't know whether I'll find a publisher or no.'[34]

Jack was also occupied at this time with the preparation of plays for his miniature theatre. Miniature stages, with cut-out actors and actresses which were pushed on and off stage with strips of card, were one of his enthusiasms, and at least two shops in London specialised in all the requirements, including the lurid texts of melodramas, often involving pirates and brigands. Jack has a collection of these. But his interest went far beyond performance. He wrote his own plays for miniature theatre and performed them for the local children. He did everything; drew the characters, mounted them on card, and coloured them. And they are magical.

They belong to a strange and now forgotten genre. Almost any successful play put on in London, if it contained enough excitement and action suited to family entertainment, found its way, in one form or another, into the miniature theatre. The expression 'Penny Plain, Twopence Coloured' derived from the way in which the printed settings and characters were issued. It was also the title of Robert Louis Stevenson's essay on miniature theatre in which the author, according to Jack, 'told people what fine things these plays were'.[35] The originator was Skelt, whose 'Juvenile Drama' consisted of a toy theatre with the texts of a collection of plays, and with the scenery and characters in a printed form to be mounted and cut out. The plays, mainly anonymous, are listed by Stevenson: *Aladdin*, *The Red Rover*, *The Smuggler*, *The Inchcape Bell*, and *Three-Fingered Jack, the Terror of Jamaica*, which comes closest to the pirate dramas which Jack was later to write. The miniature theatre was hugely influential. Stevenson was the acknowledged authority: 'What am I? What are life, art, letters, the world but what my Skelt has made them? He stamped himself upon my immaturity. The world was plain before I knew him, a poor penny world: but soon it was all coloured with romance.'

95 to 97. 'Pastimes of the Londoners', pen and ink drawings, late 1890s.

95. *Fleet Street*.

96. *A Pugilist's Funeral*.

97. *Barrow Racing*.

Stevenson was given his 'Skelt' for his sixth birthday. Jack at the same age was absorbed in his own, home-made 'Farm'. Skelt's idea and the material passed through several hands, Park's, Webb's, Redington's, and finally Pollock's.[36] In the early days, hand-colouring was used, so that purchasers had the choice of ready-prepared props and equipment. Later, printed colour vied with the uncoloured versions which adults and children could mount for themselves and then paint.

The first knowledge we have of any outside interest in Jack's plays for miniature theatre comes from John Butler Yeats, who read *James Flaunty, or, the Terror of the Western Seas*, towards the end of 1899, and wrote to Willie:

> Did I tell you about Jack's play written for his puppet Theatre? It is the prettiest and most poetical little play I ever read, 'Flaunty, or the Terror of the Western Main.' You read it in five minutes and it is only when you read the last line that the tenderness and beauty of the whole idea flashes upon you. The play is done with the most wonderful stagecraft. You and Moore and Pinero and Arthur Jones had better take lessons from Jack. I assure you the play haunts me. He must have a real gift for *construction*.[37]

98. William Butler Yeats at Coole, *c.* 1900.

Willie evidently did not like the play much, hardly a surprise, in the light of the drama which *he* was producing, and said as much to Cottie, who passed the view on to her father-in-law. He wrote to Willie in late December:

> I am greatly disappointed to hear today from Cottie that you did not greatly care much for Jack's 'Flaunty.' I do think you are quite wrong. I do want you to encourage Jack as much as possible to go on writing these little plays, which are something quite fresh and original. *If encouraged* he will I feel certain produce scores of them, each with its own *special idea and invention.* It will become a sort of speciality with Jack . . . It is too delicate for Moore . . . If Jack is not encouraged he will drop the whole thing *perhaps*. I say 'perhaps' because I know Jack never drops anything.[38]

James Flaunty was followed by *Timothy Coombewest, or, Esmeralda Grande*, which Jack wrote and played in 1900.[39] Jack wrote about it in a letter to Lady Gregory.[40] He also told her that 'nothing came of' an exhibition, planned to be held in Torquay. This was probably because he had shifted so substantially to Irish subject-matter. Jack was puzzled about the Boer War, and expressed his hopes that no friends of Lady Gregory were involved. 'I don't understand the war at all it seems that everyone has 'beliefs' about it.'

John Butler Yeats's judgment is good on the quality of the plays. Jack himself, naturally enough, valued his father's support and welcomed his understanding. Years later, in a letter to Thomas MacGreevy, referring to a comment about him having 'the Stevenson touch', he rejected totally the idea that his little plays were 'quaint' (and he put the word inside a drawing of a signpost, and added 'When all the signposts are down the one that shows the short cut to QUAINT remains.'). Then he went on, 'How much better to be like my father who had never used, or even thought, of the word in his life – and so he was able to carry on about my little play (little because it would only take ten minutes to play) James Flaunty and read it out to old friends of his own with seriousness.'[41]

His conception for the craft of the miniature theatre was original and distinctive. For all the admiration he felt for the blood and thunder of traditional dramas, his own interpretation was quite different, and in its way both masterly and – for those who read the works, or even better, perform them – enchanting. Though the stories were filled with conflicts and tension of a high order, involving violence, cruelty and death, he went out of his way to create action 'with as little movement for the figures as possible'. The essential unfolding of the plot was by dialogue. There was stage business, of course. He was inordinately proud of his stage 'business'.

> In the harlequinade of *The Playful Pilgrims or The Gamesome Princes and the Pursuing Policeman*, there was a town crier who moved his arm, and rang his bell, and a clown in the same play who smoked his pipe with real smoke. The town crier's arm which rang the bell was worked with a string which ran down his back and along the side of his slide, and the clown's smoke was blown from behind the scenes through an india rubber tube.[42]

Jack insisted that the parts be learnt. It was never good enough simply to read them. And he was conscious of the need to 'do them in different voices':

> after talking for some time in the husky voice of Captain Teach, you find that for a scene or two, all the characters are speaking their lines in the same deep notes – for the time you have acquired the throat of piracy and you must be very careful – shuler Pine must not speak with the same voice as Eldorado Gillen or James Flaunty.[43]

He built the stage to his own scale, the proportions quite different from those of the live theatre. The proscenium, which was elaborate and decorated in an old-fashioned style, was three feet nine inches wide, but only one foot ten inches high. He dispensed with lofty stage settings on the grounds that these were 'responsible for the incongruity, which we sometimes see, of the heroine and her little boy, starving in a garret, with so much top room that they could have floors put in and let the place out in flats.' His scenery was painted in watercolour on good quality paper, and then pasted on cardboard. He did the same with his cut-out characters, providing them with rigid stands and strips of card with which to push them on and off stage. The cardboard was of a dense and quite heavy quality, so that the whole structure, fixed and moving parts, was strong and durable. His painted colours were bright and vivid, and for large areas of colour he often used coloured papers which he spent the later months of the year collecting. These papers gave great brilliance to the backgrounds. The scale of the whole operation was designed so that two or three dozen people could watch comfortably.

The stage was lit with candles backed with reflectors, proper footlights, which gleamed on such props as the silver cap from a champagne cork, used as the shield carried by a mounted Arab. It always caused a warm reaction from his audience. He could not always understand what it was that appealed specially in his characters and scenes. One mounted rider always received an ovation; others were ignored. And a clown disguised as a parrot in the company of a pantaloon as a sailor man 'was also always received with honour'. Jack himself had favourites: 'The emerald in *Esmeralda Grande* which was borne aloft in the processions by four Nubians upon an oaken tray and was of the shape and bigness of a pineapple, was a pretty fine thing and much admired'.[44] This dimension – how the plays were received, and what impact the stage business had upon Jack's audiences – was of course of the utmost importance, and is possibly overlooked in Robin Skelton's criticisms, which label the first play, *Esmeralda Grande*, 'the least interesting' of the plays. It was

99. *The Whirly Horses*, pen and ink, 1903.

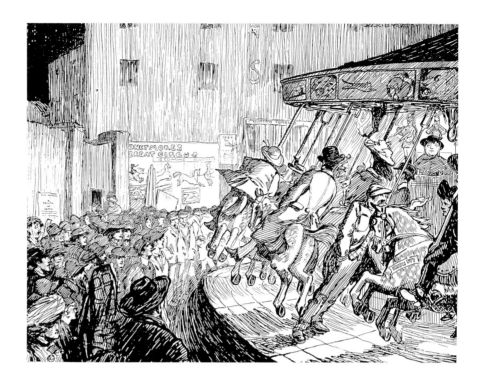

completed by Christmas 1899 and played in January 1900, and again during the summer of that year, when Lily came to stay together with their father. Jack also put it on for Harry Hall, who came on a visit then.

Jack had the utmost respect for children. One of his New Year performances is recorded as part of an entertainment put on for the National School children of Strete, sixty-five of whom sat down to tea. This was followed by the singing of a hymn, and a programme of music. 'Then came a cleverly contrived miniature circus exhibition in the Infants' Room, shown by Mr J.B. and Mrs Yeats.' And after that there was a magnificent Christmas tree. 'The children received a bun and an orange on leaving'.[45]

Jack called his circus performance for his miniature theatre, Onct More's Circus. It was played on 3 January 1901, to the schoolchildren of Stret again. The name is a joke of Jack's, 'Onct' being a dialect word for 'Once'. A poster on the wall in the background to his drawing, *The Whirly Horses*, done in 1903, advertises ONCTMORE'S GREAT CIRCUS (fig. 99). It was probably the most difficult of all his miniature theatre productions. After playing it for the Strete children – which was the equivalent of going 'on tour' – he did another showing in his own home for the Valley children, a smaller, more select band of neighbours' offspring. He played it again, in March, for his sister-in-law Polly, in April before someone described as 'Poor Indian', and to Pamela Colman Smith later that summer.

The difficulty of circus – which Jack, of course, adored as entertainment, and painted all his life – was that action could not be contained in the dialogue, except perhaps in the exchanges between clowns. It had to be physical, as the programme so clearly indicates, with the 'entry of attendants', the arrival of the Ringmaster, the 'celebrated Gonsalvas in his first jockey act', 'the Countess Castilla in her great high school act on her highly trained Arab, the Nubian Clown – Sad Alphonso'. He had two other clowns for that performance, Tuffcake and Cream, and he gave an exchange between them: 'Tuff: I am going to ask you a riddle. Cream: He's going to ask me a riddle boo boo. Tuff: How many walls make a river? Cream: How many walls? I dunno. Tuff: Then I suppose I must tell you – one if it is big enough – Now I will ask you another riddle . . . ' He pasted the details of these performances in an early nineteenth-century copy of a periodical called *The Cottage Magazine*, in which he did stencils, drawings and watercolours. The circus was broken up the following year, though not before Lily, on her visit, had taken a series of indistinct photographs with her Brownie camera.

James Flaunty, or, The Terror of the Western Seas, was published in 1901. *The Treasure of the Garden* was performed in 1902, when it was played before Harry Hall, who came on a visit in October. And *The Scourge of the Gulph* a year later. These three plays represent the high point of Jack's theatricals, though they were succeeded by other productions, not subsequently published. He put on *James Dance, or, the Fortunate Ship Boy*, on 2 January 1903, for fourteen Valley children. A year later he did *The Mysterious Travellers, or, The Gruesome Princes*, as well as *The Pursuing Policeman*, which was a pantomime, for the Valley children in January 1904. And his long creative endeavour seems to have come to an end during the following two years, with what he called a 'Gallanty Show', put on for the Valley children in 1905 and 1906.

What of the plays? To Jack they represented fun and entertainment; they sustained the cartoonist in him, but in a more sophisticated and subtle way. Real characters were created, visually vivid, but also expressive in dramatic terms. And they were embodied in living drama. It is difficult to agree with Robin Skelton's view that *Esmeralda Grande* is the least interesting. It is certainly the most substantial, running to three acts, and a with time-span of eight years. It is the story of a quest. Timothy Coombewest, a farmer's son runs away to sea, but first pledges his love for Marjorie Morning, and makes her promise to marry him when he returns in 'perhaps five years, perhaps ten – but not more than ten'. He enrols with Captain Sheaf as Cabin Boy. But Captain Sheaf is really Captain Blackbeard, bound on a treasure hunt for a large emerald the size and shape of a pineapple, buried ten feet deep in the sands of a southern Pacific island. The opening is in Sligo; the climax of the first act involves a dramatic swearing in of his crew by Captain Blackbeard: 'By the wind from Carrick-na-Gat . . . By Ben Bulbin and Knocknarea . . . By the old trade and the merchants of the old trade . . . Until our Bones are White . . . Oh-h-h-h-h-h (shudderingly).' All ends happily with the hero returning home as Captain Coombewest, he is celebrated and fêted, and marries Mistress Marjorie Morning.

James Flaunty, or, The Terror of the Western Seas, is a one-act play, in five scenes, less grand in its structure than *Esmeralda*, with characters who act without clear motive. It is set in a seaport on the coast of west Africa. It involves pirates, bribery, treachery, gallantry and shootings. The play was published by Elkin Mathews in 1901.[46] How seriously Jack felt about his miniature theatre may be seen in a letter he wrote to Lily:

> The other night I made a trial picture (you know those weird old fashioned theatrical portraits where they cut pieces out and put real velvet &c in) of James Flaunty as he appears in the show card which I did for Mr Mathews When I did it I felt it was truly lovely, indeed I hung it so that as I sank to rest my eye rested on it to the last. and so that when I woke it was all

alive oh waiting to be gazed upon. Oh dear! he has a black velvet shadowy hat a green tinsel jacket. crimson velvet breeks and a silver painted pistol and shining sword – when you come to these parts you will see him – rather I should say when you come to see him, you will be able to take in these parts.[47]

James Flaunty is the first of the plays to have come down to us with all its designs, though not in the enlarged format which was adopted later for *The Treasure of the Garden*. The changed format was perhaps in response to the popularity of the earlier plays, perhaps in response to a more practical demand: that the characters and scenes in the plays could be directly cut from the printed copy. The characters are drawn in simple, bold outline. Elkin Mathews had been the next-door neighbour of the Yeats family since 1893, living at 1 Blenhcim Road with his five unmarried sisters. They modelled for John Butler Yeats, who also did drawings of Mathews which seem to belie the fin-de-siècle mystery and romance which his books often evoke; he is shown as the conscientious, self-aware, essentially shrewd businessman he clearly was. No doubt his expression partly derives from a suspicion that the artist might well be contemplating a request for payment in cash at the earliest opportunity. Jack's own first experience of working with him was when he was asked to design, or offered to design, an invitation card for an 'at Home'.

The publication of the play, together with subsequent plays brought out by Elkin Mathews, represented further work, since there were demands for hand colouring. 'I sent back the 12 copies of Flaunty – but I didn't know whether you wanted them *fully coloured* or only the covers – so I have done half a dozen one way and half a dozen the other.'[48] Apart from all other considerations, the plays for miniature theatre earned Jack a modest income.

The Treasure of the Garden has a Sligo setting, and refers directly to the character, experience and behaviour of old Grandfather Pollexfen, his fine reputation in respect of emigrants, and the stern attitude he always maintained towards shipowners who sent passengers to sea in vessels which were not as sound as they should have been.[49] Jack's translation of piracy and sea-going adventurers into his plays presents a strange mixture of terror and sweetness. The braggart heroes of his adventures have hearts of gold. The violence in their eyes and faces, the bristling cutlasses and pistols, are belied by a softness in their actions, and mercy sometimes, and compassion. The plot is sinister, and concerns Old Henderson, who owns *The Gleaner*, an unseaworthy vessel, which he seeks to send out into the Atlantic, filled with emigrants. Willie McGowan, a former pirate, is master, reluctant to fall in with Henderson's wishes. Various scenes of skulduggery and treachery follow, involving treasure, sinking ships and death. The hard and inscrutable characters, on both the good and the bad side of the drama, became symbolic figures for Jack, and were subsequently represented in many of his paintings, stripped of course of their miniature theatre origins, but no less clearly part of a cast of powerful and mythical images drawn from the world of piracy and high sea drama.

The Scourge of the Gulph, in the play of that name, is Joe Miles, whose challenge to the threatening Captain Carricknagat provides the main action, and leads to a memorable closing line, in which 'the tenderness and beauty of the whole idea flashes upon you'. It was this which so appealed to John Butler Yeats, but left Willie unmoved. On opening the treasure chest, having shot

100. Illustrations of set designs from *The Scourge of the Gulf*, a play for miniature theatre.

the captain, Flaunty finds: 'An empty skull, a black box, a dead skipper! Have I done anything or nothing?'

The rest of Jack Yeats's miniature theatre consists of pantomime and variety, including *The Wonderful Travellers, or, The Gamesome Princes and the Pursuing Policeman*, which was played to the Valley children in January 1904, but never published. A good part of Jack's characterisation is in his drawing. His pirates are theatrical figures, exaggerated and colourful in dress and gesture, laconic, melodramatic, occasionally grotesque, his women at times innocently beautiful, at times as haughty as Gibson girls. It is memory of the Sligo Quays, of Ben Bulben, of Rosses Point, which inspires the action and the characterisation. Both he and Cottie were involved; they put on a show for the local children. It was nothing more than that.

There was a brief public response to the plays when they appeared in Elkin Mathews editions. Jack issued them in two versions, at one shilling uncoloured, five shillings hand-coloured by himself. And the *Glasgow Herald* reviewer, though he felt *The Scourge of the Gulph* captured the Stevensonian atmosphere, thought the plays far too expensive for any 'stage-struck juvenile'.[50] In fact, both as books and as plays, they fell into something of a limbo. Printed by Elkin Mathews, they were part of the world of collectable books, fine printing, limited editions, and hand-colouring. But the purpose of the books, which greatly increased their subsequent rarity, was that they should be cut up, pasted up, coloured, and turned into the physical material for the miniature theatre.

In 'Penny Plain, Twopence Coloured' Stevenson wrote: Out of this cut-and-dry, dull, swaggering, obtrusive and infantile art, I seem to have learned the very spirit of my life's enjoyment; met there the shadows of the characters I was to read about and love in a late future . . . acquired a gallery of scenes and characters with which, in the silent theatre of the brain, I might enact all novels and romances; and took from these rude cuts an enduring and transforming pleasure . . .[51]

Jack concurred. He drew on his own childhood to enrich the lives of the Valley children in Devon, and of the much wider audience for the few plays he published. The stories are slight, yet revealing. They engage our attention at the level of fable or quest. Timothy Coombewest seeks his fortune, wins his bride; James Flaunty intrigues outrageously, yet survives; Willie McGowan confronts evil, saves his honour, but loses his bride-to-be; and Joe Miles presents us with Life's only imponderable: have I done anything or nothing? His most significant hero – Willie McGowan, in *The Treasure of the Garden* – is clearly based on William Pollexfen, and is a moral tale with interesting psychological insights. Its story has deep and tragic undertones, and the reference to the world of famine, emigration, the exploitation of unscrupulous shippers and middle-men, and the ultimate horror of coffin-ship deaths, is central to his upbringing, much of his early art, and his admiration for his grandfather. Yet it is all packed up easily and put away in the toy-room or among the lumber of his childlike early enthusiasm. It lies like a tiny nugget of life, to be discovered by those who will. Most who do are the collectors enticed by the undoubted rarity of the published plays. But some design, draw, paint and enact them, living again the wanderer's dream in the ghostly Grove of Heads on the Savage Islands, or beside the Smuggler's Cave of Rosses Point, or in the tropical romance at the Happy Return.[52]

There is in these plays, and in Jack's attitude towards them, a playful escapism, however seriously he undertook their performance, and with what skill and love he designed and painted the sets, and then illustrated the published works. Indeed, he had escaped. Devon was a remote and wonderful world in which to live, and he clearly loved many aspects of it. When the outside world intruded, it was temporary. For the present, rural life sufficed.

CHAPTER EIGHT

The *Broadsheets* and John Masefield
1901–1903

The noble deeds that we did

101. Jack, *c.* 1900.

J ACK WAS IN his thirtieth year when Queen Victoria died, in 1901. He had established a comfortable and settled life with Cottie in the west of England, but spent a substantial period of time in Ireland which provided him with the material for his art. Friends and family came regularly to stay, and from time to time they travelled.

Jack made his friends among those who had a like interest in the sporting life, in music hall, in entertainment. Typical of these was Frederick York Powell, Oxford scholar, and neighbour of the Yeats family in Bedford Park since 1887 (fig. 102). Jack seems often to have led the academic – twenty years his senior – to see boxing matches in low dives in the East End, which the older man loved, just as he loved Jack himself: 'It is strange how York Powell loves him', John Butler Yeats wrote to Willie, in December, 1899. 'Whether at work or play York Powell is always in holiday humour, loving his friends without any calculation or afterthought. But staying on till 2 o'clock nearly killed us all.'[1] York Powell was friendly with the whole family, and was described by Willie as his father's 'chief friend'. He lived in Bedford Park, at 6 Priory Gardens, for more than twenty years, from 1881 to 1902, escaping to London whenever he could from the atmosphere of Oxford, which he found less than congenial. He was 'a broad-built, broad-headed, brown-bearded man, clothed in blue cloth and looking, but for his glasses and the dim sight of a student, like some captain in the merchant service'.[2] Jack called York Powell 'Yorick'. He designed a bookplate for him, showing St Francis releasing a dog.[3] York Powell was also a visitor to Coole.

York Powell took particularly to Jack and Cottie; indeed, he had known Jack since his return to live in London and study art, in 1887. In July 1896 he presented Cottie with a finely-bound and inscribed copy of *The Rubáiyát of Omar Khayyám*. He admired her art, and thought particularly highly of her illustrations to the poem, done later, now lost. Writing to her on May Day 1902, from Christ Church, Oxford, and addressing her as 'Dear Mrs Jack', he told her, 'You have done the best illustrations for Mr Omar yet done. Do some more and publish them in a little album . . . They are really adequate to Omar's strength and meaning.' York Powell was an expert linguist, and the previous year had himself translated quatrains from the Persian poet. He also accepted a gift of stencils.[4]

If Jack taught Frederick York Powell the delights of prize-fighting in London's East End booths which were tough places, York Powell helped to

102. *Frederick York Powell*, pencil drawing by John Butler Yeats, *c.* 1900.

reinforce and widen Jack's enthusiasm for ballads, songs and poetry. Two examples among many sent to Jack by York Powell represent a fine taste in both men for the essential simplicity and sentiment of romance poetry in translation. York Powell had done a version of 'Winter', by Finn Mac Cumhal, after one by Kuno Meyer:[5]

> My tidings for you; the hart is belling,
> Winter is coming; summer is gone
>
> Wind high, cold; low the sun,
> Short his course; sea running strong.
>
> Deep red the bracken; shapes are hidden.
> The wild goose has caught his winter cry;
>
> Chill has caught the bird's wings:
> A Season of ice – these are tiny tidings.

'Isn't it pretty and true?' York Powell wrote to Jack. He also sent him another quite different song: 'The pretty maid she died, she died'.[6] York Powell, whose background was very English, recognised through language and poetry the differences between the two cultures, and added a note to one of his translations from the Irish, 'The Queer Man':

> It isn't half as good as the Irish, but it's the kind of way an English peasant who knew the Irish would put it for his own people to understand. It would not do to stick more closely to it, the idioms are not English, so I have used English idiom. I think it gives the sense pretty well. It can be sung to any long-drawn droning tune, with a chorus rather gay.[7]

York Powell was responsible for Jack's brief solo exhibition in Oxford, at the Clarendon Hotel, of 'Sketches of Life in the West of Ireland'.[8] When the exhibition closed, John Butler Yeats wrote to John O'Leary: 'He has sold some things, though not many, it not being the Oxford season'.[9] The exhibition seems to have contained works left over from the March show in Dublin, but augmented with a number of non-Irish subjects and a group of stencils, which were bought by a friend of Powell's. York Powell himself was given stencils the following summer: 'Jack gave me two beautiful stencils today. they are very good: the "metal man" in the channel at Sligo, pointing out the "fair way" for ships, an iron figure of a sailor painted like a figurehead. It is charmingly felt and given.'[10]

By then York Powell had become associated with Jack on his monthly, *A Broadsheet*. The first appeared in January 1902. *A Broadsheet* brought together old friends and new. Willie, Lady Gregory, George Russell, contributed, as did John Masefield. Ernest Rhys was drawn back into Jack's circle by this new collaboration. In some respects it was a friends' anthology, in the best tradition of Bedford Park co-operative thinking. And it endeavoured also to be commercial, as the letters exchanged between Jack and the publisher, Elkin Mathews, indicate (fig. 103).

Jack and Pamela Colman Smith edited together. She was known as 'Pixie'.[11] Thomas Nelson Page wrote of her: 'The "Annancy Stories," by Miss Pamela Colman Smith, a young lady who has recently come from Jamaica to live in this country, are perhaps the most original contribution to negro folklore literature since the day when "Uncle Remus" gave us his imperishable record of "Brer Rabbit" '.[12] By 'this country' Page of course meant the United States.

103. *Elkin Mathews*, pencil drawing by John Butler Yeats, December 1893.

She stayed there briefly, travelling to London later in 1899, where she met the Yeatses, possibly through Elkin Mathews. He would have known of her work as an illustrator; he later published an illustrated book by her.[13]

They were associates in a venture which demanded a great deal of work, yielded small return, and was of very limited public appeal. It had charm and originality. Pamela Colman Smith worked with Jack for the first year, but then, in January 1903, mainly because of the burden of hand-colouring, she pulled out. Jack found the association unsatisfactory. In a letter to John Quinn he wrote:

> Between you and me and the wall, as they say, Miss Pamela Smith (though I think a fine imaginative illustrator with a fine eye for colour, and just the artist for illuminating verse) is a little bit erratic, and she being a woman I can't take a very high hand with things, so there is often a lot of bother about the numbers, and I don't like being responsible for anything that I have not got absolute control of.[14]

This is a significant pointer to Jack's character; he preferred to work in isolation, and certainly worked best when, as later in *A Broadside*, he had discretion over the total content. Lily confirmed many years later the difficulties of working with Pamela Colman Smith: 'I used to go to her studio once a month and colour Jack's picture while she did hers, only a hundred. Yet she often lay on the sofa and cried because, she said, I was bullying her and making her work when she did not feel like work.'[15] Jack told Elkin Mathews, 'I will have to go on myself. I have put with pictures by Jack B Yeats & others because I will try and get an odd drawing here & there when I can.' He particularly liked her drawings, which in style are quite close to Cottie's, and the two remained friends. Cottie's copy of *Annancy Stories* was inscribed: 'Cottie with love from Pixie Pamela May 1904', and it contained three drawings, two of 'Pixie' herself, one of a mouse.

Each *Broadsheet* was printed on thin paper with a page size of 20 by 15 inches. All the illustrations were hand-coloured; and it was published by Elkin Mathews, from his shop in Vigo Street, and sold by him as well as by his two artists from their homes. It cost '13 Pence a Month; 12 Shillings a Year. In America, 25 Cents a Month; 3 Dollars a Year.' The inspiration came as strongly from England as it did from Ireland. Jack's ideas about drama and desperation came from piracy, the fickle sea, drowning, seamen and the like, and also from the heroic image of the itinerant figure, as often the English gipsy as the Irish tinker (fig. 104). Willie was in the first number, with his 'Spinning Song', illustrated by Jack, and a scene entitled 'The Blood Bond', from *Grania*, his play written with George Moore. In Pamela Colman Smith's drawing, the king is witnessing two young men drinking from a horned cup, and joining their bloodstained hands as blood-brothers. These two men, Finn and Diarmid, were later to feature in paintings by Jack. He also did a drawing of a Pooka, the nightmare figure of Irish legend, in this case in the form of a flying horse. There were also drawings of the Back Strand Races, in Sligo, and illustrations to translations by York Powell and by his daughter, Mariella.

Jack had several motives for what he did, probably the least important being money. Mathews was a specialist printer and publisher, who produced fine books and periodicals, which on the whole were quite expensive, and in editions with small print-runs. He had published Willie's *The Wind Among the Reeds* in 1899, and Jack's first play, *James Flaunty or the Terror of the Western*

104. *A Broadsheet*, July 1903, with illustrations by Jack.

Seas in 1901, and he continued to publish Jack's work. Mathews was part of the aesthetic movement. Together with John Lane, publisher of *The Yellow Book*, he could be said to have cornered the market in aesthetic books, a cult in collecting which was associated with the work of Whistler, Wilde, Beardsley and Beerbohm. In design, illustration and content, Mathews books seem to epitomise the fin-de-siècle atmosphere of death-wish and corruption. In reality, the emphasis on decadence, which had taken society by storm with the first appearance of *The Yellow Book* in April 1894, changed substantially by the end of the century, when writers such as George Moore and Laurence Housman, and artists such as Walter Sickert, William Rothenstein, Charles Furse and Jack himself became involved. Involvement with other lovers of the arts, seen collectively, was important to Jack. So was control, as indeed it seems to have been with Pamela Colman Smith, who, having offered excuses to Jack about finding the hand-colouring too much, immediately started her own publication, *The Green Sheaf*. This was also hand-coloured, issued by Elkin Mathews, and contained works by the writers who appeared in Jack's publication during its second year, when he ran it on his own.

Willie was in the first *Broadsheet*, but then did not write again. George Russell, Kuno Meyer, Frederick York Powell, all contributed on what might be described as the 'Celtic' side. They were balanced by English subject-matter, with John Masefield the most significant working colleague. Jack himself did pirate drawings. One of Pamela Colman Smith's drawings is of 'Henry Morgan, thus sailed he'. Jack also did drawings of his related enthusiasm, the miniature theatre. His drawings of Jack Sheppard, the Highwayman, in April 1902, indicate also his love of outlaw characters. Here was the subject-matter of the ballads Jack loved, the 'Whack-fol-di-riddy-iddy-tiddy-ol-di-ray' of going thieving-O! And then the result: Sheppard sitting in straw on the back of the cart which is taking him to Tyburn, his elbow resting on his own coffin, a bottle of booze in his hand.

Love of horses and horse-racing produced a drawing of the Back Strand Races at Rosses Point, and of four men at the races walking and singing:

Come gather round, and don't make wry faces,
'Till I tell you a tale of the Cumeen races,
Of Micky Mack and John Devine,
Mulsheen Connor and Gash o' Wine.

It is interesting that this drawing, also from the April 1902 issue, dated from 1892, ten years earlier. Jack was indulging in nostalgia for the broadsheet and ballad-sheet culture of his youth in Sligo. Ballad singing still flourished in the early 1880s, in the west of Ireland in particular. Singers were arrested during the Land War for singing songs against the payment of rent, and the whole tradition was on the fringes of both society and the law. After 1880 ballad singing and the sale of broadsheets fell off.

Jack's first gypsy, who appears in the issue of May 1902, is indisputably an English gypsy, the scene taking place outside the grammar school in a Devon market town. Everyone is looking with suspicion at the dark and swarthy figure passing down the street, a man of threatening appearance, with hat and stick, looking neither left nor right. Spectators include a typical middle-class 'hiker' – the kind of comic character Jack loved drawing – the schoolmaster, farmers, schoolboys and tradesmen's errand boys. The same figure, pervaded by the same sense of physical threat, appeared later, in what was perhaps his best representation of the type. This was his 'Dark-eyed Gipsy O', a fine drawing accompanying that wonderful ballad, 'The Raggle-Taggle Gypsy, O!' though Jack's title is 'The Dark-eyed Gipsy O!'. His version has more than a note of madness in the ultimate two stanzas:

What do I care for houses or land,
What do I care for my children O,
What do I care for my own wedded lord
When I follow my dark-eyed Gipsy O!

Then she took the garment that she wore
And wound it as a head-dress O,
Saying, 'I'll eat the grass and drink the dew,
And I'll follow the dark-eyed Gipsy O.

He published much that was Irish. George Russell's poem, 'The Gates of Dreamland', was illustrated by Pamela Colman Smith. Jack's own drawing of the west of Ireland mail car, and his inevitable Sligo ballad singer, singing 'The smashing of the Van' to a group of Irish peasants, were included.[16] There was also a drawing of an old man with a stick sitting on a stone wall addressing the sky, as an illustration to a translation by Lady Gregory from the 'Repentance' of Raftery, the Blind Connaught Poet, 'whose songs are known in every Irish-speaking county of Ireland'.

> When I was young my deeds were bad, and I delighted greatly in quarrels and rows. It was better to me to be playing or drinking on a Sunday morning than to be going to Mass. I was given to big oaths, and I did not let lust and drunkenness pass me by. . . . The day is stolen away, and I have not raised the hedge until the crop Thou didst delight in is destroyed. I am a stake worth nothing in a corner of a hedge, or I am like a boat after losing its rudder, that would be broken against a rock in the sea, and that would be drowned in the cold waves.

Jack included Lady Gregory's translation from the Irish of Douglas Hyde's short poems which include his 'Old Man Walking the Roads'.[17] Jack's own copy of Hyde's book, *Love Songs of Connacht*, has an undated inscription by the author, the first four lines, in Irish, of 'The Cooleen', 'A honey mist on a day of frost, in a dark oak wood'.[18]

John Masefield appeared a number of times in *A Broadsheet*. 'A Last Prayer' was illustrated by a drawing of Jack's of the seabed; 'Port of Holy Peter' by a drawing of two men on a ship, looking at a town in the distance, the scene for much pirate adventure. Other Masefield poems used in *A Broadsheet*, and illustrated by Jack, include 'Cargoes', 'Blind Man's Vigil', and 'Theodore', for which Cottie did the drawing, signed with her monogram:

> They sacked the ships of London town,
> They burned the ships of Rye and Cadiz,
> They pulled full many a city down;
> A bloody trade the pirate's trade is.
>   But Theodore,
>   Though dripping gore,
> Was always courteous to the ladies.

Jack claimed to have found Theodore 'in old-fashioned dime novels', and knew him as the adopted son of Jean Laffitte, or so he told Henri Pene du Bois, of *The New York American*, in a letter designed to correct the rather academic view taken of his work by New York critics:

> He was the adopted son of Lafitte the Famous. I do not know if Theodore ever existed in real flesh, but I have met him so often in old-fashioned dime novels that he exists right enough for me. We think him rather a little sneak, though picturesque; and a friend of mine, John Masefield, a one-time sailor, who has a fine turn for rhyme, writes of this Theodore —
>
> > As Theodore pulled on his trews,
> > (Oh, oh, the Gara River!)
> > The scarlet trews that pirates use
> > To make the merchants shiver,

105. Detail from *A Broadsheet*, May 1903; 'Cargoes' illustrated by Jack.

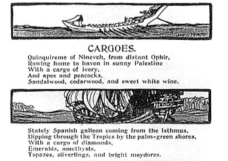

He found a purse in the lining stuck,
(Aha, the main top bowling!)
Which he had sneaked from a negro buck
The last time they were coaling.

Jack has painted him like that.[19] Theodore was a wonderfully effeminate pirate, who appears in many of Jack's drawings. In some he is wearing rouge on his cheeks. He has long eyelashes, and is shown in one drawing with his hair in a fetching little pigtail. Theodore was stylish and theatrical. He was later used to illustrate *A Broadside*. Masefield provided Jack with details of the grisly end of Theodore's protector: 'Did I tell you that I came upon an account of Laffitte's death in Honduras? They broke up his establishment at New Orleans; he sailed to Honduras; died there in penury, and was eaten by the local pigs.'[20]

York Powell wrote enthusiastically both to Jack and his father about *A Broadsheet*. 'Jack is going on broadsheeting fine' he told John Butler Yeats. And later in the same letter: 'Jack will be a great colourist some day. He has such feeling. He is a wonderful chap and so nice to do with.'[21] York Powell kept up a steady supply of verses, translations and anecdote, and kept in closer contact than any of Jack's other writers, particularly in the second year of the publication, when the artist, apart from the help he got from Cottie, was working more or less in isolation.

Returning from holiday at the beginning of August York Powell picked up the July issue and wrote immediately, praising the material, enjoying Mayo and Theodore particularly, and wishing Jack well for his Dublin exhibition. There was also contemporary Irish material; drawings of Hanrahan, and of Douglas Hyde acting in his own play, *The Twisting of the Rope*, with Lady Gregory's translation of a part of it. We see the first appearance of a theme of significance for Jack, that of the rose as symbol not just for beauty – we have seen hints of that in his childhood booklets, such as 'The Beauty and the Beast' – but also for secrecy. This is in the old Irish song, 'The Grand Conversation under the Rose'. The drawing Jack did is of Napoleon on a horse, galloping, his hand flung backwards.

A Broadsheet ended 1903 on a seasonal note with Jack's representation of Christmas mummers. The long, thin, drawing shows a group of children performing in the hallway of a house. On 22 January 1904 York Powell wrote to Jack thanking him for stencils, which reminded him of 'the Captain Cuttle, little ship sign, with the middy taking a sight of the sun with his sextant'. He had been in London, visiting exhibitions, and had stayed with Charles Conder. This artist, friend of William Orpen, Augustus John, William Rothenstein and Max Beerbohm, was then married and settled in Chelsea. York Powell visited his exhibition, and writes of Conder as though Jack knew him. The association is understandable, given the older painter's interest in theatre, his delicate, subtle, enchanting work on silk, and his decorative art in painted fans. York Powell, who died later in that same year, had been ill, and told Jack: 'I am better (since you ask, but I hate writing so much about myself and my health) and recovered my Folkestone relapse. I hope to go on better. Being with the Conders did me good. It is lovely here now and must be finer in Devon. There is a hard white frost on now, which only yields when the sun falls directly on it.'[22]

George Russell saw the point of what Jack was doing in *A Broadsheet*, and commented to Sarah Purser:

Jack Yeats and the little Carribean Pixie Pamela Mamosetti Coleman Smith, bring out a broadsheet monthly with coloured pictures. I like it. The first number has some drawings of Diarmuid and Grania and a picture of a green horse by Jack, 'The Pookha', which is splendid. The Gore-Booth girl who married the Polish Count with the unspellable name is going to settle near Dublin about summer time and as they are both clever it will help to create an art atmosphere. We might get the materials for a revolt, a new Irish Art Club. I feel some desperate schism or earthquaking revolution is required to wake up Dublin in art matters.[23]

Russell identifies here precisely the void which Jack was eventually to fill: the visual equivalent of what Willie and Lady Gregory, together with many others, were working at. Yet, as we have mentioned, Jack was guarded about the literary renaissance going on in Ireland. He was too elusive, too independent, too original, to want to be a foot-soldier in a campaign in which he had no real control, and over which the generalship lay firmly in the hands of his brother and Lady Gregory. He was undoubtedly interested. His exhibitions show a clear commitment, just as *A Broadsheet* does. But he was going to approach the matter in his own way, and in his own time.

By far the most important friendship in his life at this time – perhaps at any time – was with John Masefield.[24] Friend of both brothers, he had been drawn into the Yeats circle in the autumn of 1899. Masefield, younger than either Willie or Jack, had far greater experience of the world. He had enjoyed a happy childhood, but at the age of thirteen had left home for the Conway training ship where he trained for the merchant navy. He later sent Jack a photograph of the vessel, 'taken on our boat race day, in June 1893'.[25] He had qualified and gone to sea in 1894, on a voyage to Chile. Sent home from this trip as a result of both physical and mental illness, involving some kind of breakdown, he went off again within a year across the Atlantic. He deserted ship in the United States, and became a vagrant, taking odd jobs, reading widely, and beginning to write verse. His job when he met Willie was more mundane; he had lodgings in Walthamstow, and was a bank clerk. He wrote to the poet, asking if he could call. 'He came, told me how he had always wanted to write, and said, "What shall I write about?" I said, "Your life. Then you will find out about yourself." Upon this Masefield acted, and brought to the poet a chapter a week, and read it to him.'[26]

Jack appears to have been present at a dinner with Willie, Masefield, Laurence Binyon and Thomas Sturge Moore in January 1901. Either then, or earlier, he had told the story of having seen, in Sligo, 'an old man bite off the testicles of calves when a boy. He did one after another. It was his trade.'[27]

The friendships Masefield had with the two Yeats brothers were quite different. Towards Willie, bridging an age gap of thirteen years, the young poet was respectful, even formal. Jack was also some years older, but their friendship was founded in mutual love of the sea, children, children's games, pirates, vagabonds, ballads and sea chanties. There was a bookish dimension as well. Jack illustrated *A Mainsail Haul* with a charming drawing of two piratical characters drinking grog in a bar.[28] And Masefield dedicated his next book, *On the Spanish Main*, to Jack. And he must have had Jack in mind when he produced *A Tarpaulin Muster*, which has a lively and altogether appropriate introduction laying stress on the poor tradition of sea poetry in English

106. *John Masefield*, sketchbook drawing, 1903.

poetry, something which he, together with Kipling, though the latter to a lesser extent, remedied.

Masefield stayed with Jack and Cottie in Devon in 1901, and they made and sailed their first model boats on the Gara River that summer. There are photographs of Masefield walking along the river bank with a long stick in his hand, and fending a boat off the bank or away from the shallows. It was the first of many happy visits. Jack's love of the sea was experienced vicariously, through his friend. Like Robert Louis Stevenson, he 'loved a ship as a man loves Burgundy or daybreak', but unlike either Stevenson or Masefield, Jack's experience of the sea was confined to the journeys of his childhood and cross-channel packet-boats. Writing to Masefield after his friend had published an article called 'Being Ashore', Jack wrote: I'd like to be at sea when I read it, all but being up aloft. I who on top of the cathedral stay crouched as close as I can to the spire while the others look over the edge and tell me how they see men like flies walking'.[29] Appropriately perhaps, given not only Jack's timidity but also the fact that Masefield had abandoned the sea for writing, the enthusiasm they both had in abundance was scaled down to their shared love of model boats, pirate tales, sea shanties and theatre.

Jack, with Masefield, designed and constructed a number of different vessels, and his interest in model boats remained keen throughout his life. Among the simpler designs were sailing boats made out of cork, stone and paper, and a folding boat constructed entirely from paper. There were more robust efforts, but the life of most of their models was transient and short. As with his theatre, Jack wove the pleasure of their pastime into a romance to be shared with children everywhere; and he meant, as always, children of all ages, but having in mind particularly strong, bearded men in their twenties or fifties, or even seventies, who joked, and smoked, and drank, and yarned about their escapades around the fireside in the evenings. And he put this into written, practical, usable form, in books and articles, then and later. He also exhibited his drawings of homemade model boats, and the models themselves. He told Lady Gregory: 'I have sent to the exhibition drawings of all the home made toy boats which I had made from corks and cardboard boxes, including one I made in Coole which we called the Tata, which sailed away into the setting sun and vanished'.[30]

Their boat was the Monte, a small fore-and-aft schooner made from a flat piece of wood about five inches long, with thin wooden masts and paper sails (fig. 107). She had a string tie amidships, to hold in place a stone as ballast and keel. There was no rigging. The paper sails had holes in them, and these slipped over the mast. There was a rudder-cum-tiller stuck at an angle through the stern. Her voyage was short, sweet, varied, and ended in disaster. The stretch of the Gara River which they used ran from the narrow water-meadow below his studio towards the sea. The prevailing wind was with the current. And the Monte set sail on her first and only voyage with wind and tide: 'it was blowing a gale at the time – of course you will understand that it was not blowing a gale *to us*, but in proportion to the size of her, it must have been a gale *to her*'.[31] The Monte negotiated the hazards of Round Channel, Pirate's Leap, Bully Bowline, but then got into the wrong current, called the Blackwall Hitch, under some cliffs on the western bank of the Gara, and could have come to grief, 'and was only saved by very good steering from running straight into the very dangerous snags called the Bad Snags'. She weathered

107. *The Monte*, one of Jack's model boats, drawings in pen and ink.

108. The friendship between Jack and John Masefield produced many amusing letters from Jack, with eccentrically illustrated envelopes. They reflect their shared enthusiasm for ships, pirates, and cowboys and indians.

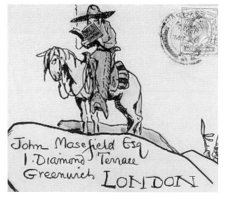

these, and crossed again the Marbley Shallows, so named 'because the stones under the water used to roll along like a lot of little marbles'. All went well until her skipper, 'like a silly', and one suspects the rueful poet was on that bank of the river, came out of Safety Cove and hit against a rock. She turned over, and that was the end of her. The poet, for his sins, wrote her epitaph:

> And now by Gara rushes,
> When the stars are blinking white;
> And sleep has stilled the thrushes,
> And sunset brings the night;
>
> There, where the stones are gleamin',
> A passer-by can hark
> To the old drowned 'Monte' seamen
> A-singing through the dark.
>
> Our bones are green and weeded,
> Our bones are old and wet;
> But the noble deeds that we did
> We never can forget.[32]

Masefield composed lines for most of the fleet, and for many other of the escapades that he, Jack and Cottie engaged in during the holidays spent together in Devon. Indeed, Pirate's Leap, a hazard on the north side of the Gara just below Jack's studio, was so named 'because a poet who had been a pirate, I expect, was thinking about a poem when he ought to have been shoving the vessel off the rocks, and so he fell in'. But it seems, from his first bread-and-butter letter that only the Monte was made and sailed on his first trip. What began then, and grew apace during later visits, was the writing of ballads. Masefield even called them the 'Cashlauna Ballads'.

Masefield wrote affectionately to Cottie, referring to himself as 'a love-sick swain', and saying how enjoyable his merry fortnight at Snails' Castle had been: 'I've been in such a whirl since I met herself that I'm not sure if the rest of the world isn't a dream, but even if this engagement goes contrary I shall still remember the merry fortnight at Cashlanna as one of the Royal Flushes in my life'. He admitted that their kindness had been of particular value, since he had been in a state of mind 'calculated to Jar a Person'. This referred to the approaching marriage.[33] He wrote every day to his fiancée, telling of his long evenings sitting with Jack and Cottie,

> The Yeatses are rare good folk in a rare pretty house, and I talked over my worship of you darling, in their pretty dining room last night, but I hardly like to tell you what they said as it is, I'm afraid, dear, too much in my favour. Darling Constance, they think this, that we ought to marry. Jack, who kept a very nice memory of you, was convinced of it.[34]

Jack drew Masefield several times inscribing each portrait sketch 'Thinking of Her'.

> We stand on a great hillside . . . and have gorse in full bloom above, and below a fine wood that drops down to a brook that brabbles [sic] continually with a noise that goes to ones heart . . . Our great delight is to build paper ships and set them afloat as targets for pebbles, and it is fine to see two such bad shots together . . . We have a wooden ship which has an engine room that smokes – real smoke . . . I shall never forget this part of

MASEFIELD AND MOBY DICK

109. *John Masefield and Moby Dick*, sketchbook drawing and watercolour, April 1903.

the world, and whenever I smell a faint smell of woodsmoke with a strong smell of primroses and wet grass I shall think of Cashlauna, and the toy boats skinning down the Gara towards the sea.[35]

Masefield, it seems, was contemplating an autobiography, for which Jack would do the illustrations, but it never came off.

Jack saw his friend off on the train from Kingsbridge, and Masefield wrote an entertaining account of various characters in the carriage, an 'Imperial Guffer', who talked throughout the journey through his hat, 'like a page of Titbits', a parson who 'jabbered a mortitious girt deal of bosh', and a pale lady who sucked on oranges. 'Tell the Skipper!' Masefield instructed Cottie, and went on to list in some detail the unremitting nonsense coming from his fellow-passengers, and the growing urgency of his desire to be able to punctuate the Imperial Guffer's jaw with a big full stop.

The Moby Dick, another of the model boats, was an approximation of a Mississippi steamboat, and built out of a flat piece of board some fifteen inches long by six across (fig. 109). She had a funnel, and a cocoa tin inside her cardboard cabin in which a fire was made out of paper and touchwood. Unfortunately, her anchor snagged in a weed, and the Moby Dick was dragged down to the bottom.

Masefield admired Theodore, and wrote a good deal of light-hearted verse about him, including his love-songs to Constanza:

My love's a duck, a dear, a sweet
And I hope no dust nor dirt'll
Pollute her neatly booted feet
Or spatter her russet kirtle

Masefield's Theodore was an object of humour among the pirates. He is depicted with a dainty nightie wrapped round him, and looking like a cherub. He is described on his knees, saying his prayers, and making people weep at the spectacle. He was a good man to dance, nifty on his toes, while the other pirates were busy 'chewing their tobacco to wind'ard, and spitting to looard.'

The vessel named after him was just a cardboard box, her lines painted on, and portholes cut in her side. 'We were in a great hurry to go out, so could only build her very badly.' What they really intended, it seems, was a big insurance claim. Masefield concluded one Theodore ballad:

And Theo says 'well it can't be cured
Its a lucky thing she was well insured'

'She caught fire suddenly – really, we set fire to a lot of touchwood and stuff inside her because we wanted to see what a ship on fire would look like on the river. And she looked splendid with the crimson flames coming out of her ports, and the reflection on the still piece of water just under the cliffs was beautiful.'

And let no landsman doubt it,
She was a gallant ship;
And her Cap. (brave man) throughout it
Kept a stiff upper lip.

Jack gives a calm enough picture, in the published version, of the way in which the Theodore was set alight. What actually happened was much more exciting. The two men were dedicated to playing their serious games. They had brass cannons, one of which was given by the poet to the painter, and they used these to bombard their model boats. Once again, Masefield put into spirited language how great it was when the crew of the Constancy, using swan-shot shells, tore into the sides of the luckless Theodore until the vessel was unrecognisable.

The Pasear was made from a green cardboard tie-box – Jack was quite a dandy in his day, and Masefield did his riverside duties dressed in a well-cut suit, with a low-crowned, broad-brimmed hat on his head. It was a two-masted, top-sail schooner, and she sailed nearly a mile, and was then left at Huckleberry Cove. Their finest vessel of all was the New Corinthian, and she was a real boat, in that the hull was a proper toy lifeboat, rigged by them with mast and sails, and given a lead keel. Liking her too much they sailed her only on a round pond called Mystery Bay, and she therefore had no adventurous voyages, her biggest excitement being her encounters with the tadpoles, which, according to Jack, tried to board her. Jack also owned a larger model sailing boat which he kept in his studio. He may have sailed her on the inner lagoon at Slapton, but if he did, he told no one.

Masefield wrote movingly of their friendship, even if his verse was often

110. Jack with model of a yacht.

111. *John Masefield at Hallsands*, sketchbook drawing and watercolour, April 1903.

parody. Everyone at this time indulged in writing in the manner of Henry Wadsworth Longfellow's Hiawatha, and Masefield was no exception.:

> Off to Perrins went the Painter
> With a package full of Broad Sheets
> And a dinky white Sombrero
> On his organ of Perception
> While the Bard, the Poet Masefield
> Threw his shadow on the Roadway
> Launa Lane, the muddy Roadway
> Close beside the Painter's Shadow
>
> Then the Pussy cat Meowa
> Laughed aloud to see the dinky
> Figures both of them were cutting
> On the Launa Lane, the Roadway
> Running muddily and greyly
> By the woodland, by the mudbank
> (Slip and bust the clayey mudbank)
> That was taking them to Perrins.[36]

The coastline which stretched out below Jack and Cottie's castle had been one of the reasons for their settling in that part of Devon. It was peaceful, beautiful, and even then the haunt of holiday-makers. But it was not just the scene of idyllic painting and ballad-making, sailing and romancing about pirate days. Commercial interests at the time provoked a serious controversy which became public and political, involving Masefield as well as Jack, who were both enraged by the ruthless, dangerous exploitation of the environment. Jack recorded in his sketchbooks the complicated and sorry story of the decline and destruction of a Devon fishing village (fig. 111).

Along the southern strip of coastline below Snail's Castle are three villages,

Torcross, Beesands and Hallsands, the last of which had always been a community engaged in seine fishing for pilchards over the offshore channel and the Skerries, a large shingle bank below sea level even at the lowest of spring tides. Seine fishing involved nets which were taken out by tuck seine boats, requiring a crew of six. They went out only when shoals were spotted, usually by a watchman on the clifftop, and the nets were paid out from the shore, around the shoal, and back in again. Then the whole village community combined in hauling in the catch.

Unlike other villages there, Hallsands is in an inhospitable situation, caught between cliffs and the shingle beach, with the houses built into the cliffside. In the 1890s the Royal Navy decided to extend its Devonport dockyard at Plymouth. 395,000 cubic metres of shingle were needed, and the man who won the tender for the construction, Sir John Jackson, was given a licence to dredge up the coarse aggregate he needed for the concrete from Start Bay, off the coast opposite Hallsands and Beesands. It was Crown property, administered by the Board of Trade, and the licence forbade 'encroachment' on the land above high water mark. But, with two hopper barges being filled on every tide, from the commencement of the work in April 1897, removing some 1,600 tons a day, it became rapidly clear that the beach was slipping into the sea, exposing the houses to danger, and removing the capacity of the fishermen to carry on their trade. The villagers objected. They sought the help of their local Member of Parliament, Colonel F.B. Mildmay. Sir John Jackson's counter-argument, that it was only a matter of time before the erosion would be made good, was accepted by the Board of Trade, undoubtedly swayed in this by the Royal Navy's needs, which were focused on the large battleships and cruisers then being commissioned.

The dredging went on; the beach slipped further into the sea. Troubled by his conscience, and aware that he had a problem on his hands, Sir John Jackson paid £125 to the village community for each of the years of the dredging, and gave also a Christmas gratuity which amounted to £4 for every male villager. By 1900 winter storms lashed in over the sunken beaches, broke down the man-made defences between the rocky outcrops on which houses were constructed, and caused property to collapse. The same thing happened in 1901 and 1902. The dredging was eventually stopped, but the damage was done. Though the final tragedy, which eventually turned Hallsands into the 'ghost' village it is today, did not occur until 1917, when storms led to the abandonment of the houses, their livelihood was gone. There was conscience money from Sir John Jackson and the Board of Trade, topped up by generous personal gifts by Lord Mildmay of Flete, as the colonel later became. But life at Hallsands was over.

Masefield wrote a poem about it in the *Speaker*.[37] 'My dear Yeats, The Hall Sands poem is out . . . It does not, of course, contain the vivid wishes for Sir John J's future happiness which I put into the first draft, but I've managed to give him a tender dig about his greed.' Masefield did, however, 'return' to Jack an earlier draft of the poem: 'You might like it for Theodore's scrapbook.' (They had evidently worked on it together.) And he told him: 'I shall get 15/- for the poem and I'm going to blue it in cannon for the fleet so that you can give a salute of guns on the wedding day if you don't happen to be in London when that joyous morning dawns'.[38]

The poem appeared with a lengthy introduction, explaining the way the village had been undermined:[39]

The moon is bright on Devon sands,
The pale moon brings the tide,
The cold green water's greedy hands
Are clutching far and wide
Where the brown nets are dried.

The controversy appealed to Jack as a cause; it was so clearly an arrogant and unfair exploitation. If it defines him in any way, it does so as a man on the side of the underdog. He is at one with Masefield in this respect, and Masefield was at one with John Synge, to whom he introduced Jack Yeats shortly after these events.

To outward appearances it seemed he lived his life at this time 'in miniature': miniature theatre, small editions of small books, esoteric broadsheet publications. Perhaps they give a slightly fey character to Jack. But as his father recognised, only the scale is small; the content is passionate, coherent, vividly realised. The plays live, even if they are miniatures. So, too, do the drawings and the writing in the *Broadsheets*. As to Jack and his model boats, who shall deny him the indulgences of friendship with one of English poetry's finest balladists expressed in this way?

Jack stored up the experiences. He had a lasting conception of epic in miniature, believing in a creative conquest of scale, so that later paintings, which depict solitary encounters between lonely men on roadways, or passing events in city streets or at country fairs, are raised to epic scale in a way that reflects back to these early enthusiasms. His mind as mature painter, which became vast in its imaginative range, did so with the material of ordinary human encounter and struggle. The same thing happened in his novels. He unfolded his life's artistic quest from these miniaturist escapades; they need to be valued for their contemporary joy and excitement, but also for what they foreshadowed. Like a geographer, he was mapping out future journeys on the table in his studio, or beside the fire with his trusted friend, Masefield, and with Cottie watching over them with an instinctive understanding that it would all lead on to something big.

CHAPTER NINE

Ireland and the United States
1904–1905

Unaffected kind-hearted genuine and sincere

JACK LED A busy and active life during the early years of the century (fig. 112). He exhibited regularly, and frequently, averaging a solo show a year throughout the first decade, combining this with his participation in numerous group exhibitions. He travelled to the United States – his only visit. He and Cottie were regularly at Coole. He published a number of books, and he acquired a small following for *A Broadsheet*. He sold watercolours, but by no means made a living from being an artist. The collectors of his work were often friends, or became so. It is tempting to see him as part of the Irish Literary Revival, even if he is on its fringes. More than any other painter, he seems to us now to have provided it with visual expression, symbol, imagery, a cast of characters, the drama of identity and fate. Notwithstanding the 'Grand Old Man' status of Nathaniel Hone,[1] in Irish art, the growing fame of William Orpen,[2] in both Dublin and London, and the self-conscious attempts by George Russell to epitomise faery and folklore strands in the Celtic temperament, it is Jack's humorous, compelling realism that seems most representative of those years. Yet we have seen that Jack was ambivalent about his commitment. His interest lay in the lives of his Irishmen rather than in the Irishness of their lives. This was to change, as his own nationalism developed, but the process was slow, dictated by his continued residence in England.

What he achieved he did from a distance, happily remaining in Devon until 1910. It was as a traveller to the country, and a visitor to its people, that he developed his skill in representing life in Ireland. From being a first-hand reporter of events, in his early period, he had become a commentator, seasoned by observation, contemplative and philosophical about motive and character. But his work still involved recording the event, capturing on the sketchbook page the crowded images and working them up into more studied interpretations of the life he saw.

His status was ex-patriate, reasoned and conscious, as if he believed that pursuing a life in art which was overwhelmingly based on the visual representation of 'Life in the West of Ireland' required him to live outside that world, visiting it for the purpose of examining, recording and representing. He did this regularly. Such visits made up his working life during the summer. He visited Coole, but measured carefully his involvement there, enjoying in his own fashion the house-party atmosphere and the friends he made. But he travelled widely elsewhere in Ireland, exploring new places, revisiting Sligo, and spending a good deal of time in Dublin.

112. Jack *c.* 1904.

The Yeats family were all being drawn back to Ireland, so that quite early into the new century, Jack, who had spent more of his childhood in Ireland than any of the others, was left the only member of the family resident in England. It must have contributed to him feeling a little on the outside at such occasions as the 'At Home' given by Lady Gregory towards the end of his 1901 Dublin exhibition, which followed his father's joint show with Nathaniel Hone. On that occasion, Jack's father and brother both spoke:

> About eighty guests were gathered together, all more or less belonging to the Irish 'Renaissance Movement,' and there was a symposium on the present state and prospects of art. Mr W.B. Yeats made a vague, lofty and mystical address on the subject. His father, Mr J.B. Yeats also spoke, and declared that the artist should have the feeling for art that a lover has for his mistress, all the world should be coloured by it . . . Lady Gregory's party was very interesting, appropriate and characteristic.[3]

The return to Ireland by his family began haphazardly with John Butler Yeats. He didn't *move* exactly. He had travelled to Dublin for his joint exhibition with Nathaniel Hone, which opened on 23 October 1901. He then had insufficient money to return to his two daughters in London. Like the later, and much greater change in his life, when he settled in New York, he was the victim of circumstance. His brother, Isaac, his friend, Dowden, and relations and other friends, provided him with lunch and dinner, he had modest lodgings, and he did some drawings which earned him a little. His indecision, aggravated by being financially compromised, was then overtaken by the changes in the fortunes of his two daughters.

Lily and Lolly were asked if they would be interested in becoming part of a craft enterprise in Dublin, managed by Evelyn Gleeson (fig. 113).[4] The invitation came from the distinguished botanist, Augustine Henry, who had already interviewed and rejected other candidates before approaching the Yeats sisters.[5] He wrote to them on 18 January 1902 asking if the idea interested them. It came at a providential time. Staying on in London held little attraction for either of the two women. One brother was increasingly in Dublin, the other firmly resident in Devon. Their father was temporarily in Dublin, and by now offered them no prospect of present or future security. If he was to be *their* liability – and there seemed no other option – then why not in circumstances where they had at least some assurance of a livelihood which suited their talents?

Not long after Henry's approach to the Yeats sisters, Jack wrote to Lily and inquired, 'Any fresh developments over the Gleeson business?'[6] And he got the reply that indeed there were fresh developments, with the Yeats family finally cutting its ties with Bedford Park and moving back to Ireland. William Murphy has explained the various published versions of how Dun Emer came into existence and of the relationships between the women involved, and has given his detailed and well-researched alternative view.[7] It is of some relevance to Jack, in that the setting up of Dun Emer was responsible for bringing together Cottie and Augustine Henry, who remained friends until Henry's death, in 1930.

The move led to an arrangement whereby Lily used the knowledge and experience she had developed with William and May Morris to run an embroidery shop. Lolly in due course deployed her artistic and design abilities and took responsibility for the setting up of a printing works. In order to

113. Evelyn Gleeson, founder of the Dun Emer Industries.

do this she needed training. She had none, knew nothing of the mechanical side of printing, hated machinery, and was afraid of sewing machines. But she took a month-long course at the Women's Printing Society, and with the courage which had sustained all the Yeatses so well, prepared for this great change in their lives.

It was an age for female determination and self-assertion. Evelyn Gleeson was a spirited creature, fired with the best of feminist intentions, capable and far-sighted. She was a nationalist, believing that Ireland should provide livelihoods for its people, but recognising that it would only do so if women of her calibre took the initiative. Willie may have been right in his belief that it all should have been thought out more carefully. But nothing adventurous in life happens if it depends on caution, and the risk was part of the enticement, not just for Gleeson who had means, but for the two Yeats sisters, without means and faced with the dismal alternative of remaining at the Blenheim Road house; waiting in fact to wait on their father into the foreseeable future.

He encouraged his daughters, particularly the fearful Lolly. Jack showed interest in the move, and in Lolly's training as a printer. Evelyn Gleeson travelled to Dublin, found a suitable large house in Dundrum, called Runnymede, changed the name of it to Dun Emer, and called the venture the Dun Emer Industries.[8] John Butler Yeats found a house called Gurteen Dhas, in Churchtown, big enough to accommodate himself, the two sisters, their cousin, Ruth Pollexfen, and two servants. It was quite isolated, in what was then mainly countryside. For the girls it was a good step to work in Dundrum, and a good step also to the tram in Rathgar. But it was near to the Churchtown railway station, on the line which ran into Harcourt Street. A second-hand printing press was bought, and Lolly chose the beautiful Caslon as their typeface. They started work immediately.

John Butler Yeats's exhibition, in the autumn of the previous year, had attracted the attention of John Quinn, a young and ambitious New York lawyer with an interest in art and literature.[9] Jack's solo exhibition opened two days later than his father's. This confused the American, who first wrote to Jack, though expressing his curiosity about portraits of John O'Leary and others. Once the situation was clarified, he made inquiries about buying one or more of the paintings and drawings which had been shown, and was offered a choice of a copy of the portrait of John O'Leary, or the actual portrait drawing of Willie done in 1899. John Butler Yeats even ventured the idea of getting Willie to sit to him again. The match between the two men could have been made in heaven, though the arrangement was less blessed as time went on.

Quinn's initial keen interest, which led to his protracted, forceful and fruitful involvement in Ireland, resulted from the decision of Sarah Purser to organise the joint Hone-Yeats exhibition. This had not been an easy project. Sarah Purser took on all the organisational responsibilities, either frightening people into submission, or simply frightening off those around her who might have helped. She even intimidated sitters like Susan Mitchell, who was sharply told her pencil portrait by John Butler Yeats would *not* be included. The artist himself did not know what role he was to play. He could get no satisfactory direction from Sarah Purser, who collected together seventy-two works by Yeats, forty-four by Hone.

Quinn came to Europe the following year, first to London, where he was

114. 'The Old Inveterate', John Butler Yeats in 1906, in the studio in St Stephen's Green.

115. *John Quinn*, pencil sketch, *c.* 1905.

met by Jack, who showed him round (fig. 115). In Dublin, Jack's solo exhibition, 'Sketches of Life in the West of Ireland', was held at the Well's Central Hall, Westmoreland Street, from 18 to 30 August, and was well-attended. The catalogue cost sixpence, and entry was threepence; combined, they covered rent and all expenses, which suggests heavy attendances. The catalogue carried a note, 'Copyright of all pictures reserved', and this was to appear regularly on all Jack's catalogues. The reviews confirm the generally favourable mood in which the show was received. The pictures which John Quinn bought included *A Tale of Piracy, Beside the Western Ocean, A Dog Watching a Seagull, An Emigrant, The Ballad Singer's Children, Willie Reilly, Fortune and her Wheel, The Man of the West* and *Simon the Cyrenian*. Jack annotated his own copy of the catalogue carefully with these and other purchases, and the prices paid. The total from that show was £106 9s. And he wrote: 'I believe I have added it wrong, I am tired, but isn't it good! gate money paid rent and printing.'

Quinn's largesse made a considerable impact on the Yeats family, and his brisk, self-confident decisiveness took him swiftly to the heart of the group around Lady Gregory. He was a naturally attractive man, though balding, and he had the self-confident authority of a lawyer. He was as tall as Jack, an inch over six feet, slim and upright, with clear blue eyes. When they met, Sarah Purser 'looked at him hungrily to paint him'.[10] He also had sex appeal. Lolly recorded him as being the only man, apart from John Synge, that Lily 'took *that sort* of interest in.'[11] And later he was to have an affair with Lady Gregory. Yet despite the generous way in which he first swept through Irish literary and cultural life during that summer, there was an instinctive feeling that his good will had to be 'tried on and tried out before the Irishmen could tell how to live with it'.[12]

For Jack, Quinn proved a mixed blessing. The first, and overwhelming enthusiasm – no one else had bought pictures quite as Quinn did; he acquired them in the kind of volume one associates with the purchase of books – was not sustained, and in later years Quinn prevaricated over his support for Jack, as he did for the Irish cause, and Irish artists generally. Even James Joyce, whose interests were protected by Quinn many years later, could have been better served, and felt slighted in particular by Quinn's decision to sell off the incomplete manuscript of *Ulysses*.[13] But in those heady early days of the century, and of the Irish Literary Revival, Quinn was a cohesive and dynamic force, energising people, and encouraging them to be tough and self-reliant.

The day after his exhibition closed, 31 August 1902, Jack travelled with Quinn to Athenry, and then by sidecar to the tiny village of Killeeneen, in beautiful east Galway countryside overlooking the flat valley of the Dunkellin River. The village is near Craughwell, some fifteen miles north of Coole. At its centre is the 'graveyard of the poets'; not only is it where the poet Raftery is buried, but it also contains a memorial to Jeremiah Callanan, Raftery's friend, whose poetry, in English, but deriving from the Irish, is justly celebrated. He died in Lisbon.[14] Jack and his American companion were on their way to stay with Lady Gregory at Coole, but went first to the Raftery *feis* that August Sunday, staying until nightfall. It was one of several such festivals to celebrate the poet, details of whose life were being discovered and published by Lady Gregory, Hyde and others.[15] It was a huge affair; Quinn recalled 'perhaps a hundred side-cars and other vehicles and five or six hundred men and women at the meeting', which was held in a field on rising

116. Sketchbook drawing showing Quinn with images associated with Coole and the Raftery feis at Killeeneen. August 1902.

Draw on him now

Jack B. Yeats
August 1902

And I'm the man that drew the two of ye

And I'm the man that came from America to hear you say the same

I'm the man that buried Raftery
I'm the man that held the candle

ground outside the village. Lady Gregory, with Hyde and Martyn, sat on a raised platform, while the two Yeats brothers, with Quinn, watched 'the spectacle' from the crowd.[16] This was Quinn's first meeting with Willie, and of course his first with Lady Gregory and Douglas Hyde. It was not until late in the evening that the party, with added guests, came home. 'It was black when the lights of Coole welcomed us. Lady Gregory got down from the car first, and, turning to me and extending her hand, said with a pleasant smile, "Welcome to Coole".'[17] Jack did small portrait drawings, on a copy of the programme, of Lady Gregory, Douglas Hyde, John Quinn, his brother and himself, and all of them signed the page.[18]

Quinn's round trip lasted seven weeks. During that time he had encountered the heart, soul, mind and administration of Irish cultural life and rebirth. He had cut his initials into the beech tree at Coole, bought the beginnings of a collection of Irish art, greatly enlarged his own library and made innumerable friends, among them the men and women whose controlling hands were on the future development of art and literature in Ireland.

Like Quinn, Jack departed in the late summer content with what he had done. His exhibition had been a success. He had travelled and met many new people. He had found a good friend and generous patron in Quinn. And he had steadily enlarged his knowledge of the country. He returned to the old pursuits, his life with Cottie in Devon, his frequent visits to London, and his friendship with John Masefield, who was now living in Greenwich.

In London, Jack continued to pursue his keen interest in 'the Low Life'. No longer the reporter, he was nevertheless drawn still to the excitement of a good programme of bouts in the Wonderland at Whitechapel, the Coffee and Dining Rooms at Bethnal Green, which offered 'Everything of the Best, Quality and Quantity is my Motto', or East End pubs like The Nag's Head, owned by Morris Abrahams, and Ye Olde Blue Anchor, whose proprietor, Herbert Faustmann had as his widely blazoned message, 'Let 'em all Come!' Everything they offered was 'celebrated' or 'renowned', from their jellied eels to their prize fighters.

When Jack went to Ireland in the summer of 1903, Dublin and other parts of Ireland were *en fête* for the visit of King Edward VII. It was his first as monarch, though he had often been before as prince of Wales; he was popular in Ireland for his love of horses, if not women. His reign as monarch, from 1901 to 1910, was relatively speaking a benign period of social and political calm in Irish affairs. The king included in his itinerary more than one visit to the International Fair at Ballsbridge, where there was a huge exhibition of arts and crafts. Jack was among the many painters whose work was on show. The king, in the course of his examination of the room, was reported to have gazed with some emotion on 'an artistic memorial picture in green and black of the late Queen Victoria. Subsequently when the King observed a colored [sic] picture of the Commander-in-Chief of the British Army he said, "There is my old friend Roberts".' This small cutting was kept by Jack, who added in pen, at bottom: 'But they dont say anything about all the other Pictures.' Jack's response was to fill this gap in as humorous a way as he could. He produced his *Panner•rammer•rammer• 0f Edward VII's VISIT to the VERY POOR OR The King among the Pictures Dublin July 24th 1903. All Highly Coloured.*[19] This is a fourteen-fold booklet depicting the king's progress through the art exhibition, starting with his majesty, dressed in green neckerchief, marked with shamrock, wearing a leprechaun hat, and traditional Irish peasant clothes, with one hand in his pocket, the other pointing at the picture on the wall exclaiming 'Bedad its meself thats in it'. The portrait shows Edward VII in military regalia. 'Boys me mother', he exclaims, before a portrait of Queen Victoria; and King Edward is shown having taken off his hat, and placed it across his breast, bowing reverently before the image of the dead Queen. 'It's me old friend Roberts' has brought the monarch full face, but with 'eyes right' towards the picture, which has the word 'Bobs' on it. The king is standing at attention, saluting. For each of the fourteen images, Jack contrived a visual joke.

Jack's real view of the British monarch's standing in Ireland is hinted at in a letter to Lady Gregory written in late July from Strete, where he was working on the October *Broadsheet*: 'Edward the VII has everyone cheering in Ireland and waving handkerchiefs and shaking hands with him. Its like after the war in South Africa when the Boers and the Britishers sat side-by-side

117. *In Frank Feeney's*, sketchbook drawing, *c.* 1903.

118. 'I want some tobacco'. Sketchbook drawing of the Barrel Man, 1903.

119. 'To get it between . . .' Sketchbook drawing of the Barrel Man, 1903.

singing each other's hymns – its hard to believe . . . I wonder what Edward VIIs reception was really like.' And he accompanied these words with a drawing of 'a Boer, an Oriental and a Britisher all singing each other's hymns at the conclusion of the Boer War'. And Jack has added: 'A few more years shall roll'.[20] Jack drew 'Boss' Croker in the Dolphin at this time, and also in the Shelbourne Hotel.[21] 'Boss' Croker was the kind of colourful, louche character to appeal to Jack, though a very different kind of American from John Quinn. He did small drawings of his friends, Padraic Colum, Fay reading his part, and Starkie.[22]

Quinn found Jack the most congenial of the Yeatses to be with, and wrote to him on 1 May 1903 to suggest that they take a walking holiday together, possibly including John Masefield, whom he had met in London. Jack agreed. Masefield was in the throes of marriage, and could neither accept the tour nor visit Coole. But Quinn came, bringing news of Willie's plays in New York, which were a great success. When it came to it, Quinn's walking tour with Jack was reduced to one week, possibly because Quinn was keen to get to Coole, where interest in Lady Gregory then detained him.[23] Jack and Cottie, however, had their own interests to pursue, visiting Coole, travelling to Sligo, and dealing of course with another solo exhibition. Their holiday took them through Mayo. It was on this visit that Jack first saw and drew the Barrel Man act in a local fairground, an image which clearly haunted him. Jack's annotations to the drawings indicate something of the savagery behind this particular circus stunt, in which the man himself faces an onslaught of sticks, disappearing down into the barrel when the going gets too tough (figs 118–19). Many years later, in *Humanity's Alibi*, the distilled experience of 1903 became an apocalyptic vision in which the daring and the courage of the lone figure rising out of the dark barrel to face a sky filled with flying cudgels, evokes the battle of the individual against the destiny he chooses for himself, no matter how insane the choice may seem to be.

Jack and Cottie returned to Sligo. Cottie features in a number of drawings. Jack also did a drawing of Charlemont, the rather gaunt house overlooking Sligo Harbour, which had been his grandfather's penultimate home.[24]

Jack and other Irish artists were commissioned to do work for the new St Brendan's Cathedral at Loughrea, in County Galway. Father Jeremiah O'Donovan, known as 'Jerry', was administrator of Loughrea parish. He was an enthusiastic member of the Gaelic League and of the Irish Agriculture Organisation Society. Deeply committed to the revival of Irish crafts, he had lectured on 'Native or Foreign Art' to the National Literary Society.[25] He was in touch with Edward Martyn, a devout Catholic, who is said to have been the inspiration for the decision to commission works by Irish artists for the new cathedral. Sarah Purser, who founded An Túr Gloine in 1903, A.E. Child, who was appointed to teach stained-glass at the Dublin Metropolitan School of Art in the same year, and Maurice Healy, were all commissioned to do stained-glass windows. Beatrice Glenavy and Catherine O'Brien were later involved in design work on the windows. A surprisingly large number of Protestants worked on the project.

Jack's own involvement was substantial, as was Cottie's. The administrator first commissioned ten banners; he extended this order more than once. Twenty-four were to be done by Jack and Cottie, and the other artists involved were George Russell and Pamela Colman Smith. Jack wrote to York Powell:

Peter

from Oyster Island

125. *St Asicus*, banner for Loughrea cathedral, designed by Jack.

We had a long letter the other day from my father. He was very cheerie in it – Lily writes every week – Lolly (Elizabeth) is doing Russell's book & Lily working at embroidering the saints – Mrs. Jack and I have designed a lot it is great fun to see them after they are embroidered . . . I wish there was a good pirate saint to do – he would look so fine with crimson breeches dyed with bullocks blood.[26]

Jack told him an amusing story which makes the concept of a pirate bishop not entirely unimaginable: 'There was a pirate once on the Mosquito Coast who shot one of his men dead for irreverent behaviour during mass.'[27] Many years later, writing to the American collector of Yeatsiana, Eleanor Reid, about the embroidery work on the banners, Jack wrote: 'My wife made beautiful drawings as the many designs for my sister's embroidery show how she felt all things through a natural sense and love of design or what is called design.'[28]

The banners, beginning with Willie's own comments, have traditionally been attributed more to Jack than to Cottie, but from this letter and the stylistic evidence of the works themselves, it would seem that Cottie played a far greater part in the design than has been credited to her. She was a designer of skill and experience; her later work for Cuala confirms the broad, well-structured sense of volume and mass necessary for embroidered and printed art, and evident in the banners themselves (fig. 125). They were designed for the sodalities of the Sacred Heart, named after different saints, and were put up in the pews to indicate where each sodality would congregate. Their clearly defined outlines, strong, homespun appearance, and powerful realism, were ideally suited to their function, and the stamp of Jack's line is the dominant feature, perhaps to the point of being a bit crude and clumsy. Before being delivered the banners were exhibited at the Dun Emer studios (fig. 126), the show being advertised in *The Irish Homestead*.

The embroidery work was a huge undertaking for Lily and the Dun Emer workshops. Lily took on the administrative work; she sent Jack a charming

Opposite, clockwise from top left: sketchbook drawings and watercolours of Coole and Sligo, 1903.

120. *Two men in caps, one in bowler, Coole.*

121. *Village Street, horse and cart, Sligo.*

122. *Harbour Bar, Sligo.*

123. *From Oyster Island, Sligo.*

124. *Peter, Sligo.*

126. Lily and 'her girls'. The embroidery rooms at the Dun Emer workshops at Dundrum.

postcard of Willie Fay acting the part of the Tramp in *The Pot of Broth* – 'This card is worth having?' – and telling him 'the banners are safely at the station and I will get them up tomorrow and have show in two days'.[29] The banners are preserved at the cathedral, for use on the first and second Sundays in the month. 'Of these it is not too much to say that they represent an entirely new departure in Irish ecclesiastical art work.'[30]

Not unnaturally, given all the commotion, Willie became involved. He wrote to Eric Maclagan:

> My brother's saints strike me as vigorous and simple, but I doubt if they are sufficiently traditional. The trouble is that my sisters are getting only three pounds a banner (or rather their school is for they have nothing to do with the commercial side), and cannot give more than 10/ of this for a design. The result is that they have had to pick, not the best possible designers, but those who will do designs for so small a sum or for the love of God.[31]

Earlier in July he had been staying in Loughrea. 'I saw Father O Donovan yesterday in passing through Loughrea. He does not like the S Patrick banner [this was done by George Russell]. He does not think it reverent. He was satisfied with the others, but you should not go on with what he calls "the hurler".'[32] Later in the year, in a letter to Maclagan, he criticised his brother's work: 'My brother has been doing banners for them [his sisters], which are I think too fanciful and modern. If the cathedral people had sense they would try them for protestant heresies.'[33]

The outcome was more original than that. 'Jerry' O'Donovan was indeed 'modern' in his outlook. He left the cathedral and the priesthood in 1904, later married, and took up a literary career. Still later he had an affair with the novelist and travel writer, Rose Macaulay. The cathedral was completed in 1905 at a cost of £30,000, but its furnishings, including the stained-glass windows, were still being completed in the late 1930s. The Loughrea banners commission attracted considerable contemporary publicity. They were illustrated in the *Art Workers' Quarterly* and progress, as we have seen, was followed in articles in *The Irish Homestead*. As one critic summed up: 'the Dun Emer banners mark the beginning, as we hope, of a new epoch in art work of this kind, wherein originality of design shall replace vulgarity and simple beauty replace tawdriness'.[34]

Willie assumed a central a role in the commission – which affected every member of the family – and his critical judgment is again voiced in respect of his brother's and sister-in-law's work. His comments on his brother's work are rare. He never regarded him as having a leading role in the collective drama of awakening Ireland to its own cultural worth, and his comments, when they did come, must have seemed arbitrary. In sharp contrast, John Butler Yeats gave out advice and critical comment with most of the breaths that left his body. This caused Lily to explode:

> I don't like your writing to Jack. You say too much. He is all right and knows what he is doing. He never drifts. Willy and Lady Gregory are both too ready to criticize and direct. They forget Jack is at the beginning and is *seven years* younger than Willy. What of Willy's technique seven years ago? They all forget this and from their pedestal direct and order others a great deal too much.[35]

Her's was heartfelt resentment. She continued: 'Don't worry Jack. He wants encouragement, and his work is beautiful and his own. When we are all dead and gone great prices will be given for them. I know they will.' She saw that Willie and Lady Gregory were critical and intellectual in their view, particularly of other people's art. Her intuition about Jack was objective. Willie's was egocentric, based on an understanding of his own ways of working rather than Jack's. As for the recipient of the letter, John Butler Yeats was still so lacking in understanding of Jack's art that he thought he should be working from the model, and for years to come he went on begging Jack, in letters, to do portrait drawings of people and events, as though Jack were still an illustrator, or had become a portrait painter. Lacking imagination in his own art, he never saw that it was an overriding dimension to his son's work. More seriously, none of them, save perhaps Lily, realised the difficulties which Jack himself had with the very idea of being criticised or directed in what he did. Imaginative, determined, perhaps inarticulate in respect of what he did as a painter, just as he was reserved about his personal ambition, the intrusion of others was never welcome.

Perhaps Willie's intrusion was least welcome of all. By 1904, with Jack an established artist and writer, having had several solo exhibitions, and having brought out the small but exquisite books which their mutual publisher, Elkin Mathews, had produced, the recorded responses from his elder brother could hardly be described as enthusiastic. He had noted in a few early letters Jack's perpetual drawing. He had appreciated the financial contribution made by his younger brother to the family income, through the early illustrations for periodicals, and had collaborated in providing stories for them, probably at Jack's instigation. He had then witnessed the first London show, and the subsequent Dublin ones, representing a real contribution to Irish culture. Yet there is no evidence of any profound appreciation. He had been cool about Jack's early skills as a dramatist, missing the point of his plays for miniature theatre, and he was to be similarly uncomprehending and essentially dismissive about Jack's later plays.

He intruded over the Loughrea commission. The banners, admittedly, were part of a family involvement in the collective art and craft work which accompanied the cultural renaissance. And others were involved, too. For these reasons, perhaps, Willie was ready to speak out. But it could hardly have been welcome. Many years later Lily also had things to say about the commission. In a letter to Sarah Purser in 1926 she told her that Jack 'despised all the men saints but St Patrick & St Laurence O'Toole . . . & Cottie despised all the women saints but St Bridget which was done by Pamela Colman Smith'.[36]

Willie's dominant position in family affairs, combined with his fame as a poet, impinged on Jack in other respects, notably in his relationship with John Quinn. Quinn was enthusiastic about the work of both men, and determined to help them both. He was involved in Willie's lecture tour to the United States, in the autumn of 1903, and sold to the magazine, *McClure's*, two stories, 'Hanrahan's Vision', and 'Hanrahan's Curse' for $100 apiece on the poet's behalf. In November, writing to Lady Gregory, Jack passed on news: 'We have just got a lot of papers with notices of Willy and his arrival, and his clothes. But of course there is not yet time to see the ones about the first lecture, I expect he will be a great success.'[37] Quinn was working at the time to secure a booking for Jack, to have a solo show in New York, and,

127. Jack and Cottie on board SS Mesaba, 1904, bound for New York.

128 to 130. Sketchbook drawings with watercolour from the New York visit.

128. *Knickerbocker Theatre.*

though nothing had been arranged, Lady Gregory had also proposed his involvement in the St Louis Exhibition, which was to take place the following year. Jack wrote to her: 'Thank you for your letter about the St Louis exhibition it would be fine if I could have a good wall space there I think the Irish American Committee would be best for me don't you? I may very likely go to New York with pictures in February Quinn talked about it when he was over, but nothing is yet decided.'[38]

Quinn did secure a booking for Jack, at Clausen's Gallery, at 381 Fifth Avenue, New York, from 28 March to 16 April, and Jack and Cottie sailed for the United States on the SS Mesaba, arriving in New York on Wednesday, 23 March (fig. 127). Pixie naturally took an interest in Jack's visit to New York in 1904 and it was probably at her suggestion that he took as his American agent William Macbeth who had published her first prints and had been her agent since at least 1897.[39]

Jack's American visit was recorded in *The Gael* for April 1904, which told of Jack visiting America 'partially in connection with his exhibition of pictures at the St Louis Exposition'.[40] The exhibition was the biggest he ever assembled. There were sixty-three works, and they covered his whole career, in England and Ireland, with many pictures deriving from his life in London and in Devon; athletics, horse-racing in Liverpool, at the Grand National, boxing, music hall entertainment, were examples of the former, while the greater number of drawings and watercolours were drawn from the series of 'Life in the West of Ireland' exhibitions on which he had based his artistic career up to then, and which had first attracted Quinn. Many of the works had been shown in earlier exhibitions, and had remained unsold. Many of course are familiar now, and highly prized, as among the best examples of the artist's work in those early years (figs 128–30).

The exhibition was not a great success, and without Quinn's own purchases, would have been a commercial disaster. He bought *A Young Man's Troubles*, *The Man who told the Tales*, *The Fair of Carricknagat*, *It Must have been an Allegory*, *The Crest of the Hill*, *Singing the Lament of the Irish Emigrant in a Liverpool Christy Minstrels*, *The American Table Cloth*, *The Car is at the Door* and *Donkey Races*. There were only two other buyers, of a single work each.[41] According to Hilary Pyle 'Some of his friends said that it came too closely on the heels of his brother's debut in the States, and that it was not advertised widely enough.'[42] Quinn was already captive. His love affair with Ireland and its artistic people was in its first state of rapture, and Jack was a beneficiary of that. But it was a quite different thing to translate such rapture into hard cash from the pockets of fellow-Americans. Hilary Pyle is closer to the truth, however, when she says that the New York visit 'was an unforgettable experience for him, of permanent value, and provided his imagination with a bottomless store from which to feed until the end of his painting and his writing life.'[43] And this is richly reflected in the sketchbooks, which also record a stern-faced patron, every inch the successful New York lawyer.

Jack was an avid reader of Bret Harte's westerns, and he picked up echoes of the America they depict in drawings of New York Indians, negroes, images of 'Uncle Sam', and the early sky-scrapers. But the real life of this tireless city soon took over. The Italian and Chinese character of New York came through in his drawings of Sicilian marionettes, in Brooklyn, and Chinese theatre, as well as music hall at the Dewey. He and Cottie took the steamer to Ellis Island, and a quite different record emerged from that trip. He drew an apple

129. *Brooklyn Bridge.*

Tug taking a barge
with shed on it along

130. *The Father
Christmas – Papa.*

The father christmas
keep Papa

as Mrs Forbes Robertson
as Ophelia

woman on the ferry, a New York policeman, wearing an English-style hat, and waiting on the landing stage. An Italian went out on the same ferry, with a guitar, to meet emigrants. Through a gap in houses, Jack did a drawing of the Statue of Liberty. When he got to the island he recorded the people coming down the gangway, with medical inspectors checking them, looking at gloved hands and at the children's legs. There is a watercolour drawing of the exit, with the sign: 'Go ahead. That's New York'.

At the end of six weeks, Quinn saw the couple off on the *SS Celtic,* and wrote to Willie, praising the younger brother in terms which the poet must have found compelling: 'He is one of the most simple and unaffected kind-hearted genuine and sincere men I have ever met and I like him more than I can tell.'[44] It is difficult to define the view Jack had of New York, in the end. He was perhaps put off by American brashness.

If Jack came back from the United States a bit disappointed in the poor sales of his work there, he would have been encouraged by the reception given to his work at the Guildhall, in London, where, under the direction of Hugh Lane and George Temple, an exhibition of Irish art had been organised. It should not surprise us, though it was an irritation to Jack, that he and his father were confused in the catalogue.[45] But one reviewer wrote: 'If one were asked to single out the most unmistakably Irish artist it would be Mr Jack B Yeats, brother of the poet. Several of his drawings are touchingly Irish, with a touch of blarney, too.'[46] And under the heading: 'A Real Irishman' the *Glasgow Herald* reviewer wrote: 'For unmistakeable Irish character – not easy to discover in this by no means specifically Celtic collection of pictures – one had better pause before some of the drawings of Mr Jack B. Yeats. His "The Rolling Donkey", on a dusty road flanked by emerald green grass, has the true note of blarney, as again has "The Star Gazer," representing the front half of a racehorse, jockey on back.'

Jack produced another delightful manuscript book, a partner for his 'Panner-rammer-rammer', called 'The ABC of Piracy', a tiny volume with the pirate, Theodore, as frontispiece, the delectable Constanza, his Spanish Gipsy woman, with her fan, as a colophon, and a tiny drawing for each letter of the alphabet, A for Aloft, D for Dancing on Air (a drawing of a man on the gallows), M for the Metal Man, U for You, and Z for Zactly. The title page had a drawing of a barrel, and Gara River as place of publication.[47]

Jack and Cottie's friends were moving on. John Masefield was married. Pamela Colman Smith had opened her own shop, and wrote to them both in a froth of excitement:

> I have a shop! Observe circular! 'The Green Sheaf' as a periodical is to be discontinued! after number 13 which will be out shortly (also no 12) – And *the shop's the thing* – Any stencils or drawings or watercolours of yours or Jacks I should be so pleased to have – on sale – at 10 per cent. You fix price – I had not heard of Lilly & Lolly's great move – of taking on all Dun Emer – good !!!![48]

Pixie made a living from dramatised story-telling at parties, and in response to a question from Cottie, told how she had been out that very afternoon at a children's party, and had been twice in the country during August, doing the same thing. But her overriding interest was the shop, and obtaining material for it from Jack:

Do you know a Cupid Horse Jack did? It was in your houses – & at a show – in Bond Street – Please will you make him do a tracing of it – & let the shop have a plate made & he colour a proof & we to sell it at 2/6 – a print? You getting 6 pence each copy sold? – I know of several people who will have it – Mathews asked me if I would get it also – I also wish to know if the Wren picture (that was used in Number 11 Green Sheaf) which we have the plate of – may we use it as a Christmas print?

It had been a very busy period for Jack. In December 1904, John Masefield, set in train another event which was to dominate the early part of the following year, and bring together two giants of Ireland's cultural rebirth. Masefield wrote to John M. Synge and suggested that he should write some articles on the Aran Islands for *The Manchester Guardian*, as well as doing paragraphs for the newspaper's 'Miscellany' column, for each of which he would be paid five shillings. Synge's reply was laconic. 'I will certainly have a shot at them with some articles and pars.' He declined the proposal that he might review for the paper, on the grounds that it took up too much time. But he promised to look into the terms which might be on offer, and subsequently modified the Aran Islands proposal, deciding instead to investigate Connemara and North Mayo.[49] The enterprise was to bring writer and artist together in a memorable collaboration.

CHAPTER TEN

John M. Synge 1905–1909

The best companion

He was the best companion for a roadway any one could have, always ready and always the same; a bold walker, up hill and down dale, in the hot sun and the pelting rain . . . I think the Irish peasant had all his heart. He loved them in the east as well as he loved them in the west . . . Synge was by spirit equipped for the roads. Though his health was often bad, he had beating under his ribs a brave heart that carried him over rough tracks. He gathered about him very little gear, and cared nothing for comfort except perhaps that of a good turf fire. He was, though young in years, 'an old dog for a hard road and not a young pup for a towpath'.[1]

This was Jack's description of his companion John Millington Synge during the month they spent together in Connemara and Mayo during the summer of 1905 (fig. 131). The two men set out on their *Manchester Guardian* commission to write and draw something of the life of the people in the areas of greatest hardship and distress in the west of Ireland.

The trip inspired powerfully committed writing and poignant, perceptive drawings. And then the two men parted. They had some later contact, including a visit which Synge paid to Jack in Devon, two years later, and several sympathetic letters which Jack wrote to Synge during the long and painful decline in his health. It would perhaps be wrong to describe them as friends, in the sense in which Jack and Masefield were friends. But they were kindred spirits, and shared a view of Ireland, and an idea of how to express it, which is somehow different from the general approach of those engaged in the Irish cultural revival of the time. And latterly there was a sweetness in the affection which is strangely moving, in the light of Synge's early, tragic death.

Their characters were not unlike. George Moore, writing of a meeting he had with John Synge, drew one of the most perceptive brief portraits of the man, and correctly associated Synge's approach with that of Jack.

As I write this line I can see Synge, whom I shall never see again with my physical eyes, sitting thick and straight in my arm-chair, his large, un-couth head, and flat, ashen-coloured face with two brown eyes looking at me, not unsympathetically. A thick stubbly growth of hair starts out of a strip of forehead like black twigs out of the head of a broom. I see a ragged moustache, and he sits bolt upright in my chair, his legs crossed, his great country shoe spread over the carpet. The conversation about us is of literature, but he looks as bored as Jack Yeats does in the National Gallery.

131. *John M. Synge,* sketchbook drawing with watercolour, 1905.

Synge and Jack Yeats are like each other in this, neither take the slightest interest in anything except life, and in their own deductions from life; educated men, both of them, but without aesthetics, and Yeats's stories that Synge read the classics and was a close student of Racine is a piece of Yeats's own academic mind. Synge did not read Racine oftener than Jack Yeats looks at Titian.[2]

Jack, in his short essay, confirms the same: 'Synge must have read a great deal at one time, but he was not a man you would see often with a book in his hand; he would sooner talk; or rather listen to talk – almost anyone's talk.'

Masefield's proposal to Synge, that he might write more regularly for the *Manchester Guardian*, was followed up by the editor of that newspaper, C.P. Scott, who wrote to him on 15 May 1905 inviting him to write a series of articles on the Congested Districts in the west of Ireland (fig. 132). The newspaper had already become involved in reforms in the area, some years before, and the funds it raised had resulted in considerable improvements, notably in the health of the people, among whom typhus had been common.

Synge was then living at 31 Crosthwaite Park, in Kingstown, south of Dublin. He was not sure what his movements would be, and had questions to put to Scott. The formalities included getting clearance for the writer to talk with officials in the Congested Districts, and Scott put Synge in touch with Mr Muldoon in Dublin, whom Synge saw the following week. 'He looks at things from a more purely political point of view than I do, but he very kindly offers to get me some introductions that will be of use to me if I go.'[3] It seems that Scott favoured what Synge described as 'the strictly orthodox National-ist' point of view for the articles, but Synge was reluctant to follow this advice: 'In my letters I could work on the lines you suggest, but I would deal with the problem independently.'[4]

Synge suggested three locations, in Galway, Mayo and Donegal.

> To do the thing at all adequately I would have to spend some time – possibly a week or more – on the North Galway Coast – south of Cliften [sic] – and about the same time in Belmullet in Mayo. There is a third centre of obvious distress in Donegal I could go on to from there if you wish . . . I was in Belmullet for a week last autumn and with another week there now I could do you a few letters that would perhaps give you all that you need.[5]

Scott responded to this by accepting Synge's broad political approach. In his memorandum of the reply to this letter, Scott noted: 'Working at the thing in the way you would intimately & trying to give the readers a sympathetic understanding of the people and the way their life is lived & to let the political lesson emerge out of that.'[6]

The relaxed approach evident in Synge's letter concealed feelings of tension which were expressed in a letter to Stephen MacKenna:

> I cannot write as I am packing to go off to the west to do articles on the Irish Distress by special commission of Manchester Guardian, an interest-ing job, but for me a nervous one, it is so much out of my line, and in certain ways I like not lifting the rags from my mother country for to tickle the sentiments of Manchester. However terms are advantageous and the need of keeping some rags upon myself in this piantic country has to be minded.'[7]

Synge concluded the letter: 'To think of you in the Rue du Luxembourg – you luxurious dog – and me chewing blighted spuds upon the quaking bosom of a Connaught bog.'[7]

Scott replied to Synge, offering him the collaboration of Jack Yeats as illustrator. He did this, it seems, on Masefield's suggestion, and before consulting the artist; he would have had some awareness of Jack as an artist since Masefield's writing had been reviewed in the newspaper by Jack, and Jack's own exhibitions had also been reviewed.

Synge welcomed the proposal. 'I should be very glad indeed to have Mr Yeats with me on my tour . . . he already knows the west so thoroughly.' Synge thought Jack might be too busy, and believed that he could do the drawings from experience he already had, and just send them to the *Manchester Guardian*. But when Scott wrote to Jack, three days later, the invitation was taken up enthusiastically:

> Your letter just come, I would be delighted to go to the West of Ireland with Mr Synge and make a set of drawings for you. I can start in a day or two. You will let me know I suppose when and where to meet Mr Synge – as I don't know his present address – also you will tell me how the drawings are wanted – whether while we are in the west or after we return – Of course I would like the latter way best, as I could then get a mass of notes and sketches and do the drawings in my studio. I hope Mr Synge's articles and my drawings may do some good, for the people of the west of Ireland are a great people.

Their distress was great also. The area came under the Congested Districts Board, set up in 1890 by Arthur James Balfour, when he was Chief Secretary for Ireland.[8] The board's purpose was to alleviate distress which derived from the fact that the stony and unfruitful land could not support a population which elsewhere might have thrived. Poverty was extensive, and in places extreme. The market operating in such a basic product as 'kelp' (a baked compound made from the burning of seaweed, and used in the manufacture of iodine), was fragile, and open to abuse by middle-men. But the work was pursued proudly by the people along the north coast of Galway Bay; gathering and burning kelp was infinitely preferable to relief work offered by the board, and supervised in a manner which caused Synge to be critical. Nevertheless, the board carried out many good and enlightened reforms. One of its objectives was the purchase and redistribution of land, and during the thirty years of its existence it acquired by purchase and then reassigned over two million acres. Inevitably, its operations, though aimed at providing help through employment, led to abuses of various kinds, and to an authoritarianism which was unwelcome among the peasant peoples of the west.

Synge's approach was political enough. He had the distinctive brand of intellectual radicalism peculiar to his Anglo-Irish Protestant landed class. He was well-informed, and had read Marx. But he had a practical knowledge of the people, not just the Irish peasants whose study was his lifelong interest, but of Irish men and women of all classes, among whom he found sufficient numbers of scoundrels to make him sceptical of any such orthodox label as 'Nationalist'. In a letter to Stephen McKenna he gave a vivid picture of his general view:

> There are sides of all that western life, the groggy-patriot-publican-general-shop-man who is married to the priest's half-sister and is second-

cousin once-removed of the dispensary doctor, that are horrible and awful. This is the type that is running the present United Irish League anti-grazier campaign, while they're swindling the people themselves in a dozen ways and then buying out their holdings and packing off whole families to America. The subject is too big to go into here, but at best it's beastly . . . In a way it is all heart-rending, in one place the people are starving but wonderfully attractive and charming, and in another place where things are going well, one has a rampant, double-chinned vulgarity I haven't seen the like of.[9]

Synge, in this letter and in other remarks at the time, touches on the complex realities of Irish life; posterity has simplified it all into the curse of British rule and the indomitable spirit of 'the Irish'; and even though Synge's interpretation of the truth may also be faulted, he does have the courage to see the problem in local rather than global terms: 'I have the wildest admiration for the Irish Peasants, and for Irish men of known or unknown genius . . . but between the two there's an ungodly ruck of fat-faced, sweaty-headed swine.' His articles were designed to explore some aspects of this, and Jack was ready to go along with the same interpretation, as his drawings show.

This question of politics, not just in Synge, but also in Jack, and, in the background, in C.P. Scott's political views and those of the paper he edited, need a further word. By his own admission, Synge was at pains to separate the way he would write from any 'Nationalist' standpoint. In the climate of the times, Jack would probably have felt the same. Scott was liberal, and so was his newspaper. 'Nationalist' meant the traditions of Parnell, which now embraced Sinn Fein. We know more about Synge's politics than we do about Jack's, at this stage. Synge displays a clear-sighted humanity which owes more to English and international roots than it does to domestic political developments. He was an admirer of Shelley, and wrote extensively about the poet's life and work, including the statement: 'With Shelley, an enthusiastic humanity *came first!*' As well as Karl Marx he read other notable radicals and socialists, including Herbert Spencer, John Ruskin and William Blake. He was that unusual Irish political creature, an Anglo-Irish Ascendancy radical, with views which wavered between socialism and communism. Jack was to follow him in this, as we shall see, and both men have suffered the distortion of their views. Synge's own class, including his close literary friends and associates, tried to suppress acknowledgement of his radicalism, or to soften it, both during his lifetime and later. More insidious, in a way, has been the overlay of cultural nationalism. The claim that Synge wrote on the side of the oppressed, in a specifically 'Irish' context, meaning one in which the forces of liberation were pitted against British rule, was a way of avoiding his much deeper-seated, more profoundly radical thinking. Though Jack's own thinking was far less developed, it is this side in Synge which impressed him during their work together, drawing them closer in the way they saw and represented the distress in the west of Ireland.

They set out for the west on 3 June 1905. They travelled to Galway by train, and then by sidecar to Spiddal. Clifden is seventy miles north-west of Spiddal as the crow flies, but infinitely more distant as the two men went, by different forms of horse-drawn transport. The land between the two towns includes some of the most beautiful but desolate countryside in Ireland. This is particularly so of the islands of the Gorumna peninsular west of Carraroe,

133. *The Emigrant*. This drawing and figs. 134, 136 to 138 are from the series of articles written by J.M. Synge which appeared in *The Manchester Guardian* during June and July 1905.

and including Gorumna itself, Lettermore, Lettermullan, Furnace and Dinish. All save the last are linked by causeways, the majority of which were constructed or improved under the Congested Districts Board. The soil is thin, the rock is everywhere visible. The grazing is poor. The fields are small, and divided by dry-stone walling. The crops, where crops were possible, were potatoes and oats. Jack depicted it in drawings which emphasise the toy-like character of the landscape; the scale is altogether tiny: tiny cottages in tiny fields surrounded by walls which the animals and people cross without difficulty.

Jack's portrayal of children is inspired by a pathos which borders on the sentimental. And the figures of the men mix the debonair with the rural. The characters depicted were not 'types'; in one instance he drew two men they actually met on the Monday on which they began their work, near Spiddal, 'one of them, by his hat and dress, plainly a man who had been away from Connemara. 'In a little while he had told us he had been in Gloucester and Bristol working on public works, but had wearied of it and come back to his country.' The theme of the returned emigrant was to feature through their travels. It emerged when Synge came to the point of summing up, at the end of their time in the west, with an article called 'Possible Remedies'. And Jack's drawing, *The Emigrant*, was a straightforward statement about the able-bodied male breadwinner having to leave for foreign parts in order to earn and send back the money needed by his family (fig. 133). A mare, with its legs hobbled, and with a foal at its flank, implies less than abject poverty, in one drawing, and the degree to which the people 'managed' is indicated in Synge's description of the 'long strings of country people driving home from Galway in low carts drawn by an ass or pony. As a rule one or two men sit in front of the cart driving and smoking, with a couple of women stretched out at their ease among sacks of flour or young pigs, and nearly always talking continuously in Gaelic.'

Gaelic was spoken widely in that part of Connemara, and Synge's command of the language was a passport for both men. On one occasion, when he gave to an old woman a few halfpence he got a 'God save you!' in English, to which he replied in Irish with a blessing. Her response was a stream of welcome and delight: 'That the blessing of God may be on you, on road and on ridgeway, on sea and on land, on flood and on mountain, in all the kingdoms of the world,' and she went on until they were out of earshot. His knowledge of the Aran Islands, and of the people there, helped also, giving him a ready entry into local gossip. Synge was the leader, and made the decisions as to where they would go and what they would do, and Jack maintained that this was decided between them on the basis that Synge was a couple of months older.

The two men were of a practical turn of mind, and the careful exploration of the realities of life among the peasants, which took tact and sympathy to uncover, went on through conversations which were put directly into the articles. Synge's second piece was built almost entirely around one encounter. An elderly man on the Carraroe peninsula, which was described to Synge as the poorest parish in the country, told them how the breeding of Connemara ponies – the only kind of horse capable of living off the poor grass, or negotiating the difficult terrain – was dying out, and that the horses they were now getting were producing foals which were then sold, reducing everyone to the use of the ass. This confined the people to the traditional

134. *Relief Works.*

134. *Relief Works.*

broad-beamed boats of the area known as hookers as a means of getting to market in Galway, a voyage of four hours in fair weather, or to the islands of Aran or Clare to sell turf cut from the mountains. The old man told them that when he was young the land was more fertile, and that there were fewer people. The making of poteen

> was a great trade at that time, and you'd see the police down on their knees blowing the fire with their own breath to make a drink for themselves, and then going off with the butt of an old barrel, and that was one seizure, and an old bag with a handful of malt, and that was another seizure, and would satisfy the law; but now they must have the worm and a still and a prisoner, and there is little of it made in the country.[10]

Their roadside philosopher, cheerful enough himself, completed the catalogue of doom by telling them that dancing and singing were dying out, that the piper never came to their cottages any more, and that all the young girls going to the special schools set up by the Congested Districts Board expressly for the purpose of teaching lace-making were saving their money in order to leave for America, 'and then away she will go, and why wouldn't she?' There was consumption and typhus, and there were 'places round about where you'll sometimes hear of a score and more stretched out waiting for their death.'

Both Synge and Yeats took particular exception to the relief work which they found on the roads into the islands, and which had been taken up with some enthusiasm by the Congested Districts Board, though it was by no means a new device. Every famine had brought relief schemes, every causeway and bridge had been built and improved and extended by both men and women under the supervision of a ganger

> swaggering among them and directing their work . . . As we drove quickly by we could see that every man and woman was working with a sort of hang-dog dejection that would be enough to make any casual passer mistake them for a band of convicts. The wages given on these works are

135. *Man from Arranmore*, chalk and watercolour on board, $14\frac{1}{2}$ x $10\frac{1}{2}$, 1905.

usually a shilling a day, and, as a rule, one person only, generally the head of the family, is taken from each house. Sometimes the best worker in a family is thus forced away from his ordiznary work of farming, or fishing, or kelp-making for this wretched remuneration at a time when his private industry is most needed . . . I have been told of a district not very far from here where there is a ganger, an overseer, an inspector, a paymaster, and an engineer superintending the work of two paupers only . . . it probably shows, not too inexactly, a state of things that is not rare in Ireland.

Jack drew the misery, and his drawings are an austere, unhappy record in which he tries to show the burdensome toil, and the heavy hand of the ganger's self-importance. The women carried heavy loads, whether of turf, or kelp, or the sixteen-stone bags of flour, and many of them did permanent injury to themselves, without knowing it. Yet again and again, it is the cheerfulness which Synge notices, the disposition to talk, laugh, tell stories, drink and smoke, and it is the fine look of them he notices, and Jack draws, 'in new red petticoats and shawls. They looked as they crowded up on the road as fine a body of peasant women as one could see anywhere, and were all talking and laughing eagerly among themselves.'

The 'Ferryman of Dinish', who took them out to the last island in the Gorumna group, inspired two fine drawings (fig. 136). They show him as wild and colourful; the stories he told them confirmed this, and became one article. They are expressive of the strange, almost magical diversity which poverty and emigration forced upon individuals such as he. Having travelled the world, serving at sea and on land, as a seaman, an interpreter for emigrants, visiting New York and Baltimore and New Orleans, working in Manchester, Birkenhead and Newcastle-upon-Tyne, and sailing to every coastal port or town in Scotland or Wales, the man had returned to row the ferry across the narrow strip of sea between the two rocky islands, and to gather seaweed for kelp. 'I got married then, and I after holding out till I was forty.' But after starting a family he lost his wife, and three cows from a disease of the brain, yet was held to his job on the island by the young children;

> If it wasn't for them I'd be off this evening, and I'd earn my living easy on the sea . . . And I don't know what way I'm going to go on living in this place that the Lord created last, I'm thinking, in the end of time; and it's often when I sit down and look around on it I do begin cursing and damning, and asking myself how poor people can go on executing their religion at all.

The man was fifty-seven. He had managed to get his son into his place, doing relief work, but the ganger had twice put him off from the employment, unexplained, and though he had been prepared to complain, he decided against, 'for what good is it harming him more than another?'

Kelp-making was of great interest to both men, and Jack drew the women bringing the seaweed in from the boats in huge loads piled up in creels on their backs (fig. 137). Trawbaun was a village on the coast opposite the Aran Islands much involved in kelp-making. Here the seaweed was hauled out of shallow water and brought in by curragh. It was laid out on the grass and walls to dry, and then built into piles in long trenches. A fire was lit (as in the making of charcoal), turning the seaweed into a molten mass. Onto this fresh supplies of weed were piled to contain the heat and prevent flames. Dense

136. *The Ferryman of Dinish Island.*

137. *Gathering Seaweed for Kelp.*

138. *Kelp-Burning.*

volumes of rich, cream-coloured smoke rose from the temporary furnace (fig. 138). This took about twelve hours. It then took three days to cool down. The hard, crusty residue was broken up and loaded into curraghs to be transported and sold. The trade was dependent on fair weather for good drying and burning, but was a reliable indigenous business, and made good profits and gave a measure of independence. A two-hundredweight sack of flour cost about one pound. Between three and five tons of seaweed were required to make one ton of kelp, and one ton of kelp earned somewhere between three and five pounds. The people had no way of checking on the honesty of the middle-men – a perpetual problem, to which Synge frequently refers – and there was dissatisfaction; but it was preferable by far to the shilling-a-day rate for relief which was a humiliation and a waste of personal and government effort.

There were difficulties in balancing the content of the articles with the drawings. Jack clearly welcomed the individuals such as the ferryman on whom he could focus a strong line of character; and the general scenes proved straightforward, though at times a bit didactic. Where he had difficulty was in Synge's quite serious analysis of the conflicting claims of different employments, the rates of housing, the quality of the cottages, the replacement of thatch by tin, and land acquisition, that is the central conflict between tradition and modernisation. Thatching was a social event, done in an idle period, involving whole communities, and often the occasion for a festival; and it had gone on for centuries. Similarly, Synge spotted the ingenuity of the peasants in working out the scale of a new building, how they would discuss for hours the proportions of a house, though 'they had never, of course, heard of proportion'. They knew how high a house should be for a certain length, and how many rafters, in order that it would look well. He thought there was great danger in losing these traditions, and that it would be better by far to support what the men and women did to earn money, so that they could decide on their own housing and other benefits, rather than imposing too rapid a set of changes, which would destroy their lives.

After completing six assignments, the two men had made their way to Clifden, the end of the stretch of the Midland and Great Western Railway which ran out through Oughterard and Maam Cross. They returned to Galway. Jack ordered a model of a hooker from Thomas Hill and Company, to be made and sent on to him in Devon.[11]

The two men then travelled north to Ballina, in Mayo, by train. They made the journey overnight, and went on from there by long car to Belmullet, a journey of forty miles which began at four o'clock in the morning. The long car was a precarious form of travel. In a letter to Masefield, Jack told him that because he was so sleepy he had to tie himself on. 'When the driver saw me apparently pitching off head foremost he roared with horror but when he saw the rope held he roared with pleasure.'[12]

It was an entirely different, but equally distressed countryside into which they travelled. The stones of south Connemara gave way to the great wastes of turf and bog in north Mayo. Instead of dry stone walls, the fields were divided by turf banks over which meadowsweet and grasses grew, and turf was used widely in the building of cottages. Jack drew the roads lined with turf, and the tumble-down cottages; he drew one strangely elegant interior, where they took shelter from the rain, with a four-poster bed, a spinning wheel, and great flagstones spread out to the divided door with the drenching rain falling beyond. Synge said this brought 'an almost intolerable feeling of dampness and discomfort'. Their initial impressions were universally dismal. The rain fell heavily, they drifted in and out of sleep as the car jogged on through the wet, and they witnessed endless scenes of depression: the wet cattle straggling on the roadsides, the people weeding their potatoes, dressed in colourless and 'draggled' clothing, unlike the homespun tweed of Connemara, and the cottages, some of which had the end of an old barrel stuck in the roof as a chimney. The cottage in one of Jack's drawings is a singularly decrepit building, its roof sagging, strings crossing it to hold the old thatch together, and the stones, door and windows set at crazy angles.

The best land was owned by the big farmers, the bogs were exhausted of turf, there was no way of replenishing and reviving the soil, and no feed for the cattle or the pigs. There was dependence on remittances. The reported speech of the people is not despairing, but phlegmatic and resigned. There were good years and bad ones, catastrophes and setbacks. The remittances were vital. When the rain cleared, and Synge and Jack went on their way, they found the Sligo boat at the jetty north of the town of Belmullet. It was the *Tartar*, a Pollexfen vessel now belonging to Uncle George. Over a hundred local men were to go aboard for Sligo, and then on to Glasgow, as harvestmen. And they would be followed by many more in the course of the week. It was a grim departure, ameliorated only by the fact that it was infinitely to be preferred to the much more permanent emigration to America, from which only a few ever returned. The men, girls and boys, all went, to pick potatoes, to make hay, to weed turnips, and they often made up shiploads of five hundred or so at a time. They usually went to Glasgow, spreading out through the Scottish and north of England countryside, sleeping in barns, and staying for a period of months, at the end of which they might, if they were careful, bring back eight or nine pounds.

Synge's vision is not unrelenting in its gloom. He draws from those he meets occasional sparks of hope and humour, and is always ready to record fragments of history, though these relate, often sadly, to famine experiences. But his message is critical, and his purpose is to expose mistakes and exploitation, often in ways which reverse the simplistic views which have grown up about Ireland's dispossession and anguish at this time, particularly in the west. He refers to the traditional view of the absentee landlord as the curse of the countryside, but himself comes to a different conclusion: 'in reality the small landlord, who lived on his property, and knew how much money every tenant possessed, was a far greater evil'. And he had a poor regard for the rent system, and the dangers of self-improvement, which either brought about a rent increase, or made it more expensive to buy out a tenancy. At the same time, in certain districts, one of which was Geesala, Synge found an active and self-possessed community, strong in Gaelic League activities, with plays being acted during the winter, and supported by a busy branch of the Agricultural Co-Operative Bank, promoted by the Irish Agricultural Organisation Society, and supported by the Congested Districts Board.

Jack saw a softer side to this, at least in retrospect, and tells a story of one of their stops in Mayo, where they paused at an inn where the innkeeper's wife talked in Irish and English. She told them she had lived in America in Lincoln's day. Her husband was little and old, and put in an odd word. 'The husband was a wonderful gentle-mannered man, for we had luncheon in his house of biscuits and porter, and rested there an hour, waiting for a heavy shower to blow away; and when we said good-bye and our feet were actually on the road, Synge said, "Did we pay for what we had?" So I called back to the innkeeper, "Did we pay you?" and he said quietly, "Not yet sir."[13]

Synge shared with Jack a love of little children and of animals, and took delight in 'the narrow paths made of sods of grass alongside the newly metalled roads, because he thought they had been put there to make soft going for the bare feet of little children'.[14] Jack later noticed Synge's sympathy with children in Bemullet on St John's Eve, 24 June:

> we stood in the market square watching the fire play, flaming sods of turf soaked in paraffin, hurled to the sky and caught and skied again, and burning snakes of hayrope, I remember a little girl in the crowd, in an ecstasy of pleasure and dread, clutched Synge by the hand and stood close in his shadow until the fiery games were done.[15]

Synge, who also recorded the same event, described it more sternly and traced its origins to Druidical rites.

The later articles, which concentrated on presenting the life inland, and the contribution of the markets, the village shops, and the general trade in the towns, placed a considerable strain on Jack, since he had to cram into single drawings as vivid a picture as he could of a whole world of activity. In his sketchbooks we find a softer and wider version of events. In Belmullet he discovered the redoubtable Mrs Jordan, who was not a subject for the *Manchester Guardian*, but did appear later in his book, *Life in the West of Ireland*. With her severe features and wire-framed spectacles, frowning over an unpaid account for which a poor peasant woman has brought in her bag of money, while a gallant local seaman stands indifferently aside, this woman was also responsible for buying the kelp (fig. 139). There was a public house off the shop, and outside its door there were shawls, suits and saddles, hanging up, while inside hob-nailed boots and hanks of rope are suspended above the woman's head.

139. *Mrs Jordan*, from *Life in the West of Ireland*, 1912.

The weather improved greatly during their travels in Mayo, and from Swinford Jack wrote of it being too hot, and sent Cottie a postcard of an Irish Jaunting Car. He apologised for not finding time to write any letters.[16] Not many local people are recorded, but Jack did promise to send copies of the articles to a Mr J.Y. Hegarty, in Bangor Erris, and duly did this.[17] They made their way back towards Dublin in easy stages, through Ballina, Swinford, Claremorris and Galway. In the hotel in Claremorris Jack did a two-page interior of the hotel sitting-room, with a portrait of Parnell on the wall, and one of Robert Emmet.

Back in Dublin, Jack stayed for a while at Gurteen Dhas with his father and sisters. He wrote to Synge on 4 July, giving him details of his final expenses, and telling him that he had sent off the final article with his own drawing. 'Tonight I cross to London and after a day or so with Masefield I go to my home. Whenever you have nothing better to do write me a letter. Letters from Ireland are greatly appreciated by us. Yours very kindly Jack B Yeats. I expect to be back in Ireland in September.'[18] Ever careful about money, he told Synge to add to their expenses seven shillings, four shillings for breakfast on the last Sunday and three shillings for a car to Harcourt Street station for the train. He remarked in a later letter on the fact that the cheque sent by Scott did not sufficiently cover what was owed. At the same time, he was more interested in the safe arrival from Galway of the model hooker which he had bought early on in their travels. And he drew the huge crate in which it came. 'It looked like a canary bird in a cage'.

Synge had enjoyed the trip and was proud of his work for the *Manchester Guardian*. He wrote to Stephen McKenna on 13 July, from Crosthwaite Park:

> I've just come home from the Guardian business. Jack Yeats and myself had a great time and I sent off 3 articles a week for four weeks running. Would you believe that? But he, being a wiser man than I, made a better bargain, and though I had much the heavier job the dirty skunks paid him more than they paid me, and that's a thorn in my dignity! I got £24.4.0 which is more than I've ever had yet and still I'm swearing and damning. However we had a wonderful journey, and as we had a purse to pull on we pushed into out-of-the-way corners in Mayo and Galway that were more strange and marvellous than anything I've dreamed of.[19]

Jack and Synge met again in the autumn of 1905, when Jack returned to Dublin for his mid-September show, both a critical and a financial success, and they seem to have gone walking in Wicklow. Miss Horniman, Jack Geoghegan, Tom Kelly, Quinn, Lady Mayo, Douglas Hyde and George Moore were all buyers at his show, and several works derived directly from the mid-summer travels in Connaught. Among these may be included *The Mail Car Driver*, *A Political Meeting*, and *The Fair at Ballinasloe*. And all of them were later used in *Life in the West of Ireland*.

The collaboration between Jack and Synge continued, this time over the book which Synge had developed out of his earlier essays and articles on the Aran Islands. As early as May 1900, Lady Gregory refers to Synge 'working at a book on Aran, & has sent an article to Harper's on it, which if taken he promises to get Jack Yeats to illustrate'.[20] This did not happen, but in September the following year, on his way to the Aran Islands, Synge brought with him to Coole the first, bulky manuscript of the book, and seems to have shown it to Willie and Lady Gregory, or possibly have left with them. By the beginning of October both had read it, and Lady Gregory wrote to Synge giving it glowing praise, and adding Willie's comments.

By 1905 Synge had made three visits to Aran, and was about to embark on a fourth. He dropped off the manuscript in November with the London publisher, Grant Richards. It went on to other publishers, including Elkin Mathews, who listened to John Masefield's praises of the text, but did not make up his mind. Then George Roberts, managing director of the new Dublin publishing firm of Maunsel, persuaded Synge to get back the manuscript and give it to him. At that stage Synge thought of illustrating it with some of the remarkable photographs he had taken. But by the end of 1905 it appears that Jack was considering doing the illustrations. There is nothing in the collected letters to explain Jack's involvement, but Synge sent him the manuscript during the winter of 1905–6, and in February Jack had already started on the drawings, and had got an agreement with Maunsel. Synge sent him his photographs taken on the island during his four trips there:

> The photographs you send are fine! and are a great help, and thank you very much for letting me have them – when I finished reading your manuscript – I was bothered to understand how you could leave such people. I wish I could live in Ireland – everyone that has any right there should be in it –

140. *The Evictions*, from *The Aran Islands*,
1907.

Masefield was here for a few days in the New Year. We sailed card board boats to destruction on the pond and on some flooded marshes.[21]

Jack's view, about those having the 'right' to be in Ireland being there, is typical of the way his mind worked around an idea, here involving obligations and duties which he himself was really so slow to take up.

The Jack Yeats drawing which became the frontispiece for the book, and a compelling, even heroic image for the kind of men they had encountered, is derived from a figure in a Synge photograph of 'Islanders on Inishere'. The man's waistcoat is dark and the shirt light in the drawing, while it is the other way round in Synge's photograph; but other details – the stance of the figure, the beard, the hat, the wide-bottomed trousers, are the same. Jack derived the figures of the two women, in *The Pier*, *The Hooker's Owner*, *Kelp-Making*, *Carrying Seaweed for Kelp*, *The Evictions*, *A Four-Oared Curragh*, *Thatching*, *Porter* and *An Island Horseman*, all directly from photographs sent to him by Synge (fig. 140). Even *The Man Who Told the Stories* and the strange figure sitting on a bollard inquiring about the heavy weight of Synge's bag – 'It's real heavy she is, your honour,' he said; 'I'm thinking there's gold there will be in it.' – is from a photograph in the package sent from Dublin to Devon and kept by Jack long after the writer's death.

The tribute paid by Jack to John Synge was unique. On no other occasion did he draw from photographs in order to illustrate another man's writing. He was probably aware of the difficulties Synge had had with the book, and recognised the impact which clear black-and-white line drawings would give.[22] Of course, he was conscious of the success of their west of Ireland venture, in terms of public reaction to the *Manchester Guardian* pieces, and the private admiration expressed by C.P. Scott. And he had clearly enjoyed working closely with Synge. He was to complete their collaboration posthumously, with the publication, and in some cases the republication, in 1911 of his drawings for the Connemara articles, together with Wicklow and Kerry drawings.

It seems that they saw a good deal of each other, though this is not reflected in the usual way, through letters. It can, however, be inferred from remarks which Synge made in letters to Molly Allgood about Jack.[23] It is clear from these that the two men met from time to time, and went walking together. Synge went to Jack's solo show in October 1906 with his mother; their names are listed in a newspaper cutting of distinguished visitors in Jack's cuttings book. Lady Aberdeen, the Viceroy's wife, bought *The Coronor's Inquest*, and Lady Dudley, who was interested in his work and later that year arranged a London show of several works from the exhibition, attended.[24] The two men also went to the Queen's Theatre together, seeing a melodrama which Jack wrote about. In one letter to Molly, written from Glenageary on 4 October 1906 Synge wrote: 'Fancy, two days more and then *Sunday*! How I look forward to it! I hope rain or Jack Yeats wont stop us.'[25] And in another, a week later: 'If you are *not* there, I'll take it you cant come and I'll go and see Jack Yeats.'[26] Synge admired Jack's painting enough for Molly to acquire two works for him; and this may have been inspired by the 1906 exhibition, which took place during the first three weeks of October, though this is not clear. In a letter from Synge to Molly, in April 1907, he writes: 'By the way if you have really ordered those pictures of Jack B Y's we must keep them, dont mind my little burst of temper – I am very grateful to you for thinking

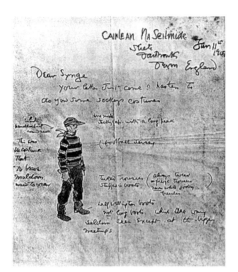

141. Letter to J.M. Synge concerning designs for costumes for *The Playboy*.

of getting them for me, but I have been getting a little bit scary about your extravagance lately that is why I blew up.'[27] No works by Jack were in Synge's collection when he died; it is not known whether Molly retained the two works 'ordered' from the artist, but in December 1907 Synge wrote to Molly: 'Did I tell you I have got Jack Yeats' sketch of the stoker framed and the glass put into the etching. I am quite proud of them, I have them in my little study and they look very nice. That is my first step towards furnishing! Nish! *I'm* as unpractical an ass as you are – that's the worst of it – fancy marrying and setting up with no furniture but three pictures and a *suggan* chair and a fiddle!'

Synge sought advice from Jack over his play, *The Playboy of the Western World*. He had completed it by the end of December 1906, and it went into rehearsal in Dublin in the new year, its first night scheduled for 26 January. In the second week of rehearsal Synge wrote to Jack for help over the entry of Christy Mahon in Act III, 'now a great hand at racing and lepping and licking the world'. The stage instruction has 'Christy comes in, in jockey's dress, with Pegeen Mike, Sara, and other girls and men'. And the tide of action is rising to the climax of the play. But what did a west of Ireland jockey wear? Synge, not a racing man, had no idea. Jack responded immediately with a letter full of drawings of jockeys. One wears a jacket, another a shirt, another a football jersey. They all wear tweed trousers, and he shows one with pink and green striped socks and no boots at all, and another in rough shoes with one spur only attached to the right foot. Jack is emphatic that white jockey trousers or high boots would be entirely wrong, except at the bigger meetings, and his advice is eventually in favour of 'the costume that the brave Muldoon used to wear'. This consisted of a home-made jockey hat with a long peak, a striped football jersey, a white handkerchief at the neck, and tweed trousers stuffed into half-wellington boots. He advised Synge: 'If the race is over he'd be well splashed with mud.'[28]

The previous autumn in Dublin, Jack had said to Synge that the Abbey Theatre should 'get some excitement to itself. Looking for excitement at the Abbey is like looking for a gas escape with a naked light.' It was an odd remark, reflecting Jack's love for melodrama, and possibly a latent distaste for the self-conscious theatre of 'national revival'. But now the excitement descended, with a vengeance. The 'Playboy' riots, on the first and subsequent nights, occasioned specifically by Christy Mahon's reference to 'drifts of Mayo girls standing in their shifts', threw Dublin into turmoil.[29] It brought Synge and his play a notoriety which scandalised the Church and the press, and represented a high point of drama. 'No great play ever had a meaner reception', wrote one early critic.[30] Jack wrote to say that 'when the excitement comes it comes severely . . . I never expected anything like this.'[31] Jack speculated on the kind of play which Synge would next write, first with a drawing of a man with a bird perched on his arm, talking to women, and captioned: 'Will it be as mild as milk?' And then with a drawing, headed 'or will it be?' showing a group of men throwing a man over a cliff. Jack would not have been conscious of the seriousness of the riots for Synge. In her diary, Sara Allgood, Molly's sister, wrote of the pandemonium on the opening night. 'We all flocked into the Green Room . . . poor Synge – white as a sheet – and some of our friends among the audience came back stage'. Of Synge in particular she added: 'I personally think it hastened his death'.[32]

Jack wrote to him of his own, quite different excitements:

Ships I think leave you unmoved, but [I] saw last Saturday what a great many people have never seen and I never saw before, a *five masted ship* under full sail – it really was magnificent – every sail on her was up and down as stiff as the board and she was whacking up the channel like a racehorse I saw her first a couple of miles off and then as she got further away I got a big telescope and brought her close up again. She would have made the old ferry man on Dinish Island scream . . . When will you be able to look us up in this part of the world?

Synge's health was giving him cause for concern, and he faced an operation at some stage during 1907. But in the spring he had more or less determined to take Jack up on his offer, and go to Devon, and on to London. He wrote to Molly: 'I am going to the doctor tomorrow and then I'll either have the operation, or go away to Jack Yeats.'[33] At the end of May Synge saw his doctor for approval. This given, he left Glendalough House, in Glenageary, took the boat from Rosslare that night, and sailing first to Falmouth, then on to Plymouth, was with Jack in Devon at 1.15 p.m. on Friday. He was met at Kingsbridge by Jack with their small pony and trap. The visit got off to a good start, but was not a success, simply because Synge's health continued to trouble him. He recalled it later in the year, when the possibility of a trip to Brittany was being considered, and he told Molly then that he hardly saw the good of spending £10 going to France: 'I have more cough now than I had when I went to Jack Yeats, and I was miserable there too ill to enjoy myself in the least.'[34] In addition to the coughing, he was suffering from a more serious complaint, that of swollen lymph glands in his neck, symptomatic of the spread of Hodgkins Disease, which eventually killed him. Yet he did get some pleasure out of Jack and Cottie's company, going for day-long walks, and admiring the simple comfort of their lives, and the evident happiness of their marriage. He wrote to Molly after his first three days in Strete:

This is a charming place, my room looks out across a little creen vally [sic], with a little water mill at the bottom, and the birds sing so loud they seem to waken me at 4 o'clock every morning. I went for a long walk along by the sea with J.B.Y. on Saturday, so that we were out all day from 11. till 7. Yesterday we puttered about, and today we are going for another long expedition after Breakfast. He is a charming fellow. I dont feel much better for the change yet, my cough is bad still, and I'm not sleeping well, or in good spirits. J.B.Y. and his wife seem a very happy couple after eleven years of it, and they must be comfortably off as everything is very nice in a simple way.[35]

The two men also seem to have discussed a further collaboration on a book of Irish types. Synge does not mention it, nor does Jack, but just before the playwright went into hospital for his neck operation, in September of that year, John Butler Yeats visited him and reported to Willie: 'I saw him the day before the hospital business and he was in good spirits, wanting to see Jack about a book on Irish types he is meditating.'[36] The prospects of such a combination, with Jack's vast visual resources of Irish characters, drawn in every part of the country, and Synge's accumulated notes of the people he met and visited on his travels, is enchanting. C.P. Scott is even thought to have offered to commission it.

Synge went on to London, and Jack had occasion to go as well, but they saw little of each other. Jack and Cottie went to the Continent that summer, and took a trip up the Rhine, writing to Synge after it. Synge had gone to Wicklow, and was staying in Bray Cottage, outside Enniskerry, mainly for health reasons, and unsuccessfully in that respect. The letter, which reveals the warmth and simplicity of the relationship between the two men, is worth quoting extensively:

> The weather was first too cold, and then too hot and now after a tearing thunder-storm that hit a building nearby twice yesterday afternoon, there has been a fog for the last six hours . . . The rain yesterday was beyond anything in my experience, on one hour and a half of it three big rivers leapt out of the hill opposite and tore the road to splinters . . . There is a magnificent four-year old youngster in the house who keeps me amused as I hear him under the door. The other night the whole family chased him for 3/4 of an hour to make him take a pill and each time just at the critical moment he managed to get under the table and begin saying his prayers when they were too pious to disturb him. Glen Cree Reformatory – that you may have heard of – is a mile off townwards – and I went through it a week or two ago and saw an admirable cake-walk danced by one of the convicts, – and a roomful of the youngsters with a hag – a lazy hag – over them knitting stockings for the institutions. When we went in the young devils – God help them – blushed scarlet at being caught at such an ungaolbirdlike employment. It is told that one of them a while ago made himself a nun's outfit – he was a tailor's apprentice – and escaped in it, and then before he was caught went round Dublin and collected £40 for foreign missions. I go back to Kingstown at the end of this week and stay there for a week. Then if I am well enough I may go to Kerry for a time. I spent a day with Masefield when I was in London . . . I hope I'll see you while you are in Ireland, I suppose you'll make a stop in Dublin on your way back. Please remember me kindly to Mrs Yeats. Yours cordially J.M. Synge.[37]

Jack, like Synge, was essentially a shy man; but unlike Synge he found difficulty in being forceful or direct. More retiring and more cautious, he seems to have envied Synge his forcefulness and his direct manner. Yet in their art they are similar. The wildness of Synge's *Playboy* is echoed in drawings such as *Let me Tear 'Un*, and the characters which appealed to both men were those who lived on the fringes of conventional life, seemed to challenge it, and managed to carry with them, wherever they went, the real stuff of existence, the 'living ginger' which so appealed to Jack. He was greatly taken, for example, by Synge's ballad, 'Danny', as violent a story as any about rural Ireland. Danny was a noted Mayo womaniser, begetting children, including twins, on the fair girls and women 'from Binghamstown to Boyle and Ballycrory', striking the priest twice at Crossmolina fair, and fighting men and boys everywhere. He was then waylaid on the road from Bangor Erris to Belmullet by twenty-nine Mayo men who attacked him. Though Danny fought fiercely, the odds were against him:

> But seven tripped him up behind,
> And seven kicked before,
> And seven squeezed around his throat
> Till Danny kicked no more.

It is possible that Synge and Yeats heard the story of Danny on their travels in Mayo. Certainly, 'the flat cross on a stone' was to be seen a mile or so out of Bangor until relatively recently, when it was broken up and used in the widening of the road. In 1908, when Jack restarted his *Broadsheet*, calling it instead *A Broadside*, he asked Synge for the poem – at that stage unpublished – and seems to have thought only *nine* men did the deed:

> My dear Synge – How is the world using you? and how is your health keeping? I am restarting the Broad Sheet which I think you saw, it was a monthly sheet with ballads (ancient and modern like to hymns) and chaste pictures by me – Have you done any ballad lately that I could print in it I would be thankful if you could let me have something – the Broad Sheet (or Broad Side which is the new name as I daresay you might expect, only pays for what it gets with 'my thanks'. Even if you'd let me have that ballad you did of the nine men jumping on the one, I think it would be too 'bloodish' for the Broad Side – at least it isnt quite that only I personally have a horror of those terrible things.[38]

Jack was fascinated by the violence as well:

> I dont think there are so many [terrible things] now I know when I was a boy in Sligo I used to often hear of fearful beatings after fair days – I saw a ticket snatcher at Windsor races once running with all the crowd behind him and he fell – and I tell you, if the police hadnt got into him quick they never would have been able to carry him away on a hurdle – they'd want to use a sack. How is the Abbey Theatre going on? and how has the going of the Fays worked? We were in London a month when my picture show (which did fairly well in a very bad season) was on and had a good time I saw some boxing and some wrestling a big affair with Russians Italians French Turks and a Negro . . . a little man behind me after yelling 'Fair Play for all' explained to his friend 'They're all a lot of furriners.'[39]

Jack wrote several affectionate and interesting letters to Synge during the summer and autumn of 1908, and they reveal his awareness of Synge's health, and his innate sympathy and kindness towards the man. Jack was no doubt hearing bad news. He and Cottie were at Coole, and were going on to Lissadell, to stay with 'Long' Harvey, who was now rector at the church in Ballinfull, the tiny village near Lissadell. During their stay with Lady Gregory they had been out to Kinvara, and Jack reported that

> a sort of sailor man sitting in a Connemara turf boat hailed me as Boss and invited me aboard I gave him a cigar, and he told me of his adventures on the deep in Norwegain and Yankee vessels, I asked him to drink also the crew of the turf boat. When we got to the grocers the sailor man invited other friends of his to roll up to the bar and drink at my expense – later on he spotted me in the yard and touched me for 2/- to pay his fine for being drunk and disorderly the week before – I was what they call an easy mark . . . After some time in Sligo we think of trying some little seaport on the East Coast Arklow perhaps – You know Arklow I think – I suppose you don't know any lodgings there near the sea.[40]

There was another letter from Coole in late August: 'How are you getting on? better and stronger I hope – I wrote to you some time ago I daresay you never got the letter. I wrote to Rathmines. There was nothing to reply to. I only mention it to show I had not forgotten you in your sickness.'[41] Synge described the letter to Molly as 'not a very interesting one'; he clearly did not welcome references to his health. At that stage the two men had not met in more than a year. But Synge wrote to Jack, inviting him to visit. Jack was staying at Gurteen Dhas with his sisters, and he wrote with a comical drawing of the crowded train they had taken from the west. 'they put the people where they could – note the pained face of representation of old county family on finding a second compartment full of third class people.'[42] The visit, however, was somewhat awkward for both men. 'I had Jack Yeats with me all the afternoon yesterday – It was a heavy day and we both seemed to find it rather hard to keep up a flow of conversation. It isn't easy when you're not very well to be suddenly confronted with a man you haven't seen for a year or so. Still I was very glad to see him, and I think he was glad too.'[43] Clearly, the joint project on Irish types had been abandoned by then.

Jack and Cottie took their time going home to Devon. They went by way of Wexford, and from there to London, where they stayed a fortnight. Later that year Synge's mother, who had been ill when Jack called, and on whom Synge had relied so heavily, died. He was dying himself, and Jack's letter, dated 6 December, and offering condolences, was the last communication between them. He wrote of a whale caught on the beach in Wexford:

> he got tangled up in the fishermans nets and they slew him as he drowned himself and they exhibited him on the beach to get money to pay for the torn net, they took £17 . . . I never knew before that whales had large round eyes – they said as they dragged him ashore they were shining – I don't want to go whaling now. Yours kindly Jack B Yeats.[44]

Synge died early in 1909. Jack wrote to John Quinn about it:

> This is very sad, Synge's death. I hoped he would have weathered it. He was so plucky and had stood such a lot of doctors work all his life. He was a fine spirit. I liked being away with him so much that time in the West of Ireland. And we had him here a week or two a couple of years ago and he was a delight – always so ready. I went out to see him when in Dublin last autumn and he thought that he would get on all right I imagined – he's a great loss.[45]

CHAPTER ELEVEN
Last Days in England 1909–1910

If I could live in my own country . . .

JACK'S DESIRE TO return and live in Ireland is expressed in his letters to Synge and also to John Quinn. He was both the product and the prisoner of his strange upbringing. Now, in his thirties, he had a life in England and a life in Ireland. His birth in London had given him pride in the city, and an affection for its people reinforced by his success in depicting them. A similar affection, similarly reinforced, had grown out of his childhood in the west of Ireland. Increasingly Ireland became the subject-matter for his work, and though he loved Sligo, it was neither wholly, nor solely the material for his work. Coole, Connemara, Mayo, Donegal, Kerry and Cork all inspired him and featured in his work, as did Dublin, Wicklow and Wexford. Travel was therefore a necessary part of his working life, as it had been when illustrating magazines.

The collaboration with John Synge changed him fundamentally. He no longer looked at 'Life in the West of Ireland', from the outside; it was becoming part of him. His Irish identity was itself an inspiration. Yet like Synge, Jack was far from being 'Nationalist' in the accepted sense, which pivoted upon a view of English rule being bad for Ireland. 'You ask what I think of the Sinn Feiners,' he wrote to John Quinn. 'Well, I don't think a great lot of a great many of the Sinn Feiners but I believe in the Sinn Fein 'idea'. I think its a good thing for its full of living ginger, and I do *not* believe in the new form of three-water groggers.'[1] The Sinn Fein idea – 'Ourselves Alone' – fitted accurately with almost everything which Jack and Synge had learnt at first hand in the Congested Districts: the importance of pride in one's own work, independence of spirit, the right to decide one's own life and activity, and the magic of the real culture of the people, dancing, music, story-telling. It had made a powerful impact on Jack and gave him a sterner sense of his own life and art.

Working with Synge, and attaching social and political arguments to living people, had transformed Jack's own view of subject matter which was already familiar to him. Instinctively, when doing a work like *The Emigrant*, at the beginning of the century, he had been conscious of the implications of the story behind his drawing; the tragedy of departure, families split by poverty and need, the awful wrench of leaving the beauty and desolation of remote districts, and with them the emigrant's own past. The effect of the *Manchester Guardian* commission had been to add to the instinctive view a rational interpretation, where time and history, folklore and health, disease, deprivation and death, all confirmed and extended the portrait of life in the west of Ireland which was already Jack's principal purpose as a painter.

If one assembles together the illustrations done for Synge, ranging from *The Ferryman of Dinish Island*, to the standing figure of *Muldoon*, together with such drawings as *The Rogue*, *The Man from Aranmore*, *A Tinker*, *The Ganger*, and *The Gaffer* the collective impact is powerful and at times threatening. Serious men are claiming serious positions in the world, whether behind the oars of a ferryboat, on the quayside, or in front of a music hall. In some cases – as in the Ferryman drawing – there is a frantic, almost mad expression in the face, and a hint of frenzy in the movements of the figure, entirely consistent with the story he had to tell of his life. That tension, which seems to run down his brawny arms and into the oars on which he hauls and the seat against which he braces his hob-nailed boots, is not always to be found in the drawings. Yet it is a singular fact that Jack rarely depicted men or women who were handsome or beautiful, in any obvious way. Many years later this aspect of his work was put to him by Alan Denson, who told him:

> In all his studies of people none seemed to have beautiful faces, although full of life and character. He gave me a very steady long look and asked me if I had read any stories by the American Bret Harte. There's one story by Bret Harte about a boy whose face was covered with freckles. In the nineteenth century freckles were not regarded as attractive, but Bret Harte liked them and reading his story you can see he loved them on children. There are ideal types of beauty in people, but I've always tended to see the liveliness of personality and character and haven't looked for conventional beauty any more than Bret Harte did in his story.[2]

He did follow some conventions. In the *Broadsheets* and *Broadsides*, for example, there are times when Jack resorts to 'types' of conventional female beauty, and in his Irish primers the children have an innate appeal drawn from the direct and simple depiction of peasant children in their simple homespun clothes, quite the antithesis of the wily, shrewd, lethal-looking east-end kids of Phil May's drawings, which are contemporary and comparable.

He said, in the September 1907 letter to Quinn quoted above, 'Ireland consists of all sorts of people. In fact, it is a nation ready to start at any time.' Orpen had the same view, expressing it in many ways, and filling the pages of his book, *Stories of Old Ireland and Myself*, with slightly teasing remarks, as though the country were being 'geared up' for some great start, or change. But whereas Orpen turned his back on the adventure of being part of it, and remembered instead the 'old Ireland, that Romantic Lady who slumbered and dreamt her way along to the music of the laughter and tears of her people,' Jack had by 1907 been transported from that view and into a quite different one.[3]

His words in the letter to Quinn closely echo those in Synge's letter to Stephen McKenna.[4]

> There are braggarts and fakirs here as everywhere else. In a word, or in a lot of words, Ireland consists of drunkards, murderers, thieves, humbugs, ex-policemen, Unionists – and honest men . . . though I know that if we had Home Rule tomorrow, for many years there would be many queer things done, as there would be among any people who had had no hand

142. Cottie's bookplate, by herself.

in governing themselves since modern ways of governing became necessary . . . If I could live in my own country I would be interested in some kind of politics. But here in England it is so strange to listen to people getting excited about things that I do not give a thrawneen about.[5]

At the same time, Jack was married to an English woman and had a life in Devon which was happy and comfortable. Every indication is that Cottie loved it there and had many friends. They both had. The quite ordinary correspondence which has survived, and which deals with local life in Strete, reveals a degree of involvement which had grown out of the permanency of their residence in south Devon.

Jack loved Cottie and depended on her. Their marriage was a powerful bond and a sure comfort. She made little of her own artistic talent in order that his should come first. She was home-maker, housewife, cook, companion, and in the end his best friend. We have less strong evidence for this than is available for his men friends. When he and Cottie were apart the letters which passed between them are filled with affection and concern. And when they were together, though it might seem too obvious a statement to set down, they did things together, enjoying as a couple the pleasure of entertaining the children of Strete and the surrounding farms. When friends write about their visits it is clear that the close harmony between Jack and Cottie has been a central part of their enjoyment. And all the members of the Yeats family repeatedly emphasised the sense they had of Jack having found contentment with an ideal wife.

She was interested in nature, wild life and wild flowers as well as the cultivation of their garden. Both of them valued knowing the great botanist Augustine Henry, and they corresponded with him long after the break-up of the Dun Emer and Evelyn Gleeson association. Jack's uncle, Isaac, in a letter from the house in Morehampton Road, wrote to Cottie, telling her that 'Meredith and Edie gave Gracie and Jenny a real nice green house – it is erected but the glass has not yet arrived, but it is promised within the next few days. We will have the crow of you unless Jack gets rich and gives you one.'[6] And he wrote to her often with advice about what to plant in the garden. 'You and Jack might imagine yourself Molly Woods and the Virginian. You should be working in your garden to prepare it for spring, all bulbs should be down now.'[7]

They kept hens. Cottie kept a careful record of the eggs laid in the same book as her lists of garden bulbs and her spring plantings of parrot tulips, auratum lilies, giant anemones and angels' tears. They had to deal with hen fights: 'Old Cough hen has been fighting, torn comb and corner of eyes.' Cottie, incidentally, wrote into her account book this 'advice for young men': 'Never give animals or anything alive to young ladies; they either hate you or marry you to get a home for the dog!'

They had a small billiard table, and both of them played. Indeed, at one time it became a nightly craze with them: 'Mrs Jack and I now play billiards every night with a patent arrangement bought at Gamages – there are pockets which screw onto an ordinary table and broad green web bands between the pockets to act as cushions its great fun. We have not made any very large breaks yet – 8 I think is the highest.'[8] Jack, of course, made his model boats, and acquired more lasting versions of the schooners and brigs he so admired.

154

143. View of Strete, *c.* 1910.

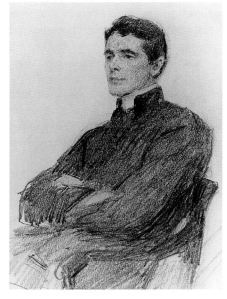

144. *Arnold Harvey*, pencil drawing by John Butler Yeats.

In the evenings they read to each other. Jack liked blood-and-thunder fiction and he tells his friend, Arnold Harvey,

> Mrs Jack is reading out 'Tom Cringle's Log' to me now, its all about Jamaica and the Gulph of Mexica[sic] – and a particularly bully book – its full of sudden death – and roaring robust humour – its date is about 1810 – what do you think of a man getting stung on the nose by a scorpion in the middle of the night and waking every one else up, to make a poultice for his nose, – and when the poultice was made and fixed, and all had again sunk on their couches, he made such fearful smothered groans in his sleep that some inventive spaniard shoved a small hollow bamboo right through the poltice onto his mouth so that he could snore through it comfortably – but it made him 'look like a sick snipe'.

The inevitable drawing accompanied the account, of a figure outstretched with bamboo sticking up, and the others looking on.[9]

Cottie was a careful and conscientious cook, and from their days in Chertsey kept a cookery book with recipes pasted in. We can form some idea of their domestic appetites from the earliest of the cuttings, though the book itself lasted Cottie until her death. We can almost savour the smells from the kitchen which must have greeted Jack as he climbed back up to Snails' Castle from his studio below, the buttered shrimps netted in Slapton Lea, the chestnut soup in autumn, the vegetarian dishes, 'cheese and nut savoury', the rummelled eggs, and the spring chicken 'latest style'. Cottie and Jack had been brought up to love puddings, and recipes for them abound; there is Leicester pudding, and Scarborough pudding, and gardeners' pudding; there are fig, and 'floating', and 'five minute' puddings, and 'Mamma's Christmas Pudding'.

Was Jack fearful that Cottie would have trouble settling in Ireland? He respected her love of Devon, the comforts, the garden and the home which they so enjoyed. And his respect for her feelings was reinforced by an innate caution and the painful example of the many unhappy parental homes of at least part of his childhood. He treated with care and patience the problem of moving, and he ensured that Cottie, over a number of annual visits, would come to know his country and be free to share in the future choice about living in Ireland. One of the troubles, for Jack, certainly during the early years of the century, was that he did not wish to live on the east coast of Ireland, and had no special affinity with Dublin. What he wanted was the west, and preferably Sligo; yet this seems to have been too great a transition for them. He went so far as to say that Dublin itself held no charms for him, that he would not give a 'thaureen' (he meant *thrawneen*, Irish for a straw) for it, claiming that he wanted to live 'somewhere in the west and by the sea'.

His friendship with Harvey reinforced this (fig. 144). As rector of Ballinfull, at Lissadell, he provided a link with the west of Ireland. He came to stay, he joined in their entertainments, there were a number of lively letters, and Harvey received and kept amusing examples of Jack's stencils, including those which he printed on his special writing paper, paper which he reserved for those who might appreciate the wit and cleverness of the drawings. Harvey and Jack had friends in common from the time when the future clergyman had acted as tutor to Robert Gregory at Coole.

Jack wrote of his father whom Harvey knew: 'The governor is going into his old studio at 7 Stephens Green the one that poor Osborne had – so Hugh Percy Lane will have plenty of room to manoeuvre his sitters in.'[10] Lane at the time was persuading artists to paint portraits of Irish men and women for the future modern gallery, and both John Butler Yeats and William Orpen were involved, though not Jack. This letter had a stencil of 'Captain Stratton', and contained one of the verses from the Masefield poem, 'Captain Stratton's Fancy', which Jack and Masefield sang together, to the tune of 'The Old English Gentleman'. And Harvey, who had attended his miniature theatre performances, was brought up to date with Jack's best effort of all:

> Last Friday Mrs Yeats gave her annual tea to the valley children and I gave them a performance on my theatre – it was an old fashioned Harliquinade with clown and pantaloon and a comic policeman, I think it amused the children more than any of the other entertainments I have given them. It really wasn't half bad, I had some working figures of which I was very proud – a town crier who rang a bell, and a figure of the clown . . .[11]

Harvey had bookplates designed by Jack. When Jack wrote about Theodore, he referred to him as Laffitte's 'third curate'. In another letter Jack wrote:

> Great excitement outside our windows this morning – an outward bound Barquentine – the pilot on the poop – the pilots boat – the vessel threw a line – the boat missed it – the Barquentine went on – the boat tried to catch her up – failed – and now the pilot wont get ashore till he reaches Cardiff – the fog above the pilots head is his language. NB I also happen to know the Pilot has a headache.[12]

Jack drew the vessel in the letter. They were staying on that occasion at Elsinore, at Rosses Point. Later, at Roger's Hotel, in Killybegs, he wrote of Donegal's special appeal, 'the most delightful country all full of twisty little corners not great expanses like Connemara.'[13]

There are times when he yearned to be in Dublin, for events such as the *Playboy* riots. In Ireland, Jack could step out proudly in the company of his fellow artists. He was appreciated by the leading figures in the Irish revival, admired greatly by some of them, and he was making a contribution which he believed was lasting. Yet he did not come. There was in Jack a reserve, founded partly in shyness, partly in doubts about what he could do other than see, draw, paint and show his work. Unlike his brother, he had no didactic political purpose to fulfil. Unlike Lady Gregory, he had no general mission on behalf of Irish art; unlike Douglas Hyde, he was not disposed to put Sinn Fein principles into his art by making the very language a statement of definition. Unlike George Moore, he had no wish to settle in Dublin in order to poke fun at what was going on there; unlike Orpen, he had no professional need to establish a practice in the city, or the financial need which, in the early years of the century, caused Orpen to teach in Dublin's Metropolitan School of Art. Jack was independent, free to go where he wished, and do what he most wanted to do; and this was to record the life around him.

He had reason to be cautious, and needed to look no further than his brother, who was involved more in theatre politics than in national affairs. In a postcard from John Masefield he got an oblique reference to this when Masefield wrote of Willie's troubles with the company. W.B. Yeats was to spend the weekend with Masefield. 'There is another row in the company, he says. Fay and Miss Allgood are quarrelling about a silly mistake of Fay's in letting his wife play *as Miss Algood*, when Miss Algood was too ill to come on. This is the sort of thing which is using your brother's best years.'[14]

Masefield, who was in his thirtieth year, seven years younger than Jack, wrote feelingly about the passage of time, and since it was Christmas Day mentioned what a melancholy time it was for him always. 'I don't seem to get any wiser as they slip by; and one gets very few when all is reckoned.' For Jack, this remark, that Time was knocking at all their doors, was a reminder. It confronted him with the sharp difference between his career and those of his brother and his brother's colleagues engaged in Ireland's cultural revival.

The biggest single disincentive to change remained the family situation from which Jack had escaped through his marriage. The move to Dublin of Jack's two sisters and his father had solved nothing for John Butler Yeats. He remained insolvent, impoverished, and a burden. He still talked endlessly, and interfered in his daughters' affairs. Jack's involvement with the commissions for St Brendan's Cathedral, in Loughrea, had taught him about the unprofitable nature of working within an arts and crafts movement, and had revealed his brother in the not altogether attractive light of business adviser to their two sisters. There was the painful reality that his two sisters and his father, now permanently established in their house in Dundrum, and committed to a life in Ireland from which none of them could easily extract themselves, were not making ends meet.

Jack recognised that his participation in his sisters' business was limited, and he understood that the delicate balance of his life as an artist would be disrupted by closer involvement with the rest of the family in Dublin. Publicly, he was seen as the recipient of *their* help:

> 'This Exhibition of his might be aptly called Yeats' Week, for one not only enjoys his pictures, but has the pleasure of meeting all the members of his talented family, who each in their own department of the 'Arts' are famous, and try all they can to help him and his charming wife to do the honours to their many friends, who make their charming exhibition quite the 'Salon' during their stay in Dublin, when every form of art and culture are discussed.[15]

The relationship between Jack and his sisters remained close and affectionate. As far as Willie was concerned, there were still difficulties. Our knowledge of them is extended after John Butler Yeats's departure for America, when all sorts of family issues are revealed through his letters: 'I would like to know about *Jack and Willie*,' he wrote to Lily, 'though I don't suppose things there will ever alter. I am perfectly certain Willie is very fond of Jack and I suppose Jack has an affection for Willie. Of course Willie irritates Jack, whereas Jack never irritates anyone.'[16]

Some attempt was made by Jack to work with Willie on theatre projects. He was asked to make sketches for the first production of *The Well of the Saints*, by Synge, which was in rehearsal in the autumn of 1905. Willie wrote to Lady Gregory: 'I am waiting on Jack's designs for Synge's play, as it may be possible to use some bits of scenery which will afterwards come in useful for Synge. Failing this I shall get Pixie Smith, who alone seems to understand what I want, to make a design.'[17]

Jack's designs, if they turned up, were not satisfactory. Instead, Pamela Colman Smith's designs, painted by Robert Gregory and Seaghan Barlow, were used. No drawings by Jack which could be construed as designs for the Synge play have survived.[18]

Jack accepted this philosophically enough. He was kindly in his attitude towards Robert Gregory, and went to see him at his work when he was in Dublin. Jack told Lady Gregory that an artist's smock, or an overall, was necessary, and showed this in a tiny sketch of her son. He reported to her on his own exhibition. As usual, many were coming to see it, few were buying. 'The public are coming to the Exhibition very well every day but the Insurance company seem to have frightened most of the picture buyers, make provision for your old age!!! buy Jack B. Yeats pictures, why insure a life, what is life without pictures, why take shares in a company, every picture, a share of the world.'[19]

Robert Gregory, who went to the Slade School of Art, got on well with Jack and Cottie and saw them in London when they visited. 'I went to Jack's show – some good things in it I think – and with Jack to see boxing one evening. He seems fairly cheerful tho' he has not sold a picture yet.'[20]

One person who might have bought on that occasion was George Moore. His admiration for Jack was deep and genuine. Lily reported on an encounter with Moore to her father: 'He told me he liked Jack's pictures so much that he had gone over and over again to the exhibition and hungered to buy, but had no where to hang them. "Give them to the National Gallery," I murmured. But he just did not hear me.'[21]

So Jack's yearning to return to Ireland was ambivalent, and this governed what he and Cottie did during the years between 1905 and 1910. There was a price to be paid for remaining in England. The confusion of John Butler Yeats with Jack, in the Guildhall Exhibition of Irish Art, in 1904, occurred again when the Irish International Exhibition took place in Dublin, in 1907, and Jack was not exhibiting at all. With his father showing no less than fourteen works, Orpen seven, Osborne thirteen (though posthumously), and W.J. Leech, Mary Swanzy, Eva Hamilton, John Lavery and Dermod O'Brien all involved, for Jack to be absent was an inexplicable blow.

From his first show, in 1897, and for the next ten years, both his London and Dublin solo exhibitions received widespread and favourable notice. His critics liked the fact that he gave them a view of Ireland. It was fresh and sympathetic; it was original and unique. There was an expectation that the vision of Ireland contained in small drawings would grow into something big. But the favourable critical attention was at heart more for the content than for the artistic range or scale. In this he was still modest and confined. An unsigned review in *The Irish Times*, in 1903, contained the following: '*Why should he insist on reproducing the tears and evading the smiles of Western Erin?* . . . Why will not Mr Yeats paint solidly in oils, and give his indubitable talent a chance to become bright and inspiriting? . . . the artist is capable of doing very much better.'[22]

That same exhibition, in the late summer of 1903, attracted a more outspoken attack from Robert Elliot: '. . . I also consider his work to be a weak kind of *happy-go-lucky link between the stronger art of certain London woodblock revivalists* and certain phases of life in the West of Ireland . . .'[23]

There were compensatory views, notably from Seumus O'Sullivan who wrote: 'Those who have followed with interest the development of Mr. Yeats' work from year to year cannot fail to find in this exhibition a broadening of treatment, a greater certainty of touch, and (most important of all) a more absolutely fearless following of his wonderful moods.'[24]

And in *The Celt*, Evelyn Gleeson, who had descended on Dublin the previous year from London, bringing with her the remainder of the Yeats family, like the contents of Pandora's box, went to the very heart of the problem which Jack faced in her comment: 'I know not with what subtle touches Mr. Jack Yeats conveys so much, for his sketches are very slight, but they are full of power – they are Irish art.'[25] She compared Jack with Count Markievicz, who had also exhibited paintings of Irish peasant life done near Sligo, and in her view 'very sympathetic . . . and most pleasing; but one sees in them the people from the outside; not all his power can approach the truth that is Mr Jack Yeats's birthright.' She concluded her notice in ringing tones: 'The Irishman of today is more alert, more self-reliant, than the same man was seven years ago; his interests are wider, his power is greater, and his outlook more hopeful; but as yet the sunshine only guilds the peaks – in the valley it still lingers as a soft twilight haunted by dim visions of the past.' Jack sent to the Guildhall exhibition of Irish art his drawing, *The Rolling Donkey*, and though he did not have the original review, he commented in his scrapbook, '*The Family Herald* !! said The Rolling Donkey was in its way the *Jem* of the collection!'[26]

It was a warning to Jack, when his brother's friend, the writer Arthur Symons, whom he also knew fairly well, wrote in *Outlook*: 'With Mr. Yeats one scarcely feels that anything very much better is to come. It is improvisation, and it is a kind of natural gift, which seems hardly to be capable of very serious cultivation.' He was reviewing the group show at Baillie's, and he made the additional point that Jack seemed to inhabit 'a child's paradise'.

Two years later, in Dublin, the *Irish Times* critic was similarly critical of Jack's uneven technical and psychological maturity: 'There is a studious crudeness about most of his work that goes far to assist the suggestion of the uncouth and bizarre in Western life . . . In many cases he has given the cartoons a distinctive touch by thick bold outlines like the leads in stained glass. Mr Yeats is apt, however, to let the style cramp him.'[27]

These views, which in summary suggest a number of defects in his art, and do so not unfairly, run through the years 1903 to 1910, both in London and Dublin newspapers. The Dublin critics labelled Jack as 'Impressionist' or of 'the advanced Impressionist school' in a pejorative way, and sought to prove this in references to his 'queer pucey backgrounds' and to the fact that 'all the paintings are gloomily coloured'.[28] He was criticised for slightness, for a heavy reliance on line, for poor colour, for limited development, for being impressionist. He was praised for his grasp of character, for his understanding of people, of the west of Ireland, of Irish scenes – in the dramatic rather than the landscape sense. There is justice in much of this. He was struggling with a less than perfect technique, brilliant draughtsmanship and good perception of character, but without the benefit of a fully realised palette and with composition that is often predictably mundane. 'He can paint an Irish scene, any Irish scene, Irishly, so to speak; others have to look out for something "characteristic," as they imagine – something with a pig in it.'[29] This is Jack as he was to remain: a powerful invoker of atmosphere, but always limited technically.

One writer in *Modern Society*, reviewing his London exhibition of 1908, had this to say: 'Here, instead of daintiness and romance, the atmosphere is mostly grim, with touches of pathos, such as help one to understand why Erin is still called the distressful country . . . these are not the things that Englishmen like to hang upon their walls.'[30]

There was another approach, more often found in London reviews and based on the idea that Ireland and the Irish people, particularly the peasants, were quaint, funny, pathetic, bizarre, unique and eccentric. They offered an inexhaustible supply of 'types', and Jack Yeats was their chief exponent. Indeed one reviewer of the same exhibition, writing in *The Court Circular* – Jack certainly attracted wide social support for his shows – made the point that Jack was the only Irish artist who painted Irish life. 'There is a singular reserve as to their country on the part of Irish artists . . . Mr Yeats's pictures show that in Ireland, as well as everywhere else, there are admirable subjects at hand for a painter who possesses discriminating vision.'[31]

These criticisms repeatedly made the distinction between his vision, and his capacities to present it. 'Now and then his types are handsomely and eminently Irish, and his sense of genre exhibited in the glimpses of a busy roadway or a crowded fair is helped by qualities of humour and perception, and an individual touch. The colouring is less satisfactory, sometimes it is rankly abusive.'[32]

Jack read the criticisms and annotated them. He kept his notices carefully in large scrapbooks. He corrected privately what he saw as 'mistakes'. He underlined both good and bad judgments. He sometimes speculated on the identities of unnamed authors. He also kept the social comment, the listings of attendances at shows, and the fashion paragraphs, which frequently noted with approval the clothes worn by Cottie, who always cut quite a dash at her husband's openings. The interviews he gave are helpful and revealing, particularly one to the *Irish Independent* in 1909. 'I can't talk art,' he told the paper. 'I work hard and live in a little village far away from those who talk art.'[33] Jack, according to the writer,

> after very successful exhibitions in New York and London (he) has come back to Dublin neither cockneyised nor Americanised but as happy and as pure as ever in his Irish pictures. 'Landscapes do not appeal to me unless they are peopled,' he remarked. And that is why he loves those rugged types, grave and gay, with which we are so familiar in his pictures and in his illustrations of Mr Synge's 'Aran Islands.'

Jack's public was protestant in the main, upper class, prosperous if not wealthy – though not, it would seem, interested in buying drawings of their tenants – and either mildly or enthusiastically interested in the cultural revival, of which the artist formed an increasingly interesting part. Lily went to the 1909 opening in Dublin, though for the first time she did not have Susan Mitchell with her. She had written an offending piece about Willie: 'Susan did not come because I was so mad with her over the article . . . she wrote an abject apology and says her career as a dramatic critic is ended and she is really and genuinely sorry to have offended us but I think she is at bottom proud of her beastly article.'[34]

On another occasion Lily returned in the usual state of social exhaustion: 'we are just back . . . our faces stiff from smiling at 250 people . . .'[35]

Constance Markievicz commented on Jack's exclusive use, at that time, of solo exhibitions:

> I do not know why Mr. Jack Yeats has not patronized the annual exhibitions much, but has confined himself mostly to 'one man shows' in Dublin and in London, and so is surprisingly little known to the general public.

His work, with its intense originality and life-likeness, seems to appeal to us with almost a shock, and to demand its just due, that is its recognition in all countries where Art is understood – as something real and new . . . The work of Mr. Jack Yeats might be compared to the work of Mr. Synge the dramatist, for both men, each through his own art, bring us into touch with and awaken our sympathies for the man of the roads . . . definitely Irish in the feeling that inspires his work. In fact, a man whose soul is part of the great National soul of Ireland, and who, therefore being absolutely honest and direct in his methods, has given us a very individual, though entirely National, vision of some Irish people and landscapes we have hitherto overlooked or misunderstood.[36]

Jack was experimenting with different media in the early 1900s. His earliest known oil was painted in 1902, a version of *Simon the Cyrenian*. About 1906–7 he was doing some more. He wrote to Quinn from Clifden to say that had been spending three weeks at landscapes, 'doing a little more in oils than usual'.[37] Hilary Pyle emphasises that the early oils were descriptive paintings, though she is perhaps not accurate in asserting that the watercolours also were.[38] He admired the technique of Goya and Morland. He was fascinated by the grotesque, as was Goya; he was fascinated by the horse, as was Morland. He owned books about both artists. He loved the intimate, domestic scene of the latter, at his best; he loved the wild, desolate landscape, peopled by unimaginable happenings of the former. And there is compelling perception in his remark to Quinn, about Goya, that 'he was the cords and strands of a painter'.[39]

But technically Jack had a hard time of it, suffering from the shortcomings of his truncated art school education. He was never adequately trained in the proper handling of oil paint. It is questionable whether he had sufficient training in draughtsmanship, either. And his approach to watercolour painting was the cautious one of the graphic artist using pencil, and adding washes and more intense areas of colour to the skilful and inventive drawings.[40]

Up to 1910 he had painted less than a dozen works in oil, none entirely satisfactory. If we try to step into the painter's shoes in 1907, and look at his output and its critical assessment with his eyes, then for all the admiration showered on him for his arresting drawings, and his visual commentary on a people and a period, the artistic grandeur is still not there. He is being admired for his undoubted ability to illustrate the Ireland of the Literary Revival; he is not being admired simply as an artist. Despite being detached from the 'movement' in Ireland, and particularly in Dublin, he has somehow been taken over by it, and is being programmed to deliver a collateral visual message about the progress of Ireland's life and spirit.

The departure from England, when it came, was a great wrench for Jack. Just how much he loved London can be gauged from the wonderful series of sketchbook drawings which date from these years, 1908 in particular, and which are full of the particular 'living ginger' of the city of his birth. From his very earliest experiences, he had been a lover of sport. While still a boy he had lost his shirt at Kempton Races, backed trotting competitors, both horse and human, and seen innumerable combats, bare-knuckle and gloved, in East End boxing booths.

Jack loved this London he would have to leave behind. For Elkin Mathews'

145 and 146. Illustrations for *The Fancy*, pen and ink, 1906.

1905 reprinting of *The Fancy* he did thirteen line illustrations which demonstrate his affection for boxing when it was bare-knuckled, open-air, and open-ended, round after round slogged out among young Regency bucks and blades (figs 145–6).[41] Its author, Hamilton Reynolds, as well as being a friend of John Keats, was brother-in-law to Thomas Hood, a hero of Jack's a we know, both in his verse and his drawings. Jack's own drawings capture that exciting period. It was probably the last time Jack and Masefield associated closely. Masefield was regularly involved with C.P. Scott (he joined the staff of the *Manchester Guardian* in 1907), and relayed the paper's editor's wishes for more black-and-white work, accompanied by articles which would be written by himself if Jack did not want to do them.

'You will see that he wants more London sketches, and accompanying articles, but he is afraid of shocking folk with anything bluggedy – my pirates live on pap, they count for nothing – so if you send a drawing of boxing you ought to make the gloves good and big like so –' (And Masefield, who did little matchstick men drawings in his letters to Jack, depicts fighters.) 'I will do what I can to write articles to your drawings, unless you would prefer to write them yourself, in which case I would gladly overlook them for you, though you write a lot better than I do, for you know the stuff and do it, while I only try to do it in a certain way . . . was jolly sorry to get back home after such a gay time with you. I wish I was back on the Gara, sailing skeps down Pontius Pilate Reach, instead of sitting here trying to write sense about the pirates . . .'

The bare-fisted days had passed away by the time Jack had become professionally involved in reporting the sport, in the 1890s. The quality of British boxing had also declined. With the coming of gloves dominance in the sport passed to the United States, and the reigning world champion – in 1894 it was 'Gentleman' Jim Corbett – took on challengers there, not in Britain. Only very intermittently was it an international pursuit in Great Britain, notably when three world championship fights took place in quick succession. Jack attended the first world heavyweight championship fought in Britain, in December 1907, when the Canadian champion, Tommy Burns, fought 'Gunner' Moir, and knocked him out in the tenth round. Tommy Burns was a highly professional fighter. He was treated insufferably by the British promoters of his fights, the National Sporting Club, and they were astonished at his arrogance in demanding half his £2,400 purse before his first fight. His second, against another British challenger, Jack Palmer, who came from Newcastle, and was well past his prime, was held at Wonderland on 10 February 1908. Jack was there also, in a packed stadium, for a fight which was to have gone for twenty rounds, with prize money of £1,000. Jack's drawings of the event record, in pencil and wash, the huge crowds outside, the scene inside, with referee and time-keeper, Palmer in his corner (he was first into the ring) wearing a Kimono-like dressing gown, and the two figures facing each other before the fight. It is a colourful, if not a unique record, Jack Palmer with his green trousers, a sash of white and orange round waist; there is a fine drawing of the commanding figure of Burns.

The third Burns fight was held in the Theatre Royal, and no less than 1,700 press passes were applied for, the ticketless public being left outside, where they listened to 'The Boys from Wexford' being sung to accompany the

147. Walter Sickert, c. 1910.

arrival of Roche. 'Minutes later a customer rushed out, moaning, "It's terrible, they're killing one another, blood everywhere, I can't stand any more." He sold his ticket for half-price – and the late-comer charged inside to discover Roche had been flattened in 88 seconds.'[42] Jack pasted into his sketchbook the programmes of the fights as well as newspaper cuttings describing them. They were the last world heavyweight boxing matches held in Britain or Ireland for many years.[43]

Jack's abilities in drawing boxing scenes, and his interest in the theatre, inspired the admiration of Walter Sickert, who became a friend (fig. 147). He was the only breakfast companion that Yeats cared to see on London visits. Both men were intensely interested in the life and bustle of the streets, and both drew and painted working men about their business as regular subject-matter. They saw a good deal of each other around 1907. Sickert certainly had a very high regard for Jack's work; what he particularly liked was a quality which he considered Jack had in common with Boudin and others, of raising the human element in any scene to the prominent position: 'He does not subject himself with any doctrinaire pedantry to painting only as much of a human being as can be "touched in" while it moves across the field of vision'; the men and women carry life and charm, and are not used 'as spots to accentuate their landscapes'.[44] There is much in common between them as painters, including their palettes during the early period of Jack's paintings in oil, their choice of subject-matter – both loved theatre scenes, horses, people at work – and in the strong and confident drawings they both produced.

1908 is the last year in which the emphasis of his detailed sketchbook work is very much on London and its sporting life. Jack was now thinking about giving it up, and he visited other well-loved haunts during the year, doing drawings of scenes on the Thames showing sailing boats and barges, and many of the theatre and music hall, seeing, among other productions, Yvette Guilbert in her long black gloves, Shaw's *The Devil's Disciple*, The London Follies at the Apollo Theatre, Harry Harris, and Elton and Edwin, comic banjo-players, at the South London Palace, and a 'nautical-farcical' comedy called *A Fair Exchange*, which had a huge and distinguished cast of music hall entertainers.

In the summer he and Cottie travelled to the west of Ireland. They spent most of their time in Sligo, staying with 'Long' Harvey at Ballinfull. Jack did wash drawings of all of them, and several watercolours of Cottie, sitting on the rocks at Knock Lane looking out to sea. He painted Harvey in his kitchen making toffee, and he did many other drawings of local people, including the local gamekeeper, Dan O'Connell.

From 1908–9 on, there is a marked change in Jack's approach. His sketch-book drawings are less 'worked up', with colour and washes, and are more *aides-mémoires*, notations of things seen, rudimentary drawings and small portrait sketches, with the working up to be accomplished in other forms. He uses pencil more; the delicate washes which are such a delight in the earlier books, are infrequent in the sketchbooks which come at the end of the decade. There are also fewer of them. This is entirely consistent with the particular kind of black-and-white illustration required for *A Broadside*, and with the slow and uncertain development of his oil painting.

The contrast between the London sketches, full of crowds and entertainment, and the rough and tumble of the boxing booths, and other sporting

163

places, and the wide open spaces of Sligo, with great mountains sweeping down to the turbulent sea, could hardly have been more pronounced. The attractions of Ireland were becoming increasingly compelling. It was to Mrs Harvey that Cottie felt able to say 'that they had lived in Devon over ten years, and that they did not know their neighbours in the slightest. It was only when they were leaving that she realised what pleasant people they were.'[45] For Cottie, the prospect must have been daunting; she knew Ireland only through Jack, and she was giving up a comfortable and trouble-free existence, as well as the close proximity of her remaining family, for the challenges of a new life in a country facing great change.

Jack was approaching forty, and his career still consisted of small-scale exhibitions, in every sense of the words. This encouraged him to paint more in oils, but he seemed to lack confidence, and progress was slow. Other events were also influencing Jack, helping him in the decision to leave Devon and move to Wicklow. One of the most significant was the departure of his father for the United States. There have been many explanations. Perhaps the most realistic — and it comes from an unlikely source — was given years after the departure, and from someone who hardly knew John Butler Yeats at all. George Yeats, the poet's wife told Stephen Spender:

> He left home after his wife had died and when his daughters were middle-aged, because there was a feeling in the air that he ought to be looked after, and he did not wish to be. 'He wanted to go on being untidy and not have people putting his things away in drawers.' So he went for six months to America, and stayed there for twenty years.[46]

George Yeats also reported to Spender how John Butler Yeats wrote innumerable letters, and used to have a desk in his studio, and 'would often get up in the middle of his work, and sit there writing one of his letters'. Spender reported Mrs Yeats saying that when Willie and Jack were young there was

> a disagreement between the old man and his sons, because he was domineering and insistent on the exact way in which everything should be done. I said, 'All the same, to judge from his letters to your husband, the disagreement was of a kind that is fruitful.' She said that yes, this was so, as long as it was confined to correspondence. When he was actually on the spot it amounted to interfering and could be tiresome.[47]

As far as Jack was concerned, his father's departure from Dublin for America removed another barrier to his own return to the city. He had left London for Chertsey, and then Devon. He had established his own terms for visits by his father to Snail's Castle, and for the visits he and Cottie made to Bedford Park. His father's subsequent move to Dublin, and residence at Gurteen Dhas, was in part responsible for keeping Jack in Devon. Now, with the move to America, the way was becoming clear for Jack and Cottie to move to Ireland. There was undoubtedly a coolness at this time between Jack and his father, expressed in a letter from John Butler Yeats to Rosa Butt:

> It is curious, but I find Willie with all his faults more lovable than Jack. The latter was too long in Sligo and so is full of ill will towards all his fellow creatures and suspicion and contempt. It is the way with commercial people . . . Jack of course sticks manfully to duty which makes him an

148. Jack in the early 1900s.

admirable fellow citizen, but then it makes him a little cold and self complacent.[48]

It was to have been just a visit. The Great Man endowed the trip with vast potential. Yet again, he was off to make his fortune. Nothing would stand in his way. By all sober judges, within the family and outside it, the move to New York was regarded as a mistake. Lily and Lolly soon became alarmed, and those closest to them, on both sides of the Atlantic, shared their concern. Less than a year after his departure, George Russell, writing to John Quinn, reveals their collective concern:

> Turning to other matters which you mention, I quite agree with you that J.B.Y. is altogether past the time for any new adventures in strange countries. His daughters want him back and are alarmed by his long absence. I think they have done their utmost to induce him to return . . . I see both the girls very often and they tell me all the news about their 'Pilgrim Father' as they call him. I recommended them to cable 'Family all dying. Come to receive last messages'. But they said he would not come for that, and I don't know what will bring him.[49]

The answer was simple enough: nothing. Notwithstanding the near-poverty of his life during many of the years spent in New York, and the yearning of his eldest daughter in particular; notwithstanding the perpetual worry associated with so much he faced; notwithstanding the financial demands he made, particularly on Willie, who, to his credit, faced up to them from a position of uncertain and by no means extravagant income from his writings and his lecturing; notwithstanding all of this, John Butler Yeats had at last found his niche. Moving to New York turned out to be the correct course of action. Independent, proud of his modest talent, free of the expectation of a demanding country and people, he lived out his years contemplating his ageing, erect, white-bearded figure in the full-length canvas of his self-portrait, a Dorian Gray in reverse. The indomitable optimist never came back, and he never saw Jack or Cottie again.

CHAPTER TWELVE

The *Broadsides* 1910–1915

No painter could belong to a country more thoroughly

DESPITE HIS IDYLLIC life in Devon, Jack was now bent on departure. He wanted to make his mark in Ireland. He sought involvement. He had defined a role for himself. He had drawn Ireland, depicted it in wash, and was now painting it in oils. He wanted to inhabit it and either possess it or be possessed by it. And this objective now governed his thoughts and actions.

The way for a return to Dublin was still not entirely clear. During their last two years in Devon, from 1908 to 1910, Jack's sisters' were involved in Dun Emer controversy. Jack's reference to 'the Gleeson business', carrying with it a faint hint of scepticism, was all too close to the mark. The four people who were involved – Augustine Henry (at a distance, but in the important role of financier), Evelyn Gleeson, and Jack's sisters – proved incompatible; the wonder is that the working enterprise lasted as long as it did. Part of the credit belongs to the long-suffering Henry, who was fond of Lolly, despite all her tempestuous acts and precipitate decisions, and he advised Gleeson to be generous. There was also the success of Dun Emer; it produced good work which impressed people, and it made the intended contribution to Irish culture and craftwork. But internally there were disagreements and rows. By 1904 it was clear the sisters would part company. This they did. George Russell worked on a new agreement. They continued under the Dun Emer trade mark, but with Lily and Lolly operating independently. Overall control remained with the principal shareholders, Evelyn Gleeson and her sister, the widowed Mrs MacCormack.

The exhibition of Irish goods in New York in 1908 was successful, with the two branches of Dun Emer operating at opposite ends of the exhibition hall; the women at that point were hardly on speaking terms. Lily remained for a time with her father, while Lolly returned to Dublin, relations with Gleeson worsening by the minute. In her sister's absence Lolly moved their part of the business into a new building, intending still to operate under the Dun Emer name. This precipitated the final break. A further agreement allowed the sisters to have the precious Albion hand press, on which their books were printed, and to be discharged of their debt, in exchange for undertakings not to duplicate activities such as carpet-making, tapestries and rugs, which were the province of the main owners.

Willie had been involved; midway through the crisis-riven early life of Dun Emer he took badly the idea put to him by Lily that he should provide funding. He told Lady Gregory of his feelings, which were confused and angry.[1] He was limited by lack of knowledge. He felt that the book publishing side of Dun Emer 'looks like a good investment,' but he knew too little about it. He was also unable to judge on the quality of the embroidery work. Like his father, he also felt that George Pollexfen might become financially involved, but this appears not to have happened. His letter to Lily was brief and noncommittal. He sent a copy of it to Lady Gregory. No further correspondence in 1904 refers to the affairs of Dun Emer; they were crowded out by the increasingly intense business of theatre. But Willie did continue to act as literary editor or director.

Unquestionably, Willie was the dominant outside influence on his sisters' affairs. This manifested itself in the field of literature, which he knew about; but he concerned himself also with the quality and viability of the other work. The difficulties of 1904 revived two years later in another financial crisis, and John Butler Yeats wrote to his son of his concern. 'If they had a little capital I believe they would work out something good. Their devotion is extraordinary.'[2] Willie fell out with his sister, Lolly, in 1906, but they resolved their differences in time for his name to be on Katherine Tynan's *Twenty One Poems*, 'selected by W.B. Yeats' which Dun Emer published in March 1907, and he then went on to publish *Discoveries* in December 1907. This was the last Dun Emer title.

There is, as one would readily expect, a marked contrast between Willie's involvement and that of Jack and Cottie. While the elder brother was concerned with making judgments and wielding the kind of power which reflected his status in the family and to an extent his public reputation, the younger brother provided help and support, and said nothing. He was backed in this, in a practical way, by Cottie. Jack became involved in another then fashionable item of printed ephemera, the bookplate. He did several for Lolly's printing side of Dun Emer, continuing to design them for the early years of Cuala, though it is difficult to produce any clear idea of when. He did individual bookplates for John Quinn (fig. 149), E.R. McClintock Dix, R.A. Anderson, S.F. Beeke-Lane and Harry Clarke. He did a bookplate for the Dun Emer Press. Willie, however, did not commission one of Jack's bookplates for his own library, using instead a design by his London friend, Thomas Sturge Moore.

Jack remained the silent witness, perhaps motivated by a desire to avoid conflict with his brother. He did receive some intimation of what was happening, indirectly, in a long and interesting letter to Cottie from his father at the end of 1906. At the time Dun Emer had, through Lady Gregory, been offered a printing contract from her one-time lover, Wilfrid Scawen Blunt, 'a fine hand-printed edition well paid for & which would take years to do – & paid for by Blunt out of a well-filled purse. . . . If this Blunt scheme comes off it will mean years of peace and comfort for Dun Emer.'[3]

Evelyn Gleeson was a woman with a volatile temper, but at heart generous in spirit. Responsible both for bringing the two Yeats sisters back to Ireland and giving a significant thrust at the beginning of the century to Irish women in the arts and crafts of the country, she also ensured that the Dun Emer Guild, as it became known after 1908, survived. It did so principally through weaving.[4]

Jack and Cottie gave permission for drawings to be made into prints, then coloured by hand and sold. The involvement was small. Seven or eight prints

149. Bookplate for John Quinn.

150. *The Strand Races: The Start*, Dun Emer print, *c.* 1906.

151. Humorous illustration for *Punch*.

Victim. "I WONDER YOU DON'T USE A SAFETY-RAZOR."
Barber. "PARDON ME, SIR, ARE YOU ONE OF THESE 'ERE CONSCIEN-TIOUS OBJECTORS?"

are recorded in the pre-Cuala period. Neither the prints, nor the lesser examples of printed ephemera, including the bookplates, are dated. As for Christmas cards, illustrated poems mounted on card to hang on walls, and calendars, these belong exclusively to the later Cuala period.[5] The most notable early prints included the popular and delightful pair, *The Strand Races*, showing the start and finish (figs 150 and 152). Among the earliest of the Cuala prints was *The Post Car*.

We can piece together the practical side of what happened during 1908, the decisive year for Cuala, which was also to lead directly to Jack's own return to Ireland. In mid-April, in the letter to Synge in which he expressed concern for the playwright's health, and in which he asked for the poem, 'Danny', he told him he was restarting 'the Broad Sheet'. Jack's apparently off-hand remark to Synge also signalled their closer involvement in Ireland. Apart from anything else, the editorial management of the details, of poems and drawings, must have been greatly complicated by doing everything by post. And Jack, who was very particular about typefaces, layout, colouring and design, would have found difficulty over not being in absolute control. His sisters started publishing *A Broadside* in July 1908.

As a precaution, and a wise one in the light of his sisters' experiences up to that point, Jack 'planned his return to *Punch* (shortly after Synge's death) to coincide with his exodus from Devon to Ireland in July 1910'.[6] From this point on the pages of *Punch* carried, with increasing frequency, his comic cartoons. They are quite different in character from his Irish drawings. Deliberately, they are lighter, and more ephemeral, in keeping with the tone of the publication. They continue the tradition of comic illustrations in which he had worked from the very first. What he had recorded in his diary of 1888 is similar to what he drew in 1910–15 (fig. 151).

Jack had sole editorial responsibility for *A Broadside*.[7] This contained, on average, three illustrations in each monthly part, two of them hand-coloured. The edition was limited to 300 copies. The colouring was carried out by staff at the press, but the main responsibility for *A Broadside* rested with Eileen Colum, Padraic Colum's sister, who had joined Dun Emer to do embroideries, and had been transferred to the press in February 1906. When the sisters started Cuala she went with them, and she devoted the rest of her life to working with Lollie on the publishing side of the enterprise. Another of Colum's sisters, Susan, worked in the press before her marriage.

A Broadside was a substantial undertaking. Jack appears not only to have

152. *The Strand Races: The Finish*. Dun Emer print, *c.* 1906.

153. *Tumblers at the Circus*, illustration for *A Broadside*, *c.* 1913.

solicited and edited written work, but also to have written ballads himself, using the pseudonym 'MacGowan' with the initials W.T. and R.E. derived from two of his Irish patriot heroes, Wolfe Tone and Robert Emmet. As we have seen, he asked John Synge, unsuccessfully, for the poem 'Danny'. And he used work by many other writers, English, Scottish, Welsh and Irish; even the American hymn-writer, Julia Ward Howe, author of the rousing 'Mine Eyes Have Seen the Glory of the Coming of the Lord', finds her place in the pages of *A Broadside*. Jack was nothing if not idiosyncratic. He chose according to the dictates of his own heart, and in response to the opportunities which words gave for drawings.

A Broadside is not in any sense just an Irish publication. The ratio of Irish writing to writing by non-Irish poets and balladeers is roughly speaking two-to-one. He used James Stephens consistently, Seumus O'Sullivan, Padraic Colum and Douglas Hyde. Single poems, like Thomas Dermody's (1775–1802), Thomas Davis's (1814–45), and James Clarence Mangan's (1803–49), indicate some drawing from the past, but in the main this is confined to the frequent use of ballads throughout the seven years. His main non-Irish contributor is his friend, John Masefield; but there is also work by Ernest Rhys from time to time. It is entirely cosmopolitan. There is none of his brother's high seriousness about its content being 'representative Irish'. There are more pirates in it than tinkers, more scenes of the sea than of the west of Ireland; and there are as many anonymous works, most of them ballads or sea chanties, as there are Irish and other poems added together.

A Broadside is a rare and beautiful publication, and among all of Jack's printed output it occupies a special place (fig. 153). In some respects it epitomises his wayward and idosyncratic character. He drew from earlier work, and republished drawings which he had used, either in *A Broadsheet*, or elsewhere. There is even, at times, a strained quality – as though the matching of a drawing with lines of verse represented a kind of cobbling together. He faced on his own the exigencies of putting together, on a monthly basis a regular visual and verbal package. The drawings themselves were offered for sale. They were uncoloured. The Cuala Press published a notice to this effect, quoting prices of two guineas for the smaller ones, three guineas for the larger, with three or four which were priced at five guineas.[8]

The prints which Jack and Cottie produced for Lolly are of a different order. *Evening* is undoubtedly the most famous of these. Colourists worked away under Lolly's direction for the ready market which existed for Jack's

169

pictures, in particular this rear view of a cantering donkey. But Jack – though all his life he loved the donkey best of all animals – used to shiver at the nightmare spectre of yet another ass cantering into the sunset.

One of the writers used by Jack for *A Broadside* was Francis McNamara, and Jack sent him a copy of *The Little Fleet*, which McNamara and his son, John, read together. 'Every time we came to a picture of the Monte capsized, he turns it upside down & tries all he can to right her. My devotions to Mrs Yeats,' he concludes with affection.[9] It also developed at this time with Padraic Colum and others. He sent *A Broadside* to his Aunt Agnes, his mother's younger sister, married to Robert Gorman, who had always taken an interest in his work. She always remembered Jack's birthdays, and took an interest in his and Cottie's life generally, sending Jack hand-knitted socks at Christmas. She was not in good health, though she put a brave face on it: 'I still keep fairly well, but the weather prevents me crawling up the garden, my only walk on fine days. The Orphan Bazaar is on today, it is St John's Parish Stall this year. Kind love to Cottie and you. A.M. Gorman.'

Agnes's marriage had not been accepted too warmly by the Pollexfen family. The Pollexfens looked down on the Gormans, and the marriage was modest by comparison with the wedding of Susan to John Butler Yeats. She later had a nervous breakdown, and was in a mental hospital from which she escaped, seeking refuge with the Yeatses at Bedford Park. She had to be 'recovered' from there, with the aid of nurses, and returned. 'In her lucid moments she was the bright, sharp, clear and affectionate woman who had been equally affectionate, if misunderstood, as a child.'[10]

In the late summer of 1910, the Yeats family as a whole lost its staunchest Pollexfen supporter when the head of the Sligo business, Uncle George, died. He had been a great figure in their lives, a friend and adviser to all of them, and a robust and lasting personality in Sligo affairs. The funeral was the talk of Sligo town for years afterwards, and Jack's sporting sympathies gave him the happy idea of sending a wreath of flowers in George's racing colours, primrose and violet. It was a Masonic funeral. The order was strong in the town. And George left a substantial estate, widely distributed. There were nine principal shares, for each of his surviving brothers and sisters, or their heirs, with the exception of William, who was in an asylum. He made a stipulation on the bequest to his sister's children, that Lily and Lolly should receive one-third each, while Willie and Jack split the other third between them. There was a further complication; Fredrick, George's younger brother, who had lived richly and rather too well, received his share in trust, for his children. The provision went to court, in order to facilitate the proving of the will, and with Jack as a willing defendant in an action brought by Arthur Jackson, who was married to his sister-in-law. The purpose, in Lily's memorable phrase, was 'to put the snuffer on Frederick Pollexfen.'[11]

The Sligo business passed into Arthur Jackson's control. Jack told Willie, while they were both in Sligo for the funeral, that it would be

harder rule now – Belfast rule. That George knew every man in his employ and had the gift of getting discipline without ever being harsh. That men would be let back, after a time, if they had done wrong and so on. That he would, as it were, degrade a carter to the ranks. He would take his whip from him and hang it on his wall – and then when the man was penitent give it back and the workmen understood this way and liked it. Every case decided as an individual case and with sympathy. Now if a man goes he will go forever.[12]

Willie formed a different opinion. He was impressed by Jackson's 'force and his kindness' he told Lady Gregory, in a second letter the next day, which also revealed that Uncle George had left £50,000, and predicted that 'the money will be divided among many, something for all who had even a distant claim'. The visit inspired memories of his grandfather, and Jack did a drawing: 'the old bearded man is standing in a Sligo street. He holds a stick, and wears a flower in his buttonhole, and is a picture of dignity and respectability'.[13]

In the meantime Jack's father had satisfactorily established his failed life in New York, and was making the best of it. He commenced what was to be a vast and rambling correspondence with Jack and Cottie. He sometimes wrote to her with complaints that Jack did not send him letters, nor did drawings to amuse or inform him; sometimes he wrote to both of them, in a mood of despair at their silence:

> I often think that it would be a good thing if you and Jack would save your money and come over here from September when the heat and the mosquitoes are gone and stay here till Novr. the climate is heavenly – there are no words too strong for its beauty . . . Jack and you would both be a great success in New York – Jack's work would be received by the artists here with enthusiasm by men like Henri and John Sloan Glacken & by Charles Fitzgerald.[14]

He put at the head of one letter a small self-portrait.

> Above is a picture of myself looking very mild – so forgive me for not answering any of your letters – I don't write because there is so much to say & so little to say – So much to tell – am I not in New York? so little to tell, because – I find it very difficult to pay my way – my last venture is lecturing, in which I have had some success – at one lecture I made 75 dollars & and at my next lecture which takes place in a few days I hope to make as much – I will send you a copy of Harper's Weekly . . . in which is an article of mine for which I have received 75 dollars – . . . I get drawings to do when I can. That is the kind of work I like best – I am very comfortable at the boarding house it is much more comfortable than the hotel.

He hoped to go home in the spring. 'People think I suppose that I must be tarrying here because I am making money – it is rather the other way – If I made some money I would go home pretty quick – I will write to you again, Every little bit of news about Jack and the work I greedily devour . . .'

Despite the busy schedule of work for the Yeats sisters' new enterprise of Cuala, Jack managed a substantial output of drawings, watercolours and paintings. He held his regular solo exhibitions in each of the years 1908–10, and in 1909 and 1910 contributed work to three other group shows, in Dublin, London and Belfast in 1909, and in London and New York in 1910.[15] Jack had been slow to exhibit oil paintings. Apart from one or two sketchy works on millboard, and *Low Water, Spring-tide, Clifden*, a view of the estuary with the hills beyond, which he exhibited in 1906, he did not show landscapes in oil until 1909, when he exhibited *Race Card Seller*. He also exhibited *A Summer Evening (in Ballycastle)*, which shows two men playing cards at a

171

round table which has in its centre an oil lamp. These two works, both vertical compositions, both containing human figures, are the first of a series which subsequently included the illustrations used in *Irishmen All*. At this stage, however, they are outnumbered by the early oil landscapes and sea-scapes, tentative and experimental works done in the open air. 'He and his wife would hire a rowboat, when they were in the West, row out to some small island and moor the boat, while he painted.'[16] In a letter to John Quinn Jack gave a dismal report on the work: 'it is no pleasure to sit on a desolate coast, perched on a damp rock, with the cold showers sweeping over you and your paint and a drop on the end of your nose'.[17]

Tentative though the early oils seem to have been, it was Con Curran's view that Jack gave up watercolour painting because the medium was perishable. Other reasons should be considered: watercolour was technically very demanding, and did not sell well. Writing of the works chosen by himself and MacGreevy for the 1945 Retrospective in Dublin, his friend claimed: 'The water-colours shown in the exhibition dated from 1898 to 1910. By that time he had become perhaps oversensitive to the dangers which threaten that perishable medium and had turned to oils.'[18] Jack had been made aware of the more limited prospects for watercolours by his New York agent, to whom he wrote in 1910: 'I am very much obliged to you for bothering about my pictures as I know you do not go in for watercolours very much. I am however getting to work in oils a good deal more now and may after a time have something to send to you in that medium.'[19]

Jack and Cottie finally moved to Ireland in November 1910, in time for his Leinster Hall solo exhibition, which opened on 8 December. Before moving in they spent some time with Lily and Lollie at Gurteen Dhas. They took Red Ford House, on the Dublin side of Greystones with a view from its windows over the Irish Sea, and with the Little Sugar Loaf mountain behind them, and to the north, along the coast, Bray Head. Quite unprepossessing, it had a sizable garden, and a greenhouse, which might have been an advantage for Cottie, had not Jack taken it over as his studio. In the grounds there was a thatched cottage, still in use. The house was then known as Cartref, and Jack, as he had done with Snail's Castle, changed the name. It was subsequently changed back again. Jack and Cottie were installed in time for the April 1911 Census, which records also a servant living in called Margaret Whitty, who was 'Roman Catholic, able to read and write'. The census also gave Jack's age, correctly, as forty, and Cottie's as forty-two.[20] He lists himself as 'artist, painter of pictures'. They are both down as Church of Ireland, and Jack as 'Head of Family'.

He later came to regard Greystones as something of a backwater, a place where they knew no one, and which in the end they were glad to leave. But Jack made it entertaining and unusual for Cottie, himself and their guests. One of these was the Irish writer, Page Dickinson, who recorded both Jack's simple, childlike sense of fun, his belief in Ireland and his love of its people.

I used to see a good deal of him, as my wife's mother lived close to his house and, during our frequent week-ends at Greystones, I spent many Sunday mornings with him and his wife. He had an amusing inmate in his house who contributed greatly to the entertainment of everyone. This was Theodore, an imaginary person, by trade a pirate . . . He was a desperate character who had lived from his early days among pirates, but in his calm moods 'seemed to remember a good home and a kind mother'. This absurd person came into all sorts of daily doings in the household. He figured on the decanter and other vessels in heroic poses, and on one Christmas morning was discovered in the bath, sailing some strange craft containing a present for Mrs. Yeats.[21]

Page Dickinson reported somewhat inadequately on Theodore to his wife, who became irritated with this imaginary character.

> Finally she said crushingly, 'I can't stand Theodore,' and added, I don't know why, 'Dickens would have hated Theodore'. I, rather surprised, could think of no suitable repartee, and finally said, 'Has it ever occurred to you that Theodore might have hated Dickens?' This ridiculous remark became a family saying and I expect my daughter will use it in years to come, without having the remotest idea of its absurd origin.

Dickinson makes the interesting observation about Jack: 'He was sensitive to a degree, and if he did not care for his surroundings, never opened his lips.'

They were to stay in their first Irish home until 1917; yet it came to mean very little to either of them. In a letter to Padraic Colum in 1918, after the second move, into the Dublin suburb of Donnybrook, Jack wrote: 'We are glad to be in Dublin, for a while at any rate. We met more friends in a month than we did in twelve months in Greystones. Greystones was neither town nor country nor suburb. Our only link with the spacey world was from the tinkers that passed along the road.' Greystones may have been chosen for Cottie's sake. It was a stronghold of Protestantism and Unionism, wealthy, stable, and rather smug. It was linked to Dublin by a comparatively efficient rail service. The view from the windows pleased Jack, and he did some drawings of shipping, though he seems to have experienced none of the excitement of the spanking, five-masted vessel which he had seen from Strete, churning its noble passage up the English Channel. Of course Jack now had easier access to the west of Ireland, indeed to all parts of the country. In addition, he could pursue in Dublin his interests in such things as theatre, music hall, sport and entertainment, and the enthralling street life which began now to feature in his paintings.

John Butler Yeats wrote to Jack: 'I am so glad you have lots of friends & that the move to Ireland is a success.'[22] And Jack himself, in a letter to John Quinn wrote: 'We are glad to be back in my own country'.[23] Their old friend Tucker Wise, whom they had known since their marriage, and who had now moved to a house near Strete, was a little more tentative. 'How are you both getting on over there? I have been out to North Mill once or twice preparing the house for our furniture. I see your old residence quite deserted and the gardens neglected . . . I hope Mr Yeats likes the change of being near Dublin – that is a great thing but of course it is not like Snail's Castle.'[24]

And George Russell told John Quinn: 'Jack Yeats is busy at Graystones (sic) now. He might be at the North Pole for all one sees of him, being so far out of Dublin, and what is worse miles from a railway station.'[25] This was not in fact true; the line to Greystones opened in 1855, with services from both Harcourt Street and Westland Row, making it reasonably convenient for the sisters, who would have travelled in to Harcourt Street from Churchtown. Greystones was the outer limit of Dublin's well constructed local system, and there would have been between six and ten trains a day when Jack and Cottie were living there.[26] He joined Dublin's United Arts Club in 1912, at a time when it was already a significant cultural force. At this time there was a strong and growing association between the arts and politics, and many United Arts Club members were also key political figures, among them leaders in the planning of the 1916 Rising. As Patricia Boylan has pointed out:

> Darrell Figgis was a writer and actor. Joseph Plunkett was a poet, involved in the theatre. Conor O'Brien was an architect and writer. Erskine Childers was a writer. Seamus O'Sullivan, a poet, was sympathetic. Susan Mitchell, writer and poet, showed where she stood in her ballad 'Gods of the Irish Protestant'. Jack Yeats was allied to the Nationalist cause if not its violent resolution.[27]

Soon established in their rented house in Greystones, Jack and Cottie began a pattern of entertaining, inviting, among others, the women who worked at Dun Emer for Lily and Lolly. They would go with the sisters for afternoon tea, and were given soft drinks, biscuits and fruit.

> We took the train from Dundrum to Bray where Mr Jack waited to welcome us. He had engaged four outside cars which took us through the Kilruddery Estate to their house . . . The lawn had been prepared for croquet and winners of the games and performances arranged by Mr Jack received small prizes that he made himself. He used fir cones, acorns, sea shells and other little things for prizes and each of us received one. I won a dice container fashioned from a large cork ingeniously cut to form a box containing two dice cubes. The lid slipped into place over the cubes and could stay closed because of the clever way it had been cut. The amount of thought and trouble he took with the prizes was typical of the Yeats family's perfection in all of their undertakings. After a beautiful tea we returned to the Bray railway station by another route in the outside car.[28]

Jack and Cottie also used to attend parties at Gurteen Dhas where Jack engaged in drawing 'moving pictures' for the women. They had a blackboard in the embroidery room, and he entertained them with a visual anecdote called 'Moving Day' which showed a cottage, with a little girl and her mother. Each would bring out packages and load them onto a cab, Jack drawing and rubbing out as the story developed:

> Finally, the woman appeared in her cloak and bonnet with a few last articles, locked the door behind her and got to the cab to start on her journey. As she stepped in, the parcels tumbled off and the cab collapsed to the ground. At this point, the horse looked back over his shoulder to see what happened. Mr Jack with a very broad smile and one large wipe of the duster, finished the amusing episode.[29]

Unlike his brother, who was ill-at-ease with almost all classes of people, Jack went out of his way to be friendly, and through his sisters instructed the girls who worked for them,

> not to pass him without recognition . . . He acknowledged seeing any of us by smiling and raising his right hand in salute, thumb and forefingers together with little finger extended . . . He had an unusual style of dress and manner of walking that distinguished him from other men. He was

tall and slightly built. His long overcoats of tweed or heavy cloth with velvet collar were fluted at the back from the waist downward, giving a slight fullness to the heels which dipped a little in front from his forward and ever so slightly sidewards manner of walking, as of a peson ascending a hill. He was good-looking with beautiful eyes, long-shaped, clean-shaven face, good skin and nice complexion.[30]

They also got on well with Cottie:

> Mrs Jack was a frequent visitor to our Merrion Square workrooms. She was very picturesque in her well-designed clothes and exquisite jewellery which suited her face and her figure of small proportions. Her house had hand-painted furniture and other hand-made articles of pleasing design which she herself invented and executed. She was always delighted to show her latest addition to any of us workers who called on an errand to her house.[31]

154. Frontispiece to *The Bosun and the Bob-Tailed Comet*, 1904.

Jack's working life took on a bookish slant during the first years after the move to Ireland. By now he had a fine body of work published, much of it in books by other people, in his own periodicals, but including his plays for the miniature theatre, as well as *The Bosun and the Bob-Tailed Comet*, and *The Little Fleet* (fig. 154). It was slight enough, 'invented for the delight of all children under ninety'. These words come from Ernest Marriott, whose book, *Jack B. Yeats: Pictorial and Dramatic Artist*,[32] was published in 1911. Marriott was also an artist, and a friend of Jack and Cottie. He had visited them in Devon, and was enthusiastically interested in both the miniature theatre and the model boats which Jack and John Masefield had sailed to extinction on the River Gara.

Marriott revived them. His little book was first read at a meeting of The Manchester Literary Club, then printed in *The Manchester Quarterly* for July 1911, and finally in book form. Its frontispiece is a drawing in profile of the four-year old Jack by his father. The book also contains a large, fold-out map of Pirate Island, charting the games played on Gara River. It depicts 'The Music', a rope from his ankle held by one of the pirates, being allowed to parade in the strand with his guitar. Other figures are engaged in piratical pursuits, which seem to include hammocks and fishing rods, barbecues and even the reading of books. No one came near to Marriott in his comprehensive assessment of Jack's work, both as artist and writer, for many years after the publication of this small monograph. He was equally enthusiastic about both.

> He has published five books dealing entirely with essentials. Together they do not weigh more than a few ounces. Placed flat on top of each other they are not an inch high. Yet within that small compass there is much of the quaint and beautiful; and I would barter a few yards of the sacred books of Eastern philosophy rather than lose from my shelves these precious five.[33]

Marriott relates Yeats in his miniature theatre to the reforms of Edward Gordon Craig, who Marriott believed had 'rid the stage of antiquarian accuracies and replaced dead pedantry with poetry'. Marriott, like Masefield, had enjoyed the rare privilege of seeing the plays acted. He had also seen a great deal of Jack's work. He knew his method. He refers to him 'filling sketch books with rough studies. Up to the present time he has accumulated over two hundred of these books.'[34] And he claims that Jack rarely made pictures of things which he had not seen actually happen.

His judgments confirm and strengthen the illustrator at the expense of the painter in oils and watercolour, 'not so well known to the general public as they deserve to be'.[35] And he gives us valuable practical detail on the transfer of black-and-white illustrations to the prints and to the pages of *A Broadside*. 'The original drawings are generally about half as big again as the reproductions except in very crowded designs when he makes them at least twice the size of the intended reduction.'[36] Jack outgrew the early admiration of Marriott, and came in time to view him slightly patronisingly. In a letter to MacGreevy, who had met him in Bath, he wrote: 'Poor old Marriott I used to see him from time to time at my exhibitions and he was always friendly. I hope he has a long retirement among the blossomy lands of the "West Countree" as he would say. The idea of "the Stevenson touch" came I expect from my having made little private plays for the toy theatre.'[37]

Edward Gordon Craig corresponded with Jack at this time, and gave some attention to plays for miniature theatre in *The Mask*, his elaborate and elegant periodical published in Florence.[38] In it Craig presented his theories about the stage, and a wide range of essays by himself and those who supported his views. Craig was living in Paris, in the Rue de Rivoli, and wrote to Jack on 12 March 1912, telling him of the forthcoming issue of *The Mask* 'devoted to the toy theatre' and asking him rather diffidently to send a word or two, explaining how and why he made theatre for his miniature stage. 'Elkin Mathews,' he added, 'has already been writ to – and asked to lend one or two clichés – should we have written about that to you? . . . It is curious that we have never met and that I have never seen your theatre at work. For I should have been a good audience – '[39]

It is indeed curious, since Craig was involved with Willie, for whom he had designed costumes for *The Hour Glass*, at the Abbey Theatre, and with Pamela Colman Smith, who was a friend of his mother and his sister. More immediately, he had in 1911 designed screens for the Abbey Theatre, used the following year in his production of *Hamlet* at the Moscow Arts Theatre. It also seems that Jack had given some unspecified help or encouragement to Craig's School for Acting, in Florence. It is uncertain whether they ever did meet; but the brief collaboration was a happy one. In that first letter Craig specifically asked Jack:

> Have you seen my screens at work at the Abbey Theatre and do they behave themselves. They have a queer way of getting sulky at times – there are days when I can do nothing with them – and the house becomes unbearable. If you have seen them at work in Dublin and could tell me something about them I should be glad. They really ought not to have been shown for a dozen years or so – and then only after a good years practice with men who understood how to take a gun off and on to its carriage – 'Jack wrote back to say that he had seen the screens in action, and that they seemed natural, and Craig wrote again: 'Yes, the screens have yet got to yield untold wonders – streets – lanes – forests – glades – roofs of London – the sea – and if only that school would hurry up the things would pour out. But alone and without wood and nails one is a little helpless. Enough, lest I rage.[40]

Craig had a profound interest in what Jack Yeats had done for the miniature theatre, and related it to his own researches, and his belief in the importance of design. He was delighted when Jack also sent him a package of material, including original drawings and designs, for the forthcoming issue of *The*

Mask, and copies of *A Broadside*, which Craig undertook to advertise in the magazine.

> I am really much obliged to you for the packets of good things – pictures – notes. And Mask shall send back the original to E Mathews as soon as reproduced. Your designs will come out in the July number. I suppose 'James Dance' may be reduced to a Mask heading? How else to get it in I don't know – If it mayn't you must write mask and say so.

In the issue for July 1912 there appeared 'How Jack B Yeats Produced his Plays for the Miniature Stage, by the Master Himself', and there appeared also an article of perhaps over-enthusiastic praise of Jack at the expense of Synge, and written by Allen Carric.

> There was an Irish dramatist called Synge who I once thought knew something about movement. I now realize that by the side of Jack Yeats Synge becomes a dreamer. Synge was never able to thrill us by a mere stage direction. Synge never translated us a thousand miles in an instant as Yeats can with his one solemn line of scenic art, 'Scene one; "The Deck of the Distant Land". Why, to have put that down just as it is settles his right to the Laurels . . . There isn't a reader of *The Mask* who ought not to secure copies of Mr Yeats' Dramas and pictures. You go out of your way to spend a pound for some dead stuff in heavy binding. Why? you get nothing. Stop doing that. Get Yeats' works. And don't forget to do your best to buy the *Broadside*. The copy for May 1911 has a superb design of Captain Blackbeard swearing in his crew. It's coloured; coloured with the sun in the heart of its maker.[41]

In addition to *A Broadside*, and his prints for Cuala, he also produced for Maunsel one of his best-known, and best-loved publications, *Life in the West of Ireland*. This book, containing no letterpress, represents clearly enough what the artist in his professional career had achieved. He was forty-one, and his main work was in drawing. The colour prints and line drawings in the book form the greater share of its illustrations. They contain the spirit of the country and of Irish people. They are a truthful, vibrant and dramatic representation of Irish life. Jack has gathered together, in the first and larger part of the book a lifetime's work (figs 155–6). The paintings are at the back, almost an appendix to the line drawings. They present an undoubtedly sombre view of Irish life and people, a foreshadowing of things to come, both for Ireland and for Jack. *The Ganger* – the same figure as had appeared in the *Manchester Guardian* illustration – is shown in even more portentous pose, grim-faced and with his eyes and lips fixed in an expression of steely, unrelenting authority (fig. 156). A witness is seen preparing to give evidence; *A Man with a Broken Head* offers another image of the hard knocks of Irish life. And, almost dreadful in the intense evil of the gaze, there is Jack's most sinister *Tinker*, a figure used in more modest form in *A Broadside*. There are more joyful subjects, drawn from ball alley sport, racing, the fair, and the coming of the circus to town. Yet even here, in a painting such as *An Occupation*, which shows an elderly circus worker, bent under the strain of feeding animals, or that haunting early canvas, *A Circus Dwarf*, the message is hardly consistent with the golden age of expectation which had so concentrated the minds of writers and artists during the first decade of the century. The vision, instead, is grim with stubborn fortitude or blank despair.

155. *The Driver of the Long Cart* from *Life in the West of Ireland*, 1912.

156. *The Ganger* from *Life in the West of Ireland*, 1912.

His long succession of solo exhibitions devoted to the theme of life in the west of Ireland had genuinely created a conscience of the race, and he maintained this steadily, eventually producing, in this book, a climax which seems to have been designed to bring to a much wider audience drawings and paintings which had delighted the small following he had of visitors to his shows. *Life in the West of Ireland* which appeared in 1912, is a summation of his work at the age of forty.

Jack wrote to his father, at the time of publication, and Willie sent him a copy of *Life in the West of Ireland* which was warmly received.'My dear Jack,' John Butler Yeats wrote, in an affectionate letter,

> It is very good of you to write to me at all, since I have been so long without writing to you . . . I wrote a long letter to Willie thanking him for that most welcome book with your illustrations all of which I know by heart. But tho' I don't write I am always thinking of you. Not a day, hardly even a half-hour passes without my thinking of you. And when I think of you I think of Cottie – both come together into my mind . . .[42]

Jack said he was sending him a copy of another book which he had illustrated. This was *Irishmen All*, by G.A. Birmingham, a pseudonym for Canon Hannay.[43] But John Butler Yeats had met Hannay in New York, and already knew of the book, and of the success of Jack's illustrations. 'He was most enthusiastic about your part in the book. – & told me about its being done without any communication passing between you – every sketch a masterpiece & every one suitable – except one –'[44] In an earlier letter, begging for word from Cottie, he had blamed himself for not hearing from her, because he had not written himself. He went on: 'I am really, though I have said nothing about it, rather lonely – very lonely – God grant I get home this summer.'[45] Jack would undoubtedly have resisted any notion of his father's return. Willie told Lady Gregory: 'Jack wont have him back . . . he says Lily wants him back just as a mother wants her worst child to be brought home . . . I thought Jack was really alarmed at the idea of my father's return. I wanted him to write to Quinn & arrange it, he & I to pay He says he always fought with my father after a week.'[46]

Jack also sent a copy of his book to Quinn, who replied giving further news of John Butler Yeats: 'Hannay's book came with your illustrations. I haven't read the book, but I like the illustrations very much.' *Irishmen All* is a book of key significance for Jack, since it resolved and crystalised much of his thinking about himself and the direction of his art, and inspired a series of figurative works which are justly admired for their study of character, their clear line, and the powerful chiaroscuro which rendered them so satisfactory as book illustrations. Jack had collaborated with Canon Hannay for some years, illustrating his short stories in pen and ink for *A Celtic Christmas*, published each year by *The Irish Homestead*. Hannay asked him to do the illustrations, based only on the chapter titles of the book, and Jack readily agreed, producing all twelve paintings in a matter of months. It was a sensible case of not confusing the painter with unnecessary detail, since Jack knew all too well exactly how to tackle such inviting Irish types as *The Lesser Official*, *The Greater Official*, *The Squireen*, *The Publican*, and others. The works, all on panel, all the same size, pleased Hannay, who wrote to Jack, 'Considering that neither of us saw each other's work the illustrations and text fit together extraordinarily well.'[47]

157. *The Police Sergeant* from *Irishmen All*, 1913.

In the twelve paintings, Jack took his own well-developed sense of line, his profound perception of character, and his love of life, and deployed them in a manner which defined his style for the next ten years. With some few exceptions. Jack's oil painting had developed uncertainly, with a mixture of generally flat landscapes and seascapes which are noteworthy for their lack of focus and their uninspired composition, and subject pictures which often appear to make a virtue out of restraint, to the point where the point itself is lost. All the glory and excitement which Jack associated with the circus, for example, seems to be suppressed in *The Circus Wagon*, which dates from 1912, and which strongly emphasises the movement, right to left, of the long line of horses, with just the first part of the wagon visible on the extreme left.

Jack's early landscapes were low key exercises in seeing and capturing the perspective of colour. They are deliberately linear and horizontal in composition, as though the over-riding requirement was faithfulness to the visible material. There is no creation of geographical drama. He resembles Nathaniel Hone in this; but where Hone managed to use the most obvious focuses in a landscape, such as the shadow of a tree, or the towering contrasts of a cloudy sky, to create great visual drama, Jack is more neutral.

With his illustrations for *Irishmen All*, Jack was *drawing* in oil paint (see fig. 157). The clear line is there. The edge of *The Greater Official*'s coat, the flagstones, pillar and steps around him, are the stuff of black-and-white illustration. Only now they are filled in with rich colour put on quite thickly, and given great depth and contrast through the paint. These characteristics are even more pronounced in *The Lesser Official*, *The Country Gentleman*, *The Politician*, *The Publican*. They are closer by far to the coloured line drawings of *A Broadside*, with sections in them of colour, defined by line, and shaded and strengthened by dark blues and browns, giving a powerful chiaroscuro effect, and reminding us not only of Jack's intense interest in, and knowledge of, illustrative techniques, but also of his experience of poster work.

Whatever the inspiration, and however the artist himself saw his work for this book, the intense deployment of his energies in the twelve paintings had a powerful impact on his vision and technique. Such immediately subsequent works as *Dust Play*, *Empty Creels*, *Here She Comes!*, *The Ash Plant Seller*, and *A Summer Day* (plate VI), all of which date between *Irishmen All* and 1914, owe a good deal of their strength to the Hannay commission, and feature as part of his stylistic equipment from now on. What also seems to have happened is that the earlier, horizontal landscape and seascape paintings, as well as the racing subjects, become more forcefully expressed through the use of figures – animal, human, or both combined – in a way which strengthens and defines his voice as a painter. It slowly becomes the rule, rather than the exception, that the dramatic focus of a picture is increasingly tied up with the presence of a living form, pregnant with action or desire, alert with the exercise of energy, or quivering in anticipation.

Con Curran probably comes closest to an accurate critical assessment of Jack's painting at this time:

> These first oils recall the woodblock and some, indeed, were intended for illustration. They are without the sumptuous and profound colour of his maturity; they do not attempt to realise the full potentialities of paint but none the less their sense of life and character, their very directness and simplicity have made them deservedly popular.[48]

In 1913 Jack participated in the Armory Show, in New York, mainly at John Quinn's inspiration. Quinn was buying French paintings and drawings from Ambrose Vollard and English work shipped to him by Jack Knewstub, Orpen's brother-in-law, who ran the Chenil Galleries in Chelsea. And Quinn rapidly became involved in the early planning of the Armory Show.

For Jack this was a significant event, both at the time, and as a benchmark for posterity. The Armory Show took its name from the exhibition venue, the huge regimental armory of the Sixty-Ninth Regiment. More conventionally it was the 'International Exhibition of Modern Art' put on by the Association of American Painters and Sculptors, which had been formed expressly for the purpose by a group of artists led by Robert Henri, Walt Kuhn and Arthur B. Davies.[49] What began as a show of American art became a vast international expression of 'Modern Art' in the widest and most radical meaning of the term. It included no less than 1,600 works, from Goya, Delacroix, Courbet, the Impressionists and the Post-Impressionists, to twentieth-century master-pieces by Duchamp and Kandinsky. And it went on from New York to the Art Institute in Chicago and to Copley Hall in Boston. A quarter of a million people paid to see it, and its impact was vast. For the United States it established the relevance and appeal of modern art for collectors, painters and sculptors, critics and dealers. The Armory Show was a significant in shifting the centre of gravity of world art across the Atlantic Ocean. It also provoked ridicule and indignation.

For Jack, involvement was an accolade, and he sold one of his five paint-ings. It put him closely in touch with the indefatigable Quinn once again, and the exchanges between the two men were warm and relaxed. But if Jack anticipated that this mark of approbation might have influenced Quinn to take him up again, he was wrong. The Armory show led Quinn still further towards international modernism, and away from Jack and George Russell, indeed away from his passionate interest in Irish domestic culture altogether.

Jack was relaxed about the whole Armory Show. Though he valued Quinn's help, which was as practical as ever, and required of him details about pricing and commissions to pass on to Davies and another organiser, Walt Kuhn, his letters were filled with other things, mainly stories about boxing, and details of the lively campaigning in Dublin to establish a gallery of modern art. 'I'll let you know,' Quinn wrote, 'as soon as I hear of the arrival of your pictures and will see that they are properly "hanged", not too close to any either high-keyed or low-spirited neighbors.'[50] Reid accurately assesses Jack's position at this time:

> Jack Yeats had the kind of originality of vision that would make his own work always 'radical'; but this was not his sense of himself, and he mis-trusted the fanfare accompanying the 'new.' He thought the wild new men were useful liberators, efficient enemies of convention, but he felt no need of their services, being, like his friend Synge, a 'realist,' a mere honest looker.[51]

Jack later wrote to Quinn: '. . . these gay souls will do good in unshackling painting. But, so far, they do not shake me in my plans, which are only to paint what I have seen happen.'[52]

His most powerful canvas in the Armory show was *The Circus Dwarf* (plate V), which he had already shown in London, the previous year, although it had been rejected by the Royal Hibernian Academy in 1912. It had attracted early critical attention. There was perceptive identification of an important Jack Yeats characteristic: 'The people Mr. Yeats is interested in are a rough, hard-bitten, unshaven, and generally disreputable lot of men. His broken-down actors practising fencing, his "Circus Dwarf" . . . are subjects no other artist would have chosen to paint.'[53]

Hilary Pyle takes a sentimental view of this work, referring to the dwarf looking 'meditatively', having a 'sad, painted face', with 'added poignancy', and the 'vulnerability of the performer'. The subject of the painting is indulging in no self-pity; he is tough, devious, a survivor. His face is neither painted, nor is it sad. Jack clearly identified the painting as his own major exhibit for New York, and that historically important event in twentieth century art.

The scale of the work was unique for Jack in 1912. In later years, the same dimensions, 24 × 36 inches, though always horizontal, became a 'standard' with the artist for major paintings, and he increased this in the late 1930s for a series of great works. He never painted another large-scale vertical work. As to the style, James White has identified the shift from drawing in oils to using the tone rather than the line to define form:

> When Yeats turned finally to oil painting around this period he relinquished his role as illustrator and began to experiment with plastic surfaces. Where previously his line appeared to follow his subjects in their activities, now the subjects take on symbolic qualities and he fashions them broad and expressive as in The Circus Dwarf 1912.[54]

Jack was unable to cross the Atlantic for the show, but excitement about it reactivated concern for his father. Word of his doings came from various sources, generally positive. But Canon Hannay, after a trip at this time, reported to Katherine Tynan that 'old Mr Yeats was living in deplorable circumstances, lodged in a shabby place, and badly nourished.' The word got around Dublin, and Susan Mitchell wrote to Quinn at once: "Is it true that he is so badly off as to give any foundation for the story?" Quinn reassured her, and the matter was dropped.' Willie offered to pay all his debts and bring him home for a season in Dublin, but John Butler Yeats declined. 'When I come home it will be for good,' he told his daughter.[55]

Jack held two solo exhibitions in 1914, the first in Dublin at the Mills Hall, the second in London at the Walker Art Gallery. Jack went to London for the show, and visited Masefield at Lollingdon, where he was now living. The show in Dublin was his first solo exhibition there since 1910. It was the first to be given any kind of extensive social comment, and the first also to record Cottie – in 'a plaid skirt with a navy-blue jacket, and a flowered silk hat with velvet brim and a high bow' – receiving the guests. She was to act as hostess for his shows regularly from 1918 on, and the illustrious listing of guests gives a social flavour of the times: Lady Carrick, Lady Ardilaun, Lady Gregory, William Jellett with his wife and eldest daughter, Mainie, Maud Gonne, Constance Markievicz, Sarah Purser, Bethel Solomons, Padraic Colum with his wife, and many others, including fellow-artists.[56]

An unnamed critic filed a favourable piece for the *Christian Science Monitor*, in Boston: 'These rough pictures (referring to present scenes of the Irish life of today) have peculiarity, strength and characterization; they are outlined thickly in black, and filled in chiefly with flat color of low tones . . .'[57]

More negatively, later in the year, a London critic complained: 'His signature is much more exact than his drawings, and [he] has no more notion of colour than, as Handy Andy says, "a Connaught cow knows about buttonin' up a shirt front".[58] Dublin, however, showed unusual sympathy after the four-year gap:

> The forty-two pictures on view represent the most interesting and the best yet seen from the brush of this clever artist . . . There is no possible doubt whatever that Mr. Yeats' art will live, and will command admiration and appreciation the more it is studied and understood . . . Those who love and understand Irish scene and character will lose one of the treats of their lives if they miss this exhibition.[59]

Padraic Colum wrote:

> No painter could belong to a country more thoroughly than Jack B. Yeats belongs to Ireland . . . It is in Irish character and in Irish streets and houses that Jack Yeats has discovered a new world for the painter – his pictures reveal the race – a race that has still vigour and personality with something of 'the playboy' in every character. Romantic Ireland is not dead and gone as long as we have Jack Yeats to look on our country and our people with patient and never indifferent eyes.[60]

Two comparisons must have been welcome to Jack. The first was Frank Rutter's comparison of Jack with William Orpen and John Lavery, two leading Irish painters working successfully in London. Rutter was an important art critic of the time. He found that neither Orpen nor Lavery displayed any perceptible Irish character. 'Their art is essentially cosmopolitan in character, not national.' Whereas Jack's works

> are Irish as 'The Playboy of the Western World' is Irish, and as 'John Bull's Other Island' is English. To compare the painter with the playwright may sound like extravagant praise, yet Mr. Yeats undoubtedly has something of Synge's power of transfiguring aspects of Irish life which would appear sordid to less poetic eyes.[61]

The comparison with Synge was made by another London critic:

> Jack Yeats, the brother of the poet, whose paintings occupy a room at the Walker Gallery, is an artist of the modern renaissance in Ireland, whose work corresponds in some way pictorially to that done by Synge in poetry. Jack Yeats, of course, has not a deep or tragic vision like the author of 'Deirdre', but there is in his work the same sense of satire and of the grotesque which is so characteristic a feature of Irish Art.[62]

In the lifetime of the Yeats family, in Jack's own lifetime, indeed in Ireland, both politically and socially, the decade, 1900–10, had about it a golden quality. It was a time of reform under a succession of benign administrations. The violence and bitterness of the nineteenth century, in almost every decade of which there had been Irish 'troubles' of one kind or another, were replaced by calmness and stability within which was held out the promise of Home Rule. Yet from 1910 on, this carefully prepared ground, this conscientious attempt to respond to a nation's demands, slowly but steadily disintegrated.

It is clear from many of Jack's own comments, already cited, that he was conscious of this positive atmosphere in the country, and anxious to play his part, even if the chosen place – Greystones – was a Protestant and Unionist stronghold. But this steadily changed, and by 1914, leaving aside completely the threat of war in Europe, Ireland was on the edge of its own civil war, a product of the Home Rule crisis. In 1910, Edward Carson had taken over as leader of the Ulster Unionists. In 1911, Asquith had introduced his Home Rule Bill, and by the beginning of 1912, the open recruitment of men to defend the Union, 'The Ulster Volunteers,' was taking place, and plans were being made to arm them. The purpose was to bring a measure of order among an increasingly violent Protestant population, particularly in the north, which led to sectarian riots in the summer of 1912. But the volunteers were also intended as an army to support any provisional government, if this became necessary.

Moderation on the other side was represented by John Redmond, leader of the Irish Parliamentary Party, who held the balance of power at Westminster. But as the Home Rule Bill continued its slow progress through the Commons, ultimately to be rejected by the House of Lords, Redmond's strength slipped away, and a new, militant spirit replaced it. 'I think the Orangeman with a rifle a much less ridiculous figure than the nationalist without a rifle,' Padraic Pearse said, and this new militancy was to be greatly reinforced by the events of 1913, when the terrible, five-month lock-out against James Larkin's Irish Transport and General Workers' Union gave birth to the Irish Citizen Army, in November 1913, led by James Connolly and J.R. White. It was followed, almost immediately, by the setting up of the Irish Volunteers, an equal and opposite force to the Ulster Volunteers, and prepared, like them, to acquire arms for the increasingly inevitable civil war over independence.

Pearse, who was addressing meetings of the newly formed Irish Volunteers, visited Dundrum, and Jack went to hear him. He was worried at the drift towards a harder political climate, and warned his sisters of the increasingly dangerous situation he saw developing.[63] By January 1914, when the lock-out finally ended, the essential shift in power had taken place, from the constitutionalists, led by Redmond, to the revolutionaries, led by Arthur Griffith. In April, 25,000 rifles and three million rounds of amunition were landed in Larne and Donaghadee for the Ulster Volunteers. In response, on 24 July 1914, the Irish Volunteers landed a smaller consignment, in broad daylight, at Howth. Troops were sent to seize the Howth arms, but without success. The soldiers, returning along the quays, were jeered at by the crowd, and stones were thrown. They opened fire, killing a man, a woman, and a youth of eighteen. The incident, which was to become the inspiration for one of Jack's more important canvases, *Bachelor's Walk: In Memory*, had a huge effect on public opinion. It greatly strengthened the standing of the Irish Volunteers, and locked Redmond into his more militant attitude, which had already, on the same day, contributed to the break-up of the conference at Buckingham Palace which had been called by the king to resolve the impasse. With the imminent conclusion of debate on the Home Rule Bill, and the inevitability of its passing into law, one or other side would have to be confronted, including their newly recruited 'armies'. But a greater conflict intervened: the outbreak of the First World War meant that Home Rule was postponed.

CHAPTER THIRTEEN

Nervous Breakdown 1915–1918

The war went on. The war was over.

158. *Padraic Colum*, pencil drawing by John Butler Yeats, *c.* 1900.

159. *The Flapper Meeting*, sketchbook drawing, *c.* 1903.

J
ack failed to sell his oil paintings in any significant number. The adverse effect of this on his career, combined with other setbacks, resulted in a nervous breakdown. There was critical acclaim for him as an artist depicting Irish life. There is almost a sense of wonder at his prodigality. 'Do the horses really prance with such exuberance?' Padraic Colum wrote. 'Is there so much sombrero in the hats the peasants wear? Do scrubby fellows tell across counters to shopkeepers such extravagant falsehoods – "nine years on the plains of Arabia and the battlefields of Europe"? Yes, in the West of Ireland there is an extravagance of movement, of gesture, of words . . . Jack Yeats reveals Ireland's most significant secret – the secret that the Irish are a youthful people.'[1] Colum was close to his subject (fig. 158). He knew the artist's work in some detail, and was, by 1914, a friend, and an early guest at Red Ford House, in Greystones. He is also committed in the same way, and in his own art pursued the same purpose. This reinforces the eloquence of his comments on Jack's feeling for Irish life.

Yet his paintings failed to sell. The public bought little black-and-white drawings, at under ten guineas a-piece. But four years after his return to Ireland, he had still not made the grade as painter. The meagre sales of his first 100 oil paintings (up to 1916) must have emphasised his feelings of failure and disillusionment as a painter. Of the six oils exhibited in 1914, from the twelve he did for *Irishmen All*, two sold, *The Farmer* (Major Lander) and *The Publican* (J.C. Miles). In general, such figurative works seem to have been less popular than his straightforward landscapes. Dermod O'Brien, that generous patron of younger painters, was catholic in his taste. He bought *A Country Jockey* in 1914, at the Dublin exhibition, a lively early racing picture, and he also bought, on the same occasion, *Looking towards Fenit*, a simple and direct work of landscape painting. *The Maggie Man* sold; *The Barrel Man* did not, though it was exhibited four times before the outbreak of the First World War, including being part of the Armory Show in New York. Of the small, gentle landscape works, put on exhibition in Dublin in 1914, *Lough Gill, Kerry, Castlegregory, Kerry, The Coast of Mayo, A Cottage at Roundstone, Tralee Bay Looking South-East, A Village Shop in Kerry* and *Iron-Roofed Cottage, Kerry*, all sold before the outbreak of war. But adding together all that he had done in oils, the total of sales amounts to about twenty paintings, spread over not quite as many years. Sales tailed off during the war, naturally enough, but immediately afterwards, though there was an improvement, the situation returned to one of only modest demand.

A good figure for comparison would be William Orpen; Irish, of the same class, and with a comparable sense of mixed loyalties – to both Ireland and England – he was, by 1914, a major success. He was seven years Jack's junior. He had made clear-cut decisions in his youth, addressing all the key technical problems, learning to draw, learning to paint, developing a personal style, and had then got on with the business of a regular and reliable livelihood which also fulfilled his deepest creative ambitions. By the outbreak of the First World War he had painted many masterpieces, and he was to paint more. He had done the opposite of Jack, as far as Ireland was concerned, placing it in a special category in his mind. Setting aside, however, the choices each man had made – and they were both leading Irish artists of their time – the comparison in terms of both market place and critical success is very marked.

We do not know what Jack's feelings about this were. There are no recorded reactions to the various exhibitions, his comments on reviews amount to little more than the underlining of passages which interested him, with occasional exclamation marks in the margin. He and Cottie lived modestly, on her private income and his earnings. It is not known what, if anything, was paid to him for his Cuala prints. Probably very little.[2]

What we do know is that *A Broadside* ended in mid-1915, and that in or about that time, Jack had some kind of nervous breakdown. The date is important. Hilary Pyle suggests that it occurred in the late spring of 1916, attributing it mainly to the Rising:

> Something collapsed inside the artist. At this time, and from now the sketches in his few notebooks are interspersed with subjective scribbled concepts either in 'dream', or 'half memory', grim faces reminiscent of Kirchner, and even some whirling geometrical abstracts which had never before come from his pencil.[3]

She also suggests that overwork contributed. 'Besides the emotional strain overwork caused Yeats's illness in 1916.'[4] But there is clear evidence in a letter from Lily to her father that his trouble – whatever its nature – had developed by the autumn of 1915, so that it could not have derived from the Rising, nor from the events associated with it. Writing of Jack, Lily says:

> he looks much better & was cheerful and talkative – he told me that the specialist had made some change in his medicine & told him that it was slow & that three months made really no perceptible difference – six very little – he could not expect to be well a year from when he got it – it is almost eight months I think . . .[5]

And this is corroborated in another, earlier letter from Lily to her father about Jack: 'Jack and Cottie came up by motor last Sunday with a police pass. Jack looking very well – I had not seen him for two months – he says he is much better but going to another doctor as he had promised you – he was to go the very week of the riots.'

A further strain had been placed on Jack for some years by a legal action involving the Pollexfen estate. This was the second time that Jack had become so involved.[6] It was significantly more complicated. His grandfather had made financial provision for his mentally-ill son, William, who had spent his life in an asylum, leaving the executors, Arthur Jackson and George Pollexfen, in control. On the death of William, in February 1913, Alfred

Pollexfen claimed, as administrator of his brother's will, responsibility for the £2,500. Alfred was also ill, and was to die in a nursing home in Bray in 1916, and the case brought by Jack and Arthur Jackson was against Alfred in the interests of the rest of the family, all of whom had legitimate claim on a share of the money. For three years Jack, with Arthur Jackson, was engaged in trying to sort matters out. Because Jack was in Dublin he carried the main legal burden. The wrangling, which involved many meetings and court appearances as well, was tedious and complex for him, and undoubtedly contributed to the strain leading to his nervous breakdown. Ironically, Alfred Pollexfen, from his nursing home in Bray, writing to Cottie in November 1915, says, 'I was sorry to hear Jack was not very fit, but hope he is better by now.' He reports also on Robert Gorman's death.[7] Jack was not well enough to attend the funeral, despite the fact that Agnes, Gorman's widow, was particularly close.

Full details of Jack's illness were kept from his father in order not to worry him, and perhaps to prevent him attempting the hazardous, wartime return to Ireland. As we have seen, Lily gave him some information. But the effect was a tidal wave of further inquiry. It led to irony and no doubt some pain to Jack himself and to Cottie, for the letters poured forth from New York, and there was growing anger at the continuing silence from the couple in Greystones:

> I will do worse than cut you out of my will – I will stop the newspapers if you do not write to me – There are some questions I would like answered – . . . How are you getting on with the oil painting? Have you started a portrait of yourself? Do you now go to the National Gallery? – once you start that portrait you will of yourself want to go and look at the portraits there – you will get so curious about them – how are you getting on in the trivial matter of paying your way. What are you reading? I hope you read Dickens. – Cottie ought to love Dickens Lately I have read several times David Copperfield = I know it by heart. He is a much bigger man than George Meredith – his heart – his humanity – is bigger . . .[8]

In March 1916, in a letter to Lily, he concludes: 'Jack hardly ever writes – which worries me not a little – I suppose however he is all right.'[9] And on the same day, writing to Jack himself, he takes up the same sad complaint:

> Why do you never write to me – & make me worry. – I think you must be in low spirits & that you have tumbled into some pits of black melancholy – Remember your Yeats and Corbet ancestors who were joyous people – with lots of sunshine in their hearts – the Middletons also were happy people. Your grandfather sometimes was gloomy – but you are mainly a Yeats & a Middleton & therefore have no excuse. I am always worrying about you – I think I worry about you more than about any one else – why I don't know except it be that you write so seldom. – & then you are the youngest. as to Cottie if she does not write oftener I will come home & upbraid her. She does not write because she is enjoying herself too much to bother about old men.

This was inspired in its guess as to the cause, but somewhat ill-judged in its references to family joy and gloom. Jack would not have agreed that he was mainly a Middleton and a Yeats. He believed he had much of the Pollexfens in him, including the gloom of his grandfather, and the melancholia of his mother, and this would have emphasised the hereditary strain in his illness. His loquacious father, determined perhaps to prod a reaction out of his son by exploring every possibility for the silence, opened another theory in early April when he put forward the idea of marital disharmony:

> I hope tomorrow to get a good letter about you perhaps from you. I think I now know why you have not put sketches in youre [sic?] letters. You have been in bad spirits. Is it the war is it your own health – or are you tired of Cottie – of course if it is the last I can't help you as Cottie might be disagreeable. – Though I admit she is generally amicable and sensible . . .[10]

John Butler Yeats also filled his letters with views delivered at great length on the British and the Americans. He was nothing if not global in his political views, and he filled pages with charming character assessments of Kaiser Wilhelm and other European leaders, often accompanied by delightful drawings. If, as is quite possible, Jack's illness was in part aggravated by the trauma of war – and there was a general perception of unprecedented doom occasioned by the world conflict – then John Butler Yeats's ignorance of the real situation led to unhelpful prognostications from New York. Fortunately, his niece, Ruth, who was then living with his two daughters at Gurteen Dhas, wrote to John Butler Yeats giving him more details, making him more fully aware of just what Jack had been going through. He immediately wrote to Cottie: 'I have just had a letter from Ruth. a very interesting letter – but from what she writes – I have become more anxious than ever about Jack – & I hope I will soon get the doctor's report . . . do be frank & serious with me about Jack – & don't try to put me off –'[11]

Faced with the need to explain, Cottie sought advice from Dr W.S. Ross, their Greystones doctor, as to what she might sensibly tell her father-in-law, and he wrote back, calmly enough:

> I think the thing to tell your father in law is that Mr Yeats has been suffering from a nervous breakdown due to overstress mental & bodily but that there's no organic disease. Also that recovery in these cases is always very slow but that he is steadily improving & will in time get all right. This is exactly how the case stands & this explanation should satisfy every one. I hope to go over on Sunday as Mr Yeats kindly asked me to do.[12]

Then, rather belatedly, it was Willie's turn. It is almost a refrain in John Butler Yeats's letters, his desire that the two brothers should come to some kind of rapprochement; in the spring of 1915 he wrote to Willie, urging closer affection between brothers: 'You will find as you get older that there is a particular value in brotherly regard – I mean between brother and brother . . . In Jack is an unsunned well of affection. He won't let the light get down into it. I fancy Cottie know all about it. There must be somebody to whom Jack unbosoms.'[13]

Willie visited the couple later in the spring. John Butler Yeats, when he heard of it, wrote to Jack and Cottie, asking, 'Did you invite him, or did he come of himself?'[14] Cottie, it seems, was quite conscientious about their relationship with Willie, now as before. As we know, she owned copies of most of his books, and those that needed to be cut in order to be read were so cut; the evidence is that she followed his work and career and was proud to be sister-in-law of the poet. When Jack's illness became a matter of general family concern, Willie wrote somewhat formally to Cottie from England:

I write to suggest that Jack see some Dublin specialist. I imagine that illnesses connected with the nerves are among the things one wants a specialist for. If you like I will write and ask friends in Dublin who is the best man. I believe that Jack would find that it is a great comfort to consult some clear-minded man who would tell him if he was doing right. Half the cure in such matters is not to have to worry about one's self more than is necessary. I imagine that all our family have some nervous weakness. It is our dangerous spot. The Yeatses never had it. We picked it up from the Pollexfens.[15]

Wisely, perhaps, Cottie appears to have ignored the offer and there is no record of Willie taking further action.

The family's view of Cottie changed. It was felt that she displayed a measure of indifference or neglect. John Butler Yeats, admittedly making his judgments from a distance, saw her as making 'such a mystery of it'.[16] Lily wrote to John Quinn: 'I agree with all you say about Jack. Cottie's answers to me are just the same as her written answers to you. What is wrong is, I think, she is just limited. I saw her in town and I lunched with her two days ago, and I talked of Jack and a specialist. She did then say what she would not say before, that she would get a specialist at once if she thought Jack was not improving.'[17] And in a later letter Lily told Quinn: 'When talking to her I always find myself being careful, going back and putting things more carefully as I see her face change and her mind close up . . . We think it is English because we can't think of anything else to call it.'[18] In Lily's view, having children would have changed this; it would have 'mixed' her more with the Yeatses.

The illness was known to all members of the family by the time of the Easter Rising, in 1916, and at that stage Jack was convalescing. Lolly was away from Dublin, and on Easter Monday, the day on which the rebellion started, Cuala was of course closed. Lily in her diary gives a vivid picture of the following weeks, describing the special arrangements which had to be made for food, and the heavy police restrictions on movement of any kind. Nevertheless, Jack made the effort:

The second Sunday Jack and Cottie and their maid Maggie came from Greystones in a motor to see if I was safe. – Maggie they sent on in the motor to Ranelagh to get news of her sister, they had been stopped many times by the police, who examined their permit . . . In the early morning as I lay awake listening to the horrible sounds from the city my heart full of anxiety and sorrow, the angelus rung from the village and Rathfarnham Convent, used to give one great comfort, it sounded so calm, so permanent, as if saying 'all this will pass but I will remain'.[19]

John Butler Yeats pestered for news well into the summer. He worried that Jack was suffering from consumption. He took grave exception to the fact that Cottie seemed to be treating him like a child. He thought Jack's health of mind was at risk, and brought up references to the supposed mental instability of the Pollexfens, 'They are anxious people.' He thought poorly of the Greystones doctor. 'The country Doctor is possibly quite at sea.'[20] And in the same letter he reported that Quinn blamed Cottie, though he himself felt that Jack was 'happy in his life with his nice kind timid Cottie a wife after his own heart'.[21]

As Jack slowly recovered, Cottie judged there to be no real need for post-mortem explanations, and failed to give details to her father-in-law. In May he wrote to Lily: 'I wonder if she thinks I am made of wood. She makes feeble jokes about Jack's illness – as if she thought that kind of thing would relieve my mind – why does she not send the specialist's report. Yesterday and today I expected a letter from her & have not been able to do any serious thinking through suspense. I have never complained of her laziness but I do now.'[22]

A collective Yeats resentment of Cottie had undoubtedly built up. It developed later into the view that she was 'stupid'. It was unjustified, and undeserved. But Cottie knew her man better than all of them. She respected his view of how things should be, and seems to have judged the actual illness correctly, of course with the help of the specialist, whose own letter, already quoted, confirms this.

Jack began to write letters again, among them one to Lady Gregory. She replied:

> I was very glad to see your handwriting, and to hear, as I had done, that you are on the mend – You must take care of yourself and get quite strong. . . . The picture of 'Young Theodore' you gave me looks so splendid in the nursery: I often think you could make a big impression in an exhibition of 'Nursery Pictures' in this style – If I do go to America again I will ask you to do me another 'Young Theodore' for Roosevelts grand-children! . . . John Quinn was well – he was much concerned about your illness.[23]

By August he was fit to receive visitors, and Lily responded to a wish from Thomas Bodkin that he might visit Jack and look at his paintings. She wrote: 'He is very much better but still has to take life quietly – therefore I would like to give him warning of visitors.'[24] Thomas Bodkin formed a collection of Yeats paintings, and remained a friend of the artist.

John Butler Yeats wrote with his usual warm affection at this time:

> It is a good morning. Such as we get weeks of in the Fall – the windows all open and quiet at the back of the house, and no squalling children since there are no children in N. York. So I naturally being in good humour which is favourable to the affection, think of you and the perfect wife. *Do* write to me. Hereafter when I have become a silent member of the Company existing only in memory, it will be pleasant to think that you have written to me many times. So do write. An old man should think of the past, but I am all interested in the future. I watch the post. I have an idea that any moment a Commission may come to me – my success at Pittsburgh has raised all my hopes and I trust myself. Do you know that often when I am in low spirits I take up your illustrations to the Hannay book, and each time I get a fresh impression of their loveliness and their actuality – and a sort of poetic truthfulness – you satirize but with such a kind heart. York Powell as you know once said you had a mind like Shakespeare's – I like also the way you 'progress'. You do not stand still – a man of genius should be like a growing boy, who is never, never, and never will be a grown up. . . . I hope you take things easy. I failed because I worked too hard. I let myself be driven by that foul witch, an uneasy conscience, which is only another name for Fear – who is the demon of life, and the great source of all or almost all its crimes and its

criminals . . . never interest yourself in anything you don't care about. This is not the rule for conduct, but is the rule for art, and for artists in their work.[25]

How appropriate the advice, though how inadequately observed in his father's case.

There are various modern theories about the nature and indeed the actual realities of what used to be embraced in the catch-all phrase, 'nervous breakdown'. It is not nervous; it is not, strictly speaking, a breakdown. Modern psychoanalysis would describe Jack's problem as a depressive episode, with depression as its over-riding component. And there would be those within the modern discipline who would subscribe to the view that the so-called 'breakdown', or more properly the episode embracing a period of depression and associated withdrawal, contained within it the seeds of healing, since they include a strong element of self-confrontation. The side effects of the depression were likely to have been a whole range of reactive attitudes, including silence, indifference towards his work, failure to correspond with people, becoming isolated, giving those closest to him a hard time, ignoring requests, invitations, queries and contacts. And some at least of these are hinted at in his behaviour. But clearly the most important manifestation was in his art, and it is to this we must give further examination.

Reverting to the year in which the ill-health started, there is an important work to be considered. Jack did not witness the tragic shooting on Bachelor's Walk by the British soldiers. But the next day he went to where it had taken place and witnessed a much slighter event which moved him deeply. 'A flower girl walking in front of Mr. Yeats took two carnations from her basket and cast them in a doorway as she passed. Glancing down, the artist saw a number of little floral offering strewn on the ground, a touching tribute from the flower girls to the victim who had been shot there.'[26]

He went back later that week and did a sketch of the railings, the wall and the shop window with a bullet hole in it. He inscribed it: 'Where the people were shot on Sunday a few paces further towards O'Connell Bridge flower girls had thrown flowers I suppose one of those killed fell there'.[27] He also did a drawing which was subsequently published in *A Broadside*, and which relates to the painting, but only in very general terms.[28]

Then he painted *Bachelor's Walk: In Memory*. In the painting Jack takes the pathos of the flower-girl's small, silent gesture, and creates a work of great poignancy (fig. 160). It has been used as a nationalist ikon, and a symbol. Earnan O. Malley, in his introduction to the 1945 exhibition singles out this painting:

> One departure of his was completely new in Irish painting, the depiction of national events. The memory of the dead makes for a tragic understanding in Ireland. It evokes a feeling of dead generations who served or have died for a common cause, their struggle echoed in each generation. The Bachelor's Walk incident is shown as a simple, but hieratic incident of a flower-girl who casts a flower outside a doorway where men have been shot down. There is restrained dignity and grace in the movement of her hand and a tenderness that evokes a sense of pity.

Rosenthal suggests that the woman is 'an archetype representing all Irish womanhood mourning the loss of their men.' Hilary Pyle, who quotes this

160. *Bachelor's Walk: In Memory*, oil on
canvas, 18 × 24, private collection. 1915.

passage with obvious approval, herself refers to the flower-girl's 'ritual gesture', and describes the painting itself as an elegy. 'A deeper dimension
entered, and the depictions of history, for instance "Bachelor's Walk: In
Memory", were fortified with a real and powerful emotion.'[29]

A great deal more has been written in comparable terms, forcing symbol of
one kind where quite another was meant, in an effort to reinforce and broaden
the quite sufficient natural appeal which the scene has. Rosenthal, for
example, describes it as

> one of Yeats's greatest paintings, . . . a major political statement, as deeply
> felt on its smaller scale, and in its relatively traditional composition, as
> Picasso's Guernica. But while Guernica is all white heat and outrage,
> violence and carnage, Yeats's painting is emotion recollected in regret and
> sorrow, and much more effective because of this. The flower seller throwing
> a single red rose onto the other flowers already left there, her pale, beautiful
> face framed by hair of the same black as her shawl, is both an individual
> woman, painted with love, and an archetype representing an Irish woman-
> hood mourning the loss of their men. In terms of technique, this great
> picture is a kind of mid-point for Yeats. The fluidity and the almost

graphically realistic imagery are those of his water colours, but the paint is, perhaps for the first time, the oil paint of a master of his medium, still conventional in texture but also free, without handcuffs and ready to go on to much more daring exploits.[30]

And John Booth, no doubt with MacGreevy, O'Malley, Rosenthal and Pyle all in mind, reinforces the symbolic interpretation: 'The painting has a powerful, resonating presence and it is not surprising that the flower girl has been interpreted as a symbol of Irish women mourning their men or, indeed, a symbol of Ireland herself, remembering the loss of her sons form emigration, war and famine.'[31]

These views are in marked contrast with what Jack himself thought about the painting. He gave an interview, in late December 1921, to a journalist specifically on the subject of whether or not dramatic national events stimulated the work of artists. The moment could hardly have been more dramatic. The Treaty had been signed days before. The tensions of achieving agreement and avoiding the terrible war threatened by Lloyd George were shortly to be replaced by the greater terror of civil war. Jack, described as 'a representative Irish artist whose vivacious presentment of Irish life and character has won him many admirers in England,' readily agreed. 'I certainly think that the work of artists over here will be strongly national in the future. I do not mean that it will be didactic. Art degenerates into propaganda when it becomes that. But it will take Irish subjects and treat them in an Irish manner.'[32]

It was a characteristic of Jack's, then and throughout his life, to receive visitors with his easel empty and his paintings out of sight in wooden racks hidden by a drawn curtain. He showed pictures, if at all, for a purpose.

As an indication of the new spirit which we may reasonably look for in the Irish art of tomorrow, Mr Yeats showed me an unexhibited picture of his called 'Bachelor's Walk'. 'It reflects an incident I witnessed just before the Easter week outbreak,' he explained. 'Some of our fellows had been shot along the quay here. A common flower woman, passing with a basket of carnations, dropped one or two of them as a memory-offering on the spot where one fell. They were her stock-in-trade, and I thought it a noble action.' Jack gave his wider view on the subject of artistic response to the political events:

'Has the Republican movement found direct expression in art yet? Scarcely at all. Only one painter, to my knowledge, has drawn on the incidents of the last few years. We have had no Sinn Fein war artist. The conditions of the conflict made that almost impossible'.

Jack does not reveal his own motive for going to the scene, and is vague about the date, locating it 'just before' the Rising, when it actually happened almost two years earlier. But the important fact, of his having witnessed the flower girl's action, and his view, that it was 'noble', is the clue to his view on such art, and also to his self-imposed limitation, of not painting subjects he had not himself seen. The nobility and feeling in the event itself is what matters and Jack's interest was in expressing the instant of human emotion and not the abstraction of 'national feeling'. Effectively, this confined his total output of 'national' art, in the political or 'republican' sense, to two canvases, neither of them outstanding as paintings, though both charged with emotional overtones.[33]

161. *The Funeral of Harry Boland*, oil on canvas, 24 × 36, Sligo County Museum and Art Gallery. 1922.

The first is *The Funeral of Harry Boland*, exhibited in the Royal Hibernian Academy in 1923 (fig. 161). Harry Boland was on the anti-Treaty side, and was a victim of the Civil War, wounded while being arrested at the Grand Hotel, Skerries, and dying later as a result. Jack attended the republican plot in Glasnevin Cemetery, and his painting became the only visual record of the event, since cameras were confiscated at the gate. It is an interesting, rather than an inspiring record of the event, its undoubted faithfulness to the actual scene again characteristic of the painter's truthfulness to what he experienced. It has been raised by critics and commentators to heights which it does not sustain. MacGreevy's eulogy sets the tone: 'In this picture Jack Yeats rose to the full height of the heroic in art and, like Gros in The Battle of Eylau, lifted the contemporary scene on to the plane of historical painting.'[34]

It is precisely because Jack did not emulate painters like Gros, whose epic works, conceived on the grand scale, were artifically posed, though wonderful in their way, that he moves us. But if he moves us in a painting such as *The Funeral of Harry Boland*, it is for reasons within ourselves rather than within the painting.

Much the same may be said of *Communicating with Prisoners* (fig. 162). which dates from roughly two years later. It depicts exactly the kind of tense event which appealed to Jack. Women prisoners in Kilmainham Gaol had broken their windows in order to talk with women outside, and the scene

162. *Communicating with Prisoners*, oil on canvas, 18 × 24, Sligo County Museum and Art Gallery. 1924.

shows, in distant perspective, the ring of faces in the high top of the tower. Its tones are low-key, but there is drama in the composition. Like the other two, it has attracted enormous critical attention. MacGreevy calls it 'out-standing'; Hilary Pyle writes of it underlining 'the paradox of such situations in war and peace'. MacGreevy, interestingly enough, misunderstood the painting. He thought it showed women communicating with men, but Jack pointed out: 'The description of the prison picture is not quite right there are women prisoners only looking from the windows. But later on, if you dont see the picture itself again, I will send you a photograph.'[35] Again, the reality is rather different and significance had been attributed where none was necessarily intended. Unlike so many of the events which appealed to Jack, and from which he drew inspiration for the often enigmatic and intriguing scenes in his pictures, these three works gain their apocalyptic reputation largely on the grounds of being identifiable in historical terms, and carrying the additional appeal – which was undoubtedly appealing to Jack as well – of pathos and a collective, national sadness.

These works fall into what Hilary Pyle describes as Jack's 'transitional style'. This is a much more sensible way of viewing him than in terms of 'periods' or 'phases'. What happened, stylistically, and it is quite marked in respect of *Bachelor's Walk: In Memory*, is that the artist moved away from the clearly defined outlines, and the bright and contrasting colours, of his pictures for the *Irishmen All* commission, to a much more muted palette and a less definite sense of line. Mass and volume, and the contrast of light and shade, replace the tighter, more literal intepretation of such works as *The Maggie Man* and *The Lesser Official*. Jack is responding to the idea of form as a more direct expression of the emotional message of the work. And he is seeking an entirely new use of colour.

The two departures evolved at different times, with quite distinct emphasis emerging. His palette changed radically between 1914 and the early 1920s. There is a jewel-like quality to that small group of completely accomplished genre and character paintings with which his career climaxed before he succumbed to his illness. The colours are parcelled out by line in the same way as jewellery deploys the setting of silver and gold to enhance the brilliance of emerald, amythyst, ruby or diamond. This is a strength, but also a limitation. And Jack never resolved the difficulty of blending and carrying over the colour. In order to do this, he resorted first to a kind of mauve monochrome deriving from the free and sometimes arbitrary mixing of primaries. In this he was seeking to discover for himself his own palette, unique and forceful, and related to the general tone and texture of the Irish landscape and climate. He did so from a very limited technical base. He had never been taught painting in oils, and this shows in works from this period, which have suffered fundamental deterioration as a result of defective technique. His art school training, patchy and interrupted, had been governed by the restless line and the urge to draw. Indeed, that was a domestic need as well as an urge, and it took him away from learning the essential laws of oil painting, including any conventional understanding of the properties of colour.

The twentieth century has produced innumerable artists finding their own colour, and flouting all traditional conventions. Jack was one of the earliest. But the trial and error was a significant factor during this period of the Great War and afterwards. And it is governed, to a considerable extent, by the pitfall of mixing primaries and ending up with a range of different shades of mauve. Training, and colour conventions, as acquired by Yeats's contemporaries, Leech, Swanzy, Orpen, and by the masters he knew in his early years, Hone and Osborne, created a balance of bright light falling on clothes, trees, buildings and other scenes. And they managed, within this constraint, to deliver a convincing enough portrait of Ireland, though, in the case of most of them the attractions of other countries, with more sun and a different light, proved overwhelming.

There is a tendency towards monochrome in his work of this period. *Empty Creels, A Summer Day* (plate VI), *The Public Speaker, A Cake Cart at the Races, The Riverside (Long Ago), Dublin Newsboys*, are dominated, though not exclusively, by shades of warm mauve and of different greys. And it is too frequent, and too dominant a trait to be excused in terms of it being representative of the light and atmosphere of Ireland, whether rural, urban or coastal. The reality is of an artist moving, tentatively towards the creation of a palette of his own. He wanted a colour range comfortable to work in, convincing for his audience. The 'transitional style', referred to above, is in large measure devoted to this question. Its resolution, in the mid-1920s, was achieved with difficulty.

163. *The Greater Official*, oil on panel, 14 × 9, private collection. 1913.

Side by side with the huge matter of colour, there is the question of line, and how line could be resolved into mass and form. There is no line. That is one of the fundamental truths about nature, and it has to be absorbed and understood by the artist, who may then use the *convention* of line, as Jack did in his early work, or meet in more subtle ways the evolving revelation. And gradually Jack, after decades devoted to the use of line, was learning this lesson, and preparing himself for its greater implementation in his work. There is light and shade; there is volume and shadow; there is bright colour and muted, dark colour. But the edge of that large, generously-cut, orange-coloured coat worn by *The Greater Official* and painted by Jack in thick brown outline, is the work of a draughtsman whose first instinct is to define the territory rather than realising the subtleties of tone and colour perspective (fig. 163). The process of doing this could be said to have started with *Bachelor's Walk: In Memory*, or with several other canvases dating roughly from the same time. It is imprecise, and uncertain. It was extremely difficult for a painter so comprehensively and ruthlessly a practitioner of line from his very earliest work, to move away from it. He does not abandon it. That lies a long way into the future. But he reinforces it steadily with mass and volume, creating statuesque figures, such as the flower-girl and the little boy, or the three jockeys in *Before the Start*, or the left foreground group of side-car and figures in *A Westerly Wind*. In these and many others, Jack is deploying light and shade, and painting up the focus in tonal rather than linear terms. And the process is slow, and uncertain. He had limited resources of training. He had a conviction about his own unique grasp of Ireland, strongly rein-forced by those who admired his art. And he had determination to go on, notwithstanding the setbacks, both critical, commercial and personal, which characterised these years.

Something of the difficulty and struggle may be inferred from the fact that, between 1914 and 1918 the number of Jack's paintings fell dramatically. Of course it did so, in part, as a result of his illness; but it may also be attributed to the causes of that illness, insofar as they have been correctly inferred, and the exploratory nature of his canvases during these years. In the year in which war broke out he not only had the two exhibitions mentioned in the previous chapter, but exhibited with the Royal Hibernian Academy, becoming an associate the following year. And during the period of the war he submitted paintings to a number of group shows. But he did not hold another solo exhibition until 1918. Nor would his output have justified it. Dating of works at this time is uncertain, but it seems clear that between the autumn of 1914 and the end of 1918 he produced just over twenty oils, while in 1919 alone he painted fifteen, and in 1920 he painted seventeen.

War preoccupied everyone, as the relentless tidal-wave of death swept over Europe. John Butler Yeats's view of it, from the distance of New York, was decidedly republican. 'England humiliated would not mean for me the end of the world,' he wrote to Jack early on. 'I could survive seeing her taste a little of that humiliation which she has considered it her mission to inflict on everybody else. After all I am an Irishman first and a British citizen after.'[36] A fortnight later he wrote again, condemning the speech which John Redmond had made, urging Irishmen to enlist and fight on the British side:

in order to mark their gratitude to England for a home rule that is so incomplete it is an insult . . . Of course I hate German militarism and hope it will be crushed. But it is not for Irish nationalists to rally to the help of England when she is quite resolved to refuse them everything for which they ask.[37]

Quinn very quickly decided that in a serious conflict between England and Germany he would have to back England. And in due course John Butler Yeats followed the advice of his friend and patron. Lily's preoccupation with the war was directly related to the unbridgable gulf of the Atlantic Ocean separating her from her father. His exile seemed permanent. She wrote to Quinn:

> I appreciate very much what you say about Papa. Not only do I love him as my father but as my greatest friend. When I think of his age and the distance he is off I cannot keep away my tears, and then the thought of the sixty years of hard struggle he has had for the money that never came! He doesn't know what a success he is, how fine his work is, what a big man he is.[38]

In another letter, describing a performance of Synge's play, *Riders to the Sea*, where people around her sobbed through the performance, she gave a quite different view of the impact they all felt from the war. 'Death all about us – so many we hardly mention it when we meet, partly because most one meets have sons or brothers at the front.'[39]

Dublin and New York were divided by German U-Boats. Dublin was troubled by insurrectionary disturbances and threats. The Great War had embroiled the United States, and, though its eventual outcome was no longer in doubt, the massive and once-invincible German war machine was guaranteed to ensure further bloodshed on a huge scale. All of this made Quinn increasingly conscious of the burden he had to bear, in respect of this old man, and the fact that he was answerable to children who were themselves middle-aged. He would have liked to have persuaded them earlier to bring their father home, and he was to begin the process as soon as the Armistice was signed, when, of course, it was really too late.

Quinn was important to the family on account of taking responsibility for John Butler Yeats. He was the main source of dispassionate information about their father, usually through Lily, and a cool and reasonably detached version of events was necessary as John Butler Yeats approached his eightieth year. Other Quinn ties, notably with Jack, changed in character. The warm early friendship had lost its intimacy. It was still friendly enough at the outbreak of the First World War, but Quinn did not buy from either of the two 1914 exhibitions, and only wrote to inquire about them on New Years' Eve: 'I hope that you had a good exhibition. I suppose this war interferes with the sale of sketches and of books and of pictures but I hope it won't pinch you.'[40]

He heard of Jack's illness, but it did not prompt any correspondence. And in due course he heard of Jack's departure from Greystones after his recovery, in 1917. Jack and Cottie moved to a house in Marlborough Road, Donnybrook, near to Uncle Isaac Yeats, and two aunts.[41] The terraced house, built in 1861, is generously proportioned, with ornate plasterwork in the two reception rooms, and three quite sizable bedrooms, one of which, looking out over the long, narrow garden, was Jack's studio. He decorated the wallpaper on the insides of the shutters with landscapes seen through narrow archways. It was not the only decorative work; the house had previously been owned by Terence de Vere White's family, and he records his mother's dismay when Cottie had the William Morris wallpaper stripped, and the walls painted in 'hideous colours'.[42] The house was less than two miles from St Stephen's Green. Jack had found Greystones lonely. The physical isolation, and the reserve of the people, had come at a bad time. He told Padraic Colum of meeting more friends in a month than they had done in a year in Greystones, and went on to say how much he enjoyed walking along the canal: 'It was an honour to think that every step was a step nearer the west. Where ever I am I always want to walk towards the west. As well as from a desire to get to an ocean coast, from a wish to be going with the sun.'[43]

Quinn wrote to Jack in October:

One of your sisters has written to me that you were moving closer to Dublin. I imagine the change will be a very pleasant one. I quite agree with you about the advantage of moving. It does help one to destroy 'irrelevant' and useless hoards. Not a day goes by that I dont clear up something in my office or apartment.[44]

Quinn was obsessively clearing out his office, and devotes a whole paragraph to details of this. Tentatively, Jack had offered to send photographs of paintings, clearly in the hope that Quinn might resume collecting his pictures.

Thanks for offering to send me photographs. You say 'photographs of my picture'. I wish you would send me photographs of several of your things, marking on the back of the photographs the title, size and price. Your father is quite well and although he looks whiter and a little thinner than he did some years ago I think he will get through the winter all right. He comes up to lunch with me nearly every Sunday, and I dropped in to see him last Thursday evening.

Though the request for photographs of more than one painting was encouraging, Quinn's response was negative, in part due to ill-health and on 29 January 1918, he wrote:

I received on December 5rh your letter of November 1st with the photographs, which I thank you for sending to me. I was very glad to hear from you . . . Under the circumstances, I cannot write to you about your pictures or make an offer to you for them or do anything about them. The doctor says that the period of convalescence will be a period of a month or six weeks. The operation will probably take place in New York. Later on I hope to get back to work and then I will take up your letter and write to you. You will understand, I am sure, my feeling about not closing with you for one or two or three of your works under the present circumstances.[45]

Jack suffered a blow to his esteem which seems to have affected him considerably. The 'Man from New York', with whom his relationship had once been so warm and encouraging, had become increasingly interested in Modernism. Quinn was now involved in an espousal of the struggles of writers like Ezra Pound, T.S. Eliot, and above all James Joyce; in his collecting of pictures he was becoming enamoured of French painting. It was to be five years before they corresponded again. The reference to Willie's marriage is, perhaps, an appropriately abrupt introduction of this event in the story, since it came

164. *George Yeats*, pencil drawing by John Butler Yeats, 1920.

about in precipitate circumstances, with the family only meeting George Yeats after the wedding (fig. 164). Willie, up to late August 1917, still entertained hopes of marrying Maud Gonne. He had asked her in the summer of 1916, on a visit to Normandy, and had discussed marriage with her daughter, Iseult. On 7 August 1917, he went to stay again with Maud Gonne and Iseult in Normandy, and this time proposed to Iseult. He was refused. Six weeks later he proposed to George Hyde-Lees and was accepted. The marriage took place on 20 October. He did not visit Ireland until the following spring.

Lolly, in a letter to her father, describes the event:

This is Wednesday and on Saturday Willie and his wife came to Dublin – they telegraphed from Chester to say they were crossing and would come out to us on Sunday evening, asking us to get Jack and Cottie . . . all worked out beautifully . . . We like George *greatly* – she looks older than her years. I think it is the marked features – a very large nose – her hair is reddish brown – very waving and curling and worn low over her ears – she has a good deal of colour and very nice eyes – blue – a charming expression – you feel that she has plenty of personality but that her disposition is so amiable that she does not often assert herself – not from inertness but because she is happiest in agreement with the people around her – this is the impression she gave us – she has gaiety and is I am sure intuitive – she would fit in anywhere – *Cottie* at first was a little self-conscious but George was so nice Cottie was soon quite at ease – and not afraid the new sister in law would try to supplant her with all of us. I think *Cottie* just felt nervous and fussed up; but all this evaporated in a few moments and we were all at ease. Willie and Jack and Cottie and George walked off to the Dartry tram together at 11 o'clock to get the last tram.[46]

Jack summarised the end of 1918, and this dark phase in his life, as briefly as ever he summarised a crisis and its resolution: 'The war went on. The war was over.'[47] During the war years he had been made an Associate of the Royal Hibernian Academy, in 1914, and a full member the following year. This elevation delighted Jack's father. 'When I get back we will be a family interest & swamp the Academy – & then we can toss up on whether you or I shall become presidents.'[48]

CHAPTER FOURTEEN
A Dublin Man 1919–1922

The roots of every art must be in the country of the artist

This wintry weather I like to be down on the Quays to see the old decrepid retired seamen, polishing their shoulders and the walls, and catching any little glint of sun they can in their little pale eyes. They hug themselves to think how well they have managed to never have to go to sea anymore. They forget, though they know it well, that there is no such thing as an aged seaman afloat where the tall ships are.[1]

Jack was fifty when he wrote these words, in the winter months of 1921, and they evoke the simple nature of his life as it then was. And so it was until its end, thirty-five years later. He became the quintessential Dublin man. The city was the centre of his universe, its people the heroes and the heroines of much of his art. With the exception of occasional visits to England and the holiday trips he made in summer time, he lived a Dublin city life.

The pattern of his day was settled, from the undisturbed morning in his studio which, if it went well, lasted through the afternoon, though rarely later than four o'clock. He was a tidy and methodical man, and when he had finished his painting for the day, he cleared everything away. The unfinished canvas was placed in a storage rack against the wall, and a curtain drawn across. The brushes were cleaned with old newspapers, and his materials put away in his painting cabinet. It had belonged to his father. The timely departure for New York of John Butler Yeats, at the end of 1907, had coincided with Jack's increased interest in oil painting. When it became clear that his father would not be returning, and the studio in St Stephen's Green was given up, Jack had inherited this and other bits and pieces, including the easel which he used for the rest of his life. His way of working remained the same virtually until he died; whatever fine frenzy may have stirred his emotions and inspired his conception of a painting's subject, in practical terms he was ordered and calm. So that the shift from smooth brushstrokes in the oils of the 1920s to violent, stirred impasto and vivid splashes of colour in later works, were all embraced within a calm and ordered existence.

He walked a good deal. The house which he and Cottie had taken in Marlborough Road was close to the tram routes; but it was also a comfortable distance from the centre of the city, and Jack walking was a familiar sight. His tall figure had become leaner as a result of his illness, and the bone structure of his face, which in later years was to become quite cadaverous, gave it a stern authority. His gaze was clear and direct, yet softened by a kindly expression. He walked with a long stride using unfrequented routes, just for the curiosity of it. But there was a purpose and design in all that he did. Little things mattered. He made lists of where he was going. He visited shops to pick up packages by pre-arranged agreement, and expected everything to follow the arrangements he had made.

He dressed well. He bought all his clothes from the best of the Dublin outfitters, and had accounts with Walpole's, in Wicklow Street, with Tyson's at the top of Grafton Street, with Callaghan's, and with a number of other tailors and outfitters. The names are like elegies of a past lost forever; he chose Morley's pure wool underwear for winter, but sea island singlets in summer; he wore Callaghan's Wool Pants, and also 'Balbriggan Longpants', and sometimes 'Braemar Wool Pants'; his shorts were taffeta, his singlets Aertex, his shirts 'Kingsway' and 'Vyella', as were his pyjamas. He was worried about catching cold. 'Arthur Power remembered . . . his long ample greatcoat (which) hid any hint of the hot water bottles he was said to wear, slung around his waist, to keep him warm in cold weather'.[2] He kept his handkerchiefs in an embroidered holder made by Cuala, and almost certainly embroidered by Lily.[3] He was big, took a $17\frac{1}{2}$ sized collar, his pants were size 48 and his singlets 46. And when the clothes were old they were turned to good account; in a notebook he records, 'Old shirts for paint rags'.

He entertained, generally on his own, and in his studio. The harmonious and companionable life with Cottie went on, but increasingly, in the period immediately after the First World War, and from then on until her death, they each had their own sets of friends, and pursued visits and engagements separately. Cottie was an essential part of his life. They were a couple at all formal occasions. Among others, they entertained Lily and Lolly, and went to Gurteen Dhas for the regular parties and other entertainments. They also took the sisters out. Lolly records a visit when Jack and Cottie took her and Hilda to the Royal Dublin Society Horse Show on the Four Shilling Day, 'to jumping enclosure expensive tea + all the proper things – we got home at 8 o'clock'.[4] Earlier Lolly wrote of one of their Monday parties:

> Cottie quite well again + they both say '*it was a very good party*' – I had a note from Cottie today + she says in it 'You are both splendid hostesses + everybody so happy' Jack and Cottie are going to London on Tuesday week. Cottie to her mother at Kew Gardens Jack to some Hotel – Cottie seems quite well again she looks far better than Jack does – but he never looks well in great heat.[5]

They went to the theatre together, to exhibition openings, and to receptions and parties. But Jack the artist was visited by friends, by collectors who sought his work, by other painters and writers, and by the growing circle of admirers. And these people, many more men than women, came to him, and were seen only by him. He served sherry, whiskey – always Irish – and, according to Niall Montgomery, a friend in his later years, an undrinkable concoction which Jack fondly thought was brandy, but which his guest knew was not.[6] On certain occasions, Cottie brought in tea. It was all rather formal. Jack did not have a telephone. He communicated by letter, and he expected to be written to by people who wanted to meet or see him.

His taste in entertainment was as eclectic as ever. He still liked everything, from circus and music hall to modern, avant garde, experimental theatre. He became a regular guest at Abbey Theatre First Nights, presumably arranged by his brother or by Lady Gregory, and kept all his programmes for these openings, which provide a comprehensive history of the plays at this theatre during the period 1920–30, when he went to more than 100 First Nights. Yet he was not on intimate terms with theatre people. Among his friends was the architect, Joseph Holloway.[7] They corresponded from 1921, and their friendship – as was the case generally with Jack's friends – was long-lasting.

Jack sometimes attended Lady Gregory's 'Gort Barm-brack suppers'. She had instituted these in the Abbey Theatre's premises in Camden Street, used for rehearsal, when her play, *Twenty-Five* was in preparation.

> The Gort Barm-brack was a huge cartwheel of a fruit-cake, filled with the richest ingredients, made specially by her own bakers at Gort for the casts of any of her new plays. It was a huge affair of several pounds weight and tradition had it that it usually took two to carry it. Wrapped around with silver paper, bits of candied peel and glacé cherries sticking out all over its shiny surface, it held a place of honour on a table near the stove.[8]

Sara Allgood, in her autobiographical memoir, gives the dimensions: 'it stood about twelve inches high and about fifteen inches in diameter'. It lasted several days. On one occasion Lady Gregory records: 'Jack Yeats very appreciative, that pleased me best.' And in her Journal she several times referred to Jack and Cottie coming to the theatre in terms of affection and deference.[9] At a performance in April 1924, of her play, *Brigit*: 'I was near Jack Yeats, he liked it all through; the Christ especially pleased him, and the last Act. He came with me to the green room between second and third Acts.'

He loved ballads, and collected them all his life, buying them from street traders and from ballad-singers, some of whom were still offering them outside places of entertainment in the late 1940s. He records in his 1889 diary buying a ballad sheet; and in his large collection he writes on one of them, 'bought outside the Abbey Theatre, 1946'. But there is no record of him going to singing pubs or to other establishments where ballads and patriotic songs might have been sung. They were often sung in theatres, during the intervals between the first and second halves of musical or vaudeville productions, with the words projected onto a screen.

Quite obviously, gallery openings were important, and he seems always to have enjoyed them. Right to the end of his life he went to group and solo exhibitions, often seeking out the work of obscure and little-known artists, and going out of his way to acknowledge and encourage. He celebrated his full recovery and return to solo exhibitions, with his 1918 Dublin show at the Mills Hall in March, well before the end of the war. And it was well attended. Cottie received the guests, and a social diarist wrote of her in 'a navy coat and skirt trimmed (with) braid, and a black hat brightened with a flame-coloured heron osprey'. The guest list has changed somewhat since 1914, and new names include Oliver St John Gogarty, Thomas Bodkin, Susan Mitchell, James Stephens, Edward Martyn, together with many who were already collectors, or at least supporters (fig. 165). A cartoon of the artist appeared in *The Dublin Evening Telegraph*, showing him alert and quite youthful.

He was increasingly active as a member of the United Arts Club; so much so that as early as 1921 he was jointly proposed by Francis Cruise O'Brien and the club's manager, Mrs Duncan, for honorary membership.[10] Others proposed at the same time included Lady Gregory, Susan Mitchell and James Stephens, giving some assessment of how Jack compared at the time. As a

165. *Edward Martyn*, by Sarah Purser, oil on canvas, Hugh Lane Municipal Gallery of Modern Art, Dublin, *c.* 1899.

MR. JACK B. YEATS

166. Cartoon of Jack by Shemus. May 1923.

167. W.T. Cosgrave, on right; with him is General Sean McKeown, known as 'The Blacksmith of Ballinalee', and Surgeon McArdle, a noted physician at St Vincent's Hospital.

member of the club he was 'agreeable and amusing when occasion demanded, but capable of reading quietly in a corner and creating an aura of "Please do not disturb" around himself and of gliding away, and out, as if invisible'.[11]

There is virtually nothing in his work during the five cataclysmic years, 1918–23, which refers to the War of Independence, the Black and Tans, the Treaty, and the Civil War. He did not seek out the aftermath of events, as he had done with the episode on Bachelor's Walk, in 1914. He was not inspired to paint rallies, public meetings, funerals, or memorial celebrations.[12] He portrayed no one of political significance, and avoided painting events, either directly or indirectly connected with the five most profoundly shattering years for Ireland of the twentieth century. Neither then, nor later, did he refer directly in his painting to the birth of his own nation. And whatever views he had about politics – and they were often outspoken and direct, and decidedly republican, with a mixture of Fianna Fail and Left-wing ideology – he did not let them intrude on his artistic output. He was not inspired by politics, by political violence, by national achievement, by class struggle, or by party differences.

An example of how he felt is given by his reaction to the two-day national strike 'against the refusal of the authorities to abide by the agreement to recognise the status of the political prisoners in Mountjoy Prison'. This strike was in support of a hunger strike by prisoners. The men were released, and no tragedy occurred. During the public strike institutions like the Royal Hibernian Academy remained open, but Jack closed his exhibition for the period.

There are many episodes which indicate his staunch nationalist views, but which should be read in the context of his life rather than his art. A particular *bête noire* was W.T. Cosgrave (fig. 167). Quite late on Jack asked his nephew, Michael, whether he had he seen a profile of Cosgrave in *The Irish Times*. Then he added: 'Next thing you know they'll be doing one on Sadleir and Keogh'.[13] Later, according to Niall Montgomery, Jack came to despise de Valera almost as much, referring to him as 'that fellow from 42nd Street'.[14]

However, anyone reading Thomas MacGreevy's extended essay on the artist, *Jack B. Yeats: An Appreciation and an Interpretation*, might be excused for thinking the opposite. One-third of the book is devoted to a consideration of Jack's paintings in the context of politics; and an attempt is made to imply political views, and to suggest some kind of involvement between Jack's growing up and his art, and the Irish nation's struggle for independence. It simply does not exist. MacGreevy suggests that Jack was somehow aware of agrarian unrest as a tiny child, and that his subsequent representation of 'Life in the West of Ireland' was the expression of that awareness, developing and growing as Jack himself grew. The evidence is of a different development, in which experience slowly built up an understanding of many different strands of human motive which were clothed in emotional purpose often too deep to fathom, long before any political cloaks were thrown over them. It is a mistake to make politics the starting point. It was anything but, in any of his work. But for MacGreevy, for complex reasons, politics became increasingly important, as if he needed to prove his own allegiances to Ireland, and after 1932, by extension, to 'Fianna Fail' Ireland. Unfortunately, he used Jack for this purpose, and Jack became an extension of his own romantic wish fulfilment. Ironically, Jack was pro-Fianna Fail anyway.

But the effect of MacGreevy's interpretation of Jack Yeats as a hero of Irish artistic nationalism influenced other writers, and created a collective conviction about Jack which is in need now of reassessment. Thomas MacGreevy was undoubtedly of great importance to Yeats. The relationship, which began as early as 1922, but developed more substantially in the mid-1920s, was most significant, and lasted for the rest of Jack's life. It is best understood if the quite different personalities are compared. MacGreevy, voluble, eloquent, dogmatic, and trading on the fact he was closer to Jack than anyone else, became his 'spokesman'; whereas Jack, taciturn, elusive and retiring, seems content to have been represented by his friend. Inevitably, as a result of this, certain general views and interpretations, emanating from MacGreevy, need to be treated with caution, while perhaps some of Jack's own statements on art need to be treated with greater attention and respect, as are his views on issues generally, which he was not slow in putting before the public, frequently through interviews with journals and newspapers. He had a sympathy with the press, having lived at least part of his working life in their company.

Contrary to a widely held perception of Jack, he did comment about art and other artists. In the course of explaining his own solitary approach, and that of many other Dublin painters, he gave an account of how things operated which included references to the only other living Irish artist with a London reputation, William Orpen. 'Of course we have nothing like a school over here'; he continued,

> There is the Arts Club, but only a very few painters belong to it. There is the Hibernian Academy, where we hold meetings periodically. But for the most part we work singly over here. There is no rendezvous in Dublin, for instance, like the Café Royal in London, nor is there an artist's quarter like Chelsea. Some years ago Orpen had a school over here, but he did not remain long enough to influence style to any great extent.[15]

Jack was vocal at this time about many things in addition to art. He could be outspoken and controversial. He took particular exception to the tasteless addition of illuminated advertising to what he already considered an atrocity, the ugly iron loopline bridge that cut across the view down river and concealed Gandon's nobly proportioned Customs House. He recalled his father's opposition to the new bridge.

> Has Dublin's artistic sense been developed since then? Well, I think so. I'm sure it has. And I believe, too, that the appreciation of Dublin's beauties is stronger among ordinary people than they themselves realise. The danger of a thing like this is that it may come into being before people understand what it means to them, and their artistic perception, now subconscious, will receive its full shock when what has caused it is irrevocable. I consider it of course a scandalous thing to have the bridge there at all. I wonder if there would now be strength enough among Dublin people to start an agitation for its removal . . . It might be possible. At any rate, I believe, that eventually – not at the moment, but eventually – the country will be enlightened enough to remove the bridge.[16]

Jack loved the River Liffey, and was familiar with it from Islandbridge, where he used to go and watch the rowing, down to the tidal reaches below the Custom House. He painted it in many guises, including a view, *From the Metal Bridge*, down towards the reviled loopline bridge, though the railway link is decently obscured by distance, and by the more elegant arches of the Carlisle, or O'Connell Bridge.

He entered into the sprawling, haphazard arguments surrounding Hugh Lane's pictures, the Municipal Gallery, and the provision of art gallery facilities generally for the people. On the campaign to have the Lane Pictures returned to Ireland, Jack did two posters.[17] It was a controversy of much prominence, and one destined to go on for some time, involving his brother and Lady Gregory. He focused on a proposal then current, for the State Apartments in Dublin Castle to be used as the Municipal Gallery of Modern Art, and he rejected it, not from experience – since he had never been there – but on the simple grounds that a gallery's prime requirement was light, and the light should come from above. This meant a single storey building. What was required was space, not height, and he envisaged a gallery eventually forming the four sides of Merrion Square, all the paintings well-spaced, and hanging at natural horizon height. There would be easy and frequent access.[18]

His views on art were truthful, direct, and frequently quite profound. Later he became reserved about comment on other painters, and elusive about his own art. Still later he became silent. But in the years immmediately following his recovery from his illness he was forthcoming, and there is much published material. Indeed, the evolution of a philosophy of art may be construed from his correspondence, his interviews with journalists, ultimately in his writing about himself, and his single recorded lecture on art.

The popular press, in the 1920s, wanted people's views. Painters, like other performers, were frequently interviewed about their art. Jack did not escape, and his scrapbook contains many cuttings which demonstrate a strange role for him, that of spokesman or commentator on artistic issues of the time. In his correspondence with Quinn he also discussed art, and he did so with Thomas Bodkin.

The moving spirit within the United Arts Club, Mrs Duncan, persuaded Jack to involve himself in the organisation of an exhibition. Roger Fry's exhibitions in London, of Post-Impressionist art, had caused an enormous stir in art circles everywhere, and the educational fervour about bringing Continental paintings to the notice of collectors and artists, as well as the general public, was strong in Ireland. Mrs Duncan suggested such a show, to be held in the club's premises, and Jack helped.

Quinn wanted to persuade Jack of the merits of modernism. This provoked a lengthy discussion between the two men on the rival merits of the amateur and professional instincts in the artist. Jack was an unredeemed and permanent amateur, decrying the professional instinct in the artist, and dismissing Conrad as 'one of the professionals'; 'He has too much respect for the authority of convention and not enough for truth.'[19] Jack's ideal of the amateur, among writers, was George Moore. He read T.S. Eliot at Quinn's suggestion, and found him 'amusing'. Jack went on to develop his crucial distinction:

> The novelist, who respects his workshop more than life, can make breasts heave, and arms wave, and even eyes flash. But he cannot give his people pulses. To me man is only part of a splendour and a memory of it. And if he wants to express his memories well he must know that he is only a conduit. It is his work to keep that conduit free from old birds' nests and blowflies. Man cannot invent. When he thinks he is inventing he is only

stirring with a wooden spoon. All of this is obvious to many people. But they forget it every now and then. There need be none of this stirring in painting, and that is why painting is greater than writing. Painting is direct vision and direct communication.[20]

Two years earlier Jack had painted *The Old Ass*; and sold it for £50 in 1919, a higher price than was normal for small-sized oils. Thomas Bodkin had wanted to buy it, but it seems he could not afford it. Jack had respect for Bodkin; he wrote: 'I would like to sell the picture to you: for I would like it to be in your possession more than in most people's.' It went instead to Captain Gough, who had married Robert Gregory's widow. Jack sent a reproduction to his father, one of the rare occasions when he seems to have satisfied the perpetual appeal for images.

> I am more than delighted with that picture of the Ass – it is beautiful – a sort of joke with poetry at the back of the joke . . . it was only after some time that I discovered it was in oils – In water colour you can suggest but to paint in oils demands a complete technique – I am now quite satisfied that you have come into your own – I showed it to several people here & their delight was instantaneous and abundant.[21]

Jack needed to be provoked into speech and opinion. He seems rarely, if ever, to have offered his own views without some kind of stimulus. It could well be a journalist, though he expressed himself more wittily and at greater length with those whose views he trusted or admired. By 1921 Jack and Bodkin were seeing quite a bit of each other, and in April, following a discussion about old masters, Jack wrote to him:

> I understood at once, when you spoke again, that you were not thinking of the material mellowness of the old masters . . . About those dear old masters – most of them tried to paint only what was; not what they saw, a few followed 'fancy'. Many of them made 'pictures'. These were the most wretched. And a very few followed truth, which is a different road for any man, but especially for the painter . . . Painting has never yet taken its true place as the freest and greatest means of communication we have. If you have nothing else to do next Saturday afternoon the 23rd come and see me. I knock off work at 4 o'clock.[22]

He is briefer in comments to journalists, but he still revealed in his own fashion what he thought about art, what his essential objectives were, as well as his inspirations. 'I never make up my pictures. All my people are people I have actually seen. That is desirable, I think, because human nature is capable of infinite variety, and unless I went straight to life for the types I draw I should be in danger of using always my own particular "set" of performers.'[23]

In Jack's views generally about art, there was undoubtedly a process of gestation during the period from 1918 into the early 1920s, a period in which he resumed regular solo exhibitions, with at least one each year from 1918 to 1923.[24] Its most obvious practical expression was in the shift in his output, and in the strength of certain canvases, of which one might most notably identify *The Dawn – Holyhead, A Westerly Wind, A Dancer, Singing The Dark Rosaleen, The Circus, Tinkers – Early Morning, The Island Funeral* and *The Circus Proprietor* (figs 168–9). These works span five years, and seem to define Jack's search for tension, event, expectation and yearning. The *Manchester Guardian*

art critic, writing in 1919, and indicating clearly his familiarity with Jack's earlier involvement with the paper, seemed to hit on an essential truth: 'There is something shadowy and fugitive about all this artist's work, as if each picture were a good-bye to something.'[25] It was not a state of artistic achievement smoothly concluded. Other critics observed the uncertainty and difficulty of what the artist was trying to do, and expressed views on this, and views on his national idealism and on the Irishman attempting to express the character and definition of the new country. Darrell Figgis, for example, stressed this:

Jack Yeats holds an individual position to-day in Irish art. One need not press the word Gaelic too far in the natural association of certain interpreting ideas to see in his work a national quality that no other word could so easily describe. The very qualities of our national speech are the qualities of his work. Both are concrete and real and vividly picturesque – the more picturesque, in fact, because they are so concrete and real.[26]

Two critics took up the issue of the treatment of his subject-matter being surbordinate to the subject itself, finding limitations in this. 'He has no definite manner; he adapts his manner to his matter, and this is at once a source of strength and a limitation.'[27]

These drawings by Mr Jack B Yeats are very vigorous and clear-cut expressions of Irish life. Mr. Yeats, however, claims that he subordinates 'manner' to 'matter.' Either this would mean that Mr. Yeats has no manner, which is not true, for his manner is most distinctive, or it would mean that each new 'matter' creates spontaneously in him that technique for itself. And Mr. Yeats is quite a pronounced stylist. I think I would rather look at his pictures than listen to his theories. When he is painting Irish sporting subjects he is racy, descriptive, and amusing. But his landscapes are rather dull; perhaps over them he has more time to theorise.[28]

In *Everyman* the heading of an article emphasised Jack's directness:

Art without an 'ism': 'There is, indeed, more than a hint of genius in a good many things in this exhibition. It is, one feels, the painting of a man who has got something that he particularly wishes to say, and not that of a man who has evolved or borrowed a theoretically interesting language, and is more anxious to show how well he speaks it and what a good language it is, than to express anything in particular by its means.'[29]

In a more colloquial vein, the editor of *Ireland's Own* questioned him about his changing style. '"Yes," he replied, "we must change from year to year, and we must paint that which is in us".'[30]

Jack was invited to lecture to the Irish Race Congress, in Paris, in January 1922. He accepted, and it forced him to bring his views on art to some sort of resolution. He chose as his subject a very general theme, 'Modern Art'. This was subsequently published as *Modern Aspects of Irish Art*.[31] The Irish Race Congress was a six-day affair held in Paris during the last week in January 1922. It had taken almost a year to organise, and the general intention was to forge links between Irish people around the world, and then 'decide how best such a central machinery can be set up as will enable the Irish abroad to assist in the reconstruction of the Motherland'.[32] But by the time of its opening it had been overtaken by events of the most momentous kind. The Dail had met

172. Eamon de Valera; he is seen here in the early 1920s, with political colleagues, including Sean T. O'Kelly, who later became the second president of Ireland (right) and Sean MacEntee (left) and P.J. Ruttledge.

in the first half of January to ratify the Treaty. After nine days of debate, much of it fiery and acrimonious, the vote in favour had been carried, sixty-four to fifty-seven. Eamon de Valera then refused the presidency of the Dail, warning of 'internal strife'. Arthur Griffith became president, and Michael Collins head of the provisional government.

It is remarkable that de Valera not only arrived for the Race Congress but remained for much of it, chairing sessions and participating in debates (fig. 172). Among the quite specific set of purposes for which it had been called, all broadly concerned with gaining independence, there was at the head of the list a commitment 'to put a stop to the excesses of the British troops in Ireland by securing their withdrawal'. This thorny dimension of Ireland's outstanding and unresolved severance from Britain was debated during the week. The congress was international, with delegates coming from Irish organisations in every continent, including obscure delegates from China. Eamon de Valera, who was president of the congress, was leading a delegation from Ireland of those who were in opposition to the Treaty, and this matter also became an issue during the week-long series of debates.

The central point – which was to remain critical for much of the rest of the twentieth century – came to a head on the Wednesday, 25 January, when the congress was invited to debate the following motion: 'To assist the people of Ireland to attain to the full their national ideals, political, cultural and economic'. The words 'to the full' – which carried huge implications, both in the light of immediate past history, but more significantly in the light of what already overshadowed the future – were introduced by an Australian delegate, P.S. Cleary, from New South Wales. The best part of a day's debate revolved around this single word, 'full'. The true significance of the addition – relating, as it did, to the idea that the Treaty had settled for an incomplete form of independence – did not wholly emerge. But in no sense did this inhibit involved and tortuous discussion.

For Eamon de Valera, who had left behind him in Dublin the threat of 'internal strife', which was soon to spill over into bloody civil war, dominated this Paris forum, and he used it to forge political links with Irish people in different parts of the world. Jack was in good company, with his brother giving a lecture on 'Lyrics and Plays of Modern Ireland', and with Douglas Hyde, Evelyn Gleeson and the musician Arthur Darley among the contributors on cultural subjects. Both brothers spoke on Monday, 23 January, Willie in the afternoon session, Jack at 8.30 in the evening, followed by a concert of Irish music. The event took place in the Salle des Fêtes of the Hotel Continental.

Eamon de Valera, clearly recognising the importance for his own future of the international dimension, sought to forge an organisation which they finally decided to call 'Family of the Gael' (Fine Ghaedheal) with its motto: 'Greater than all telling is the Destiny that God has in store for Ireland'. Jack had little or no role after the opening day. It is not known what he did or even whether he stayed on in Paris, travelled to Dresden, or returned home. Willie was accompanied by his wife, George. Cottie was probably with Jack, though there is no confirmation of this. No sketchbook records Paris at that time. But he did exhibit in the Exposition d'art Irlandais, at Galerie Barbazanges, which opened at the end of the week, on the Saturday.

Modern Aspects of Irish Art is a strange little document, little more than a pamphlet. It contains the name of no artist, living or dead. Its references to Ireland are brief enough, and they are related to Jack's broad dismissal of the past. In a sense he is presenting pure philosophy. He believed that civilisation itself had become jaded and slavish, and that the pull of science had taken people away from nature.

> There is a country more ready than any other to lift painting into its rightful place, and that is Ireland, this land of ours. Because here we have not too many false traditions about painting to get rid of, and so we have an open mind, and the foolish civilisation of the cities and the love of money for the sake of money has not as yet stolen us away.[33]

His own deep nationalism had developed, by 1922, into a clear-cut conviction that,

> when painting takes it rightful place it will be in a free nation, for though pictures speak all languages the roots of every art must be in the country of the artist, and no man can have two countries; and this applies with greater force to the artist than to anyone else, for the true painter must be part of the land and of the life he paints. The artist may travel all the roads of the world and may paint pictures of what he sees, but he can never be part of these roads as he can of the roads of his own land. His pictures will tend to be nothing but the dead skins of what he sees.[34]

He dismissed the influence of art from other countries, expressing particular reservation about Paris and London.

> There are some fine artists in Ireland now whose feet are on the right strand, but there is room for many more, and those others may come from all the different corners of Ireland. But we must look to ourselves for the springs of our art. We must not look to Paris or London for a pace-maker. London can only give us what she has learnt from Paris, and a lead from Paris is particularly dangerous for a young artist, because Paris is the home of the very science of fashion, and true painting has nothing to do with fashion.[35]

Jack's words parallel his own development, his emergence from uncertainty into certitude; they are also in keeping with the theme of the congress. Listeners like de Valera, uncertain of the attitudes of Jack's brother towards what he and his political colleagues had achieved, perhaps even more uncertain about what they were to contemplate in the immediate future, would have been reassured by Jack's dedication to the new State. Few of them would have been familiar enough with his art, however, to see the identification which Jack appeared to be making between himself and those who, in a variety of other disciplines, were all facing the same challenge – metaphorically speaking – the blank canvas. Only this can explain the extraordinary approach adopted, an attempt to dismantle prejudice about the elitism of art, expel ignorance, challenge groups and movements, and restore to the centre of his and their thinking the reason and purpose of pictures. He stressed particularly 'the memory' and 'the moment', twice referring to them: 'A picture which is true is the memory of a moment which once was as it appeared to the artist.'[36] 'The true artist has painted the picture because he wishes to hold again for his own pleasure – and for always – a moment, and because he is impelled – perhaps unconsciously, but nevertheless impelled – by his human affection to pass on the moment to his fellows, and to those that come after him.'[37]

What he despises is the idea of artists keeping themselves apart, as 'a wonderful and mysterious race', and ordinary people playing into their hands by feigning an ignorance for which they should be as ashamed as if they were to say, 'I suppose this is a fine day, but I don't know anything about days'. Jack conceived of the painter as someone capable of breaking away from the rules of art by taking the side of nature, and he saw all art historically as 'the old lazy bondage of the rules' punctuated by breakaway groups or episodes when the dominance of nature was restored. He was later to develop this broad concept. But at the Paris congress he confined himself to the general theory. All other paintings, all art, should be forgotten when we are looking at a fresh work, since what is already in the memory represents a barrier between nature and the viewer. 'We should think of the picture before us and of the scene it represents, and if the artist succeeds in making us feel that we are present, looking at the scene and feeling about it as he felt, then the picture is a success. If the feelings of the artist were free and noble, then our feeling will be free and noble.'[38]

The 'false picture' is the opposite of this, a painting done from other pictures, even when nature is present, the painting done to display skill or cleverness, or even the attractiveness of science (he cites Futurism and Vorticism as examples, the only schools mentioned) – 'science is easier to follow than life. One can learn science from a handbook.'[39]

Jack saw the danger of racial exclusiveness in the arts, and expressed his views on it in terms which are also instructive in the context of Ireland, and his own future. For the artist who settles to work in his own country there was the danger that he would become

> easily satisfied with his own efforts, and to be content to hop from the ground to his perch and never use his wings . . . The painter who works in the land of which he is a part need not build a wall about himself . . . Those painters who have the affection for their own country and their own people will paint them best. The roots of true art are in the affections, no true artist stands aloof. This land is full to the brim of all things that lend themselves best to pictorial memory . . . Every house and street has been made by the hand of man and so carries some of the spirit of man . . . I think the two most beautiful pieces of man's handiwork are the old-fashioned plough and a sailing ship.[40]

The lecture dealt with certain practicalities – the teaching of art, the familiarising of children in their schools with the simple skill of drawing – and it concluded with an alarming object-lesson for his sophisticated, international audience, 'get some paper, a good black pencil' . . . and communicate. Jack's message was magical in its childlike simplicity, so imbued with nature, with seeing, with the emotional response to what is seen, that it is quite impossible to gauge its impact. But it is a remarkable distillation of his mind, a comprehensive statement about his art to which other comments he made, then and later, fit with an integrity and coherence which epitomises his truth.

If the timing of the Irish Race Congress in Paris was inconvenient for Eamon de Valera, it turned out to be more climactic for the two Yeats brothers than they could have imagined. Within a week of its conclusion, their father died in New York, and this powerful, towering influence on both of them ended his lifelong expositions on life and art (fig. 173). There had been some warning from the great man himself that his departure was

173. *John Butler Yeats*, self-portrait, oil on canvas, 1908–22.

imminent; late in the summer of 1921, John Butler Yeats sent Cottie and Jack a letter with an imagined drawing of their supposed pets, a cat and a dog, and with the enigmatic message: 'I am the last the smallest & the least important of the dark – after me will come the radical – I go to sit at the feet of the great men & the great angels & tell them my story – dear Jack my beloved – farewell –'[41]

It was not quite farewell, since even at that late stage there was still talk of him coming home. But it did intimate that this promised return was in doubt. 'I shall be very glad to be home for Xmas – for by that time my portrait will be an accomplished fact – and I am in great hope – that being among Quinn's pictures it will hold its own . . . and bring me a little posthumous reputation the thought of which will smooth my last hours –'[42]

Still later he wrote to Jack: 'Forgive me for not coming home – I am kept here by certain things that must be done – These finished – I will come with much happiness & be a cherished antique – & be put on my shelf & carefully dusted every morning – with a good fire – so that the temperature be right – and nothing to harm my frail porcelain . . .'[43]

Jack's father enjoyed his last Christmas in New York. There had really been no intention of returning. He told Quinn at the end, 'I will not leave America.'[44] His final illness was brief. He died on the evening of 3 February 1922. The next day Jack wrote to Lily:

I got your sad telegram last night and went round to Uncle Isaac and to Aunt Fannie. My wishes as to the burial arc as yours and Lolly's – I will telegraph to Willy, and see to the Irish papers today. His passing was as he would have himself wished with intellect unimpaired. Cottie's and my love to you both. Jack B Yeats.[45]

Above his deathbed was the still unfinished self-portrait which had kept him on the other side of the Atlantic. 'In the end it happened as you feared, in exile,' Jack wrote to Quinn. 'Like most fine talkers, I think he had a simple nature which flowed on. Talking is not such an usurpation as writing, which becomes mortised into a man's soul. Truthfully painting does nothing but reveal.'[46] Quinn handled all the details of John Butler Yeats's last illness, death and burial with great care and sensitivity. He wrote frequently to all of them, consulting over details, while at the same time hating this side of the business.

I dread illness, suffering and death more than anything. But when the thing came with your father, I went through with it. Your father knew that I had sincere affection for him, and I believe that he had a like affection for me, though at times he did weave a web of fiction, or what he would call romance, which was pure or impure fiction, about me. For example, he was never able to make a good drawing of me, though he tried it many times. He always made me look like a young Priest, just out of Maynooth; no lines, no modelling of the face. He was an affectionate lovable man. His talk was more interesting than most books, more brilliant, more amusing. He never preached or cared to instruct or to improve. He followed the gleam. Down to the end, life was still full of interest and mystery. And now that he has sunk into his dream, there ought to be no regrets.[47]

Jack was becoming increasingly self-assured and confident in his own life, happy in the new home in Donnybrook, and surrounded by admiration and affection. Wider family affairs were in better order in the post-war return to normal life, though his sisters then, and for the foreseeable future, were to be faced with a hard and exacting struggle to survive. He continued to help them, though he was less than completely happy about the demands of Cuala on his time. But in personal ways he was supportive. When he learned that Lily had suffered a recurrence of her boils, he paid for a week's stay at a hotel in Malahide and packed her off there. Lolly remarked on it:

> She goes on Friday – Miss Boston goes with her – Jack is treating Lily to the week . . . Jack came over to dinner with us on Sunday last Cottie like Miss Boston had caught a chill – she had to have the doctor – but she is better now – We thought if Jack came to us she could have what every woman is supposed to love 'something on a tray'. Jack was in great form + talked away about all sorts of things always taking some quite whimsical view of things – we gave him an excellent dinner lamb. mint sauce. *salad* + so on + coffee afterwards + Maria brought in cups of tea before he started home + gave him a huge bunch of lilac for Cottie.[48]

Despite the restored confidence and sense of authority, Jack remained at heart inscrutable, and enigmatic. These were his over-riding characteristics. He kept himself to himself, reserved his council on everything, divulged no secrets, expressed his opinions deliberatively in a cautious flow of words. Yet he determined his own fate in a clear-cut way. Lolly wrote: 'He has lately put very high prices on his pictures, but he always knows what he is about – or at any rate it is no use discussing prices with him. He goes his own way, and apparently sees his own road clear before him.'[49]

CHAPTER FIFTEEN
Modernism and the Issue of Style
1923–1930

The memory of a moment

WILLIE BECAME a patrician in the newly formed Irish Free State. Jack became a radical. Willie supported the Treaty, Jack opposed it. For many years it stood between them, and the separation it created was strengthened by the Civil War which followed. In the new Ireland, their paths diverged. Willie was made a member of the new Senate. Jack became deeply critical of the government led by W.T. Cosgrave. And the antagonism between them against which John Butler Yeats had fought throughout his life continued for the remainder of the decade and on into the 1930s.[1]

The separateness of the two brothers' lives was based on difference, rather than on animosity. Both were dedicated to Ireland, its life, its culture, its art. Both were civil to each other, and indeed moderately interested in each others' careers. Both were also dedicated to family ideals and had a strong sense of ancestry. Both loved and supported the two sisters. But each interpreted the history of their country in his own way, and they differed profoundly in the ways in which they wanted to become involved in politics and public affairs.

Willie was now a poet with an international reputation. In November 1923 he won the Nobel Prize for Literature, 'for his always inspired poetry, which in a highly artistic form gives expression to the spirit of a whole nation.' Indeed it was at the time 'said to be a tribute to the new Irish Free State'.[2] Jack was unsurprised at the award. He wrote to Quinn: 'I think he should have had it some years ago.'[3]

Jack was now a Dublin man and saw the city's social and political affairs in unpretentious terms, as any citizen might. In contrast, his brother's views were a loftier affair. He was not above lecturing his compatriots, viewing Ireland and himself from the outside. Jack became interested in party politics, and he kept himself well-informed by regular reading of newspapers and talking with friends. He had strong views on the issues of the day. By nature a radical, and in politics republican, in the heightened atmosphere of post-civil war Ireland, this had a distinct meaning best explained in the context of events.

The Civil War had run its bitter course during 1922 and the first half of 1923, with two 'governments' for Ireland, one of them, 'provisional', led by Eamon de Valera, and including the gaoled Liam Mellowes as Minister for Defence. Despite pleas to the Roman Catholic Hierarchy, the Church had

174. William Butler Yeats and his family, late 1920s.

175. Erskine Childers.

condemned the murder and assassination which had 'wrecked Ireland from end to end'. And the government itself had been encouraged to enforce the severest measures which included military committees to deal summarily with possession of arms, ammunition or explosives. The principle of exemplary execution was embraced; in reprisal for the assassination of Sean Hales, a distinguished West Cork military leader during the War of Independence, the government decided to execute Rory O'Connor, Liam Mellowes, Dick Barrett and Joe McKelvey. These deaths shocked the anti-Treaty side into a swift abandonment of acts of violence. Jack's revulsion against this act of the Free State government alligned him politically with those opposed to it.

He faced what undoubtedly was a defining moment, politically speaking, with the court decision to execute Erskine Childers (fig. 175). Jack was one of many individuals outraged by the choice of Childers as a republican scapegoat under the new Emergency Act, and he wrote to W.T. Cosgrave: 'I urge you to hold your hand and not to execute Erskine Childers, I write to you in the name of humanity and in the name of sober judgement.' Childers was shot on Friday 24 November 1922.[4] Across the letter a Cosgrave assistant scrawled: 'The man you plead for had neither Humanity nor Sober Judgement'.

It is difficult to conceive of any section of the community unaffected by the Civil War; indeed, its impact ran through families and businesses, even intruding into the affairs of Cuala. Lily records a raid on the premises in May 1923 when she saw a man with a bit of hawthorn in his buttonhole jumping the wall, followed by another man, and when she went into the printing press, it was full of men. They were reading type, looking at manuscripts, and they then announced that theirs was 'a raid by military orders'. They asked for two girls by name, and took them away in a lorry. '"Thank God Miss Lolly wasn't here!" was Lily's first thought, and when her sister arrived she said the same — "I would have bitten somebody!"' The truth was that the two Yeats sisters knew that two of the girls were mixed up with the I.R.A. and had tried, unsuccessfully, to persuade them to give it up. 'They turned up again about six weeks afterwards & seemed to have had a very good time in prison. We never asked them a word about it, nor did they tell us anything about it.'[5]

In August 1923, Jack and Cottie went to Coole. Willie was busy at the reconstruction of Thoor Ballylee, his 'Tower' nearby, and George with the children, Anne and Michael, had been to stay. On 6 August Lady Gregory wrote in her journal:

> Jack Yeats and his wife have been here a week. Hearing he was a Republican I have been trying to get at his point of view, which seems not far from my own, though he would not reason at first, said 'I want a Republic because I would like it' . . . I said the Republic will come when the Colonies demand that for themselves. But he doesn't think 'that is the right way for it to come'. But he would not fight for one and thinks the Government have done and worked well, but that the initial fault was accepting the Treaty.[6]

Though it took a further six months for the Civil War violence finally to be brought to a conclusion, the executions were widely considered to have hastened the end. The last of the military executions took place in June 1923. In September Lady Gregory was in Dublin, and visited Jack, who showed her his painting *The Funeral of Harry Boland* and also *The Wave*. 'Jack thinks the men responsible for the executions cannot stay in the Government or even in the country. But I told him how there had been as great a bitterness between the North and South in U.S.A., and they had come together. W.B.Y. says the leaders in gaol all mean to fight again if they get out.'[7]

There was an echo of the political division in the arts, though it is not related to party loyalties. Much of the debate continued to centre on modernism, and Jack came down on the side of the modern movement in art, though he did so in a conciliatory way. Effectively, he established a position which straddled modernism and academicism; he was determined to maintain his position as a member of the Royal Hibernian Academy while at the same time being a member of what was probably the longest lasting of the forums for modern art in Ireland in the first half of the twentieth century, the Society of Dublin Painters. He was a founder member, and one of the three signatories – with Clare Marsh and Paul Henry – to the original lease. He exhibited with the society from its opening show, in August 1920 and had three consecutive solo exhibitions there from 1921–3. One of the paintings shown in the second of his solo exhibitions was *Bachelor's Walk: In Memory*.

The small group of artists who dominated the exhibitions of the society during the first ten years or so, included much of the best and original in painting talent in Ireland.

> From the beginning the Society of Dublin Painters became synonymous with the best of avant-garde painting in Ireland and until the early 1940s, when the Irish Exhibition of Living Art was established, its members were at the forefront of developments in Irish art. The Society espoused no collective aesthetic, but rather sought to foster a spirit of broad-mindedness and sympathetic understanding in young artists of promise.[8]

Brian Kennedy stresses Jack's modernism, challenging Thomas MacGreevy's broad claim that Jack was the champion of nationalism in art, and not concerned with modernism. Paul Henry was the moving spirit behind the foundation of the society, with his wife, Grace.[9] Jack was able to joke about the Dublin Painters. Years later he recalled that 'some woman wanted to call us the Gween Gwoup.'[10] But he was happy to be a member. 'I wanted to have an exhibition every year. It was a cheap way of getting a gallery. There were no galleries in Dublin before that time.'

Within modernism itself there were problems, and a major controversy erupted when Mainie Jellett, in 1923, exhibited her first abstract paintings. Some painters at the time placed a strong emphasis on art representative of national identity. A further dimension was given by the founding, later in the 1920s, of the Academy of Christian Art, which was the creation of George Noble, Count Plunkett, who had been Minister of Fine Arts in the First Dail. This institution was *exclusively* for Roman Catholics, much of its members' energies directed towards church design and decoration. At that time Jack himself was going through a transition in his thinking. Returning some photographs to Bodkin which had been sent back from *The Studio*, he refers to the progress in his work which they demonstrate: 'A little change from the works of the star student of the provinces with his little bosom torn between his provincial shame and his ancient South Kensington inhibitions'.[11]

Oskar Kokoschka became an influence on Jack probably from this time, and not just in his art, but in his approach to life (fig. 176). Such influences are generally eschewed, almost as though their presence might represent a contamination of Jack's purity of inspiration; and in the case of the Austrian painter the later and mutual admiration is emphasised at the expense of the earlier association between the two men, one of them much more famous than the other. Jack may first have met Kokoschka in the early 1920s, in Dresden.[12] This meeting, if it happened, could have taken place in the early part of 1922, after the Race Congress in Paris. The two men differed fundamentally in their private lives, the tempestuous nature of Kokoschka's bohemianism, his love affair with Alma Mahler, and his vigorous involvement at the centre of an artistic group, contrasting sharply with Jack's gentle, even placid marriage and his creative isolation. But the two men shared many characteristics. They were both writers as well as painters. They both came from an 'arts movement' background, in Kokoschka's case Jugendstil and Secession, in Jack's the 1890s Elkin Mathews tradition of fine printing, decorated and illustrated books, and the world of William Morris which was followed by his part in Dun Emer and Cuala. They were both intensely interested in theatre, and both were playwrights. The early drawings of both men were often mannered, and well-suited to reproduction, in Jack's case in illustrations and prints for Cuala, in Kokoschka's to the picture postcards which were produced for sale by the Wiener Werkstätte.

At this time, in the early 1920s, Kokoschka, despite being much younger than Jack, had travelled further in both emotional and creative experience. He had fought in the First World War, and had been seriously wounded. He had exhibited in Berlin and Dresden, and was a leading figure in the Dresden circle of Hasenclever, Lücken and Neuberger, and had worked on opera with Paul Hindemith. His painting was free, liberated, intensely rich and sensuous, and with a magical release of colour. Werner Haftmann writes' in this period he painted with a spontaneity that expressed his extraordinary visual sensibility. A magnificent series; the landscapes are poems, records of the experience of a wandering poet-painter whose vision is alive with dramatic feeling . . . but it is a psychic eye.'[13] How much Jack saw, and how long he

176. Oskar Kokoschka.

was with the younger man, is not known. But it is at least possible, and at best appealing, to attribute at least some of the feeling of release that can be sensed in Jack's palette and his composition at this time to the impact of the other man. Kokoschka's own words throw further light on the similarities between the two men. At the age of fifty he wrote:

> It took me twenty years to grow up; I have spent thirty trying to keep outside the society which I have observed and painted. My profession, which taught me to trust only in my eyes and what they have seen, has developed in me the instinct of always sensing, at the right time, any danger of the painter being dragged over to his subject's side. My constant subject: society . . . When I was born the national exchequer held only devalued gulden notes. Very early on, therefore, I learned to be independent and to work for my living . . . I was interrupted . . . with my call-up to the World War. But I did not have it in me to shoot down supposed enemies who were personally unknown to me; so I saved some Russians' lives by taking them prisoner, for which I was decorated. I also received a head-wound and a punctured lung. Nevertheless, I did not feel that I had done enough for culture, and I decided to return to my previous vocation. I painted.[14]

Jack both liked and admired Kokoschka, sharing his view of society and of the ambivalent position occupied by the painter. Kokoschka spent his adult life 'trying to keep outside the society which I have observed and painted,' and yet coming to the conclusion that the very thing he avoided was his 'constant subject'. In this, Jack was like his friend.[15] The first Yeats-Kokoschka meeting was followed up by further encounters, before the end of the decade, when Kokoschka visited Ireland, which he did in both 1928 and 1929. He called at the United Arts Club and Harry Kernoff recalls also that Kokoschka, who reputedly had acquired a financial backer, 'travelled in style'. As well as staying in Killarney, where he painted landscapes, he also painted a picture of Dun Laoghaire. He was received hospitably in the bohemian Dublin of the period, made welcome at Jack's club, and was happy to paint in the city and in the west.

Jack was in favour of a regular subscription by the United Arts Club to the German art magazine, *Die Jugend*, and supported a proposal to this effect by Doreen Vanston, a painter member who was a contemporary of his, Post-Impressionist in her style.[16] He was less enthusiastic, artistically speaking, about Paris. In a rare reference to another painter, he said at this time: 'Picasso would be more thrilling to his time and generation if he had jumped straight out of Spain without the use of Paris.'[17] There is evidence of an interest also in the Belgian painter, James Ensor. Jack owned a brief monograph on him, in the series, Les Artistes Nouveau, given him in 1929 by Lady Gregory.[18] Many of his attitudes on art and culture were channelled through his club, which at this time was a powerful and dynamic centre for the promotion of cultural ideas, particularly under the direction of Mrs Duncan. Jack, as we have seen, was a committed member, and served on its general committee between 1923 and 1926. 'He was always ready to support a good Club cause.'[19]

Jack could be both solitary and gregarious. The United Arts Club, as well as being of cultural value, was to Jack a place for light-hearted entertainment, and encounters with people who were not necessarily deeply involved in art.

There were even some of a raffish disposition, whom Jack took to, and in whom he may have seen some of his own wilder characteristics. An obvious example was Tom Casement, Roger Casement's brother, an immensely colourful character whose life revolved around the Arts Club, which he had joined in November 1920. His earlier experiences would have appealed to Jack. He had fought in the Boer War, beach-combed in Africa, and had sailed in his early days on clipper ships to the Antipodes. He was generally hard up, had a prodigious thirst, and he swore terribly. He liked women. He had married, while in Africa – possibly in his respectable days, when he was British Consul in Portuguese East Africa – but his wife had grown bored with his simple attitudes. He courted, in one way or another, most of the women members of the Club. To Mrs Campbell he wrote romantic little notes, repeating, unfortunately, endearments which had been used with other women members.

He appealed to Jack in another context. He had returned to Dublin with a plan for the Irish Coast Life Saving Service, which was in fact adopted by the government, and Tom Casement was appointed its first director. He operated the service from a basement in Fleet Street, with a retired sea captain called Captain Foster as his assistant. The two were 'characters'; so much so that Denis Johnston used the Captain and Tom Casement as 'Captain Potts' and 'George' in his play, *The Moon in the Yellow River*. Both there and in their real lives, the two men could quite easily have stepped from a Jack Yeats painting.

The solitary side of Jack's life, largely self-imposed, and the result of a shyness and diffidence which may be traced back to early childhood experiences, was off-set by his growing self-awareness, some aspects of which are reflected in the modest newspaper fame and attention which came to him from his exhibitions. He also wanted someone to interpret, analyse, explain him. And he found the appropriate acolyte in Thomas MacGreevy. MacGreevy was more than twenty years Jack's junior. He came from Tarbert, in County Kerry, and was a commissioned officer in the Royal Field Artillery in the First World War. He fought in the battle of the Somme, and was twice wounded. He worked for a time in the National Gallery in London and then went to Trinity College in Dublin, where he read history and political science. Jack wrote to MacGreevy as early as 1919 in response to a query about his work. In it he made brief reference to the *Irish Statesman* and to Joseph Hone, already known to the family for his book on Willie to which both Jack and his sisters appear to have contributed.[20] But it was not really until MacGreevy had completed his studies that the friendship between the two men developed.

MacGreevy was instinctively controversial, and had become very much a man-about-town in Dublin. He had gleaned some command of modernism, both in poetry and art, and this was first expressed in a trenchant attack on Dublin critics over their savaging of Mainie Jellett, who was then, and remained for twenty years, the most advanced avant-garde artist in Ireland, and the country's first and easily most important painter of abstract works. MacGreevy's article appeared in October 1923.[21] In the same month MacGreevy and Thomas Bodkin were locked in public combat, in a complicated argument which included – though only marginally at first – Jack's merits as an artist. The row has all the signs of being deliberately manufactured by the younger man. Bodkin was already a highly prominent figure in art generally. He had been central to the campaign for the recovery of the

Lane Pictures, and was also employed as secretary for the Commissioners for Charitable Donations and Bequests. He had written an article in the *Irish Statesman*, in late September, on Nathaniel Hone, containing the injudicious superlative, 'No Irish painter, living or dead, has equalled, much less surpassed, the purely aesthetic quality of his art.'[22] There is a measure of truth in the claim; there is pure magic in Hone's painting, unaffected by the addition of any narrative or genre persuasiveness, and his landscape and seascape masterpieces do occupy a supremely admirable place in Irish art. But the unqualified remark gave MacGreevy an opportunity for which the tone of his letter suggests he had been waiting. 'I venture to write with reference to one statement,' he wrote to the editor, quoting Bodkin's unequivocal claim.

> To let Mr Bodkin's statement pass without comment is, I think, to leave ourselves open to the charge of under-rating the genius of a living Irish painter who, at his finest, leaves Hone where the man of genius leaves the man of talent, where Giorgione leaves Bassano, where Watteau leaves Michel. In drawing, in colour, in design, there has not, I believe, been any Irish painter whose work is as unerringly right, as rich and as delicate as Mr Jack Yeats's. No Hone that I have ever seen could, I think, equal, much less surpass, the aesthetic quality, the impressive design, the massive movement, the fine colour, of Morning After Rain, in the last Jack Yeats exhibition here.[23]

The eulogy continued, unrestrained. Hone was described as dull, slow-blooded, not often impressive, whereas 'there is not a square inch of a good Jack Yeats picture that is not quick with life and beauty'. No foreign artist, MacGreevy claimed, 'has painted at once quite like Jack Yeats and as well', and he threw in for comparison, Bonnard and Breughel. His concluding paragraph has several masterly twists to it, and is worth quoting in full:

> I have no doubt that Mr Bodkin appreciates the qualities of Mr Yeats's work, and I am sure that he will understand the impulse on my part to enter a caveat against his dictum. It is not that I want to argue with him – one cannot argue about such things, it is not that I am so impertinent as to think that Mr Yeats's work needs defence or explanation. Mr Yeats's work will look very capably after itself for many centuries to come. It is merely that I want to testify that I am one of those whose aesthetic faith, so far as Irish artists are concerned, is not Mr Bodkin's.

Bodkin, in his reply, trod carefully on thin ice, but held to his main contention, and in doing so expressed clearly the distinction he had made between Hone and Hone's type of art, and the unique voice of Yeats:

> No one could claim for Mr Yeats that his concern was chiefly for form. A list of the titles of his pictures would be sufficient to show that he is profoundly concerned, in almost everything he paints, to express ideas and opinions, to record emotions and experiences that have nothing whatever to do with the purely aesthetic quality, and may often, indeed, impede its expression. That Mr Yeats does show in his pictures an aesthetic quality of high order should be apparent to everyone. It is, certainly, apparent to me; yet I still feel justified in saying that Hone, as an artist, was pre-eminent in that one respect. This opinion must not mislead Mr McGreevy into

177. *Portrait of Cottie*, oil on canvas, 24 ×
36, private collection. 1926.

suggesting that I asserted Hone's general superiority over Mr Yeats. I am
not given to such sweeping and odious comparisons.[24]

Earlier, in the long letter, he writes of being flattered at MacGreevy sparing
his time 'from rhapsodising on Ronsard and pontificating on Picasso' – a
possible reference to his article on Mainie Jellett quoted above, and an
undoubted reference to MacGreevy's status as a tyro-poet – to correct his own
modest views. And he describes him as 'the self-constituted and super-
sensitive champion of Mr Yeats'.

It is a fair description of what MacGreevy became. Jack undoubtedly
contributed to it, often guiding MacGreevy and exercising a control over
what he said and wrote which would have been inconceivable with other
friends, such as Curran and Bodkin, who were more level-headed. Cottie was
fond of MacGreevy. Perhaps she divined, from the start, how critical a voice
he might well become in defence of her husband's art. When Jack painted his
portrait of Cottie (fig. 177), which was a Christmas present, he wrote:

Mrs Yeats sends you every good wish for Christmas. I have painted her
portrait for a Christmas present to her 24 inch × 36 inches. I have
numbered it 1. and now I think I am prepared to paint ten more portraits
of people who interest me in some way, for a £1,000 a piece so if you know
anyone who is willing to pay that sum and chance being turned down as

unsuitable and the bargain called 'off' by me roll them up. This is neither bluff or impudence. But I would be in misery and would sink beneath the bog if I became a portrait painter. But I am ready to take on that limited number, if I pick them myself the heirs of the 10 would be on velvet.[25]

Cottie added her own note to the letter: 'The portrait of me is wonderful, a wonderful piece of painting, you can imagine how proud I am to have it, my very own! Love + best wishes from Mrs Jack.'

The close friendship with MacGreevy, which much later led to a kind of 'management' of Jack's life and affairs, including his friends, did not at this stage interfere with other friendships. Bodkin, after the controversy – in which, of course, Jack had played no direct part – remained a regular correspondent, and indeed a collector of his work, acquiring in 1919 a drawing, *Die We Must*. This had appeared in one of the *Broadsides* to accompany lines of verse written by 'Wolfe T. MacGowan', Jack's pseudonym. Bodkin wanted to know the identity of the writer, and on two occasions suggested to Jack that it was Masefield. Jack denied this, but was unprepared to divulge more: 'Here are the verses "Die we must" you will see they are signed Wolfe T. McGowan so I cannot say that they were written by Masefield,' he wrote in 1919.[26] When Bodkin raised the matter again, five years later, Jack was still playing his cards close to his chest, though with an amusing hint at the truth: 'I think I may have given you the wrong impression that the verses "Die we Must" were signed by Masefield in the Broadside. All I can say about them is that they were given me as by Wolfe T. McGowan. Someday we may find out the author on the road of Famous Shades – where they are as fond of their sparrows as of their eagles.'[27]

Jack's output expanded substantially in the 1920s. From the personal crisis which he had faced, in his mid-forties, Jack seems to have blossomed into a sprightly, adventurous, talkative, extrovert fifty-year-old, determined to demonstrate his vigour and inventiveness in the years which faced him, and to be part of modern art on his own terms. This lasted unchecked during the productive 1920s, sustained him through the dramatic stylistic changes in the closing years of that decade, but then went wrong. His output as a painter fell quite dramatically in the early 1930s, a fact which may be explained superficially by his activities as a writer. But it may not be as simple as that. It seems that his switch to an entirely different art form – a switch he treated with the utmost seriousness – may in part have derived from a sense of disappointment at the adverse criticism which his developing style as a painter attracted. And there were changes also, in the middle years of this period between the two World Wars, in his public attitude. He became less open and extrovert, more elusive.

He co-operated with James Sullivan Starkey,[28] who, as Seumas O'Sullivan, founded *The Dublin Magazine* in 1923. The leading article in the first number was on Jack, written by Masefield, and the frontispiece was the recently completed portrait of Jack by Estella Solomons, Starkey's wife.[29] She had undertaken the painting in the spring of 1922, and Jack was sitting to her in April of that year (fig. 178).[30] Both she and her husband were republicans, though Starkey was more moderate in his views. The event was an obvious celebration of Ireland's leading painter.

Choosing Masefield to write about Jack was a mistake. Jack had developed quite literally out of recognition since the days of their enthusiastic and

178. *Portrait of Jack Yeats*, Estella Solomons, Sligo County Museum and Art Gallery. 1922.

childlike friendship, sailing model boats along Gara's rushing stream. Jack told Starkey: 'I am sure Masefield would write something though I have not seen him for years. Why do you not write about my pictures yourself.'[31] Masefield himself responded to Starkey by saying he was 'proud to write something about Jack Yeats'. It might have been better to have called in MacGreevy, though he was not then experienced or well-known enough as a writer. For a more dispassionate assessment Thomas Bodkin would have been a sensible choice, or even Sickert. Though Masefield struck a truthful note, praising Jack for his 'romantic view of a toiler's life and amusements . . . He delights in whatever delights the heart of his race . . . Nearly all his best paintings commemorate someone vivid who has lived by his hands in a rough world', the article is vitiated by Masefield's evident failure to keep up with Jack's more recent work. He writes, to a large extent, from memory or from second-hand information. He picked one painting, which he thought represented the very essence of Jack's mind.

> It represents a big, flat, floating buoy in Sligo Harbour. On the top of this buoy are three or four intent little boys playing cards or knuckle bones, or some similar game. I feel sure that in his mind, Mr Yeats is usually out there upon the buoy playing knuckle bones in Sligo Harbour, and when his mind comes ashore, its joy is to talk with those old pilots who filled his boyhood with romance . . . Perhaps all that any artist ever does is to make significant in after life things that were delightful in childhood. Mr Yeats is always making significant the delights of his days at Rosses Point.

The article was illustrated with prints supplied by Jack. He was later to acquire some notoriety for his strict views on the use of reproductions of his paintings:

> I have got '*The Bog Road*' from the photographer and I send it to you with *The Cake Cart, Approaching Rosses Point Early Morning* and 'The *Bather*' all of which should produce all right I also send *Croke Park Dublin Singing my dark Rosaleen* But I do not think a satisfactory black could be made of it. Perhaps you could ask the block maker.[32]

Approaching Rosses Point, Early Morning is a seascape with figures in a rowing boat, and *The Bog Road* depicts two men 'at turf'. In the Croke Park painting three men are lined up to sing this disguised rebel song, making the painting vaguely 'political', and in *The Cake Cart*, dating from 1918, and showing a woman at a racecourse selling food, the subject, though it fits in with the concept of amusement, is treated in solemn terms.

The *Dublin Magazine* article pleased Jack, and Starkey sent him the September issue as well. Jack responded by inviting the poet to call on him, but he did not subscribe to the magazine. It was a useful contact, however, and when Jack's books began to appear, *The Dublin Magazine* received them well, and used extracts from some of them.

In January 1924, following Jack's solo exhibition at the Gieves Art Gallery of Paintings of Irish Life, Sickert wrote:

> Forgive me for saying that I think your exhibition superb. It fulfils my theory that there can be modern painting. Life above everything The movement of the figures true & felt & the landscapes, water, sky, houses ruffling like flags in support of them. I cannot find adequate words. I must

226

speak about them at a lecture I am giving at the Royal Institution 21 Albemarle Street on Thursday at 5.[33]

Jack's reception remained uneven. He entered *The Liffey Swim* as a sporting work in a competition held in association with the VIIIe Olympiade in Paris, in 1924, and won the silver medal (fig. 179). Much admired at the time, the work was subsequently put into the Royal Hibernian Academy in 1925, and shown in London and Liverpool the following year. The swim took place each year between Guinness's Brewery and Butt Bridge, and was a popular event, with the quayside all the way along the river, north and south, crowded with spectators. *The Liffey Swim* was noted as a departure away from 'Connacht's tinkers, ballad singers, wild-looking horses and asses'.[34] It was also praised for its 'tremendous vigour': 'The Dickensian touch of exaggeration makes Mr Yeats's pictures exhilarating. If you had one in your room you would never wish you were dead; you'd look at it and give life another chance.'[35] There was a rumour that an attempt was made to steal the painting, and there were references to it as the only truly 'Irish' picture in the annual summer exhibition. There is a cutting referring to 'the prize-winners in the Olympic Art Competition – including Mr. Jack B. Yeats, the Irish artist – will receive their awards at the same time as the athletes'.[36]

Jack exhibited in New York and Rome in 1924, in Pittsburgh in 1925, in New York, London and Liverpool in 1926, and in Liverpool again in 1927, all in group shows, and he held two solo exhibitions a year in 1924, 1925, 1927 and 1929, and single solo shows in the intervening years. It was an astonishing level of work, and it earned him much praise. But it also met with notices of uncompromising condemnation. This was particularly so with his London show at the Gieves Gallery in Bond Street in January 1924, which included *Approaching Rosses Point*, *Early Morning*, *A Ballad Singer*, and two paintings of market-day subjects, *Market Day, Mayo* and *Market Day, Evening*.

Jack went to London for long enough to see 'every picture exhibition now on show in London', as he told a *Freeman's Journal* columnist on his return, early in 1924. He had last shown in the city in 1919, and before that in 1914, so the event provoked references to changes in his style, and uncertainties with his medium. And repeatedly the point is made that the artist's vision is his strength, not wholly supported by his competence in colour or composition. 'The glamour Mr Yeats casts over life is poetic, a glamour of the spirit. His painting is now and then so crude as to border on amateurishness. Whilst his compositions are generally pleasing, his brush-work is shallow and flat and careless. His colour, too, is dirty and depressing, or impossibly theatrical.'[37]

The writer singled out *Approaching Rosses Point, Early Morning*, which had been illustrated in *The Dublin Magazine*, as the best picture, and then in conclusion reverted to the central theme of his review:

> I enjoyed this exhibition in other senses than artistic. It gave me back no very small part of my youth, when all eyes were turned on Ireland in search of great creative figures. The family to which Mr Yeats has the honour to belong played a noble part in the emancipation of that country, and these pictures gave me the pleasure of an intimate diary of one to whom I was joined in youth by spiritual kinship.

And in the *Evening Standard* another reviewer wrote: 'I like Mr Yeats best when he is thinking about Ireland rather than about paint', while in the

179. *The Liffey Swim*, oil on canvas, 24 ×
36, National Gallery of Ireland. 1923.

Illustrated Sunday Herald he was compared unfavourably with Augustus John,
whose 'formidable technical mastery' is set against the fact that Jack 'is far less
happy with oils than with the simple medium of pen and ink'.[38] And in a
notice of the London exhibition in *The Irish News*, the message appeared in yet
another form:

> His merit lies in the freshness of his vision, and the spontaneity of his
> statement, which disdains all conventional devices of picture-making. He
> does not search for the picturesque, and does not trouble with composition.
> That his pictures have the balanced distribution of masses which make
> for good design is probably due to instinct rather than to deliberate
> planning . . . Mr Yeats allows nature to compose his pictures.[39]

Other works which understandably attracted attention at this time included
*The Breaker Out, Sligo Bay – Early Morning, O'Connell Bridge, Girls and Boys, In
Galway Town*, all shown in the 1925 solo exhibition in Dublin, all mentioned
in George Russell's extended and important critical survey.[40] In it he dealt with
a central problem in Jack's art, the seemingly simple yet fundamental question
– does it come off? As an artist dealing, as so often he claimed, with the
remembered moment, there is a point of failure or success where all the colour,
all the structure and composition, all the feeling and passion are of no avail if
the final result fails. Even judging that, which Russell attempts, is fraught with
difficulty. What one is addressing is personal and subjective, even if, through
the medium of public criticism or debate, the view can be tested. George
Russell, by now one of Jack's most experienced colleagues among Irish artists,
and a sympathetic and experienced critic over more than twenty years,
addressed this point in detail, and posed for himself the central question:

> I confess I wonder how in some of these impressionist paintings, in spite of
> a looseness of touch, a lack of precision in the form or feature, a precise
> emotion is created in the onlooker. It may be that he paints more for the
> imagination than to the eye. They will not bear close inspection by the eye,
> but they bear a concentration of attention by the mind. We ask ourselves

what is it is significant in these impressions, and we cannot often answer, no matter how deeply we are moved. We look at a crowd and ninety-nine times out of a hundred it is opaque to us. We feel nothing about it, but in some rare moment, we do not know why, the crowd becomes significant, symbolic in some obscure way, and we are thrilled by a sudden affinity between the seer and the thing seen. Now Jack Yeats almost always starts a picture because he has such moments and can convey to us his own emotion. Not always.[41]

Russell described *A Glass of Port* as a work which was meaningless to him. And he contrasted it with *The Breaker Out* which made him feel 'a vivid emotion'. And he went on to suggest that Jack faced a real problem in the matter of scale, and was at his best in the smaller paintings. 'In the larger canvases he does not increase intensity with increased size. Indeed they tend to become a little painty and empty. We demand more knowledge than Jack can give us in the larger paintings.'[42] The brief critical essay stands as clear and correct today as it did then, and may be widely applied to the problems presented by the overall oeuvre, and by the more specific issue of success in the smaller works, and the problem of emptiness or diffusion of effort in some of the larger canvases.

A number of important issues about Jack's art are raised centrally by Russell and more marginally by other critics writing at the time. And there is no reason to suppose that Jack did not accept there was uncertainty in his accomplishment, and unevenness of performance; the vision was certainly there, but its realisation was flawed, either by technical limitation or simply by bad painting. Waves of sentimental adulation built up over half a century, and unchastened by objective judgment, have distorted the contemporary reality, which was of a lively and varied critical reaction which was often quite severe, and quite sensibly so.

It became much more severe in the late 1920s with the dramatic changes in his palette, and in the freedom with which he applied paint to the canvas. He liberated himself, in terms of colour. He applied paint more freely and more generously. It became a prodigal expenditure, the heavy impasto, the slapping on of bright layers of colour, the literal use of the third dimension – that of physical, measurable depth. His vision remained consistent. What we can talk of is the actual application of paint. This changed dramatically in the second half of the 1920s, and changed again later, and indeed went on changing and adapting, even if the 1920s change represents a more signifi-cant watershed than later ones. And he paid a price for his revolutionary development.

His use of colour became more adventurous, its application at times reckless, particularly the primaries. Blue, yellow, red, together with a strong mid-green, inspire him to the laying on of whiplashes of paint, squeezed in abundance directly from the tube and then vigorously attacked at points with the palette-knife.[43] Even so, subject-matter remains the motivating force; it is the mood of the event which the artist is capturing, and not a response to materials, much as he took delight in the volume of paint and the creation of its final texture and shape on the canvas. Style, as it might have been defined in colour combinations by an artist with a more conventional or academic training, meant little or nothing to Jack. He would have seen such an approach as a form of artistic prison to which he was being sentenced for the crime of not having followed through the terms of his own artistic apprenticeship. From the very beginning he recognised that he was working from a standpoint of relative ignorance in the use of oil paints; it was intentional, and he never sought to rectify it. And his mature view was governed by this fact. He was perpetually at odds, both with convention, and with the normal and natural development of the technically sophisticated painters whose works crowded the walls of so many galleries in which Jack, from time to time, hung his own works.

There is disagreement about the dating of these changes. Terence de Vere White is more emphatic than most. 'His breakaway from conventional painting took place in 1927. For more than ten years he suffered almost complete neglect.'[44] Earlier in the same passage White suggests:

> Yeats had arrived in the Academy in a Trojan horse: he was elected for his west of Ireland scenes in water colour in the manner of a gifted illustrator: when he had graduated in oils, his pictures, in the main, retained their illustrative character. Then, quite suddenly, when over fifty years of age, he began to paint in an expressionistic style in which the drawing was implicit, so that he might have freedom to express through colour, rather than form, his vision and his dreams. The only thing that is modern in Yeats's painting is the licence he takes to depart from conventional representation. The whole tendency of modernism is to escape from literary values. In Yeats's painting an idea – tragic, fantastic, poetic, nostalgic – is always at the core of his painting.[45]

This consideration of medium, line and colour together is also at the heart of another perceptive friend's view, that of Earnan O'Malley:

> It was, I think, a lucky chance when he found a number of his early watercolours destroyed by damp. This accident made him think more in terms of oil and he began to experiment. Then continued a long period in which definition became gradually more colourful and his essential bent, that of a colourist, more emphatic. By the year 1921 he had reached the limits of his expression in this manner . . . Jack Yeats found his world in a greater feeling for the emotional use of paint, as it were, escaped its mould to become an end in itself. It is hard to explain a change in direction, but one of the factors may have been the heightened sensibility which could result from the tension of life during the struggle for freedom in Ireland . . . His work no longer dealt with a perception of countrymen in relaxation or at ease in a folk-lore tradition. His figures now enter a subjective world in which they are related to the loneliness of the individual soul, the vague lack of pattern in living with its sense of inherent tragedy, brooding nostalgia, associated with time as well as variation on the freer moments as of old.[46]

When John Rothenstein, director of the Tate Gallery, met Yeats he asked him:

> Why it was that the artist's vision developed all but invariably in the direction of increased generalisation and his handling of paint in that of breadth. 'I believe,' he replied, 'that the painter always begins by expressing himself by line – that is, by the most obvious means; then he becomes aware that line, once so necessary, is in fact hemming him in, and as soon as he feels strong enough he breaks out of its confines.'[47]

Rothenstein, with less authority, dates the change differently:

About the year 1922 Jack Yeats himself, like a rocket emitting a shower of multi-coloured sparks, burst suddenly out of the linear system which had served so well the racy, touching narrative painting of his early and middle years. This change was accompanied, or more probably occasioned by a change in the focus of his poetic vision. The characteristic subjects of the earlier years are lucidly defined, such, for example, as the beautiful incident of the girl throwing a flower into a doorway where a man has been shot. The later subjects are less specific, less firmly fixed in time and space, and they are suffused by a poetry which is not the less passionate on account of its abstraction.

Jack had to contend with a critical approach which included the following: 'Last year, when he adopted a new style, his admirers and critics were doubtful that he was going to improve by the modern sweep of his brush. This year they were able to understand him better.'[48] More seriously, he did receive constant attention, and it did deal with the practicalities of applying paint, with what one critic sensibly described as 'executive restraint', equally sensibly calling for more of it.[49] And this was before the new riot of colour in the mid-1920s. The show which immediately followed the London exhibition, and was held in Dublin at the Engineers' Hall, provoked a *Freeman's Journal* critic to write of 'three stages' in Jack's art, and of developments and expansion. This was for a show in which *A Riverside (Long Ago)* was the dominant work and Jack chose to be photographed in front of it at the opening (fig. 180). It is a romantic work, set at evening time, and showing two lovers about to embark for a trip on the lake as the boat-owner prepares his craft. 'The old man, in whose boat generations of lovers have spent evenings on the lake, eyes his latest clients as they stand together on the landing-stage, with sympathetic and friendly critical interest.' The work is pervaded by tristesse, and in this it resembles Watteau, with its sense of fleeting happiness within the irrecoverable moment.

He bewildered art critics, and the more established they were, the more they needed to reach for an artistic thesaurus. Clive Bell is a case of the critic trying to find a category in which to put his subject, and failing lamentably with Jack. Reviewing his first show at Arthur Tooth's Gallery, in 1925, he wrote:

Mr Yeats belongs to a school which, so far as I know, possesses no name, unless it be 'the school of 1899'. About that date appeared several gifted painters who, emerging from impressionism, did not come directly under the influence of Cézanne or Seurat . . . and the Tate ought certainly to possess one of them. The Free State, I understand, takes a proper pride in its artists; may a mere Sassenach presume to draw its attention to two living Irish painters whose work is far above the ordinary, Mr Jack Yeats and Mr Roderic O'Conor.[50]

The Tate Gallery had been considering the acquisition of a work by Jack Yeats, and might have been influenced by Clive Bell, though so timely is his remark, made in April 1925, that it is equally possible Bell had an inkling, when he wrote, that the purchase had already been made. Whichever it was, the Tate Gallery bought the delightful oil, *Back from the Races*, at the Arthur Tooth Gallery exhibition, and the director, Charles Aitken, made a request

180 *A Riverside (Long Ago)*, oil on canvas, 24 × 36, Ulster Museum, Belfast. 1922.

which sparked off an exchange with Jack which was, and still remains, of considerable importance.

> Mr Tooth tells me you were enquiring if I would transfer the copyright of my little picture 'Back from the Races' to the Trustees of the National Gallery. What do you usually do in such a case. Do the trustees pay the artist for the copyright. Or does the artist just transfer it to them. What use would the trustees be likely to make of the copyright. I am not a great believer in broadcasted reproductions of pictures. I know it spreads a diluted pleasure in pictures. But I think when anyone sells a picture they should rest on the memory of it. If they buy a little photograph of the picture as they go out, that little photograph stands between them and the picture.[51]

Aitken replied immediately:

> In the past we have practically had no funds to buy living artists' work. The Chantry Fund bought chiefly popular subject pictures where the copyright had a considerable money value, though I fancy this is less so now. At Muirhead Bone's suggestion we are now trying to acquire the copyright where we buy, in fact we shall I think make it a condition of purchase shortly. It is of no great money value in most cases, but in a national gallery the public should have the right to official reproductions and to copy if it wishes. It saves a great deal of trouble and correspondence though most artists at present consent to allow reproduction in all our official publications and to let students copy. I do not think that in the case of your little picture the copyright has much market value, but I thought I might as well begin the new plan as we were buying it. The Liverpool Gallery appears to do so. Students require records of pictures, even if such reproductions have no great aesthetic value.

Jack wrote back on 5 May, giving Aitken 'permission', but not assigning the copyright: 'Thank you for your clear letter of April 30th and I agree to let the gallery have the right to reproduce the picture in their official publications and for them to allow students to copy.' Aitken assumed the assignment of copyright in this:

> I am obliged to you for your letter which I take it I may regard as an assignment of copyright in 'Back from the Races'. I do not think there is any money value in this particular copyright but it is a convenience to us to have it and I think artists might regard the honour of being purchased for a National Collection as a sufficient return, even if there were some money value. I told my trustees yesterday of your kind consent to my proposal and they wished me to express their thanks.

The director had assumed too much. On 9 May Jack wrote:

> In reply to your letter of May 7th No I do not assign the copyright of 'Back to the Races' to the National Gallery. I agree to let the gallery have the right to reproduce it in their official publications and for the gallery to allow students to copy. I am not thinking about money and I will agree to reproduce the picture myself, or allow anyone else to, without the consent of the National Gallery. Galleries do not honour painters just as painters do not honour what they paint. They acknowledge.

181. *Before the Start*, oil on canvas, 18 × 24, National Gallery of Ireland. 1915.

This uncompromising and unequivocal reservation of copyright, which had been adopted by Jack from the time of his earliest exhibitions, when his catalogue had always asserted the fact, had been learnt in the hard market place of his many early drawings done for publication. And it may be assumed that he retained this same view from then on. There is no correspondence in which he *does* assign copyright, and he remained cautious in the extreme about the reproduction of his work. He accepted the need for it in articles about him, but he was against anything which encouraged either commercial exploitation, or the unthinking substitution of a postcard for the real thing, erecting that barrier which stands between viewer and picture.

However, with regard to this 'diluted pleasure', in one area he had, of course, done precisely this, and on a substantial scale. This was in respect of his sisters and Cuala. Here he had assigned copyright, and he regretted it, and wished he could reverse it. In a letter to Willie, later in the same year as the Aitken correspondence, he wrote:

> I know you are doing a great deal for Lilly and Lolly and it is very good of you. But I can do no more. The last two or three drawings for prints I have given them against my will. These reproductions are a drag, and a loss to me in my reputation . . . If I had the ready money I would try and buy up the copyrights of all the prints of mine which Cuala publishes. It is not any question of personal dignity . . . You say that my painting is now 'great'. Great is a word that may mean so many different things. But I know I am the first living painter in the world. And the second is so far away that I am only able to make him out faintly. I have no modesty. I have the immodesty of the spear head.[52]

This is a rare moment of truth between the two brothers, and represents a powerful claim and an impressive expression of self-confidence. It is almost necessary to remind ourselves of the disparity in age and fame between the two brothers which Jack attempts to scale. It is as if he sets aside Willie's statement about Jack's greatness, substituting for it an entirely appropriate personal claim that he was 'the first living painter in the world'. It is as though his confidence, shaken during the 'middle years' of his early fifties, is now massively restored, never again to be disturbed.

He wrote also at this time to Lolly, terminating the arrangements which had been made for reproduction of illustrations from *A Broadside* as new Cuala prints. One of these was *The Hurley Player*, which means that the transfer of black and white illustrations published in one form during the period 1908–1915 were being reprinted from the blocks ten years later as hand-coloured prints for regular and widespread sale. Jack, as revealed in his letter to Willie, was conscious of the cheapening of his reputation for which this steady distribution of prints was responsible. His early care for the correctness and density of the hand-colouring could not be sustained. Nor was it; the differences to be found, even in early and late examples of work in the period between the wars, is marked. The mechanical printing process, for coloured images was not satisfactory for Jack.

Jack's fierce pride in his work, his aggressive sense of 'ownership' of what he did, the actual physical 'life' of each painting, was growing and developing. He wrote at the time:

> I understand all you say about mens early work But the picture is different

from all the arts. I have never yet stood up free and I object to carrying anything on my back even the incompletely embalmed shell of my youth. I agree nothing can be appraised by a footrule except a footrule and as far as I am concerned I am ready to recognise the wisdom of youth . . . Right painting is no translation . . . I have been running with my head loose for two or three years now and my work is as I wish it to be. I do not do any illustrations now and I have only a mild piano interest in the illustrations I have done in the past.[53]

It is not recorded if Jack ever put to James Joyce the interesting theory about literature, that it was 'translation', but there did develop at this time an association between the two men, and Joyce bought two paintings from the solo exhibition which Jack held at the Alpine Club, in London, in 1929. First evidence of the artist having a view on the writer comes from Lady Gregory, who records in August 1925 when Jack and Cottie were visiting her,

> Jack thinks Joyce a bigger man than Synge, though he thinks Synge 'had a great deal to let off' and might perhaps have done finer things had he lived. I think he had done his best. Deirdre has less of power than the rest. He thinks some parts of Joyce very fine indeed, though some revolting . . . Dublin he thinks was what absorbed him, his enemy, his obsession. I told him of his bitterness at not having been recognised earlier as one of the big writers here. He thinks that is because of copies of *Dubliners* having been collected and burned (which I had not heard of) but I think it was earlier than that . . . Jack says the over use of the National spirit, the insincere use of catchwords is like the turning of 'Beauty to Prostitution'.

Jack may have felt a bit restricted by the way in which his art was so regularly compared with Synge's, which in the conventional sense was 'dated', if by nothing more than the fact of Synge's death, in 1909. Reviewers repeatedly attempted to 'explain' Jack's individuality by reference to Synge, as happened in a 1920 review of the Royal Hibernian Academy in which Jack showed *Market Day, Mayo* and *The Dark Man*:

> Mr Yeats is as original and as unmistakably Irish as Synge . . . For all his preoccupation with primitive life, Synge was sophisticated in his artistic delight in the selection of language and situation. The charm of Mr Jack Yeats lies largely in the unaffected naiveté of his scenes. His countryfolk are superb as they stand before us invested with the boyish glamour of their associations.[54]

Sean O'Casey came to stay at Coole while Jack and Cottie were still there (fig. 182). He had just finished *The Plough and the Stars*, and Lennox Robinson and Willie had indicated their liking for it. Lady Gregory herself read and liked the first act, and then read it to the evening gathering of Jack, Cottie and its author, 'and they liked it, a fine opening, but tragic'. Lady Gregory noted setbacks and difficulties for herself, including the 'tepid reception' given by Jack, Cottie and Sean O'Casey to her play, *Dave*, when she read it out, and her growing deafness – 'I lose a good deal of talk when not addressed to me'. She nevertheless records, 'Jack and his wife enjoyed their visit and seemed happy all through . . . and I am glad Coole still gives so much pleasure.'[55]

Jack's enthusiasm for Joyce was reciprocated (fig. 183). Joyce said of the painter, 'Jack Yeats and I have the same method'.[56] The works which Joyce

182. Sean O'Casey.

183. *James Joyce* by Wyndham Lewis, pencil drawing, National Gallery of Ireland. 1926.

bought were two oil paintings, *Porter Boats*, and *Salmon Leap, Leixlip*,[57] and are directly related, in subject-matter, to what he was writing at the time, his last long work of fiction, *Finnegans Wake*, which has for its central theme the River Liffey, 'Anna Livia Plurabelle'. As one would expect, their remarks about each other, and about each other's work, are epigrammatic and brief. They shared a common dislike of literary and artistic conversations. Jack liked to listen, Joyce liked to talk of other things – music, people, money and sex – but not about art. One art critic who visited him and commented at length on the merits of one of the Jack Yeats paintings, was cut short by Joyce who told him, 'There are great silences in that picture, Mr. M—.'[58]

Joyce and Jack did not correspond directly. Communication, such as it was, went through MacGreevy, who, after a time with Lennox Robinson, obtained an appointment in 1926 at the Sorbonne as English Reader and made contact there with James Joyce, an association which lasted until the writer's death. By the end of the 1920s Joyce was sending to Jack, through their intermediary, extracts from 'Work in Progress', which was to become *Finnegans Wake*:

> The extract from Anna Livia Plurabelle has just come please thank Joyce for having it made for me. It is lovely and wonderful and it makes me proud and happy to see the resemblances between this writing and my painting especially my later painting and most particularly in that sentence beginning 'By that Vale Vourclose's? Lucydlae' There is a reason I am sure why they should be alike. But I get headaches from reasons I get new ones for everything everyday and they all fit perfectly where I want them too I think Reasons are very little use down here on the sod. But up aloft, just after St Peter shuts the gate gently on us, with us within, we will be as happy as lambs throwing little round reasons from hand to hand until they roll over the side and flop down into Hell and I thank you for your notes.[59]

MacGreevy saw Joyce regularly, and Joyce got him additional literary work on the avant-garde magazine, *Formes*. The British Institute was less forthcoming. This was all reported to Jack, who advised him: 'If you think it will bother you to be like the new-old model steamboats which go where the lilt takes them with steam produced from solid white spirit in their centres and crying "woof poof" all the way round, But if you look forward to being in your oneness then it is good.'[60] Jack also directed MacGreevy towards America, telling him, if he could not achieve publication in the English art magazine, *Apollo*, he should consider transatlantic avenues for his work. The man blocking MacGreevy seems to have been the art critic, D.S. McColl, and Jack described him as 'one of those unfortunates who engage themselves to lower the temperatures and clog the speeds and cry loudly from Pay Day to Pay Day'.

Their correspondence relates to Joyce in other details, among them the confirmation by Jack that his 'porterboats' were the Guinness barges which brough the drink down the Liffey to have it loaded onto the cross-channel steamers for shipment to England. Joyce responded to the information by sending 'the porter-barge passage' from Finnegans Wake,' and Jack wrote to MacGreevy, 'and tell him . . . I am very pleased he likes the second picture and that it looks well where it hangs'.[61]

The Alpine Gallery show, in 1929, took place in what was, for Jack, 'the biggest Gallery I have had for myself in London. So I will have room to hang my pictures not "high' but "wide and handsome".[62] George Bernard Shaw, with his wife, was among guests at the opening, Mrs Shaw taking back entirely the view she had expressed the year before, at the Arthur Tooth Gallery exhibition, that Jack had 'gone mad'. Jack wrote: 'This year she said she had made a complete mistake and retracted. So one day Bernard Shaw came with his namesake Aircraftsman Shaw. Both thrilled with the pictures, but in themselves they both seemed to me a little *piano*.'[63] Jack was debonair and happy at the triumph this show represented over past adversity, and one newspaper columnist noticed him 'swinging down Bond Street . . . with a peculiar rhythm of his own' and with a carnation in the buttonhole of his 'rough tweed suit'. Another columnist referred to his carnation and the 'Irish metal ring' on his finger. Willie's wife, George, wrote enthusiastically about the decision of the Contemporary Art Society to buy a painting for £100, and then added: 'He is in great form and not bitter. Don't tell anyone I said so, but he does blossom in the London atmosphere. I had an extraordinarily enjoyable lunch with him yesterday. It is one up against the Pursers that London is buying his later pictures.'[64]

An inner confidence was increasingly immunising Jack from the kind of reviews which expressed regret over the passing of precisely the kind of work which he had been trying to shake off for years. Those who remember Mr. Jack B. Yeats' jolly pictures of Irish and pirate life will be disappointed with his exhibition at Messrs. Tooth's.'[65] And he bore now with equanimity the association of his painting with his brother's poetry. 'J.B.Yeats Paints What His Famous Brother Writes Of' was the heading over a piece in which the critic wrote of 'pictures of shadowy figures crossing a rolling country' . . . 'I can't say I actually saw them' he confessed to the *Daily Sketch* yesterday. 'but I felt they were there, or else I shouldn't have painted them. The sky is more like a lantern in Ireland.' he said. 'Being an ocean island, the clouds are thin, and the light filters through softly, with perpetual change, in a way you can never forget.'[66]

It was not the Alpine Gallery exhibition, but the solo show in Dublin, later that year, which attracted one of those cosy, friendly, fireside chat interviews which Jack appears, from the content, to have handled with his characteristic patience and charm: 'I like to be a human being first and a painter afterwards':

> In any case, the people I like to paint become very self-conscious if they know they are being sketched. So I have either to sketch them furtively or carry their faces in my memory until I get home. You see, the faces immediately lose life if the people know they are on show. I like to get about in the crowd and be one of them – see them in their natural humours . . . a painting is not a vehicle for anything at all except itself. It is the memory of a moment. In other words, the eye is coming into its own . . . The first man who breaks fresh ground in an art . . . is very often a genius. He is honest, he is worthy of admiration. And the more shackles he breaks the more healthy it is for the art: it is a sign that it is moving, that it is alive. The innovator frees our eyes and adds considerably to our eye-pleasure. Formerly we had got used to certain combinations of colour; some were 'nice' others were 'nasty'; the nice ones made us feel well, the others made us feel sick. It takes the innovator to teach us that the combinations of colour are infinite.[67]

CHAPTER SIXTEEN

Career as a Writer 1931–1935

I began to jettison my memories . . .

THE JACK YEATS whom the world has now come to admire, is the Jack Yeats of the paintings from the end of the 1920s. The dramatic change which had occurred gave him renewed youth and vitality. It gave him strength, and a new-found independence. James Stephens wrote, in June 1930:

> Here something that seems absolutely incredible has occurred, for Jack Yeats has sloughed his past as a snake sloughs its skin. If ever an artist seemed indissolubly wedded to his own style, and to a peculiarly personal idiom, one would have said that Jack Yeats was such an artist . . . Jack Yeats's painting today does not remind one, even distantly, of any painting that he ever did before; nor does it remind one of any other painting whatever: It is young and fresh and daring and is of a surpassing vitality and virtuosity. It could now be held that, as his brother is our greatest poet, so he is our greatest painter, and that he is an artist of whom not only Ireland, but the whole world, must take note.[1]

He gloried now in paint. Colour was triumphant, line virtually abandoned. It was as if, through the spirited subject of individual pictures, he had embarked, towards the end of the decade of the 1920s, on a new riotous leap forward in self-discovery by way of a new language in paint. It was a riotous language, not always coherent, not always under control. And there were times when he was not completely content with its liberated grammar, much of it of his own making.

His paintings still did not sell at all well. He told Lady Gregory that his solo exhibition in London, in the midsummer of 1930 'had a very fine press, the best I ever had. But business is small.'[2] And however valiant and determined he may have been about what he did, a little thorn of doubt still pricked his flesh. It made him do other and different things, and to become in himself more eclectic, more elusive. But it did not alter his purpose nor check the glorious artistic energy which came to inspire his new works.

Lady Gregory's loyalty to both Jack and Cottie had been a reliable constant in their lives since the beginning of the century. She was a most thoughtful woman, always practical in her generosity. She recorded in her journal at this time: 'The fat little turkey given me by the O'Byrnes looked so tempting that I had it roasted, and sent to Jack and Mrs. Jack Yeats.'[3]

The grand old lady of Gort was failing, however. Still anxiously working for the return of the Lane paintings, still busy with Abbey Theatre affairs, still in constant correspondence with Jack's brother, she records more and more frequently her own fatigue, the effects of the cold, preventing her from sleeping, and her rheumatism. She was stoical; despite temperatures which froze over the lake, she declined to have a fire in her room. The sending of the turkey was in fact her last communication with Jack.

The change in Jack's painting coincided with a move into the centre of Dublin. They were obliged to leave Marlborough Road in 1929. They did not wish this, but the owner of the house wanted to sell, and they only wanted to go on renting. They took a first-floor flat on the corner of Fitzwilliam Square and Fitzwilliam Place, the window of Jack's studio looking north, down the broad street between elegant Georgian terraced houses into Merrion Square (fig. 184). He wrote to MacGreevy: 'We like our new place here. The studio window does not look on the wide ocean but down wide Fitzwilliam Street. Anyway the wide ocean can be worn like the Andeans Poncho by making a round hole in it and putting your head up through it from below.'[4]

He began to develop his career as a writer at the end of the 1920s, and it inevitably took attention away from his painting. His painting output during the 1930s dropped substantially. He held fewer solo exhibitions, though he did spread himself more widely in group shows. He did not date works, but he kept good records of his pictures, and from these his output can be reasonably chronicled. Thus, in the 1920s, he painted thirty-five oils in 1924, fifty-one oils in 1925, seventeen oils in 1926, thirty-six in 1927 and twenty-five oils in each of following three years. He then dropped to just five oils in 1931, thirteen in 1932, one in 1933, four in 1934, eight in 1935, and then thirty-three in 1936. For the rest of the decade his output was in single figures. Given that his life work consisted of more than 1,100 oil paintings, some of these years display distinctly frugal yields.[5]

Painters address the problems connected with their income in different ways. Indeed all artists have profoundly distinct and often eccentric attitudes to money. Orpen, for example, went for sales, in the form of portrait commissions, at the expense of all else in his career, and paid a heavy price for it. Mainie Jellett virtually dismissed the idea of sales, and kept herself alive through a bit of teaching and by living at home. She pursued a rigorous purity of statement, and exploration of abstract theory in painting, which also cost her dear. Sickert painted with rich, full-blooded energy, and met head-on the demands of the English market, which he was able to satisfy, in the process making a fair living out of his art. Kokoschka struggled; so did Ensor.

With Jack, there is more than a hint of parsimony in his overall approach to cash. He was always conscious of, and sensitive about, his own limited financial success. There were several quite deep psychological constraints upon him, beginning with the most obvious and deep-seated one of all: the collective family poverty which had prevailed throughout his childhood. Poverty in early life, once known, is never forgotten. Despite the financial security deriving from marriage, his own early experiences appear to have set up the further constraint of having to earn a respectable share of their needs as a couple. He also attempted this through a variety of non-painting pursuits. Though initially his marriage absolved him from financial obligations to the rest of the family, placing a greater burden on Willie's shoulders for a time, Jack did resume contributions to his sisters, and it is clear that this was a burden he bore without demur.

184. 18 Fitzwilliam Square, Dublin where Jack and Cottie moved to in 1929.

239

He pursued his semi-secret life as a regular *Punch* cartoonist, using the pseudonym, W. Bird.[6] He kept up the work, with its regular income, between the two World Wars. He never referred to it. Lily recognised Jack's hand in the cartoons, and confronted Cottie with the fact of it, making her 'so red and embarrassed she had to tell'.[7] And she told Quinn: 'Everyone now sees through the W. Bird myth, but I have not heard of him yet as having acknowledged it'.[8] On one occasion, through an oversight occasioned by a brief period during which the two Yeats brothers were both living in Fitzwilliam Square, a monthly payment went by mistake to his brother's address, and was opened by Willie. He sent it directly to Jack, with apologies. But Jack was greatly put out. Willie had known of Jack's work for *Punch* since the beginning of regular contributions, in 1910, so it was perhaps the revelation about the amount of money that peeved him. Jack made his annoyance known to the postman.[9] It is revealing that Jack felt the need to keep up such regular work as cartoonist. It bestowed no benefit apart from the modest income for which he had no apparent need. He occasionally made oblique reference to the work; when Bryan Guinness referred to these cartoons, Jack told him: 'I suppose a little bird told you?' He made similar comments to others; increasingly it was an open secret.

In re-embarking on a literary career at the end of the 1920s he was perhaps motivated by the need for an extended, wider platform, and one which might gain him fortune to give material substance to his fame. So he wrote a novel, and called it *Sligo*.[10] He made a joke of the idea of it yielding him a fortune: 'I believe when this book is all sold, and I join those millionaires, that I will be able to promise you not to be a too fastidious one.'[11] At the time, writers who were at all successful made money, in sharp distinction to painters, whose struggles were invariably difficult, to the point that they provided the writers with romantic subject-matter for some of their fiction. Jack, in the light of his limited sales, set practical store by his books, and though he joked about the possible income, at the same time he took very seriously the prospect of real wealth.[12]

Sligo is unlike any other novel. If it belongs in any genre, it is that of the tale, though without the fictional framework to be found in the later books. The 'tale', in literature, has an ancient and definable set of characteristics; it relies on coincidence, deals with journeys and with death, is not realistic but is concerned with marvellous and mythic events. It presents a succession of incidents of equal weight, and is told 'in a flat tone', and 'can only be stopped; it does not end'. 'The teller of the tale doles out incidents, piling them one upon another using the "And then . . . and then" pattern.'[13] In the case of *Sligo*, the 'tale' is more autobiographical, and closer to a memoir. It is constructed as a chronicle and runs towards no climax and this is generally the case in Jack's writing.

His fictional style parallels that of his painting. Event is paramount, but what is less often stressed is the degree of coherence *between* paintings, as if the viewer enters a Jack Yeats territory not unlike the magical world of fable – or the literary tale whose ingredients are outlined above – and then goes on a journey. This could consist of embarkation in a boat, arrival on the shores of an island, a meeting there with a woman singing a song, a climb up a hillside, the appearance of another figure who leads on down towards a shore or a jetty, a fresh journey over water to another land, where a white horse awaits ready to carry the traveller across a landscape where he comes to a circus or a town or a fair or a battle. It does not greatly matter what the sequence is, nor the fabled nature of the experience. The outer world has been cut off from these events, making them into adventures, and investing them with coherence and credibility, while at the same time linking them all together. The interdependence in Jack's art is that of a narrative in which climax has been replaced by sequence, one event after another, each of them inviting us to become involved, and invest whatever is happening with the additional excitement of our interpretations. It is tempting to invoke the idea of the dream; the literary tale is perhaps the closest literature comes to a formal recreation of the dream.

Sligo begins on a hillside in Sligo, overlooking Lough Gill. 'Church Island', is named by the narrator, who recounts an event from a summer regatta on the lake, when the editor of one of the two Sligo weekly newspapers, stepping across from the gunwale of one rowing boat to another, fell into the water. We are swept on again to another vision, of 'long cars with unicorns of three horses', and post-cars which 'rattle the rambling stones of the Mail Coach road, as they come down the hill in the dark with staggering plunges . . . Good Boys, going early to school, crossing the bridge where the brown fresh water flows into the salt.' This is the young Jack Yeats, on the bridge across the Garavogue, in the heart of the town, on his way up the Mall to his first school. This is what Jack elsewhere calls the shedding of ideas. It is also the staining of the reader's mind with the indelible substance of memory. Jack picks on the purpose and place of happiness, imagines the setting sun, over Sligo Bay, wild and tattered, glowing down and glistening. The glow is in the words. They light us into the corners of the house in Sligo turned into a stable for a great stallion which 'fathered a handicap horse which won money for the boys of that town'.[14]

As we know, he loved all things to do with the sea, the spacey eyes of the sons of it, the women who watched men sail off upon its stormy surface, the pilots who guided the ships home again, and especially the old songs sung about it, 'any old song which has the true mournful sweet strain of other days to it. There is something that never dies while grass grows and water runs: and white early mornings mortise themselves into memory while water runs, while tide flows and ebbs.'[15] His narrative suggests a wayward journey, his hand slack in the water, letting slip from its grasp first one idea, then another, to float on or below the surface of his words. The characters, drawn from memory, come and go. The names are transient. He tells good stories. 'At the same time I write this Book because I want a couple of million (pounds) quickly, and as it may be the last book written in the world it should have a very large sale.' Jack explains the book's title. A melodeon player met on a train found out that he was making notes for a book and told him to call it Sligo, the only town in Ireland the traveller was never in.

Despite its rambling format, perhaps *because* of its rambling format, *Sligo* is full of delights and enticements. It pleased its first critics, on the whole, though its author told Lady Gregory: 'One cross critic of *Sligo* said it was a "re-Joycing and not a rejoicing"'.[16] The cross critic was Victor Neuberg, and he had a point. He saw the book as part of the misshapen, pygmy progeny of *Ulysses*, and its author as lacking in discipline and indulging in wanton eccentricity: 'It is impossible to make head or tail of the gist, drift, and significance of the grotesquely realistic study called *Sligo* . . . When Mr. Yeats spells "rejoice" with an "i" he will give us the goods. May it be soon.'[17]

With *Sligo* he embarked, as he approached sixty, on a serious writing career which was to last until the mid-1940s, and which produced in all seven novels and nine plays. As far as the press and public were concerned, his writing was received with polite admiration but with limited understanding. It failed to capture the imagination, and though it provoked attention and speculation about his purpose and intent as a painter, it failed almost completely to enter the realm of popular fiction. Given that he was using a far commoner kind of language than the language of paint, it might be anticipated that the books would be more easily understood than the paintings. But this was not so then, nor has it been later. All his books remain difficult to read or understand, and have a limited following. Readers still admire the first novel more than the rest, as they did in the 1930s. The plays are rarely performed. They are frequently judged to lack dramatic focus, and their casual dialogue means slow dramatic action. The later books present increasingly difficult problems of theme. Niall Montgomery, who was a close friend of the artist, and a regular visitor to his At Homes throughout the 1940s and 1950s, was invited to Canada to take part in an inter-university seminar in Irish studies, and to lecture on Jack's prose and plays. But he replied: 'I couldn't guide anyone towards Mr Yeats's writing because I don't understand it.'[18]

Sligo and the other novels are not any easier to understand than the paintings. Jack is, and remains, 'difficult'. We are prevented, for very obvious reasons, from looking at *Sligo* as though it were a painting. It is equally difficult to view it as a novel. Jack says, 'In it I explained that my reason for writing was to jettison my ideas. And that is, I believe, the true reason for all the books I have written.'[19] But he phrased it slightly differently elsewhere: 'I talked about Tin Can Racing before, in another book, the book where I first began to jettison my memories which were filling up too well cabin and hold.'[20] The idea is appealing, but the concept that memory can be managed in the constructive way outlined by Jack is open to question. His was a fantasy view of the nature of creativity in writing, and he included in it a portmanteau approach to words and ideas which undermines the thrust and drive which books require.

Like Joyce, he disparaged conventional prose: 'This word business is nearly played out unless some new language blossoms to give a few new mouthfuls.' He uses words well. There is a flow and a pattern to the language, a liveliness and colour, with images tendered in profusion, and ideas offered up in rapid succession. This is consistent with his method of composition, about which little is known, though we have a clear view of the composition of a later work, *And to You Also*, for which Jack listed many pages of single-subject ideas, giving them blue ticks as they were incorporated in the book.[21] *Sligo*, even more than the novel which followed it, *Sailing, Sailing Swiftly*, conforms to this approach. Critics recognised the fact: 'It is as though Mr. Yeats had a brainful of memories and flew them in the face of his readers like flags on a gala-day – all shapes and colours, strung up anyhow, flip-flapping gaily in the breeze.'[22]

In the view of John Purser, who has written a distinguished and detailed analysis of the prose works and the plays, Jack

avoids any development of character. This is what makes his narrative so unusual and also what gives it its unity. We are so stuck with the convention that events are only made coherent through the perceptions of a human that we expect always to have the events in a narrative presented to us as part of a person's life history with some clue as to the periods of both the memories and the memorising . . . the events in Sligo shine out more truly on their own account, following one another by verbal associations or by characterstics they hold in common with each other, rather than with the life of the author.[23]

Well and good, for the events, or for the memories, as Purser describes them. But novels need more than unity, particularly if the price paid for it is the absence of character. The adventure of a lively mind is the subject of memoir, or of memory. And we know that memory is crucial to Jack in every painting he painted, every creative concept he had. But part of the essence of fiction is the comprehensive transmutation of memory and the past into a new and living present from which the writer tries to shed identity and the source from which he creates. Even if there is but one character, and that character unnamed, fiction still requires that we identify with him or her, and follow fortune through space or time. This identification, with the things which then befall whoever it is, produce what we call 'action', and without it a novel is not a novel. Instead it becomes something else. There is a valid argument for considering *Sligo* as an autobiography of eccentric genius. Willie understood it in that way, a judgment deserving respect. But if accepted, it makes more difficult the position occupied by the remaining books.

Sligo is winsome, appealing, provocative and memorable. Those who love Jack can hardly fail to enjoy the snippets of life which are delivered in fresh and stimulating language. And it is of particular import to learn them in respect of the man himself, no matter what the guise or action. The privacy of his imagination, more revealing perhaps than the privacy of his ordinary toiler's life, is slipped out in brief opinion or observation. We grapple with the paradox of this man who loved horses.

> I was generally on the ground looking on, and you didn't require your trousers strapped down for that . . . But I seem to have been constantly standing in stables admiring horses with the clothes thrown off their quarters, and listening to wise talk about them . . . or with people who rattled ashplants in hard felt hats to make horses show themselves off.[24]

Willie wrote Jack a friendly letter, praising *Sligo*, and calling it,

> a most amusing, animated work, showing more of the true mind and life of Jack Yeats than Jack Yeats' biography will ever show. It is the best of talk & the best of writing and at the top of a fine fashion. I think of James Joyce's linked associations. 'My new book is about the night & I have had to put language asleep' he said to me a few days ago.[25]

He told his brother he was sending his book to a friend who was the adopted daughter of a cardinal and immensely wealthy. He hoped she would 'talk of it & of you'.

Lady Gregory also loved the book: 'I don't know when I have had such delight in reading a book as in yours. I finished it last night and am about to begin it again.'[26] And Cottie's friend, Elsie Henry, wrote to tell her, 'Sligo is pure Delight! And I shall make several friends happy with it on birthdays and Xmas. Sligo is the first thing I've been able to read, and please tell Mr Yeats that every page was a keen pleasure.'[27] The book also appealed to Sarah Purser, who wrote about missing Jack, and finding the book when she came home, and wanting Jack and Cottie to call for her Tuesday At Home.

> The book is all about races & boxers & ships & oddities – all things along with Dickens I fervently hate. & still I keep on reading it through & up & down with *great* pleasure and admiration – it is so like you & so unlike any other book in the world. It must be a satisfactory thing to be yourself and unlike people on the stage the colour of the light thrown on them. – Some day *soon* I expect to be quite wealthy & able to produce 'crinkling' notes & treat myself to a good picture Cdn't speak of it yesterday before folk. Truly you mustn't go on painting more & more interesting things or I shall never be able to choose. . . . I shall get you to explain the more cryptic passages some day.[28]

Jack sent a copy to his old friend, John Masefield, who had been appointed Poet Laureate in succession to Robert Bridges. Masefield thought W.B. Yeats should have had the post, 'I saw your brother 2 or 3 weeks ago at Rapallo: he is pretty much himself again. I feel that he ought to have had the laurels, and none would have rejoict [sic] more than I had they been given to him.'[29] Though he wrote from Boars Hill, near Oxford, he was on his way to Liverpool, and wanted Jack to come over and attend a boat race on the Mersey. 'I'll hope to see you at the South End of Liverpool Landing Stage at 1 p.m. on Saty. I shall be wearing a blue and red bow tie.' The shy friend of Jack's youth was now a confident and popular poet, perhaps the best-known in Britain, prolific and appealing. Jack did not apparently go over for the race. But Masefield read *Sligo*. 'Many thanks for your jolly book. I took it out & read it through as soon as it came, with the feeling that I was having a long talk with you . . . I had a poem sent to me the other day. In the last stanza, the poet said: "Soar on, blithe dove"' meaning me. I say to Sligo: "soar on, blithe book".'[30]

As a writer, engaged 'at the top of a fine fashion', Jack felt most at home in his exchanges with MacGreevy, and their correspondence during 1930 is rich with literary chat, and a growing intimacy, as well as mutual understanding. During the early part of the year MacGreevy had sent to Jack examples of his own poetry, as well as of Joyce's writings, as they had appeared in *transition*. MacGreevy had sent a copy of the magazine to Lennox Robinson, who had promised to send it on to Jack, but failed to do so until written to. Eventually, Jack was able to express his enthusiasm to his friend:

> It is only now I am able to write to you and say how much delight I got from all your lines in 'Transition' Robinson always forgot to send it on or wanted it a little longer for himself. And I was not able to get a copy in a book shop here. So I wrote to Lennox and got it. Some of your lines shake my mane of course more than others but all are to me like roweling with a plain-ring spur I daresay people are right if they think you would not have written so if Joyce had never written. But the gate does not matter so much if it opens on to the praries roll or perhaps these gates are watergates opening onto the wide ocean. How is Joyce himself?[31]

The poem was heavily influenced by T.S. Eliot, also by Joyce:

> The long poem was begun a year before I left Dublin and finished a little after I left . . . People think probably rightly that its Joyceish but actually I have the illusion that its pictures I'm most influenced by. You are certainly behind Red Hugh as behind even more certainly the enclosed

which I am not sure you ever saw – it's four or five years old – and several others.[32]

He reported that Joyce was asking after Jack, and that Nora had done up her drawing room, rehanging Jack's paintings.

Jack's modernist instincts in literature, as in his painting, were welcome to MacGreevy. In 1926, MacGreevy had published a poem called 'Dysart'. In 1930 it was republished in a New York journal, and MacGreevy chose to 'rechristen' it 'Hommage à Jack Yeats'.[33] Jack was pleased enough; 'I thank you very much for renaming "Dysert" as a "Hommage" to me and I am right glad but my head remains untarred. I get Hommage the way Bread and Porter gets it and a good way too.'[34]

At the time, MacGreevy was himself writing his first book. It was a study of T.S. Eliot's poetry. It had been commissioned by Charles Prentice, an editor at Chatto and Windus responsible for a new series of monographs on writers. Prentice was a friend of Richard Aldington, at that time MacGreevy's closest companion in Paris, and both men did work for Prentice. They even persuaded him to commission a Proust monograph in the series from the much younger Samuel Beckett. MacGreevy wrote telling Jack of his own book, asking him if he knew Eliot's work, and seeking approval to include reference to his painting. 'I know Eliot's poetry,' Jack replied. 'I have a book given me by John Quinn, and I am glad to have you say something about my work in your book.'[35] Jack had almost certainly become acquainted with Eliot's writing while MacGreevy was fighting in France; Quinn had seen to that, and Jack had copies of works by both Eliot and Pound, given him on their publication. He also owned the first published drafts of *Ulysses*, in *The Little Review*, also given to him by Quinn. When the book arrived he expressed his pleasure in a letter to MacGreevy (fig. 185):

I am delighted to have your book. It is full of the most intelligent brilliancy – you have a whole time brain and with it you will be clattering down the dove cotes and making the doves stop cooing and come out and stand up, and take a view and I thank you very much for what you say about my work I think your bright bird is too large for the Eliot cage.[36]

In the event he was right. The book is polemic. It savages numerous English writers, describing Shaw as 'emasculate', and it attacks vigorously such things as the 'passionless, fastidious would-be aristocratic, Nonconformist Liberalism' of the period, and identifies Willie as 'the only great poet writing in English', a curious back-hander in a monograph on T.S. Eliot. The references to Jack come buried within a highly controversial, if somewhat obscure passage where MacGreevy is being deliberately contentious about Ireland and England, and berating Eliot for his dismissal of some of Willie's poetry about fairies as coming from 'the bog'. He then, in parentheses, explains the loveliness of Irish bogs:

There are stretches of bogland – in Ireland at least, I do not know the boglands of Great Britain and France – that seem to me to be as lovely in their own unpretending way as any operatic Italian or grandiose Spanish landscape I ever set eyes on. Mr Jack Yeats, who, in his attitude to his art, is the Cézanne of our time, and not the less so for the fact that his radiant genius is utterly different from that of Cézanne – has more than once achieved the perfect expression of their loveliness in paint.[37]

185. Thomas MacGreevy, *c.* 1950.

245

Digressions and non-sequiturs run through his *Eliot*, but it is MacGreevy's anti-English sentiments which predominate. There is also a great deal about Joyce, who is used as the principal point of comparison – 'Mr Joyce is happy, while Mr Eliot is, so far, only resigned'. MacGreevy was in a position to know more about Joyce's happiness, at that time. Possessively and not without a hint of pride, MacGreevy reported:

> We married Giorgio Joyce the other day. It was good fun and the Registrar took Mrs James and me for the bride and groom! Which pleased J.J. who is very proud of her and she was looking particularly elegant. To celebrate the mistake she and I sang *The Harp of Tara* as a duet at a party afterwards. I spend Xmas evening with them. I hope you and Mrs Yeats will have a happy and a rich Xmas. I think of you often and am now looking forward to seeing you soon. Affectionately always, Tom McGreevy.[38]

Then MacGreevy ventured to introduce another, more obscure writer to his friend:

> My last years colleague and my successor Samuel Beckett is still in Dublin for a little while. He's a nice fellow the nephew of Cissie Sinclair. I told him to introduce himself to you from me if he saw you but I suppose he hasn't done so. He lives at Cooldrinagh, Foxrock. It would be a charity to ask him round one afternoon and show him a few pictures and drop all the conversational bombs you have handy without pretending anything. But the luck will be all on his side, he says very little, especially at first, and you might find him not interesting, so don't do it unless you feel like doing nothing one day. Joyce does like him however, and I'm genuinely fond of him tho' he's maddeningly young . . .[39]

MacGreevy's suggestion introduced a new and important figure into the painter's life, one who would be there to the very end, their friendship becoming increasingly rich and mutually rewarding. Beckett's indebtedness, in the early years, was very considerable, and can be traced in his prose-writing, his understanding of theatre, and his views on art generally. Jack would have been sympathetic to the idea of a meeting. Cissie Sinclair was a spirited figure in Dublin bohemian life, known to Jack through her art. She certainly influenced her nephew Sam, as did 'The Boss' Sinclair.[40] Like her nephew, she was a Beckett misfit. The family fortune, derived from successful building and contracting, and vested in land and property, was used to educate two of her brothers as prominent physicians, while Beckett's father entered the business instead of going to Trinity. Dublin gossip had it that there was 'at least one bohemian per generation' among the Becketts, and in marrying Sinclair she carried this tradition almost to the point of a family breach. Her close, lifelong friend was Estella Solomons, who had painted Jack's portrait in the early 1920s, and she was friendly also with Beatrice Glenavy. In her early days as a painter, this would have brought her into regular contact with William Orpen, and the rowdy set which surrounded the artist up to and including the first year of the Great War, including 'The Boss', a fellow-reveller with Gogarty.

Jack and the young Samuel Beckett became close friends, but the process was slow to evolve, in part because of Beckett's own wayward attitude (fig. 186). He was a shy man, easily young enough to be the painter's son, and was in awe of him; moreover, he was governed by the inertia which later siezed on

186. Samuel Beckett, *c.* 1930.

his characters. He had a taste for shebeens and low dives where he drank, sometimes to excess. But Beckett did read *Sligo*, and that summer returned to Dublin, where he took up an appointment as assistant in French at Trinity College. He did not immediately call on the painter, though he told MacGreevy, 'I want to inflict myself on Lennox Robinson & Jack Yeats, for a moment, but so far m'en manque!'[41] On another occasion he told MacGreevy he did not have the courage to call on Jack.

In the late autumn, Jack wrote to MacGreevy, 'I was very glad to hear from you. We had just been asking about you from Sam Beckett who called here on Tuesday. I liked him . . .'[42] Samuel Beckett was bowled over by the encounter, and MacGreevy reported on the young man's uncharacteristic enthusiasm:

> Beckett wrote me about his visit to you. I'm glad you liked him. He was completely staggered by the pictures and though he has met many people through me he dismissed them all in his letter in the remark 'and to think I owe meeting Jack Yeats and Joyce to you!' He's got a good sense of values all right. A good lad though still younger than he'll be yet – if he can manage to avoid the fate of poor Geoffrey Phibbs, but I think there's no fear of his thinking any downtown jewess from New York has 'the greatest intelligence in Europe.[43]

There is a prophetic irony in part of what MacGreevy wrote. Though Beckett did not marry until the end of his life, he liked women, and did have a torrid affair with an American heiress from New York, Peggy Guggenheim. During the course of their relationship, Beckett put forward to Peggy the idea of including Jack among the modern artists in her gallery. At the time she was planning to open a gallery in London. Her early preference was for old masters, but Beckett told her,

> one had to accept the art of our day as it was a living thing. He had two passions besides James Joyce. One was Jack Yeats and the other a Dutch painter, Geer van Velde . . . and he wanted me to give them both exhibitions. I could not refuse him anything, so it was agreed. Jack Yeats luckily realized that his painting was not at all in line with my gallery and let me off.[44]

Beckett paid an early tribute of his own to Jack, which reflected his views on the importance of contemporary art, when he sent him a copy of his first book, *Proust*. It was inscribed: 'For Jack from Sam Beckett heepishly. 23/3/31.'[45] Later inscriptions were even more terse; *More Pricks than Kicks* was inscribed, 'for Jack Yeats from Sam Beckett, May 1935', and the same wording used eighteen months later on *Echo's Bones*.

In the early 1930s Beckett's constant friend was Georges Pelorson. The two men had first met in Paris, during the two-year period when Beckett was *lecteur* at the Ecole Supérieure Normale, and Pelerson his only student in English studies. Their relationship had been rather stiff and formal to begin with; but then Pelerson discovered Beckett's interest in Joyce, and Beckett discovered his student's interest in the surrealist poets. Beckett, having got to know Joyce through MacGreevy, had then become involved with Lucia, Joyce's daughter, who had a romantic interest in him. This was not reciprocated, but it did cause problems. As part of Beckett's attempts to disentangle himself, he used Pelerson as a chaperone for himself, to Lucia's dismay and anger. He did not tell Pelorson, which added to the Frenchman's bewilderment; but their own friendship survived. Pelerson then preceded Beckett to Dublin, where he had a Trinity appointment as exchange lecturer. Unwittingly, he found himself again placed in slightly embarrassing circumstances, when he called on Beckett's parents in Foxrock, and let slip details about the early book of poems, *Whoroscope*, which Beckett, apparently deliberately, had not sent to his mother. On Beckett's own return, they became constant companions, and would dine together, on omelettes, if the Frenchman was cooking, on scrambled eggs if it was Beckett's turn.

Beckett wanted to share his enthusiasm for Jack Yeats with his closest friend at that time, and the two decided to call round. Their first visit, on 25 January 1931, was on a Sunday, an occasion when Jack was not receiving. But they went back again the following Saturday – which was then Jack's At Home day – and 'had two entirely delightful hours looking at a lot of pictures we had not seen and talking. He wanted a definition of cruelty, allowing that you could work back from cruelty and original sin. No doubt. But I dont think it is possible to define cruelty . . . Can one imagine a fine art of cruelty? The old question!'[46]

Now that he was in Dublin permanently, Beckett kept in touch with Jack, and early the following year invited him to a curious and specialised theatrical evening, the performance of three short plays in French in the Peacock Theatre as part of the annual programme put on by the Dublin University Modern Languages Society. In spite of his limited command of the language, Jack, who was trying at the time to learn Irish, went along, and in his usual methodical way, added the flimsy programme of the event to his collection. One of the three plays, *Le Kid*, has been treated as Beckett's first recorded work for the stage, but was in fact the work of Pelerson. The text has not survived, but we know a good deal about it. It was a short, one-act farce, based on Corneille's *Le Cid*, with Beckett playing the part of the hero, Don Diègue, clutching an umbrella instead of a sword, and wearing a bowler hat which he raised every time the king was mentioned. The three plays put on together were reviewed in *The Irish Times*, and also in *T.C.D. A College Miscellany* in so patronising a way that Beckett then wrote for that weekly college journal a one-page dramatic burlesque entitled 'The Possessed'.

From this period on Jack took an interest in Beckett, and this led in turn to a greater interest in Trinity College, and particularly its sport, which he now followed quite closely. Beckett played cricket for the Trinity XI. Jack was a friend of Captain Shaw, on the administrative staff, and of H.O. White, in the English Department, later to be its professor. Samuel Beckett became a frequent though irregular visitor to the flat in Fitzwilliam Square when he was in Dublin during the 1930s, and had the unusual distinction, particularly attractive to Jack, of being both avant garde in his artistic views and a sportsman of undoubted ability and sustained enthusiasm.[47]

In 1930 Jack exhibited again at the Alpine Club Gallery in London. He stayed at Garland's Hotel for about a fortnight, and lunched with one of his London admirers, Walter Sickert. 'He was full of fun and had some good claret a rumbling round the tumblers.'[48] He received even greater critical success than he had enjoyed the previous year. Favourable comparison of his work with that of Kokoschka appeared in *The Spectator*, and to Kokoschka *The New Statesman* added Daumier, Ensor, Rouault, Chagall, among moderns, and invoked classical masters as well – Rembrandt, Rubens, Watteau and Goya.

They were invoked, said the critic, T.W. Earp, to place Yeats 'among those artists who have used a maximum, instead of a minimum, of the means which their art supplies in order to express their vision.'[49] At least two of those named, Watteau and Goya, were admired by Yeats himself, and have often been mentioned to help explain his painting.

Jack told MacGreevy that, as far as press coverage was concerned, the 1930 show in the Alpine Club Gallery was ' the best I ever had for quality and quantity,' but that 'financially the exhibition will (even when a belated straggler or two may have made up their minds) be a very small affair'. Jack had been warned that it was 'the worst year ever known to man', but was light-hearted in reporting the gloom-laden warning, and was touched at MacGreevy's concern. 'You mustnt bother about my pictures. I would be delighted if you could give them a push along to the pasture – do so whenever you get a chance but you are not to let them trouble your mind – Especially and your own ships not coming home.'[50]

It was a grim time. Unemployment in Britain stood at more than two million. The Nazi Party in Germany was making massive electoral gains. Stalin was carrying out heavy purges in the Soviet Union. There were riots in India, an unsuccessful republican rebellion in Spain, and growing troubles surrounding the Cosgrave administration at home.

MacGreevy's 'ships' were of every sort. He was trying to write and sell a play, a libretto, poetry, and articles on literature and on painting. He was also still trying to write his 'fantastic' play. In this he shared in the shuffling tread of those tramping armies of writers who crowded each other off the boulevards of Paris, filled the cafés and bistros when they had the price of a coffee, and believed that the world was young and entirely in their favour. In response to MacGreevy's request for photographs of paintings which he could use to support anything he might write about his friend, Jack developed further his opposition to the use of reproductions. He felt that writing about art should be writing, and nothing more. He deplored the trend in art books, of their being filled with illustrations, and looked to a day when 'no article of importance of any kind will show a single reproduction of the pictures the article talks about'.

These letters to MacGreevy give a vivid picture of Jack's mind at this time, and of his clear and colourful feeling for words: 'You are lucky to have smelt sun in any south coast. It has been very thin and wirey and seldom here since three years went aft and now a boiling bath every morning is a something of a substitute. However hot it is one of my toes is enough to take the kick out of it.'[51]

He was in fact working on a second book, *Sailing, Sailing Swiftly*, and striving to make it more of a true work of fiction. But, though he reduced the number of paintings he did, this should in no way be seen as a loss of confidence, or an uncertainty about his own vision and technique. It seems mainly to have been a response to market circumstances. To an admirer in New York who had sent him American press clippings about his work he wrote, as he had done with MacGreevy, of the fine press given to his 1930 exhibition in London, adding: 'My painting has, the last few years changed in a way which would I believe excite and delight my father were he here.'[52]

At the time of his 'successful' London solo exhibitions, in 1929 and 1930, at the Alpine Club Gallery, the reception he was getting in Dublin was increasingly perplexed and negative. Among other attacks were the highly

187. 'The Man who tried to get the hang of a Jack Yeats picture', *Dublin Opinion*, May 1929.

188. 'Mr Jack Yeats paints a picture', *Dublin Opinion*, May 1930.

visual ones which appeared in the Dublin comic weekly, *Dublin Opinion*, which seems to have had an annual jamboree of artistic chauvinism, with cartoons regularly entitled 'Our Annual Gallery of Rejections from the R.H.A. Exhibition', and invariably including a scribble for a work by Jack. There were other attacks; one showed how 'Mr Jack Yeats paints a picture (As imagined by our irresponsible artist.)' and 'The Man who tried to get the hang of a Jack Yeats picture', in which the gallery visitor drives himself insane before the canvas, and is taken away by guards in the direction of an 'asylum' (figs 187–8).[53] But it went deeper than that. One of the side-effects of the regular chaffing of him was that his 'new' style was represented as deliberate obfuscation. Terence de Vere White writes well of this, and concludes: 'Jack B Yeats is as simple as his brother was splendid. And if he lacks pomp he has dignity.'[54]

White also refers to 'neglect'. It is not the *mot juste*. Throughout his whole life as an artist, Jack never suffered serious or permanent neglect; he simply failed to evoke the kind of recognition he felt was his due. And what he was doing was not understood. Every show he held was covered in the press, and generally speaking was covered handsomely. No artist, from his earliest days as a painter, rivalled him in terms of public interest, no doubt in part because of the unwished for relationship with Willie. The very fact that he pursued a solitary road as a painter, relying predominantly on solo exhibitions rather than group shows, and ensuring that the focus of those shows was Irish life in all its variety, created a special intensity in coverage.

In some respects he was, in the short-term, his own worst enemy. Increasingly he gave up explaining himself, and his earlier willingness to talk with the press, and give opinions on art, his own and that of others, gradually disappeared. He also declined public speaking engagements, except those in the convivial company of fellow members of the United Arts Club. On one occasion, asked to give a lecture, he replied: 'I am very sorry to have to say I cannot lecture for you. I have nothing prepared. Indeed I dont want to be a lecturer at all. I want to be one of Gods creatures.'[55]

From time to time he simply had to put up with ignorance and what seems to have been a deliberate misunderstanding, a mild form of that traditional Irish begrudgery. The art critic of *The Irish Tatler and Sketch* put it thus:

> We've got to figure this thing out. How did it happen? We are all agreed that Mr Yeats used to paint pictures in the good old days which were highly individualised but none the less excellent portrayals of Irish life and character. Has some ill-advised leprauchaun shown him a page from the book of the Modernists, and advised him that it was simplicity itself to go and do likewise?

The reviewer then advised modernism as a route which Jack might follow, since only three of his works had quality. 'A bewildered connoisseur who was trying to do justice to the show approached us and whispered with bated breath, "I've discovered a way of looking at them which makes them look like something. Stand off at a distance and look at them sideways!".'[56] The reviewer in *The Nation* declined to deal with several works 'simply because to the present writer they are incomprehensible'.[57]

Dublin begrudgery – a propensity for which the city is famous – is evident in the sustained, if relatively mild, teasing which went on and on, relentlessly, through the 1930s. It is perhaps most obvious to us in some of the cartoons. More substantial, in Jack's eyes, must have been the controversy and the publicity which surrounded his painting, *The Liffey Swim*, when it was bought in 1930 by the Haverty Trust.

This fund for art was set up under the will of Thomas Haverty, whose father, Joseph Patrick Haverty, was a nineteenth-century Irish artist of some distinction. His son made sufficient money to be able to leave a sum of £10,000 to endow the annual purchase of Irish works and encourage Irish art. The trust started its activities in 1930, and Jack's painting was not only the first work acquired, but was, for many years, the most modern, though Jack disparaged the comparative conservatism of the choice: 'The Haverty Trust Committee have bought my "Liffey Swim" as their first purchase. I hoped they would have taken something wilder but there were some cold feet.'[58] His expectations were perhaps excessive. The Haverty Trust, in its emphasis on Irish art and artists, was remarkably enlightened and innovative. It was less *avant garde* than the Friends of the National Collections of Ireland, for example; but the Friends dealt in international works, in the main, seeing their role as one of enlightenment within Ireland through the purchase of works by international modern artists.

The Liffey Swim was not immediately destined for the National Gallery, which, in any case, was not permitted to hang the works of living artists. It became part of the collection in 1931. Before that, the Haverty Trust sought to lend the painting, 'through the National Gallery of Ireland', to the Municipal Gallery of Modern Art. At the time, the director of the National Gallery was Thomas Bodkin, and he, together with Dermod O'Brien, were, ex officio, the trustees. A third ex officio trustee, the Lord Mayor of Dublin, was yet to be elected. At the time, civic government was in the hands of the city commissioners, who nominated John Reynolds, curator of the Municipal Gallery, to act in place of the Lord Mayor. The selection committee was differently composed. It included the Lord Mayor of Belfast, among others. Reynolds sat during the summer, and then, when the new Lord Mayor took up office, an attempt was made to have Reynolds accompany him to meetings of the Haverty Trust, to advise. This was blocked by other members, and Reynolds then took umbrage at the method chosen by the Haverty Trust for making the painting available to the gallery. He believed that the Municipal Gallery was the 'natural home' for modern art, and that *The Liffey Swim* should have been given direct to the city's gallery, and not 'through the National Gallery of Ireland'.

The trustees were legally and morally right in what they did. There was no special disposition in its terms towards Dublin's modern gallery, which in any case enjoyed limited respect, since the generosity of Hugh Lane in founding it had in no sense been equalled by any civic generosity in funding its buildings or collections. It was only now, almost thirty years since Lane had initiated the Municipal Gallery plans, that serious moves were in train for the reconstruction of Charlemont House, in Parnell Square, as a permanent home for the civic collection; and even then the progress was slow. The loan was refused. The painting was then lent to the Crawford Gallery in Cork, and eventually became part of the National Gallery's permanent collection. John Reynolds was at pains to ensure that Jack would not be offended; indeed there was no special reason for this, nor was he upset.

Early in 1932 the Cosgrave government fell and Eamon de Valera came to power. Consideration was given by the new administration to the possibility of making Jack Minister for Fine Art. Lady Gregory, made aware of this by the journalist, Kathleen O'Brennan, wrote to Frank Gallagher, editor of *The Irish Press*.[59] Kathleen O'Brennan had been working hard on Jack's behalf, and told Lady Gregory: 'Jack has made every sacrifice for his principles all through the years and he is very popular'.[60] De Valera had created a Ministry for the Fine Arts at the time of the first Dail, and had appointed Constance Markievicz to the post. With independence, the idea had lapsed, but now seemed a possibility once again. In soliciting Lady Gregory's help, Kathleen O'Brennan needed a respected voice at the heart of the cultural establishment, but one politically acceptable to Fianna Fail:

> Most of the present Ministers are friends of mine, and I am assured if the post is made the portfolio will be offered to Jack. He is very modest and will never look for anything for himself and he is unaware that I have been working on his behalf. If you have not yet written to Mr de Valera perhaps you would say a word about including a Minister of Fine Arts in the Cabinet and I know the proposal of Jack's name will be acceptable, especially coming from you.

Lady Gregory was the ideal person. She was more radical in her nationalism than Willie, and close, politically speaking, to Jack. But she was weak and ill. She wrote in her journal at the time of having to be helped to move from her bedroom, 'Such wasted days these seem', and in the end she played no part in the event. She died in May, within two months of the appointment of the new government. De Valera made no such appointment. Jack, mercifully, was spared the heartbreak and the wasted time such a job might have imposed on his energies. But the exchanges indicate his sympathies with the anti-Treaty side in Irish politics, and hint at the esteem in which he was held by Fianna Fail.

By the autumn he was scheduled to have exhibitions in either New York or Paris. It turned out to be New York, where he had two solo exhibitions in 1932. Jack had submitted works fairly regularly to group shows in New York, but had not had a solo exhibition there since 1904, when he had made his only transatlantic journey. He showed in various group exhibitions in the 1920s, notably with the Society of Independent Artists, and then, in 1930, at the Helen Hackett Galleries. But in December 1931 the owners of the Barbizon Hotel in New York opened a Museum of Irish Art and its first group show included work which Jack had submitted. The following year he had two solo exhibitions in the city, one in the Ferargil Galleries, the second in the Barbizon, both of them well reported in the press, with generous reviews.

The Ferargil Galleries' show was a bad experience. They failed to sell the thirty-seven works he sent, and passed on the paintings to the dealer, Patric Farrell, who was also director of the new, and short-lived Museum of Irish Art, in the Barbizon Hotel. He failed to make sales. All Jack's subsequent efforts to get the paintings sent back were ignored, and it was not until James A. Healy, the New York stockbroker, became involved, finding an effective lawyer to act on the artist's behalf, that the matter was sorted out. Jack valued the pictures in America at $18,500, a serious sum; and it was a worrying problem, since it had to be handled at such a distance.[61] Jack mentioned nothing of this to members of the family.

Willie was in America at the time of these shows, having just completed a tour, reading and lecturing, and was trying to raise funds for the Irish Academy of Letters. He attended a farewell reception at the December group exhibition before departing for Ireland, and spoke there about his brother in terms which were represented as 'tales out of school'.

> Jack was always last in school. It was because he was painting – but grandmother used to say it was because he was too kind-hearted; he didn't want to hurt the other boys' feelings by getting ahead of them. He has a remarkable visual memory, once painting a portrait of a man who had been dead for thirty years.[62]

It was an inaccurate, silly view of Jack, who was never the benign dunce suggested. Willie also expressed a preference for his brother's earlier work; he liked, he said, to 'recognise pictures as soon as he saw them'.

Sean Keating also exhibited in that December show, as did Power O'Malley, George Russell and Charles Shannon, whose portrait of Willie, painted twenty-five years earlier, was on loan to the museum. Several portrait drawings by John Butler Yeats were included. For a New York show, the coverage was extensive. It was a time of substantial pro-Irish feeling in the city. The singer, John McCormack, and the Irish composer, Hamilton Harty, were at the exhibition, and later were guests at a dinner given for Willie.

Jack read of all this from afar, collecting evidence of recognition, and was pleased at having extended his impact as a painter at a time of economic recession. *The New York Times* art critic, Edward Alden Jewell, wrote perceptively about Jack's 'veritable poems in pigment', tackling the central stylistic questions of high and florid impasto, 'sheer capricious magic', and 'original musings on the phantasmagoria of the human soul . . . musings at once turbulent and full of passionate splendor'.[63] At a time not particularly marked in America for the appreciation of modernism, Jewell showed understanding of Jack's passionate sense of purpose. Farrell, described Jack's 'phantasma-poetic pandemonium of moods and emotions'.[64] Jack's difficulties in getting his paintings back from Farrell provoked a strong sense of injustice and an abiding hatred of anything which smacked of duplicity or dishonesty.

He valued greatly these reviews of work exhibited abroad, and set them against the misunderstandings at home. As his style became liberated, his brushwork and handling of paint more adventurous, his colours more vivid, his use of primaries more extensive, he continued to face negative reaction. Signe Toksvig, who lived and worked in Ireland for ten years from 1926, and visited his and other shows of paintings, records in her diary, 'I also went to [the] Hibernian Academy. Many pictures nearly all 'a la maniere de-' Don't believe they work hard enough. But Jack Yeats is original, anyhow. Still, you'd have to build a house around one of his.'[65] A cartoon in *Dublin Opinion*, in May 1931, sustained the magazine's disposition to make fun of him by depicting the artist himself at the Royal Hibernian Academy saying 'I wish I'd brought a catalogue along. I wonder which of my pictures that is.'

Bregazzi was a Dublin frame-maker, and did carving and gilding in the Italian style. He knew Jack's work, and told Signe Toksvig to go and see his solo exhi¹ ition in the Engineers' Hall:

> 'sure 'tis like a conglomeration of snakes' he said. He thought pictures ought to be intelligible and was speechless at these. Well, we were surprised to find something in them, even before Yeats came in and kindly explained them to us. I was struck by one blue picture. A Dublin bridge, a boy talking to a girl, but all like fantastic dreams, yet with a very haunting quality and full of deep fresh colours. But one ought to have a poem by the brother accompanying each picture. And when *one* picture that looks like a palette before being cleaned is called 'the old corner' and explained as 'some faces seen in the elemental plane' from the balustered corner of a Dublin hotel – why –. Or another similiar one as the dream of a man of Sligo in Pittsburgh. Or another as a Republican funeral. He could tell you a novel about each one. All are representational pictures, save the mark! A certain gallantry in his demeanor. Is he *fumiste*? No. *Fou.* No.-?-[66]

But Jack was still deeply immersed in another art form. As John Purser makes clear, a great deal of his literary output can be dated to the first half of the 1930s. In addition to *Sligo*, Jack's next novel, *Sailing, Sailing Swiftly*, together with *The Careless Flower*, *The Amaranthers*, and several plays, including *The Deathly Terrace*, *Apparitions*, *The Old Sea Road*, and *Rattle*, were all written before 1935.[67] It is perhaps of interest that at this time, at least half a century after his first purchases of miniature theatre material from the shops which specialised in the cardboard structures, the cut-out characters, and the scripts, we find Jack in correspondence with the firm of B. Pollock, of Hoxton Street, ordering a selection of 'drop scenes' and settling his account for 4s. 6d.

In general, the paintings of these years are not among the artist's most distinguished works, but the five-year period did conclude with one of his

189. Jack participated conscientiously in the work of artistic organisations. He is shown here on the Royal Hibernian Academy's Hanging Committee judging the annual entries. *Irish Independent*, March 1935.

most powerful works, *About to Write a Letter*. Other paintings reflect his comparatively solitary movements. He went on long walks at this time, both in the mountains and along the Royal and Grand Canals, which ran out of the city north-west and south-west. *Turf on the Canal, By the Canal, Canal Water, Canal near Ashtown, Canal Bridge*, were all painted in or around 1930–2. And there were a number of paintings of Dublin interiors, pubs, a reading room, domestic settings, and street scenes, including views along the quaysides of the Liffey, which he constantly visited during his rambles through the city. He received two medals for his painting at this time. The Dublin Aonach Tailteann gave him a silver-gilt medal in 1932 for *Music in the Train*, a painting which dated from ten years earlier, and the same organisation gave him a second silver-gilt medal for *Darrynane*.

Sailing, Sailing Swiftly, which appeared in 1933, is better than *Sligo* as a novel, though the comment again raises questions about how we define Jack's idiosyncratic writing. It has pace and action. There are characters who stay before us for several pages at a time. Events pile up. Happiness is sought and found. We pass from one generation to the next. And death takes its toll. We begin in a railway carriage, where two friends, Thady O'Malley and Jasper Newbigging are travelling to a spa town in England, in the 1860s. Jasper is an English horse-dealer, Thady a partner in a Mayo coaching business. Mayo helps to give the title to the book, since it comes from the last line in a ballad which Thady sings to his companion. 'And I sailing, sailing swiftly from the County of Mayo' are the faintly melancholy thoughts which all ballads deliver up to those who sing them, which is the why and wherefore of ballads.

Thady is an unconscious bachelor; Jasper has slipped the net on countless occasions. Harrogate is the spa town where they lace the waters with 'a slash of whiskey', decanted into a medicine bottle. They parade the town's pavements with cigars. It is Jasper's intent to find a suitable wife for O'Malley, though the Irishman declares himself too busy for such things, and he brings him to the town's bookshop run by Annette Dunaven, whose heart stops in her throat, and whose fates fail to defend her, at the sight of the man from Mayo. The two men meet the girl in the park, and Jasper promotes the mutual interests of the lovers, while Thady sings sweetly of sailing to Mayo, to the consternation of the 'hobbling string of invalids'. Annette is introduced to the intriguer, Jasper, as 'the future Mrs O'Malley, the future Queen of Mayo'. The honeymoon is in London, and includes eating whitebait in Greenwich. Then both men die.

The first heart of the story dies with them; the second travels to Mayo with Annette O'Malley, who, in her widow's weeds, takes on the look of Lola Montez. Alone in another railway carriage she weeps sad tears for her lost husband, thumps the cushion of her seat with her white fist, and sings of sailing swiftly to Mayo. Engulfed by Thady's uncles, Daniel in particular, who walks her to the edge of the Atlantic, she then returns to England where her son, Lawrence John, is born. There now enters another character, Edward Devinne Tarleton, but catastrophe strikes again. Scarlet fever carries Annette down to her cold grave. Her son goes to work in London, designing furniture. He studies at the South Kensington Museum. At work he meets Sally Belfield, a polisher of furniture whose smile, among all her colleagues was 'always the first, the clearest and the best'. We expect the inevitable. It does not transpire. Sally goes on holiday, and marries another. Larry, as he has become in his grown years, is desolate but stoic. He meets Sally's friend, Miss Gown. His work prospers, his salary goes up. And the story shifts now into its final phase, with Larry's and Uncle Ned Tarleton's lives pursued through East End boxing halls, among the Corinthians, in roller-skating rinks, in early cinema performances of Wild West adventures. Larry marries his employer's niece, Ellaine, and they have two children. They buy a small car, and Ellaine leaves her husband at the station every morning. The Great War transforms the furniture factory into one for munitions. 'The war went on. The war was over.' And Larry was a wealthy man. The son of his former love, Sally, now dead, returns. The two men travel together to Southampton, and there, on a tender, a child loosens a barrier, and Larry goes overboard. Though rescued, by a stoker, who 'clove the spumy waves with a shaking, shaggy paw, and a brow like crumpled iron', he dies, and the story ends at Uncle Ned's bedside, with the last memory, of Larry's daughter, Celia, sending Tarleton into a quiet sleep.

This strange story is a chronicle of days, spanning sixty years or more, three generations, two countries, war and peace, love and death. It undulates, the pace is constant, but the tale shifts its focus endlessly, and it is in this that both its merits and its defects lie. Hilary Pyle says of *Sailing, Sailing Swiftly*, that 'the events . . . leave the impression that the tale has not ended yet'. The mythic content has been extensively explored by Norah McGuinness, and John Purser has explained the allegorical meaning, which concerns the difficult and doomed relationship between England and Ireland. Hovering behind this overt confrontation – represented by the marriage of Thadeus O'Malley and Annette Dunaven – are battles between nature and commerce, between an old world of horses and horse-trading, and a new world of manufacture and motor travel. The English novelist, Norah Hoult, described it as 'a pet book', and it was warmly praised by other writers.

Jack's own life, his experiences as an artist, his familiarity with art and design, boxing and Greenwich, money and security, horses and travel, uncles and children, spill over into the anecdotal sifting through different lives and fortunes. Memory is drawn upon, and then dissolved. The riches of imagination are dissipated, and the story sails swiftly to its end. The book was in a style at odds with its times, and with contemporary fashion in fiction. Nevertheless, it was well-received. Jack's friend, Lennox Robinson, who had included the ballad about Mayo in an anthology from which Jack had taken it, wrote: 'And then a year or two ago he wrote a book called "Sligo" and I bought it and could not read it, and last year I bought "Sailing, Sailing Swiftly" and I can read every word of it and only wish there were fifty thousand more words in it to explain it. The book is so original that it is impossible to explain it.'[68]

CHAPTER SEVENTEEN
'Lives' 1936–1938

. . . all dripping with pencil and chalk lines . . .

JACK EMBARKED ON a new series of sketchbooks in the 1930s. He called them 'Lives'. They are unlike anything else in his work, and stand as a solitary and rare monument to the workings of his imagination, expressing the feelings in his heart about his own life and what he had created. In a painter who had so little to say about himself, and increasingly, as his career progressed, said what he did say in elusive and puzzling ways, there is in this collection of drawings an extensive and magical self-expression which comes close to explaining his approach to art (fig. 190).

'Lives' does this through its visual narrative. We see individual paintings reflected in tiny sketches, hinted at, explored, and related one to another. At the same time, we 'read' a sequence of events or images which offer a loose narrative. 'Lives' grows and expands from early, tight, multi-subject pages, to single broad drawings of just one event. As painter, he has reversed the practice of a lifetime, whereby the images were gathered in street or market-place, recorded in the sketchbooks, and used in his paintings; here, the pages draw from his memory and the experience of his working life. They have become the realisation of his art, and not its starting point. Something similar has happened to him as story-teller. The drawings in 'Lives' are narrative in the way his books are narrative, a succession of images without climax but with a flow of movement running through individual pages and from page to page, even from book to book, for the total work consists of no less than seven volumes of drawings. He achieves a creative transmutation, from the static singleness of the moment, with no before or afterwards, which is peculiar to painting, towards the progression of narrative idea, the movement through a tale or story, a sequence of events, peculiar to writing. He comes near to achieving the virtually impossible synthesis of two quite different art forms.

For the seven volumes of drawings, when finished, Jack fashioned a rough cardboard cover and wrote on it: 'Finished about 1939'. 'Lives' was clearly started in the early 1930s, and was well advanced by 1936, at which stage Jack already envisaged it as a book. In that year Jack moved from Heinemann to a new publishing firm, Routledge, where his work was handled by T. Murray Ragg. Their correspondence continued until 1945. When it started Jack was still expecting Heinemann, who had published *The Amaranthers*, to bring out his next book, and told this to Ragg, who had met Jack before and who now asked if he might be interested in producing a book about donkeys. This was to be: 'An informal book in which you could express your love for

190. Illustration no. 5 from Book I of 'Lives'.

the donkey in scrapbook fashion. Won't you reconsider the idea and see whether, on jotting down a few paragraphs, some sort of intimate, informal testimony to the donkey does not take shape in text and pictures.'[1]

The idea did not appeal at all; Jack put forward the idea for a quite different book:

> I have a book, a wild one, on the way. It is of drawings only. I think it would be called *Lives* and would have about 200 pages. There would be no story of any kind. Though figures would appear in some cases a few times. There would be no explanations. I send some 18 pages and I hope you will want to take a gallant chance.[2]

Ragg considered this, mentioning his belief that 'the Anglo-Saxon has precious little wildness in his nature', and came back with a refusal: 'I am afraid I have to write and tell you now that we cannot see our way to publishing your book "Lives" of which you sent us some specimen drawings. The cost of reproduction of the book would be very high and this, and its strangeness and wildness, make it impossible for us to see it as a business proposition.'[3] He sent back the drawings.

Jack was philosophical about the refusal:

> I cannot blame you at this time for not being being able to publish the book. I know its wildness seems much stranger than the wildness of any other book which you have seen of mine. I believe, as the world turns along, the people will enjoy, sometimes, the unpepsinized event presented to them between the finger and the thumb, which picked it out for them, all dripping with pencil and chalk lines, and the colours would have added greatly to the cost of *Lives*. But they gave me, I thought, more limberness than pen and black ink could.[4]

'Lives' was rarely shown to anyone. No one commented on it during his lifetime. Those who have seen it since his death have been captivated by the freedom of expression, the wonderful movement in the figures, and the rich diversity of subject-matter, contained in more than one hundred large drawings in mixed media.

He worked, often on the same page, in conté, crayon, pencil, pen and ink, and to a lesser extent gouache and watercolour. And he progressed from a dazzling array of characters and events, in the early drawings, to a spare and empty stage, peopled with spectres and abstract shapes at the end. Who can say what he intended? Could Jack himself? Perhaps all that can be ventured, in a tentative way, is that the 'Lives' are the lives he witnessed; and that they are also his own life or lives, in their fragmented multiplicity (fig. 191).

The echoes of the past are constant and powerful. Jack does not simply revert to the imagery of his own youth, the sporting London of the 1890s, the market and racecourse life of Sligo at the end of the nineteenth century and into the twentieth; he goes further back, to the regency bucks and the Corinthians, to the romantic world of theatre as expressed in the plays of Dion Boucicault, and to the magical, mythical violence and adventures of pirates, their victims, their barrels of brandy and their treasure. In later drawings he introduces mythological subjects. Predictably, the most frequent image of all is the horse. The second most frequent image is also familiar: throughout Jack's paintings we have so often the figure of the man alone, contemplative, entrapped, beleaguered by dark thoughts, confronted by inexpressible chal-

lenges. He peoples his early drawings with examples. He produced some of his
more memorable large watercolours on the theme of solitary self-examination,
patience, fortitude, sadness and resignation, all compellingly focused within a
single figure. And this figure, almost always a man, often of middle or later
years, frequently of humble or marginal pursuit, features in 'Lives' as the
embodiment of an alternative stillness and questioning to Jack's own.

His favoured characters include the singer, with his or her audience. Jack
was fascinated with the creation of music and its performance. No painter has
so magically captured the striving, breathless anticipation, the skill and
timing, that mixture of energy, memory, judgment and gift which produces
the melifluous ballad, the music-hall song, the party piece. Jack, like James
Joyce, saw the artistic value of it. His singers are not the great ones. Their
stage is the drawing room, the bar, the parlour, the fairground, and the
audience is held only by the talent. His niece, Anne, recalls that he 'would
sing music hall songs, or snatches from them' while talking about them. And
he kept a vast collection of ballads.

Jack's early adult plays belong to this period in his life, and represent a
new direction. He crossed a threshold, from being an avid theatre-goer to
attempting the role of dramatist.[5] He began this process with the three plays
which he published in *Apparitions*. In their structure they have the common
general theme of the 'literary tale', raising questions about the quality of their
dramatic action, and giving them the character of chronicle plays. *The Old Sea
Road* is full of characters, but limited in its action. It takes place on the road
of the title, which lies above the village of Cahirmahone, and leads to the

neighbouring village of Jacksport. Its climax, which is presented as a practical joke, involves Ambrose Oldbury, who has already tried to deceive the people of the first village into thinking that an earthquake has destroyed the second village. He draws all his money from the bank, burns it, and then takes drink and dies, carrying off with him, as a fellow-victim, Michael the Song, though for no apparent reason.

Reason and purpose, the twin dynamics of all effective theatre, are absent. We have Nolan and Dolan on stage at the beginning, both with the christian name John, both roadmenders who have stepped from the oppressions depicted by Jack for Synge, in the Connemara of 1905, into the Irish Free State, where, according to the play's first stage direction, 'there is a lark singing overhead for a while'.[6] Nolan, marginally more dynamic, shatters the action into various directions by invoking America, 'the Home of the Brave', his own love of drink, 'the bright breeze that blows o'er Erin's Isle', and his own determination to get a short, neat one to reinforce himself. Leaving Dolan singing 'With me hi fol de diddle I do', he goes to the village and back, but fails to get a drink. This feat of suspended action strains at the outset our suspension of disbelief.

It is no surprise when Nolan and Dolan, who might have scraped a sentence or two out of Flann O'Brien, and who endow Samuel Beckett's imagination with a historic authority, shoulder their shovels, and are then replaced by a new character, Julia and her teacher, led on by the silent postman, who does not speak until well into the second act. Nolan and Dolan return to hold things up for a few additional speeches, adding to Ambrose Oldbury's repertoire of practical jokes the story he spread about the Grand National being stopped because a brewery had burst, flooding the course. We discover no reason for the existence of two roadmakers, Nolan and Dolan, nor for the schoolteacher, Josephine Curran and her star pupil, Julia. Act Two introduces new characters, a chain-smoking young man called John Dwyer, and Michael the Song, and they then debate the relative attractions of the two villages. There is a dispersal of characters, and the two main protagonists, Ambrose Oldbury and Michael the Song, are left in a long scene together in which Ambrose speculates on the possibility of having a few practical jokes left.

Norah Hoult, who greatly admired *Sailing, Sailing Swiftly*, said of the plays in *Apparitions*: 'They are rather as if the later and odder Mr. James Joyce had slightly influenced an Irish road-mender named Nolan with a weakness for practical jokes and more than his share of the Irish talent for irrelevancy.'[7]

Worse came from other reviews. 'In constructing them (*Apparitions*) their author has ignored most of the accepted ideas about theatre craft. He . . . hardly troubled to make them playable.'[8]

> The plays give the impression of having been begun without the end clear in view, as if the dramatist allowed his whimsical imagination too great a licence, and in a multitude of ideas his themes seldom properly take shape. It may be the method, or one of the methods, of genius; Mr. Yeats may be a genius, but at the moment at least I think he is only partially inspired. At the same time, his originality and lively imagination are undoubted.[9]

Cottie's mother died in 1934. Cottie went to London, and stayed on to look after her sister. As usual the couple exchanged affectionate letters. This was always the pattern when they were apart. In the context of Jack's marriage,

Terence de Vere White raises the tangential but important question of sensuality, which he claims was entirely absent from his art.

> There is no hint anywhere of sensuality in Jack Yeats's paintings. His mind remained always in the condition of Robert Louis Stevenson's stories. Stevenson himself lamented that he had not broken through the convention of reticence and written more intimately about women; but I am convinced that Yeats had no desire to paint even an academic nude. He was romantic through and through.

Jack did not echo Stevenson's lament, and would not have equated White's view about sensuality with an understanding of women. Women in his paintings sometimes end up looking like Cottie. Yet Jack could as often produce brassy blondes, and with a painter's eye he favoured yellow hair for at least some of his women; at times he treated this choice as a symbol of strength. Beyond this contrast he does not delve into the nature of women. The normal profile is of a restrained, pensive expression, unemotional. There is no great variety of expression or gesture. There is little characterisation.

He never gossiped about women; indeed the word seems inappropriate of his conversation generally. But Cottie had a different reputation. The sisters found it not always safe to talk to her, for she might repeat confidences. Lily wrote to Ruth: 'I like Cottie greatly, and she is reliable and kind and the best of wives, but I don't tell her anything I don't want repeated.'[10] This Yeats reserve may have been reinforced by an earlier judgment which Lily refers to in a letter to John Quinn: 'When talking to her I always find myself being careful, going back and putting things more carefully as I see her face change and her mind close up.' Lily felt there was nothing in her behaviour directed against the Yeatses personally. 'She is just the same with her own people. We think it is English because we can't think of anything else to call it.'[11]

Jack never uttered anything coarse. And he was unhappy about womanising and infidelity. On one occasion White and Jack were talking about the character of Don Juan. The association of ideas invoked the name of a literary figure of the time who had a reputation for love affairs, which led on to the unhappy outcome of homes being broken up. Jack said of him: 'A man like that feels nothing. His aim is to perfect his art so that he has to use the least possible effort in collecting a woman. I think he has reduced it to the lifting of an eyebrow.'[12] The person concerned was Stephen Gwynn. It is perhaps of interest that Gwynn's wife was one of Cottie's friends and is recorded at her Wellington Place address, and also at 7 Pembroke Road, where the Gwynns lived later.[13] As White points out, Willie was preoccupied with sex in the later years of his life, 'but Jack gave every appearance of being oblivious to it; and, if I were called upon to testify, my evidence would be that there had been one woman and only one in his long life'.[14]

Jack and Cottie moved in theatrical and literary circles. Though he had long since ceased to write for children, he responded positively to his old friend, Padraic Colum, for whom he did illustrations for *The Big Tree of Bunlahy*, and when Patricia Lynch asked him to illustrate *A Turfcutter's Donkey*, he produced fifteen free-flowing drawings.[15] A near neighbour was Joseph Holloway, the eccentric and long-winded architect of the Abbey Theatre (fig. 192). Mid-way through the 1930s they saw much of each other, and on one occasion met at an experimental theatre in Capel Street.

192. Joseph Holloway depicted on the jacket of his *Irish Theatre*. Vol. 1.

I met Jack B. Yeats and Mrs. Yeats at the Torch Theatre on Monday last. Jack has taken quite kindly to the old melodramatic plays at the little theatre, and told me he had been to see many of them. A drama built around the career of Wolfe Tone was the piece on the bill; its author, a fine old Irish actor, Frank Dalton, died only a fortnight ago. He actually conducted the first rehearsals of the play. He was 85 – a truly grand old man![16]

On an earlier occasion, Jack called round to Holloway's home, in Northumberland Road. There was a strike on at the time, but Holloway makes the point that it had no effect on Jack:

The strike doesn't affect him as he always walks where he wants to go . . . He was lately at the Gate, but not at Othello. He was sure that MacLiammoir would make a success of the title role; he had McMaster's style. Yeats didn't know till I told him that Hilton Edwards and Coralie Carmichael had been members of McMaster's company. And so he chatted on most entertainingly and interestingly all the while. He is first rate company. He wore his long overcoat and soft felt hat and looked quite a character.[17]

His appearance, the fact that he walked everywhere, his knowledge of Dublin, his curious mixture of amiable approachability and austere reserve, made even his simplest habits noteworthy. Gossip-writers observed and described the Jack Yeats people knew and saw in the streets. One wrote:

Mr. Jack B. Yeats is one of the keenest observers I know . . . You may meet him any afternoon wandering through the city; for he tramps for miles and knows every street and sign in Dublin. He presented me with a list of all the old signs which adorn the business houses in the principal streets and along the quays. . . . He tells me that of late he has abandoned his weekly tramps through the mountains. He made it a habit of taking this weekly holiday, and often did thirty or twenty-five miles in the day. On these occasions Mrs. Yeats took her holiday also, and visited her friends. What an amicable arrangement. No fear of Mr. and Mrs. Yeats ever getting on each other's nerves; for they understand the ideal of missing each other and then returning with fresh interest and with a story to tell.[18]

The marriage worked well. Independent lives, divergent energies, separate groups of friends, quite different interests, a lively curiosity about each other's doings during the day, evenings spent companionably, frequent outings together, a shared passion for theatre. By the mid-1930s, Cottie was in her sixties. She was a small woman, and her health had been affected by emphysema, giving to her chest and torso that slightly barrel-shaped stiffness associated with the disease. But she kept herself well, dressed carefully, even with a certain measure of flamboyance. 'She kept herself young for his sake', according to Terence de Vere White. She wore quite striking hats. Her dark hair was cut in a fringe. And she was always ready with comment and observation, though almost exclusively on the subject of Jack and his work.

Despite this concern, their closeness, her passionate interest in everything he did, and her own professional background as an artist, she was not told about his work. Lily refers to him treating his pictures 'as if it was counterfeit coin he was making'.[19] When he sold some work in New York, Cottie only found out through Lily who had been told by John Sloan when he was paying a bill to Cuala. Cottie planned to 'have some fun with Jack over it'.[20] Of course when Cottie did know how much Jack received for a painting, she was just as secretive about it as he was. 'He and Cottie are so deep and dark they do not say if he sold one big or small, ' Lily told Ruth, and when it was 'a big-priced picture' Cottie said 'she wasn't sure of the price'.[21] Lily knew nothing of Jack's finances. 'Jack is so mysterious you never know. He may be looking for 6d or he may have a good bank account.'[22] In another cutting from the same year, taken from the *Irish Independent*, we read:

> Not even Mr. Yeats's wife realised that he was writing a novel in the intervals of painting shut up in his studio until it was completed. Not that he was making any secret about it. On the contrary, it never occurred to him to talk about the thing until he was certain that he had brought it off. Jack Yeats has the modesty of the really great artist.[23]

Jack kept a vast collection of theatre programmes. He went very often and to every kind of production. At one performance of a thriller, based on an adaption of a Bulldog Drummond story by Sapper, Jack approached Holloway and told him: 'I am enjoying the piece. All the tricks and thrills to create thrills are being used with effect'. On another occasion, when at a production of Louis D'Alton's *To-morrow Never Comes*, Yeats remarked to Holloway, 'None of your highbrow stuff about that – just an ordinary thriller.'[24]

Dramatists' skills failed to rub off. A lifelong exploration of almost every kind of theatrical production, music hall, miniature theatre for children, circus, pantomime, melodrama, the abstruse early antics on stage of Samuel Beckett, the classical thunderings of Anew MacMaster and the prodigal artifice of Micheal Mac Liammoir: set against the gentle, placid, wayward plots of his own plays, which never seem quite to take off and have never been revived, we are presented with a conundrum.

There are two detailed studies of Jack's writing, by John Purser and Norah McGuinness, which explain his inspiration and ideas with considerable success.[25] In addition, Robin Skelton has written perceptively on his plays. Nevertheless, these studies are not entirely convincing in the way they tackle such central problems as dramatic action in the plays and the sustaining of interest in the fictional characters. Jack's characters offer a Yeats 'universe' (according to Norah McGuinness), or a theory of deception (according to John Purser), or a schema of pre-ordained behaviour (according to Skelton). And all three writers explain his motives, elucidate his obscurity, counter the bewilderment with which critics generally address his novels and plays. But we are still left with the kind of view expressed by Ernest Blythe about his plays generally: 'These quaint rambling compositions had a strange charm and indeed reminded one of certain pictures which delight the eye and intrigue the mind, ' while at the same time either not being suitable for performance, or being treated by directors as 'gimmicks'.[26]

Norah McGuinness's stated position is that 'Yeats is a nationalist writer in many important ways'. And she goes on: 'Previous critics have overlooked the relation of Yeats's writing to Irish events which had a strong influence on his work. Yeats was an Irish nationalist, at once a contributor to the Irish Rising and one of its victims. Both before the 1922 Treaty and after it, Irish nationalism affected Yeats's writing.'

She claims further that Jack ran *A Broadside* 'to contribute to the nationalist consciousness-raising'. And she claims of Jack's speech to the Race Congress that it 'shows the influence of his political ideals on his aesthetic ideals'. All of these statements are interesting, and intellectually provocative. Some of them may even be true. But there is little supporting evidence. Jack was almost certainly a nationalist, as were the vast majority of his contemporaries, including his brother, whose expression of nationalism was so different from Jack's. Jack was undoubtedly *some kind of* nationalist. And he was a writer into whose work nationalist views and attitudes are injected at a number of levels. Yet even to call him a 'nationalist writer', implying that his nationalism, in certain ways, inspired his writing, begins a process of special pleading for which the evidence is virtually all circumstantial, and dependent on reinterpreting the works to bring them into line with the thesis.

Skelton's point of view is again quite different. He identifies certain thematic constants – the deaths of key characters, the presence of the 'much travelled stranger whose arrival on the scene sets off a chain of events', characters caught up in a pattern of destiny – and he sensibly stresses Jack's claim that 'human intentions are pointless: we are prisoners of a will greater than our own: we can only, if we are wise, accept what life brings us and live as much by chance as by choice'.[27]

John Purser presents other and different problems, not least unravelling, challenging, correcting and extending the views of Norah McGuinness. Profound in his familiarity with the Irish people, and Irish history, he approaches Jack's writing with understanding and sympathy, and with a ready appreciation of the meaning behind both novels and plays. His admiration is unstinting, but his view contains special pleading. He recognises that Jack's writings have failed consistently to impress, putting this down to misunderstanding, and to an inherent and deliberate obscurity. Coupled with the 'unconventional and innovative' nature of his writing, there are two further, compelling arguments about Jack: 'He is in the shadow of himself as a painter. He is in the shadow of his brother as a writer.' Yet Purser places him in 'the forefront of Irish letters', as does Robin Skelton, and argues his case persuasively. And he judges Jack alongside four major figures in twentieth-century Irish literature – Synge, Joyce, Beckett, and his brother Willie.

Purser dates the first three plays, published as *Apparitions,* to 1932. Yet Jack had clearly finished *The Old Sea Road* early in 1931, and possibly in 1930. It was given to Lennox Robinson, for production at the Abbey Theatre, and Robinson read it to Willie, and then sent it on to Lady Gregory, with a note: 'Alas, I am afraid it is no use. It is a painted play, all nice pictures. I read it to W.B.Y. last night & he agrees that it is not worth the playing, but you must read it.'[28] Lady Gregory came to the same conclusion:

193. Sketch for Act One, *The Old Sea Road.*

I began it with faith & hope – but alas my grief it gives but shadowy figures passing the road – and then destroying that shadowy life that is in them with laudanum – for no reason save perhaps boredom. And they have not been sufficiently alive at any moment to make one feel interested even. I am very sorry – would risk myself, getting Jack to the rehearsals to see its empty spaces. I daresay the Gate Theatre may do it, they don't mind what they splash on or how they splash it – living I think on little Mac Liammoirs boundless energy. The Abbey is too self conscious – to much 'in the stern and proud procession of eternal things' to take risks lightly – having a 'character' to keep up![29]

It is difficult not to agree with these judgments. Robinson's description of the play as 'painted' is predictable, and it is hardly true to claim that it is 'all nice pictures'. It clearly is not, with a static, flat set, unchanged throughout the action, and a reliance on stage directions which require much changing of the light, from morning to evening, and the difficult sound of a skylark as part of the background without making any contribution to the action. But his judgment coincides with Jack's own strong sense of composition, demonstrated in drawings of how he wished the characters to be placed. The characters are interesting, and have some appeal, but they do not interact.

The same is true of *Apparitions*. It is wilfully static. *Apparitions* is a play in one act. Jack had to defend it.

> I meant it to be performed on a stage surrounded by the audience. In the middle of the stage is an oval table, on which is an inkstand. Seven chairs are placed around the table. It is a coffee room in a hotel. I wanted to make an experiment when I attached such stage directions to the play. But there is no one who will put such an experimental piece on the stage. Such a play is not fit for the stage in Ireland, to say nothing of England.[30]

The Old Sea Road is ostensibly in three acts, thought its length is no greater than *Apparitions*. *Rattle*, the third play to be published in that first collection of three, is twice as long as the other two. Its complicated plot involves the sale, by the Gardeyne family, of its riverside and wharfing properties, and consideration, by Edward Golback, whose family are in-laws, of other property in distant Pakawana. Through Act Two the rather flat drama of the family's future fortunes runs side by side with the growing importance of Ted's Pakawanaian inheritance. The unresolved affairs of the Gardeyne family are abandoned in Act Three. This shifts to a wooded glade in Pakawana, and concerns two characters, Edward Golback and Doctor Canty, who are on their way to the city. A minor civil war is threatening. Ted speaks in expectation of his own death, summarising his life. Shots ring, and Ted is mortally wounded. Ted Golback, the eventual hero of the play, having enunciated some of its most moving sentiments, dies. It is a not unfamiliar Jack Yeats resolution of plot, reminiscent of the the death of Captain Carricknagat, at the end of *The Scourge of the Gulph*, with Miles expressing that strange epitaph: 'An empty skull, a black box, a dead skipper! Have I done anything or nothing?'

Rattle is the fullest play of the three. John Purser and Norah McGuinness detect significant thematic meaning. McGuinness attaches importance to a familiar twentieth-century interpretation of inequality and exploitation by the Ascendancy. Actions by Gardeyne ancestors in the eighteenth century are described as 'unjust'. They are accused of 'frivolity'. And inevitably the dreaded word, 'colonialism', comes to the surface. John Purser is of a different view, in respect of Pakawana, investing it with a multitude of roles, as an equative Ireland, as a symbol of Empire, as an emblem of India. And he explores these undoubted parallels. Both writers touch on the Pollexfen-Middleton prototype for the Gardeyne-Golback wharfing enterprise, but are reluctant to place it at the centre of the action, where it clearly belongs. The inspiration for the play comes from Jack's much-loved grandfather, William Pollexfen, and the extended family.

Ted is close in character to Jack. He is torn between two worlds, two countries, two loyalties. When he remembers the uncle grasping two

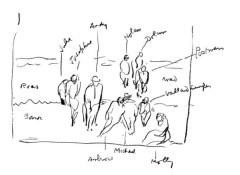

194. Sketch for the position of players just before a policeman enters in the last scene of *The Old Sea Road*.

presents, he is remembering Uncle George Pollexfen. When he recalls the childhood uncertainty of not being told where he was going, he is expressing the instability of his youth, saved from chaos by his doting grandparents. And when he tells Doctor Canty, in respect of the possibility of there being art galleries in the capital of Pakawana, 'You may not need such aids to civilisation. You may have only what you yourselves like, ' the voice is that of the elderly playwright and painter, looking upon the early 1930s outcome of an Irish cultural revival which has largely failed, and from which so many practitioners have fled away.

Jack displays harmony and sweetness in the writing of these plays. And there are parallels between the plays and the fiction, in that the same waywardness, which seemed to work tolerably well in *Sligo*, is transposed into dialogue in the plays, but with results which are far less easy to accept. At one point in *Rattle* Christie says: 'We are all being rather ridiculous'. Unfortunately, it is true. And certain critics of his trilogy felt the same. 'Mr. Yeats's style, which although extremely irritating, owing to his distressing syntax and lack of punctuation, is redeemed by a fair quantity of really good and vivid word-pictures of places and people'.[31]

Jack and Samuel Beckett were good friends by this time. Beckett preferred seeing the painter on his own, and made disparaging remarks about the Saturday 'At Homes', and about other visitors. He refers to Professor Fearon 'grinding out mots', and to Sarah Purser 'scuttling along the treetops', on one particular visit. On another, Dermod O'Brien brought Henry Tonks. O'Brien pontificated about a painting of a waterfall, but 'Tonks was beautiful, decrepit & pleasant, very willowy & Honeish, full of George Moore, Rowlandson & Sickert'. Beckett was also, it seemed, an avoider of Cottie. 'I went round to JBY last Saturday week, found him all alone & Mrs invisible with a 'acking corf,' he wrote to MacGreevy.[32] And on another occasion: 'Yesterday afternoon I had Jack Yeats all to myself, not even Madame, from 3 to past 6, and saw some quite new pictures.'[33] They shared a liking for long walks in the country. Both men were fairly cadaverous, and the appearance of them on the roads must have been of two lean and hungry figures, the older man with his habitual broad-brimmed hat, the younger with short hair swept back. Beckett was still diffident about Jack, and sometimes records setting out to call on him and then changing his mind, and taking a tram ride instead. Beckett even records one of those all too familiar, tangled dreams, about *not* getting to an appointment 'for a long walk by the sea with Jack Yeats'.[34] Beckett brought his brother-in-law, Boss Sinclair, to see Jack'. They found him 'all alone with his pictures deployed. Boss was enthralled.'[35]

Beckett also was enthralled, particularly by a Sligo painting called *Morning*,

almost a skyscape, wide street leading into Sligo looking west as usual, with a boy on a horse, 30 pounds. If I had ten I would beard him with an easy payment proposition. But I have not. I let fall hints here that were understood but not implemented. But I have not given up hope of raising it. Do you think he would be amenable to instalments. It's a long time since I saw a picture I wanted so much. I ran into him again yesterday in the library, but he was uneasy & looked ill and wouldn't have a drink.[36]

While Beckett's mouth was watering over *Morning*, Jack was slipping a word of advice into his ear for MacGreevy, that he should apply for the directorship

195. Thomas Bodkin, *c*. 1950.

of the National Gallery. The job was poorly-paid, part-time, and unsupported by any properly trained staff structure. Thomas Bodkin, who had taken over from Lucius O'Callaghan in 1928, had attempted to have the post made full-time, and to have more staff appointed. He failed, resigned, and went to the Barber Institute of Fine Art, in Birmingham (fig. 195). Jack's advice, through Beckett, was discreet enough, and Beckett told his friend 'not to fail to apply'. In the event George Furlong became director, and remained in the position for fifteen years.[37]

Beckett's early hints to Jack about *Morning* bore fruit. In May 1936 Jack raised the subject with him, and Beckett borrowed ten pounds as a first instalment, 'the remaining £20 to follow God knows when, ' and secured the picture, which hung for a time in his Trinity rooms.[38] Beckett also loved *Low Tide,* describing it as 'overwhelming'.[39] He came to love another work, *A Storm*, which he called 'the fuchsia picture'. Having reservations about it at first, because of its 'artificial excitement', he told MacGreevy he liked it much better the second time he saw it.

Jack's friendship with the younger writer continued to flourish. Beckett's mother, a powerful woman who took a keen interest in her son, met Jack for the first time at Goff's Donkey Show, in July 1936. Like Jack she liked the beast, and had a donkey herself at Cooldrinagh. She remarked to her son how sad and ill he looked. Jack himself was concerned at Beckett's health: 'He enquired was there anything wrong with me, and advised 5 miles walking daily whether it was mental or physical. I thought, the ice is breaking at last.'[40] In the spring of the following year, Cotrie and Jack went out to tea at Cooldrinagh, where they got on well with Beckett's mother. On another occasion Beckett himself drove them, together with Joseph Hone, out to Foxrock, apparently to see Mrs Beckett's donkey. 'I think it went quite well. Mother was as completely natural and at her ease as the donkey was and didn't allow Joe's remote mumblings to disturb her. Cotty had a penetrating basin hat and everything was jolly. Jack admired his pictures.'[41]

It seems, according to a letter in July 1937, that everyone was delighted with *Morning*. Jack was selling paintings, and obviously telling Beckett about this. Bryan Guinness bought one at thirty pounds, and *The Little Waves of Breffny* was sold to a London collector. *While Grass Grows* was acquired by the Haverty Trust and presented to the Waterford Municipal Art Gallery. It was at this time, inspired by the picture, *In Memory of Boucicault and Bianconi*, that Beckett made the observation, 'JBY gets Watteauer & Watteauer'.[42]

What did Beckett mean? And what was Jack? He was familiar with various expressions of modernism in the period between the two World Wars, including abstract Cubism, the style followed by Mainie Jellett, who lived near him in Fitzwilliam Square, and Evie Hone. Jack has often, and wrongly, been characterised as unsympathetic. This view is based on the much-quoted, and indeed misquoted, remark about Albert Gleizes, 'Who the blazes Gleizes?'. Victor Waddington used to tell the anecdote, as did R.R. Figgis, interpreting it as a supposed expression of Jack's impatience with modern art generally, which in the 1930s meant modern *French* art. The story came from an encounter between Father Jack Hanlon and Jack, after the artist had attended the younger painter's first celebration of Mass. It is also given in Hilary Pyle's biography: 'In his slow deep voice Yeats pontificated afterwards on French art, so influential on his contemporaries. "They're all talking about French art. They're all saying who the blazes is Glazes (Gleizes)".'[43]

196. Terence de Vere White.

Jack knew who Gleizes was, from the early 1920s. He often saw Mainie Jellett, and had discussions about art with her. He never pontificated, least of all about art. And French art, regrettably perhaps, was far from influential on his contemporaries, with the exception of a handful, whose work he generally admired. The disparagement, if it was such, may have been directed more towards the speaker of the words than towards the French painter.

Another example of his apparent indifference towards the icons of modern art is contained in his brief outburst, recorded by Terence de Vere White, during a luncheon in Dublin where a visiting lecturer on modern art was being entertained. Jack Yeats was, as usual, a silent witness. The conversation soon became tedious, since the visitor

proved himself a crashing bore and the luncheon was an unhappy affair. Only one of the company exerted himself and the others sat around while the visitor and his local accomplice pontificated about this and that. In the course of their conversation the name of Cézanne came up. They talked about him a great deal in a rather self-conscious way. When they drew breath, Yeats made his first contribution to the conversation: 'Cézanne, Cézanne, Cézanne, sez you.' It was also his last. After so epitaphic an utterance the party could only break up.[43]

The implication in both instances is of impatience, if not dismissal, a view emphasised by Terence de Vere White, who suggests that Jack is not 'much interested in the work of others, ancient or modern'. Such a view, however, is not consistent with Jack's views and behaviour. He expressed his opinions quite forcefully in the context of art exhibitions held in Dublin throughout his active life in the city and he endeavoured to attend most of them. He was also supportive of the work of his younger contemporaries. And he took seriously the efforts made by many people, during the period between the two World Wars in particular, to educate and to encourage an understanding of modern art. He was at one with people like Figgis, who saw how crucial it was at this time to create a new and independent culture for the country which would not be excessively chauvenistic. Above all, he was always interested in the unusual and the new. It was pretension that made him suspicious.

Many of his attitudes on art and culture were channelled through the United Arts Club which became his habitual watering place, at times almost a second home. After the move to Donnybrook, and even more after they took the flat in the same street, just two hundred yards away, he went there almost daily. 'It is remembered that this tall thin figure could fold itself into a chair beside some shy or lonely soul for a moment's chat which left a warm feeling of comfort.' He once made an after-dinner speech in faked French which fooled everyone, but his forte was the epitaph as his contribution to club entertainments. He wrote epitaphs for several members.[44] He later sent Thomas Bodkin a selection of these, one of them for Bodkin, adding that he thought they sounded better than they looked:

In the gallery of his Nation
killed by his occupation
Bodkin lies,

In his prime
At ninety-nine.
And the bolt which
Pierced his heart
was winged with Charity
And tipped with Art.

Under no stones
Nor slates
Lies Jack B.
Yeats.
No heaped up rocks
Just a collection box.
And we thought a Nation's folly
Would like to be jolly
And bury in state
This singular Yeat.
But they were not so inclined
Therefore if you've a mind
To slide a copper in the slot
'Twill help to sod the plot.[45]

The artist Brigid Ganly has confirmed how well Jack performed on these occasions. She remembers at one exhibition feeling that she had to say something about his paintings, and how difficult it was. The subject was sometimes hard to understand, and it was hard also to talk about paint or about the light in the canvas. He stopped her, however. 'There's no need to say anything.' At home it was his habit to serve her with a glass of marsala. He was neither shy nor withdrawn, she says, but lively and aware. When in the company of old friends he could let his hair down, and deliver a varied and colourful account of himself. He did not sing in public. And his recitation was of the lightest kind; in addition to epitaphs, he made up fairly low-grade doggerel on subjects such as the disturbing noise of dustbin men in the early morning.[46] But it was amusing, and she remembers him as 'companionable, witty, always kind, and a brilliant entertainer'. A painter herself, she held Jack in the highest regard as an artist, and quotes with approval Cottie's view that he saw visions. 'Jack would see things that Willie Yeats would give his ears for.'[47]

CHAPTER EIGHTEEN

Death of William Butler Yeats 1939

Far more human than his brother . . .

THE DIFFICULTIES JACK encountered as a writer during the early 1930s caused his output as a painter to fall dramatically as we have seen. It was a deliberate and serious change of direction, and his expectations were high. But his novels, which enjoyed brief attention, could not be considered successful; his plays, as we have seen in the last chapter, even less so. And the wonder is that his determination was so well sustained. His practical difficulties increased with publication of *The Amaranthers* in 1936. This pivotal work provoked a leading English critic of the day, Herbert Read, to describe Jack as a 'Surrealist'. It was a judicious observation; more so than his painting his writing is more revealing of a certain belief in the principles of Surrealism. As a movement it is quintessentially reflective of the creative arguments which bubble out of that unstable and rebellious period between the two World Wars.

Surrealism is an attitude of mind. As an artistic movement its strength and diversity lay in the fact that it imposed no conditions or rules comparable to those governing abstract Cubism. Certain of its beliefs and characteristics may be applied to Jack. Appropriately perhaps, the first and most obvious is the fact that Surrealism is both a painter's and a writer's movement, and attracted the whole commitment of mind and spirit, so that the art produced by the Surrealist artist was the expression of his overall 'style' through thought and philosophy, behaviour in life, and aesthetic beliefs. At the heart of Surrealism lies objective chance, in other words inexplicable coincidence. This is central to reality, which is never an orderly system of events controlled by logical thought. Of nothing is this more true than certain actions in his drama, and, to a lesser extent, the fiction.

When one considers this quiet painter in his Dublin studio, in his sixties, producing wordy and static plays and idiosyncratic novels, keeping silent about his work, listening to his friends and visitors, and making odd and mildly dismissive remarks on the passing phases of modern art, it is difficult to sustain an argument in favour of him having any association with a movement as dramatic as Surrealism. Yet in his declared abandonment of memory, his eclecticism, his evident reliance on images which so often have a dream-like inspiration, and the powerful symbolism of certain conjunctions of people, challenges, ideas, events and moments, it is difficult to imagine how the vortex of Surrealist inspiration did not affect him. He is not *like* other Surrealists. But then other Surrealists are not like each other. There is no clear

197. Jack and Cottie, *c.* 1935.

relationship between René Magritte, Max Ernst, Alberto Giacommetti, Salvador Dali, André Breton or Joan Miro. And the history of Surrealism itself is punctuated by the phenomenon of its members joining and leaving the movement, taking from it such ideas as were useful, exhibiting under its mantle, and then developing beyond it.

In reviewing *The Amaranthers*, Herbert Read was reminded of the French writer, Philippe Soupault, and regretted very much the absence of 'literary life' in Britain, against which movements such the 'Surréaliste' movement might exist and develop. 'Our real need is for more consciousness and mutuality among our poets and painters, so that from their sympathetic activities, their movements, a wider public consciousness might grow and learn to place the individual work in a coherent frame of references.'

In the more intimate circumstances of artistic life in Dublin, this mutuality to some extent existed, not least in the life of the United Arts Club. Jack responded to it, and may well have absorbed from other satirical writers such as Eimar O'Duffy, Lord Dunsany, and possible James Stephens, the style and attitude which gave Read his unusual view of Jack's inspiration. He was aware that in labelling Jack 'a surrealist' he would not be thanked. He quotes extensively a passage notable for its *non sequiturs*, to prove his point.

> The book is a magnificent satire, an irrational and hilarious farce written with the greatest verve and wit. It may, at times, suffer a little from a particularly Irish kind of waggery, but even its grammar is transcendent. Neither the style, nor the humour are the same as Sterne's, but I know no book which comes so close to the unique and immortal qualities of *Tristram Shandy*.[1]

The 'Amaranthers' of the title are members of a private club. They take their name from the amaranth, an imaginary flower, immmortal, never fading. A woman 'with a yellow mop head, short hair, with glossy, duck-neck green and violet tinges' – clearly a female who has stepped out of a painting – is on an island, working as a secretary for a railway speculator. His speculation is rapidly terminated, she leaves for the unspecified city, and there she witnesses a police raid on the club occupied by the Amaranthers. The members, including one who is a government minister in the state which takes this action against his club, manage to escape with their possession, but are seen by the young woman, who then effectively blackmails the minister into giving her a job – 'I only want forty-five dollars a week certain'. Only at this point in the story is her name revealed: Dolores Gray. This sub-plot then comes to an abrupt end when the minister and his new English section library secretary die in an assassination. This part of *The Amaranthers* is written a little in the manner of Graham Greene.

We next encounter James Gilfoyle, a shy, tense figure with a modest shareholding in South American railway shares. When the dividends on these fail, he travels to the country in which the railway has been built in order to obtain redress, and his journey is one of adventure, a familiar theme. Gilfoyle travels the railroad at the company's expense, becomes involved in a film-making project, and in the wake of a hurricane finds himself enrolled in a mercy mission to a hard-hit island. It is the island of the Amaranthers. The conclusion is an apotheosis for the club members and for James Gilfoyle. It encompasses, in a single paragraph, the charm of Jack's writing, the insouciance, the vivid language, the lack of concern about normal fictional demands, and the underlying thread of surrealist thought: 'But the garlanded engine took Brenner, Fagan, Dowd, MacGann, Malone and James Gilfoyle, with laughter on the footplate and laughter in the creamy coach. Up, up, up, the bold mountain to the town on the rock shelf where the Great Man's hand, though more tremulously than when James last saw it, was still capable of signing a contract up there in the skies, ether, clear or speckled, just as you like.'[2]

Was Dublin's United Arts Club in Jack's mind when he wrote *The Amaranthers*, about a secret society of congenial souls, fuelled by an assortment of highly-coloured, high-powered drinks and bent on enjoying life and its amazing melodramas? There was speculation to this effect among members at the time of the book's publication.[3] Thomas Bodkin wrote the following lines in a United Arts Club song at the time:

> So come ye 'Amaranthers' all and drink a toast to him,
> And let it be as long and strong as is 'The Liffey Swim . . .'[4]

The reception given to the book, between its publication, in March, and Herbert Read's review in *The Spectator*, was very mixed. Jack particularly liked Read's review, and told Beckett, who also praised it in a letter to MacGreevy. Writers wanted Yeats to be 'writerly', if he was going to step into their profession, rather in the way that art critics want painters to be 'painterly'. But their taste could not embrace the manner of Jack's delivery. C. Day Lewis concluded that '. . . Mr. Yeats' style depends so largely on using the extraordinary word wherever the ordinary one would be expected that his 'fine writing' becomes too often just finicky writing.'[5] Another critic invoked two figures of importance and influence in Jack's development as an artist, and also in his writing, but without resolving their impact. 'Except that Mr. Jack Yeats's style in prose is as distinctively his own as his style in painting, I would be tempted to say that if J. M. Synge had written a New Arabian Night to follow on R.L. Stevenson's this would have been the book.'[6]

In one further, undated and unidentified cutting the lack of structure is condemned: 'It reads like a private joke or a half-waking dream; a chaotic flow of mental imagery lacking any conscious control. It rejects the common necessities of plot, characterisation and realism; punctuation and grammar go by the board; and it has no beginning, no middle and no end. It is just "tale . . . signifying nothing".'[7]

Among serious examinations of his work, an essayist in the *Times Literary Supplement* wrote:

> In its incongruous mixture both of objects and beings as well as its abrupt transitions the fantasy brings us the sensation of the dream. Only in a dream should we expect to find a primitive island, which appears to be in the west of Ireland, with a skyscraper of its own. The dream-like quality is intensified by the fact that, although the island has a flourishing industry in illicit spirit and is guarded by quicksands, it is less than half a mile from the tram and railway termini of the mainland. The Surrealiste (sic) effect of the whole is increased by Mr. Yeats's peculiar style, for he follows the inflections and expressive tones of good conversation rather than the less arbitrary conventions of ordinary writing. But it would be a mistake, perhaps, to identify the method of this fantasy with Mr. Yeats's experimental phase in painting. He is obviously content to ramble fancifully and to fulfil unconsciously that unwritten law which forces the wanderer in bush or desert to describe a circle.[8]

Samuel Beckett also reviewed *The Amaranthers*, for the *Dublin Magazine*.[9] He asked Seumus O'Sullivan to let him do it, and told MacGreevy he got it 'by return of post'. The allowance of 500 words was hopelessly inadequate; he was looking for 2,000. 'I wrote review of *Amarenthers* for Seumus. Only 500 words, I was tired & it is bad. I compared him with Ariosto.'[10] He described Jack's process as 'analytical imagination', quotes at least two passages which are not unlike descriptive writing from James Joyce, but rejects all easy labels, of allegory, symbol, and satire. 'The Island is not throttled into Ireland, nor the City into Dublin, notwithstanding "one immigrant, in his cups, recited a long narrative poem".' And Beckett demonstrates his close reading of Jack's work with an observation about a stage 'suggestion' from *The Old Sea Road*: 'The sky, sea and land are brighter than the people.' Perhaps most tellingly, Beckett avoids any linkages between the book and Ireland. He was already becoming seriously resistant to the idea of being an 'Irish' writer, and was pressing his case, as we shall shortly see, in respect of others, notably Jack.

MacGreevy wrote to Jack admiringly of *The Amaranthers*, and Jack replied: 'I thank you very much for the fine things you say so well about "the Amaranthers" I am proud and fond of all the personages of all kinds, in that book, so anything good you say about them, or their countries pleases me.'[11]

Jack must have been reassured enough by the reception given to *The Amaranthers* to go on to write three more novels. *The Amaranthers* was published by Heinemann in 1936. Jack sent them his next novel, *The Charmed Life*, in mid-summer 1937, but Heinemann turned it down. Herbert Read told Ragg, of Routledge, that sales of *The Amaranthers* had been poor, but he expressed at the same time his own enthusiasm for the new book, and advised Ragg to offer for it. Ragg wrote to Jack:

> Read has told me how highly he thinks of it – in fact I have read his report to Heinemann about it; and this, together with my knowledge of you and my remembrance of 'The Emeranths' and 'Sailing, Sailing Swiftly' encourages me to write to you and ask whether you would send the new novel to me . . . Our policy is only to publish very few, and they must be novels of real distinction. Nothing would please me more than to have a novel by you to publish in the spring of next year.[12]

Jack, in the meantime had offered it to Faber. It came back with the worst of messages for the writer: 'a kind and long letter. They all seem to delight in it – but they write of "the bed of Procrustes with which novels have now to be fitted in order to sell". Its an "apple pie" bed to me. I have the greatest pleasure in sending the book to you.'[13]

The response was enthusiastic. Ragg decided before he had finished reading the book that he wanted to publish, and offered Jack the usual terms of the period, though with a small advance, even for 1937.[14] Jack quibbled over the details, and his high expectations were indicated by the demand he then made:

> I am satisfied with the terms you suggest except that, though I do not see my work appealing to a very large public, still, I would like to feel that, if you did have that fortune, I would get a larger royalty – So I suggest that that I should get 20% on from 6,000 to 10,000 copies, and over 10,000 copies 25%.[15]

The high expectation was not to be realised.

276

It was later in the same year that Jack recommended to Ragg Samuel Beckett and his novel, *Murphy*:

> A friend of mine, Sam Beckett, has the manuscript of a novel 'Murphy' which is to be submitted to your firm. I have not seen it, but his other novel I read and I thought it the real thing. There was inspiration in it. It was published a year or two ago. and I daresay by now the public readers have crept under its inspiration. But even if this has lept away in front of that, perhaps the hour has come when the public dunderheads can be induced to stoop their noses to something more alive than the old printers-ink-aniseed-bag. – 'something to read the same as the last' I write to ask you, if you cannot read Becketts MS yourself just now, to give it to some open minded reader.[16]

Ragg read the book himself, while ill in bed, and liked it enormously. He decided straight away that he would publish, but added the sombre warning: 'I am afraid there is no doubt that it is far too good to be a big popular or commercial success. On the other hand, like your own book, will bring great joy to the few. Thank you very much for introducing it to me.'[17]

The Charmed Life appeared in 1938. The book has a pair of principal characters; they are called No Matter and Bowsie. No Matter, through whose 'voice' the stream of anecdotes and half stories emerges, is named as a mark of innate deference to the invisibility of the story-teller. Nothing about him is strange. 'In fact, a washing away of strangeness was his long suit. He had, at times, without any effort as far as anyone could know, a way of almost floating into the invisible. He was there. He wasn't there.'

For close on three hundred pages he is certainly there, the mellifluous flow of his words linking the diffuse and fragmentary together. Is he as near as we get to Jack himself? His presence is a blank mirror into which the other main character, Bowsie, stares, rather bleary-eyed. No Matter monitors Bowsie's behaviour, attempts to tidy him up a bit – there are fascinating insights into late thirties standards in dry-cleaning, with Bowsie's suit smelling strongly of petrol, used to remove stains – and there is a near-drowning of the same slightly unkempt character. And because No Matter is 'first-person', the temptation to identify him with Jack is strong. But when Bowsie says, of wild and open spaces: 'I go in without a ticket, except a complimentary one. I give myself that one. I am Eternity's fool, and we neither understand each other. We don't have to,' it, too, sounds like Jack speaking. The phrase itself, 'travelling through life without a ticket', became a slogan, used frequently as a description of his own experiences. Do we have two alter egos, conversing with each other? If that device fitted with Jack's creative method, it would seem so. But it is more complicated than that. Other figures slip in and out among the loosely-woven strands of yet another tapestry of Irish talk. There are the Devanys. There is the Judge, and Hound Voice, John Devine and Small Voice.

The stories reflect the imagery which must have filled Jack's visual memory, and to which, in his writing, his words are so cleverly and often so refreshingly linked, so that individual phrases can be compelling, as when he describes stiff-legged men as being 'agile as angels in clouds', or Devany, after learning of his early rescue from drowning, being 'very thankful to all who baptised him with romance'. The material covered is the material of the painter's own life, his smoking, given up eventually on account of health; his

198. *A Dusty Rose*, oil on panel, $9\frac{1}{2} \times 14$, private collection. 1936.

interest in horses, circuses, lakelands and water, the life of the sea, the racecourse, and America.[18] He uses again, though with greater subtlety than before, the oldest structure of all in the telling of his tale, that of the journey. The journey has an end, both physically, by the sea, and in terms of character, in the death of Julia and the near-drowning and departure of Bowsie. There is a psychological ending as well, as they talk of death at dusk. The three hotels and the three locations mark three stages in the journey, with two characters consistently accompanying each other on their way. *The Charmed Life*, as John Purser and Norah McGuinness have persuasively argued, achieves its aims more effectively than the other books.

The book was well received. Kate O'Brien reviewed it for *The Spectator*: 'I put *The Charmed Life* at the top of the class this week because, although it is often turgid, sometimes maddening, and occasionally just plumb silly, it is nevertheless a work of imagination, airy, non-pedestrian, and taking its full share of "freedom and scope".'[19]

From *The Daily Express* it provoked a pen-portrait: 'Jack Yeats comes from Sligo in West Ireland, is sixty-one, white-haired and high of brow. Chief work is landscape painting. He believes in fairies, reads a lot of poetry, likes playing darts, watching circuses, listening to birds singing. Adores donkeys.'[20]

Willie liked it better than *The Amaranthers* and referred to it as:

My brother's extreme book . . . He does not care that few will read it, still fewer recognise its genius; it is his book, his 'Faust', his pursuit of all that through its unpredictable, unarrangeable reality least resembles knowledge. His style fits his purpose for every sentence has its own taste, tint and smell.[21]

Inevitably, the displacement of one activity by the other affected his output as a painter. As we have already seen, the flow of oils during the late 1920s – thirty-six in 1927, twenty-three in 1928, twenty-five in 1929, and twenty-four in 1930 – fell dramatically. The overall total for the next *five* years – 1931–35 – was only thirty-one, less than one year's work, in 1927. There then followed, in 1936, a sudden burgeoning of expression, with thirty-three oils. And this was followed, shortly after, with the commencement of his late, large-scale output as well. Indeed, a harbinger of this was given by the succession of major works in 1936, all 24×36 inches, and including *Donnelly's Hollow, In Tir na n-Og*, and *They Come, They Come!* His drop in output is reflected in the fact that he had a Dublin solo exhibition in 1931, and then not again until 1939.

If the output was lean during these early years of the decade, it had a character of intimacy and sweetness which is most appealing. This is perhaps best exemplified by the series of Rose paintings, works of great loveliness and of an intensity of feeling which impressed many people.[22] He wrote of the project to Thomas Bodkin: 'I painted the other day a new subject for me – a rose. I painted the rose alive, and then followed it into the ante room of the Roses' shadowland, and painted another little panel of it departing. But theres nothing piano about it, nor yet fussy diegame.'[23]

He showed them to Beckett, who called on him one Saturday in mid-September 1936. At that stage, three out of the four canvases had been completed. Beckett gives as the title of the first in the sequence, *Tyranny of the Rose*. This equates with *A Rose*, in Hilary Pyle's Catalogue Raisonné, but she writes there of a possible 'fifth rose painting which has not since been traced'.

199. *A Rose*, oil on panel, 9×14, private collection. 1936.

279

Jack refused to communicate anything about them to Beckett, whose own view is that the main transition comes with the third painting, *A Dusty Rose*, which the artist moved off the mantelpiece and placed 'on a table with the room all round. So that 3 is less of a flower than an interior.'[24] Though not a sequence as such, it is clear that Jack saw them united by their central subject-matter, new to him (figs 198–9). Among the important works painted during the 1930s was his large canvas, *Death for Only One*, which was first exhibited at the Royal Hibernian Academy in 1938 where it was seen by Ernie O'Malley. O'Malley and his wife came up from their home in Newport, County Mayo, in April 1939, wanting to buy the painting. Jack described it as 'of a dead tramp lying on a headland with another tramp standing by – and a dark sea and dark sky'.[25]

He wanted to be more widely known. We can see this from the correspondence with MacGreevy. The idea for a book about himself had been on his mind for many years, and he had been approached by the Talbot Press, a reasonably successful and prolific Dublin publishing firm. In 1936 he first raised the idea with Thomas MacGreevy. Though it took ten years to reach fruition, the two men repeatedly discussed the project.

> Years ago, the Talbot press in Dublin were looking for someone to do a book about my painting with a lot of reproductions. But they didnt find anyone who seemed suitable . . . Would you think of editing such a book yourself suggesting it to Chatto and Winders[sic] or Cape or whatever publication you thought. Especially one who would produce some cash. I have plenty of early water colours and oils and a thick bookfull could be got together without touching at all on illustration work or line drawing. You would not want to write panorama show man descriptions of my paintings nor personal notes about the hats I wore. But just your own ideas associated, in ever so slight a thread of a way, with everything brought about by a brush on paper or canvas . . . It might be a good moment to find a publisher so I suggest it now. But if the plan seems a creepy nuisance to you dont think anymore about it anyway first of all you would have to let me know . . . I expect this plan would not count exactly as *my* book.[26]

MacGreevy responded enthusiastically. Chatto and Windus had published a book by MacGreevy on T.S. Eliot in 1931, quite short, and suggestive of what might be done about Jack. He worked on the project and some time towards the end of 1937 showed Jack a draft. MacGreevy wanted to have the book published in England, not necessarily related to any exhibition.

Jack was not an easy man with whom to collaborate. He had a great deal to say, and particularly did not like being described in the draft as Anglo-Irish:

> 'Anglo-Irish' means, to my ear, one brother tea planting in Ceylon, Ethel married to a rubber planter in Siam, and Doreen, married to a decent chap who has tried sheep farming in New Zealand. Or perhaps it means, the Big House or The Little Big House at the back of my mind. Perhaps Yeats, the name, is not what is usually meant by 'Anglo'. Its likely mispronounced 'Goats', a goats head is our crest. The crest also (when it cant be refined into an antelopes head) of the Gore, or Gower families and Gower is Gabhan = a goat. and when the fierce lad, who edits the 'Catholic Bulletin', wants to be extra chop nasty to my brother he calls him 'Pollexfen Yeats'. Pollexfen,

my mothers name, is not Anglo, there is only one in the London Directory and I think I know who it is. But it might easily be some spot name for a celtic place = the pool of clearwater. An old uncle of mine would have it that the Phoenicians – tin men – brought the name to Cornwall. He said nothing about Helens big thumbed brother. I dont want to pull this stuff about being more Irish than the Irish, making the Brogue roll. No I belong to those who belong to a spirit land . . . I think on page 13, where you begin 'It would be doing a disservice to Jack Yeats' you begin further down the page to do a disservice to me, and all who walk where I walk. Those who have elected to step upon the slippery clouds. If they are ever to have the shackles taken from them, and their heads tossed free, by anyone but themselves must be considered as walking all abreast in conversation perhaps and all those Grand Conversations are over the Rose. But that is enough. Those who take the risk of standing with the immortals stand where all are equal, no caste. There is no arithmetic in Heaven.[27]

The work progressed despite the extensive commentary. He wrote to his friend early in 1938:

I said from the first that you were to feel absolutely free in writing about my work. But as you ask me for them, here are some notes that may, or may not, come as useable suggestions to you. The description of the prison picture is not quite right there are women prisoners only looking from the windows. But later on, if you dont see the picture itself again, I will send you a photograph . . . I think perhaps 'Anglo-Irish' is a pivot point in your essay . . . Must I never look with the eye of affection on anything that grows, or moves, or is still. Only paint the solemn angular or the rigid curtains of grandeur. I know you dont wish that. But here is where a crown colony civilization like the British can never produce sunlight only moor's gloss . . . I would wish you to give the donkey a more respecting adjective than 'stubborn'. I, myself, never use 'Donkey' or 'Ass' as a term of human derision. The Donkey, without great aggressive strength has had to repose himself on what defence he owns. The blood horse was made by man, by selection. The Ass selected himself. The wild ass of the foothills is still the finest type of ass alive. Now in this essay, after all, I am satisfied that you, if you wish it so, do not undot an i or uncross a t. Will you yourself see Ragg at Routledges about the book?[28]

Jack was unsure how to procede, worried about reproductions. He told Ragg of MacGreevy's book. Jack told Ragg he did not want

an elaborate album with imitations of the paintings . . . My idea of a proper book of a man's pictures is that it should be illustrated by sketches made of the compositions . . . Not humbug notes *for* the pictures . . . but honest notes *of* the pictures. And the people told that they have in these a rough idea of the picture. But not a near substitute for the event. The Voice of the eternal. But not a gramaphone record of it.[29]

It was turned down as not profitable enough and the material returned. The project was suspended, and the book did not appear until after the Second World War. But MacGreevy did much of the groundwork at this time, and, as well as discussing it in detail with Jack, consulted with Samuel Beckett. The exchanges are important. They reveal Beckett's insights into Jack's work, but also into his own. The debate on Jack's art is between two men intimately familiar with the work. According to Deirdre Bair, MacGreevy showed the draft of the book to Beckett while he was convalescing in the Hotel Liberia, after having been stabbed on the streets of Paris by a pimp. This was early in 1938. But the MacGreevy correspondence reveals that the book was partly written as early as 1936, when Jack showed Beckett photographs which could possibly be used for illustrations, and Beckett wrote to MacGreevy asking him to tell him more about it.

It was an ill-fated project, both then and later. Part of the problem was that Jack saw it as a joint affair, himself consulting with the Society of Authors about terms and payments. He seems to have been obsessed, as with his fiction, about the large sums of money which might be gained from such a venture. This placed unnecessary strain on his friend. It surprised Beckett, who told MacGreevy, 'I am sorry you haff bin haffing such trouble with the finances of it. Was it necessary to drag in the Authors' Assoc. or whatever it is? Could it not have been a private arrangement between you and him more fair to you?'[30]

Beckett took trouble over the book. He read it through twice, and then wrote, commending it in general terms, particularly the first eighteen pages, in which he did not think a syllable needed changing. He thought particularly well of MacGreevy's examination of Jack's integration of figures and landscape. At the time of Beckett's letter, the artists with whom MacGreevy compares Jack included Le Nain, Chardin, Millet, Courbet. They provide a framework. But in further writing, they subsequently changed, and Rembrandt, Titian, Perugino, Claude, Corot, Constable, are all invoked, all with reason. Beckett's own modest proposal is to add 'Le Douanier' Rousseau. He then makes the point that MacGreevy had taken up his now famously over-worked reference to Jack growing 'Watteauer and Watteauer' in a way quite different from Beckett's own intentions, which were philosophical rather than literal. It does not take from the writer's view; indeed, one of the best passages in the MacGreevy essay is the one dealing with the Watteau comparison. And Beckett commends it. But it *is* different.

Beckett's analysis of MacGreevy's handling of history and nationalism is important. He took exception to the presentation of Jack in nationalist terms. He uses the word 'construit' to preface a sensitively reasoned argument. MacGreevy, as a historian, gives more credit to circumstance; Beckett, as a writer, gives more weight to the natural evolution of the 'general psychological mechanism' of the creative person. They move as they develop, from the particular, the 'local', to the more eternal and universal themes. How true this is of Beckett's own writing, and of Jack's.

Beckett was himself angered at the time because his own novel, *Murphy*, which was shortly to be published by Routledge, was to be accompanied by publicity material which stressed his 'Irish genius', and his 'Celtic waywardness'. Deirdre Bair claims that 'the merest suggestion that he was an "Irish" writer enraged him.'[31] This material referred to him as 'Sam', a shortened version of his name which he deplored, at least in public use, and the wording was modified.

Beckett is clearly unhappy with MacGreevy's attempts to relate Jack's development, particularly pre- and post-1916, with events in Ireland and to extrapolate a nationalism which is inappropriate. He also finds the overall argument top-heavy for the essay's essentially brief and limited scope.

I received almost the impression for example, as the essay proceeded, that your interest was passing from the man himself to the forces that formed him – and not only him – and that you returned to him from them with something like reluctance. But perhaps that also is my fault, of my mood and of my chronic inability to understand as member of any proposition a phrase like 'the Irish people', or to imagine that it ever gave a fart in its corduroys for any form of art whatsoever, whether before the Union or after, or that it was ever capable of any thought or act other than the rudimentary thoughts and acts belted into it by the priests and by the demagogues in service of the priests, or that it will ever care, if it ever knows, any more than the Bog of Allen will ever care or know, that there once was a painter in Ireland called Jack Butler Yeats. This is not a criticism of a criticism that allows as a sentient subject what I can only think of as a nameless and hideous mass, whether in Ireland or in Finland, but only to say that I, as a clot of prejudices, prefer the first half of your work, with its real and radiant individuals, to the second, with our national scene. Et voila . . . God love thee, Tom, and don't be minding me. I can't think of Ireland the way you do.[32]

There are moments when Beckett and MacGreevy appear to be fighting for the soul of Jack Yeats, by way of his art and his nationalism. Jack is somewhere in the middle, not as strongly against his own Irishness as Beckett was against his, and caring more about the Irish people than Beckett appeared to care. He shared MacGreevy's enthusiastic interpretations and accepted that MacGreevy had to decide his own criteria.

Jack received letters from Beckett after the Paris stabbing episode in 1938, and wrote to MacGreevy, reporting on Beckett as 'fairly cheerful but has pain though he is going along all right'. Apart from the wounding, Beckett was enjoying Paris, and stayed there. He was obliged under French law to pursue the case against his would-be assassin, Prudent, and found himself sitting beside the man he was to accuse. He asked him why he had done it, and was told, 'I don't know'. The man got two months in prison, where he was showered with presents from his *poules*. Beckett's own book, *Murphy*, published at this time, yielded small funds. Jack went off to Sligo for the funeral of Arthur Jackson, the husband of Alice Pollexfen, the youngest of his grandparents' family, who had been running the Sligo business. Jack ended the letter, 'so the oldest event takes us back to our childhood paths'.[33]

In the summer Beckett called on Jack and Cottie. Jack had been busy '. . . painting various bends of time. One is a Helen launching a ship herself.'[34] Beckett saw the painting and was greatly taken with it. The figure of Helen made him think of the Venetian painter, Jacopo Bassano, not because of similarities in treatment of figures, but because of 'some extraordinary tendancy & distinction of handling'. He also thought of Delacroix. He was profoundly impressed. He wrote of Jack's courage and his depth, achieved in an absolutely natural and unrhetorical way.

Jack saw Beckett off to Paris. Beckett came back to see his mother for a month in the summer, but had effectively settled in Paris, moving such things as his collection of books and his bicycle with him. He was clearly not likely to see Jack as often as had been the case through the 1930s. 'He concluded his letter to MacGreevy: 'Taking leave of me on the step he said "It must be 6 or 7 years since I first walked out of this house with you to buy the evening paper and 6 or 7 years should mean a lot to me, but they don't seem to & it doesn't matter".'

There has been confusion about the second half of that sentence. Beckett's biographer suggests that it was Beckett referring to the years not having mattered, but in fact it was Jack, who had passed through one of the more difficult periods in his life, one which had been partly shared by the much younger man, who was now so close a commentator on his art, and so deep in his general understanding of the painter.[35]

A short-lived venture in the second half of the 1930s was *A Broadside*, restarted by Cuala in 1935, and repeated in 1937, though now with W.B. Yeats, together with Dorothy Wellesley, as joint editors, and Jack listed merely as one of several illustrators. Willie wrote to Dorothy Wellesley in 1937, saying how delighted he was with the new *Broadside*: 'My brother has got to perfection the old-fashioned highly ornamented Dublin hotel or tavern where such men would gather after a Parnell celebration.' He was referring to an illustration to his own poem, 'Come gather round me, Parnellites', which appeared in the issue for January 1937 (fig. 200). Four men, two of whom have faces like thunder, raise their glasses to toast their leader, in an expressive late drawing filled with the drama and emotion which his great name conjured. 'Every man that sings a song,' the poem says

> Keeps Parnell in his mind,
> For Parnell was a proud man,
> No prouder trod the ground,
> And a proud man's a lovely man
> So pass the bottle round.'

But the admiration for Jack's work was no indication of the real relationship between the two brothers. Politically, at this time, they were still far apart. As early as 1933, Willie had become involved, though briefly, with the Blueshirt Movement in Ireland, and generally displayed right-wing tendencies which were seriously at odds with Jack's left-wing views, and his Fianna Fail-style republicanism. They saw little of each other. The Yeats children, Anne and Michael, did not really come to know their uncle during the 1930s, when they were growing up. Michael feels he never knew him at all well; Anne believes that she only came to know him when she had finished her education, and had become involved in two of Jack's favourite activities, painting and theatre. But in fact Jack sent her a Christmas present in 1938, well before his first play was accepted. It was the Worlds Classics edition of Bret Harte, and as well as sending her seasonal greetings he wrote: 'I send you these stories of Bret Harte's because all my life they have stood to me for romance. If Bret Harte had never lived there would have been no San Francisco, no Golden Gate, no Los Angeles, No Hollywood, No California at all. And California is still California, California, The Queen of Comeallya. And I am your affectionate uncle Jack B Yeats.'[36]

By this stage, Willie's ill-health had taken him away from Ireland. He had suffered bouts of ill-health since the late 1920s. In 1929, while staying in Rapallo, in Italy, which for a time became a second winter home, haemorrhaging of the lungs brought on an illness serious enough for Willie to make an emergency will, witnessed by Ezra Pound and Basil Bunting. And he had renewed serious illnesses in 1935, causing collapse, and again in 1936. From

200. Illustration for *A Broadside* 'Come gather round me, Parnellites', pen and ink, 1937.

then on his visits to Dublin virtually ended. He ceased also to read Jack's growing output of literature, and wrote to Edith Shackleton Heald to tell her: 'now that I have created nothing for a good many days and have ceased to read my brother and Milton I begin to feel that I can face my fellow men again'.[37]

He did return home, in June of 1938, mainly to sort out Cuala Press and Abbey Theatre affairs. And this was the last occasion on which the two brothers met. Jack later recalled thinking him 'full of mental vitality with a few years left to him'.[38] And he told MacGreevy of their last meeting: 'My brother suffered very little towards the end. When I spent an hour or two talking with him, at Rathfarnham . . . he was full of vigour of Spirit.'[39] But the vigour of spirit failed; the years had run out. George was with her husband, in the south of France, staying in a small hotel outside Roquebrune, overlooking the Mediterranean, when he made his final answer to 'the singing-masters of my soul'.

There were extensive tributes, worldwide. A great poet had passed away, a controversial voice from his earliest days, and combative to the end, there was nevertheless a feeling of fragmentation and uncertainty at the end. Among the tributes there was, understandably, a formal one passed by the United Arts Club: 'At this meeting the Committee desire to place on record the sense of loss felt by the Committee and all the members of the Club on the death of Mr

201. Jack Yeats and William Butler Yeats, in 1933, standing in front of Gurteen Dhas, the house from which their sisters ran the Cuala enterprises.

W.B. Yeats, one of the Club's Honorary Members. A copy of this resolution to be sent to Mrs Yeats and to Mr Jack Yeats. Passed unanimously.'[40]

Willie seemed not to have belonged to Ireland during his closing years, and to have been ravished by uneasy voices and conflicting arguments. He remembered, in *Last Poems*, to designate how and where he was to be buried. And the poems deal also with eternity and posterity, with the effect of both the future and the past upon the present. The summary is relevant to Jack: between the eternity of a man's soul, and the eternity of his race, he lives and dies many times. The partings are brief, since mortality binds together again. Man's instincts are to fight, and to create. Let those who will pursue them.

W.B. Yeats's soul and spirit may have transcended time, but the gathering of his bones in conformity with his last wishes was a clumsy and protracted affair. His body was consigned first to a chapel in the steeply sloping cemetery of Roquebrune. Under French law it required clearance before being moved, and there were no obvious ways of bringing it home. The assumption, however, was that the delay would not be prolonged, and when George Yeats returned to the children in Rathfarnham it was in the expectation that her husband's body would soon follow her. It was necessary to make arrangements for the burial. In anticipation of this, and shortly after her return, Jack travelled with George Yeats and the two children to Sligo, on Wednesday 8 February, to choose the site for the grave. As the senior male in the Yeats family he had assumed the traditional position as its head, and his voice, from then on, was the deciding factor in all family decisions. It is Anne's view that her mother would have regarded as entirely correct the handing over of formal decisions to the eldest male in the family. But in reality, she feels, the actual decisions would have been hers. They all stayed in the Great Southern Hotel, and the next morning went out to Drumcliff churchyard to see the site chosen for the grave. Everything that was done 'carried out in letter and in spirit Willys wish'. In the church was a tablet to Jack's own great grandfather's memory. 'Parson John Yeats' (1774–1846), rector of Drumcliff, had fathered a dozen children, and had ministered for many years in this parish, nestling under the great mass of Ben Bulbin.

Characteristically, Jack went off by himself on what he described as 'my Rip Van Winkle walks round the corners of Sligo'.[41] 'After dinner in the hotel I walked into the town & though it was rather a drip drip night, the Garavogue was rolling over his weir to the sea as if he had lately been filling himself with strong rains . . . I was round the town this morning after breakfast and will likely go out again presently.'

He stayed two nights, lunching with Oliver Edwards on the Friday before taking the mail train back to Dublin. He included instructions to Cottie in his letter telling of his return: 'I'll only be hungry enough for a little supper.' He renewed acquaintance with someone he had sailed with on the west coast: 'One figure from the past – (the not so distant past) – recognised me and spoke to me – Frank Feeney from Rosses Point the son of old Frank (who you saw the first time you came to Rosses Point). This younger Frank was engineer on the *Tartar* when we sailed on her from Ballycastle to Belmullet.'[42]

Jack attended the memorial service in St Patrick's Cathedral in Dublin, but he did not go to England for the service, a month later, on March 16, in the church of St Martin-in-the-Fields. However, he was concerned to alert people to it while at the same time being diffident about placing old friends under obligation. He wrote to MacGreevy, giving details:

There may be some people, who could go, but may know nothing about it . . . I would, myself, send them a line. But they might then feel bound to go. That would embarrass them so will you, if you have the opportunity, tell any friend of mine. I will not be able to be over. The 16th of March is also the Centenary of my fathers birth. When they were arranging the date of course they did not know that.[43]

There was another death at the time, which briefly ruffled the life of the United Arts Club, and was then forgotten. It provoked from Jack, in the same letter, an oblique reference to his own death: 'The last curtain, when it does come down, will be so tattered, that it will not be able to be used under the excuse that it is a mantle of decency.' He was led to these thoughts by the suicide of Tom Casement, Roger Casement's brother, who stepped into the Grand Canal, at Mespil Road. His body, dressed in pyjamas and dressing gown, was recovered near Baggot Street Bridge. Jack was fond of his wild ways and sad at the unfortunate episode of suicide. During the 1930s Casement had become something of a club bore, perpetually there, perpetually drinking, swearing, and getting into scrapes. He had been given honorary membership, but had then resigned, on some kind of protest, thinking that his honorary membership would protect his long-term access. It did not. He found himself out in the cold, in more ways than one, deserted by former friends, no longer tolerated in his regular watering places, and desperately hard up. He was kept in his Burlington Road lodgings by a Northern Ireland relation, and a small fund organised by Beatrice Glenavy, and subscribed to by club members, gave him weekly resources. No doubt Jack was a subscriber. Casement's grave at Dean's Grange was paid for by his sister. After his death the lifeguard service he had founded subscribed for the gravestone, some nine hundred members around the coast giving sixpence each.

Many explanations have been offered of the relationship between the two Yeats brothers, many interpretations of their political differences, their huge divergences of character and belief. They were very different in their outlook, and they were not close in their adult lives. They saw the world quite differently. Where Jack boasted of travelling without a ticket, Willie not only always had one, but ensured that it was first class. Yet Jack admired his brother, both as poet and man, and stoutly defended his character and his actions. And there is something perceptive and intensely moving in the reply to a question about the poet from Monk Gibbon:

> I once said to Jack Yeats, as we sat together in his studio, something about the arrogance which W.B. could display on occasions. And in his entirely gentle and oblique way Jack came immediately to this brother's defence, hinting that it was a result of the humiliations which the poet had had to share in his youth, when family cash was always short and fame still very far off.[44]

Willie had borne the not inconsiderable burdens of being the eldest of the Yeats children from early youth, literally until the end of his life, and had still been dealing with the Cuala Press financial difficulties within months of his own death. Jack, the silent observer, and perhaps, in the end, the more ruthless artist of the two, had observed and understood, and stood to his brother's defence after the poet's death.

Jack expressed his retrospective thoughts on his relationship with his

202. William Butler Yeats, towards the end of his life.

203. Ernest Blythe.

brother in a letter to William Rothenstein: 'Of late years I had longer talks with my brother than perhaps I ever had. We sat at our ease on opposite sides of a milestone on the grass verge of a road. And, simply, the innocent grass grew over the turnpike and it wasn't a turnpike any more. My brother's spirit and his imagination were as full as ever they were to the very last.'[45] The turnpike had lain between them for many years, perhaps even back to childhood and early manhood. No two brothers, in art or literature, were more drawn together by family or national circumstance while at the same time being so emotionally or psychologically different. One reads with relief this bare but moving recollection of reconciliation.

Willie's death however had a practical advantage for Jack. During Willie's lifetime, the Abbey Theatre had failed to put on any of Jack's plays, which had regularly been submitted, and read, since the early 1930s. Willie's role in the relevant decisions was probably marginal; and when he did judge on his brother's work the judgements seem to have been objective and professional. But they do appear to have coloured the general view. The view taken of Jack, as a playwright, was patronising. He was recognised as a national figure, with a dedicated following among art lovers. And there was some recognition of his merits as a writer. Ernest Blythe records that most of the Abbey Theatre directors 'felt that Jack Yeats's plays had some sort of quality and were not indisposed to try one of them on the public, partly as a gimmick and partly in the hope that Jack Yeats's name and his fame as a painter might draw substantial audiences to the theatre for a week or so.'[46]

Blythe himself admired the work (fig. 203). But there had always been the serious problem of Willie. We saw how Jack's first play, submitted in about 1930, and read by Lennox Robinson, Augusta Gregory and his brother, led to general agreement that it simply would not do. This view prevailed with his other plays, and even hardened. Towards the end of the 1930s, when his fame had increased and he had published both plays and novels, the same veto was applied: 'When the proposal was made at a Board meeting, however, W.B. Yeats pronounced firmly and curtly against it.'[47] Perhaps Jack's scarcely veiled criticism of Willie's *The Word upon the Window Pane* had something to do with this.

The text of *Harlequin's Positions* was first sent to the Abbey by Jack in September 1938. In April 1936 Jack told MacGreevy he had also sent it to Tyrone Guthrie and had mentioned in his letter the possibility of Charles Laughton playing a part, presumably that of Alfred Clonboise.

> I havent heard from Guthrie yet about the play. He said anyway that Laughton was liable to be dilatory. I had not begun building any great hopes. And I hadn't been spreading any advance news of possibilities. The slipt lip dreads the cup. I try to be only talkative about the thing done. Guthrie cheered me a little because he did not treat my play as just mad wren's nest making in a cloud, and only two or three other producers had as much ordinary sense.[48]

The decision to put it on appears to have been made immediately after Willie's death. There is a letter from Jack to F.R. Higgins:

> Thank you for your letter of yesterday. tho I never received your previous letter. I know that my play *H.'s P.* is describable as an experiment. But I hope it may prove a successful one. And I will be very glad that your

204. Ria Mooney and Sean O'Casey at the dress rehearsal of *The Plough and the Stars*, in the summer of 1926. She was his choice to play the part of Rosie Redmond. He inscribed the photograph for her: 'Be clever Maid and let who will be good.'

Experimental theatre should produce it. With all good wishes to Mrs. Higgins and yourself, Jack Yeats.[49]

The chosen venue, once his brother's embargo was removed, was the Abbey Experimental Theatre, which had been formed in 1937, and played in the Peacock Theatre. It had opened with Mervyn Wall's first play, *Alarm Among the Clerks*, a witty comedy set in the Irish Civil Service. The whole enterprise was run on student labour and volunteers, with the blessing of the main theatre, which made available the premises, cash for scenery, and a young man to act as stage manager.

The play was directed by Ria Mooney (fig. 204) and Cecil Ford. She was also responsible for management, and she has written enthusiastically about the period and the various experimental ventures she undertook. She was under the impression that *Harlequin's Positions* was Jack's first play, and from her first reading of it formed the view – perhaps an exaggerated one – 'that this brother of W.B. Yeats could have contributed as much to the Irish theatre as he did to Irish painting'.[50] Anne Yeats designed and painted the sets. Jack did sketches to guide her, and though they are rough and diagrammatic, they are filled with furniture and props. He dwells lovingly over detail, including 'glass globe with snow storm on holly green mat'. Because the venture was 'experimental', the actors expected Jack to become even more involved. They invited him along, thinking that he would tell them about the play, and instruct them as to how he wanted it played, 'but he said he was content to leave it in their hands completely. "The play was strange and disconnected and might be subtle, but seemed simple on the surface," Miss Fitzgerald said'.[51]

From photographs it is clear just how rudimentary the production was. Yet it had many interesting aspects; Clonboise for example was played by a youthful Wilfred Brambell, later famous as Steptoe in 'Steptoe and Son'. The part-amateur, part-experimental approach suited Jack. He went frequently, and by the end of the production, which was extended, felt he was among friends, though in fact he knew no one at the outset, apart from his friend Ria Mooney and his niece. He kept a programme signed by all the cast, and the end-of-production party, which was also photographed, shows among others the Abbey's managing director, Ernest Blythe.

There are some themes in *Harlequin's Positions* common to Jack's other writing during the decade. One of the characters is an orphan who owns a piece of land on which the town's forthcoming cinema is to be built, thus providing her with money and 'a gold ticket to admit me any time'. There is the South American interest: Alfred Clonboise, a central character, has lived there, and his return to Portnadroleen to rediscover relations, precipitates the action. Two relations, Rose Bosanquet and Claire Gillane, have a nephew, Johnnie Gillane, whose father, serving a five-year term in prison for fraud, dies half-way through. The theme of the play swings in a new direction when orphan Annie, on whose inheritance of land the cinema is to be built, decides to travel; the Second Porter announces, at the start of the act, 'This was a sudden plan they made to go travelling'. This part of the play takes place in the railway station – even a railway engine draws in – and is dominated by the Station Guard and First and Second Porter. Warning comes of an unspecified war. The journey, initially to Liverpool, but then by boat to South America, is abandoned. The principals from the first three acts disappear. And the play concludes in the hands of the station staff and an apple woman who has returned from market.

'It is a play of war's alarms' Jack wrote to Ria Mooney. The play opened on 5 June 1939. It was scheduled to run for one week, but was so popular with the public that it was extended for a second. Ria Mooney was enthusiastic, and proud of how she had produced it.

I taught my students to speak his plays with intelligence and conviction, within the characterisation given them by the author, and with no more than the minimum movement necessary . . . Nothing should distract attention from the play as conceived by the writer . . . Words and character-drawing are the first requirements for the interpretation of Jack Yeats.[52]

It seems to have been an entirely happy and satisfying experience for him. 'My play came to an end at the Peacock Theatre on Saturday night. It was on an extra week – making the fortnight. The people that produced it, and acted in it, did it beautifully and the more I saw it (four times) the more I liked it. And they were all very nice to me – the old wag-of-the-wall.'[53]

The reviews in Irish newspapers expressed bewilderment. A fellow playwright, Donagh MacDonagh, writing 'A Dublin Letter' for an America journal, described it as a

highly colored and rather Cocteauesque interpretation of life in an Irish country town. There is a great deal of fantastic, original and often hilarious talk, but what all the talk is about no one, least of all the characters, knows. Within its own framework however 'Harlequin's Positions' is fine entertainment, it is only when one examines it from the coldly logical standoint of a rainy street that the whole thing begins to see like a great gob of unedited subconscious torn out whole and living and left to ramble about the stage.[54]

The Peacock Theatre had its own café, and it was a popular meeting-place. One reviewer described reaction there:

Play dissection is as important as play-going in Dublin. So after the show many of his friends sat about the café, hunched over tea and coffee, trying to think up some highbrow explanation. 'But what does Mr. Yeats think of it himself?' I asked. 'Oh,' said a friend, 'he's probably sitting at home breaking his sides with laughing at the lot of us.'[55]

Not so. 'My play was beautifully done, produced and acted, and whenever I was in the theatre . . . the audience were listening, quietly when they should, and laughing when they should, and I believe were happy and free of care.'[56] MacGreevy congratulated him and Jack wrote back: 'It had its own queer success.'[57]

At the end of the 1930s Jack had a solo exhibition in Dublin, the first in the city since 1931, and also had work in the IBM exhibition of contemporary art in San Francisco in the summer of 1939. Sean Keating was the only other Irish artist to be included. They were nominated by George Furlong, the director of the National Gallery of Ireland, and they 'represented' Ireland. This was stressed by the company. Furlong received a letter telling him that IBM would purchase all the works exhibited, and it was expected that they would be 'typical of Eire and representative of its life or scenery, or both, but this is a matter that would be left entirely to you and the Artists concerned'.[58] The company gave to each participating artist a large bronze medal in a black hinged case lined in deep plum-red velvet.

The Dublin exhibition was held in Jack Longford Contemporary Picture Galleries, in South Leinster Street. John Manning Longford,[59] with his partner, Deirdre McDonagh[60], had started the Contemporary Picture Galleries in 1938. Though Victor Waddington is remembered for his lifelong promotion of Jack's work, to the exclusion of all others, Longford played a part which reflects great perception at a very difficult time. Stephen Rynne, who was perhaps the outstanding art critic of the 1940s in Dublin, wrote of him: 'Longford was a fine connoisseur and a picture vendor – head and shoulders above all his kind in Ireland at that time. No one did more for contemporary art or showed a better appreciation of good Irish artists than the gentle Longford.'[61]

Allowing a gallery director to represent him was a departure for Jack, in that, for the first time in Dublin, he was allowing others to organise his solo shows. Characteristically, he told MacGreevy: 'I send you the catalogue of the exhibition of paintings which has been made, so sportingly, by Miss Deirdre MacDonagh and J.M. Longford. If you know of anyone coming over here who would enjoy the Exhibition you will, I know, be kind to let them know of it now.'[62]

He had had other solo exhibitions, two of them in New York, in 1932, and two in London, in that year and in 1936. In addition, by this stage in his career he was widely in demand for group exhibitions in Britain, Ireland and the United States, for which, it must be added, he had numerous paintings.

McDonagh and Longford had already engaged Jack's support for their new venture, and had included him in a group show, their 'Loan and Cross-Section Exhibition of Contemporary Paintings', which was held in October 1939. This quite remarkable show brought together Irish and international work of great range and quality. The meaning of the title was that continental works from private collections in Ireland made up the loan section, while a 'cross-section' of works by Irish artists made up the rest of the show. Bonnard, Braque, De Chirico, Derain, Dufy, Gleizes, Gris, Lhote, Kisling, Marquet, Pechstein, Picasso, Signac and Vlaminck were in the loan section, with paintings many of which have since become important works in Irish public collections. There were British artists such as Gertler, Sickert, Steer, Tonks and there was work by Orpen. And the Irish artists included the best from every style and discipline, from abstract artists to the president of the Royal Hibernian Academy, Dermod O'Brien, who liked Longford, gave his venture staunch support, and bought paintings generously, as he had always done.[63] Jack's first solo show followed immediately after, in November 1939.

The association between Jack and the Contemporary Picture Galleries, was productive, but short-lived. The two partners had opened specifically to show avant garde work. Modernism had been promoted persistently during the previous two decades, the abstract branch of it led by Mainie Jellett and Evie Hone, but with many other styles boasting artists of real talent. In general these artists had been forced to organise their own shows, and a centre for these had been the Dublin Painters' Gallery, in St Stephen's Green. Jack, of course, was part of this group, though only in its early years did he take advantage of the gallery space to show work. What Deirdre McDonagh and

205. Louis MacNeice.

Jack Longford offered was professional organisation and backing, a relatively new and obviously very valuable kind of support, and new to Dublin, where the idea of an intermediary being able to make a living by dealing in pictures mainly on a commission basis was highly adventurous and full of risk.

Louis MacNeice's visited Jack late in 1939 (fig. 205):

I remember from this Dublin of the Fall a number of hilarities, of happigoluckiness, of tangents away from reality. One afternoon I went round to Jack Yeats's studio – the tidiest studio possible, a high eighteenth-century room with elaborate mouldings on the cornice. Yes, Jack Yeats said, he found them a great standby; when he had nothing to do he just watched those mouldings, all of them were animate. See there, he said, that is the Pompadour, that is Elizabeth Barrett's little dog, and these are some little men having a walking race. He gave us Malaga and with a deft oldmaidish precision squeezed some drops of orange into each glass. An old lady present, who collected modern French paintings, was talking about her childhood in Ireland – how many carriage-horses they had, how many carriage-horses the neighbours had, how many hunters. 'But now,' she concluded sadly, 'now there are no neighbourhoods.' . . . Keats said that he could subsist for ever writing poems and burning them. There is something of this about Jack Yeats. Far more human than his brother, he has never bothered with publicity, has gone his own way developing a manner of painting which seemed very outre to Dublin, slashing the paint on thick but with subtle precision, building up obscure phantasmagorias, combining an impressionist technique with a melodramatic fancy.[64]

CHAPTER NINETEEN

The Outbreak of War 1940–1942

Days of Wrath

JACK WAS CELEBRATED as Ireland's leading painter from a comparatively early stage in his career. Such recognition was related more to what he did in the early years, than how he did it. From the beginning of the century, powerful voices, including those of Lady Gregory and George Russell, identified in his drawings the extent to which he embodied Irish nationality in his work. They praised this because it conformed with the artistic movement which dominated those years and to which they adhered.

Quite properly the emphasis of this artistic movement was on the literature. But no art form was untouched. The different strands of Irish artistic self-discovery, the recovery of a lost past, the celebration of contemporary heroes and heroines through portraiture, and a fresh look both at landscape and at genre subjects, grew and developed to an unprecedented degree, and in a manner which was neither aggressive nor repetitive. Jack was part of this. He portrayed the life of Ireland in a simple and direct way, with the emphasis on event and with no attempt at caricature. At each stage in his development he ignored his contemporaries, and did not compare his work with what others were doing. He started exhibiting when two outstanding Irish painters, Nathaniel Hone and Walter Osborne, were the leading figures. Jack hardly knew them. Nor did any others have much contact with him. For a certain period of time, up to the outbreak of the First World War, the outstanding Irish artist was William Orpen. Technically brilliant, he shone on a larger, world stage. He deliberately sought to outclass all around him. But he did not resolve a conflict of loyalty between England and Ireland and could in no sense challenge the identification with Ireland which gave Jack his unique position. In the 1920s and 1930s, despite difficulties, Jack enhanced his position as the embodiment of his country; from being seen as its leading painter he gradually became accepted as its greatest artist.

There was a comfortable, if deluded, idea in Ireland, that visual art was largely the prerogative of a middle-and upper-class culture, with its leadership largely in the hands of Protestant and Ascendancy people. There had never been hedge-schools in painting. Catholic Ireland, at least, had risen up to express itself through verbal and not plastic achievement. The reality was more complicated and to Eamon de Valera's credit he showed considerable sympathy for art. He in fact contemplated studying at the Metropolitan School at one stage, and he had several student friends.[1] But his poor eyesight prevented him pursuing this discipline. He supported advanced, modernist art, such as

206. Jack, *c.* 1940.

that of Mainie Jellett, who during the late 1930s received two government commissions to decorate Irish pavilions at international fairs and exhibitions.[2]

The 1930s ended for Jack, as it did for the country, on a note of disillusionment. Despite all his expectations for *The Charmed Life*, expectations shared by Ragg, the book sold poorly. In the autumn of 1938 Ragg wrote to him: '"The Charmed Life" has sold to date 680 copies. I am afraid this will be disappointing to you as it is to us; indeed, it had as good a press as any book which we ever published, but in spite of that it has, as you will seem a comparatively insignificant reading public.'[3]

Jack offered him the typescript of *The Careless Flower* to read again, suggesting that there was 'more bone in it' than in *The Charmed Life*. Ragg had seen it some five or six years earlier. 'Here is "The Careless Flower"', Jack wrote.

> I have not been writing anything for a long time. I am just now going to correct the typewritten copy of a play I wrote over a year ago. When it is corrected it will begin to follow other plays of mine, sitting on the doorstep, of the heart, of any play producer, who seems to have one with courage to it. None of my plays have ever smelt footlights yet.[4]

Ragg declined the book. He and others at Routledge felt it would make even less impact than *The Charmed Life*, and was more wayward. Jack replied to his letter:

> I suppose the only way the book will be published will be when I chance to drop it on the desk of a publisher who has lost his memory and makes a start, with a clean slate, with my book. You miss bone in The Careless Flower and I dislike bone in a book. Most times I think its just glue. Because there is no bone it isnt necessary that the thing is just jelly. There is no bone in a wave of the sea.[5]

Ragg did send Jack a copy of Samuel Beckett's *Murphy*. Since the book came from the publisher, Jack's copy of *Murphy* was uninscribed, but into it he later pasted Beckett's poem, 'Saint-Lo 1945'.

War was declared in September 1939. Early on, Jack's personal judgments, reflected in his paintings, were far-sighted and anguished. *Tinker's Encampment: The Blood of Abel*, first exhibited at the Royal Hibernian Academy in 1941, was based, according to MacGreevy, on the Gospel reading for St Stephen's Day, a passage from Matthew 23 which comes at the end of the great climax of warnings and denunciations following Christ's ride into Jerusalem. Scribes, Pharisees and hypocrites are castigated for the blood they shed, and for their persecutions (fig. 207).

These were sombre days, and the atmosphere was pregnant with expectation. Ireland's neutrality was a frail thing. It had been so described by de Valera, who was all too well aware from other European experiences that a declared neutrality could easily be overthrown by a powerful aggressor. But he was adamant in his determination to hold out firmly against both sides, and this was grudgingly recognised by the German and British Ministers in Dublin. The German Ambassador, Hempel, reported to Berlin in May 1940: 'De Valera, in my judgement, is still the only recognized political leader of large stature who has the nationalists firmly in hand.'[6] He made it clear that German intervention in Ireland would meet with strong Irish resistance which de Valera would lead.[7]

207. *Tinker's Encampment; The Blood of Abel,* oil on canvas, 36 × 48, private collection. 1940.

Jack was deeply moved by Lolly's death, on 16 January 1940, from heart failure. Lolly had become very ill the previous December, and was moved into Sir Patrick Dun's Hospital, with congested lungs on 14 December, when Jack went to see her. 'I think she was unconscious when I saw her in the hospital that night. But she has, so far, made a recovery and her heart is standing up well.'[8] According to Gifford Lewis Lolly's heart trouble had been overlooked, and she was suspected of nervous disorder for so long that little attention was paid to symptoms of heart disease. She had been treated for neurasthenia, off and on, since 1916. Lily, quite wrongly, claimed after her death that her sister had only suffered the one illness, at the end of her life. But then Lily, according to her biographer, 'was deeply uninterested in her sister's life and remembered none of the details of her sister's childhood or its illnesses'.[9]

Lolly was buried in the churchyard of St Nahi's Church, the old church at Churchtown, and there was a mishap at the service. The undertaker's men placed the coffin awkwardly on the trestles, and during the service it fell to the ground with a crash. Anne Yeats remembers thinking that this was Lolly, characteristically, having the last word. She was sitting beside her uncle. Jack was far from amused. 'All through her life she brought with her the gaiety and the quickly troubled spirit of a young girl, so it seemed to me. I am glad she did not have much pain or that for long.'[10] She had been closest to Jack in age and at Cuala had been responsible for printing his work. The President of Ireland, Douglas Hyde, who knew Jack and Cottie well and was fond of both of them, wrote a sympathetic letter to Cottie. 'Please tell Jack how sorry I am at his loss. I am sorry for Miss Lily Yeats too, though I did not know either of them at all well.'[11]

There were many messages. When John Masefield wrote to Lily he emphasised the impact Lolly had had on Willie: 'We always felt that you and your sister did very much to make your brother what he was, and to keep the Irish movement linked with the progress of the arts rather than with violent political upheaval.' There was no mention of Jack.[12]

Jack was Lolly's executor. The bulk of the property remained with Lily, at Gurteen Dhas, but there were certain bequests to deal with. She left paintings to the Friends of the National Collections of Ireland. These were all passed on to Sarah Purser, who had founded the Friends, in 1924.[13] If Jack himself was beginning to feel something of a senior citizen among the men and women artists of Ireland, he was still comparatively youthful compared with Sarah Purser, doyenne of Irish art and Jack's patron when he was starting out as a young man. He saw her socially, at the 'At Homes' in Mespil House, the 'Days of Wrath' as they were called by her great-nieces and great-nephews. She was still active in the affairs of the Royal Hibernian Academy, to which Jack remained loyal. And she was on the Board of Governors and Guardians of the National Gallery of Ireland, where her contributions were as clear and precise as ever. On one occasion he described her at Mespil House: 'as quick minded as usual, and holding the last few stragglers for a few more minutes talk – which you know was generally good talk'.[14]

Jack himself had been appointed a member of the Board of Governors and Guardians of the National Gallery of Ireland in November 1938, and served until his death.[15] He joined a group which, in addition to Sarah Purser, included Sir John Lavery and the sculptor, Oliver Sheppard. An early concern of the Board was security, in the face of war, and a special meeting was held to discuss this. Eamon de Valera requested that a recent gift to the nation by the Italian Government of a painting by di Chirico should be put on display for a six-month period.

Another member of the board was Edward A. McGuire, an amateur painter and successful Dublin businessman, who came to know Jack through board meetings, but also as fellow-guest at Sarah Purser's 'At Homes'. He was rich enough to buy Yeats's paintings:

I bought quite a number of his new-style works following visits to his studio in Fitzwilliam Place . . . His new idiom was regarded by many as rather eccentric and caused raised eyebrows among the RHA elements, who were firmly in the Academic tradition. I frequently met him roaming the streets of Dublin wearing a waisted long overcoat and black hat with turned-down brim, and he always stopped for a short discussion about life and living, especially Dublin life. On the occasion of Sarah Purser's 90th birthday, a dinner was given in the Shelbourne Hotel, and Jack Yeats proposed the toast to her. It was a really memorable occasion. He excelled himself in a speech which was completely 'off the cuff'. He rambled on with thoughts and ideas as they came to his mind on the subject of Sarah's age, ideals and many achievements in the world of Irish painting. he evoked a fairyland atmosphere which he revealed at other times in his paintings. Everybody who heard him was fascinated and sorry when he finished.[16]

Jack was good at attending board meetings. He occupied the chair only once, that role being generally fulfilled by Judge Murnaghan, and he witnessed the recital of many deaths among fellow artists, Sheppard, Dermod O'Brien (fig. 208), and Sarah Purser among them, and new figures joining the board, including Evie Hone. These were days of poverty for the gallery. Its allowances for purchase and upkeep of pictures were halved when Jack joined, and the records show many offers of painting for sale to the gallery, at modest prices, being turned down. The future benefactor, George Bernard Shaw, who

208. Dermod O'Brien.

209. Hélène de St Pierre.

210. Niall Montgomery.

was to transform this situation on his death, was in correspondence at the time of Jack's appointment in respect of the full length statue of himself by Troubetsky of which he wanted a copy made for London.

The early days of the war brought confusion and uncertainty, but above all, for an island community, it cut the country off. There are poignant messages contained in the brief entries in Jack's appointments book where he writes on a page under the letter B: 'Sam Beckett called December 29 1938; Called July 12 1939; Called August 24th 1939.' He was not to see his younger friend again until the conflict was over. And in the summer of 1939 Jack was visited by others from abroad who would not return until after the conflict, or, in some cases, not at all. David H. Green, the Harvard scholar then working on J.M. Synge, and on honeymoon, visited Jack on 20 July 1939: 'He collecting particulars about JM Synge's narrative work – I gave him Apparitions and Sligo – Wife was a Miss Healy – parents from Clonakilty.'[17] A visitor in the spring of 1940 was Henry Silvy, an expert in French art who was attached temporarily to the French Legation. His visit carries the brief post-script: 'He was killed in Italy 1944.' After the fall of France a young Frenchwoman who had luckily been in Dublin, Hélène de Grosourdy de St Pierre (fig. 209), called on Jack from her temporary home in Malahide. She was studying to be a painter, came in the company of Jack's dealer, Jack Longford, and eventually married an Irish lawyer.

Niall Montgomery became a regular visitor (fig. 210). He was an architect by training, but with wider capabilities as writer, artist, wit, raconteur. He was well-read in modern literature and a notable Joyce scholar. He met Jack through his parents. His father was the first official film censor, appointed in 1923. He was also chief engineer to the Post Office. His mother was a rather forbidding woman, with a literary inclination, and a taste for lionising people. Both of them had known Jack for many years, and Niall Montgomery's first encounters dated back to childhood. He was a frequent, if reluctant companion for his mother when she attended 'At Homes'. Jack was well-disposed towards the young, and was aware of the excruciating agony for children of being at such adult gatherings; he went out of his way to alleviate the boredom. Once the painter wrote: 'Though we were not boys at the same time in Dublin still when he walked on the edge of the quays of Dublin I walked on the edge of the quays in Sligo. And so I think, we, every little while, spoke the same language and that is an experience that gets hourly more rare.'[18]

Niall Montgomery married in 1939. Their first child, Rose Mary, was born in 1940, and is referred to in many of the early letters. Niall was as formal as his older friend, exchanging letters and cards, and often responding to the small decorative sketches on Jack's missives with drawings on his own replies. 'There is never a beautiful line without hope in it,' Jack wrote in reply to a 'fine' Christmas card, which he said he was proud to have. And though the Montgomeries and Yeatses lived close enough to each other, there is a correspondence reinforced with drawings which indicates a blossoming friendship. Letters during the early 1940s were often accompanied by humorous verses, newspaper cuttings, and other ephemera. 'Many thanks for sending me these verses and letting me keep them. In this crooked tongued, woolly eared year of a half snuffed candle, such ringing innocence is a cork balk in a murky sea. I send a little cutting that may amuse your father as well as yourself.'[19] Quite early on, Montgomery sent Jack a collection of his pieces, broadly about architecture, and they provoked this response:

Many thanks for letting me have the enjoyment of reading these brilliant papers – I respect them for their genius and because I respect myself for finding . . . ideas which satisfy me. They would make grand lectures – quietly, and slowly delivered, so that your hearers didnt get tangled in themselves with the good things coming so close on each others heads. I think architecture is a splendid peg in which to hang shining thoughts . . . Your mind is not lined with twigs or feathers. Or bricks and mortar.[20]

Early in 1943, Niall Montgomery's younger brother, Seamus, died of tuberculosis. Though feared, it was painful for the whole family, and Jack sent his own and Cottie's sympathies, together with a letter for James Montgomery, who died a matter of ten days after his son. The second death remained on Jack's mind through the spring. In June he wrote: 'Very few days go by that I do not think of your father and often, such is vanity, because I have heard or thought of something I would like to tell him. To let some puny wit glow an instant in the shine of his generous and larger wit.'[21] The comments were accompanied by an invitation to call. When *Ah Well* was published, Montgomery sent a copy to Jack Sweeney, at Harvard, and a friendship developed between the two Jacks, which then blossomed out to include James Johnston Sweeney, who in turn with his wife, became Fitzwilliam Square visitors.[22]

Jack's old friend, Thomas Bodkin, director of the Barber Institute of Fine Art in Birmingham since 1935, was cut off from easy access just at a time when he needed Jack's help. He had finished a book, *My Uncle Frank*, and, wanting a frontispiece and possible illustrations in the text. A lengthy correspondence about this provoked from Jack some delightful asides.

I have been at Robertstown a few times, and a little way round it and I think it is a lovely part of this country I remember, one time, seeing a kennel cart passing through the village, with the body of a poor old dead horse stretched on it. And for a long while the cart and the poor old shaking legs could be seen. weaving their way through. The plain of the old bog, a fallen leaf to grow into a nosegay, a dead horse to feed hounds, to hunt foxes, for the edification of ladies, and fierce young men, and red faced old ones, and the glory of paid huntsmen and whips, and the honour of the Horse Show, and the improvement of live horses, and the encouragement of breeches makers, and boot makers in Dame street, and for the rubbing together of the hands of the bald-faced salesman in Combridges while he sold dashing hunting prints by Snaffles and Edwards to men who imagined themselves to be the spiritual descendents of Tony Lumpkin.[23]

Jack welcomed news of the book, which was clearly more about nephew than uncle: 'I am very glad to hear that you are writing a book – and that it is about your youth – and that you think I might make a picture of some kind of it.'[24]

The manuscript of *My Uncle Frank* was delivered and Jack's response was enthusiastic: 'I think yourself and your uncle were very lucky in knowing each other. Your book has its own vivid setting and requires no other illustrating. But it will give me a great deal of pleasure to do a frontispiece for you, and any other smaller drawings I can, if the publisher should see his way that way.'[25] He suggested a landscape, in oils if there was time for it to dry. But

211. Frontispiece to *My Uncle Frank*.

the enterprise was modest, and the publishers, Robert Hale, felt that a Jack Yeats illustration would be prohibitively expensive. In the end it came down to a line drawing as frontispiece (fig. 211). Bodkin suggested his uncle standing on the lawn in front of the house, but Jack did a spirited drawing of Uncle Frank in a trap, his favourite horse, Black Jack, its ears pricked forward, emerging from an archway, the Hill of Allen in the distance and the swallows wheeling in the evening air. Bodkin was also delighted when Jack told him: 'I dislike the idea of any author being out of pocket over a book so pay me £5, or any part of it that your terms with the publisher make a proper possibility. And see that the block maker keeps the original drawing clean and returns it to yourself as I want you to have it'[26]

Bodkin had left Dublin in protest about his treatment as director of the National Gallery. As Professor of Fine Art at Birmingham University and first director of the Barber Institute, a position he held until 1952, he was outstanding. His acquisitions for the institute, over a seventeen-year period, created from nothing a distinguished group of old masters at a time when few institutions were willing or able to devote time and intelligence to such investment.

Bodkin was lucky to be published at all. As far as Jack was concerned, his correspondence with Ragg at Routledge fell off in the early years of the war. In the summer of 1940 he wrote to say that he had seen no copies of *The Charmed Life* in the shops, and Ragg replied: 'The book business is just about dead now, and has been stagnant ever since the war began.'[27] They did not correspond again for two years.

For those living in Dublin there were compensations for the growing isolation, as the war became increasingly serious. Instead of becoming a dreary and restricted neutral state, Ireland attracted an interesting cross-section of ex-patriate talent, and there was a rich and diverse domestic flowering of artistic activity. Exhibitions were held frequently, and there were controversies about art and Modernism, about religious art and decadence. The artistic community were suspected of containing 'spies'; Brian Boydell, the composer, recalls police surveillance on himself and friends.

Nor was artistic life entirely confined to Dublin. Robert Wyse Jackson, a Church of Ireland clergyman and friend of the painter, who later became Bishop of Limerick, organised in the late summer of 1940 that city's annual art exhibition and wrote to Jack.

> I did not know that he disliked group shows, and in all innocence I wrote to explain what we were at and to ask him to exhibit . . . Yes, he would exhibit, and he thought that as he had not exhibited previously in Limerick, we might like to have one picture from each of three periods . . . The last day of the show had come and we had had very few sales. Nobody in Limerick at that period of the war had any money; and we all had a bill which did not at all look like being paid by percentages on sales. I was on duty in the gallery that last day when Mrs. Tom Clarke, Madge Daly, and her sister, came in. It was a shame, they thought, that Limerick should let itself down by not buying. 'For the reputation of the city,' said Madge, 'I'll buy one.' 'So will I,' said each of the sisters. That is how, on the very last day, I sold our three Yeats pictures. I have heard from time to time over the thirty years since then, how much pleasure they gave.[28]

But the dominance of the capital city concentrated attention there.

Representatives of both Allied and Axis powers occupied legations, and it became one of the few capitals in Europe where all sides were in evidence. Behind the scenes the government favoured the Allied cause; much was done to ensure that at every level Britain was helped, and Germany hindered. German spies in Ireland were arrested and detained for the duration of hostilities; there is no record of any British agent held in captivity. Diplomats indulged their interest in the arts. John Betjeman, appointed in January 1941 as press attaché to Sir John Maffey, the British government representative in Ireland, vigorously pursued a cultural relations role.

Ireland had abolished the position of governor general and had then introduced a new constitution. No appointment replacing the governor-generalship was made between 1936 and 1939, and it was only in November of that year, two months after the British declaration of war against Germany, that Maffey, a retired English diplomat, was brought back and sent as 'British Representative' to Dublin. Under normal circumstances he would have been the British High Commissioner. This was the rank of British representative in British Commonwealth countries; but, though Ireland had not formally left the Commonwealth, the idea of a British High Commission was unacceptable. Nor could he come as British ambassador, since Ireland, to the British, was 'Eire', or the Irish Free State, while to the Irish, following the enactment and coming into force of the 1937 Constitution, it was the Irish Republic. Britain was reluctant about recognising it as such, due to Northern Ireland. As if in contradiction of much of this, Ireland had a High Commissioner in London, John Whelan Dulanty.

This might all seem a long way from Jack's life as a painter. In fact, it bore directly on it. Betjeman, an enthusiast for Irish life and culture, became an agent in the interest of Irish artists, among them Jack himself. Betjeman saw himself to be in direct competition with Hempel, the German Minister in Dublin. Germany's diplomatic relations with Ireland were on a more even keel than were Britain's, and Hempel had already seized an initative in the field of the arts. Shortly after arriving in Dublin, Betjeman wrote in one letter to Kenneth Clark: 'Your visit will be invaluable . . . and you will be satisfying the craving for attention that there is in artistic and literary circles in Dublin. At present the German Minister has rather a monopoly of art and gave a dinner to old Jack Yeats recently.'[29]

212. John Betjeman.

Betjeman was no stranger to Ireland (fig. 212). He and Maurice Bowra had stayed with Pierce Synnott, 'a wackily-dressed and eccentric undergraduate with whom Bowra was in love', as early as 1926, and he described Ireland as 'the most perfect place on earth'.[30] He visited the country regularly, and knew many of its artists and writers. But the circle he generally moved in was the titled world, of Lord Dunsany, Lord Longford and the Marquess of Dufferin and Ava. This was a fraternity not well-known to Jack, though it must be said he had in his invitation-lists for exhibitions a good line in aristocrats. Through close friendship with the painter, John Piper, Betjeman had become a friend of Kenneth Clark, the director of the National Gallery in Trafalgar Square, and he quickly involved Clark in Irish affairs, asking him over to Dublin to lecture, to which Clark promptly agreed (fig. 213). He also sought his help in finding a London gallery which might show the work of Nano Reid, and asked Clark to put on an exhibition in the National Gallery of Jack's paintings.

Just before St Patrick's day Betjeman had tea with Jack: 'He was very good

213. Kenneth Clark in 1940s.

214. William Nicholson.

value. A man to talk to', he wrote to John Piper, 'but I miss you very much. There's no one else to fire one with enthusiasm.'[31] He had by then written a formal letter to Kenneth Clark on the subject of 'Art Liaison in Eire', which he described as 'a ridiculous title for this letter, but it helps the Registries'. Betjeman seems to have been on a three-month trial in Dublin, renewed for a further three months in April; 'worse luck', he told the Pipers.

When Kenneth Clark came to lecture, he 'worked very hard with the Irish and created the most wonderful impression and talked to Dev for two hours'.[32] He met Jack, and saw sufficient of his work to be persuaded. The indefatigable Betjeman introduced him to other Yeats enthusiasts, including R.R. ('Bobs') Figgis and Con Curran. Some time after his return to England, Clark proposed the exhibition, through Betjeman, who saw Jack in July to tell him. It was not to be a solo exhibition, but a joint venture, with the English painter, William Nicholson. It was not to take place until early the following year. At that time, as a result of the war, the permanent collection had been moved to Wales for safe-keeping, and the National Gallery had become a place for concerts and other cultural events, including exhibitions by living artists. Perhaps surprisingly, since he always preferred exhibiting on his own, Jack promptly agreed to an exhibition shared with Nicholson. He told Joseph Hone: 'I used to admire every painting I saw of his years ago.' He even took exception to the fact that their works were being hung in separate rooms in the gallery, on the grounds that 'any point of view where we are the same is hidden'. The judgment to keep them separate was probably wise. The blaze of colour from Jack's work of the 1930s, which predominated in the show, would have clashed with, or perhaps swamped the muted tones of Nicholson's still life paintings. Despite this, they were a well-matched pair; and their origins in the black-and-white tradition were emphasised by the decision to hang together their drawings and prints in a shared room, thus bringing together the strong impact of the *Broadside* illustrations with Nicholson's incomparable poster designs and book illustrations.

Clark wrote a forceful and entertaining introduction to the catalogue, referring to the youth and independence of both Nicholson (fig. 214) and Yeats (they were, respectively, sixty-nine and seventy), and suggesting that, by the time they reached ninety, 'they will be reckless'. Then he clearly reflected, and went on: 'Not that Jack Yeats could be much more reckless than he is.' Jack's noncomformist qualities, his extravagance of style controlled and shaped by his vision of contemporary life, and his transformation of light into colour, are all stressed in the short essay.

Colour is Yeats' element in which he dives and splashes with the shameless abandon of a porpoise. And colour knows no laws: it is the language of the free, the passionate, the impulsive, the intoxicated. We follow Jack Yeats breathless and a little drunk; and then when the roof is just about to blow off and the floor to heave under our feet, we pass into the rooms of William Nicholson.

Clark attributes to Monticelli and Mancini – two artists whose work he had so recently seen in Dublin's Municipal Gallery – an influence on Jack, but points to the difference in the Irish artist's anchoring of all his work in the contemporary life of street scene and marketplace.

The great poet, his brother, said that he wished to write ballads which should be on the lips of men who could not read, and finally achieved in a direct vernacular utterance, having passed through labyrinths of myth and learning. Jack Yeats was there in a leap, and in one way reversed his brother's development, for his early work is in the style of popular ballads, and often actually illustrates them, whereas his later work is symbolist in its use of evocative colouring and is certainly not intended for the dull average eye.

Clark felt that 'anything could happen' in a Yeats painting, and that he was capricious; but the essay, in which the lion's share is given to Jack, glows with admiration.

In reality, Clark was more reserved about Jack's talent. In introducing him in a catalogue for a show which he himself had instigated, clearly it was incumbent on him to admire. But in an article he wrote for Cyril Connolly, to be published in *Horizon*, the director of the National Gallery expressed views which offended Jack, to whom recognition was long overdue. 'Always the pull-back', he told Terence de Vere White.[33]

Clark's article in *Horizon* fell into the predictable trap of invoking the comparison between the two brothers, but is otherwise not entirely unfair. It stresses, for example, the swiftness of Jack's mastery of myth and symbol, compared with Willie's longer and more difficult journey, but then suggests that the poet's work had a certainty which the painter lacked. Very much to Jack's annoyance, his work as a *Punch* cartoonist was used to demonstrate his badness as an artist. Clark concludes with the understandable claim that Jack, as a painter, ended up with greater artistic integrity than artists such as William Orpen, who were more gifted men.

The exhibition was opened by Ireland's High Commissioner, John Dulanty, on New Year's Day, 1942. A telegram sent by Clark to Jack in Dublin suggests that he did not go over for the opening, but many friends were there, including Bryan Guinness, who had lent pictures, and Winston Churchill's wife, Clementine. The event, essentially very formal and attended by rather grand guests (Queen Elizabeth, mother of the present British monarch, was in the habit of attending National Gallery functions), was not without its humorous side. John Dulanty was given a high stool in place of a rostrum, and climbed rather nervously on to it. He kept his eyes fixed in trepidation on the distant floor, plunged one hand into his pocket, and with the other made a constantly circling motion, the forefinger outstretched. The newspapers at the time reported his speech from the text which had been distributed. But John Dulanty was not the man to be constrained by printed versions of what he intended to say. 'I can ask for a drink,' he told the assembled company,

> but I don't have the language of art. Perhaps there ain't no such language. I don't know. But what I know about Yeats is that he is a major artist, and member of a distinguished family who are all against the mechanical. His sisters even made printing unmechanical with the Cuala press, which they set up to provide a setting for their brother's wood-cuts. The father, also a painter, lived like a lot of nice people I know. He was always hard up![34]

Dulanty provoked increasing laughter with his remarks. 'If he painted an ass, whether it was an ass on two legs – if ye can have a two-legged ass – or an ass on four legs, you could be sure it would an *Irish* ass.' Jack, according to

215. Bust of John Dulanty.

Dulanty, had once sent a number of his paintings and drawings to London to be sold, and for a time they had been in the High Commissioner's office. 'The office cleaner,' he told the assembled company, 'a nice decent body who hasn't a god's idea about art, took a fancy to two of the drawings, and asked if she could buy them by shilling installments weekly.' This, said Dulanty, was a true tribute to the artist's work.

Down from his improvised podium, the High Commissioner, 'a smallish man with a large head and a thoughtful face', inserted his thumbs into the armholes of his waistcoat, and murmuring in his rather low voice, expanded still further on the qualities of Irish life, Irish art, and Irish hospitality. The effect was contagious. William Nicholson, who was at the opening, became expansive about his own painting, and in particular about what is perhaps his most famous canvas, *The Hundred Jugs*.

Everybody tries to count them which is more than I have ever done. My son (the painter, Ben Nicholson) was painting a jug – and taking an awful long time about it. What's the use, I said to him, of painting *one* jug? You ought to paint 100. Then there'd be something to look at! Then it suddenly occurred to me, The Hundred Jugs. Ah, that's a fine title! So I began to assemble all the jugs about the place. And one of them was the milk-jug which got upset and was a fine chance for the cat, so he's in the picture too. You never know what will happen when you're painting a picture.[35]

The light-hearted aspect of the London show spread to Dublin, where Brian O'Nolan, writing under his newspaper pseudonym of 'Myles na gCopaleen', had fun at everyone's expense, quoting for readers of *The Irish Times* a review in *The Architectural Review*:

I notice a review of London's Clark-sponsored Yeats-Nicholson National Gallery show. 'Jack Yeats' (listen to this my god) 'is more dashing, more "modern," least effective in his Dufy manner and most effective in a subdued key.' Do you mind the withering cuteness of that? Dufy is a smart water-colourist, his paintings are 'amusing', 'comment' on 'the contemporary scene,' his 'sense of decoration' is 'infallible'; in a word, he's the sort of man that works for *Vogue*. If the critic said that Mr. Y. is least effective in his Sir Joshua Reynolds manner, it would be more mystifying, and, therefore, smarter – and it would be just as intelligent. Or if he cut out the reference to Mr. Dufy altogether, and wrote 'quay' instead of 'key,' he might have something. The less eccentric spelling of Dufy is Duffy, of course. He is a good Fermanagh man. Cf. Anton Dolin of the Leipsiger Lepschule. How about a campaign to secure the return of the Duffy and Van Gough pictures to Ireland. They're ours by right, aren't they? I often talked about the pair of them to A.E.[36]

There was a gentler aspect to O'Nolan's writing, and a genuine feeling for Jack. He retold an oriental legend in his *Irish Times* column, claiming it had come from Jack:

Some thousands of years ago (long before the ironical word 'civilisation' was heard of) a little Chinese painter painted what he thought was his masterpiece. It was an enormous picture showing a wide and savage river flowing by, with stepping-stones crossing it to the other shore, where dim mysterious caves could be seen at the foot of a beetling cliff. The little painter held a little party and invited all his friends. They praised the picture and went to considerable trouble to be polite. Nevertheless, the little painter knew that they did not like it, not in their inner hearts. This made him very sad. He bowed his head and said nothing for a long time. Then he moved slowly over to the picture, hopped up on the first stepping-stone, ran nimbly across to the other side of the river, disappeared into one of the caves and was never heard of again.[37]

There is no doubt that the National Gallery exhibition had a profound effect on public interest in Jack, more in Ireland than in England, though the reviews in England were exceptionally favourable. The simple, unflattering truth was that English recognition counted more than the limited praise given to Jack by Irish critics. The full blast of publicity woke everybody up to the fact that Ireland had a painter whose work mattered in England. Irish critics had treated Jack with the utmost seriousness, their interest comprehensive and extensive, though their judgment was a bit negative towards his work in the late 1930s. Nor did English critics suddenly wake up to his existence; they had been reviewing his solo exhibitions since the end of the previous century. The difference with the National Gallery show was that it shifted the focus away from the circumscribed realm of private galleries and art critics writing for collectors and enthusiasts, and placed it firmly in the mainstream of public notice.

The reviews were not universally favourable, by any means. Several critics gave the lion's share of their attention to Nicholson. Others expressed quite serious reservations about Jack's work. Maurice Collis wrote:

> They are alleged to reflect the artistic frenzy which overtook him in his middle age. They purport to convey a strong emotion and seemingly are meant to be a blaze of colour. But they do not convey any more emotion than does a player who keeps his foot on the loud pedal and beats the piano like a madman, as he rolls in his seat. As to their supposedly flaming hues, it is a curious fact that in many of them, when you stand back, as you are supposed to do in order that the eye may digest the impasto, the colour, which a close inspection of the dabs and slashes of pure red, blue and yellow reveals is really there, refuses to carry and the picture goes a dirty grey.[38]

The art critic of *The Connoisseur* wrote of Jack as:

> an Irishman through and through, whose impulsiveness seems to us often to result in incoherence. A voice kept constantly at screaming pitch is apt to get out of control . . . we think of all sorts of extraneous things – a jumble of coloured silks, spun glass and sugar sticks exploding in spontaneous fireworks . . . But often the paint seems to have run amok and a technique no doubt admirably suited to sunsets, volcanic eruptions and tornadoes is, we feel, less perfectly attuned to commoner themes and those scenes of work-a-day life to which Yeats frequently applies it . . . Who, for instance, would have guessed what *Going to Wolfe Tone's Grave* is about without its label?

But Raymond Mortimer, Herbert Read and John Piper (no doubt encouraged by Betjeman and by Kenneth Clark) reviewed the show in glowing terms. Piper, writing for *The Spectator*, drew together the names of Sickert, Nicholson and Jack. They were united by a common genius for illustration, according to Piper, and he displayed a good knowledge of the relationship between Jack and Sickert, quoting Sickert's recommendation: 'He is doing what I would like to urge young painters to do: painting the life of his own country.'[39] And Piper's own judgment on the show is warmly expressed: 'His paint and his colour are personal and exciting, and he has shown that a great Irish painter can remain Irish without being lost: which nobody else has proved in this century.'[40]

Herbert Read was even more specific in linking Jack with Sickert, quoting from the 1924 lecture to the Royal Institute in which Sickert spoke of Jack's abilities in blending the action of people with the framework of landscape:

> Sickert goes on to point out a technical achievement in his painting which only another painter could have discovered so easily and expressed so clearly: 'Much of our modern landscape has an imported air, and the figures are tucked away in corners. They are seldom *doing something* in the landscape. Instead, the two elements should be knit together both psychologically and pictorially. The novelists know how to use landscape as part of the things that people feel and do. Yeats' landscapes are solidly constructed and occur behind figures which are active. In his picture "Westerly Wind" there is a jaunting car with a child in it. The centre of the focus is the child's inspired little face and golden hair, its eyes full of wonder. Behind it, and seen as though one were looking at the child, is a luminous street scene, an integral part of the whole composition.' If this were true eighteen years ago, it is still more obvious in the artist's recent work, which shows an astonishing development in freedom and fusion. In pictures like 'Jazz Babies' (1929), 'From Portacloy to Rathlin O'Beirne' (1932) and 'A Room in Sligo' (1935), the paint is slashed on in a frenzy which can only (in technical jargon) be called 'expressionist', and it is to expressionist painters such as Oskar Kokoschka that we must go for an adequate comparison. Yeats' vitality is nowhere so near the organic reality as in his paintings of horses; there is one small picture in the exhibition, 'Here comes the Chestnut Mare', which has all the frantic energy of Delacroix' famous picture of a horse frightened by a storm. In his painting of human figures Yeats has something of the intensity, though not the monumentality and spiritual depth, of Rouault. But then Yeats, who is an Irishman, does not pretend to a tragic sense of life; his daemon is rather the comic spirit, as his novels, even more undeservedly neglected than his paintings, sufficiently prove. I am aware that Yeats had a brother; it is a public misfortune if it prevents people reading the fantastic revelry of *The Amaranthers* or *The Charmed Life*.[41]

Read adds Kokoschka's name to that of Sickert. Raymond Mortimer did the same, though with more reservation:

> In his later work gusto for the thing seen is drowned in gusto for the means of expression. Whether he has felt the influence of such painters as Kokoschka I do not know – he may well have invented on his own similar methods. (Van Dongen, I fear, is another painter of whom he sometimes reminds me.) He paints like an expressionist, and uncongenial as I find this way of painting, I can see in Mr. Yeats's work a startling virtuosity. His painting is luminous and succulent, but I do not find it expressive. The cadenzas have no formal context. Exuberant, voluble, slapdash, Mr. Yeats

cannot be accused of burying his talent, but does he not dissipate it rather recklessly? . . . It may be, however, that Mr. Yeats is not the careless, improvising rhapsodist he appears, but like James Joyce, so absorbed by his medium, that he neglects the content. Whatever the cause, these paintings seem to me as empty as they are brilliant.[42]

One painting in particular appealed to Kenneth Clark, and he later bought it. It was *Rose in a Basin*, and hung in the doorway leading from the Yeats rooms into the Nicholson rooms. One reviewer wrote: 'It may have been coincidence or placed there by intent, but it is a gesture. In its charm and delicate sensitiveness to colour, this appealing pink rose, lying in running water in a white wash bowl, makes a perfect handshake between the two painters.'[43]

CHAPTER TWENTY

Painter Triumphant 1943–1945

Work of a very great master

THE NATIONAL GALLERY exhibition was a watershed, confirming publicly Jack Yeat's own growing sense of immortality. There is little doubt this had developed during the previous ten years when he was largely neglected and extensively mocked. Terence de Vere White has written of this in a rich and splendid tribute:

> Anyone who is foolish enough to think Yeats insincere has never met the man. W.B. Yeats cultivated a poetic manner deliberately . . . He was conscious of the poet's mission and proud of his calling. And in part what seemed like arrogance was only self-protection. The world is not over-kind to poets. Jack B. Yeats is as simple as his brother was splendid. And if he lacks pomp, he has dignity. He is a man with strong prejudices but he has a sense of veneration as well. He does not share popular enthusiasms and his heart does not respond to copy-book maxims or the fine sentiments of leading articles. His idols are not the idols of the market place. He is not taken in by shibboleths or fashionable sentiments. In this he is sometimes almost independent to the point of perversity. But of what is noble and brave in man or beast he is more appreciative than anyone I have ever known. He accords to all things their proper dignity. And this is apparent in his manner which, though kind and easy, is not without a certain ceremoniousness.[1]

He had a real sense of slight at the lifelong public preference for his brother's art over his own. Lily frequently wrote of how he was 'rather put in the shade by his big brother'.[2] Murphy records two examples:

> In late 1937, a little more than a year before WBY's death, another American lady on a visit to Dublin 'gushed up' to Jack and said she had longed for years to meet him. Hardened by decades of misidentification, he tried to steer her in the right direction. 'It must be my famous brother,' he replied. 'No,' she said. 'It is you, and you are just as famous.' Jack, unprepared for such a response, managed only a lame reply, 'Well, he has kept his hair and I haven't.[3]

And again in the early 1950s, on Grafton Street: 'Two American tourists were being shown about Dublin by an Irish friend . . . "Oh," the first woman responded, "are you related to the famous poet named Yeats?" The other woman noticed how JY's face stiffened, the muscles in his tight jaw working.'[4]

Terence de Vere White is one of the few commentators on Jack and his life who demonstrates real understanding of Cottie. He writes of her fierce pride in him with admiration.

> But she found it hard to suppress her indignation at the tardy recognition his work had received. She said, on one occasion, that when he was dead, she would burn any pictures in his studio so that they should not fall into the ungrateful hands of those who had neglected him. But any painting of his was far too sacred in her eyes for that, and I knew that what she said was only an expression of her love for him.[5]

In the autumn of 1942 the United Arts Club decided to give a special dinner for the painter. Jack had been made an honorary member in May 1942. It was an event often proposed, and therefore suitable for discussion in the 'mootery', the establishment of which had been one of Jack's more light-hearted proposals for the improvement of the club, a place giving scope for the inexhaustible capacity members had for discussing changes which never came about. Eventually this one had. The dinner was given in October. It was an evening crowded with event. Thomas Bodkin had written an ode to Yeats which Brendan O'Brien, whose father, Dermod O'Brien, was president both of the Royal Hibernian Academy and of the club, sang. O'Brien, who was married to Kitty Wilmer, a painter and a supporter of Mainie Jellett, had a fine voice, and the applause he received was loud and long. Another song had been written for the occasion by an amateur poet called C.F. McLaughlin, but known in the club as the Gunman, and this was sung by the Irish composer, Freddie May. There were speeches, lots of them! And more songs; and a row or two. And through it all Jack and Cottie sat in evident, immense happiness. 'Mrs Yeats was quite unashamedly shedding the happiest of tears, delighted with the honour done to dear Jack.'[6]

The fireworks came from the speech given by the club president, Dermod O'Brien, in proposing the toast to the guest of honour. Long before, Thomas Bodkin had conferred on O'Brien the title, Perpetual President of the Arch-Insulters' Guild. And unintentionally, since O'Brien admired Jack's work, he lived up to his reputation that evening with a succession of *faux-pas*. He produced a copy of one of Jack's *Broadsides*, and then, having made a point about the early drawings, threw it down on the table at the end of a sentence. R.M. Smyllie, editor of the *Irish Times*, was annoyed by this treatment of 'something which was almost a Bible to me for many of my early years', and grunted his disapproval, though he was disinclined to make any serious issue of the supposed slight. Smyllie knew O'Brien well. O'Brien then went on to point out that Jack had been refused associate membership of the Royal Hibernian Academy, and that the subject-matter of his art revealed Jack's own style and personality, a point demonstrated by O'Brien with examples such as 'the circus and the circus clown . . . the slob in the public house . . . the loafer'.

These references in particular enraged T.C. Kingsmill Moore, a barrister and later a judge, who had brooded his way through the speech, and who now got to his feet. He was determined to breach all good behaviour and the traditional club constraint about rudeness, and declared straight out that 'he was going to embarrass the guest of honour', and take on the club's president. As it happened, Kingsmill Moore, a passionate lover of fly-fishing, had been at odds with Dermod O'Brien over fishing rights owned by O'Brien in the west, so that his resentments were deep-rooted.

216. Frontispiece to *And to You Also*, published 1944.

217. Illustration from *And to You Also*, published in 1944.

Jack himself then intervened. He indicated to O'Brien that he would like to speak. 'Mr Moore said he would embarrass me,' Jack told the company, 'and he has done so. I am embarrassed by all the kindness I have received here tonight. I am always being embarrassed because no one, I believe, has ever received more kindness all through his life than I have.' His speech turned the occasion, which threatened to become unruly, into a gracious and memorable evening.

In response to the poem, Jack sent Bodkin a copy of his new book. It made Bodkin even more homesick than he was. On the details of the evening, which he had received from Isa McNie, the secretary of the United Arts Club, he had been sworn to secrecy; he felt his own contribution had been rushed. 'To do you due honour I would like at least a month in which to ponder and polish a fitting ode.'[7]

The 'new book' was *Ah Well*, which had a subtitle, 'A Romance in Perpetuity'. It is a short book, just ninety pages, and full of charm. Episodes from it first appeared in *The Bell*, a Dublin literary magazine edited by Sean O'Faolain. Then Jack sent it to Ragg, at Routledge, suggesting that its shortness – 'a book of only 28,000 words' – might be a recommendation. Ragg and Herbert Read read it, and there was an immediate and favourable response. Jack declined to illustrate: 'I am very glad that yourself and Mr Read like Ah Well for I am proud and happy about the book. But it should never be illustrated.'[8] Jack once again made provision for higher royalties should the book's sales exceed 7,000 copies, and in the letters exchanged the months before publication he demonstrated a close interest in design and punctuation, expressing a horror for pages littered with inverted commas. When, eventually, at the time of the United Arts Club dinner, Jack received his 'advance', apparently paid on publication, his income tax was ten shillings in the pound, the amount received £12 10s.

He sent off the typescript of his next book, *And to You Also*, the following summer. Again he was asked to illustrate. This time he agreed to do so.

> I am glad that yourself and Herbert Read like And You Also I think you know that the suggestion of illustrating my writings makes me feel miserable, and that I write with one side of my brain and paint and draw with another side. But I see the difficulty about the size of the book, and I would be willing to make a number of drawings, which would have to be wild, free, and without any but the most slender connection, with the text. How many drawings should there be . . . ?[9]

Jack himself called the book by the shortened title, which Ragg took up, only to be corrected in a later letter. The production timetable was slow, but Jack was happy about it, and proud when it was published. 'You have turned it out as a beautiful little book to look at. If I find I can read it with as much enjoyment as I look at it I will be on top of the grass indeed.'[10] He sent Ragg a present of two drawings. He clearly believed that the drawings in the book had helped sales: 'Drawings may have had something to do with the better sales of *And to You Also* over *Ah Well*'[11] (figs 216–17).

Despite the gloomy events of the Second World War, foggily reported in the pages of *The Irish Times* through a miasma of censorship, this was a happy time for Jack; he had come into his own. He was celebrated in London and famous in Dublin. His painting had revived. His books were published and were also successful. *And to You Also* sold out. Ragg wrote that it 'went along nicely and has now gone completely – in other words, we are sold out of the first edition.' In the spirit of war-time rationing which then prevailed, there was first a reduction to six copies to each bookshop, and, when those had gone, booksellers were offered back-copies of *Ah Well*. Of this title 1,500 copies had been printed; Routledge had 'not yet succeeded in selling one thousand to the best of my knowledge. On the basis of this evidence we printed only one 1,000 copies of *And To You Also* and to our surprise when the travellers had copies and began to take orders these came to well over 1,000 copies.'[12]

All of this was profoundly gratifying to Jack. Socially, he had become the doyen of the arts, without losing any of his charm, nor his humility. In a letter to Lily he describes his and Cottie's increasingly glamorous social life:

> We went to a good and pleasant lunch at the provosts on Friday to meet Julian Huxley and Propus MacMillan Miss Purser Mr Grove White Sir John Keane, Lord Dunsany and Lady Dunsany, Gray (the U.S.A. Minister) and Mrs Gray and Fearon Sir John Maffey and Lady Maffey I had been to the opening meeting of the Philosophical Society the night before. Queue from the door of the Dining Hall to entrance gate of Trinity. I suppose the greediness of listeners-in who love to see the owners of voices.[13]

Earlier, his play, *La La Noo*, was performed for the first time at the Peacock Theatre, and in his correspondence with Ragg he tells of a 'Large and enthusiastic audience, and, in spite of the strangeness – nothing looks so strange as innocence – the 4 papers gave it good notices.'[14] He also received many letters from people who had seen and liked it, including the young artist, Louis le Brocquy. Holloway wrote of it to a friend who was a playwright:

> although it wasn't a play at all, the dialogue was so richly poetical and withal natural when falling from the lips of a publican and stranger and a group of eight women tourists. Brian O'Higgins as the 'Publican' spoke his lines so naturally and effectively that he carried the talk to a successful end.[15]

Ragg wondered if Jack had pursued the possibility of a show in London, but Jack though it too Irish in its characters; instead, he mentioned two earlier plays:

> But I have two plays <u>The Deathly Terrace</u> a long short play and <u>The Silencer</u> a short long play which some years ago I worried many English producers with and only Norman Marshall for the 1st, and Tyrone Guthrie for the second got up to the production fence when something interfered with their plans. Now if you know of anyone who would be likely to take a chance on these plays I would be delighted to send them.[16]

George Yeats wrote to ask Jack if Cuala might publish *La La Noo*, offering a £10 advance and 15 per cent royalties. He replied 'It makes me happy to have Cuala publish "La La Noo" . . .'[17]

If his writing was going well, his painting was doing even better. From the early 1940s on, we discover a quite extraordinary pattern in his output. It was as if the National Gallery exhibition in London, and the recognition which came with it, gave him a new and apocalyptic vision of himself, his output became prodigious. Apart from anything else that he did – and he did much – he crammed into the next fifteen years, from the age of seventy to the age of eighty-five, no less than half his oil paintings, more than 500. And among these are many of his grandest statements about humanity. Yet the two years which ended the 1930s, and the two years at the beginning of the 1940s, had been the leanest of his whole career.[18] In 1938 he had produced just three canvases; four in 1939, including two truly major works, *High Water – Spring Tide*, and *A Morning Long Ago*; in 1940, five canvases, among them, *Tinkers' Encampment; the Blood of Abel*; and in 1941, five works, including *Now* (plate XI).

Arthur Power, a fellow member of the United Arts Club and a painter who got on well with Jack, treated the transition as a matter of style, when it was one of inspiration and the lean, threatened fire of old age:

> What was vigour before now became almost a frenzy. It seemed as though he felt that his pictures had not represented him fully, and that he sought to extend his expression by bringing them to the highest pitch. In his violence he tore down all convention, ripped up form and colour, and produced a tremendous blaze. In this he may be compared to Joyce in literature, except that Joyce was a bitter cynic, while Jack Yeats is a wild romantic.[19]

He was an old man, yet he responded to what was, in effect, both national and international praise of a high order, with all the intense, imaginative energy of youth. For some years he had thought much about his reputation, and of how he would be seen by posterity. Towards the end of the 1930s it seems, in what he painted, that he reached out for a grander design, a more noble expression of life, a vision of the human condition that completely transcended his search for personal immortality through his art. And in order to achieve it fully, he augmented the scale and design of his canvases.

Dimension in his work was important. He priced his canvases according to their size, a time-honoured approach through the centuries. And when he embarked on the late, large-scale works, paintings which now represent the heart of his overall output, it was not done in response to the reception given to his show at the National Gallery in London; it was already in train by then. But it seems that this show and the critical impact reassured him, since his work from this time took on an assurance and confidence which was indeed apocalyptic. Furthermore, he seems also to have been gifted with that energy in old age which was a Yeats characteristic, and which inspired the late poetry of his brother, and the remarkable energies of his father.

We have two important developments at this time, side-by-side. Firstly, we become aware of a larger vision, a greater sense of grand design and universal purpose. And it can be generally related to the size and scale of his works. Secondly, there is the later and striking acceleration in his output. From the five works painted in 1941, Jack jumped to twenty in 1942, to forty-two in 1943, and then to seventy-nine in 1944, seventy-five in 1945, and seventy-seven in 1946. Many of these were large canvases; some, his largest. In all, between 1937 and 1953, he painted twenty-three canvases in the dimension 36×48 inches or larger. Several were 40×60 inches: *Leaving the Raft, There is No Night, Shouting, And Grania Saw this Sun Sink, The Basin in which Pilate Washed his Hands, Grief, Glory* and *My Beautiful, My Beautiful!* (plates XV–XVI) Of course they matter in absolute terms because scale

312

matters. They matter in the context of Jack Yeats because size was important to him.[20] This is true at the mundane level of pricing; true also in the sense that great statements demanded large-scale works. Nor was it simply a matter of size. The larger canvases changed the ratio between height and width; the dimensions 36 × 48 inches alter the visual impact from the more familiar sizes used by the painter. There is greater height in relation to width in these large canvases than there is in the other three dimensions he regularly used, 24 × 36 inches, 18 × 24 inches, and 9 × 14 inches.

The largest size of all gives to the composition of the paintings a loftiness which tends to alter its character. There is greater space for the sky in the Tate Gallery painting, *Two Travellers* (fig. 218). The full compass of a great outdoor theatre or stadium is enhanced by the height in *Now*. And in *The Basin in which Pilate Washed his Hands* there is a contemplative, reflective character endowed by the scale of the work and its shape, and by the wonderful composition, rising to a peak in the centre, and carrying upward our sense of wonder. In many others of the group – *My Beautiful, My Beautiful!*, *Glory*, *And Grania Saw this Sun Sink* – the grandeur of scale is a significant element in the composition, and then in the impact of the work. He knew there was a very limited prospect of selling these large-scale canvases, or even the previous largest size, his 24 × 36 inch canvases, and this seems to have both sobered and released him. The wife of one collector recalls the mouth-watering titbit of information, that, in about 1943, she was passing the Waddington Galleries in South Anne Street, and saw three paintings lined up across the window, *Bachelor's Walk: In Memory*, *Communicating with Prisoners*, *The Island Funeral* (see chapters 13 and 14). They were all priced at £30! Because of the war, and because her husband had gone away to fight, she decided she could not afford to buy them.[21]

Both scale and numerical output are side issues, though recording them has something to tell us about artistic energy, ambition and self-confidence, as well as the vision and inspiration. These were apocalyptic years. And all the time Jack expanded his energies and produced a remarkable body of new and sensational work.

Jack Yeats's measured purpose in these works is there for all to see. And though it may seem at first somewhat perverse to be approaching his art in terms of the scale of it rather than perhaps the chronological ordering, this is the true glory of such works as *Now*. There is embodied in this canvas the accumulated inspiration of a lifetime's love of the stage, the circus and the world of entertainment. Just as much as his brother, Willie, and in some senses even more so, Jack was imbued with the magic of theatre from childhood on. Of all the Yeats children, he had the greatest propensity to act. And he was, as we have seen, a lifelong addict of all live performances, boxing matches, pantomime, circus, and the unending offerings of Dublin theatres over a period of half a century. In *Now* he brings the wealth of experience to a pregnant climax, divorced from particulars, reduced to essentials. On the left of the painting, expectation; on the right, contained energy. The standing figure leans slightly, giving a line of white which points upward to the half-circle of light above the auditorium. Both here, as well as in the standing figure above the horses, and the widening perspective on the extreme left, the importance of the shape of the canvas, with its lofty vertical space, becomes fully apparent.

Now provoked great interest, when shown in the Royal Hibernian Academy in 1942 and was singled out by Mainie Jellett for its technical and artistic excellence, and also its 'quality of nationality'. It was an emblem of 'dignity and distinction' in an environment (the Academy) which, she warned, 'must not shut its doors to life'. She declared that it showed 'how a large picture can be full of brilliant colour and artistic feeling'.[22] Despite the great interest, then and later, *Now* did not sell, and was in the artist's studio at the time of his death.

Mainie Jellett had chosen a magnificent example, both in painting and in personality, for her polemic against the inclusive deadness of the Academy's traditions. She was firing the first shots in a war between the old and the new, and it would lead to the setting up of an alternative annual group show for artists, the Irish Exhibition of Living Art, which was first held in 1943. Jack had initially been reluctant to become involved but Anne, his niece, was a member and the assistant secretary of the committee of the new movement, and she asked him to send in work. At its inception, it was of great importance to the Living Art committee to have Jack's sympathetic involvement. He did not readily submit to other group shows, with the exception of the Royal Hibernian Academy, after 1940, except those arranged by Victor Waddington, the majority of which were in Great Britain or further afield, though we have seen other exceptions. As it happened, the reception given to the new modernist, Living Art exhibition in general, and to his own work in particular, confirmed him in his decision to become involved. And he marked approvingly a newspaper report about the impact of the show on a group of primary school children:

> A surprise for some of the committee was the popularity with the children of the works of Jack B. Yeats, Mainie Jellett, and some other painters, whose work is so remote from the representational that many adults find them difficult to understand. On the whole, this difficulty meant nothing to the children. They accepted these pictures as pictures; if they did not understand them they were neither disappointed nor irritated – they are used to encountering the incomprehensible.[23]

It was at this stage that Jack formed the professional relationship with the dealer, Victor Waddington, which led to a number of solo exhibitions, and which was to last to the end of his life. The first of these was in November 1943. Waddington was to represent him in a quite new and comprehensive way for the next fourteen years, and the bond between the two men was uniquely significant for both (fig. 220). Victor Waddington was a dealer inspired by a love of art, a good eye, and a capacity for emotion which added an extra dimension to his professional capabilities. He could move people, he could *make* them buy pictures. This talent for persuasion was hypnotic, and it was deployed in the interests of those artists he truly admired. He allowed himself only a small stable of Irish painters of whom Jack Yeats was unquestionably the prime figure. For a period of perhaps twelve years, he brought to art in Dublin a professionalism which was impressive. And he made the general public aware of Jack as the leading painter of the day.

Their relationship did not start so propitiously; Leo Smith (fig. 221), who worked with Waddington, was the first of the two to recognise Jack's potential. Waddington had started dealing in the more conventional of the Academy painters, including Keating and Kernoff. E.A. McGuire, an amateur painter and Dublin businessman, says that Waddington at first

220. Victor Waddington with Jack, *c.* 1953.

221. Leo Smith.

had no use for, or understanding of, the post-Impressionist movement which sprang up among artists studying in Paris after the war. At the time when Jack B. Yeats made his departure into what was known as his new expressionist style, it was Waddington's partner, Leo Smith, who first recognized its merit. Later, when Yeats' new work began to attract attention, Waddington recognized not only the artistic value of his paintings but their financial potential as well. He moved his shop across the street to a larger premises and established what could deservedly be called a gallery and therein he built up his name and fame as the patron of the modern, as distinct from the Academic, painting idiom.[24]

McGuire claims that the arrangement between Waddington and Yeats to market his pictures brought two very good businessmen together. And he points out that Jack's own one-man shows became especially important

Everybody who was anybody was invited to the fashionable openings and people vied with one another to make a purchase of a recent Jack Yeats at increasingly high prices . . . Jack Yeats was no mere dreamy artist; he was financially competent as well. Waddington's Anne Street Gallery proved to be very successful and regular exhibitions were held there.[25]

McGuire's own painting was much influenced by Yeats's technique and plastic use of paint.

The tactile feeling of the paint itself, bringing an element of sculpture into the act of painting, always fascinated me. Myles na gCopaleen, the Irish Times columnist, once remarked, 'It is well for Ned McGuire he can paint a Jack Yeats in one afternoon.' Another amusing remark about my painting was made by Nano Reid. I called at the Waddington Gallery one afternoon to collect a little picture of mine of a cricket match (later owned by Terence de Vere White), which I had left to be framed. It was ready, but Waddington had put it in his shop window with some Jack Yeats pictures. As I sat in a dark corner of the shop, Nano walked in and said to Waddington, 'That little picture of a cricket match is one of the best Jack Yeatses I have seen'.[26]

Victor Waddington was born in London in 1906. His father was a mathematician, who taught in Aberdeen University and his mother was German. In his early manhood he engaged in bare-knuckled boxing-booth fights in order to earn money and indulge his love of art. On one occasion he tried to buy a painting by Monet with the proceeds of two fights. In the course of that early set of brutal experiences his nose was broken, the lid of one eye damaged, and when he came back to the dealer, the painting had been sold. He began an apprenticeship in the hotel business, but then in the mid-twenties moved to Dublin. He travelled around Ireland working in retail. He became friendly with a furniture-maker named Nathan Levine, and married his daughter, Zelda, at the end of the 1920s. They had three children; Max, born in November 1932, Leslie in February 1934, and Theo in November 1943. By the beginning of the 1930s, Waddington was dealing in art, and he may have known Jack Yeats from as early as 1931. Much of what he did in those early years involved travel. He put on art exhibitions in different parts of the country, and it was only well into the Second World War that he set up in Dublin. His assistant Leo Smith was with him for eleven years, before setting up on his own in 1944. Jack was then exhibiting with Longford. Jack's transfer

– from Contemporary Picture Galleries to Victor Waddington's Galleries – took place before Longford's tragic early death from a fall, in September 1944 (believed by many to have been suicide). It is not known why Jack moved, but he held his first show with Waddington in 1943.

It was always a formal, professional relationship, in which Waddington managed the painter's business affairs, took over the framing of pictures, took and delivered them from the studio in Fitzwilliam Square, and kept careful accounts. These were set forth in typed letters which began, 'Dear Mr Yeats'. The artist always wrote in reply, 'Dear Victor Waddington', and signed himself, as he did indeed to his brother and other family members, 'Yours kindly Jack B. Yeats'. The formal note is an admirable one for a lasting friendship. It was accepted between the two men that *all* works by the artist would be handled through Waddington. This had not, apparently, been the case with Jack Longford, and with any previous gallery owner Jack had simply operated a single-show agreement. With Waddington, his professional affairs were placed permanently in the dealer's hands.

However, behind the strict proprieties a warm friendship developed, and Waddington became part of the inner circle of younger visitors to Jack Yeats's evening encounters. The painter's social life by this stage was more or less dominated by Thomas MacGreevy, whose social status was enhanced by his relationship with the painter. MacGreevy liked it to be thought that nothing was done in respect of Jack Yeats without his approval. Yet there were times when evading his dominant and presiding wisdom was in order, and both Terence de Vere White, who was then close to the artist, and Waddington, were of this view.

In the absence of MacGreevy, a different, more light-hearted atmosphere prevailed. Waddington was a busy and hard-working man, with a young family to educate. He paid Jack late afternoon visits to deal with his affairs, and these encounters were naturally private ones. If they later became extended with the arrival of other visitors – and the artist had a busy diary full of meetings – then the change from formal to informal took place. Cottie rarely, if ever, attended either these soirées, or the earlier afternoon tea. Leslie Waddington, who went quite frequently to visit Jack in his father's company, recalls that Cottie used to bring tea in then disappear. In the evenings Jack served madeira, sherry, whiskey or malaga with orange peel. Anne Yeats remembers having madeira and cake, as does Brigid Ganly.

The end of the war saw the winding up of the friendship between Jack and his publisher. Ragg wrote in September 1944 that he fortunately still had a house in which to hang the two drawings given him by Jack, and that 'the dangers and risks through which we have been passing, now happily seem to be coming to an end – but perhaps that is tempting providence too much!'[27] Ragg wrote his last letter to Jack the following summer:

It is nice to be able to write to you now that a measure of peace has returned and I do hope that we may see you over in London before very long. Meanwhile, I have heard a rumour that tea is short in Ireland and that you and your wife are connoisseurs of tea and have a special favour for Earl Grey's. I hope therefore that you will not consider it impertinent to send you this packet of Earl Grey's tea which my wife has been able to get in London. It will indicate in a very small way my respects for your work and the pleasure that the two drawings which you gave me give me every day.[28]

222. One of William MacQuitty's photographs; he was the only person Jack Yeats allowed to photograph him at his easel.

Jack's friends came from every kind of background, and he had a liking for adventurers, one of whom was William MacQuitty, whose father was owner of the *Belfast Telegraph*. Maurice Craig, the poet and historian, was a friend of Jack's and brought MacQuitty to visit. This was during the war. MacQuitty had led an exciting life in India and the Far East, as pilot, banker, soldier, beachcomber, and chronicler of strange and terrible events, including the 1931 Cawnpore Massacre. MacQuitty believed that his varied and adventurous life appealed to Jack Yeats 'living and experiencing real life vicariously, and constructing its realities for his paintings from memories or from encounters with others'.[29] MacQuitty had returned to Belfast at the outbreak of the Second World War, and become a film-maker there and in London, mainly producing wartime propaganda films. He visited Dublin in 1943, and indulged in the exciting round of social life which included dining at Jammet's and the Dolphin, going to the Gate Theatre, and forgetting about the war. He met Victor Waddington, and, either through him or another friend from Northern Ireland, Paddy Falloon, not only Jack, but the architect, Michael Scott, and the sculptress, Hilary Heron. He bought his first Jack Yeats painting, *The Sailor's Last Return*, and met the artist. He remembers asking Jack for advice, – and to confine it to one sentence – about what he should do with his life. 'After a long pause Jack said, "Ah, well." Then he gave me a copy of the book, which he signed.'[30]

Although their conversations were based on the younger man relating his adventures abroad, MacQuitty remembers them both talking hard to each other. There was a complete character contrast: MacQuitty the man of action, much-travelled and with a wealth of worldly experience, Jack contemplative and elusive, waiting to be told stories and then responding to them. 'His look was very penetrating. He had cold eyes. He could see right through you to the back of your head.'[31]

In 1944, when Victor Waddington had been formally associated with him for only a year, Jack painted a haunting 'portrait' of him, called *Sleep* (fig. 224). Not a portrait in the formal sense, it is simply a record of a visit made one afternoon. At the time, Victor Waddington was immersed in work on behalf of the Jewish victims of the Nazi Holocaust, and with his business placing heavy pressures on him there were times when he arrived at the studio, or at Portobello Nursing Home, too tired to stay awake. Jack supported his work on behalf of the Jews, and paid silent respect in painting the picture, which he gave to Waddington. He took an interest in his children. He also responded to the light-hearted wit of George Waddington, Victor's brother, who helped in the gallery and dealt with framing.

He continued to be interested in Anne and Michael Yeats (figs 223 and 225). Anne had already been involved in the production of his first play at the Abbey Theatre, *Harlequin's Positions*, doing the sets from his rough designs. Michael, on the other hand, away at school, had seen very little of his uncle, and it was not until he entered Trinity at the beginning of the war, to read modern history and political science, that the two had any contact. Unknown to Jack, Michael had developed quite strong sympathies with Eamon de Valera and his party, Fianna Fail. These dated back to his days at Baymount Preparatory School, where, at the age of ten, in defiance of schoolfriends and family, he declared himself 'A Dev Man'. And he was to remain staunchly Fianna Fail thereafter.[32] The decision was in marked contrast with the ethos of Baymount, where the pupils would, if anything, have been pro-Cosgrave,

223. Anne Yeats in 1947.

224. *Sleep*, oil on canvas, 14 × 18, private collection, 1944.

225. Michael Yeats in 1947.

their anti-de Valera feelings strengthened with residual Southern Unionist sympathies. It would also have been against the grain of the family's feelings about politics. Michael's father, during those uncertain years, was, in varying degrees, right-wing in his politics, and an appointee to the Senate by the Cosgrave-led government. And his mother, who was English, during Michael's schooldays remained loyal to Willie's sentiments. Even more remarkable was the fact that this early pro-de Valera stance prevailed throughout his time at St Columba's College in Rathfarnham, the most Unionist and Protestant school then to be found in the 26 Counties, where support for Fianna Fail would have been a hanging offence.

This unregenerate young Dev man took to politics in Trinity. He became auditor of the College Historical Society, and gave as his inaugural address a paper on 'The Small Nations'. His list of guest speakers was ambitious. At the top of it was Eamon de Valera, closely followed by Jan Masaryk, then one of the leaders of the Czechoslovak government in exile, and its foreign minister.[33] Michael Yeats invited his uncle to attend the meeting, and Jack promptly accepted. It was more difficult getting the platform together. Michael Yeats went to see Eamon de Valera, who said he would attend the meeting if Masaryk accepted. Masaryk agreed, but then was faced with the problem of a visa. Neither Britain nor Ireland wanted difficulties to develop, or for there to be any protests or demonstrations. Unbeknownst to Michael Yeats de Valera organised that Masaryk would be allowed to travel to Dublin, thus ensuring his own appearance on the platform in Trinity College.[34] The Provost of Trinity College, Alton, hearing of the meeting, asked Michael Yeats to go to de Valera and invite him to dine on the High Table at Commons, before the meeting, and he went on the college's behalf to issue this invitation. This use of a student intermediary, between the college and the government in Merrion Street was indicative of the guarded view Trinity

226. Father Senan Moynihan.

took of 'the great Irish world outside'. In the event de Valera came only to the meeting. Being an inaugural it was held in the large Examination Hall, which was filled to capacity, with many people outside. And it attracted enormous public attention. Jack attended both the meeting and a dinner afterwards, and his nephew remembers him drawing sketches on the menu. Another of the platform speakers was Owen Sheehy Skeffington, an outspoken radical teacher in the French department and a lifelong friend of Samuel Beckett.

In 1944, Faber brought out a selection of John Butler Yeats's letters, edited by Joseph Hone. In the circumstances, the title chosen, *J.B. Yeats: Letters to his son W.B. Yeats and Others 1869–1922,* was insensitive.[35] Jack had in fact co-operated with the editor, having letters typed, and suggesting editorial cuts. He had a vast store of letters, both to himself and to Cottie. The letters are full of John Butler Yeats's opinions, reflect his wide reading, and the alert and curious mind. Hone, of course, had been through the letters to Willie during the period immediately after the poet's death, when he was busily at work on his *Life*. This was published in 1942.[36] It is understandable that the vast majority of the letters he chose for publication were those sent by the portrait painter to his eldest son. For Jack, however, it was a reflection of the wide fame his brother's name enjoyed, compared with his own more limited standing.

Though Victor Waddington had been associated with Jack for a relatively short period, he was determined to get him wider recognition. He had a powerful ally in Father Senan Moynihan, the editor of *The Capuchin Annual* (fig. 226)[37]. Father Senan, as he was universally known, played a significant role in public education about Irish art. He wore the traditional Franciscan brown habit, with its distinctive *capuche*, and his face, with its pointed, renaissance beard, became a familiar sight at social and artistic functions, almost as though he officiated as private chaplain to the men in power. He started his annual in 1930, a big, bulky, soft-backed book, up to 200 pages in length, and containing all sorts of articles printed on semi-glossy pages, and with extensive illustrations. It had a standard cover, in brown, with an illustration of St Francis, and it became the leading Catholic publication on Irish art and culture. It was a remarkably well-balanced annual, its purpose assertively nationalist, but in the most generous and positive way. Father Senan ran the offices of *The Capuchin Annual* from an upper floor in Capel Street, above the hatter's and outfitter's shop owned by the Lemass family. Sean Lemass was a close friend, and Father Senan moved in a circle which was intimate with Eamon de Valera and other government ministers. There was clear allegiance to Fianna Fail, and the annual enjoyed de Valera's support.[38]

Its first article on the artist, 'Three Historical Paintings by Jack B. Yeats' and written by MacGreevy, had appeared two years earlier. The paintings in question were the three which had stood, earlier in the war, side-by-side in the window of Victor Waddington's gallery priced at £30 each. They had subsequently been bought as part of a Capuchin collection which hung in the office where Father Senan spent virtually all his time. The works remained there until the 1960s.[39]

Father Senan was the obvious choice for chairman of the committee to organise the Jack Yeats National Loan Exhibition, which was planned early in 1945. Its huge committee, of more than fifty people, included two government ministers, the Ceann Comhairle, or 'speaker', of the Dail, and gallery and museum directors from as far away as New York and Pittsburgh.

Having seen this project set in motion, Waddington then mounted a private Jack Yeats show in March, a kind of warming up, or curtain-raiser for the year's main event. He had the exhibition rooms in his gallery enlarged specially for the Yeats show, and this was referred to in newspaper reports as a 'tribute' to the artist. Jack showed twenty-three works, among them *Near a City Long Ago, The Breaker Out*, and *The Little Sister of the Gang*. The total amount asked for all the paintings was £2,920, with *Near A City Long Ago*, at £300, one of just three at this, the highest price. Stephen Rynne judged it the modern masterpiece of the show, and it was one of the first to sell. Indeed, within minutes of the gallery doors opening £2,000-worth of paintings were sold, and the press made quite a to-do about the public's keenness to buy. Jack, rather perversely, mounted in his scrapbook an enthusiastic eulogy from Theodore Goodman beside a *Dublin Opinion* cartoon, showing a wealthy collector, with a fat cigar in his mouth, pointing up at a wall covered in pictures in ornate frames, and saying, 'Sometimes, as I said to Halligan of Paper Fasteners Ltd., I feel like sellin' five or six o' them an' buyin' one Yeat [sic.]'. *Dublin Opinion* had been consistently anti-Yeats, publishing many cartoons over the years which described, in various amusing ways, how difficult it was to understand the artist's work. This one was the first to switch the emphasis to the growing taste of businessmen for a Yeats, usually as a symbol, not of their cultural judgment, but of their wealth. It is a situation which has changed very little since.

Cottie was firmly established as hostess at Jack's solo shows. In press photographs she is always present, quite evidently at the heart of the event, her pride in him clear from her smiling expression. This time due to illness, she had not been at the opening of the show. C.P. Curran (fig. 227) wrote to her

> I don't want you to tell Jack, but since you were not at the opening of the show today I must tell you most plainly about the attendance. It was not that it was more than ever friendly and appreciative but that everyone was very conscious that they were in the presence of the work of a very great master. At no other show was I so aware of this feeling of real respect.[40]

The usual things were said by the usual critics. What was different was the emphasis on money and collecting. The artist appeared in the usual photographs, looking a bit grim, the result of the awkwardness he felt at such occasions; but looking also an old man, his eyes a bit sunk, their expression sad, the great domed cranium virtually bald, the mouth severe, and the lines in his thin face drawn. He wore his tie with an unusually large knot in it (a habit which both Waddington and Leo Smith later copied). This was decidedly not the fashion of the times. Roses were not yet in flower, and in his buttonhole he had a large red carnation.

The bold Stephen Rynne wrote the liveliest review of the exhibition, irreverently referring to *The Breakfast Room* with an aside about another famous painter of interiors: 'Turner used to slap up these sort of interiors in water colours'. Others he described as 'Very Spooky', 'A trifle, but a happy conceit', 'No, not pulled off'.[41] 'Yeats', he said, 'is still a very young old man: "And your young men shall see visions: and your old men shall dream dreams".' Jack did both.

227. C.P. Curran.

CHAPTER TWENTY-ONE
Death for Only One 1945–1947

The artist has no age

COTTIE RATHER SHYLY pointed out to Elizabeth Curran that the great 1945 retrospective exhibition of Jack's work very nearly coincided with their golden wedding anniversary. 'She said it with such joy. Through the whole business of finding and selecting work for that show none of us had given any thought to the personal dating coincidence.'[1] No one had noticed. The event also very nearly coincided with Jack's own seventy-fifth birthday, and if notice was taken of that, nothing was made of it. Here was an old man, in the full floodtide of his belated yet prodigious energy, glorying in his own strength of purpose, in the golden glow of his own imagination, and yet standing very nearly alone.

As people waited in a lengthening queue outside the National College of Art for the National Loan Exhibition, the secretary of the organising committee went out to tell people that catalogues would soon be arriving and that the doors would shortly open. To her surpise she found Jack queueing up with everyone else. 'Oh, Mr Yeats,' she said, 'You shouldn't be here, but inside.' He replied: 'But I'm enjoying it so much, hearing all the comments about myself.'[2]

He was being honoured by his country, as its greatest living painter. It was his friends, not the State, honouring the artist. He was fortunate to be surrounded by people who had ensured that his work would be known, admired and bought, and who now created a tribute to him in his seventy-fifth year. Unlike the London exhibition with Nicholson, held in the National Gallery in Trafalgar Square, this was neither in the National Gallery nor the Municipal Gallery of Modern Art, but in the rougher environment of the National College of Art, beside Leinster House, in Kildare Street.

The National Loan Exhibition opened on the afternoon of 11 June 1945. The Very Reverend Dr Patrick Browne, president of University College, Galway, spoke first and in Irish, claiming Jack as one of 'the classicists of Ireland'.[3] 'Not alone did he paint Irish people and Irish scenes, but he imbued them with the soul and the thought of Ireland.' Jack sat beside Eamon de Valera with members of the government and the committee grouped around to hear the tributes. MacGreevy spoke about Jack's art, stressing its 'outstanding interpretation of some of the most glorious and exciting periods of our history, the last fifty years. In titles, in subjects, in treatment, it was intensely Irish.'

This nationalist interpretation of the artist was expressed in other ways.

228. *Irish Independent* photograph of the 1945 National Loan Exhibition.

229. Earnan O'Malley.

One might have expected the strongest reflection to have come from Earnan O'Malley (fig. 229), who wrote a long introduction to the catalogue, and whose claim to republican fame rested on exploits during the Rising, the War of Independence, and the Civil War. Yet his extended explanation of Jack's life and work is a model of balanced interpretation. His tribute is more moving than MacGreevy's. He understands paint better. He interprets Jack in an entirely natural and relaxed way, giving a narrative of the early childhood days in Sligo. 'Great roaring winds sweep in from the Atlantic to drench the land with spray, soften the intention, weaken will and perseverance.' And he writes no less perceptively about the towns, particularly Sligo, to which sailors, tinkers, small farmers, countrymen, dealers, ballad singers and beggarmen, came in alert and excited anticipation about what they would find, what they would make, and what they would spend.

O'Malley knew Yeats well. They were good friends, and would have remained close, only O'Malley lived much of the time in Mayo and abroad. Louis MacNeice recalls meeting him on a visit to the painter's studio:

> Ernie O'Malley was there too, sipping his Malaga quietly. A legendary figure from the Irish Revolution, who had run Michael Collins's intelligence service, who had been riddled with machinegun bullets, he was now, while still young, living in retirement in Co. Mayo with an American wife and growing his own vegetables. He had a great deal of charm but, unlike most Irish who have charm, was neither flamboyant nor noisy. A Gaelic scholar, he was sceptical about the use of Gaelic. And sceptical about Irish politics. But not embittered . . . He and Jack Yeats and I went out into the street together, a great wide Regency street bathed in a warm grey and ending in a mountain vista. An old woman offered us violets. Jack Yeats bought us each a bunch. As we walked away he told us the old woman's history. He knew the history of all the beggars in Dublin.[4]

O'Malley, having given much thought to Jack as a stylist, identifies and explains the dual growth in experimentation and vision. His is a piece of simple and unstrained writing which glories as much in the 'persuasive paint' as it does in the visionary, subjective world of the later canvases, with their brooding nostalgia, their inherent tragedy. O'Malley, who in a sense appears briefly on the field of Yeats's exegesis and then vanishes again, understood that 'philosophic isolation amongst an indifferent audience who resent an artist's new direction', and he teased out, from knowledge of the artist during the difficult years of misunderstanding, neglect and mockery, the inner purpose, Jack's 'quality of mind in paint'.

> He brings a fresh experience to each canvas he paints; his individual work cannot be judged in terms of previous work but in the individual canvas one looks at. That demands alertness of mind and an unprejudiced, innocent eye. He is a romantic painter who through memory has made notes all his life of material which has stirred him by its emotional significance. These notes may remain unused for years but they have been sifted in his unconscious. When he calls on them he can recollect his original impressions, organise his perceptions through an enlargement of that experience, and create a work of art.

O'Malley enjoyed an intimacy with the artist which allowed him to debate style and technique. The passage in his essay on the act of painting takes us closer than anyone to that 'homogeneous surface . . . where his handling of knife or brush seems to be by instinct'. Among the O'Malley paintings were several from the time shortly before the exhibition, and it is the technique of these he understands so well, writing of the familiar emphasis on a limpid, lightning-swift chiaroscuro, and on the use of almost bare canvas, right down to the basic priming to enhance the luminosity of light.

> At times, impatient with the brush to commmunicate his feelings for the richness and charm of pigment and his sheer joy of its expressive power, he employs the palette knife to give swiftness and vigour to the immediacy of his emotions. Seemingly unrelated colours directed by this urgency create an orchestration due to his unerring taste in colour harmony; and in a form of evocative magic, make a direct impact on the mind.[5]

Father Senan paid tribute in a brief essay written in Irish and inspired by childhood memories of learning the language through the primers which Jack had illustrated at the beginning of the century.

> I shall only say this: Yeats is one of the great 'painters' of this world. He won fame and respect not only at home in Ireland, but also in lands abroad, without ever lessening the 'Irishness' which he laid bare from the beginning of his work. He created his pictures here in Ireland and in them he drew in sketches and in colour the lives and life of our own people. The history of the country and the qualities of the Irish people can be seen in many of his paintings. We should therefore be grateful to God that there is among us a man who can, finely and clearly, portray our country's history and the essence of our nation to today's Irish people and to those of the future and to the people of the world.

Of course huge notice was taken of the show, and many tributes appeared. Daniel Corkery was in puckish form when he began an article, 'No, too much has not been written about the Jack Yeats exhibition. The promoters have been thanked, certainly not thanked too much.'[6] And he went on to expand on a favourite theme, the discovery by Irish artists 'that the Irish scene in all its moods and tenses was worth while'. For any artist to have achieved this revelation for himself was, in Corkery's eyes, welcome; but for someone 'from the Ascendancy side of our people' there was an innate blockage to be overcome. 'They lack, almost naturally, one might say, that gift of mind which of all others is most necessary to the writer or artist who would find his matter in ordinary flesh and blood – tenderness; tenderness, which is the fine flower of reverence, that angel of the world.'

Sensitivities about the Irishness of the occasion were widely evident. In one review it was stressed that Ireland was not only honouring Jack Yeats, but honouring herself as well, because she is showing that as a nation she appreciates his art. And the same reviewer went on to stress that ninety per cent of the works on show were owned by Irish people living in Ireland. C.P. Curran, Elizabeth Curran, Maírín Allen, Monk Gibbon, James White, all reviewed the show. Arthur Power, reviewing it for *The Irish Times*, said, 'some of the pictures are good and some are not so good', and went on to refer to the paint being 'often meaninglessly dragged about and tortured without purpose'.[7] Monk Gibbon wrote:

> He seems far more deeply rooted in the living tradition of the West . . . he

230. *G'Morrow; Strawberry*, watercolour and pencil on paper, $5\frac{1}{2} \times 3\frac{1}{2}$, 1903.

licks his lips with quiet relish, now as always, over any theme that suggests Ireland, ragged Ireland, devil-may-care Ireland, the Ireland of circus tumblers and tipsters and amateur jockeys, the Ireland that, if it believes in any virtues, believes in the 'wasteful virtues', to use a phrase of his father's.[8]

He was justly celebrated in the many press tributes. His work now sold, whenever it was available. It was suddenly fashionable to own a Jack Yeats, and a new and not entirely welcome fame fell upon his head and shoulders, like petals of spring blossom after a long and cruel winter. He became a living legend, and a 'National Treasure'.

The P.E.N. Club gave a dinner in his honour at Jury's Hotel. It was hosted by James Starkey ('Seumus O'Sullivan', editor of *The Dublin Magazine*). Proposing the toast to the guest of honour, he told his audience he had been conquered by Jack's art long before. At the age of twenty-three, working on the *United Irishman* for Arthur Griffith, he reviewed the August 1903 exhibition 'Sketches of Life in the West of Ireland'. He went, he saw, he was conquered. One picture in particular, he told his audience, stuck in his mind. It was called *G'Morrow, Strawberry*. What appealed to him, he said, was that the subject was seen as if through the eyes of a child. Indeed, this seemed to characterise the whole exhibition, and was the outstanding characteristic in the artist's work.

Jack made a gracious reply. Overwhelmed by all the tributes, he began by telling his audience that, instead of addressing the P.E.N. Club he should have been running for President of Ireland, 'With the "Big Three" making his claim for the commodious house in the Phoenix Park.'[9] What he was meant to speak about was his career and his travels, yet there was little enough to say. Indeed, of the many places he had been in, the most satisfying of them all was 'Hy Brazil'.[10] Other speakers included Victor Waddington and Brigid O'Brien. She was there in place of her father, Dermod, who was too ill to attend.

It seems that Jack went home and looked up the review. Sure enough, it singled out *Goodmorrow (sic) Strawberry* for 'the glee, the sheer childish glee' of it and another work, *A Pony Cupid*. Jack still had the watercolour in his studio. He wrote on the back of it, 'To Seumas O'Sullivan President of the P.E.N. Club with all thanks for a most happy dinner', and sent it round to his friend as a gift. It is a wonderful little drawing, showing a baby donkey rearing up to touch noses with a large carthorse. It remained in the Starkey family until 1971, when it was lent to the Sligo Museum, later becoming a gift to the collection (fig. 230).

The National Loan Exhibition closed at the end of July. To coincide with the event Victor Waddington published MacGreevy's essay on the artist.[11] Beckett reviewed it for *The Irish Times*, and called it 'the earliest connected account of Mr Yeats's paintings'. MacGreevy particularly wanted Beckett to review the book for *The Irish Times*, and to do so favourably, which Beckett strongly resisted on the grounds that their friendship was well known. In the end Beckett went ahead with the review, taking issue with MacGreevy's interpretation. In the gentlest of ways, Beckett implies that there would be alternative views. He clearly stood between two valued friends, the author of the book and the painter. Beckett examines in some detail, and with a lengthy quotation from the essay, the MacGreevy interpretation of Jack as 'the first great Irish painter . . . the first to fix, plastically, with completeness and for his time finality, what is peculiar to the Irish scene and to the Irish people. This is the essence of his interpretation, and it permeates the essay in all its parts.'

Though Beckett praises his friend's writing on Jack's art, and describes it as 'art-criticism of a high order', he disagrees profoundly with it. 'The national aspects of Mr Yeats's genius have, I think, been overstated, and for motives not always remarkable for their aesthetic purity.' And he goes on to question the use of criteria other than the aesthetic grounds which he himself sees as central and exclusive. The artist's importance has to be sought elsewhere than in his 'sympathetic treatment of the local accident'. There then follows the much-quoted passage, worth giving in full:

> He is with the great of our time, Kandinsky and Klee, Bellmer and Bram van Velde, Rouault and Braque, because he brings light, as only the great dare bring light, to the issueless predicament of existence, reduces the dark where there might have been, mathematically at least, a door. The being in the street when it happens in the room, the being in the room when it happens in the street, the turning to gaze from land to sea, from sea to land, the backs to one another and the eyes abandoning, the man alone trudging in sand, the man alone thinking (thinking!) in his box — these are characteristic notations having reference, I imagine, to processes less simple, and less delicious, than those to which the plastic vis is commonly reduced, and to a world where Tir-na-nOgue makes no more sense than Bachelor's Walk, nor Helen than the apple-woman, nor asses than men, nor Abel's blood than Useful's, nor morning than night, nor the inward than the outward search.[12]

Though he did not include this in the review, Beckett, who saw Jack for the first time after a gap of five years, in the summer of 1945, resumed walking with him, and asked him: 'Did he feel his work had changed and in what way? He finally replied: "Less – (long pause) – conscious".'[13]

Other reviewers endorsed the MacGreevy approach, notably the lengthy notice in *The Times Literary Supplement*.[14] But in general the absence of any serious consideration of the painter's technique by MacGreevy was criticised, as were the reproductions, some of which, notably of later work, were judged 'incomprehensible'. As black-and-white illustrations of the period, they are clear enough, and number twenty-one, from a 1902 watercolour to several large oils from the 1940s. Jack himself had been responsible for the small scale of reproductions. 'I myself liked best the idea of small reproductions of pictures, which recall the picture as against larger reproductions which, the bigger they are, the more they become like a featureless ghost staggering in front of a picnic party sheltering on a rainy day in a ruined home of other years.'[15]

That great warhorse of Irish art, Dermod O'Brien, who had presided over the Royal Hibernian Academy from 1910, and over the affairs of the United Arts Club for almost as many years, died in October. His death coincided with the annual general meeting of the academy, and all members turned up to pay tribute. It was Jack's At Home day, and he wrote to Con Curran to warn him. On account of his busy year, there had been several missed Thursdays, and he told Curran, 'I would not like any friend to meet a closed Door'.[16] Cottie wrote to Dermod's son, Brendan, and to his wife, Kitty Wilmer O'Brien, and

Jack called on them; they both sent flowers. Dermod O'Brien had always greatly admired Jack's work. Kitty told him that her father-in-law 'would remark "I wonder what Jack has for us this year".' And she reminded Cottie of the way Dermod's face had lit up when Jack arrived at the painter's birthday dinner in the Arts Club, earlier in the year. Jack wrote a tribute for *The Irish Times*, headed, simply, 'Dermod'. It was much appreciated by the family.[17]

Earnan O'Malley brought John Rothenstein, director of the Tate Gallery, to see Jack on 6 December 1945.

> The climax of the afternoon was provided by two large and elaborate pictures, the first of which represented a theatrical performance seen from the wings, the second two travellers in a wild Sligo landscape. This last, to my thinking, is one of the most unquestionable triumphs of Jack Yeats's manifest though undisciplined and flickering genius. No hint is given of the identities of the black, dishevelled figures or of the occasion of their encounter, yet certain human values are mysteriously asserted: most positively perhaps those of human dignity and independence, of faith in Providence as opposed to carefulness and calculation, and the imaginative as distinct from the rational outlook upon life. Although, look as we may, our ignorance of the identities of the two figures is not dispelled, we are certain that they live according to these values that they consider the lilies (or whatever their Sligo equivalents may be), and that they take no thought for the morrow . . .[18]

Rothenstein was encouraged to make a choice between the two paintings (the theatrical one was *Now*), and chose *Two Travellers* for the Tate Gallery. It was shown at Wildenstein's in London the following spring, in a solo exhibition of Jack's work, the first after the war. Another meeting followed, and the painter got on well with the dynamic, even fiery gallery director. Jack sent a gracious thank-you note to O'Malley for 'introducing him to the picture'. The painting, though not the first Yeats oil acquired by the Tate, swiftly became the gallery's most famous example by the artist, and reproductions have been sold around the world. It was painted in 1942, but was not in the National Loan Exhibition.

Rothenstein wanted to write about Jack, and persuaded O'Malley to take him back for a second visit.

> 'Here's a picture I thought you might care to see,' the artist said, bringing out from behind the screen a longish landscape, seen, as it were, from the imaginary back of a black horse, whose determined head and energetically curving neck projects into the foreground. The landscape is flat and, marked with an occasional dune, it stretches seawards. Grass covers it almost entirely, soft, springy grass that must tempt the hooves even of the most ancient horse. 'I used often to ride along this track', he said, 'when I was a boy' and he traced its course with his forefinger lovingly. Often and with absorbed interest he spoke of the past, of his boyhood and youth.[19]

He submitted work to quite a number of exhibitions. With Victor Waddington now handling all the details, in 1946 Jack exhibited at the Atkinson Art Gallery, in Southport. He was invited to send work to the Royal Scottish Academy Galleries, in Edinburgh, to be part of the 52nd exhibition of the Society of Scottish Artists. Paintings of his were part of a special centenary exhibition to celebrate Thomas Davis and the Young Ireland Movement in the National College of Art. And he was in two London exhibitions, the Wildenstein solo show of his work, and the Leger Galleries winter exhibition.

The painting, *Now*, which Rothenstein had passed over in favour of *Two Travellers*, was shown in the Atkinson Art Gallery exhibition, in Southport. It seems to have attracted attention, even notoriety, on account of its being the most expensive work in the 55th Exhibition of Modern Art at the gallery; it was priced at £600. The art critics of the local weekly newspaper, *The Guardian* , referred to Yeats 'having risen rapidly into favour of late' and the *Southport Visitor* suggested 'there would be a buyer at £600 before the Exhibition closed on September 7'.[20] No buyer emerged, then or later. But the art critic went on to record an interpretation of the painting: 'Note . . . the conductor with baton raised, the orchestra about to burst into music, and the chariots to charge into the arena. "Now" is the psychological moment.'[21]

In April 1946, the Irish poet, Donagh MacDonagh, published in *The Irish Times* a fine tribute, entitled, simply, 'Jack B. Yeats':

Love of the dusty rose
Blooming above the Square
Lights the whole studio
And singer, fisher, clown,
Horseman and saddled horse
Surge through the winter air . . .

The women by Liffey side,
The pig-buyer home from the fair,
The horse taking time in his stride
Are dead . . .
But they and the sailors of Sligo
Are bright in a memory where
Colour condenses in light
And the starved rose blushes again.[22]

In July, Dublin University conferred on him the honorary degree of Doctor of Letters. He had always thought of himself as 'a Trinity man'. Willie had been conferred with the same degree many years before, in 1922.[23]

Jack's election a year later to University Club on St Stephen's Green strengthened the association with Trinity. The United Arts Club had become less congenial since Dermod O'Brien's death. Brigid Ganly attributed this to the craze among members for contract bridge. Two Trinity friends, Professor H.O. White, who was professor of English, and Captain J.H. Shaw, who was college bursar, put him up for the club – 'Occupation – Painter' – and he was elected. He used it regularly thereafter, and remained a member until about 1953.[24] He was popular, if at times enigmatic. One member recalled him appearing in the bar looking decidedly put out and staring silently at the assembled members for so long that they all fell silent as well. 'Are you looking for something, Mr Yeats?' he was asked. He paused and stared round the room. 'I am looking for the truth,' he said. 'I cannot find it anywhere.' He paused again. 'I think Liam Wicklow is sleeping on it upstairs.' And he turned and left the room.[25]

He was at this stage a quite forbidding figure to those who did not know him, though always a man of seemingly infinite charm to those who did.

Robert Wyse Jackson recalls his uniquely old-fashioned manner and appearance: 'My own memories of him were the late ones of a deaf and lonely old man in the Club, head to one side, charmingly courteous. He had an archaic sea-captain air, dressed as he always was in a square-cut nautical-looking navy jacket and large loose black tie.'[26]

He took a keen interest in Trinity sports. He was on the House and Gardens Committee of the Dublin University Boat Club, which held annual regattas at Islandbridge. He supported the club with annual subscriptions, and attended committee meetings in the College. He also went to parties out at the boat club on the Liffey, and was a guest at trial eights dinners. On regatta days, members of the club were deputed to entertain him, and the physician, Alan Browne, recalls the faint feeling of intimidation this task inspired. Jack was unfailingly friendly and polite; but silent as well, and the obligation to make conversation and try to keep him amused, while walking up and down the banks of the river, had the usual effect of totally silencing his youthful escort. On one occasion, Browne remembers, a race was heading down towards the boathouse and the finishing line. Jack commented, pointing to the Phoenix Park bank, 'That crew is going to win.' 'How do you know?' Browne asked. 'They are dressed in primary colours,' Jack replied. 'The pure colours cut through the air quicker.' And they did.[27]

Jack felt at home with writers who were dominant voices in the 1940s, Sean O'Faolain and Frank O'Connor. The former, in particular, whose reputation had been firmly established through his editorship of *The Bell*, started a literary group in June of 1946 of which Jack was a member. Called the Russell Circle, its members met to have lunch together once or twice a month at one or other of the justly renowned eating places in Dublin. These included the Russell Hotel, on the corner of St Stephen's Green, the Bailey restaurant, in Duke Street, and the Dolphin Hotel. Jack's Trinity college friend, H.O. White, was a member, and also from Trinity, the historian, T.W. Moody. Other friends included the artist, Sean O'Sullivan, C.P. Curran's daughter, Elizabeth, and Frank O'Connor.[28]

An even racier group of friends became known to Jack through his niece's career in theatre, and her work among painters, including several left over from White Stag Group days, during the war. Anne, for example, did the sets for the production at Austin Clarke's Lyric Theatre of Donagh MacDonagh's verse play, *Happy as Larry*, and she wrote a card to Cottie from the Dublin Zoo; she was there painting wallabies, and the card showed crocodiles. 'It's a grand play and should play well I think. Uncle Jack has three lovely paintings in Waddington's window this last two weeks – They are big ones . . .'[29]

The solitary figure who had stalked his way through the decade of the 1930s, his paintings unsold, his talent frequently mocked, his energies dispersed into fiction and drama, and his output faltering and falling off, had been a classic example of the isolated artist. This was now profoundly altered. He was surrounded by friends and supporters, and by constant recognition. From Edinburgh, at the time of the Scottish Academies show, Thomas Bodkin wrote to tell him how well the works had been displayed. Then the president of the Society of Scottish Artists, Dr Elder Dickson, wrote to fill in the details; the lecture which Bodkin had given had been 'magnificent', and the audience had been held 'enthralled'. Bodkin, in his letter to Jack, had spoken rather gloomily about growing old, and being unable to find time or energy to write his memoirs. 'Pipe down on age,' Jack told him.

Don't be any age. It will be long years until they can get in your way. But if you begin, as Shaw did, drawing attention to his birthdays when he was only in the eighties, you will land yourself, as he has, on the slab of a tomb. Sitting there interrupted every time he speaks by the cry of 'Hear the great unburied one! Isn't he just wonderful! Ain't he cute' The Artist has no age.[30]

But the predator, Time, stalked Cottie. Four years older than Jack, she had been ill on a couple of occasions in 1946 and in mid-February, 1947, she woke one morning unable to speak; she was gravely ill with heart trouble. Companion throughout his long life, who had shared so closely in his difficulties and triumphs, whose tears had so readily flowed, both in sympathy for setbacks, and in overwhelming joy at all his successes, was to part from him. Dr Honor Purser came to see her, and she went into the Portobello Nursing Home on 14 February 1947. Jack wrote to MacGreevy: 'She is comfortable. I saw her for a few moments today, her head seems clear, and her speech is better. If you could come and see me here between six and seven this evening or between nine and ten at night I would like it for I am very down & I am yours kindly Jack B Yeats.'[31]

Cottie was weak; she made no recovery. But she lasted for several weeks more, Jack calling to sit with her every day, and trying to face the awful emptiness which loomed ahead. He depended much on MacGreevy. On 25 March he intended to go over to see Brendan and Kitty O'Brien, but instead cancelled when Honor Purser called on him to tell him: 'Hope has gone – That my dear is just slipping slowly away. She has no pain and is at peace. So if you are well and not engaged come in, if only a little while to sit with me. There will be plenty of lonely times to come but by then I will have stiffened myself.'[32]

In fact she lived through the greater part of April. Often, she was aware of him only for minutes, and would then grow tired and fall asleep. But she still managed to respond to messages, and loved receiving letters. Jack told people to write to her, and many did. So much was this so, that Sunday became a rather bleak day because there were no postal deliveries. Jack went to the trouble of asking MacGreevy to write a letter, and then send it in another envelope to the matron, Miss O'Sullivan, and instruct her to hand it over 'on Sunday morning and not before'.[33] He was to round up other friends, and ask them to do the same. 'It would be good of you and cheering for Mrs Jack, and I am your friend, Jack B Yeats.' The long patient hours at her bedside did indeed stiffen him. He managed the death and the Mount Jerome funeral with fortitude. Beckett, who was in Dublin for the funeral, was asked back with MacGreevy afterwards by Jack.[34]

Jack told people of her death in the simplest way, and since he walked everywhere around the city and often met people, this happened on the days immediately after her death. The Abbey actress, Ria Mooney, recalled her own encounter:

One of my clearest and most moving memories of him is of an accidental meeting. I was waiting for a bus at the old stopping place at the Grafton Street end of St Stephen's Green, when he suddenly appeared before me and said quietly: 'I'm finished now.' My smile of greeting turned to one of puzzled query. 'My wife has just died,' he said, and walked quickly away. Two weeks later he wrote (to Hertha Eason) in a more composed mood: 'Masefield told me to remember that 'the hearts of those who are dead are finished with sorrow'. I think to everyone left on earth who has lost some one there are three great words for ever-and-ever-and-ever. My dear one is 'finished with sorrow'.[35]

He felt unable to return to the flat, and remained on in the nursing home. Ria Mooney, who had been taken completely by surprise, went to visit him there with a bunch of spring daffodils, which gave him great delight. She was by then a good friend of Jack's. She had produced his first play; she was to produce his last. And she also owned two oil paintings, which she bought from Victor Waddington, paying in instalments of a pound or two whenever she could afford it. Before she died, she donated both works to the Sligo Museum.[36] She had fond memories of Cottie.

Perhaps the most perceptive tribute to Jack's wife was written by Terence de Vere White:

> I was always moved by the delight Mrs. Yeats took in her husband. They had been married for half a century; but she was thrilled by him as if they had but lately returned from the honeymoon. I don't remember our ever talking about anything else. She said he was a very happy person and forever singing to himself. He liked to go to afternoon service at St. Patrick's to join in the hymn singing. She felt resentment *for* him, I divined. She did not, as do so many wives, echo his opinions. She always gave me the impression that she was confiding in me. Once she took me out of the studio to show me a painting he had given her. She was as excited as a child with a wonderful new toy. She was also proud of a portrait he had painted of her (in his later manner). It was the only portrait he had ever painted, she said.[37]

Cottie's passing left him emotionally bereft. It had some impact on his art, though the extent of this is difficult to gauge. It is said that he stopped painting, and then resumed again with *The Great Tent has Collapsed*. Hilary Pyle claims that 'Yeats did little work about this time'.[38] And he had been faced with the sad preoccupation of Cottie's last illness during the months of March and April 1947. Pyle suggest that in that painting he creates 'an experience of deep, irreplaceable loss, and the fortitude required to meet it'.[39] The evidence for the painting expressing a bleak and devastating event is convincing enough. Yet his output did not falter during 1947. He produced seventy paintings in that year, including half a dozen of the large sized canvases, 24×36 inches. And in 1948 his output went up to more than eighty canvases. In work terms, then, the death of his wife, for which her general state of health had prepared him, may even have enhanced the flow of creation.

It changed the pattern of his life. He required greater care from others. Choosing to remain at the Portobello Nursing Home, immediately after Cottie's death, was obviously a wise move, emotionally; who wishes to face the myriad reminders of a shared life? And these certainly filled the empty apartment in Fitzwilliam Square. But it offered wider scope for Jack, now in his late seventies, and he instituted a pattern of moving into Portobello for extended periods, and venturing out to visit his studio, or simply to go on errands to the city. He wintered in the nursing home, arriving in mid-October, leaving again in March. Sometimes, if he caught a chill, had a chest complaint, or simply felt down, he would return there. And he formed a bond of friendship with the staff, particularly the matron, Miss O'Sullivan.

Cottie's death resulted also in greater reliance on his friends. Bill MacQuitty remained in touch with the artist, and came to take photographs. Jack was 'like Christ being scourged, and at the same time being told to smile'. He looked gaunt, thin, ascetic, and was bundled up in his winter coat, even in the studio. MacQuitty asked him to be photographed at his easel, and Jack told him: 'Everything on my easel is sub rosa,' and declined. But then he agreed to be photographed at the easel writing. 'So he took a notebook and a thick stubby pencil and was thus photographed.'[40]

Jack talked with MacQuitty about his paintings, including *People Walking Beside a River*, a work MacQuitty loved. 'Are those on the left side of the painting the living?' MacQuitty asked him, 'and those on the right the dead?' Jack replied that he had never thought of it like that. It is an interesting interpretation, reinforced by Hilary Pyle, who says 'The river is the gulf dividing the living and the dead in a landscape which looks much the same on both sides, except for some black cloud in the sky over the procession. On the opposite side the sky is light and bouffant.'[41] She also suggests that one figure might be Cottie, another Willie. But in a letter about the painting to MacQuitty, Jack wrote: 'They are not painted from actual people, or from standard types. They are just people who walked into my imagination. I generally begin a picture in the distance and come away forward and let the people walk in . . . I would like to think that you are able, as I can, to stand within the picture – on the ground.'[42]

Jack also told him that his style of painting 'allows you to get to the *joints*'. MacQuitty was interested in technique, but found it difficult to get specific information from Jack. He felt there was great passion in his paintings, but also that he did them very swiftly, and his absolute rule, about not letting anyone see him at work was to avoid any break in the rapid flow of his painting. MacQuitty also felt that inside him 'there was a turmoil, a passionate appreciation of what was going on. You see depths of prescience. But there is containment. He wouldn't answer any questions about his art or his paintings or his methods. He was a quiet man. He had a dignity which kept some people at a distance from the real man underneath.' And he speculated that Jack 'may have been very wild'.

MacQuitty went on visiting Jack after the photographing session, which produced photographs justly famous for their sympathy and revelation. He always used to bring a bottle of sherry to the Portobello Nursing Home when visiting Jack, and talked to him about the films he was making. But the artist was not greatly interested in film.[43] Jack agreed to be godfather to MacQuitty's third child, Miranda.

Jack did two radio interviews at this time, one of them with the youthful Eamon Andrews, who had a difficult time persuading the painter to say anything. He invited Jack to talk about his paintings. 'I'm not at all fond of talking about my own nor other painters' work, I never lecture about painting, I don't even interrupt at lectures – but I enjoy hearing other people talk.' He then asked about how Jack started his career. 'I'm afraid we're in difficulties there again because I'm against the giving of personal details . . . anyhow my start was earlier than I remember. I know I was drawing at an earlier date than I can recall.' 'We'll pass that one,' Andrews said, 'but what would you say to me now if I tell you that there are several of your paintings that I just don't understand?' 'I would say you could not possibly understand all of any painting of mine . . . There is only one art and that is the art of living. Painting is an occupation within that art and that occupation is the freest of all the occupations of living. There is no alphabets, no grammar, no rules whatever.' Andrews concluded by suggesting to Jack that he might have advice for the young artist. 'No, there is no advice I could give. I gave up giving advice years ago . . . I never found it a success.'[44]

Late that autumn at the invitation of the BBC Jack travelled over to London to be interviewed for radio by his friend, MacGreevy. It was his first trip out of Ireland since before the Second World War; it was to be his last. MacGreevy, who had been at pains for so long to assert Jack's nationalism, now in a lengthy introduction presented him as an international voice. It was done with what appeared to be great prescience; the MacGreevy manner was grandiloquent. Like some major domo he struts verbally into sight, speaking of homage:

> to one of the creators of modern Ireland . . . communal, or even national import of a great artist's work . . . No true artist, let alone a great artist, who can give expression to an immensely wide range of ideas and moods, belongs wholly to one community or nation. His point of departure must be the life in which he shares, the life of the people amongst whom he lives . . . as an artist Jack Yeats belongs not only to Ireland, which is his country and mine, but to the whole world.

Jack did not know quite what to tell his listeners. He had been invited by MacGreevy just to speak about his paintings, and was not asked any questions. He identified affection as the greatest food on which the painter lives, and he referred to the 1945 loan exhibition and the fact that, however much other people enjoyed it, none enjoyed it as much as himself. He denied being any kind of prodigy, though he claimed to have been 'an infant draughtsman of a kind'. And he then demanded of MacGreevy that he ask him questions, since his own talk 'would bore us both, and you all'. MacGreevy was not apt at questioning. Instead, he engaged in a descriptive account of Jack living in Sligo, doing exams, drawing all the time, then moving to London. Without any question at all this then triggered a stream of reminiscence about the London of Jack's boyhood. He came, he said, to the city his mind crowded with Sligo images. These, very simply, were of two kinds — horses and sailors. He remembered himself back in London town at the turn of the century, high up on the coachman's seat at the front of a knife-board bus. The coachman is tucking the great leather apron around his knees, and he is snuggling up close to him in the wind or the rain. 'To get on the top of the knife-board bus and to sit there was a perilous business because there were really ladders at the back and when you were on the top you had to sit down quickly because otherwise your balance was very high and you felt that you would fall off.'

Jack told of taking a market cart up from what was then called 'the West Country', but was in fact no further away than Berkshire. He travelled through the night, just for the experience, and felt cold and stiff. The cart drivers slept; the horses knew the way, and kept to the kerb, and knowing when to stop they woke their drivers at 'The Maid of Honour' in Kew, 'just as everybody wakes on a steamboat when the engines stop'.

He told his listeners of his love of boxing. He described the tiny ring and talked of his days reporting on sport. MacGreevy suggested a link between Sligo and London, but there was no link.

> Boxing and these things had nothing to do with Ireland at that time. What I saw was London . . . the old town of London . . . not the city. That's the time before they made the Kingsway and places to sell fountain pens . . . But at the same time I was always keeping in touch with the West of Ireland . . . every year I spent two months at least in the West by the Atlantic where I took up again my childhood's days.

He described the journey; it was important, he said, to let the boys carry his suitcase to the boat, to pay them the sixpence; it mattered to them and it was unkindly to scold them. He was feted on board *The Liverpool*, because it was his grandfather's boat, 'I'd climb aboard . . . to find the cabin alight and the steward glad to see me and the Captain would come down and greet me and I was more or less stepping again on my own country.' The passage was sometimes stormy; 'my small stomach got harder with the years'. But then the Atlantic motion gave way to the calm in Sligo Bay, 'subdued and altered and then you were sliding up to Sligo past the Rosses Point with its long low white houses and a few bigger ones all shining in the morning sun'.

The interview turned towards Jack's writing, and his plays and novels are discussed, mainly by MacGreevy, to Jack's bemusement: 'You speak beautifully, and kindly about my work . . . I have always held that affection was the greatest attribute any painter or writer can have. I'm not a writer in the ordinary sense but when I write I have affection for the things I write about and when I paint I certainly have affection for everything I paint.' [45]

He stayed in London for three weeks. There was no Cottie to write to. We know nothing of those days, and he returned to winter and then spring in the Portobello Nursing Home, and a resumption of his painting for 1948, the single most prolific year of his whole life as an artist. MacGreevy was painstaking in his care of Jack, among other things arranged a gas ring for him in his studio so that he could make tea. MacGreevy insisted that the ring, instead of being on the ground, should be two feet up, so that Jack would not have to bend over too far and be in danger of falling into the fire.

From Cottie's death on, Anne and other members of the family were more closely involved in Jack's affairs. His niece in particular visited him often – though always by written invitation to which she was expected to reply in kind. Both she and her mother were, to a certain degree, amused by MacGreevy's endless fussing over Jack, and the fact that he talked endlessly. So much was this so, that his voice in the nursing home, heard through the walls of Jack's room as a continuous monologue, was often mistaken for the radio. George Yeats was one of the few people who had the nerve and directness to take him to task, both for his long-windedness and his opinions. 'Come off it, Tom!' she would say; and he did. Privately, within the family, MacGreevy was known as 'Painsy'. It described his profoundly painstaking attitude towards Jack. But it actually embraced another MacGreevy characteristic: he always complained about his health. The sobriquet came from an unlikely source: the hymn by Cecil Frances Alexander, 'There is a green hill far away,' and the verse:

> We may not know, we cannot tell,
> What pains He had to bear,

But we believe it was for us
He hung and suffer'd there.

Willie's widow, George, had reservations about MacGreevy because of his curiously compartmentalised life. Each phase was put into a compartment; when it was over, MacGreevy moved on, and in the process he closed off the past. This was crucially the case in respect of MacGreevy the modernist writer and poet. When he became director of the National Gallery of Ireland he became conservative and something of a snob. George Yeats used to say that he 'lived by the Almanach de Gotha'.[46] His close intimacy with Jack will always be a puzzle.

CHAPTER TWENTY-TWO

Last Years 1948–1957

Repose and calm

JACK BECAME RESIGNED to old age, increasingly a silent witness to the passing of friends and admirers. He listened; they talked. He smiled; they offered him words of encouragement and praise which made him smile all the more. He was protected by their kindness and concern for him. He revelled in the variety of company, from his young niece starting out in her professional life to the old companions who had been with him from earlier years. The closest of them had all departed – his brother and one of his two sisters, and of course Cottie. But the next generation, Michael and Anne, were now more closely associated, as indeed was George Yeats.

Her husband's remains were brought back to Ireland in September 1948. Though he had died in 1939, it was not until then that the formalities, interrupted by the war, were completed. It was George's wish that a boat small enough to travel up to the quay in Sligo be used to carry the coffin from the south of France, but in the end the corvette arrived in Galway on 17 September. It was handled inefficiently. George Yeats expressed herself quite forcibly to MacGreevy who had been dealing with the government on the family's behalf, telling him she had asked Val Iremonger, in the Department of External Affairs, 'to arrange that no further information should be given out until final arrangements were settled'.[1] Co-operation promised by Sean MacBride was not given. 'I am afraid this will all upset Jack terribly . . . I had a letter from Jack this morning saying that he did not want us to have the fatigue of a train journey and that he would arrange a car to call here whether he himself went to Galway or not.' The sending of the body from France seems to have been handled badly too. After remaining in the chapel at the Roquebrune cemetery for five months, the coffin was brought down the hill, preceded by a Roman Catholic priest, a boy-cross-bearer, and two files of French soldiers. An eye-witness recalls: 'After twenty minutes a car was heard racing up the hill. It crashed in on the still square . . . stopped, and Commander McKenna of the Macha, M Bernoit, attaché to the French Ambassador in Dublin, and Mr Sean Murphy, Irish Ambassador to France, stepped out.'[2] The motorised hearse, with silver-metal plumes on its roof, then took the coffin to Nice. A French military band, with drums, saxophones, clarinets and tubas, met it there, and it was finally handed over. Irish naval service personnel from the corvette, the Macha, nervously took charge. It was the first time the Irish navy had been outside territorial waters. The vessel put to sea at noon and set sail for Galway, the French priest from

Roquebrune blessing it as it departed. It took eleven days, and the vessel was escorted by the British Naval frigate, H.M.S. Childers. The little corvette sailed into Galway Bay, 'the wind behind her full of rain'.

The State funeral offered by the inter-party government was declined. It might have been different if de Valera had still been in power. Jack, who was at the quayside with his sister-in-law and her children, particularly disliked ceremony and had wanted the funeral to be a quiet one. However, he went on board the Macha to thank the crew looking thin and gravely serious. The coffin was then driven to Sligo, where it waited in front of the Town Hall for an hour, with a colour party surrounding it. Pipes were played, and muffled drums. All the shops in the town closed. And eventually, in the afternoon, the long funeral cortège moved off to Drumcliffe. The crowds were immense. When the Yeats family arrived at the graveyard a way had to be forced open for them. The service was taken by the Revd. J. Wilson, rector of Drumcliffe.[3] Eamon de Valera attended, a politician welcome in the eyes of both Jack and his nephew, Michael.

It was a great literary and theatrical event, with many poets present, among them Louis MacNeice and Austin Clarke, and theatre people from the Abbey and the Gate, led by Lennox Robinson (fig. 231), Micheal Mac Liammoir and Ernest Blythe. There were friends of Jack's: Ria Mooney, James Starkey, Ernie O'Malley and Maurice Craig, who has written his own account of that wet day in the west of Ireland:

> The journey to Sligo was uneventful. We looked in at the Great Southern Hotel and saw only Lennox Robinson sitting at the bar. We went straight on to the Imperial Hotel and there was Lennox Robinson sitting at the bar. (Lennox Robinson, immensely tall and thin, was not a man easily mistaken.) By now the expected time of arrival of the cortege was at hand, so we joined the crowd in front of the Town Hall . . . On the Town Hall steps stood all the notabilities, Lennox Robinson at the back, towering conspicuously over the rest . . . We decided that if we were to have any hope of getting anywhere near the graveyard on those narrow Co. Sligo by-roads we had better leave the official party to get on with their ceremonies and start at once. As a result we were able to park close by and walk to the churchyard. Standing by the grave was Lennox Robinson . . .[4]

In the *Picture Post* photographs, Maurice Craig is captioned 'son of Lennox Robinson'. One comment heard at the time, but unreported, came from an unidentified local man standing behind Craig at the graveside, who said to the man beside him: 'But why pay 3s 4d for them, when I can get them for 2s 11d wholesale?'[5]

The many photographs of Drumcliffe churchyard confirm the crush and confusion around the grave. It was a grey day. The rain which had followed the corvette into Galway Bay had, by afternoon, become general. The top of Ben Bulben was obscured in mist.

In January 1949 Lily died. 'I thought she would stay with us keeping memory green a little longer', Jack wrote to Hertha Eason. 'She was so brave and full of cheerful interest . . .' And he described her as 'the last but one of a small band'.[6]

Now he was the last of all. In his letter to Niall Montgomery who had written in sympathy at Lily's death he referred to his understanding of what

231. *Lennox Robinson*, by James Sleator, oil on canvas, 36 × 24, Abbey Theatre, Dublin.

232. Scene in Drumcliffe Churchyard on the afternoon of the return of the body of William Butler Yeats to Ireland. Jack is on the extreme left, holding the umbrella; then, left to right in a group: Michael Yeats, Thomas MacGreevy, Anne Yeats (obscured) and George Yeats, in profile.

it meant 'when someone goes away and takes away with them a store of memoires of mutual affections'.[7] Tall and thin, his expression gaunt and his gaze cold and forbidding, he painted and talked with his friends. He continued to be interested in his niece's career. On one occasion, at the annual Irish Exhibition of Living Art, he approached her through the crowd, both hands outstretched. He took hers in his own, and said: 'I used to be regarded as the brother of the poet; from now on I shall be thought of as the uncle of the painter.' He sent her sums of money to help her in a career which he had every reason to know was among the most precarious there is. As well as painting, she worked in the theatre; here also pay was miserly and haphazard, so that the life she was living produced virtually no cash at all. Her friends were the actors, directors, designers and other artists known also to Jack; he felt at home hearing of their doings, and was unfailing positive and encouraging.[8]

There is great charm in the letters he wrote to her, and in the diffidence with which he offered what were, in those days, quite generous sums of money.

My Dear Anne – Here is a little autumn cheque to wish you a happy autumn. I don't know if you are already on your travels: but if you are I hope you are getting pleasant days, with sunshine, and a gentle breeze coming from the surface of the sea. Even if you are a long way from the sea you get it. The plan is to remind you that however horrid the sea may behave in the winter you are to understand that it is only old symbolical, conventional, exercises in hate and I am your affectionate Uncle Jack.[9]

Both Anne and her mother were kind and attentive, and used to send him flowers; Anne gave him small presents. He was lonely for family comfort, a different kind of companionship from that of his male friends. His invitations to Anne were still always by letter, instructing her to call for him at the flat, when they would walk down to the University Club on St Stephen's Green, and have lunch, or merely to call in for tea. She was never offered alcohol. Anne at this time travelled as much as she could afford. She visited Edward Gordon Craig in Paris, and had lunch with him; she went to Italy, and to other European countries. And from these places sent postcards back to him.

The last play of his produced during his lifetime was *In Sand*. It was put on at the Peacock Theatre on 19 April 1949. He gave a short curtain speech: 'I hope I have succeeded tonight in putting a little salt on the tail of the Peacock. To those of you who have not liked the play, I can only say, 'Ah! Well . . . !' To those of you who have liked it, may I say, 'Ah Well, indeed!'

In Sand has a theme summarised in Jack's own phrase, 'Belfries rot and tumble down in decay, or men's ears grow sluggish to the sound of oft repeated bells . . .' He believed that he was primarily in Ria Mooney's debt for the quality of the production. He wrote to her: 'I know that you have trained the players all and MacGowran the producer as well and *In Sand* was trained and guided by you. Indeed I know it is you who have got my plays on at all and now with *In Sand* you have got the newspaper men to believe . . .'[10]

For whatever reason, according to Ernest Blythe, Jack's plays

> were warmly received by somewhat atypical audiences, members of which saw or professed to see things in them that were hidden from ordinary theatregoers. When it was found that one of them was too long and would have to be cut, to let the final curtain come down before too many people had rushed from the auditorium to catch the last buses, an actor averred that cutting would be quite easy. All that was called for, he declared, was to determine roughly what number of words had to come out to bring the play down to a convenient length and then to calculate how many pages they would fill. Thereupon ten, twenty, or fifty pages, as might be appropriate, could be taken at random and simply torn out, without audiences either noticing the joins or being conscious of gaps in the narrative.[11]

Blythe, whose involvement with the Abbey Theatre was never entirely happy, recalled that the general feeling among the directors of plays was that Jack Yeats's plays had some sort of quality. They were 'not indisposed to try one of them on the public, partly as a gimmick and partly in the hope that Jack Yeats's name and his fame as a painter might draw substantial audiences to the theatre for a week or so'.[12]

Jack was probably aware of these views on his talents as a playwright. He came, in the end, to have limited patience with his own writing. *In Sand* was adapted for radio, and broadcast by the BBC. A proposal was made to revive the broadcast, shortly before his death. On hearing it, Jack told his dealer, Waddington, 'They're trotting this out . . . I wish they'd forget this stuff . . . They should remember me as a painter.'[13]

By the end of the 1940s he was spending more time in the Portobello Nursing Home. It had become a second home for him, though he maintained its 'temporary' status. He wrote about his health, and the seasons, particularly to his niece, Anne:

> I agree spring is in the offing and with ordinary luck we may be able to entertain it. but I hope we wont have to entertain another old spring like

the one we had last year which lasted, with snufflings and moanings, until Hallows Eve. I would like to see you very much. I have not got out yet. Will you come and see me at 5.30 Friday next the 12th. I am glad to know about the Irises and the daffodils, and the grand stickiness of the chestnut buds.[14]

He wrote on one occasion, 'I wish this cat and mouse winter would go away and make way for one of our own special springsummerautumn insofar seasons which we understand.'[15] The cat and mouse reference sparked off a painting of a cat, which Anne sent him.

Stephen Spender visited Jack in March 1950, in the company of Dr Park, the Trinity College librarian:

His room was bare – three chairs, a table, with bottles of whisky and brandy, luggage piled up on top of a cupboard, a wash basin. Nothing on the walls except a conventional calendar with a coloured photoprint of two horses. Jack Yeats was up to receive us. He is bald, has a long, country-man's face, very pale after a winter indoors, with eyes bright as chips . . . He asked us what we'd drink; Dr Park said sherry, I whisky. He poured at least a quarter of a tumbler into my glass, and while he was pouring Dr Park his sherry, I poured half my whisky back into the bottle. Some of it went over the edge of the neck and, sliding down, made a damp ring on the tablecloth. 'Ah,' he said, 'you've been pouring back your whisky. Nothing is ever poured back that doesn't notice.' At first the talk was rather sticky, but soon he was telling anecdotes of his father whom he called 'the governor'. He said 'the governor' spoiled his paintings through having too long a working day and painting when he was tired. 'It was all very well for the Pre-Raphaelites, who painted in every leaf and every brick, they could devote whole days to painting leaves and bricks. But my father was aiming at a kind of effect on which you can only concentrate for two or three hours a day, so he spoiled his work'.[16]

233. Jack wearing his award from the French government, c. 1950.

Jack was made a member of the French Legion d'Honneur in 1950, one of relatively few late honours bestowed on him, but one which gave him great pleasure (fig. 233). Professionally, he had a growing number of successes to celebrate, carefully managed by his incomparable dealer, Victor Waddington. Waddington was something of a bon viveur, even in those austere days. Celebratory dinners were usually held in Jammet's Restaurant, opposite the Provost's House, at the end of Nassau Street. This renowned eating place combined excellent food, deep and capacious cellars, and an antiquated menu written in a French which most clients were obliged to learn specially in order to eat well. Here is one: 'Le Saumon du Pays fumé aux Aromates' or 'Les Natives de Galway sur Neige' with 'Tartinettes de pain noir' started the ball rolling; then came 'La croute au pot comme chez-soi' before a main course of 'Le Poussin Caprice, Celeris au Beurre, Pommes Mignonnettes'. 'Les Crêpes Suzette' concluded the meal. This was accompanied by a 1947 Chablis Moutonne, a 1943 Pommard, Clos de Chateau, and a 1917 Port. This particular dinner was given expressly for Jack, who did drawings on the menus, which were then signed by the guests. The restaurateur himself, Louis Jammet, joined the others, among them Victor Waddington and his brother, George, Richard McGonigal, and R.R. Figgis, both of them Yeats collectors, Patrick Hall, a fellow artist, Serge Phillipson, a collector who later became a governor of the National Gallery of Ireland, Father Senan and MacGreevy.

Jack now earned a comfortable living from his art. He was also happy with his personal arrangements, and the time spent in his nursing home on the canal.

He wrote wittily from 'Cell 27', his room overlooking the water at Portobello, describing his nurses as 'wardens' and telling Victor 'as an old inmate, an old hand, I would advise you to *pretend* to want to be obedient, as you will be quite unable to deceive them. You will find yourself falling gently into a willingness, which means repose and calm.' For Jack Yeats this was the only future to contemplate, and he did so with equanimity. His great life was drawing to a close. He had fulfilled his huge task on earth, creating worlds of Irish comedy and sadness in his paintings, a multitude of characters in his writing, and gathering in his wake a great band of friends and admirers. His 'children' – which is how he thought of his paintings – were still largely unsold. A great body of work was there, waiting to be summoned by posterity. And in his company, during those closing years, he could count on 'the Yeats Man' – as Victor Waddington now regarded himself – to take charge of the process by which his reputation would be enlarged and confirmed. The greater part of this was to be achieved after Jack's death. And Jack, in his methodical way, made provision for it in his will. Much was in train in the last decade of his life, and Waddington became increasingly central to this activity.

Waddington wanted to promote an international reputation for Jack, and worked hard to organise exhibitions which were not exclusively, and at times not even primarily designed to promote sales. Jack wrote a charming letter to one buyer, under the impression that he had somehow talked the man into acquiring his painting, *A Soldier of Fortune*:

> I'm bothered about you both: and it is not right that I should be bothered about such nice people. Will you tell me truly – yes I know you will – did you intend to get a painting of mine when you came to see me or were you influenced by my old talk about loan Exhibitions? I was talking in general and not in particulars for in my own case – the three large loan Exhibitions of my pictures have been indeed most useful to me in hard cash.[17]

Jack had held very few solo exhibitions outside his Dublin and London shows. These had become irregular and much fewer in number during the 1930s, compared with the previous decade. Apart from the show he shared with William Nicholson in the National Gallery in London in January 1942, there was a ten-year gap between the London solo exhibition in 1936 and his first post-war show at Wildenstein's in 1946. This was followed by two important English exhibitions, both in 1948, at Temple Newsam House, outside Leeds and then at the Tate Gallery. Across the Atlantic there was a similarly small number of shows during this period. Then came a small but important retrospective which toured North America.

This was the most ambitious of all Jack's solo touring exhibitions, and unparalleled in the fact that it travelled for a full year in the United States and Canada, during 1951 and 1952. It could be described as pivotal, but only perhaps in its *intention*. The show, travelled from place to place and had some impact, but in certain respects was ill-fated. Jack himself was responsible for placing it under handicap. Waddington took charge of it, and went to the

United States for the exhibition's first showing in Boston, at the Institute of Contemporary Art in April 1951. Kokoschka probably put up the original idea to the director of the institute, James S. Plaut. He had known Plaut at the time of his own exhibition in the gallery in 1948, when he had also lectured there on art. Plaut had travelled to Dublin, either in 1949 or 1950, to talk with Jack and begin preparations. He wrote to MacGreevy:

> I dare say that Victor Waddington has already appraised you of our earnest desire to have you prepare a text for the catalogue which will accompany the exhibition. There is no question in my mind that if we were able to prevail upon you to write on Yeats for the exhibition, we would have secured the cooperation of one of Mr. Yeats' closest friends and the most knowledgeable and distinguished writer available anywhere on the subject.[18]

The problem was Jack had decided against reproductions in the catalogue. MacGreevy , meanwhile, had been told that the Yeats exhibition would be treated in the same way as those of the two previous artists who had benefited from similar shows in the United States – Munch and Kokoschka – and that he was free to write up to ten thousand words. And he was directed towards an essay which would reflect his 'close and intimate association with the painter', and contain biographical anecdote. At the same time, there was to be 'disinterested criticism'.[19]

A great deal of care and preparation went into the show. Plaut made another visit to Dublin, saw MacGreevy, as well as Jack, several times, and then offered MacGreevy £50 for the essay, giving him a deadline of mid-December 1950. Waddington went to great lengths to help MacGreevy in viewing the works which were being shipped to the United States. MacGreevy was late, however, and sent off the essay only by the end of the following January. With it he sent a very formal letter, granting publication rights in the United States, subject to a payment of $300, together with tax, and demanding the essay's early return if it proved unsuitable. Plaut, however, with his assistant director, Frederick S. Wight, had, in the face of Jack's refusal to have illustrations reproduced, decided against making the essay part of the catalogue. They had tried to arrange publication in various American journals, including *Atlantic Monthly* and *Harper's Magazine*, but without success. No one wanted it without illustration. In the event it had to be returned to MacGreevy.

The burden of presenting him in the United States fell on Plaut's shoulders. He produced a one-page essay mainly of reminiscences about meeting Jack in Dublin. Jack was seriously put out. By the time he received the catalogue, the Boston show had just a week to run. Plaut had failed to check the contents of the essay with the artist, and they contained all sorts of things of which Jack disapproved. Plaut had written rather gushingly about visiting the painter on

> a shivering, drizzly February evening in the high-ceilinged room overlooking the Square, which has long served him as a studio and, since the death of his beloved wife, as salon and bedroom besides. To huddle – as every foreign visitor does in the Irish winter – before the anemic flame of the small gas stove, and to feel oneself unfolding to the warmth of great talk and good whiskey . . .

343

This, and much else besides, was uncongenial to Jack, including what Jack described as a 'botched' telling of a story about a foreign actress travelling in a train with an Irishman. Jack wrote to Waddington: 'I am sad – though I cannot say disillusioned. I am sure Plaut thought everything he said in his foreword would please me. And I daresay he took trouble to give me what I would like. It is all too late. Let the man think I am pleased but I hope no Plaut will get a chance to try and please me anymore.'[20]

Jack asked Waddington to cut out the date of his birth: 'I wish particularly that all the personal bits about me were cut . . . There is something you can do and that is have the year of my birth and any information as to my life cut out completely in all future catalogues.'[21]

Waddington appears to have taken decisive action. A new introduction was written and used in the catalogue for the other galleries, and the show toured for more than a year in Washington D.C., San Francisco, Colorado, Toronto, Detroit and New York. Waddington, who travelled with the paintings, reported back on the critical reception in letters which gave Jack great pleasure, but which also caused him alarm about Waddington's health. His dealer was clearly under strain, and repeatedly the artist cautioned him to take care of himself, and to rest.[22]

The whole United States venture proved unsuccessful, in terms of establishing the kind of international reputation which both Jack and Waddington believed overdue. Jack failed to appreciate that people wanted to know about his life. Since none of this was now contained in the catalogue, visitors read a slightly gauche account of a visit to a wayward painter in Dublin. Jack's belief that reproductions came between the individual viewer and the painting was a further handicap. Blocking *all* illustrations, including postcards and posters, seemed perverse.

The critical response was disappointing. American critics did not understand his work. They were perplexed and antagonistic. One correspondent writing to MacGreevy remembered 'some of the stupidities that appeared here during the Retrospective Exhibition – too bad he can't draw figures, and things like that'.[23]

In the end Jack remained philosophical about it all. Waddington's strenuous work inspired deep affection and trust between the two men. Letters came from the United States sometimes on a daily basis, and Waddington drew careful charts of the galleries, indicating where each picture had been hung in relation to the rest, so that Jack felt moved to write, 'I was proud for my paintings' sake'.[24] He went on, in what was a long and kindly letter:

> I want to say that I agree with every point where you made a stand. the result may be a little slow in coming about: but I know that it is the best for all of us, including the American people to realise that the man who goes to a Banquet will enjoy it better if he doesnt expect the banquet to be the same as the printed menu, which he got somewhere, and brought with him.

In his own subtle way Jack was standing by the principles of a lifetime, that what mattered most of all in the world, for the painter, was the unprejudiced, unrehearsed, unprogrammed encounter between each work, and the person standing in front of it, receiving its silent communications. And on the occasion of the last opening of the American tour, Jack went out to celebrate:

At 7 o clock on the opening day MacGreevy and I were down in the Spa Hotel Lucan sitting down to dinner we rose our glasses and drank good fortune I said 'how will we drink' and MacGreevy said 'good luck to Victor Waddington and to the Exhibition' and so we drank . . . and with all good thoughts and good wishes I am your friend Jack B Yeats.[25]

In contrast, the critical view of him was a great deal better at home, even at times sensational. In *The Sunday Independent* of 14 October 1951 the headline appeared: 'Art Story of the Week: £6,000 SALES IN A FEW HOURS'. The story went on:

Nothing like it has ever happened before in Ireland. The paintings are by Jack Yeats, now generally recognised as one of the greatest painters in the world to-day. They are on exhibition at the Victor Waddington Galleries. . . . Admission is free. The public should not miss seeing them. Out of 21 exhibits, 16 were bought almost immediately after the show opened on Thursday afternoon. Some of them will go to England. Two of those unsold were 'The Basin In Which Pilate Washed His Hands,' and 'Grief,' each priced at £2,500, a new high figure at an Irish art show. An exhibition . . . is being held in America at present. He is a brother of W.B. Yeats, Ireland's famous poet.[26]

There is increasing emphasis in his later letters, whether written from the nursing home or the flat, on his health. He became afflicted with lumbago during the cold winter of 1952–3. He told MacGreevy about his aches and pains, and their treatment, and mentioned being visited by Joseph Hone and Niall Montgomery, to whom he sent a few cards for his London exhibition at Wildenstein's. He now spent more time in the nursing home; less in the studio. Portobello Nursing Home was reasonably close to St Patrick's Cathedral. Jack had always enjoyed the services there, and from time to time went to sing at Evensong. He still walked a good deal and from time to time now still painted. His euphemism for it was: 'I have again got paint on the end of my nose, and am much improved in every way – the bile pain driven away – for always (I hope).'[27]

In early February 1954 Jack Yeats held his first solo exhibition in Paris. It was an exciting occasion for him, a moment keenly anticipated. It was held at the Galerie Beaux-Arts, at 140, Faubourg Saint-Honoré. Waddington went for the hanging. There had been help from the Irish ambassador, Con Cremin. Friends and collectors travelled over to Paris for the opening. Waddington took care to send a diagram showing the position of each picture. What appealed most of all to the painter was the reaction of fellow artists.

Your description of the effect of the exhibition is exciting to me. The painters particularly gave me great pleasure. With all their natural faults of self-centredness (which painters must always have because their work is absolutely personal) I have always held to the belief that the painters were fairer to each other than the people of any other occupation.[28]

Among the friends who attended was Beckett, who assiduously brought others to see the exhibition. Waddington reported on this, to which Jack replied: 'I would have liked seeing Sam Beckett, the late bloomer, in his glory'.[29] The painter Bram Van Velde, a close friend of Beckett's, visited at least ten times. Others included Georges Duthuit and Jean-Paul Riopelle. Beckett gathered essays in homage to Jack, and these were published in the

234. Niall Montgomery's daughter, Rose Mary, at an exhibition, *c.* 1950.

April 1954 issue of *Lettres Nouvelles*. Duthuit, in the end, did not contribute, but Pierre Schneider and Jacques Putman did, and of course Beckett himself. 'Of my own hommage I can only repeat what I said to you already, that it is nothing more than an obeisance, and a clumsy one. I cannot write that kind of thing and I only hope JBY will not be too disappointed + that he was not looking forward to a weightier text.'[30]

Jack wrote to Beckett on 22 March; in June Beckett arrived for his usual summer visit to Dublin, staying until September, and visiting Jack several times, often in MacGreevy's company. On 26 October, Jack moved into the Portobello Nursing Home, his 'winter quarters'. Niall Montgomery,who had come to know Beckett quite well by this time, was a frequent visitor, and he brought others to see Jack. Jack took an interest in the architectural work the younger man was doing, and also in his family. He knew the young children, and his letters are filled with questions about them, with references to their pretty dresses and bright eyes. Montgomery had bought his first Yeats painting at the solo exhibition in the autumn of 1949. For the young architect it was a moment of the greatest excitement, and he spoke of a twenty-one gun salute to it. 'I am glad you have that picture. It might have, quite easily, gone to some one who would only have any feeling for 10% of the people in it,' Jack wrote.[31] The painting was *Reality*.

Yeats allowed himself to be bullied, as he put it, by the nurses. 'The early winter threatening colds', he wrote to Victor Waddington, 'have a way of going into winter quarters in the head, throat, and chest of their victim.'[32] And on another occasion he told him: 'Nurse Arthurs is acting fairly enough and not being too severe on such transgressions as walking in a cold corridor without permission.'[33]

Although Portobello was almost his permanent home now, He still led a busy life. His taxicab account with Dubtax shows him on a typical day in February 1954 going from the nursing home to Grafton Street, where he shopped for clothes, and visiting the galleries, and calling at Fitzwilliam Square and Clare Street. No less than twenty oil paintings date from that year. Major canvases included *In Glory, That We may Never Meet Again*, and *Horse Without a Rider*.

The young writer Alan Denson called, and discussed the artist's best-known characteristics: his need to paint alone, and his dislike of photographs. Jack explained: 'Only by seeing the picture could its mood and meaning reach into the viewer. I queried this as the need to catalogue any artist's works would best be served by photographs. The subject tailed off. I had the impression he was not wholly convinced of the wisdom of his own ban on reproductions.'[34]

Denson, an outspoken young man but well-informed, had seen the National Gallery show, and expressed his disappointment with Thomas MacGreevy's 1945 essay on the artist. This was greeted with silence, though Denson visit to the National Gallery exhibition gave Jack great pleasure. Nevertheless, Jack went to extraordinary trouble for his young visitor, and the first impressions remained with him always:

What struck me forcibly then, as on all my visits to him, was the artist's concentration with his eyes, watching me all the time as we entered the big room. In those days my face immediately registered my reactions to events. Mr Yeats had displayed the summer's pictures for me. All round the room

347

were his latest masterpieces of colour rhythmically bound into evocative patterns. A marvellous display of artistic energy still creatively alive, prophetic, symbolising pictorially whatever theme had engrossed him. He asked which works of his I knew, and was delighted to know I was familiar with 'Two Travellers', at the Tate Gallery, and was equally delighted to know I had seen the National Gallery retrospective.[35]

On a later visit they discussed music, and agreed in a belief that rhythm was common to all the arts.

Other friends he saw at the time included Brigid Ganly, Terence de Vere White, Serge Phillipson, Patric Stephenson, a fellow painter, Mrs Sheila Beckett, Lennox Robinson, and his oldest friend, Harvey, now bishop of Cashel. He read a lot. In February 1954 he bought Bernard Berenson's *Italian Painters of the Renaissance* and Chiang Yee's *The Silent Traveller in Dublin*; and he bought two copies of his brother's *Collected Poems* to give away to visitors.[36] He was an annual subscriber to *Whitaker's Almanac*. He regularly took *The Irish Times*, and the two Dublin evening papers, *The Evening Mail* and *The Evening Herald*, as well as the *Daily Graphic*, for which once, long before, he had done illustrations. On Sundays, he read the *Sunday Independent* and *The Sunday Times*. He had a journalist's taste for news, a love of stories – the eccentric ones he kept in numerous cuttings boxes and files – and he liked also the illustrated papers, taking regularly *The Sphere* and *The Irish Times Pictorial*.[37]

He was now greatly honoured in Ireland, and fulfilled in his work. He had spent more than half a century depicting the life and adventures of his country; he had realised its myths, embodied its deepest feelings; in visual terms he had recreated it. But it was a small country, on the fringes of Europe, and a new country from which the majority of writers and painters, including Jack Yeats's father and, for periods of time, his brother, had departed to seek fame and fortune elsewhere. With notable exceptions there was no international dimension to Jack B. Yeats's standing as an artist.[38] From his first exhibition he had sold some paintings. He had gone on selling some of them for the whole of his life, and had a large following at home of those who loved his art. But the sales had been a measured reflection of a small country's cautious and reserved admiration for its most loyal artist, and his studio still bulged with the works of half a century.

Nor was there much likelihood of change. Ireland's fortunes were at a low point. There were many who thought pessimistically about the country's future, and considered that its achievements, just over thirty years after independence, had failed to match the high aspiration of those writers and artists, Jack among them, who had drawn value and belief from the cultural renaissance in which they had all been involved. High emigration, poverty, trading isolation, a diaspora of talent which was constantly leaching intellectual and moral strength, had demoralised the nation. It seemed to have run out of ideas and purpose.

Of immediate significance for the painter, however, was the position faced by his dealer, Victor Waddington. In 1953 he was profiled in *The Irish Times*, and gave his view that 'Dublin, more than any city in Europe, is destined to become the centre of painters and art-lovers from all over the world. "Already," he says, "many people come here just to see Ireland's paintings".' And the account given of his life and work, twenty-seven years during which he had 'backed his own judgment, and, so far, he claims that he has never made a major mistake', was an inspiring story.[39] It would have seemed, to the reader of these words, that Victor Waddington was doing well. The reality, however, was different. In those difficult years for the country, he had in fact come to the conclusion that his own career, as a gallery owner working in Dublin, had failed.

He had separated from his wife, Zelda, in 1946, and Mabel Spiro became his partner, and later his second wife. She also, to a considerable extent, was Waddington's 'backer'.

Characteristically, Jack Yeats maintained a separate correspondence with her which was affectionate and thoughtful. To some extent Mabel Spiro took over Cottie's role, in respect of exhibitions, taking care of flowers, and other details. She also was in the habit of sending flowers to Jack, both in his flat, and in the Portobello Nursing Home. There were times when he would arrive there, and find that bowls full of lily of the valley – which he loved – had been arranged in expectation of another period 'in care', or, as he would have it, 'in prison'. It is often through these letters that the painter's very real admiration for Victor's flair and intelligence as a dealer may be best seen. He felt he could tell Mrs Spiro of her partner's genius, something which he could not express directly.

For some time Waddington had discussed with Yeats the extension of his business to London. He envisaged a London gallery as an extension of his Dublin one, which would remain the headquarters of his business. But it was an unreal aspiration. Over a period of nine years, since the Second World War, Waddington had consistently lost money. He computed his losses at on average £80 a week, £4,000 a year, £36,000 over the full period up to that time, a huge sum for the 1940s and early 1950s. The loss had been fed by other business ventures, the total profits of which had gone into the gallery. And he had been helped by his partnership with Mabel Spiro. The whole experience had undermined Waddington's health. He was due to have an operation on his neck, which would take him to London anyway. Psychologically, he felt crushed by the burden of what he had had to bear and by the constant and demoralising losses.

Yet the decision was an enormous wrench.

> I have always thought to make Dublin a centre . . . to this end I have backed exhibitions at home and abroad. I have paid out enormous sums in doing all this . . . sums higher than commissions covered; but always went on doing so in the hope that someday Dublin would be a place people would come to because of painting . . . and that people in Ireland would learn and so back their painters and my gallery.[40]

Yeats contemplated this with equanimity. He had faced neglect and disappointment himself, and his disposition was stoic. The evidence for commercial failure was incontrovertible. Yet the commercial aspect had never seriously worried the artist, and at other levels the work which Waddington had done for Yeats's art had transcended the indifferent market, had given the painter his livelihood and his freedom, had spread his small but secure name among many proud owners of pictures, and had undoubtedly given him happiness. Now, in his eighties, his concern was with posterity and his 'children' – the many canvases which crowded his studio picture racks – and his many sketchbooks, drawings and watercolours. Waddington told him: 'I hope that I personally will continue to be your personal agent and representative. Both here and internationally I believe that I am the Yeats man'. Yeats concurred, and pledged his continued support.

Jack had three years to live. His output in 1954, of twenty canvases, was reduced the following year to sixteen, the last of which was painted in October. He painted no more. He made his will in November 1955. He left virtually all his personal effects to Anne, his niece; the exceptions were his 'old silver ring with bearded face', which he left to Niall Montgomery,[41] and a portrait drawing of his sister, Lily, by his father, which was to go to a gallery chosen by his executors. Any pictures hanging in his flat were to go to Anne, who was to share equally with her brother Jack's copyright. His executors were his solicitor, Perceval Browne, and MacGreevy. He gave to both of them, and to his friend, Con Curran, the right to choose from his works a canvas, 24 by 36 inches. All other paintings and drawings were to be sold, the proceeds forming part of the residuary estate, which was divided into six equal shares. With the exception of one of these shares, which went absolutely to MacGreevy, all of the others were sub-divided. Whether or not Jack knew it, the arrangement made it virtually inescapable that the selling of his substantial studio of unsold paintings, watercolours and drawings would be carried out under the pressure of a range of bequests involving no less than twelve named beneficiaries.

Jack, of sound mind when he set out these details, was equally clear-sighted when he gave his last solemn injunction:

> AND I DECLARE that it is my wish that no photographs or reproductions of any kind be made or published of any of my paintings or drawings, and that photographs or other reproductions of any of my paintings or drawings already made there shall be no publication and no further copies shall be made.

He signed the Will in both forms of his name, 'John Butler Yeats' and 'Jack B. Yeats'.

In 1956, contact was renewed with an old friend, Oskar Kokoschka. An American called Bridgelove had called on Jack in Dublin and had then acquired in London a print of *Two Travellers*, the Jack Yeats painting in the Tate Gallery. He had gone on to Villeneuve, in Vaud, Switzerland, to see the Austrian painter. Kokoschka wrote:

> You can imagine how lovingly we both, and my wife, who later joined us, talked about you. To enhance the pleasure of your spiritual presence, he had the good idea to bring your painting with him, you know that one with the two men meeting in the country on a heath or dale, one with hat, the other one with ruffed black hair and leery eyes, but the air was so much Irish and the tension between the two so vivid, that one could spin the yarn on and on for oneself without a verbally written story to support it.[42]

Kokoschka learned that Jack was in a nursing home and had stopped painting, and he wished him a comfortable hibernation. He was planning a trip to London, anyway, and suggested that he might come on to Dublin to see his old friend.

> Please, after having had your rest, let your unruly soul for another turn out in the wonderful world of your sagas and take up painting again! You alone

can in painting today tell such touching stories! Have a wonderful New Year in good health and spirits! We drank your toast with good whisky, the young American and I.[43]

Kokoschka addressed the envelope: 'Jack B. Yeats The Great Painter (may-be the last!)' and sent it care of Victor Waddington. Later he did fly to Dublin, with his wife, Olda, and they were met at the airport by Victor, who brought them to see Jack.

The artist's last days were filled with the undiminished comfort of friendship. His diaries are crowded with the familiar names of regular visitors and a few new people.[44] He kept a record of his financial affairs. He was still renting, on a monthly basis, the apartment in Fitzwilliam Square, and the payment of rent for this is recorded, as are his gifts to his niece, Anne, to Mrs Dunne, who looked after the flat, and to his sister-in-law, Polly, to whom regular gifts were sent. And the sums of money received from Victor Waddington are also recorded. Into the pages of his 1953, 'Irish Office Diary' from the Crow Street firm of Alex Thom, is laid a sprig of rosemary, 'for remembrance'. Had he abandoned the earlier idea of shedding memories?

One of his later visitors, in the autumn of 1956, was Brian O'Doherty. Recently qualified as a doctor, he later became an artist. He recalls his medical judgment: 'He bore his physical tribulations with great patience. Once when he was feeling pretty low, he allowed as how he couldn't taste his food. Casting a young doctor's eye on him, I recognised that fatigue of the very old to whom the idea of permanent rest is not unattractive. As he used to say to McGreevy "Old age is not funny".'[45]

O'Doherty had been introduced to Jack by Dr Eileen McCarvill, who taught at University College, Dublin, was herself a considerable collector, with several Yeats works, and had been a friend and supporter of Mainie Jellett. He wrote a detailed and perceptive account which is worth giving in full:

The matron introduced me to an old man, grey and frail, who rose like a grand seigneur from a deep chair. He turned somewhat shyly and gently gave me his hand. The room was hazed with sunlight through a high window which overlooked the canal. A chair was ready for me in the sunlight. He lay back, half-sideways, in the easy chair, in shadow. On an occasional table a little behind him to his left, was a lit table lamp, curious on a day of full sun. A table to my right, with two bottles of whiskey, a bottle of sherry and some glasses, half-separated us. He apologised for the glasses which looked more medicinal than for tippling. He spoke in a rather monotonous voice, running sentences together as if he couldn't wait to stop and deliver the proper accents to his narrative. I thought this was an infirmity, but later realised that it was because he had so much to say.

The profusion made him forget what he was saying as he thought of what he was going to say next. His voice ran on trying to catch up. He began by speaking of water and a memory of swans on the canal. The sunlight coming over my left shoulder made the rest of the room look unsubstantial, and he, just out of its range, partook of this. The first thing I was able to get hold of – I was somewhat overwhelmed since I admired him greatly – was the extraordinary frankness of his glance. The irises were rimmed by a white ring as they sometimes are in old age. The upper lashes were white, the lower ones absent. He poured a glass of sherry for me, and

some whiskey for himself with a deliberate economy of movement. I noticed that his hand – his painting hand – was quite steady. He toasted me and drank. I was aware of a mild ceremony that had been repeated many times before. He wore a thin, checkerboard dressing gown, left open, as was the jacket underneath. Two of the five waistcoat buttons (second and fifth) were open, pushed by a healthy paunch. A leather watch-chain crossed the waistcoat. A large yellow handkerchief hung down from the right hand pocket of the dressing gown. The left hand pocket appeared empty. From the white collar of a striped shirt a wonderful black cravat was tied in a large knot. A large opal tie-pin was stuck in the knot. The collar fell forward to expose an old man's neck.

On the third finger of his left hand was a huge mitred ring. Since his chair was rather low, his knees winged out a little from his feet, which remained close to each other, buckled into black slipper boots. The forehead was nobly domed, with a semicircle of scar above the right eyebrow. Two feathery grey wings of hair brushed back on either side. The astonishingly frank – even youthful – gaze made one forget his age, though the age was patent in the rest of the face. The white skin was delicate, translucent to the veins beneath. The nose was straight and generous; from the nostrils, two delicate lines curved towards the side of the mouth, to lose themselves in a little flurry of cross-hatches where two spare jowls supported a small square chin. A generous lower lip protruded like his brother's.

Age most clearly revealed itself in the cockatoo movement of the tongue over the lower teeth as he searched occasionally for a word. He was slightly undershot by a strong jaw. When he turned his head I was struck by the subtlety of the silhouetted lines of forehead, cheek, nose, lip. When still and listening, his head could have been cast in fine-bone china . . . I remember the voice – light and gentle but very clear – to this day.[46]

On a second visit, on St Valentine's Day, 1957, Brian O'Doherty did a pencil drawing (fig. 237).

The *New Statesman* art critic, John Berger, visited in the summer or autumn of 1956 and wrote revealingly; his short essays are models of how to address the inextricable mixture of life and art so central to the 'arch-romantic', one of the terms Berger used to define Jack. He was much taken with the idea of 'an event' being central to the painter's work, and a reflection of Irish circumstance, particularly the west of Ireland. Yeats, he says, seems too 'mobile' – 'until one has watched the West coast of Ireland. And watched is the word, for the landscape there is a fast series of events, not a view – an unchanging structure. The land is as passive as a bog can be. The sky is all action.'

This idea of an event was presented to Berger by Jack in another way: 'A painting is an event. And that's what that old Gamp Fry – do you still read him? – a grey-minded man and a timid painter too – that's what he never understood. You can plan events, but if they go according to your plan they are not events.'

The same idea, of the painting as a single event, also reinforced Jack's objection to the use of reproductions of his works; he believed that the event was turned into a process, or a reference, losing all its spontaneity and surprise. Not surprisingly, when publishers offered accuracy and faithfulness of line and colour, Jack's reply was: 'The better they are the worse they are.' By the time Berger wrote, of course, precisely what Jack had tried to prevent was happening and the situation was to get progressively worse. After his return home, Berger wrote:

> In your canvas called Discovery – the explorer has had to enter the cave, walk past the last lights that circle and fly as though they were moth and candle in one, and go even further, nailing a scarf of shadow – but then suddenly in the explorer's close-up face it is the spectator who makes the discovery. Perhaps all art's rather like that. But many must be richer for the discoveries they've made through your being the explorer – I among them.[47]

Beckett called several times in the late summer and autumn of 1956. *Waiting for Godot*, after long and disappointing delays and frustrations, had begun to make its mark. It had been first performed in Paris, in 1953, then in Berlin, Munich and Miami, coming to London in August 1955, and to the Pike Theatre in Dublin in October of that year. It was published in English by the Grove Press, in New York, in 1954. Jack was lent a copy by Andrew Ganly in November 1955. Though the play ran in Dublin, at both the Pike and the Gate Theatres, and in the Gas Company Theatre in Dun Laoghaire from

238. Jack in the 1950s.

October 1955 through to June 1956, Jack was unable to see it. He did read the play. He wrote to Eleanor Reid: "Waiting for Godot" keeps along being played here. I have only read it, but everybody seems impressed. Certainly the Easy Guffaw has been stifled at the throat from the first.'[48]

One correspondent, Fred Reid, was slightly annoyed at the absence of Jack's name from the growing list among critics of influences on Beckett:

It is interesting to see Beckett trundled about in the same carriage with Joyce, Kafka, and Sartre; but I've my own notion of his indebtedness. I say that ' Godot' is just a Beckettsian 'Old Sea Road', with Gogo and Didi passing for John and Michael; only the latter did 'go'. And the itinerant Molloy and Malone are simply Bowsie or Jimmy Gilfoyle or Oliver J. Gaw, immersed by Beckett in esthetique du mal or the mystique de la merde and offered anew to the world. But for my part I had rather that Beckett had exchanged his own flat and literal style for that metaphorical style of his master Jack Yeats.[49]

A brief inscription on 26 October, in his large diary for 1956, reads 'To Portobello'. It was the last time he was to make the autumn move into winter quarters. There is scant record for a month or so of any activity, or indeed of visits, and he may well have been too ill. But then in December there is a sudden flurry of activity, and the month's pages are mainly filled with a record of gifts and payments and the listings of people to receive Christmas cards, which he usually sent out in profusion, and almost always to his own design with a drawing quite primitively reproduced in blue line, often of a Pegasus.

His lifelong delight in printed ephemera, which had caused him to fill boxes and sketchbooks with the oddest mixture of paper, card and photographic fragments, also inclined him to keep a collection of the Christmas cards he received, among them a card in 1955 from Bryan and Elizabeth Guinness, announcing an addition to their family and enclosing a photograph. Jack had written in admiration of *A Fugue of Cinderellas*, and Bryan wrote: 'My book will be propped up in my estimation by your liking it and my estimation will be propped up by the image of that newspaper man booming down the table and the curate shouting back and yourself scattering them after setting them up.'

Bryan Guinness had bought paintings from Jack since the 1930s, building up one of the finest collections of his work in private hands. They had become good friends. Among others, Beckett sent greetings: 'This plain card to bring you, from my heart here, warmest greetings, warmest wishes for Christmas and for all the days of 1957. Ever your affectionate friend, Samuel Beckett.'[50]

He spent the Christmas of 1956 at Portobello, and in the New Year, filling out his fresh pocket diary, he entered Portobello House as his home address. The only written *aide-mémoire* was for his chest medicine, Trinitrin. Anne made her customary visit on the first Thursday in the year, and from then on came each week. His diary is filled with other visitors. An autograph hunter came to see him in February. He changed nothing. He maintained his pattern of hospitality to the end. His friends viewed this event calmly. Beckett, who was in London for rehearsals of *Endgame*, wrote to MacGreevy: 'If the end came I wd. do my utmost to get over though it will be difficult. Rehearsals at a very difficult stage.'[51] The change in Beckett's fortunes had made him the centre of a busy life as a dramatist; nevertheless, through these middle years of the 1950s his letters to MacGreevy rarely fail to mention Jack, to whom he often sends 'remembrances'.

Jack's handwriting became weak and uncertain. There are strange little squiggles on the page. In February he saw his niece, Anne, on two successive days, and his doctor came frequently, as did a specialist and friend, Honor Purser. Ria Mooney was a frequent visitor, and old but infrequent callers, among them Joe Hone, Amy Patricia Pyle (mother of the Trinity professor, Fitzroy Pyle, and grandmother of the Jack Yeats scholar, Hilary Pyle), and H.O. White, the Professor of English in the university.

He planned to go home on 27 March, and recorded this intention. Niall Montgomery was to call and take him out of the nursing home. Instead, as Montgomery told Mervyn Wall, he was with Jack the night before he died. On the next day he was due to give Anne a gift of £50. In fact he had weakened on the day before Montgomery's visit, and Miss O'Sullivan, who ran the nursing home, summoned Anne and MacGreevy. They spent that day and the next with him. Jack was holding his niece's hand, and she is sure that he knew he was going to die. He turned to her, and said: 'Goodbye, Anne.' Then he died quite peacefully. Nurses came in, and they and MacGreevy recited the Lord's Prayer.

The funeral service was held two days later, on Saturday 30 March, in St Stephen's Church at the end of Upper Mount Street. Beckett wrote to Mary Manning: 'I tried to get from London to Dublin for a few hours to see Jack Yeats into the warm earth, but couldn't manage it in the rush of last rehearsals.'[52] The church was filled to overflowing. Alfie Byrne was Lord Mayor at the time, and sat in the rector's pew at the front. The service was held by Canon Carter, who had known Jack in his curate days in Sandford parish. There had been no pre-arrangements, save that Jack himself had asked his solicitor Perceval Browne to arrange the funeral at St Stephen's Church. This had been his and Cottie's parish church, though in more recent years he had preferred going to services in St Patrick's Cathedral. Canon Carter had in fact been unaware that Jack was a parishioner. Lord Longford read the lesson. Jack's lifelong friend, Bishop Harvey, also rang to ask if he could take a part in the service, and this was agreed, as was the participation of the Archbishop of Dublin, George Otto Simms. St Stephen's Church at the time had a brilliant young musician as its organist, Julian Dawson, and the large choir turned out for a fully-robed service under his direction.

Canon Carter invited Alfie Byrne to walk with him behind the coffin. As the Rector and the Lord Mayor set off down the aisle of the church, Alfie Byrne whispered to Canon Carter that an assembly of politicians had gathered outside. In those days Roman Catholics in Dublin were not allowed to enter Anglican churches. Terence de Vere White and MacGreevy were exceptions among the pallbearers; these also included Victor Waddington and Browne. They all now descended the steps into Mount Street. There on one side of the road stood Eamon de Valera and the members of his newly elected government, and on the other side stood John A. Costello, William Norton, and the former members of the second inter-party government, which had fallen from power the week before. They held their hats and bowed in silence as the coffin appeared. One government minister, Erskine Childers, a protestant, had been in the church and now joined the government group.

Victor Waddington wrote of Jack's death to an American friend:

Mr. Yeats died peacefully and in the end I think was glad to go. He was himself right to the end and had a very distinguished funeral, as you might expect. In his coffin he wore the ribbon of the Legion of Honour of which, as you know, he was an officer. I miss him very much as I saw him every week and sometimes oftener and for many years he had been my wise and good friend.[53]

Jack was buried at Mount Jerome cemetery, in the same grave as his wife, Cottie. Eamon de Valera, who had known the painter for more than thirty years, was at the graveside, and Canon Carter read the Office of Committal.

Psalm 39 is appointed for the Order of Service for the Burial of the Dead. It contains the words: 'He heapeth up riches, and cannot tell who shall gather them.' It is a fitting epitaph for the artist. Jack had indeed heaped up the untold riches of his art, as he had of his personality, his kind heart, and his strength of purpose. He was the last of his generation of Yeatses to go, and in a poem written some years later, Thomas Kinsella celebrated the event in a brief but wider recollection of what this meant, referring to Jack and Eamon de Valera together in one poem, entitled 'The Last'. It captures the spirit of both of them in fleeting recollections, that of the artist on Baggot street, gazing with aged eyes from under his broad-brimmed hat; the other is imagined, blind and alone, after a government meeting.

The conjunction of the two very different giants of their period, and the word used to describe them, is emblematic of their worth, their purpose, their common bond. For they did forge the spirit of their times. Jack was identified, in both his work and his life, with the country he loved and with the city he had made his home and his inspiration. He had been happy in it. Lifelong happiness is a hard matter to define; yet in Jack's case the evidence is comprehensive. He lived out the rich fulfilment of a multitude of expectations, and he died at peace.

He had delighted children with his miniature theatre, amused and puzzled people with his books, startled them with his drama, and enriched them with a vast output of drawings, watercolours and paintings in oil. And in his life and friendships there was contentment. Yet like the gentle secrecy of the figure in his painting, *The Folded Heart*, there was an overwhelming privacy about this man. He had got through a long and successful life without the gross intrusions of the vaunted reputation, the mindless idolatry. For another thirty years there would be a succession of art critics affecting to have discovered him, and presenting themselves and their interpretations of his work in revelatory terms. Yeats would have smiled, and nodded. And perhaps he might have said, 'Ah, Well!'

Colour Plates

I *Memory Harbour*, watercolour and crayon on card, 12 × 18, 1900. A miniature and foreshortened view of Rosses Point, this watercolour depicts one of Jack's favoured places during his childhood. The comfortable and familiar life of the village is presented in sharp contrast to the perpetual mystery of the sea, embodied in the foreground figure.

II *Boxroom*, sketchbook watercolour, *c.* 1900. The development of Jack's skills as a watercolour artist was greatly enhanced by the many intimate sketchbook studies done in Strete; their quality was never equalled by later sketchbook studies which generally became *aides mémoires* for later works.

III *Apples*, sketchbook watercolour, 1897.

IV *The Missus*, sketchbook watercolour, *c.* 1900. This is one of the relatively few sketchbook studies by Jack of his wife.

V *The Circus Dwarf*, oil on canvas, 36 × 24, private collection. 1912. This is a major early work, expressive of Jack's taste for rough, hard-bitten and disreputable men. See pp. 181–2.

VI *A Summer Day*, oil on canvas, 24 × 36, private collection. 1914. Jack painted a number of early scenes from the west of Ireland; they provide a cast of characters on whom he drew for later, less realistic paintings and also for his plays and novels. See p. 180.

VII *A Summer Evening, Rosses Point, Sligo*, oil on panel, 9 × 14, private collection. 1922. In his records Jack refers to this painting as *Girls Dancing*.

VIII   *Water Play*, oil on canvas, 9 × 14, private collection. 1924. Jack observed and painted children from the early days in Devon to his time in Fltzwilliam Square.

IX *A Palace*, oil on canvas, 24 × 36, 1933. The Café Royal in London is the subject of this painting, but it was owned by Louis Jammet, the Dublin restaurateur, and hung in his establishment, in The Blue Room, where Jack sometimes dined.

X   *A Rose Dying*, oil on canvas, 9 × 14, private collection. 1936. One of a group of 'Rose' paintings which were of considerable importance to Jack, and much admired by Samuel Beckett. See pp. 278–80.

XI *Now*, oil on canvas, 36 × 48, private collection. 1941. Although drawing on memories from the beginning of the century, this painting is filled with a dynamic expectation and depicts Jack's lifelong enthusiasm for entertainment and the theatre. See pp. 313–14.

XII *Glory*, oil on board, 14 × 18, private collection. 1946. Jack's lifelong interest in the circus in expressed here, as it had been thirty-four years earlier in *The Circus Dwarf* and in many other canvases; the figure may be a remembered portrait of Johnny Patterson, a famous Ulster clown.

XIII *The Old Days*, oil on canvas, 24 × 36, private collection. 1942. Like *Now*, this painting was based on a recollection from his London days, and was discussed in Jack's BBC interview with Thomas MacGreevy. See pp. 334–5.

XIV *Freedom*, oil on canvas, 14 × 18, private collection. 1947. A glorious, uncomplicated painting expressive of one of the artist's earliest and most abiding enthusiasms.

XV   *The Sport of Kings*, 9 × 14, private collection. 1947. As with *Freedom*, the sense of excitement here is supremely expressed.

XVI *The Basin in which Pilate Washed his Hands*, oil on canvas, 40 × 60, private collection. 1951. An enigmatic, late canvas, one of less than ten of this size. See pp. 311–13.

XVII *The Hero Worshipper*, oil on canvas, 18 × 24, private collection. 1955. Another constant inspiration in Jack's art was the flamboyant, solitary figure, here depicted in a work from the end of his life.

Epilogue

In 1996 *A Farewell to Mayo* fetched £730,000 at auction. In the aftermath of that sale, the Million Pound Yeats was predicted for the not too distant future. The painting, 24 × 36 inches, and not therefore in the largest category of Yeats painting, had been in the collection of the English actress, Vivien Leigh. In that same year *Leaving the Raft* (40 × 60 inches), which had sold ten years earlier for £30,000, fetched £600,000. Many other startling prices, records in their day, testify to the steady growth in a Jack Yeats market. And it shows no sign of abatement.

In Dublin and London, public auctions of Irish art are not seen as complete without works by Jack Yeats in them; and few self-respecting wealthy collectors, either interested in Irish art, or coming from an Irish background, would be happy without a Jack Yeats in their collection.

He has been collected since his death; and though the prices realised publicly over four decades show an astonishing appreciation in value, they need to be put into art market contexts. During the 1960s, for example, *A Summer's Day* fetched £3,800, *On the Old Racecourse, Sligo* £2,000, and *Landing Cargo* £1,600. These are all 24 × 36 inches. *A Summer's Day* was auctioned exactly ten years later, in 1975, and fetched £8,400, while by far the highest price of the 1970s was £15,500, for *A Palace*, also 36 × 24 inches in size. As early as 1972 *By Streedagh Strand* (24 × 36 inches) fetched £9,500, and in 1978 a smaller work, *The Stevedore* (14 × 21 inches), fetched £11,500. In very general terms, an equation between size and price emerged: paintings 9 × 14 inches were worth around £2,000; 14 × 18 inches up to 18 × 24 inches, £3,500 to £5,000; and in the mid-1970s £8,500 was paid for paintings 24 × 36 inches.

There was a steady climb in values during the 1980s, very much a growth period in art generally, and a period during which a new type of Irish collector, the successful and seriously wealthy Irish business tycoon, entered the market, with predictable results. Even so, between 1980 and 1985 the two paintings 24 × 36 inches, *Jazz Babies* and *Paris Comes to Judgment*, fetched £14,000 and £12,000 respectively, and it was not until 1986 that prices began to climb dramatically. Two of Jack's largest canvases were sold, *Leaving the Raft* (40 × 60 inches) for £30,000 and *Shouting*, the same size, for £70,000. In 1989 *The Harvest Moon* caused a sensation when it was sold at public auction for £280,000. But this event was followed by a general market setback, and it was not then until 1994, with *The Haute Ecole Act* fetching

£200,000, and *Reveille* fetching £150,000 (both 24 × 36 inches), that things began to recover. In 1995 two smaller works set new records again: *Singing 'The Dark Rosaleen', Croke Park* (18 × 24 inches) went for £450,000, and *The Sea Captain's Car* (same size) fetched £320,000.[1]

Market considerations are important for a number of reasons. They ensure interest, and interest leads to careful research and cataloguing. There is a record of Jack Yeats's huge output, of oils, watercolours and drawings, and there is a balance in favour of the collector, in that few enough of his works are in permanent public collections. It is still relatively easy to buy a Yeats, and who shall say whether or not he is overvalued when the trend in market value has been unswervingly upwards over the past forty years?

But there is a negative side to this assured and structured framework of research and investment security. It tends to undermine critical assessment generally, and to encourage an almost mechanical acceptance of valuation-by-size. There are recognised variations; qualitative judgments are applied, and certain works enjoy special interest and approval. The intrusion of the market – which places a high premium on paintings depicting horses in motion, for example – distorts a good deal of critical judgment and what used to pass for connoisseurship.

Among the issues not widely faced about Jack Yeats is the fact that he was an uneven painter, quite capable of painting bad canvases, of burying minor themes in large-sized works which are then overblown and boring, of composing without much sense of structure and form, and of allowing the exuberance of his thick impasto to create problems for posterity which are far from resolved. These aspects have not been helped by the indifferent critical attention and understanding which his works have had over the years since his death.

Despite the recognition and admiration which became widespread during the last fifteen years of Jack Yeats's life, he died in possession of a considerable number of paintings and with his professional life largely unexplored. Only two critical works existed, Thomas MacGreevy's monograph and the small book by J.W. Marriott. Some perceptive articles had appeared during his lifetime, but he was an obscure figure except among a relatively confined following in Ireland, mainly in Dublin.

A few dedicated people sought to rectify this. Victor Waddington, his dealer, bought piecemeal the contents of his studio, and established the artist's position among collectors through a series of exhibitions in London. On a smaller scale, Leo Smith in the Dawson Gallery made the same efforts in Dublin. It was a painstaking labour, not without risk. 'The Yeats Man', as Waddington saw himself, placed unswerving trust in the idea of Jack Yeats's greatness, but met with a good deal of indifference and adverse criticism; as did Leo Smith.

The painter has not been well served critically. The case is made, in the preceding pages, for judging Jack in terms of contemporary critical assessment. After his death – and it is a common problem with all artists – a degree of distortion entered criticism, but aggravated in Jack's case as critics wrestled with his 'Irishness'. There was a tendency among writers to present themselves as 'discovering' him, interpreting his nationalism, often isolating him as 'special' in his own country, and expanding on something which Jack himself felt – that he did not fit in. These attitudes were often at the expense of just looking at his paintings.

The conflict of views which had been explored between Beckett and MacGreevy in the mid-1930s was reintroduced. Unfortunately, the shadow cast by MacGreevy was stronger than Beckett's. And this difficulty was aggravated by another; Irish art more generally had such a limited impact, that Jack was seen by many people for much of the period of the twentieth century as the *only* serious Irish painter. His work received a disproportionate amount of attention, too much emphasis on how Irish he was, and too much interpretation of the nationalism which people read into simple visual statements about the human condition.

Hilary Pyle has given virtually her whole professional life as art historian to Jack Yeats, researching and writing on every aspect of his output, and cataloguing his paintings, drawings, prints and illustrations with a wealth of invaluable detail. She has been Jack Yeats's most dedicated exponent. Wisely perhaps, she has described and recorded, rather than criticised his vast output. And we are greatly in her debt for the prodigious work done in discovering and cataloguing his works.

There has been remarkably little attention to the technical side of his art. Brian Kennedy has written well about the later paintings, the vulnerability of the heavy impasto, the problems of cleaning.[2] But in general, expertise of this kind is to be found among distinguished restorers, like Kenneth Malcolm, and those dealers, like Victor Waddington's two sons, Theo and Leslie, whose lifetime's occupation has been the handling of the artist's work. Their father's success in establishing for Jack Yeats a posthumous international reputation, which was by no means easy, has had some questionable results.

Jack's works are widely known. There are innumerable books, record covers, magazines, CDs and general bric-a-brac bearing Jack Yeats images. His works have attracted more money than sense or understanding within the collecting fraternity. The interest in his work, even within the National Gallery of Ireland where a more even approach might have been expected, is disproportionate to that of many other Irish artists. And the distortion resulting from these trends is likely to continue.

Amaranthers	Jack Yeats, *The Amaranthers*, London and Toronto, 1936
ATYA	Jack Yeats, *And to You Also*, London 1944
BP Letters	*Letters from Bedford Park: A Selection from the Correspondence (1890–1901) of John Butler Yeats*, edited by William Murphy, Dublin (Cuala Press) 1972
Boylan	Patricia Boylan, *All Cultivated People*, Gerrards Cross 1988
Collected Plays	*The Collected Plays of Jack B. Yeats*, edited by Robin Skelton, London 1971
Connemara	*Synge and the Ireland of his Times by William Butler Yeats with a Note Concerning a Walk through Connemara with him by Jack Yeats*, Dublin (Cuala Press) 1911
'Education'	John Butler Yeats, 'The Education of Jack B. Yeats', *The Christian Science Monitor*, Boston, Tuesday, 2 November 1920
Foster	R.F. Foster, *W.B. Yeats: A Life, Vol. I, The Apprentice Mage*, Oxford and New York, 1997
Four Years	W.B. Yeats, *Four Years*, Dublin (Cuala Press) 1921
Gregory Journals	Lady Gregory, *The Journals, Vol. I, Books 1–29*, edited by Daniel J. Murphy, Gerrards Cross 1978
JBY Archive	All Jack B. Yeats documents in his possession at the time of his death were preserved by his niece, Anne Yeats. In November 1995, they were presented to the National Gallery of Ireland.
John BY Letters	*John Butler Yeats, Letters to his son W.B. Yeats and Others – 1869–1922*, edited by Joseph Hone, London 1944
Lewis	Gifford Lewis, *The Yeats Sisters and the Cuala*, Dublin 1994
LYS	Lily Yeats scrapbook, in the Michael Yeats Archive (see Yeats Archive)
MacGreevy	Thomas MacGreevy, *Jack B. Yeats – An Appreciation and an Interpretation*, Dublin 1945
McGuinness	Norah McGuinness, *The Literary Universe of Jack B. Yeats*, Washington 1992
Murphy	William M. Murphy, *Prodigal Father*, Ithaca and London, 1978
Purser	John Purser, *The Literary Works of Jack B Yeats*, Gerrards Cross 1991
Pyle	Hilary Pyle, *Jack B. Yeats: A Biography*, London 1970
Reid	B.L. Reid, *The Man from New York: John Quinn and His Friends*, New York 1968
Reveries	William Butler Yeats, *Reveries over Childhood and Youth*, London 1916
Scrapbook I	Jack Yeats scrapbook, 1891–1925. Unpublished collection of press cuttings. JBY Archive
Secrets	William M. Murphy, *Family Secrets*, Dublin 1995
Sligo	Jack B. Yeats, *Sligo*, London 1931
Synge Letters	*The Collected Letters of John Millington Synge, Volume I*, edited by Ann Saddlemyer, Oxford 1983
TCD	Library of Trinity College, Dublin. MS call number is given
Watercolours	Hilary Pyle, *Jack B. Yeats: His Watercolours, Drawings and Pastels*, Dublin 1993
WBY Letters I	*The Collected Letters of W.B. Yeats, Vol. I 1865–1895*, edited by John Kelly, Associate Editor Eric Domville, Oxford 1986
WBY Letters II	*The Collected Letters of W.B. Yeats, Vol. II 1896–1900*, edited by Warwick Gould, John Kelly and Deirdre Toomey, Oxford 1997
WBY Letters III	*The Later Collected Letters of W.B. Yeats, Vol. III 1900–1904*, edited by John Kelly and Ronald Schuchard, Oxford 1994
Wade	*The Letters of W.B. Yeats*, edited by Allan Wade, London 1954
Yeats Archive	All Yeats Family documents, unless otherwise stated, are in the possession of Michael Yeats

NOTES

CHAPTER ONE

1 There were six children in all, two of whom died in infancy. William Butler Yeats, the eldest, was born 13 June 1865; Susan Mary (known as Lily) was born 25 August 1866; Elizabeth Corbet (known as Lolly) was born 11 March 1868; Robert Corbet was born in March 1870, and died, in the same month, in 1873; a daughter, Grace Jane, was born after Jack, on August 1875, and died the following May.

2 Murphy, p. 35.

3 McGuinness, p. 2.

4 Murphy, p. 35.

5 John Butler Yeats to Rosa Butt. 3 October 1918. Bodleian Library, Oxford. Rosa Butt (1838–1926) was the daughter of Isaac Butt (1813–79) one of Ireland's great Protestant nationalists, and founder of Home Rule.

6 'The Pollexfens of Sligo', by William Murphy, draft typescript, 1968, p. 11.

7 Lily to Ruth Lane-Poole (née Pollexfen, a cousin) 22 October 1928. Foster, p. 7.

8 John Butler Yeats, *Early Memories*, Dublin (Cuala Press) 1923, p. 89.

9 JBY Archive.

10 LYS.

11 *Four Years*, p. 62.

12 Quoted from a letter to Isaac Yeats which John Butler Yeats wrote 29 December 1915, fifteen years after Susan's death. JBY Archive.

13 John Henry Foley (1818–74), Irish sculptor, responsible for part of the Albert Memorial. Richard Doyle (1824–83), illustrator for *Punch*; he did the design for the cover of the magazine which was not replaced until the 1950s.

14 *Four Years*, p. 52.

15 Murphy, p. 63.

16 John Todhunter to Edward Dowden, 27 September 1869. TCD, MS 3417/55.

17 Todhunter to Dowden, 14 January 1870, TCD, MS 3417/60.

18 Murphy, p. 77.

19 It was from the name of this dock that James Clarence Mangan adopted the name Clarence. He did so unilaterally. It was not given at birth.

20 *Reveries*, pp. 90–2.

21 *John BY Letters*, p. 49. The letter is dated 1872. Isabella Pollexfen was an art student.

22 John Butler Yeats to Susan, 6 December 1872. Yeats Archive.

23 *Sligo*, p. 8.

24 Ibid., p. 12.

25 *Reveries*, p. 53.

26 LYS.

27 Ibid.

28 LYS, 'Odds and Ends', a sketchbook of further memoirs (Yeats Archive).

29 Psalm 109 is a psalm of revenge and anger which almost amounts to being a prolonged curse against an unnamed individual, the leader of a gang of merciless enemies and persecutors. It is a complex invocation, thought by some to have Davidic origin, by others to be the work of a representative of the poor and oppressed. It has a personal ring to it; it is a cry of suffering provoked by actual circumstance, and, though one can only conjecture as to what these were, they seem to have been a conspiracy involving false charges and the perversion of justice. The crucial question – as to why it was marked for permanent censorship – concerns the possible role played by William Pollexfen, on his first arrival in Sligo, meriting this strange attitude.

30 LYS.

31 William Pollexfen was affiliated for membership of the Freemasons on 4 November 1852, just twenty years after first arriving in Sligo. See R.W. Arthur Jackson, *Freemasonry in Sligo 1767–1867*, Sligo 1909. Arthur Jackson, who was married to William Pollexfen's daughter, became the Provincial Deputy Grand Master. George, his brother-in-law, Jack's uncle, was also a leading Freemason.

32 *Reveries*, pp. 4–6.

33 William Pollexfen's father was the Barrack Master in the fort at Berry Head, Torquay, then the town garrison. His mother, ten years older, was born in 1771. She came from Wexford. After retirement as Barrack Master the couple moved down the coast to Brixham, where they owned sailing vessels engaged mainly in coastal trade. Mary Pollexfen died there in 1830, aged 59. Anthony, died three years later, aged 52, and was buried at Brixham Church. Earlier members of the Pollexfen family came from Kitley Manor, Yealmpton, also in Devon, where they had been since 1470, and William Pollexfen owned a print depicting the house, which hung in his two Sligo homes. The name means 'the farm on the gentle river', and the river in question was the Yealm, which flows into the sea east of Plymouth.

34 Lewis, p. 8. Gifford Lewis has made a notable contribution to our knowledge of the Pollexfen family, and its distinction in law and

economics during the seventeenth century. It was a family of some distinction thereafter, so much so that the Calmady family, linked to the Pollexfens in 1698 by marriage, used the Pollexfen name for girl children, though it was abbreviated to Polly. According to Lewis, the marriage of closely related Pollexfens was not unknown.

35 The term is used by Lily, see LYS.

36 Ibid.

37 William Pollexfen (1811–92) married Elizabeth Middleton (1819–92) in 1837. Their children, were: Charles (1838–1923), George (1839–1910), Susan (1841–1900), Elizabeth Anne (1843–1933), William (1844–6), John Anthony (1845–1900), William Middleton (1847–1913), Isabella (1849–1938), Frederick Henry (1852–1929), Alfred Edward (1854–1916), Agnes Middleton (1855–1926) and Alice Jane (1857–1932).

38 LYS.

39 *Reveries*, pp. 51–2.

40 See below, Chapter Eight.

41 *Reveries*, pp. 16–18.

42 LYS.

43 Ibid.

44 Ibid.

45 LYS.

46 It also still stands, though many of its fine points have been obliterated by its inclusion in the larger complex of the Nazareth House nursing home and home for the elderly.

47 Herbert Spencer (1820–1903) English philosopher and social thinker. His principal work, *A System of Synthetic Philosophy*, had begun appearing in 1862.

48 Murphy, p. 84.

49 *Reveries*, p. 3.

50 Ibid., p. 4.

51 Ibid., p. 7.

52 Murphy, p. 86.

53 *Reveries*, p. 9.

54 Willie to RLS, 24 October 1894. *WBY Letters I*, p. 404.

55 The surviving members of the family, Anne Butler Yeats, and William Michael Butler Yeats, retain the name, as does William Michael's eldest son, Pàdraig Butler, though not his daughters.

56 The magazine was founded in 1833.

57 LYS.

58 'JBY Memoir I', a manuscript autobiography, undated, but written before 1918. It is quoted in Murphy, as part of his excellent introductory chapter, together with other important sources.

59 Murphy, quoted (p. 31) from 'JBY Memoirs'.

60 J.B. Yeats *Early Memories*, Dublin (Cuala Press) 1923.

CHAPTER TWO

1 Murphy, p. 105.

2 A fuller account of Bedford Park is given later, see below p. 382, when Jack returned to live there during his art school studies.

3 John Butler Yeats, 'Education'. The reference to the Farm being brought to 'seaside holidays' rather than to Sligo, seems to date the establishment of this habit firmly in 1879, and would suggest that it developed between Jack's sixth and eighth birthdays.

4 Lily to John Butler Yeats, 26 May 1917. Yeats Archive.

5 LYS.

6 Lily to J.M. Hone, 21 February 1942. Texas. The earlier quotation is from a letter, Lily to Ruth, 23 September 1925. Yeats Archive.

7 LYS.

8 This was to have many additional artistic associations during the course of the next hundred years, becoming the home of the Society of Dublin Painters on its formation in 1920, and a place where Jack briefly exhibited.

9 LYS. The story was told to Lily by Arthur Jackson, who had been sent to Sligo by his office in Belfast to attend the funeral. He afterwards married Pollexfen's youngest daughter, Alice, moved to Sligo to work in the firm, and became its new driving force after Pollexfen's death.

10 'Education'.

11 Jack MacGowran, Preface to *In Sand*, Dublin 1964.

12 Pyle, p. 14. The information came from Mark Franklin. Susan Mitchell (1866–1926) was a distinguished and witty Irish author, whose satiric portraits of contemporaries, *Aids to the Immortality of Certain Persons, Charitably Administered* (1908) are rightly celebrated. She wrote a study of George Moore. She knew the Yeats family, and stayed with them in 1900, after Jack's marriage.

13 Ibid., p. 15.

14 Yeats Archive. Copy in NLI Microfilm P7545. The first of these two letters is dated 1883. The second is dated 31 May 1884. The others are about this time.

15 Jack to Lily, 31 May 1884. Yeats Archive.

16 To Lolly, 17 May 1886. Yeats Archive. Copy in NLI P7545.

17 Jack to Lily, April 1881. Yeats Archive. Copy in NLI P7545.

18 'Education'. Frederick York Powell (1850–1904), professor of modern history at Oxford, was a student of languages and also lectured in law. He became president of the Irish Text Society.

19 Ibid.

20 Ibid.

21 Jack Yeats interview with Eamonn Andrews, 10 October 1947, Radio-Telefis Eireann Archives.

22 Jack to Lily, 8 July 1886. Yeats Archive. Copy in NLI P7545.

23 LYS.

24 Ibid.

25 Ibid. It must be remembered that, although Jack was at Merville all the time, between 1879 and 1887, the other children, as well as Susan, and, less frequently, their father, continued to visit.

26 Ibid.

27 Ibid.

28 LYS.

29 'Education'.

30 Francis S. Walker (1848–1916) was born in County Meath, and received artistic instruction at the Royal Dublin Society and then at the Royal Hibernian Academy School, where he won a travel scholarship which took him to London. He found work as an illustrator with *The Daily Graphic*, and *The Illustrated London News*, both publications in which Jack's work later appeared. He subsequently produced a body of graphic work, including 12 mezzotint engravings to illustrate *Killarney's Lakes and Fells*, by F.S. Walker, with poems edited by Edmund Downey, London 1902.

31 The drawing, which measures 2.5 × 1.5 inches, is in pencil and blue crayon, cut out and pasted down onto board. JBY Archive.

32 JBY Archive.

33 'The Beauty and the Beast' is in the National Library of Ireland, MS The booklet, 16 pp., stitched with green cord, is inscribed:

'By Jack Yeats July 1885 given to his sister Lollie July 14th 1885'. Only eight pages carry watercolours. 'The Pasha', is the same size, on 12 pp. Again, eight pages are illustrated, but since two of these both carry two drawings, it is the fuller of the two stories. It is undated, and inscribed: 'Given to Lillie (sic) by Jack Yeats. He did not use 'Junior' ever in his name – though it appeared in his baptismal certificate – and the B., with full point instead of 'Butler', which later distinguished him from his father, does not appear at this stage.

34 'Education'.

CHAPTER THREE

1 *Jack Yeats as a Boy*, by John Butler Yeats. National Gallery of Ireland, No. 1142. 61 × 51 inches. Unsigned. Presented by the sitter in 1947.

2 Jack Yeats kept diaries for 1888 and 1889. The first of many references to sitting for his father – suggesting an oil painting, not a drawing – is for 7 January. He records his art school studies, his pastimes and reading, his holidays in Sligo in the summer of each year, and his early commissions for *The Vegetarian* and other publications. The diaries are also filled with drawings. Yeats Archive.

3 *Jack B. Yeats*. 61 × 51, signed indistinctly, and dated 'c. 1895'. National Gallery of Ireland, No. 4040. It was presented in 1972 by Victor Waddington. The drawing, signed and dated 1899, is in the collection of Mr Michael Yeats.

4 One of the outstanding aspects in John Purser's book, *The Literary Works of Jack B Yeats* is the exposition of Jack's Christian principles.

5 Murphy, p. 131.

6 Ibid., p. 130.

7 Quoted in the 'Centenary Programme for Olympia', Earls Court, 1986.

8 *The Times*, 1 November 1887. Editorial.

9 From an undated draft in typescript of his essay, 'Why there are artists'. Yeats Archive.

10 A distinction should be made between the first, early drawings, and the later, masterly studies which were probably inspired by the return visit of the Wild West Show, in 1892. Those five years, understandably enough, brought about a complete transformation in Jack's capacities as an artist, and we shall see this in a number of later examples, which demonstrate the wonderful combination of unchanged love of the subject, with complete mastery of its presentation.

11 Jack kept his early programmes, from 1892 and 1907, though not the programme from the first show. He also kept a cutting from *The People's Weekly* (a Dublin publication) of 5 October 1946, which contained a centenary tribute to Buffalo Bill, written by Edward J. Foley, and a detailing of 'the real facts' about Cody's career, written by Frederick Watson.

12 Lily Yeats, 'Return to London 1887', from LYS.

13 Ibid.

14 Jack himself gave this information to an *Irish Times* journalist, for a profile in *The Irish Times Weekly*, 3 August 1914.

15 Jack gave to Thomas Bodkin, in a letter of 8 January 1918, the details of his art school training. See TCD MS 6946/1352–1352.

16 Jack to Lady Gregory, 22 November 1903. Letter in Christie's Sale, Dublin 1994.

17 Harry Furniss, *Confessions of a Caricaturist*, London 1901, Vol. I,

p. 9. Harry Furniss (1854–1925) was a fellow-Irishman, born in Wexford, the son of an English engineer. He was at school with George Bernard Shaw (see *Collected Letters*, London 1988, Vol. IV, p. 728) where he produced a *Schoolboys' Punch*, depicting their headmaster, Henry Parker, who saw and liked it, and encouraged Furniss. He worked for A.M. Sullivan's Irish version of *Punch*, then moved to London, and, when Francis Cowley Burnand became editor of *Punch*, in 1880, Furniss started working for him, joining the staff, though not in a salaried capacity.

18 *WBY Letters I*, pp. 70–3. The letter dates from mid-June, 1888.

19 Murphy, p. 159.

20 I am indebted to Mary Brennan Holohan for this suggestion.

21 Letter to Sarah Purser, 9 September 1888 (University of Victoria Library).

22 Ibid. The letter contains a drawing at this point of two lines of racegoers facing each other with fists and riding crops raised in anger.

23 'Jim jams' was a slang term, at that time (1885 OED) for *delerium tremens*.

24 John Pollexfen, an uncle who was married to Mary Jane, and was a sailor, lived at Blundell Sands.

25 Lolly's diary, October 1888. Yeats Archive.

26 Hilary Pyle, in her first bibliography (*Jack B. Yeats: A Biography*, London 1970), updated in subsequent publications, lists Yeats's contributions to illustrated papers; many of his early drawings in *The Vegetarian* were illustrations to articles and poems, including 'A Legend' by his brother. *The Vegetarian* was 'a weekly paper for the promotion of humanity, purity, temperance, health, wealth and happiness'.

27 *WBY Letters I*, p. 59, letter of 11 April 1888. The name is given there as 'Rolly', possibly a shortened form of Hall's second name, though he was known to Jack as Harry Hall (see below).

28 *The Vegetarian* first appeared in 1888, so that Jack's association with it was from the very beginning.

29 *WBY Letters I*, pp. 70–3.

30 Pyle records only one drawing for 1888, and only two in 1889.

31 The Vegetarian Society was the oldest and most important in England, though it was based in Oxford Street, Manchester. There were several smaller societies in London, and a London association, as well as a Vegetarian Federal Union, in Farringdon Road, London, though whether this was in existence in 1889 is uncertain.

32 Harry Reginald Holland Hall, known as 'Rolly' (1873–1930) was the son of Sydney Prior Hall (1842–1922) and became an archaeologist. His father was painter and illustrator, and also a friend of the Yeats family. He formed 'The Brotherhood' with John Butler Yeats, Ellis and later George Wilson. He was a contributor to the *Graphic*, and bought Jack's work at exhibition. Harry Hall remained a friend of Jack Yeats into the mid-1900s. The Halls were neighbours of Francis S. Walker, whose portrait drawing by Jack is the earliest surviving work by the artist. S.P. Hall did courtroom sketches for *The Graphic* of the Parnell Commission (1888–90), where allegations published by *The Times*, based on letters forged by Richard Pigott, were successfully refuted by Charles Stewart Parnell M.P. Drawings in National Gallery donated by Harry Hall 1927. Martha Jowitt had previously been governess to the children.

33 Lolly's diary, Monday 10 September 1888.

34 Ibid.

35 Randolph Caldecott (1846–86) Thought he had died two years earlier, Caldecott was a major influence on British illustrators at

the time, and one of the seminal figures in Jack's life as an artist (see below).

36   We can date these drawings exactly, since Jack records in his 1889 diary for Saturday 16 February: 'drewed did little hunting sketch a penny plane or 2d coloured'.

37   Its founder was Jonathan Thomas Carr (1845–1915) one of a family of ten noted for their radical opinions, their involvement in the arts, and their disposition towards politics. And he set out to provide a self-contained community, complete with church, shops, a club, a tavern, schools, and – more or less – its own railway station. He bought his first parcel of land, 45 acres, in the mid-1870s from the Bedford House estate. This had been the home of Dr John Lindley, a distinguished botanist and Fellow of the Royal Society, who had died in 1865. He had also been secretary of the Royal Horticultural Society which at one time had its gardens at Chiswick. Carr bought land piecemeal, and the immediate success of his revolutionary scheme can be measured from the fact that by 1883, just seven years after the start of the project, he had acquired 113 acres. Well before that, the aesthetic character of the venture had been clearly defined. The most obvious and lasting expression of this is in the architecture. Bedford Park coincided with the Queen Anne Revival, and is a clear and unified expression of that distinctive style, with its half-timbering, its sharply-pointed gable roofs, and its variety of design. A good account of the development and ethos of Bedford Park is to be found in *The Early Community at Bedford Park – The Pursuit of 'Corporate Happiness' in the First Garden Suburb*, by Margaret Jones Bolsterli, London 1977.

38   There are several good accounts of the development of the Chiswick School of Art, including the relevant pages in Bolsterli. I am indebted to Carolyn Hammond, Librarian for Local Studies at the Chiswick Library, in the London Borough of Hounslow, for bringing to my attention the unpublished essay by J.T. Fielding, 'Chiswick Polytechnic and the Evolution of Technical Education in West Middlesex', which was written in 1881. This gives an excellent account of the development of the school and its later history, long after the departure of the Yeats family from Bedford Park. The school was destroyed by flying bombs in 1944, rebuilt after the war, survived to celebrate its 1981 centenary, but was then closed the following year as part of 'educational rationalisation'.

39   Mark Glazebrook, in 'Some Artists of Bedford Park', *London Magazine*, June 1967, gives an interesting account of the artists involved, both with the art school and Bedford Park generally. The essay was republished in a combined pamphlet and catalogue to accompany an exhibition held in St Michael's vicarage, during Bedford Park Festival Week, 10–18 June 1967.

40   Letter to Sarah Purser, 2 December 1888 (University of Victoria Library).

41   Jack to Purser, 24 December 1888 (University of Victoria Library).

42   'Ye Pleiades', NLI MS 12160.

43   See Hilary Pyle, *The Different Worlds of Jack B. Yeats*, Dublin 1994, pp. 57–8.

44   MacGreevy, p. 10.

45   Pyle, p. 32 and p. 3.

46   The history is immense, and the literature vast. The particular vein tapped by Jack Yeats, however, has received less than its due share of attention.

47   Randolph Caldecott was the son of an accountant, and first sent his drawings to London Society in 1870, just after Henry Blackburn had taken over as editor from James Hogg.

48   Simon Houfe, *The Dictionary of British Book Illustrators and Caricaturists, 1800–1914*, London 1978 (revised 1981).

49   JBY Archive.

50   Hugh Thomson (1860–1920) was an Irish artist, from Coleraine, and mainly a book illustrator.

51   Philip William May (1864–1903) was the finest comic illustrator of the 1890s, and a worthy successor to Cruikshank, Leech and Charles Keene. He was the son of an engineer, from a family of landowners; he started as a scene-painter, became a caricaturist, and was enormously successful.

CHAPTER FOUR

1   Jack's diary for 1889: 'T.J. & J. Smith's Small Scribbling Diary Interleaved with blotting paper. Gilt letter 1889. Bound in limp cloth, one and sixpence.' At the beginning, on the pages for memoranda, John Butler Yeats has done two sketches of Susan. Evidently the diary was in the father's possession, not in Jack's.

2   Murphy, p. 161. He cites a remark made to Quinn in April 1919, referring to the 'incessant humiliation', the memory of which still burned in him, thirty years on. Yet in May Quinn was able to say to him: 'I congratulate you upon having learned to live so many years ago, so early in life, and having lived each day.' (See Reid, p. 391, letter of 23 May 1919.)

3   Lolly's diary, entry for 3 December 1888. She wrote in red above the entry 'Red Letter Day' and recorded that it was done in his 'best costermonger style'.

4   W.B. Yeats, *The Wanderings of Oisin*, London 1889, the poet's first book. It was published by subscription, with many friends helping Willie to make sales and get reviews. His letters at the time are full of detail about his efforts to promote the book. It contained 'A Legend', the poem illustrated by Jack in the *Vegetarian*, but not republished in later collections.

5   Jack's diary for 1889. Entry for Monday 28 October. Yeats Archive.

6   W.B. Yeats, *Autobiography* – First Draft, edited by Denis Donoghue, London 1972, opening paragraph.

7   See Chapter Two, n. 30.

8   Lolly's diary, 23 September 1889. Joseph Pennell (1860–1926) was born in Philadelphia and died in New York, but spent much of his working life in London, where he was part of the Whistler circle. He worked for *The Graphic*, just at this time, and also for *The Illustrated London News*. Sir James Drogmole Linton (1840–1916) came from nearby Barnes, and was a successful historical painter. His best work as an illustrator was done for *The Graphic*. He had been knighted four years earlier.

9   Lolly's diary, 2 December 1888.

10   Jack's diary, Thursday, 14 March 1889.

11   Jack's diary, 26 April 1889.

12   Louisa, Duchess of Cambridge, had a morganatic marriage in 1840 to Queen Victoria's uncle, George William Frederick Charles, the only son of George III's seventh son, who was the first duke. The Duke of Cambridge was a considerable public figure with a distinguished military career, including service in the Crimea; he became a field marshal, and was commander-in-chief of the army. Though in difficulties with his political masters, and notably the secretary of state for war over army

reforms, he was a popular general and the funeral was a splendid public occasion.

13 The 20th Middlesex (Artists') Rifle Volunteer Corps.

14 Ellen Terry (1847–1928) became Irving's leading lady in 1878, and created a succession of great Shakespearean interpretations, beginning with Ophelia and ending with Volumnia (*Coriolanus*) in 1901.

15 Jack to Sarah Purser, 7 June 1889.

16 Jack's diary for 1889, entry for Tuesday, 8 January. Yeats Archive; a photostat copy is in the National Library of Ireland. Herbert Beerbohm Tree (1852–1917) was another of the great figures of the English stage. His production of *The Merry Wives of Windsor* was at the Haymarket, which he leased for ten years from 1887. Ellen Terry later acted with Tree in his revival of this play.

17 It is a 'remembered' drawing, as far as can be judged. No sketchbooks survive from the 1880s, and Jack was later to distinguish quite carefully between work done on the spot, and drawings done from memory.

18 Louis Claude Purser (1854–1932) was Dublin University professor of Classics, and Trinity College bursar. He was the brother of the artist, Sarah Purser. Murphy suggests that he was 'powerfully attracted' to Lolly, but there is no evidence for this. See below, Chapter Eleven.

19 Lolly's diary, 14 October 1888. The detective was Newcomen. Richard Mansfield starred in the dual title roles. T.R. Sullivan adapted Stevenson's *Dr Jekyll and Mr Hyde* for the stage.

20 Lolly's diary, 29 October 1888.

21 Lolly's diary, Monday 21 January 1889.

22 Lolly's diary, 24 December 1888.

23 John O'Leary (1830–1907) was a supporter, rather than a sworn member of the Fenian Movement. His strong nationalist sentiments brought imprisonment and banishment. He was a strong influence on W.B. Yeats, and sat to John Butler Yeats for a splendid portrait now in the National Gallery of Ireland.

24 Lolly's diary. She adds to this description her opinion, that Maud Gonne was really calling on Willie.

25 Lily's diary (Yeats Archive). George Bernard Shaw (1856–1950) the Irish playwright, was relatively unknown at this time, except for his witty conversation, and his protest speeches at demonstrations. Willie first met him at the Morrises on 11 February 1888 (See *Collected Letters*). Robert Bontine Cunninghame Graham (1852–1936) writer and politician, was much more famous at the time, and had been imprisoned after Bloody Sunday, 1887.

26 *WBY Letters I*, p. 111. William Morris (1834–96) was a towering figure in English literary, political and philosophic circles, and had selected Willie for friendship and patronage on the merit of his writing and talk.

27 Rose was Roseanna Hodgkins (1848–1930). She joined the family in 1884, and remained with the two sisters until her death.

28 The story is told by Charles Johnston, a schoolfriend of Willie's, who gave a glowing picture of the happy, generous, artistic atmosphere in the Yeats household. See Foster, p. 30, and note.

29 Foster, p. 62.

30 Katherine Tynan, *The Middle Years*, London 1916, pp. 31–2. See *WBY Letters I*, p. 12, n.

31 John Butler Yeats to Lily, summer 1904. Published in *John BY Letters*.

32 Padraic Colum, *The Yeats We Knew*, Cork 1965. The book contains the Thomas Davis Lectures broadcast on Radio-Telefís Eireann in the summer of W.B. Yeats's centenary year. Other contributors were Francis Stuart, Monk Gibbon, Ernest Blythe and Austin Clarke.

33 Letter to Rosa Butt, 4 December 1907. Bodleian Library, MS.

34 Letter to Isaac Yeats, 1 August 1921. Yeats Collection.

35 Willie to Katharine Tynan, *WBY Letters I*, p. 72.

36 Murphy, p. 80.

37 *WBY Letters I*, p. 190, 10 October 1889.

38 Lolly's diary, 8 December 1888.

39 Dr Charles Edward Fitzgerald (1843–1916) was Surgeon Oculist in Ordinary to the Queen in Ireland, and a good friend to John Butler Yeats. He commissioned from him portraits of himself and his children.

40 Lolly's diary 8 December 1888.

41 See Pyle, pp. 177–7, 190–201. She lists chronologically the artist's original contributions to these and later publications, as well as giving his commissioned drawings to illustrate articles, stories and poems by other writers, including his brother and his sister, Lolly.

42 Drawing signed and dated 1891.

43 BBC Interview, with Thomas MacGreevy, BBC Third Programme, November 1947.

44 'Circus' scrapbook, Yeats Archive.

45 *Paddock Life*, 3 May 1892. Signed Jack B Yeats.

46 Diary, Sunday, 6 January 1889. Yeats Archive. Copy in NLI P7547.

47 *Secrets*, pp. 277–8. The reference to hiring a specialist is recorded in a letter from Lily to Ruth, 15 October 1934.

CHAPTER FIVE

1 Yeats Archive. Murphy gives an excellent account of this, pp. 164–6.

2 SMY diary, 2 August 1895. Yeats Archive.

3 Ibid. 4 October 1895.

4 See Murphy, pp. 164, 576. Murphy interviewed cousin Ida, the daughter of Isabella Varley (née Pollexfen), who recalled – admittedly seventy years later – the distinction between the brothers.

5 See Murphy, p. 162.

6 'An Irish Race Meeting', *Daily Graphic*, 29 August 1890. The drawing was accompanied by a letter signed 'J.B.W.' describing the event.

7 Ernest Rhys, *The Great Cockney Tragedy*, London 1891. This was Jack's first illustrated book.

8 The review, publication not traced, is pasted on its own into page one of Jack's cuttings book for the period 1891–1925.

9 Ernest Rhys (1859–1946) first met Willie at one of William Morris's Sunday evening 'at homes' in May 1887. Rhys was then editing the Camelot Series in which W.B. Yeats's *Fairy and Folk Tales of the Irish Peasantry* was published. Yeats in his turn was responsible for introducing Rhys to his wife, Grace Little. It is also possible that Rhys, who later worked for the publisher, JM Dent, was responsible for getting the commission for John Butler Yeats to illustrate Defoe's works. Rhys seems to have been the originator of the enormously popular Dent series, the 'Everyman's Library'.

10 *WBY Letters I*, pp. 255–6. The Katherine Tynan letter ('early July 1891') is undated.

11 'Education'.

12 Israel Zangwill (1864–1926) published his first and probably his

greatest novel, *Children of the Ghetto*, in 1892. He also wrote plays, but then dedicated his energies to helping the leader of the Zionist movement, Theodor Herzl.

13 Jerome Klapka Jerome (1859–1927) came from humble origins in the east end of London, his father having been an unsuccessful ironmonger. He published *Three Men in a Boat* in 1889, but had previously published humorous pieces on the theatre, and had been an actor.

14 These appeared in the issues of 10 January and 28 March 1891, Vol. IV of *The Vegetarian*. See Pyle, p. 189.

15 See below, pp. 132–51.

16 *The London Illustrated News*, 10 September 1892. p. 335.

17 Oliver Elton (1861–1945) was a university teacher, first in Manchester, then in Liverpool, and the author of several works, including his most famous, *A Survey of English Literature*, in six volumes. He wrote *Frederick York Powell: A Life and a Selection of His Letters and Occasional Writings* (1906), in two volumes, and in 1944, the year before he died, he wrote the Preface to Hone's edition of *John BY Letters*.

18 John Butler Yeats to Lily, 10 June 1892. Yeats Archive. The letter is quoted in *BP Letters*. Murphy wrongly dates the letter 1894.

19 Ibid.

20 Ibid.

21 Letter to Willie, September 1892. See *John BY Letters*.

22 Jack Yeats, 'When I Was in Manchester', *Manchester Guardian*, 1932.

23 'Education'.

24 'Monograph the 44th – A Black-and-White Artist – Jack B. Yeats' in *The Bohemian* 'about 1895'. JBY Archive. The dating is Jack's own.

25 Monk Gibbon, *The Masterpiece and the Man*, London 1959, p. 33.

26 John Butler Yeats to Lily, 26 June 1894. Yeats Archive.

27 1 August 1894. Yeats Archive.

28 Lily to Lolly, 24 August 1894. Yeats Archive. Copy in NLI.

29 Card in Yeats Archive, dated Easter Day, 21 April 1946. Jack also did a painting called 'A Jar of Scent', possibly inspired by this occasion.

30 Ernest Terah Hooley (1859–1947) was regarded as a financial genius. He speculated in shares in some of the great companies, including Humber, Raleigh, Singer, Dunlop, Schweppes and Bovril.

31 Jack to J.C. Miles, 24 January 1896. Miles lived in Great Yarmouth, and remained a lifelong friend. It was with him that Jack and Cottie went on their Norfolk Broads holiday. See below, Chapter 7.

32 *Chums* belonged to the Cassell group of publications, *Sporting Sketches* was a Harmsworth publication.

33 Scrapbook I. The cutting, accompanied by a small head of the artist, appears with two other 1895 press clippings at the beginning of the book.

34 Lily's diary, 21 August 1895. Lily kept only one proper, day-to-day diary during her life, 1895–6, with a few additional later entries. This is to be distinguished from the large volume of recollections, in the form of essays about family members and events.

35 Lily's diary, 11 and 13 October 1895.

36 The later cartoons were done exclusively for *Punch*, beginning in November 1910 and finally concluding in 1948, though the last is an isolated example, his work for the magazine effectively ceasing in 1941. See Pyle; see also below, pp. 168, 240.

37 Interview in *The Irish Times*, 22 February 1929, after his return from his London exhibition at the Alpine Club.

38 The house still stands, with further subsequent changes made to it. The studio is now a ruin. I am indebted to Mr F.W. Blackwell for help with details.

39 Letter to Lily, March 1896 (Michael Yeats).

40 Arthur Symons (1865–1945) was a poet, and friend of Willie's, a member with him of the Rhymers' Club. When Willie left home, in 1895, it was to move into shared yet separate accommodation with Symons.

41 John Butler Yeats to Lily, 20 September 1896. *BP Letters*.

42 John Butler Yeats to Lily, 16 July 1896.

43 It was a rule of the company, the shares in which were held by members of the family, that they could only be sold within the family.

44 Lily's diary records, 15 April: 'Willie's "Secret Rose" out last week & Jack off to his castle to work for his exhibition in the autumn'.

CHAPTER SIX

1 *The Critic*, December 1897.

2 *The Daily Chronicle*, December 1897.

3 *The Dublin Telegraph*, December 1897.

4 *The Morning Post*, December 1897.

5 *The Admiralty and Horse Gazette*, December 1897.

6 *The Illustrated London News*, December 1897.

7 *The Globe*, December 1897.

8 *The Sun*, December 1897.

9 *The World*, December 1897.

10 *The Birmingham Gazette*, December 1897.

11 I am indebted to Wendy Board, who lives near Snail's Castle, for this information. The window was subsequently removed.

12 Lady Isabella Augusta Gregory (1852–1932) writer and key figure in the foundation of the Irish Literary Revival. She befriended Jack early in his career, and provided supportive and influential encouragement in his work, buying pictures and promoting him.

13 John Butler Yeats to Lady Gregory, 2 August 1898. Published in *BP Letters*.

14 Murphy suggests that Jack and Cottie visited Coole for the first time in 1898, *Secrets*, p. 285, but there is no evidence for this. They did certainly go the following April.

15 The plaque on the monument, placed there much later by the National Graves Commission, talks of the troops fighting for 'dear Old Ireland', and of Teeling and his soldiers sharing 'an honoured place with our patriot dead . . . like their successors, the Fenians, the Invincibles, the men and women of the Tan War and those who have died fighting British Oppression to this day, have given their lives for the Liberty of Ireland and the ideals of Irish Republicanism. "Ireland unfree shall never be at peace" P.H. Pearse.'

16 Earnan O'Malley (1898–1957) was studying medicine at the time of the Rising, in 1916, and fought in it. He was later wounded in the War of Independence, and later still, at the time of his re-arrest during the Civil War, received twenty-one bullet wounds and went on hunger strike. He recovered from near-paralysis, became a writer, and published, in 1936, one of the great accounts of the period, *On Another Man's Wound*.

17 Jack to O'Malley, 29 June 1939. Cormac O'Malley.

18 From *The Pall Mall Gazette*, February 1899. The review is signed 'R.A.M.S.'

19 Jack must have been particularly pleased to have Douglas Hyde's name mentioned. Hyde (1860–1949), later to be Ireland's first president, was, like Lady Gregory, one of the founding figures of the Irish Renaissance. 'An Chraoibhin' was his *nom de plume*, and it meant 'the delightful little branch'.

CHAPTER SEVEN

1 Jack to Lady Gregory, 14 March 1899. New York Public Library, The Berg Collection.

2 Jack to Lily, 31 March 1900. Yeats Archive. NLI P7545.

3 Edward Martyn (1859–1924) playwright, from a wealthy Catholic land-owning background in Galway county. He was, with Yeats and Moore, a founder of the Irish Literary Theatre.

4 Standish O'Grady (1846–1928) historian and novelist, called variously the Herodotus and 'prose Homer' of his country, and 'father of the Irish literary revival'. Sir Horace Plunkett (1854–1932) was the pioneer of agricultural co-operation, and ran the Department of Agriculture and Technical Instruction in Ireland, an important public service body governing economic and educational development at the beginning of the twentieth century.

5 Any cursory examination of the indices of the main histories of the period will show the enormous gap in attention between the two brothers. One particular and typical example is telling: In James G. Nelson's *Elkin Mathews – Publisher to Yeats* (meaning W.B. Yeats, of course), *Joyce, Pound*, Madison, Wisconsin, 1989, Jack is noted and covered, but without mention of *A Broadsheet*, and with no real attention to the fact that he knew Mathews better than any of the others, and worked for much longer, and more closely, with the London publisher than almost anyone else covered in Nelson's survey.

6 *Irish Independent*, 19 May 1899. Jack has annotated it: 'Mick Manning, I think', and has marked those passages which deal with the intense feeling and emotion.

7 George William Russell (1867–1935) is known also by his pseudonym, 'AE', which was given him unwittingly by a printer trying to decipher the latin pseudonym, 'Aeon', which he used on an early article. Poet, painter, mystic, and influential journalist and editor, he was perhaps the earliest critic fully to appreciate Jack's purpose in his first exhibitions.

8 *Lady Gregory's Diaries 1892–1902*, edited by James Pethica, Gerrards Cross 1996. 8 April 1899, p. 221.

9 Jack Yeats to Edward Martyn, 24 April 1899. Copy in JBY Archive. *The Countess Cathleen*, by W.B. Yeats, was first performed in the Antient Concert Rooms, Dublin, on May 8.

10 John Butler Yeats to Miss Marsh, 10 May 1899. *BP Letters*. Clare Marsh (1874–1923) came from county Meath, and was a painter who studied under John B. Yeats when he taught for a time at Miss Manning's studio in Merrion Row. She later visited him in New York, staying for six months. She was a close friend of Mary Swanzy, and they exhibited together.

11 Letter to Lady Gregory, 19 May 1899, from the *BP Letters*.

12 John Butler Yeats letter to Lady Gregory, 26 August 1899. *BP Letters*.

13 Letter to Lady Gregory, 27 May 1899. *BP Letters*.

14 Jack to J.C. Miles, 3 January 1903. I am indebted to Mr Tim Vignoles for the text of this and other Miles letters.

15 Jack to Lily, 23 June 1900. Yeats Archive.

16 4 January 1900, ALS (?), New York Public Library, The Berg Collection. Quoted in 'Away', by Deirdre Toomey, *Yeats Annual Number 10*, London 1993.

17 Letter to Isaac Yeats, 1 July 1915. Yeats Archive.

18 Jack to Susan Yeats, 3 December 1899. NLI P7545. Yeats Archive.

19 Ibid., 30 December (no year).

20 *Lady Gregory's Diaries, 1892–1902*, 18 February 1900, p. 241.

21 Ibid., 19 February 1900, p. 241.

22 Jack to Lily, 23 June 1900. Yeats Archive.

23 *Lady Gregory's Diaries 1892–1902*, p. 253, entry for 7 March 1900.

24 Jack to Lady Gregory, letters of 5 and 9 March 1900. New York Public Library, The Berg Collection (letter of 9 March was from Bedford Park). Jack's copies of Mark Twain titles are in Yeats Archive.

25 Jack to Lily, 14 April 1900. NLI P7545.

26 Jack to Lily, 6 April 1900. NLI P7545.

27 Ibid.

28 Ibid.

29 Jack to Lily, 3 June 1900. NLI P7545

30 Jack to Lily, April 1900. NLI P7545.

31 Quoted by Joseph Hone in *John BY Letters*, p. 63. Letter dated 1900 (during the June visit of Jack and Cottie).

32 Letters to Clare Marsh, July 1901, from *BP Letters*.

33 Letter to W.B. Yeats, 29 August 1901, from *BP Letters*.

34 Jack to Lily, June 1900. NLI P7545.

35 'My Miniature Theatre', essay published in *The Collected Plays of Jack B. Yeats*, edited by Robin Skelton, London 1971. 'A Penny Plain, Twopence Coloured', by Robert Louis Stevenson, is in *Memories and Portraits*.

36 It was from Pollock's Toy Theatres and Toy Museum in Monmouth Street, in the 1950s, that I last bought a collection of plays, settings and characters, together with an illustrated reprint of Stevenson's essay, and details of Miss Redington and her father, and of Benjamin Pollock, who died in 1937, and whose little shop in Hoxton Street was closed in 1944, after air-raid damage.

37 Letter to Willie, December 1899, from *BP Letters*.

38 Ibid.

39 See Skelton, *The Collected Plays of Jack B. Yeats*. Skelton, on grounds of quality, places *Esmeralda Grande* first in the order of composition, and writes, 'The story lacks that ironic power which is characteristic of the later plays.' The letters quoted here, from John Butler Yeats and to Lady Gregory, would suggest that *James Flaunty* preceded *Esmeralda Grande*.

40 Jack to Lady Gregory, 23 December 1899.

41 Jack to Thomas MacGreevy, 6 August 1940. TCD MS 10381/163.

42 'My Miniature Theatre', p. 18.

43 Ibid., p. 18.

44 Ibid.

45 From the *Strete Parish Magazine*, February 1901.

46 Charles Elkin Mathews (1851–1921) was a publisher chiefly famous for *The Yellow Book*, which first appeared in April 1894. See below, Chapter Nine.

47 Jack to Lily, 21 March 1902. NLI P7545.

48 Letter to Elkin Mathews, 20 March 1903. Since the copies were printed with uncut pages the work of full colouring would have been tedious. Jack developed a simple approach, using three

colours – Lake Carmine for Nance's skirt and Flaunty's breeches, a bluish green for the sea and some touches of burnt umber, he was able to meet his publisher's requirements.

49   Jack B. Yeats, *The Treasure of the Garden*, London 1903.
50   *Glasgow Herald*, 5 December 1903, unsigned review. Reviews of *The Scourge of the Gulph* also appeared in *The Manchester Guardian*, *The Daily News* and *The United Irishman*.
51   Robert Louis Stevenson, 'Penny Plain, Twopence Coloured'.
52   Skelton and McGuinness both write well of the plays, combining the enthusiasm they deserve with scholarship and insight.

CHAPTER EIGHT

1   Frederick York Powell (1850–1904) was Regius Professor of Modern History at Oxford and also president of the Irish Texts Society. He was an expert in folklore, particularly Icelandic sagas, and it was at this level that Willie's own friendship with Powell developed. With George Moore, York Powell collaborated in the catalogue for the joint exhibition of work by Nathaniel Hone and John Butler Yeats, organised by Sarah Purser and held in Dublin 23 October-3 November 1901.
2   *Four Years*, p. 6.
3   See Hilary Pyle, *The Different Worlds of Jack B. Yeats*, Dublin 1994, p. 297.
4   The book is one of the volumes in Jack and Cottie's library; stuck in the back is a note from Powell written on Christ Church, Oxford, writing paper in 1902, beginning 'Dear Mrs Jack', a term used by Jack himself, and widely at the time by others, thanking her for stencils.
5   Kuno Meyer (1858–1919) was a Celtic scholar, born in Hamburg, and devoted throughout his life to the study of early Irish literature. His version of 'Winter' was published in *Four Old Irish Songs of Summer and Winter*, 1903.
6   This ballad appeared in the *Broadsheet* for February 1902. Sarah Purser was then at 11 Harcourt Terrace, where she was still living in 1905.
7   Oliver Elton, 27 December 1901. This ballad, sent only days before the appearance of the first *Broadsheet*, may have been offered for publication. It appeared in *The Irish Homestead* December 1901. Jack did illustrations.
8   The exhibition ran from 24–29 October. No catalogue has survived, but Lady Gregory's son, Robert, bought *Honest Man*, and Jack Geoghegan, a friend from Dublin, bought *He's the Finest Horse from the Rosses to Rathmullen*.
9   *BP Letters*, 29 October 1900.
10   Frederick York Powell, letter to Oliver Elton, sent from Bedford Park, 12 July 1901. See *Frederick York Powell: a Life and Selection from his Letters and Occasional Writings*, edited by Oliver Elton, 2 Vols, Oxford 1906, Vol. I, p. 324.
11   Pamela Colman Smith (c.1878–1955) was originally from Jamaica, and then lived in New York, where she published her *Annancy Stories* in 1899. In that year she moved to London.
12   Thomas Nelson Page, *Introduction to Annancy Stories, By Pamela Colman Smith*. Published by R.H. Russell, New York 1899.
13   Pamela Colman Smith, *The Golden Vanity* and *The Green Bed, Words and Music of Two Old English Ballads, with Pictures by Pamela Colman Smith*. London (Elkin Mathews), 1903.
14   Jack to John Quinn, 15 December 1902. Foster-Murphy Collection, New York Public Library.

15   Lily to Ruth, 15 November 1937 (postscript added the following day). Yeats Archive.
16   'The Smashing of the Van' (also known as 'The Manchester Martyrs') referred to an incident in 1867, during the Fenian rising.
17   Douglas Hyde (1860–1949) was one of the founders, and the first president, of the Gaelic League, the cornerstone movement for the revival of the Irish language, and central to the Irish Literary Revival, as were his writings and translations.
18   *Love Songs of Connacht*, Collected, Edited and Translated by Douglas Hyde, London and Dublin, 1893. The publication of this book was a milestone in the Irish Literary Revival. Hyde's first meeting with Jack may have been in Dublin or at Coole in 1899. He was certainly at the opening of his Dublin exhibition in 1901.
19   From *New York American*, article by Henri Pene du Bois. The article refers to his visit 'last year', dating it 1905. JBY Archive.
20   From one of two letters from John Masefield in envelope dated 20 January 1931. JBY Archive.
21   Elton, *Frederick York Powell*. Letter of 30 June 1903, Vol. I, pp. 377–8.
22   Ibid. Letter to Jack, 22 January 1904, Vol. II, p. 419.
23   George Russell to Sarah Purser, 5 March 1902. Quoted in Alan Denson, *Letters from AE*, New York 1961. p. 39.
24   John Edward Masefield (1878–1967) poet, and later England's Poet Laureate. He was born in Herefordshire, and had an idyllic childhood before going to sea. He published more than fifty volumes of verse, twenty novels, eight plays and other prose collections. His first book, *Salt-Water Ballads*, contained one of the most famous lyrics in the English language, 'I must go down to the sea again'.
25   JBY Archive.
26   From *Adventures in Biography*, by Willard Connely, London 1956, cited in *WBY Letters III*, p. 54.
27   See *WBY Letters III*, p. 15.
28   John Masefield, *A Mainsail Haul*, London (Elkin Mathews) 1905.
29   Letter from Jack Yeats to John Masefield, 25 March 1906. Jack was at Snail's Castle, Masefield by then living in Greenwich, at 1 Diamond Crescent. The letter was illustrated with Wild West characters – another mutual enthusiasm. Sold by Christie's, in Dublin, 29 June 1994.
30   The exhibition was in Edinburgh. Jack wrote to Lady Gregory on 19 February 1907.
31   Jack Yeats, *A Little Fleet*, London 1909. The book, published by Elkin Mathews, has unnumbered pages. It contains a map, and drawings of each of the vessels in their fleet, drawn diagramatically, to instruct young people in making their own versions.
32   Ibid. Jack owned a longer, manuscript version of the poem which provided interesting additional information about the Monte, that she was a 'first-rate', that her skipper was none other than James Flaunty, and that she flew the Yankee flag. There was an extra verse:

> Our ribs are bent and stove in
> Our sightless eyes are dark
> But we remember rovin'
> Aboard the 'Monte' bark.

33   In 1903 John Masefield married Constance de la Cherois-Crommelin, from Cushendun in County Antrim. They had a son and a daughter, who was Jack's godchild.
34   Masefield to Constance, April 1903. Quoted in Constance

Babington Smith, *John Masefield: A Life*, Oxford 1978, pp. 79–80.

35 Ibid., pp. 80–1.

36 John Masefield, manuscript ballad in the JBY Archive. Perrins was the publican in Strete.

37 See letter, John Masefield to Jack Yeats, 16 May 1903. JBY Archive.

38 Ibid.

39 *The Speaker*, 16 May 1903, p. 163.

CHAPTER NINE

1 Nathaniel Hone (1831–1917) was a leading Irish landacape and seascape artist of the late nineteenth century. He came from a distinguished family of artists, dating back to the eighteenth century.

2 William Orpen (1878–1931) was a brilliant Irish genre and portrait painter who established a successful practise in London but maintained regular teaching and portrait commissions in Dublin until the First World War. He came from an Anglo-Irish family which had first settled in Kerry in the seventeenth century.

3 *The Figaro* (3) November 1901, item in Jack's cuttings book.

4 Evelyn Gleeson (1855–1944) was the daughter of a doctor, Edward Moloney Gleeson, who later founded the Athlone Woollen Mills. She became the beneficiary of a trust fund, giving her modest financial independence. But she also became responsible for her widowed sister, who had two small daughters. Her friend, Augustine Henry, helped to set in train the plans to establish a workshop in Dublin, motivated additionally by the idea that it would be healthier.

5 Augustine Henry (1857–1930) was a distinguished botanist, and has given his name to many plant species. But he trained as a medical doctor, and served in China, working for the Custom Service. His first collection of plants, numbering a thousand, and sent to Kew, was regarded as the most important to come out of that country. He met at Queen's College, in Galway, Evelyn Gleeson's brother, Jim, and later, after his first wife's death, befriended the family.

6 Jack to Lily, 10 May 1902. Yeats Archive.

7 See *Secrets*, pp. 84–144.

8 Dun Emer ('the castle of Emer') was named after Cuchullain's wife, who was interested in needlework and embroidery, rather in the folk or myth tradition of Ulysses' wife, Penelope.

9 John Quinn (1870–1924) was a New York lawyer of Irish descent, his father was from Limerick, his mother from Cork.

10 Reid, p. 3; but quoted originally in Joseph Hone, *W.B. Yeats: 1865–1939*, London 1962, p. 183.

11 Lolly to John Butler Yeats, 19 March 1921. Yeats Archive.

12 See Reid.

13 See Bruce Arnold, *The Scandal of Ulysses*, London and New York, 1991 and 1992.

14 Antoine Raftery (1784–1835) was blinded by smallpox, and lived out his life in the Gort region of County Galway. His most famous lyric begins: 'I am Raftery the poet/Full of hope and love . . .' and ends: 'Look at me, my face to (the?) wall/Making music for empty pockets.'

15 The *feis*, or festival, involved competitions in story-telling, dancing, singing and playing music, and went on all day. Lady Gregory and Douglas Hyde were judges.

16 John Quinn, 'Lady Gregory and the Abbey Theater', in *Outlook*, 16 December 1911, p. 16.

17 Ibid., pp. 917–18. See also Colin Smythe and Ann Saddlemyer (editors) *Lady Gregory Fifty Years After*, New Jersey 1987, where the occasion is described in Daniel J. Murphy's essay, 'Dear John Quinn'. Murphy implies that they were all asked to stay that night! It is inconceivable. Quinn, and the others, must have been invited earlier.

18 The Berg Collection, New York Public Library.

19 JBY Archive. The panorama, or 'panner-rammer-rammer' is $50 \times 3\frac{3}{4}$ inches, bound in stiff rough brown covers, which are decorated with a caricature of the king, and Jack's monogram. It is painted in watercolour and gouache.

20 Illustrated letter, 28 July 1903; Christie's Sale, Dublin, July 1994, Lot 86.

21 Richard 'Boss' Croker (1841–1922) the son of a British Army veterinary surgeon, was born in Clonakilty, County Cork, but emigrated to the United States as a child, and became a powerful, Tammany Hall boss, hence the name, succeeding 'Honest' John Kelly, and accumulating a large fortune. He was not accepted by the British racing establishment, and settled in Dublin, transforming a modest house in Sandyford into a mansion, with racing stables and its own racecourse. It is now the British Embassy residence.

22 Padraic Colum (1881–1972) an Irish poet, was an early friend and supporter of Jack. He wrote of him in American publications, see below. Walter Fitzgerald Starkie (1894–1976) was an author, and an authority on Romany gipsies. There were two Fay brothers involved in the Abbey, William George (1872–1947), character and comedy actor, and Frank (1870–1931), an accomplished speaker of verse.

23 Quinn was later to have a passionate love affair with Lady Gregory, but not until the spring of 1912.

24 Charlemont, looking even more gaunt than ever, still stands in bleak isolation, overlooking the upper reaches of what was once Sligo Harbour.

25 The lecture was given in Dublin, 25 March 1901.

26 Manuscript letter from the collection of Eleanor de Bretteville Reid (1909–93) sold at auction, San Francisco, 9 June 1994.

27 Ibid.

28 Catalogue for Reid sale, see note 26.

29 Postcard Lily (at Dundrum) to Jack (at Strete) 2 February 1904. Yeats Archive.

30 Reviewer in *The Irish Homestead*, 13 February 1904, p. 134, quoted in Paul Larmour, *The Arts and Crafts Movement in Ireland*, Belfast 1992, p. 154. A very detailed survey of the work is to be found in *Watercolours*, pp. 121–5. A lively contemporary account, by Edward Martyn, is to be found in his Introduction to *Robert Elliott, Art and Ireland*, Dublin (1903).

31 *WBY Letters III*, p. 410. 31 July 1903. Eric Maclagan (1979–1951) read classics at Christ Church, Oxford, and published poetry. He subsequently became an expert in ecclesiastical embroidery, and in 1905 joined the Victoria and Albert Museum department of textiles.

32 Letter to Lily, 19 July 1903. *WBY Letters III*, p. 401.

33 Ibid., p. 460, letter of 5 November 1903.

34 *The Irish Homestead*, 13 February 1904, p. 134. Quoted in Larmour, *Arts and Crafts*, p. 156.

35 Lily to John Butler Yeats, 27 July 1904. Quoted in Murphy, p. 267.

36 Letter from Lily to Sarah Purser, 5 January 1926. NLI, MS

10,201(23/3). The two which Jack admired were by George Russell.

37 Letter from Jack to Lady Gregory, 22 November 1903. Sold at Christie's, Dublin, 29 June 1994, Lot 88.

38 Ibid.

39 See Joan Coldwell, 'Pamela Colman Smith and the Yeats Family', in *The Canadian Journal of Irish Studies*, November 1977, Vol. 3, No. 2, pp. 30–1.

40 *The Gael*, April 1904, p. 151.

41 A Mrs Byrne bought Number 60 (*The Shores of the Lake*) (HP has *Edge of the Lake*), Mrs Jarvis Number 20 (*Old John*).

42 Pyle, p. 85.

43 Ibid., p. 86.

44 Reid, p. 21.

45 The Loan Collection of Pictures of the Irish School was held at the Guildhall Art Gallery, London, 31 May to 23 July 1904. A.G. Temple was the director of the art gallery and author of the catalogue. He gives a description of the event, the thirteenth such exhibition, all of which had had a very considerable impact on artists. Temple describes the background to the event in his book, *Guildhall Memories*, London 1918.

46 *The Daily News*, 31 May 1904.

47 Jack B. Yeats, 'The ABC of Piracy', unpublished, 1904. Miniature book, $2\frac{1}{2} \times 1\frac{3}{4}$ inches, mauve stiff covers. Yeats Archive.

48 Letter from Pamela Colman Smith to Cottie Yeats, 31 August 1904. The letter is signed 'Pixie'. JBY Archive.

49 John Masefield to J.M. Synge, 15 December 1904. Synge's reply was two days later. Both published in *Synge Letters*, pp. 96–7.

CHAPTER TEN

1 Jack B. Yeats, 'With Synge in Connemara', Dublin 1911. In *Connemara*.

2 George Moore, *Hail and Farewell, Volume III, Vale*, London 1914, pp. 197–8.

3 Letter from J.M. Synge to C.P. Scott, 22 May 1905. In the John Rylands University Library of Manchester. Muldoon was the parliamentary representative for the district.

4 Ibid.

5 Ibid.

6 C.P. Scott 'Extract of reply to Synge', 26 May 1905. MS 126/66 in Rylands Library, Manchester.

7 *The Synge Letters*, pp. 111–12. Letter sent from Crosthwaite Park and dated 30 May 1905. ('Piantic' is Synge's anglicisation of an Irish word for 'painful, *troublesome*, difficult', as in a problem, a bad road, a bad day; see Patrick S. Dinneen *Irish-English Dictionary*, first published 1904, the standard work.)

8 Arthur James Balfour (1848–1930) became Chief Secretary for Ireland in 1887. In the year following his setting up of the Congested Districts Board, 1891, he became leader in the Commons of the Conservative Party, and pushed through the Land Act in that year, which legislated for the Land Purchase Scheme. His brother, Gerald (1853–1945), was Chief Secretary for Ireland from 1895 to 1900, and extended the provisions of the legislation in a further Act of 1896. George Wyndham (1863–1913), who had been private secretary to A.J. Balfour in Ireland, became Chief Secretary in 1900. The work of these three men was highly significant in the relief of distress, and in the general reforms of the administration of the country.

9 Stephen McKenna (1872–1934) a journalist and a nationalist, was the friend of Maud Gonne, John O'Leary and John Synge, whom he met in Paris. His great work was the translation of the works of the neo-Platonist, Plotinus.

10 From 'Between the Bays of Carraroe', Synge's second article. See J.M. Synge, *Collected Works, Vol. II, Prose*, Edited by Alan Price, Gerrards Cross and Washington, 1966, pp. 293–4.

11 The order seems to have coincided with a catalogue of disasters for the company. There was a fire, and Mr Hill, the senior partner, met with a bad accident while motoring. Details were offered in a vivid postcard from Thomas Hill to Jack, showing the fire, with members of the Royal Irish Constabulary putting out the flames. Postcards, which at that time were just ten years in existence, were used widely, and to great effect, as a means of sending up to the minute news. Jack and other members of the family were frequent users.

12 Jack to John Masefield, 28 June 1905. From Christie's sale, Dublin, 29 June 1994, Lot 77. Jack wrote from Feeney's Hotel, in Swinford.

13 *Connemara*, p. 41.

14 *Connemara*, p. 40.

15 Ibid.

16 PCs. Jack to Cottie, June 1905. JBY Archive.

17 PC JY Hegarty to Jack, 22 December 1905, thanking him for the articles, and promising to preserve them. JBY Archive.

18 Jack to Synge, July 1905, written from Gurteen Dhas. TCD MS 4424–6/188.

19 *Synge Letters*, p. 116.

20 *Lady Gregory's Diaries, 1892–1902*, Edited by James Pethica, Oxford 1996, p. 268.

21 Jack to Synge, February 1906, written from Strete. TCD MS 4424–6/237.

22 Synge's original photographs, sent to Jack, are in the JBY Archive. For corroboration see J.M. Synge, *My Wallet of Photographs, The Photographs of J.M. Synge arranged and introduced by Lilo Stephens*, Dublin 1971.

23 Molly Allgood (1887–1952) was the leading Abbey Theatre actress of her time, playing Pegeen Mike in the first production of Synge's *The Playboy of the Western World*, in January 1907. She and Synge became engaged, but his death forestalled the marriage.

24 *Irish Society and Social Review*, 20 October 1906.

25 *Synge Letters*, p. 213.

26 Ibid. p. 215.

27 Synge to Molly, 25 April 1907. *Synge Letters*, p. 334.

28 Jack to Synge, 11 January 1907, from Strete. TCD MS 6225/1.

29 The line correctly reads 'drifts of chosen females standing in their shifts', but Willie Fay, playing Christy, and already noted by Synge for his poor memory for his lines, substituted the more directly identifiable 'Mayo girls'.

30 P.P. Howe, *J.M. Synge: A Critical Study*, London 1912, p. 75.

31 Jack to Synge, 19 February 1907, from Strete. TCD MS 4424–6/304.

32 Sara Allgood, unpublished autobiographical memoir (in the possession of her niece Mrs Morton Hague, Oakland California), NLI P.6486. Sara (1883–1950) was Molly's elder sister. She records the fact that Miss Horniman, who made possible the early life of the Abbey, gave a make-up box to every actor and actress, complete with the 'Rabbitfoot', 'which no actor would dream of being without in the theatre'.

33 Letter, Synge to Yeats, 12 May 1907. *Synge Letters*, p. 342.

34 Synge to Molly, *Letters to Molly: John Millington Synge to Maire*

O'Neill, edited by Ann Saddlemyer, the Belknap Press of Harvard University Press, Cambridge, Massachusetts, 1971, p. 183.

35 Synge to Molly, from Cashlanna Shelmiddy, in Strete, 3 June 1907. *Synge Letters*, p. 365. The letter was written at six in the morning.

36 John Butler Yeats to Willie, September 1907. Quoted in *John BY Letters*, p. 100.

37 Synge to Jack, undated, but late summer of 1907. JBY Archive.

38 Jack to Synge, from Strete, 14 April 1908. TCD MS 4424–6/ 427.

39 Ibid. No Synge verses appeared in *A Broadside*.

40 Ibid.

41 Jack to Synge, 23 August 1908. TCD MS 4424–6/46.

42 Jack to Synge, 22 September 1908. TCD MS 4424–6/472.

43 Synge to Molly, 24 September 1908. *Letters to Molly*, p. 282.

44 Jack to Synge, 6 December 1908. TCD MS 4424–6/493.

45 Jack to Quinn, 5 April 1909. Not in Reid; but see John Booth, *A Vision of Ireland: Jack B Yeats*, Nairn, Scotland, 1992, p. 69.

CHAPTER ELEVEN

1 Letter to Quinn, 16 September 1907. New York Public Library, The Berg Collection. Quoted in Pyle, p. 91.

2 Alan Denson, letter to the author, September 1994, recalling a conversation with Yeats in the early 1950s.

3 William Orpen, *Stories of Old Ireland and Myself*, London 1924.

4 See above, Chapter 10.

5 Letter to Quinn, see above, n. 1, Pyle, p. 91.

6 Isaac Yeats to Cottie, 10 January 1905. JBY Archive. The letter is written on the headed notepaper of the Dublin Artisans Dwelling Company. Isaac Yeats (1848–1930) was its secretary. He was the younger brother of John Butler Yeats, and a graduate of Dublin University.

7 Isaac Yeats to Cottie, 23 November 1903. JBY Archive.

8 Jack to Harvey, 16 November 1904. Harvey Family Collection.

9 Jack to Harvey, n.d. Harvey Family Collection.

10 Jack to Arnold Harvey, 10 January 1904. Harvey Family Collection.

11 Ibid.

12 Jack to Arnold Harvey, n.d. Harvey Family Collection.

13 Ibid.

14 Masefield to Jack, 25 December 1907. The card was written from New College Cloisters, Oxford, though Masefield was then living in Maida Hill West, and gives his London address as well.

15 *Irish Truth*, October 1906.

16 John Butler Yeats to Lily, 25 August 1909, quoted in Murphy, p. 348.

17 Willie to Lady Gregory, 24 November 1905. See Foster p. 326.

18 For a brief account of this, and of some of Robert Gregory's other theatre designs, see *Stage Design at the Abbey Theatre*, catalogue for an exhibition in the Peacock Theatre, July 1967.

19 Jack to Lady Gregory, 11 October 1906. Christie's Sale, Dublin, 29 June 1994.

20 This was at the February 1905 group exhibition in Baillie's Gallery, in Bayswater. Jack showed with three other artists. See *Lady Gregory Fifty Years After*, edited by A. Saddlemyer and C. Smythe, New Jersey 1987, p. 365.

21 Lily to John Butler Yeats, 2 November 1909. Quoted in Murphy, p. 362.

22 *The Irish Times*, 5 September 1903. The cutting is in the artist's own scrapbook (Yeats Archive), and the underlining is his own in this and following quotations.

23 *Dublin Leader*, 5 September 1903. Robert Elliott (1863–1910) was a trenchant and outspoken art critic who earlier that year had been involved in a lengthy controversy with John Butler Yeats, whom he accurately criticised for his 'artistic hermetics'. He disapproved of the 'artist in isolation' theory, and described John Butler Yeats as 'uncertain . . . he seems to have lost himself . . . artists like Mr Yeats gradually become involved in a kind of maze, where the unending walls are shadowy portraits of the painters they admire.' See *WBY Letters III*, p. 349.

24 *United Irishman*, September 1903. Seamus O'Sullivan is identified by Jack in a manuscript note beside the review.

25 *The Celt*, September 1903.

26 Scrapbook I. Robert Gregory owned *The Rolling Donkey*.

27 *The Irish Times*, 11 May 1907.

28 Both comments in *The Irish Times* review of the 1905 exhibition.

29 From a typescript, unidentified. Yeats Archive.

30 The 1908 exhibition was entitled 'Pictures of Life in the West of Ireland' and was held at Walker's Art Gallery, in Bond Street, from 3 to 29 February. It was his only solo show that year, and indeed the only showing of his work in any exhibition.

31 *Court Circular*, February 1908.

32 *Pall Mall Gazette*, February 1908.

33 *Irish Independent*, 11 May 1909. The article was illustrated by four drawings, two of them illustrations for *The Aran Islands*, *An Island Man*, and *Carrying Seaweed for Kelp*. The other two were *The Jockey* and *The Tinker*, both mentioned favourably by the writer.

34 Quoted in Lewis, p. 83.

35 Lily to John Butler Yeats, 7 December 1910. Lewis, p. 94.

36 Constance de Markievicz, 'Developing New School of Irish Art', *The Gaelic American*, New York, 1909.

37 Pyle, p. 106.

38 Ibid., p. 105.

39 Jack to Quinn, 16 September 1907. New York Public Library, The Berg Collection.

40 Hilary Pyle clearly divides his life as an artist into three periods: 1888–97, black-and-white illustrations, pen and ink; 1897–1909, watercolour sketches and paintings; 1909–55, oil paintings. And she reinforces the division between the first two periods with two separate books, one on drawings, pastels and watercolours, the other on cartoons and illustrations. It creates a slightly artificial view of the artist progressing through sections of his life.

41 *The Fancy*, by John Hamilton Reynolds, Elkin Mathews, n.d. (1905). With a Prefatory Memoir and Notes by John Masefield, and Thirteen Illustrations by Jack B. Yeats. *The Fancy* was first published in 1820, over the pseudonym, Peter Corcoran.

42 Rob Mee, 'Heavy Mob Rumble Back to Britain', *The Independent*, 24 September 1994.

43 The next world heavyweight fight was Georges Carpentier against Gunboat Smith, at Olympia, 16 July 1914. It is not certain that Jack attended, but he did keep a souvenir programme of the event. JBY Archive.

44 Walter Sickert, 'Mr Burrell's Collection at the Tate', the second of two articles which appeared in *The Southport Visitor* on 19 April 1924. Republished as 'Manet, Boudin and Monticelli' in *A Free House! Or the Artist as Craftsman, Being the Writings of Walter Richard Sickert*, edited by Osbert Sitwell, London 1947, p. 47.

45 Pyle, pp. 98–9.

46 *Stephen Spender, Journals, 1939–1983*, London 1985, pp. 103–5.

The visit, which coincided with a visit to Jack Yeats (see Chapter 22) was on 13 March 1950.

47 Ibid.

48 John Butler Yeats to Rosa Butt, 4 December 1907. Bodleian Library.

49 George Russell to John Quinn, 1 October 1908. See *Letters from AE*, edited by Alan Denson, London 1961, p. 65.

CHATPER TWELVE

1 Letter to Lady Gregory, 8 February 1904. *WBY Letters III*, p. 547.

2 *JBY Letters*, p. 75.

3 John Butler Yeats to Cottie, from The Studio, St Stephen's Green, Dublin, 19 November 1906. Yeats Archive.

4 The enterprise outlasted its founder, who died in her house, Dun Emer, in Dundrum, in May 1944. Even then, her niece, Katherine MacCormack, continued with the enterprise, and was able to write in 1953 of more than half a century of the 'vision and self-sacrificing love for Ireland' which had inspired her aunt. See Liam Miller, *The Dun Emer Press, later the Cuala Press*, Dublin 1973, p. 54.

5 Hilary Pyle, *The Different Worlds of Jack B Yeats*, Dublin 1994, provides an invaluable detailed summary of the printed work.

6 Hilary Pyle, *Cartoons and Illustrations*, Dublin 1994, p. 41.

7 *A Broadside* was folio in format, the page size 11 × 7½ inches. It was printed on cartridge paper made at Saggart Mill, in County Dublin, west of the city. This mill made the special paper used by Cuala for books and prints, but the quality and weight of the paper for *A Broadside* is different. The first issue was published by Dun Emer, the other eighty-three by Cuala. It was sold by annual subscription of twelve shillings. Blue portfolios, decorated with a small coloured print of a pirate with a mandolin, drawn by Jack, were issued to contain the parts.

8 Much later, in a Cuala prospectus for January 1918, after *A Broadside* had ceased publication, the drawings were on offer, from Jack's own home, at five and ten guineas each.

9 Francis MacNamara to Jack, postcard, 8 December 1909. Yeats Archive. MacNamara's daughter, Caitlin, married Dylan Thomas.

10 See Murphy, p. 183.

11 *Secrets*, p. 398.

12 Letter to Lady Gregory, 28 September 1910. Wade, p. 552.

13 See *Watercolours*, p. 166, No. 708. 'Portrait of William Pollexfen'.

14 John Butler Yeats to Jack, 3 November 1909. JBY Archive. He was staying at 317, West 29th Street.

15 His Dublin solo exhibitions were in the Leinster Hall in 1909 and 1910. (When he next had a Dublin show, in 1914, it was in the Mills Hall.) His London solo exhibitions were at the Walker Art Gallery in 1908, and then not until 1912. The group shows were: Dublin – Aonach (1909) and then the RHA from 1911; Belfast – Belfast Art Society, 28th Annual Show (1909), Industrial association (1911); London – Allied Artists at the Albert Hall (1909), the Whitechapel Art Gallery, Shakespearean Memorial Theatrical Exhibition, and Allied Artists (1910), and Allied Artists again (1911); New York – Macbeth Gallery, Group Exhibition. The Macbeth Gallery was run by Jack's agent, who was also Pamela Colman Smith's agent.

16 Pyle, p. 106.

17 Jack to Quinn, 21 May 1909, New York Public Library, Berg Collection, quoted in Pyle.

18 Con Curran, 'The Yeats Exhibition', *The Capuchin Annual*, Dublin 1945, p. 105.

19 Jack to William Macbeth, November 1910. Quoted in Pyle, p. 106.

20 Census, 15 April 1911, Form Number 13, Public Records Office, Dublin. Much has been made of the difference in age, with as much as eight years mentioned.

21 Page L. Dickinson, *The Dublin of Yesterday*, London 1929, pp. 65–6.

22 John Butler Yeats to Jack, 30 April 1912. JBY Archive.

23 Jack to Quinn, quoted in John Booth, *Jack B. Yeats*, Nairn, Scotland, 1993, p. 76.

24 Postcard. 9 June 1911.

25 George Russell to Quinn, 13 February 1911. See *Letters of AE*, edited by Alan Denson, Abelard Schuman (?), 1961, p. 73.

26 I am indebted to Harry McCarthy for these and other details of railway services used in the book.

27 Patricia Boylan, *All Cultivated People*, Gerrards Cross 1988, pp. 84–5.

28 See, *I Call to the Eye of the Mind: A Memoir*, by Sara Hyland, edited by Maureen Murphy, Dublin 1996, p. 87.

29 Ibid., p. 87.

30 Ibid., p. 126.

31 Ibid.

32 Ernest Marriott, *Jack B Yeats His Pictorial and Dramatic Art*, London (Elkin Mathews) 1911.

33 Ibid., p. 14.

34 Ibid., pp. 12–13. This accurately reflects the artist's output. Hilary Pyle records more than 160 sketchbooks up to and including 1911, and she makes the point that he both sold and gave away sketchbooks, many of which have not been traced.

35 Ibid., p. 13.

36 Ibid.

37 Jack to MacGreevy, 6 August 1940. TCD MS 10381/163.

38 Edward Gordon Craig (1872–1966) was the son of the architect, E.W. Godwin and the actress, Ellen Terry, inheriting great skills as an artist from the former, and his love of theatre from his mother. He designed, edited and illustrated *The Mask*, as well as writing extensively for it.

39 Edward Gordon Craig to Jack, 12 March 1912. Craig wrote from Rue de Rivoli, in Paris, where he later moved from Florence.

40 Craig to Jack, 22 March 1912. JBY Archive.

41 Allen Carric, '*Captain Jack B. Yeats: A Pirate of the Old School*', *The Mask*, July 1912, p. 45. Allen Carric was Edward Gordon Craig's son.

42 John Butler Yeats to Jack, 30 April 1912. JBY Archive.

43 G.A. Birmingham, *Irishmen All*, London 1913. James Owen Hannay (1865–1950) was educated at Haileybury and Trinity College, Dublin. He entered the Church, using the pseudonym for his writings, which became so popular from 1908 onward that he produced a 'G.A. Birmingham' novel almost every year. He was rector of Westport, County Mayo, from 1892 until 1913, when a play based on one of his novels caused riots in the town, and a boycott on him as rector, when his authorship was identified. He then left Ireland. The book was published in October.

44 John Butler Yeats to Jack, 4 December 1913. JBY Archive.

45 Ibid., 5 February 1913. JBY Archive.

46 Willie to Lady Gregory, 28 January 1911, Berg Collection, New York Public Library.

47 Jame Owen Hannay to Jack, 15 September 1913. JBY Archive.
48 Con Curran, 'The Yeats Exhibition', *Capuchin Annual* for 1945, p. 105. He was referring to 'early' in the context of the 1945 exhibition, which showed oil paintings from 1910 on.
49 Walter Kuhn (1877–1949), an essentially conservative painter, though much influenced by the Fauves; Arthur Bowen Davies (1862–1928), a man of wide cultural interests, and great enthusiasm, who became the main moving spirit behind the Armory Show; Robert Henri (1865–1929) was a pupil of Thomas Eakins and a member of The Eight, a group of painters who exhibited together in 1908 and were opposed to the National Academy of Design. One of the group, John Sloan, was a friend of John Butler Yeats.
50 Quinn to Jack, 17 January 1913. Quoted in Reid, p. 142.
51 Reid, p. 151.
52 Jack to Quinn, 15 December 1913. Quoted in Reid, p. 151.
53 Star newspaper, 16 July 1912, article by A.J. Findberg entitled '*Art and Artist Life in the West of Ireland*'. The other works shown by Jack in the Armory Show were *The Political Meeting*, *A Stevedore*, *The Barrel Man*, *Strand Races*, and *The Last Corinthian*.
54 James White, Introduction, *Jack B. Yeats. A Centenary Catalogue*, National Gallery of Ireland, Dublin, 1971.
55 Murphy, pp. 414, 417–18.
56 *Irish Society*, 28 February 1914. JBY Archive.
57 *Christian Science Monitor*, 24 February 1914.
58 *Pall Mall Gazette*, 'An Irish "Impressionist"', late 1914, n.d. JBY Archive.
59 *Irish Society*, 28 February 1914.
60 Padraic Colum, 'Some Irish Characteristics – All Racy of the Soil', *Dublin Evening Mail*, 24 February 1914.
61 *The New Weekly*, n.d.
62 'Modern Irish Art' (? By Edward Storen), *The New Witness*, 7 July 1914.
63 Joan Hardwick, *The Yeats Sisters*, London 1996, pp. 183–4.

CHAPTER THIRTEEN

1 Padraic Colum, 'The Art of Jack B. Yeats'. *T.P.'s Weekly*, 18 July 1914.
2 Anne Yeats is sceptical as to whether anything regular was paid by her two aunts to Jack. They had the use of his work for reproductions; he retained copyright, and sold, when he could, the originals.
3 Pyle, pp. 118–19.
4 Ibid., 119–20.
5 Lily to John Butler Yeats, 5 June 1916. (Quoted in Lewis, pp. 137–8.) This would put it back to September 1915.
6 See above, p. 170.
7 Alfred Pollexfen to Cottie, 7 November 1915. Alfred's younger sister had married Robert Gorman, a miller, who notwithstanding 'bad arteries', had been in the habit of 'getting up early and going to fairs'. His death had been sudden.
8 John Butler Yeats to Jack, 16 December 1915. JBY Archive.
9 1 March 1916. JBY Archive.
10 John Butler Yeats to Jack, 7 April 1916. JBY Archive.
11 John Butler Yeats to Cottie, 11 May 1916. JBY Archive.
12 W.S. Ross to Cottie, 3 June 1916, from Clonsilla, Greystones. JBY Archive.
13 John Butler Yeats to Willie, 2 April 1915. JBY Archive.

14 John Butler Yeats to Jack, 16 June 1915. JBY Archive.
15 Willie to Cottie, 22 July 1916. He was then living at Stone Cottage, on the edge of the New Forest, in Sussex. The letter is typed, on plain copy paper.
16 John Butler Yeats to Lily, 2 May 1916. JBY Archive.
17 Lily to Quinn, 16 March 1916. Berg Collection, New York Public Library.
18 Lily to Quinn, 28 March 1916. Berg Collection, New York Public Library.
19 Lily's diary. JBY Archive.
20 John Butler Yeats to Lolly, 25 March 1916. NLI MS31,108 (19).
21 John Butler Yeats to Lily, 28 March 1916. NLI MS31,108 (19).
22 John Butler Yeats to Lily, 12 May 1916. NLI MS31,108 (19).
23 Lady Gregory to Jack, undated letter. JBY Archive.
24 Lily to Thomas Bodkin, 18 August 1916. Quoted in Pyle, p. 120.
25 John Butler Yeats to Jack, 19 August 1916. Yeats Archive, quoted in *John BY Letters*, pp. 228–9.
26 1932 press cutting, from an unidentified American publication. Scrapbooks, JBY Archive.
27 Sketchbook No. 189. JBY Archive.
28 *A Broadside*, February 1915, *The Scene of a Tragedy*. The drawing shows a man, a woman and a small boy looking at two crosses with 'R.I.P.' marked on a junk-shop wall.
29 Pyle, pp. 117, 119. *Bachelor's Walk, In Memory*, formerly private collection, now missing.
30 T.G. Rosenthal, *The Art of Jack B. Yeats*, London 1993, p. 26.
31 John Booth, *A Vision of Ireland: Jack B. Yeats*, Nairn, Scotland, p. 80.
32 Trevor Allen, 'A Talk with Jack Yeats: Art and Drama Under Sinn Fein,' *Westminster Gazette*, 21 December 1921.
33 See Chapter Fourteen for an examination of Jack's lecture, *Modern Aspects of Irish Art*, in which his own form of 'nationalism' is given some verbal expression, and is discussed.
34 MacGreevy, p. 26.
35 Jack to MacGreevy, 6 January 1938. TCD MS 10381/151.
36 John Butler Yeats to Jack, 1 September 1914. JBY Archive.
37 John Butler Yeats to Jack, 17 September 1914. JBY Archive.
38 Lily to Quinn, 10 December 1917. Quoted in Murphy, p. 474.
39 Lily to Quinn, 4 May 1915. Quoted in Reid, p. 217.
40 Quinn to Jack, 31 December 1914. JBY Archive.
41 Isaac Yeats (?) etc.
42 Terence de Vere White, *A Fretful Midge*, London 1957, p. 117.
43 Colum to Jack, 26 June 1918. Berg Collection New York Public Library quoted in Pyle, p. 121. The stretch of the Grand Canal linking the estuary of the River Liffey with the main water route across Ireland to the River Shannon, is half a mile's distance from Jack's new home in Donnybrook.
44 Quinn to Jack, 14 October 1917. JBY Archive.
45 Quinn to Jack, 29 January 1918. The letter was much read. Unlike Jack's correspondence generally, which has been little-read by scholars, this letter is folded, creased, torn, pasted together, and is possibly missing certain parts of the text, which may deal with illness. No letters from Quinn followed for a period of four years.
46 Lolly to John Butler Yeats, 13 March 1918. Quoted in Lewis, pp. 142–3.
47 *Sailing, Sailing Swiftly*, London 1933, p. 143.
48 John Butler Yeats to Jack, 14 August 1915. JBY Archive.

CHAPTER FOURTEEN

1 Jack to John Butler Yeats, 1921. Yeats Archive.
2 Boylan, p. 130.
3 A peach-coloured, embroidered holder is in the Cuala Box, JBY Archive, with an embroidered view signed in the texture by Lily.
4 Lolly to John Butler Yeats, 12 August 1921. NLI P7545.
5 Lolly to John Butler Yeats, 7 July 1921.
6 Maurice Craig remembers the drink as something called 'Mountain Malaga'; it came from Kelly's in Upper O'Connell Street.
7 Joseph Holloway (1861–1944). The Holloway Diaries are in NLI, containing a very large amount of unedited material.
8 See *Lady Gregory Fifty Years After*, edited by Ann Saddlemyer and Colin Smythe, p. 25. The description is quoted from *The Spendid Years*, by Maire nic Shiubhlaigh, Dublin 1955.
9 See Gregory Journals, entries for 18 March 1921, 9 March 1924, 16 April 1924.
10 In fact he did not become an honorary member until 1941.
11 Boylan, p. 130.
12 *The Funeral of Harry Boland* was one exception; he did sketches of the funeral of O'Donovan Rossa, but no painting.
13 William Nicholas Keogh (1817–78) was a judge, born in Galway, whose successful career as a barrister led to his appointment, successively, as solicitor general, attorney general and then a judge. He tried the Fenian leaders in 1865, and later was much vilified, becoming a symbol of treachery. He took his own life. John Sadleir (1814–56) was a lawyer, banker and politician, later in life engaging in serious frauds which, when discovered, led to his suicide. Mr Merdle, in *Little Dorrit*, by Charles Dickens, is modelled on him.
14 The information comes from Hilary Pyle's papers, quoted in Purser, but not used by her.
15 'A Talk with Jack Yeats – Art and Drama under Sinn Fein' by Trevor Allen *Westminster Gazette*, 31 December 1921.
16 'The Blot – Loop Line Bridge Atrocity – Jack B. Yeats's Views – Hope Structure Itself May be Removed.' *Evening Telegraph* (Dublin) 23 February 1921.
17 See Hilary Pyle, *The Different Worlds of Jack B Yeats*, Dublin 1994, p. 313.
18 'Mr Jack B. Yeats: His Grandiose Ideas Of a Gallery in Merrion Square', *Freeman's Journal*, 7 October 1922.
19 Jack to Quinn, 17 November 1920. Quoted in Reid.
20 Ibid.
21 John Butler Yeats to Jack, 9 December 1919. JBY Archive.
22 Jack to Bodkin, 16 April 1921. TCD MS 6946/1358.
23 'Mr Jack B. Yeats and His Art', in *The Daily Express* (Dublin) 12 October 1919. The two-column article is signed 'R.S.W.'
24 In 1918 he also exhibited in New York, in a group show at the Penguin Club. In 1919 he had solo shows in Dublin and London, selling well in Dublin (13 out of 41) and less well in London (4 out of 29). 1920 saw the first exhibition of the Dublin Painters, at the gallery which his father had occupied, in St Stephen's Green, as well as a solo show. At solo exhibitions during the next three years he exhibited a total of 69 oil paintings.
25 *The Manchester Guardian*, 12 May 1919.
26 Darrell Figgis, 'Jack Yeats' Pictures', *The Nationalist*, 3 May 1919.
27 *The Daily News*, 7 June 1919.
28 *The Observer*, 1919 (no month given).
29 R.W. Fletcher, 'Art without an "ism"', *Everyman*, 7 June 1919.
30 *Ireland's Own*, 2 March 1921.
31 Jack B. Yeats, *Modern Aspects of Irish Art*, Dublin 1922. The published lecture became one of a series.
32 *Freeman's Journal,* 18 January 1922.
33 *Modern Aspects*, p. 4.
34 Ibid.
35 Ibid., p. 5.
36 Ibid., p. 2.
37 Ibid., p. 3.
38 Ibid.
39 Ibid.
40 Ibid., pp. 5–6.
41 John Butler Yeats to Jack, 26 July 1921. JBY Archive.
42 John Butler Yeats to Jack, 15 October 1921. JBY Archive.
43 John Butler Yeats to Jack, 8 December 1921. JBY Archive.
44 Quinn to Willie, 28 November 1921. Yeats Archive.
45 Jack to Lily, 4 February 1922 (actually Jack wrote 1921). Yeats Archive.
46 Jack to Quinn, 21 February 1922. Quoted in Reid.
47 Quinn to Jack, 4 May 1922. JBY Archive.
48 Lolly to John Butler Yeats, 24 May 1921, NLI P7545.
49 Lolly to John Butler Yeats, 16 February 1921, NLI P7545.

CHAPTER FIFTEEN

1 Anne Yeats, the painter's niece, growing up in the period between the two World Wars, recalls how vague the notion of Uncle Jack was; he did not impinge on their lives; he did not visit, was not invited to meals or parties, and only really came to know her and her brother, Michael, after Willie's death.
2 Asa Briggs, *The Nobel Century*, London 1991, p. 33. The description of the poetry is from the citation.
3 Jack to Quinn, 18 December 1923. Quoted in Reid, p. 585.
4 See *Zeal of the Convert*, by Burke Wilkinson, Gerrards Cross 1978.
5 Lily's diary. Yeats Archive.
6 Gregory Journals, pp. 470–1.
7 Ibid., p. 476, 16 September 1923.
8 S.B. Kennedy, *Irish Art and Modernism 1880–1950*, Belfast 1991. p. 20. The book was published to coincide with an exhibition with the same title, held in the Hugh Lane Gallery in Dublin (20 September to 10 November 1991), and at the Ulster Museum (22 November 1991–26 January 1992).
9 Other founder members, in addition to Jack, were E.M. O'Rourke Dickey, Soumarokov Elston, Letitia Hamilton, Clare Marsh, Sir Frederick Moore, James Sleator, Mary Swanzy and James Willcox. Three of these, Willcox, Moore and Elston, left the society after the first show, and they were replaced by Mainie Jellett, Charles Lamb and Harry Clarke, all of whom strengthened its standing, and increased the experimental character and the breadth of styles. The Society of Dublin Painters was modelled on the Fitzroy Street Group in London, following its rules. It had its own gallery at 7 St Stephen's Green, with which Jack was very familiar, since it had been his father's studio from the death in 1903 of Walter Osborne, another of the artists who had occupied it.
10 Conversation with Brian O'Doherty, and in letter to the author, 18 October 1995.
11 Jack to Thomas Bodkin, 11 May 1921. TCD MS 6946/1370.
12 See Boylan, p. 131. She dates the meeting 'between the years 1919 and 1924'. It is disputed, however, by Kokoschka's widow, Olda Kokoschka, who wrote to Theo Snoddy, in 1973: 'My

husband met Jack B. Yeats through Mr V. Waddington in Dublin around 1950–1. I cannot tell you exactly. We were at his studio and saw many paintings. Yeats was a very correct, charming person. I remember that we went to a regatta together. I think my husband had great sympathy for his work and for the man himself. We read somewhere that Yeats was an influence on Kokoschka. That is not true and would be hardly possible as Kokoschka hardly knew his work before we came to London, just before the war broke out.' See Theo Snoddy, *Dictionary of Irish Artists: Twentieth Century*, Dublin 1996, p. 567. Quite apart from the tenuous evidence of the Dresden meeting, Kokoschka visited Dublin and the west of Ireland, and painted in these places, as well as being entertained at the United Arts Club.

13 Werner Haftmann, *Painting in the Twentieth Century*, 2 Vols, London 1961 (Revised Edition 1965).

14 Oskar Kokoschka, 'How I See Myself', essay of 1936, reprinted in *Kokoschka, Early Drawings and Watercolours*, London 1985, p. 23.

15 See n. 12 above, p. 567.

16 Boylan, p. 53.

17 Jack to MacGreevy, 8 December 1925. TCD MS 8105/1–34. MacGreevy had asked him whether he had seen Picasso's Three Cornered Hat scenes.

18 The book is inscribed, 'With affection and good wishes for his birthday and all that follows it, from A Gregory, Coole, August 29, 1929'.

19 Boylan, pp. 130–2.

20 Jack to MacGreevy, 21 March 1919. TCD MS 10381/102.

21 MacGreevy, 'Picasso, Maimie (sic) Jellett and Dublin Criticism', in *The Klaxon*, October 1923.

22 *Irish Statesman*, 27 September 1923.

23 Ibid., 18 October 1923.

24 Ibid., 25 October 1923.

25 Jack to MacGreevy, 22 December 1926. TCD MS 8105/1–34.

26 Jack to Thomas Bodkin, 15 May 1919. TCD MS 6946/1355.

27 Jack to Thomas Bodkin, 31 March 1924. TCD MS 6946/1359.

28 James Sullivan Starkey (1879–1958) acted in Willie's *On Baile's Strand*, on the Abbey Theatre's opening night, and reviewed Jack's 1903 exhibition in Dublin, for Arthur Griffith's *The United Irishman*. He founded *The Dublin Magazine* in 1923, and edited it until 1958.

29 *The Dublin Magazine*, August 1923, Vol. I, No. 1. Estella Solomons (1882–1968) trained in the RHA schools under Walter Osborne, then at the Metropolitan School of Art, and later in London with Orpen and in Paris. She was a member of the revolutionary women's movement, Cumann na mBan, was involved in the Rising, and then took the anti-Treaty side, hiding men on the run in her studio.

30 Jack to Estella Solomons, 19 April 1922. TCD MS 4632/522.

31 Jack to James Starkey, 9 May 1923. TCD MS 4632/545.

32 Jack to Starkey, 6 June 1923. TCD MS 4632/549.

33 Walter Sickert to Jack, no date, but c. 1924. JBY Archive.

34 *Cork Examiner*, 6 April 1925.

35 *The Sunday Independent*, 17 May 1925.

36 Unidentified, undated, Yeats Archive.

37 *The Referee*, 13 January 1924. Unsigned review. JBY Archive.

38 12 January and 6 January 1924, respectively. JBY Archive.

39 *Irish News*, 14 January 1924.

40 *The Irish Statesman*, 18 April 1925, p. 178.

41 Ibid.

42 Ibid.

43 Among the paints which were in Jack's paintbox at the end of his

life were the following: Naples Yellow, Chrome Yellow, Vandyke Brown, Mid-vermillion tint, Cadmium Yellow Deep, Prussian Blue, Lemon Yellow, Carmine Tint, Emerald Green, Burnt Sienna, Scarlet Vermillion, Raw Sienna.

44 Terence de Vere White, *A Fretful Midge*, London 1957, p. 116.

45 Ibid., pp. 111–12.

46 Earnan O'Malley, 'The Paintings of Jack B. Yeats', in *A Centenary Gathering*, edited and introduced by Roger McHugh, Dublin 1971. p. 68.

47 John Rothenstein, 'Visits to Jack Yeats', *New English Review*, July 1946, p. 43.

48 *Irish Weekly Times*, 12 March 1927.

49 *Birmingham Post*, 22 January 1924, of the Gieves Gallery exhibition in London.

50 *The Studio*, April 1925.

51 Jack to Charles Aitken, 30 April 1925. The correspondence, Jack's letters, fair-copies of what he sent, and Aitken's originals received, are in JBY Archive. The Tate Gallery does not have the correspondence in its Yeats archive.

52 Jack to Willie, 31 October 1925. JBY Archive.

53 Jack to Blakie Murdoch, 9 and 13 August 1927. TCD MS 10318/4–5.

54 *Athenaeum*, 23 April 1920, 'The Arts in Ireland'.

55 Gregory Journals, pp. 31–3.

56 Frank O'Connor (see Richard Ellmann, *James Joyce*, Oxford 1983 p. 702).

57 Ibid. Wade, p. 764 and Gregory Journals are additional sources for this remark. According to Pyle, neither of the paintings has been traced, though she illustrates a work sold at Slane Castle, by Sotheby's, in 1979 which might well be the second of the two named works, and was painted two years later. See her *Catalogue Raisonné*, nos. 325 and 386.

58 Ellmann, *Joyce*, reporting an interview in 1952 with Frank O'Connor.

59 Jack to MacGreevy, 4 April 1929. TCD MS 10381/105.

60 Jack to MacGreevy, 3 April 1929. TCD MS 10381/104.

61 Jack to MacGreevy, 11 May 1929. TCD MS 10381/107.

62 Gregory Journal, Vol. II, p. 408, 12 March 1929.

63 Ibid. 'Aircraftsman Shaw' was T.E. Lawrence (1888–1935) who changed his name to Shaw in 1927.

64 George Yeats to MacGreevy, 14 April 1926. TCD MS 8104/37.

65 T.W. Earp, in *The New Statesman*, 27 March 1928.

66 *Daily Sketch*, February 1929.

67 'Mr Jack B. Yeats and His Art', by 'R.S.W.' *The Daily Express* (Dublin) 12 October 1929. The interview and the essay resulting from it, were part of a series, 'Distinguished Irishmen – XXIII.'

CHAPTER SIXTEEN

1 James Stephens; interview with Fitzhugh L. Minnigerode, *The New York Times*, 22 June 1930.

2 Gregory Journals, Vol. II, p. 539. Monday 14 July 1930.

3 Gregory Journals, Vol. II 3 January 1931. The confusion of quotation-marks is Lady Gregory's.

4 Jack to MacGreevy, 13 March 1930. TCD MS 10381/108.

5 Readers are referred to Hilary Pyle's detailed catalogues for fuller information on Jack's yearly output.

6 Jack did cartoons for *Punch* from 1910 to 1941, and once in 1948. 'During the period when he worked solely as a black-and-white

artist, Yeats contributed to Punch only once' 9 May 1896, Pyle, p. 138.

7 Lily to Quinn, 5 April 1915. Berg Collection, New York Public Library.

8 Lily to Quinn, 10 December 1917.

9 Jack lived at 18 Fitzwilliam Square from 1929 until the final years of his life, which he increasingly spent in a nursing home. In 1932 Willie bought Riversdale, in Rathfarnham, on the Whitechurch Road, half a mile from the Yellow House, but was unable to move in directly, and rented a top-floor flat in the Solomons' house, 42 Fitzwilliam Square.

10 *Sligo*.

11 Ibid., p. 127.

12 There is clear evidence of this in the series of letters between himself and Ragg, of Routledge, who published his later books. See below, Chapters 17 and 18. All Ragg-Yeats correspondence is in the University of Reading Library.

13 Mary McCarthy, 'Novel, Tale and Romance', in *The New York Review of Books*, No. 30, 12 May 1983, pp. 49–54. It is quoted in McGuinness, p. 97.

14 *Sligo*, p. 15.

15 Ibid., p. 30.

16 Gregory Journals, Vol. II, p. 539. Monday 14 July 1930.

17 *Sunday Referee*, 7 July 1930.

18 Niall Montgomery to Robert O'Driscoll, 9 September 1970. Montgomery Family Collection.

19 Jack Yeats, 'Irish Authors: 36', in *Eason's Bulletin*, Dublin, 5 October 1948, p. 3.

20 *ATYA*, p. 5.

21 Notebook for *ATYA*. JBY Archive.

22 *Liverpool Post*, 25 June 1930. Article signed 'A.M.A.'

23 Purser, p. 128.

24 Ibid., p. 64.

25 Willie to Jack, 15 July 1930. The letter was sent from the flat on the top floor of 42 Fitzwilliam Square. In the move he had forgotten to write and thank his brother for the gift of the book.

26 Lady Gregory to Jack, 9 June 1930. JBY Archive.

27 Elsie Henry to Cottie, 29 June 1930. JBY Archive.

28 Sarah Purser to Jack, 9 June 1930. JBY Archive.

29 Masefield to Jack, 15 May 1930. JBY Archive. Yeats, of course, being Irish, could not have been appointed.

30 Masefield to Jack, mid-June, 1930. The letter refers to 'next Saturday, 14th' (of June).

31 Jack to MacGreevy, 13 March 1930. TCD MS 10381/108. The poem is entitled 'Cron Tráth na nDeithe', and appeared in *transition* on 18 November 1929.

32 MacGreevy to Jack, undated letter. Yeats Archive.

33 On later publication it appeared with the title translated into English. But the French version is the one given to Jack at the time.

34 Jack to MacGreevy, 26 December 1930. TCD MS 10381/113.

35 Jack to MacGreevy, 29 November 1930. TCD MS 10381/112.

36 Undated, but the book is dated 1931. TCD MS 10381/114.

37 Thomas McGreevy (the spelling is as published), *T.S. Eliot – A Study*, London 1931, p. 19. The book was published as part of a series called 'The Dolphin Books'.

38 MacGreevy to Jack, undated, but February–March 1930. JBY Archive.

39 MacGreevy to Jack, undated, but February–March 1930. JBY Archive.

40 Frances Beckett (1880–1951) was originally known as Fanny, but was named Cissie by her four brothers, the eldest of whom, William Frank, was Samuel Beckett's father. She studied at the Metropolitan, and then went to Paris, before exhibiting regularly with the RHA from 1901–8. To the dismay of her well-to-do family, she married, in 1908, the penniless son of a Jewish painter, William Abraham Sinclair, known as 'The Boss'. A succession of children interrupted her career as an artist.

41 Beckett to MacGreevy, TCD MS 10402.

42 Jack to MacGreevy, 29 November 1930. TCD MS 10381/112.

43 MacGreevy to Jack, 22 December 1930. Yeats Collection. Geoffrey Phibbs (1900–56) was a Sligo-born poet. His family came from Lisheen, on the southern side of Knocknarea. He was ensnared by a young woman, and in self-defence, partly on Frank O'Connor's advice, he married Norah McGuinness (1901–80) a Derry-born painter living in Dublin. The marriage had failed at this time, and Phibbs had fallen for Laura Riding, Robert Graves's mistress, who was the 'downtown jewess'.

44 P. Guggenheim, *Out of this Century: Confessions of an Art Addict*, London 1979, pp. 163–4.

45 JBY Archive. Jack's library formed part of the Anne Yeats bequest to the National Gallery of Ireland.

46 Beckett to MacGreevy, TCD MS 10402.

47 For a fuller account of *Le Kid* and *The Possessed* see Douglas McMillan and Martha Fehsenfeld, *Beckett in the Theatre*, London 1988, which contains the full text of *The Possessed*. It was however republished twenty years earlier in *T.C.D. A College Miscellany*, with an interesting note on Beckett, recalling a 'Valentine' offered to him in the edition of the magazine for 12 February 1931: 'An exhausted aesthete who all life's strange poisonous wines sipped, and found them rather tedious'.

48 Jack to MacGreevy, 14 July 1930. TCD MS 10381/111.

49 *The New Statesman*, 5 July 1930.

50 Jack to MacGreevy, 14 July 1930. TC MS 10381/111.

51 Jack to MacGreevy, 29 November 1930. TCD MS 10381/112.

52 Jack to Mrs E Dox Becker, 11 August 1930. TCD MS 8105/1–34. She sent him an intriguing little cutting from The *New York Times* of Sunday, July 27, which commented: 'Mr Yeats habitually paints from a mental condition in which a turn of the head or a gesture of the hand is remembered for the rest of his life . . .'

53 *Dublin Opinion*, May 1929, May 1930, June 1930.

54 Terence de Vere White, *A Fretful Midge*, London 1957, p. 116. His views are further expanded in an essay in *A Centenary Gathering*, edited by Roger McHugh, Dublin 1971.

55 Letter to Mrs Tulloch, 19 August 1927. Private Collection. It was not a snub to a stranger's request; Jack knew Mrs Tulloch well enough to accept, in the same letter, her invitation to supper the following Sunday evening.

56 *The Irish Tatler and Sketch*, May 1931.

57 *The Nation*, 2 May 1931.

58 Jack to MacGreevy, 26 December 1930. TCD MS 10381/113.

59 Lady Gregory wanted Gallagher's endorsement of the idea before she wrote giving her own views. She believed Jack would be excellent for the job. Kathleen O'Brennan was a journalist, and lived at 44 Oakley Road, Ranelagh. Gallagher had been editor of *An Phoblacht*, the revolutionary paper founded by Sinn Fein, and the voice of the Irish Republican Army.

60 National Library of Ireland, MS Department No: 21210.

61 *Secrets* gives details of the correspondence between Jack and Healy, p. 308.

62 *American*, 30 December 1932. Article was headed: 'Yeats tells on his Brother'. JBY Archive.

63 *New York Times*, 31 December 1932.

64 Introduction to the catalogue for Jack's exhibition at the Ferargil Galleries, New York, March 1932.

65 *Signe Toksvig's Irish Diaries 1927–1936*, edited by Lis Pihl, Dublin 1994. p. 314, entry for 17 April 1935. She was married to the novelist, Francis Hackett, and took an active part in the cultural life of Dublin during these years.

66 Ibid., p. 105. Entry for 30 April 1931.

67 For a detailed examination of the chronology of Jack's writing, the best guide is Purser. He suggests that *The Deathly Terrace*, though not published until after Jack's death, may have preceded *Sligo*, and was written in any case between 1929 and 1931. Similarly, he dates *The Careless Flower* to 1933, though it was not published until 1947, and *The Amaranthers* to 1933–5, published in 1936.

68 Lennox Robinson, 'A Year of Irish Fiction', in *The Bookman*, August 1934.

CHAPTER SEVENTEEN

1 T.M. Ragg to Jack, 8 January 1936. Routledge Archive at the University of Reading. I am indebted to Professor Jim Knowlson for drawing my attention to these letters. All Ragg-related material is at Reading.

2 Jack to Ragg, 11 January 1936.

3 13 and 23 January 1936.

4 23 January 1936.

5 Jack's theatre enthusiasms are hard to summarise, though many are evident in the large number of paintings with a theatrical theme. He admired Dion Bouccicault (*c.*1820–1890) the author of *The Shaughraun*, and painted a large 'memory' canvas celebrating the playwright; he thought *She Stoops to Conquer* by Oliver Goldsmith (1728–74) 'a drowsy old bore', and records having seen it 'not so very long ago'. He was at the first night (22 February 1926) of an Abbey Theatre production of the play, with Barry Fitzgerald as Tony Lumpkin ('a hobgoblin to me'), Eileen Crowe as Kate and Shelah Richards as her companion, Nevill.

6 In one of his sketchbooks Jack has a drawing of two shops, side by side, one with the name Dolan over the door, the other owned by Nolan.

7 Norah Hoult, *The New Statesman*, 26 August 1933.

8 Review in *The Liverpool Post*, signed 'C.V.C.' July 1933.

9 *The Oxford Times*, 4 August 1933. Review by Peter Quince.

10 Lily to Ruth, 19 March 1934. Yeats Archive.

11 Lily to Quinn, 28 March 1916. Berg Collection, New York Public Library.

12 Quoted by Terence de Vere White in 'The Personality of Jack B. Yeats,' in Roger McHugh, editor, *Jack B. Yeats, A Centenary Gathering*, Dublin 1971, p. 43.

13 Terence de Vere White interview with the author, January 1994.

14 'The Personality of Jack B. Yeats,' p. 43.

15 Padraic Colum, *The Big Tree of Bunlahy*, London 1933; Patricia Lynch, *A Turfcutter's Donkey*, London 1934. Jane Cunningham, writing of Patricia Lynch (1900–72) in Hogan's *Dictionary of Irish Literature*, London 1996, says: 'If one has any reservation about Lynch's underplayed, minor, but genuine talent, it would only be the mild surprise about the extraordinary amount of eating in her books. With Maura Laverty, she must be one of the most food-obsessed writers in all of Irish literature.' Jack's drawings do not reflect this, however.

16 I am indebted to Robert Hogan (editor of Joseph Holloway's *Abbey Theatre – A Selection from his unpublished Impressions of a Dublin Playgoer*, London and Amsterdam, 1967). The quotation comes from *Irish Theatre* (full). Vol. II, p. 44, and refers to Thursday, 20 June 1935. Frank Dalton was old enough to have acted with Dion Boucicault, who left Ireland for New York in 1872, when Dalton was 22.

17 Ibid., p. 44. 20 June 1935. Eileen was Holloway's niece, and lived at Number 30. Ellen was his maid-servant.

18 Katherine O'Brennan, 'Echoes of the Town', *Irish Press*, 29 March 1935.

19 Lily to Quinn, 5 April 1915. Berg Collection, New York Public Library.

20 Lily to JBY, 14 June 1921. Yeats Archive.

21 Lily to Ruth, 20 March 1928, and 29 July 1925. Yeats Archive. The painting, on the 1925 occasion, was *The Pilot Boat*.

22 Lily to Ruth, 14 February 1936.

23 Ibid.

24 Holloway, *Irish Theatre*, Vol. III, pp. 24, 31.

25 Purser and McGuinness. Readers are referred to these two books for more detailed assessment of the artist's writing than can be given here. John Purser, moreover, deals extensively and argumentatively with Norah McGuinness's views, as contained in her thesis of 1984, for the University of California, which then became her book.

26 Ernest Blythe in *The Yeats We Knew*, edited by Francis McManus, Cork 1965, p. 68.

27 'Introduction' to *Selected Writings of Jack B. Yeats*, edited by Robin Skelton, London 1991, p. 13.

28 Gregory Journals, Vol. II, p. 612, 27 April 1931.

29 Ibid.

30 Shotaro Oshima, 'An Interview with Jack Butler Yeats', in *A Centenary Gathering*, p. 55 (the visit took place on 7 July 1938).

31 *New York Times*, 25 February 1934.

32 Beckett to MacGreevy, 29 January 1935. TCD MS 10402.

33 Beckett to MacGreevy, 5 May 1935. TCD MS 10402.

34 13 May 1933. Beckett writes about 'two queer dreams'; the other about flying down a hill with his professor, Rudmose-Brown.

35 Beckett to MacGreevy, 18 January 1935. TCD MS 10402.

36 Beckett to MacGreevy, 29 January 1935. TCD MS 10402. The painting was acquired in 1996 for the National Gallery of Ireland collection.

37 MacGreevy eventually succeeded Furlong in 1950. An account of the directors of the National Gallery, and their contribution, is to be found in James White, *National Gallery of Ireland*, London 1968.

38 It was shown in the Royal Hibernian Academy exhibition, in 1935, and bought by Judge Creed Meredith for the Municipal Gallery. Hilary Pyle claims (*Catalogue Raisonné*) that it was presented in 1937; yet Beckett knew early in 1935 that it was going to the gllery.

39 Beckett to MacGreevy, 7 August 1936. TCD MS 10402.

40 Beckett to MacGreevy, 7 May 1936. TCD MS 10402.

41 Beckett to MacGreevy, 5 June 1937. This would have been *Morning* and the Sligo watercolour (unidentified).

42 Beckett to MacGreevy, 23 July 1937. TCD MS 10402.

43 Pyle, p. 160.

44 Terence de Vere White, *A Fretful Midge*, London 1957, pp. 117–18. Though told as though there himself, Terence de Vere White, in a later interview, says that his source was R.R. Figgis. He also identified several of the people who were present,

including C.P. Curran but the only lecturer he referred to was Sir John Pope-Hennessy. See White, 'The Personality of Jack B. Yeats', in *A Centenary Gathering*, p. 46.

45 *All Cultivated People*, pp. 52–3.

46 Jack to Bodkin, 22 February 1933. TCD MS 6946/1380.

47 See above, Chapter Seventeen.

48 Interview with the author, January 1995. Brigid Ganly is the daughter of Dermod O'Brien, a founder-member of the United Arts Club, and for many years its president.

CHAPTER EIGHTEEN

1 Herbert Read, 'The Surrealist Novel', *The Spectator*, 31 July 1936. Read reviewed the book, which had been published months earlier, because of its 'very special qualities'. He felt Jack had been overshadowed by Willie, and damned with faint praise in the publicity blurb, which spoke of him as 'better known as a painter than as a writer'.

2 *Amaranthers*, p. 273.

3 Boylan, p. 241.

4 Thomas Bodkin Papers. TCD 6913/24.

5 C. Day Lewis, 'Fantasy and Fine Writing', June 1936. Source of cutting not traced.

6 Review signed 'R.E.R.' and entitled 'Notable Novelists' in *The News Chronicle*, 1 May 1936.

7 The cutting is the earliest, dated 24 March 1936. The incomplete quotation from the last Act in *Macbeth*, with its phrase replaced by parenthesis, no doubt for legal reasons, expresses the real view of the writer: 'it is a tale,/Told by an idiot, full of sound and fury,/Signifying nothing.'

8 *Times Literary Supplement*, April 1936.

9 Samuel Beckett, 'An Imaginative Work!' *Dublin Magazine*, July–September 1936. Jack's friend, Fred Reid, said to him many years later: ' "Godot" is just a Beckettsian "Old Sea Road", with Gogo and Didi passing for John and Michael; only the latter did "go". And the itinerant Molloy and Malone are simply Bowsie or Jimmy Gilfoyle or Oliver J. Gaw, immersed by Beckett in esthetique du mal or the mystique de la merde and offered anew to the world. But for my part I had rather that Beckett had exchanged his own flat and literal style for that metaphorical style of his master Jack Yeats.'

10 Beckett to MacGreevy, 23 May 1936. TCD MS 10402.

11 Jack to MacGreevy, 29 April 1936. TCD MS 10381/133.

12 Ragg to Jack, 15 July 1937. Reading Library, Routledge Archive.

13 Jack to Ragg, 2 August 1937. Ragg 'detected' the hand of Morley, of Faber, in the reaction to the book, when he was told about it. Reading Library, Routledge Archive.

14 Ragg to Jack, 9 August 1937. The advance was £25. Royalties were 10% on first 1,000, and so on. Reading Library, Routledge Archive.

15 Jack to Ragg, 11 August 1937. Reading Library, Routledge Archive.

16 Jack to Ragg, 22 November 1937. Reading Library, Routledge Archive.

17 23 November 1937. The negotiations were undertaken on Beckett's behalf by George Reavey.

18 Jack smoked up to the period of the Second World War, when his niece remembers him having two kinds of cigarette in a little mahogany box with four legs. He used a cigarette holder.

19 Kate O'Brien in *The Spectator*, 11 February 1938.

20 *The Daily Express,* 29 February 1938.

21 W.B. Yeats, *On the Boiler*, Dublin (Cuala Press) 1938. p. 36.

22 *A Rose, A Dusty Rose, The Rose Dying*, and *The Rose in a Basin*, were all the same size (9 × 14 inches) and, according to Hilary Pyle, were all painted in 1936, though not of the same flower. The last of them was owned by Kenneth Clark, Director of the National Gallery in London. *The Rose Dying* was owned by Father Jack Hanlon, from whose mother's garden the dying rose was picked by the artist. When she asked him, could he find nothing better than a dying rose, he replied: 'This is what I want.'

23 Jack to Thomas Bodkin, 31 August 1936. TCD MS 6946/1386.

24 Beckett to MacGreevy, 19 September 1936. TCD MS 10402. Beckett was thrilled to be on his own, and to have this compelling expression of Jack's own view of his work. Beckett's detailing of the order of the three paintings is different from that given by Pyle in her *Catalogue Raisonné. The Rose in a Basin*, not yet painted at the time of this encounter, could well date from 1937, or even 1938, as it is listed in the Tate Gallery catalogue of 1948, rather than 1936.

25 Jack to MacGreevy, 12 April 1939. TCD MS 8105/31. He added a drawing in the margin of his letter. Hilary Pyle writes, in her *Catalogue Raisonné*, that the painting 'suggests the period of the Troubles in Ireland about fifteen years before'. There is no evidence for this.

26 Jack to MacGreevy, 29 April 1936. TCD MS 10381/133.

27 Jack to MacGreevy, 6 January 1938. TCD MS 10381/151. Jack's Irish is faulty; *gabhar*, not *gabhan*, is a goat.

28 Jack to MacGreevy, 6 January 1938. TCD MS 10381/151.

29 Jack to Ragg, 27 June 1938. Reading Library, Routledge Archive.

30 Beckett to MacGreevy, 31 January 1938. Quoted in Deirdre Bair, *Samuel Beckett*, London 1978, pp. 281–2.

31 Ibid., p. 281.

32 Ibid., pp. 281–2.

33 Jack to MacGreevy, 6 February 1938.

34 Jack to Ragg, 13 September 1938. Reading Library, Routledge Archive.

35 Beckett to MacGreevy, 5 August 1938. TCD MS 10402.

36 Yeats Archive.

37 Willie to Edith Shackleton Heald, 15 March 1938. Wade, p. 907.

38 Jack to Alan and Madeleine Stewart, 6 February 1939, shortly after Willie's death.

39 Jack to MacGreevy, 18 February 1939. TCD MS 8105/1–34.

40 Boylan, p. 202.

41 Jack to Cottie, Thursday, 9 February 1939. He actually wrote two letters to Cottie on that one day, the second to tell her that the mail did not reach Westland Row until 7.30 p.m. and that this would mean he would get home at eight o'clock. Clearly he walked from the station up to Fitzwilliam Square.

42 Jack to Cottie, Thursday, 9 February 1939 (second letter).

43 Jack to MacGreevy, 8 March 1939. TCD MS 8105/1–34.

44 See *The Yeats We Knew*, edited by Francis McManus, Cork (?) 1965, p. 46.

45 Jack to William Rothenstein, 6 March 1939. Houghton Library, Index of English Literature MSS.

46 See *The Yeats We Knew*, p. 68.

47 Ibid.

48 Jack to MacGreevy, 29 April 1936. TCD MS 10381/133. Tyrone Guthrie (1900–71), English theatre producer, who was then at

the Old Vic. Charles Laughton (1899–1962) was also at the Old Vic, and exclusively involved in theatre, playing leading parts, rather than character parts, which became his speciality later, after he had begun to put on weight.

49   Jack to F.R. Higgins at the Abbey Theatre, 4 January 1939. The earlier letter was addressed to Eric Gorman.

50   Ria Mooney, 'Players and the Painted Stage: An Autobiography', edited by Val Mulkerns, published in two parts, in George Spelvin's *Theatre Book*. The references to Harlequin's Positions are in Part One, in Vol. I, No. 2, Summer 1978, pp. 110–12.

51   Holloway, *Irish Theatre, Vol. III*, p. 25. The actress was Josephine Fitzgerald. I am indebted to Robert Hogan for help with these references from Holloway's vast journal.

52   Ibid., p. 111.

53   Jack to MacGreevy, 20 June 1939. TCD MS 8105/1–34.

54   Donagh MacDonagh, writing in the *Saturday Review of Literature* (New York), 19 August 1939. MacDonagh (1912–68) was the son of Thomas MacDonagh, one of those executed in 1916. His best-known play was *Happy as Larry*.

55   Anna Kelly, 'Around the Town', *Irish Press*, 16 June 1939.

56   Jack to Ernie O'Malley, 29 June 1939.

57   Jack to MacGreevy, 24 July 1939. TCD MS 8105/1–34.

58   Undated letter, Furlong Collection, U.C.D.

59   John Manning Longford (1911–44) was a Dublin University undergraduate, studying medicine there and in Edinburgh before giving up all ideas of a career as a doctor, and turning to literature and art. He died after a fall, in September 1944.

60   Deirdre McDonagh was a pseudonym for Moira Pilkington (1897–1970) who was born in Tyrrellspass, County Westmeath, and educated in France, where she acquired an interest in modern art. In 1920 she married T.H. Hinkson, son of the writer, Katherine Tynan Hinkson (1861–1931), but in 1929 the marriage failed. As well as pursuing art – she was an amateur painter – she also acted at the Gate Theatre.

61   Stephen Rynne, 'Tea with Jack B. Yeats 1940', *Eire-Ireland*, Vol. 7, 1972, p. 106, quoted in S.B. Kennedy, *Irish Art and Modernism – 1880–1950*, Dublin and Belfast, 1991, which contains the best short essay on the Contemporary Picture Galleries.

62   Jack to MacGreevy, 9 October 1939. TCD MS 35.

63   Interview with the author, January 1995.

64   *The Strings are False*, by Louis MacNeice, London 1965, pp. 213–14.

CHAPTER NINETEEN

1   Eamon de Valera interview with the author, September 1968.

2   For details of this and other developments in the arts, involving growing respect for all branches of the visual arts, see the author's *Mainie Jellett and the Modern Movement in Ireland,* New Haven and London, 1991.

3   Ragg to Jack, 27 October 1938. Reading Library, Routledge Archive.

4   Jack to Ragg, 13 September 1938. Reading Library, Routledge Archive.

5   Jack to Ragg, 27 November 1938. Reading Library, Routledge Archive.

6   *Documents on German Foreign Policy*, 1918–45, Ser. D., ix.423.

7   *Eamon de Valera*, by Frank Pakenham, Earl of Longford, and Thomas P. O'Neill, Dublin 1970, p. 362.

8   Jack to MacGreevy, 19 December 1939. TCD MS 36.

9   Lewis, p. 180.

10   Jack to Bodkin, 5 February 1940. TCD MS 6946/1391.

11   Douglas Hyde to Cottie, 25 January 1940. JBY Archive.

12   John Masefield to Lily Yeats, 29 January 1940. JBY Archive.

13   Jack to Sarah Purser, 15 May 1940, NLI MS 10,201 (23)/3. There was also an early George Russell watercolour.

14   Jack to Bodkin, 18 January 1941. TCD MS 6946/1400.

15   The appointment was for a period of five years, from November 29. At his first meeting, on 1 February 1939 a vote of sympathy was passed on his brother's death. Willie had been a member of the board for some years.

16   E.A. McGuire, Unpublished Memoir, Private Collection.

17   Both entries from address book, JBY Archive.

18   Jack to Niall Montgomery, 1 June 1943. Montgomery Family Collection. Niall's father had died earlier, on 14 March 1943.

19   Jack to Niall Montgomery, 20 August 1940. Montgomery Family Collection. The cutting concerned G.B. Shaw.

20   Jack to Niall Montgomery, 12 September 1941. Montgomery Family Collection.

21   Jack to Niall Montgomery, 1 June 1943. Montgomery Family Collection.

22   Jack Sweeney taught at Harvard; James Johnson Sweeney became curator of the Guggenheim.

23   Jack to Bodkin, 5 February 1940. TCD MS 6946/1391.

24   Ibid.

25   Jack to Bodkin, 3 June 1940. TCD MS 6946/1394.

26   Jack to Bodkin, 15 June 1940. TCD MS 6946/1396.

27   11 July 1940.

28   Robert Wyse Jackson, 'Two Doodles by Jack B. Yeats', *The Irish Times*, 16 August 1972.

29   Betjeman to Kenneth Clark, 14 March 1941. *John Betjeman, Letters: Volume I, 1926–1951*, edited and introduced by Candida Lycett Green, London 1994, p. 282. Jack also tried to persuade Clark to do something for the painter, Nano Reid, possibly finding her a London gallery, though in fact she had exhibited in London during the 1930s at Lucy Wertheimer's gallery.

30   Ibid., p. 19.

31   John Betjeman to John Piper, 17 March 1941, *Letters*, p. 283. There is a nice Freudian slip in the reference to Jack as 'a man to talk to', always an acceptable quality to anyone with a great deal to say, as Betjeman certainly had.

32   Betjeman to Piper, 26 May 1941.

33   Terence de Vere White, 'The Personality of Jack B. Yeats', in *Jack B. Yeats, A Centenary Gathering*, edited and introduced by Roger McHugh, Dublin 1971, pp. 37–9. This essay, written more than twelve years after *A Fretful Midge*, gives a more sober account of the reception of Jack's art at the time of his London show.

34   The published version of Dulanty's remarks made no reference to drink. This was reported to Sligo readers in a letter to *The Sligo Independent*, 17 January 1942, from Fred Saunders, who had been given the text of the speech, and had attended the event. He was an old school-friend of Jack's. He described the speech as 'intensely sympathetic'.

35   Report in the *Overseas Daily Mail*, 10 January 1942, article entitled 'A Wanderer Returned'.

36   'Cruiskeen Lawn', by Myles na cGopaleen, in the *Irish Times*, 13 January 1942. Myles na cGopaleen, alias Flann O'Brien, was Brian O'Nolan, or O Nuallain (1911–66), a civil servant whose sustained wit and verbal dexterity has produced some of Ireland's funniest writing.

37 Cruiskeen Lawn, *The Irish Times*, 1941 (no detail available of day or month).

38 Maurice Collis, writing in *Time and Tide*, 10 January 1942.

39 There was pathos for Jack in Sickert's death coming just a few days after the opening of the joint Yeats-Nicholson show in London.

40 John Piper, in *The Spectator*, 9 January 1942.

41 *The Listener*, 8 January 1942.

42 *The New Statesman*, 10 January 1942. The article, on 'London Exhibitions', was unsigned. Jack has pencilled 'Raymond Mortimer' beside the review.

43 *The Connoisseur*, February, 1942.

CHAPTER TWENTY

1 *A Fretful Midge*, London 1957, p. 116.

2 Lily to Ruth, 17 March 1925. Yeats Archive.

3 Lily to Ruth, 28 November 1937. Yeats Archive.

4 Murphy, pp. 265–6.

5 *A Fretful Midge*, p. 117.

6 Boylan, pp. 209–10.

7 Bodkin to Jack, 11 November 1942. TCD MS 6946/1402.

8 1 March 1942.

9 Jack to Ragg, 25 September 1943. Reading Library, Routledge Archive.

10 Jack to Ragg, 2 September 1944. Reading Library, Routledge Archive.

11 Jack to Ragg, 26 December 1944. Reading Library, Routledge Archive.

12 Ragg to Jack, 25 November 1944. Reading Library, Routledge Archive.

13 Jack to Susan Yeats, 2 November 1942. NLI MS 173.31,177.

14 5 May 1942. Reading Library, Routledge Archive. The one-night production was on Sunday 3 May.

15 Holloway to T.C. Murray, 4 May 1942. HELEN.

16 1 June 1942. Reading Library, Routledge Archive.

17 Jack to George Yeats, 5 August 1942. Yeats Archive.

18 These details are taken from Hilary Pyle's catalogue, which is a careful and thorough account of the artist's output. Its chronology includes the delay of up to six months imposed by Jack on paintings before he accepted that they could go out from his studio.

19 Arthur Power, 'The R.H.A.', in *The Bell*, June 1943.

20 Paintings in the two largest dimensions include: *Helen* (1937); *High Water – Spring Tide* (1939); *A Morning Long Ago* (1939); *Tinkers' Encampment; The Blood of Abel* (1940); *Now* (1941); *Two Travellers* (1942); *Nil Sceach I Mbeal an Chuain/Another Chance* (1944); *Above the Fair* (1946); *Leaving the Raft* (1949); *There is No Night* (1949); *Shouting* (1950); *And Grania Saw this Sun Sink* (1950); *Queen Maeve Walked upon this Strand* (1950); *The Wounded Actor* (1950); *The Basin in Which Pilate Washed His Hands* (1951); *Grief* (1951); *The Music of the Morning* (1951); *A Rose Among (and) Many Waters* (1952); *He Will Not Sign* (1952); *Glory* (1952); *Tales of California Long Ago* (1952); *My Beautiful, My Beautiful!* (1953); *Eileen Aroon* (1953). 10 out of the 23 are in public museums or art institutions. For further details, the reader is referred to Hilary Pyle, *Catalogue Raisonné*. A discussion of scale in Jack Yeats's painting is to be found in the author's introduction to Jack B Yeats, an exhibition of oils, watercolours and drawings at the Royal Hibernian Academy, in Dublin, February 1995.

21 Mrs Somerville-Large, in conversation with the author, January 1995. Her husband, Becher Somerville-Large, an ophthalmologist, was a collector of paintings, and owned, among other works, the beautiful late canvas by Jack Yeats, Confidence.

22 Mainie Jellett, 'The R.H.A. and Youth', in *Commentaries*, May 1942. Her purpose in the article was polemical, and she used the example of Jack's work to emphasise the deadness of academic painting, and the life and energy within 'Modernism'.

23 Dublin *Evening Herald*, 1 October 1943.

24 E.A. McGuire, Unpublished Memoir. Private Collection.

25 Ibid.

26 Ibid.

27 Ragg to Jack, 26 September 1944. Reading Library, Routledge Archive.

28 Ragg to Jack, 12 July 1945. Reading Library, Routledge Archive.

29 Interviews with the author, 1993 and 1994.

30 Ibid.

31 Ibid.

32 Michael Yeats (b. 1921) took his degree at Dublin University, and then studied law at the Kings Inns. He was a Fianna Fail senator, and represented the party in the European Parliament, becoming a vice-president in 1973.

33 Jan Masaryk (1886–1948) was the son of the Founder-Preisdent of Czechoslovakia, Thomas Garrigue Masaryk (1850–1937). He was a diplomat and his country's envoy to London, where he became a popular figure, making wartime broadcasts. He returned to Prague in 1945, and died three years later in suspicious circumstances, having tried unsuccessfully to prevent the Stalinisation of his country.

34 The uncertainty over guests led Michael Yeats to overload his platform. John Betjeman was involved over the arrangement of visas, including one for Charles Stewart Parnell's secretary, Henry Harrison, then 78 years old. In the circumstances Betjeman wondered if a delay in the issuing of a visa might not be 'diplomatic', and this occurred.

35 Joseph Hone, *J.B. Yeats: Letters to his son W.B. Yeats and Others 1869–1922*. London 1944.

36 Joseph Hone, *W.B. Yeats 1865–1939*, London 1942.

37 Father Senan Moynihan, O.F.M. Cap. (dates?) *The Capuchin Annual* ranged widely in its content over most aspects of Irish culture, reached a circulation of 25,000, and sold well in the United States and Canada.

38 See Brian Kennedy, *Dreams and Responsibilities*, Dublin, n.d. (1990), p. 33.

39 In 1960 the Yeats paintings, together with other works by the artist which Father Senan had bought, were lent to Sligo, and after that were sold. Nora Niland, then the Sligo County librarian, and curator of the art collection, was sensible enough to buy works, including *The Funeral of Harry Boland* and *The Island Funeral*. Father Senan personally owned *The Bargain*, a watercolour of 1910, *Market Day*, a watercolour of 1906, and *The Star Gazer*, a watercolour of 1900.

40 C.P. Curran to Cottie, 1 March 1945. JBY Archive.

41 Stephen Rynne, 'The Jack B. Yeats Show', *The Leader*, 10 March 1945, p. 9.

CHAPTER TWENTY-ONE

1 Elizabeth Solterer (née Curran), correspondence with the author.

2 Interview with Mrs Solterer, March 1995.

3 Patrick Browne, or Monsignor Padraic de Brún (1889–1960), was a distinguished priest and Celtic scholar, translator of numerous classical texts into Irish.

4 *The Strings are False,* by Louis MacNeice, London 1965, pp. 213–14.

5 *Jack B. Yeats National Loan Exhibition, National College of Art,* Dublin, June–July 1945, p. 16.

6 Daniel Corkery, 'Jack B. Yeats Once More', *Irish Monthly,* September 1945. Daniel Corkery (1878–1964), a writer and schoolteacher, was intensely nationalist, and inspired a widespread and passionate awakening of interest in Ireland's Celtic heritage, and in the beauties of Gaelic poetry. His most influential book was *The Hidden Ireland,* but he wrote fiction and plays also and was a distinguished amateur watercolour artist. His collection of short stories *A Munster Twilight,* is an Irish classic.

7 *The Irish Times,* 12 June 1945.

8 Monk Gibbon, 'The Paintings of Jack B. Yeats,' *The Irish Times,* 9 June 1945.

9 *The Irish Times,* 11 June 1945. Douglas Hyde had ended his first term as president, and, for health reasons, declined to run again. There was a contest. The Big Three were Sean T O'Kelly, who succeeded Hyde, and was the first of a succession of Fianna Fail presidents, elected while serving in political office, Sean MacEoin TD, nominated by the Fine Gael party, and Dr Patrick McCartan, an independent Republican candidate.

10 'Hy Brazil' was the mythical kingdom of Breasal, High King of the World, and was supposedly located south-west of Ireland. It became visible to human eyes only once every seven years. When explorers discovered South America they thought they had found it, and gave the name Brazil to the new country, or so goes the popular explanation. The other speakers were: Rutherford Mayne, Maurice Walsh, Joseph Hone, Francis Kelly, D.L. Kelleher, Miss May Morton (from Belfast P.E.N. Club), Austin Clarke, and C.E. Kelly, editor of *Dublin Opinion.*

11 Thomas MacGreevy, *Jack B Yeats: An Appreciation and an Interpretation,* Dublin 1945. It came out in two versions, at 12s 6d and 7s 6d, and was printed by the Three Candles Press, in Fleet Street, run by the printer, Colm O Lochlainn.

12 Samuel Beckett, 'MacGreevy on Yeats', *The Irish Times,* 4 August 1945.

13 Samuel Beckett quoted in, Gordon S. Armstrong, *Samuel Beckett, W.B. Yeats and Jack Yeats: Images and Words,* Lewisburg, London and Ontario, 1990.

14 'A Painter of Ireland', *The Times Literary Supplement,* 18 August 1945.

15 Jack to Eleanor Reid; no date, but not earlier than the 1950s, since there are references to Beckett's *Waiting for Godot* being produced.

16 Jack to C.P. Curran, 16 October 1945.

17 Kitty Wilmer O'Brien to Jack, 18 October 1945, together with second, undated letter. JBY Archive.

18 John Rothenstein, 'Visit to Jack Yeats', *New English Review,* July 1946, pp. 42–3.

19 Ibid., p. 43.

20 *The Guardian,* 1 June 1946; *The Southport Visitor,* 7 June 1946.

21 *The Southport Visitor,* 7 June 1946.

22 *Irish Times,* 27 April 1946.

23 The citation quoted Lessing and Horace on the interchangeability of poetry and painting, invoked Willie's name. 'He, alas, is no longer with us; but today we confer the same distinction on the painter, whose pictures of Irish life and landscape, whatever the particular theme may be, are equalled by no living man.' The tribute was written by William Bedell Stanford, Public Orator of Dublin University, and a friend of the artist. Another friend of the artist, Fitzroy Pyle, father of the Yeats scholar, Hilary Pyle, had made the initial proposal on Jack's behalf. Jack was in good company. Others who received honorary degrees on the same day included Alexander Fleming, the discoverer of Pencillin, and James Owen Hannay ('George Birmingham') with whom Jack had collaborated in illustrating *Irishmen All.*

24 I am indebted to the Secretary of the Kildare Street and University Club (the amalgamation of two clubs which were separate in Jack's day), Mr F.G. Yoakley, for this information.

25 *The Truth* was a religious magazine of the period. I am indebted to the barrister, Ralph Sutton, for this anecdote.

26 Robert Wyse Jackson, 'Two Doodles by Jack B. Yeats, *Irish Times,* 16 August 1972.

27 I am indebted to Alan Browne for this anecdote. His father was Jack's solicitor. His parents, who knew the painter well, were left a painting of their own choice in Jack's will, and Alan Browne, with his mother, went to the studio and chose *The Hour of Sleep.*

28 See Maurice Harmon, S*ean O'Faolain A Life,* London 1994, pp. 175–6.

29 Anne to Cottie, 17 April (?1947) (date of production). Postcard, Yeats Collection.

30 Jack to Bodkin, 30 October 1946. TCD MS 6946/1416.

31 Jack to MacGreevy, 15 February 1947. TCD MS 60.

32 Jack to MacGreevy, 25 March 1947. TCD MS 64.

33 Jack to MacGreevy, 18 April 1947. TCD MS 65.

34 See Norah McGuinness, p. 143. Source given is M.G. Rose, in *Eire-Ireland.*

35 Quoted Pyle, p. 168.

36 The paintings are *The Mountain Window* (a view of Ben Bulbin) and *He Wins.*

37 Terence de Vere White, 'The Personality of Jack B. Yeats,' *Jack B. Yeats: A Centenary Gathering,* Dublin 1971, p. 41.

38 Pyle, p. 168.

39 Pyle, *Catalogue Raisonné,* Vol. II, p. 788.

40 Interview with the author, 1994.

41 *Catalogue Raisonné,* Vol. II, p. 793.

42 Jack to MacQuitty, 18 March 1948. Quoted in Pyle, *Catalogue Raisonné,* Vol. II, p. 794.

43 William MacQuitty moved on to feature films after the wartime documentaries, and was responsible for the first film about the sinking of the Titanic, *A Night to Remember.* (MacQuitty had been at the launching of the Titanic, in Belfast, in 1911.)

44 Interview Eamon Andrews with Jack Yeats, 10 October 1947.

45 BBC Interview with MacGreevy, Third Programme, early November, 1947.

46 Anne Yeats interview with the author.

CHAPTER TWENTY-TWO

1 George Yeats to MacGreevy, undated. TCD MS 8104/86.

2 John Ormond Thomas, *Picture Post,* 9 October 1948. His photographer for the assignment was Haywood Magee.

3 Other churchmen present included the Right Revd. A.E. Hughes, Bishop of Kilmore, Elphin and Ardagh, and J.C. Beresford, Dean of Elphin. The Revd. J Hunter, from

Castleknock; J.S. Frazer, Sligo; J. Anderson, the Bishop's chaplain, and headmaster of Cavan Royal School were also present.

4   Maurice Craig, *The Elephant and the Polish Question*, Dublin 1994, pp. 38–9.

5   Interview with the author, April 1995.

6   Jack to Hertha Eason, January 1949. Quoted in Pyle, p. 168.

7   Jack to Niall and Mrs Montgomery, 26 January 1949. Montgomery Family Papers.

8   Anne Yeats worked extensively in the Abbey, Gaiety and Olympia theatres. Directors and other artists with, or for whom she designed or painted scenery included Anew McMaster, Helen Hooker O'Malley (who made her cry; she was married to Earnan O'Malley); and Ralph Cusack. She knew many of the actors and actresses: John Stephenson, Ann Clery, Hilda Brosnan, Cepta Cullen, Dan O'Herlihy, Sheila May, Freddie and Wilfred Brambell. Anne records: 'he had the biggest collection of dirty stories I'd ever heard'. She also acted herself, and was in charge of crowds.

9   Jack to Anne Yeats, 25 September 1951. Yeats Archive.

10 Ria Mooney, 'Players and the Painted Stage,' Part One of her Autobiography, in *George Spelvin's Theatre Book*, Vol. I, No. 2, Summer 1978, p. 112.

11 Ernest Blythe, (Title), from *The Yeats We Knew* edited by Francis MacManus, Cork 1965, p. 68.

12 Ibid.

13 Marilyn Gaddis Rose, 'Mixed Metaphors; Jack B. Yeats's Writings', in *Jack B. Yeats A Centenary Gathering*. Marilyn Gaddis Rose is referring to a personal conversation with Waddington, in London, 31 August 1966.

14 Jack to Anne, 10 March 1954. JBY Archive.

15 Jack to Anne, 21 February 1955. JBY Archive.

16 *Stephen Spender, Journals, 1939–1983*, London 1985, pp. 103–5. The visit took place on 13 March 1950.

17 Jack to James B. Lane, 7 June 1949. Copy, NGI/VW Collection. The couple kept the painting, apparently for more than twenty years.

18 James S. Plaut to Thomas MacGreevy, 18 September 1950. TCD MS 8149/18.

19 Ibid.

20 J.S. Plaut, director of the Institute of Modern Art in Boston, argued successfully for the change from 'Modern' to 'Contemporary' in the gallery's name.

21 Jack to Victor Waddington, 23 April 1951. Waddington Archive.

22 The same exhibition, with Plaut's introduction, went to the following galleries: Phillips (Washington) 10–30 June; M.H. de Young Memorial Museum (Golden Gate, San Francisco) 1 August–15 September; Colorado Springs Fine Arts Center (Colorado) 8 October–4 November; Art Gallery of Toronto (Canada) 16 November–23 December; Detroit Institute of Arts (Detroit, Michigan) 4–31 January, 1952; Knoedler's (New York) 12–29 February; National Academy, (Fifth Avenue, New York) 27 May–June 21.

23 Anna Russell to MacGreevy, 8 April 1959. TCD MS 8149/92.

24 Jack to Waddington, 31 May 1952. NGI/VW Collection.

25 Ibid.

26 Cutting in Jack's scrapbook. JBY Archive.

27 Jack to Waddington, 25 May 1951. NGI/VW Collection.

28 MacGreevy, 'The Art of Jack B. Yeats', TCD MS 8149/26. On the cover is written 'Prepared for the Boston Exhib. of J.B.Y. – 1951 but not used.'

29 Jack to Victor Waddington, 6 February 1954. Waddington Archive.

30 Beckett to MacGreevy, 15 April 1954. TCD MS.

31 Jack to Niall Montgomery, 29 December 1949. Montgomery Family.

32 Jack to Victor Waddington, 3 November 1952. Waddington Archive.

33 Jack to Victor Waddington, 6 February 1954. Waddington Archive.

34 Letter to the author, from Alan Denson, 8 July 1994.

35 Ibid. The first visit paid by Denson was on 30 September 1954, at 4.30 in the afternoon, corroborated in Jack's diary with a brief entry.

36 Account with Hodges Figgis, March 1954. JBY Archive.

37 Account with Bill Duigan's, of Merrion Row, January, 1954. JBY Archive.

38 Oskar Kokoschka is generally cited as an international painter who knew Yeats the man, and understood and admired his work. The example is solitary.

39 *Irish Times*, 28 March 1953.

40 Draft of letter to Jack B. Yeats, 19 June 1954. JBY Archive.

41 At Jack's death the removal of the ring was overlooked. The nurse who attended him at the end was not instructed, and it was left on the artist's finger. When Niall Montgomery was told he was far from being upset. Had he been consulted, he said, he would not have permitted its removal.

42 Kokoschka to Jack, 13 November 1956. JBY Archive.

43 Ibid.

44 He used a system, which he had probably followed over many years, though earlier diaries are lost, recording in a large desk diary his appointments, letters sent, visitors who actually came and sometimes what he might have said by way of promise or undertaking. But he also had a pocket diary, more personal in its details. He used a symbol, a capital Z, possibly to indicate when he slept, and other symbols, a capital O or just an oval shape drawn in the margin, and also a capital T; the meaning of these is obscure. Inside the back cover of his larger diaries he pasted two envelopes; in one there were his visiting cards with address, in the other without.

45 Brian O'Doherty, letter to the author, 18 October 1995.

46 Ibid.

47 John Berger to Jack Yeats, 30 September 1956.

48 Eleanor Reid correspondence; sold at Christie's, 1992.

49 Undated letter, JBY Archives.

50 All cards in JBY Archive. He received cards from Brigid and Andrew Ganly, Liam de Paor, Maurice Collis, the architect and painter, Raymond McGrath, and from Norah McGuinness. Ernie O'Malley and his son, Cormac, sent a card drawn by Cormac, and Father Senan sent Christmas wishes, as did Con Curran's daughter, Elizabeth, who was now married and living in Washington. He received a card from the staff of the National Gallery of Ireland. Jack MacGowran, the actor who had directed *In Sand*, sent him greetings.

51 Beckett to MacGreevy, 23 March 1957. TCD MS.

52 Samuel Beckett to Mary Manning, Paris, 24 April 1957. Present whereabouts unknown. Beckett was very upset. In another letter, to MacGreevy, he explained the difficulties, and then added: 'I had always promised to myself that I wld. go to Dublin on that occasion.' TCD MS 5 April 1957.

53 Waddington to Fred Reid, 12 June 1957. Private Collection

Epilogue

1   I am indebted to Ian Baird, Fine Arts Correspondent of the *Irish Independent*, for his analysis of Yeats prices over the past forty years.

2   See Brian Kennedy, 'The Oil Painting Technique of Jack B Yeats' in *Irish Arts Review, Yearbook 1993*, Dun Laoghaire, County Dublin, 1992, pp. 115–23. Kennedy was then assistant director of the National Gallery of Ireland. In an earlier article, in *Apollo*, March 1991, pp. 193–5, he had alerted scholars to the problem in language that was regarded as alarmist, suggesting that some of the late works were 'falling apart'. The two articles have encouraged a programme of restoration work with many owners of paintings, notably the National Gallery of Ireland, details of which are given in the first article cited here.

NOTE ON ILLUSTRATIONS AND PHOTOGRAPHIC CREDITS

Jack's opposition to the photographic reproduction of his works has long been compromised, the copyright holders arguing that changes in technique and quality allow for this. Though he was emphatically opposed, as his will indicates, he did make the theoretical exception when such illustrations were for study purposes, and this is recorded in correspondence with the director of the Tate Gallery, quoted in this book.

All works of art illustrated in the book are by Jack Yeats unless otherwise stated. Dimensions are in inches. Copyright in the works of Jack Yeats belongs to Michael and Anne Yeats, and I am grateful for their permission on the works reproduced here. The works of John Butler Yeats are now out of copyright.

The approach adopted here to illustrations may be briefly stated. Apart from colour plates, illustrations, as nearly as possible, are located where they are mentioned or where they are relevant to the story. In some cases later drawings which refer to earlier events appear out of chronological order. The Yeats images used in the book have been collected over a long period, and it has not been possible in all cases to trace ownership and obtain permission for use. Apologies are made for any omissions in the credits.

I am indebted in particular to Rex Roberts, whose work on Yeats archive material is an indispensable aid to all students of the subject.

Unless otherwise stated, he is the source for all Yeats Archive family photographs as well as for many of the photographs of works by Jack now transferred to the National Gallery of Ireland. Theo Waddington and Leslie Waddington made available to me the Yeats photographic archive started by their father, Victor Waddington. Hilary Pyle also made available images of individual works, as did the National Gallery of Ireland; these included works from the collection, as well as other works.

I am grateful to the following for additional illustrations:

Abbey Theatre, 232; Christies, 42; Grace Duncan 203–4, 229; Roy Foster 10, 26; Getty Images 213; Robert Hogan and the National Library of Ireland 192; Houlton Picture Library, 32; Hounslow Library Services: Chiswick Library 41; Hugh Lane Municipal Gallery of Modern Art 165; Irish Embassy 215; Irish Independent 167, 172, 186, 195, 226, 228; The Irish Times 185; Michael Purser and John O'Grady 37; Jim McGarry 13; © MacQuitty International Collection 222; National Gallery of Ireland 30, 58, 179, 181, 183, 219, 235; National Library of Ireland 8, 9, 28, 192; Anthony O'Brien 208; Rose Mary O'Brien 210, 231; Brian O'Doherty 237; Sligo County Museum and Library 161–2, 171, 178; Leo Smith's Estate 221; Tate Gallery, London 218; Ulster Museum, Belfast 180; University of Victoria, Australia 43. Other photographs belong to the author.

Paintings and published works by Jack have been indexed alphabetically.
Page references to illustrations reproduced here are in **bold**.

Abbey Experimental Theatre (Peacock Theatre), puts on *Harlequin's Positions*, 289, 318
Abbey Theatre, 147, 150, 176, 203–4, 238, 263; WBY and, 285, 338
'ABC of Piracy, The' (miniature ms book by Jack), 130
Aberdeen, Lady (Viceroy's wife), buys painting, 146
About to Write a Letter, 254, **312**
Abrahams, Morris (East End promoter), 122
Academy of Christian Art, 220
Aegeon, Miss (Chiswick Art School friend), 58
Agricultural Co-Operative Bank, 143
Ah Well, A Romance in Perpetuity (Jack's novel), 298; publication of, 309–10
Aitken, Charles (director of Tate Gallery), on Jack's copyright, 231–4
Aladdin, 91
Alarm Among the Clerks (play by Mervyn Wall), 289
Aldington, Richard (novelist), 245
Allen, David (publicity company Jack worked for), 60
Allen, Mairin (art critic, committee of National Loan Exhibition), 325
Allgood, Molly (actress loved by Synge), Synge mentions Jack in letters to, 146–50, 388n.23, 156
Allgood, Sara (actress, Molly's sister), 147, 388n.32; on Gort barm brack, 204
Allingham (Chiswick Art School friend), 58
Allport, Miss (Willie's typist), 57
Almanach de Gotha, MacGreevy's supposed dependence on, 336
Alpine Club (London), Jack's exhibition there, 1929, 235, 236–7; 1930, 248–9
Alton, Ernest Henry (Provost of Trinity college), 319
Amaranthers, The (novel), 254, 259, 273; Read's review of, and summary, 274–5; possibly modelled on United Arts Club, 275; sales poor, 275, 305; 1942 dinner for Jack, 308–9
American Table Cloth, The, formerly *The Yankee Table Cloth*, 80, 128
And Grania Saw this Sun Sink, 311, 313
And to You Also (novel by Jack), 242, **309**; sent to Ragg at Routledge, 309; sold out, 310
Anderson, R.A., bookplate for, 167
Andrews, Eamon (broadcaster), interviews Jack, 333–4
Annancy Stories, 102
An Túr Gloine (stained glass enterprise, founded by Sarah Purser), 123
Aonach Tailteann, Dublin, 255
Approaching Rosses Point, Early Morning, 226, 227
Apollo (art magazine), 236
Apollo Theatre, London, 163
Apparitions (play), 254, 261, 262; copy given to David Green, 297

Aran Islands, The (book by Synge, illustrated by Jack), 160
Aran Islands, 131, 140
Architectural Review, The, 303
Ardilaun, Lady, 182
Ariel, or the London Puck (comic paper), 51–2, 59, 60
Ariosto (Italian poet), 275
Armory Show, New York, Jack exhibits at, 181, 186
Armstrong, Mrs Cecil Frances (hymn-writer), 335
Armstrong, Sir Thomas (Head of Art at South Kensington), 41
Art Workers' Quarterly, 126
Arthur Tooth's Gallery (1925 show), 231, 237
Arthurs, Nurse (at Portobello Nursing Home), 346
Ash Plant Seller, The, 180
Asquith, 184
Association of American Painters and Sculptors, formed for Armory Show, 181
Atholl Academy, Isle of Man, 13
Atkinson Art Gallery, Southport, Exhibition of Modern Art, 328–9; *Now* shown, 329
Atlantic Monthly (US periodical), 343

Bacalieu (a Pollexfen vessel), 12
Bachelor's Walk: In Memory, 184, **192**; Jack's views on 191–3, 196, 198, 219, 313
Back from the Races, 231; copyright in, 233–4
Bailey Restaurant, Dublin, 330
Bair, Deirdre (Beckett biographer), 282
Balfour, Arthur James, sets up Congested Districts Board, 135, 388n.8
Ballad Singer, A, 227
Ballad Singer's Children, The, 120
Barber Institute of Fine Art, Birmingham, Bodkin as director, 268, 298
Barbizon Hotel (New York), Museum of Irish Art at, 253
Barlow, Seaghan, 157
Barrel Man, The, 123, **123**, 186
Barrett, Dick (Irish anti-Treaty politician), 218
Basin in which Pilate Washed his Hands, The, 311, quality of, 313; priced in 1951 at £2,500, 345
Bassano, Jacopo (North Italian painter), 223
Basterot, Comte de (early patron), 37
Bathers, The, 226
Battle of Eylau, The, painting by Antoine Jean Gros, 194
BBC, broadcasts MacGreevy interview with Jack, 334–5; broadcasts, *In Sand*, 340
Beardsley, Aubrey, 104
Beauty and the Beast, The, 26, 27, 28, 380–1, n.33
Beckett, Frances 'Cissie' (see Sinclair)
Beckett, Gilbert A. (author), 46

Beckett, Mrs May (mother of writer), 269

Beckett, Samuel, 245, **246**; MacGreevy introduces to Jack, 246, 265, 266; uncomfortable visitor to Jack's 'At Homes', 268; his mother meets Jack, 269; compares Jack with Watteau, 269; reviews *The Amaranthers*, 275; insights into Jack's work, 281–2; the Paris stabbing incident, 282; working with MacGreevy on Jack's behalf, and questioning views on nationalism, 282–3; angered at being described as 'Irish', 282; depth of friendship with Jack, 283–4, 294; calls on Jack before outbreak of war, 296, 320; reviews MacGreevy's essay in *The Irish Times*, but takes issue with viewpoint, 326–7; at Cottie's funeral, 331; at Paris exhibition, 345–6; visits Jack in Dublin, 346; visits in 1956, 353; Jack aware of his growing success as playwright, 353–4

Beckett, Mrs Sheila, 348

Bedford Park, move to house there, 18

Beeke-Lane, S.F., does bookplate for, 167

Beerbohm, Sir Henry Maximilian 'Max', 104, 107

Before the Start, 198, **232**

Belfast Telegraph, 318

Bell, Clive (English art critic), on Jack's 1925 London show, 231

Bell, The (Dublin periodical edited by O'Faolain), extracts published from *Ah Well*, 309, 330

Bella (servant at Merville), 24–25

Bellmer, Hans (Polish-French painter and graphic artist), Beckett compares with Jack, 327

Berenson, Bernard (art historian), read by Jack, 348

Berger, John (writer, art critic), 353

Bernoit, M. (French diplomat in Dublin), 337

Beside the Western Ocean, 120

Betjeman, Sir John (English poet, diplomatic representative in Ireland), 299–300, **299**

Big Tree of Bunlahy, The (book by Colum illustrated by Jack), 263

Binyon, Laurence, 108

Birmingham, George A. (pseudonym for Canon James Owen Hannay), 171, 178–80

Blake, William, read by Synge, 136

Blueshirt Movement (Irish Right-wing political movement), 284

Blunt, Wilfrid Scawen, 167

Blythe, Ernest (manager of Abbey Theatre), 265, 288, **288**, 289, present at Drumcliffe when WBY's body returns, 338; view on Jack's plays, 340

Blythe sisters (Sligo teachers), 21

Bodkin, Thomas, 190, 204, 207, 208, 220; row with MacGreevy, 222–4; relationship with Jack, 225, 226; director of National Gallery of Ireland, 251; resigns, 268; Jack's epitaph on, 270; on *The Amaranthers*, 275; tells him about 'Rose' paintings, 278; Jack illustrates *My Uncle Frank*, 298–9; writes ode to Jack, 308, 309, 330

Bog Road, The, 226

Bonfire Night, 128

Bonnard, Pierre, 223, 291

Bone, Sir Muirhead, 233

Booth, John (writer on Jack Yeats), 193

Borthwick, Nora (author of Gaelic primers illustrated by Jack), 60, **60**

Bosun and the Bob-Tailed Comet, The, 175, **175**

Boston, Miss (friend of Lily), 216

Boston Pilot, The, 55

Boucicault, Dion, 260, 395n.5

Boudin, Louis Eugene (French painter), 163

Bowra, Maurice (Oxford academic, friend of Betjeman), 300

Boydell, Brian (Irish composer), 299

Boylan, Patricia, writer on United Arts Club, 174

Brady, Father (priest at Carrignagat), 79

Brambell, Wilfred, 289

Braque, Georges, 291, Beckett compares with Jack, 327

Breaker Out, The, 228, 229, 321

Breakfast Room, The, 321

Bregazzi (Italian gilder and framer in Dublin), 254

Breton, André (Surrealist artist and writer), 274

Breughel (Bruegel) Pieter (the elder), 223

Bridgelove (American visitor, friend of Kokoschka), 350

Bridges, Robert (English poet), 244

Brigit (play by Lady Gregory), 204

British Institute (Paris), 236

Broadsheet, A, 58, 86; prepares for, 89, 102–8, 122, 149, 153

Broadside, A, 150, 153, 163, 168–70, 390n.7, 176–7; ends publication (1915), 186, 225, 234; restarted, 1935, and 1937, 284, 308

Brown, Frederick (South Kensington professor), 34

Browne, Alan (Dublin gynaecologist), entertains Jack as Boat Club student, 330

Browne, Perceval (Jack's solicitor, father of Alan), made joint executor with MacGreevy, and bequeathed choice of a canvas, 350; arranges funeral, and pallbearer at, 355

Browne, Dr Patrick (president of U.C.G.), opens National Loan Exhibition, 323

Bunting, Basil (English poet), witnesses WBY's will, 284

Burchett, E.S., 41

Burns, Tommy (Canadian boxer), 162

Butt, Isaac (founder of Irish Home Rule party) 6, 15, 379n.5

Butt, Rosa, 2, 379n.5, 164

By the Canal, 255

Byrne, Alfie (Lord Mayor of Dublin), attends Jack's funeral, 355

Café Royal (London), 206

Cake Cart at the Races, A, 196, 226

Caldecott, Randolph (illustrator), 40, 381n.35, 43–4

Callaghan's, men's outfitters, merchants with whom Jack dealt, 202

Callanan, Jeremiah John (poet), 120

Cambell, Beatrice (née Elvery, later, Lady Glenavy, Irish artist), *see under* Glenavy

Campbell of Islay, 10

Canal Bridge, 255

Canal near Ashtown, 255

Canal Water, 255

Capuchin Annual, The, 320

Car is at the Door, The, 128

Careless Flower, The (novel), 254; offered to Ragg and refused, 294

Carmichael, Coralie (Dublin actress), 264

Carr, Jonathan Thomas, 40, 382n.37

Carr, Joseph Comyns, 41

Carric, Allen (writer on Jack for *The Mask*), 177

Carrick, Lady, 182

Carrying Seaweed for Kelp, 146

Carson, Edward, 184

Carter, Canon (rector of St Stephen's), takes Jack's funeral service, 355

Casement, Sir Roger (nationalist, public official), 222, 287

Casement, Tom (Roger's brother, friend of Jack), 222; his suicide, 287

Cashlauna Shelmiddy, *see* Snail's Castle

Cassells (publishers), 51

Castlegregory, Kerry, 186

Cawnpore Massacre, 318

Celt, The, 158

Celtic Christmas, A (annual in which Jack illustrated Hannay's writing), 179

Celtic Twilight, The, 58

Cézanne, Paul, 231, 245

Chagall, Marc, 248

Chantry Fund, 233

Chardin, Jean Baptiste Siméon, 282

Charmed Life, The (novel by Jack), published, 277; perhaps his best, 278; poor sales of, 294, 305

Chatto and Windus (publishing house), 245, 280

Chevalier, Maurice (French comedian and singer), 66

Chestnuts, The (at Chertsey, Surrey, Jack and Cottie's first home), 63–4

Chief Problem, 137

Child, A.E., 123

Childers, Erskine (writer and anti-Treaty politician), 174, 218, **218**

Childers, Erskine (son of anti-Treaty politician, and Fianna Fail Minister

under de Valera), at Jack's funeral, 355
Chiswick School of Art, 34, 40–1, 41, 382n.38, 55
Christian Science Monitor, 182
Chums (magazine Jack worked for), 64
Churchill, Clementine, 302
Circus Dwarf, The, 177; in Armory Show, 181–2
Circus, The, 208
Circus Proprietor, The, 208
Circus Waggon, The, 180
Clark, Kenneth (director of National Gallery, in London, later Lord Clark), 301; Jack's National Gallery joint show, with Nicholson, 300–3; meets de Valera, 301; offends Jack, 302; buys *Rose in a Basin*, 306
Clarke, Austin (poet and playwright), 330; present at Drumcliffe when WBY's body returns, 338
Clarke, Harry, does bookplate for, 167
Clarke, Mrs Tom, 299
Claude, Lourrain, 282
Clausen's Gallery (New York venue for show), 128
Cleary, P.S., 212
Clifford Gallery (Haymarket), Jack's first exhibition, 67, 68–71, 77
Cloncurry, Lady (early patron), 37
Coast of Mayo, The, 186
Cody, William ('Buffalo Bill'), 32, 32–3, 34; scepticism about his exploits 52–3
Coe, Henry E. (architect), 32
Collected Poems (by WBY), bought by Jack to give away, 348
College Historical Society (Dublin University debating society), 319
Collins, Michael, as head of Provisional Government, 212
Collis, Maurice (English critic), adverse review, 304
Colum, Eileen, poet's sister who worked for Cuala Industries, 168
Colum, Padraic, 49, 123, **185**, 387n.22, 168; published by Jack, 169, 173, 182, 183, 185, 200; Jack illustrates *The Big Tree of Bunlahy* for Colum, 263
'Come Gather Round Me, Parnellites' (poem by WBY), 284, **285**
Comic History of England, The, 46
Communicating with Prisoners, 194–5, **195**, 313
Conder, Charles, 107
Congested Districts Board, 135, 136–40, 143
Connoisseur, The (art magazine), review of Jack, 304
Connolly, Cyril (English writer), publishes Clark on Jack, 302
Connolly, Ellie (servant at Merville who loved Willie), 25
Connolly, James, leader of Irish Citizen's Army, 184
Conrad, Joseph, 207
Constable, John (English painter) 282
Contemporary Art Society, 237
Contemporary Picture Galleries (Dublin art gallery in 1940s), 291, 315
Coole (Lady Gregory's home), 82
Corbet, Jane Grace, 16
Corbet, Robert, 3
Corbett, 'Gentleman' Jim (world boxing champion in 1894), 162
Corkery, Daniel (Irish writer), 325, 399n.6
Corneille, Pierre (French playwright), 248
Coronor's Inquest, The, 146
Corot, Jean Baptiste Camille, 282
Corscadden, Mrs (purchaser at first exhibition), 71
Cosgrave, W.T. (leader of Irish government, 1922–32), 205, 217; fall of his government, 252, 319
Costello, John A. (leader of inter-party government), outside church at Jack's funeral, 355
Cottage at Roundstone, A, 186
Countess Cathleen, The (play by WBY), 85
Country Gentleman, The (in *Irishmen All*), 180
Country Jockey, A, bought by Dermod O'Brien, 185
Courbet, Gustave, 181, 282
Court Circular, The, 160
Cow Doctor, The, 80
Craig, Edward Gordon (theatre designer), 175–6, 390n.38; Anne visits in

Paris, 340
Craig, Maurice (historian, writer), 317; present at Drumcliffe when WBY's body returns, 338; described as 'son of Lennox Robinson', 338
Crawford Gallery, Cork, 252
Cremin, Con (Irish diplomat, ambassador in Paris), 345
Crest of the Hill, The, 128
Croker, Richard 'Boss' (from Cork, became union boss in U.S.), 123, 387n.21
Cruikshank, George (caricaturist), 58
Cruise O'Brien, Francis, 204
Cuala, 125; setting up separate Cuala Industries, and Cuala Press, 168–70; effects of Civil War on, 218–9, 220; Jack's arrangements terminated, 234; WBY to settle affairs, 285; Lolly's responsibilities, 295, 302; publication of *La La Noo*, 310
  See also: Yeats, Elizabeth Corbet ('Lolly'); Yeats, Susan Mary ('Lily'), Gleeson, Evelyn; Russell, George; Henry, Augustine; Jack
Cullen, Cardinal, 1
Curran, Constantine 'Con', 172, 180, 224, 301, 321, 327, 330; bequeathed a painting by Jack, **321**, 350
Curran, Elizabeth (daughter of C.P., secretary for National Loan Exhibition), 323, 325, 330

Daily Graphic, The, 43, 51, 58, 348
Dali, Salvador (Surrealist painter), 274
D'Alton, Louis (Irish playwright and novelist), 265
Dalton, Frank (Dublin actor), 263
Daly, Madge, 299
Dancer, The, 208
'Danny', ballad by Synge, Jack's interest in, 149–150, 168
Dark Man, The, 235
Darley, Arthur, 212
Darrynane, 255
Dasher, The (Pollexfen's vessel), 11
Daumier, Honoré, 248
Dave (play by Lady Gregory), 235
David Copperfield, 187
Davies, Arthur B. (American artist), 181, 391n.49
Davis, Thomas (Irish poet), published by Jack, 169, 328, 329
Dawn – Holyhead, The, 208, **209**
Dawson, Julian (musician), plays at Jack's funeral, 355
De Chirico, Giorgio, 291, 296
Department of External Affairs, Dublin, and return of WBY's body to Ireland, 337
Derain, André (French painter), 291
de Valera, Eamon, 205, **212**; at Race Congress, 212, 217; comes to power in 1932, 252–3, 293, 296; attends Michael Yeats paper in TCD, 318–19, 320, 323; at the return to Ireland of WBY's body, 337; outside church at Jack's funeral, 355
Death for Only One, 79, 280
Deathly Terrace, The (play), 254, 310
Denson, Alan, 153, disapproval of MacGreevy essay, and on Jack's enthusiasm, 346–7
Dermody, Thomas (Irish poet), published by Jack, 169
Dervins (family friends), 55
Delacroix, Eugene (French painter), 181, 283; Sickert compares Jack with, 305
Devil's Disciple, The (play by Bernard Shaw), 163
Dickens, Charles, 187
Dickinson, Page (Irish writer), 172–3
Dickson, Elder (president of Society of Scottish Artists), 330
Die We Must, owned by Bodkin, 225
Discoveries (by WBY), last Dun Emer title, 167
Discovery, 353
Dispensory Doctor, The, 80
Dix, E.R. McClintock, does bookplate for, 167
Dog Watching a Seagull, A, 120
Dolphin Hotel, Dublin, 318

Donkey Races, 79, 128
Donnelly's Hollow, 278
Doran, John, 4
Dowden, Edward, 6–7, 17–18, 118
Doyle, Richard, 6, 379n.13
Dr Jekyll and Mr Hyde (play, after Stevenson), Jack and family attend, 47
du Bois, Henry Pene, 106
du Maurier, George (early patron), 37
Duchamp, Marcel, 181
Dublin Evening Telegraph, The, 204
Dublin Magazine, The, 225, 226, 227; publishes Beckett's review of *The Amaranthers*, 275, 326
Dublin Metropolitan School of Art, 123, 156, 293
Dublin Newsboys, 196
Dublin Opinion (satirical magazine), mocks Jack's art, 250, *250*, 254, **321**
Dublin University Boat Club, Jack an honorary member, 330; members of committee, 330
Dublin University, confers honorary degree, Doctor of Letters, 329
Dublin University Magazine, 16, 380n.56
Dublin University Modern Languages Society, puts on *Le Kid* with Beckett in it, 248
Dublin University Philosophical Society, 310
Dubliners, The (by James Joyce), 235
Dubtax (Dublin taxi firm), Jack's account with, 346
Duchess of Cambridge (funeral of), 46, 382–3n.12
Dudley, Lady, helps Jack, 146
Dufferin and Ava, Marquess of
Dufy, Raoul, 291, 303
Dulanty, John Whelan (Irish High Commissioner in London during Second World War), 300; speech opening Jack's show with Nicholson, 302–3
Dun Emer Industries, 118, 125, 130; incompatibilities and difficulties, 166–8, 390n.4; Jack entertains staff of, 174, 220
Dun Emer Press, does bookplate for, 167
Duncan, Mrs, manager of United Arts Club, 204, 207, 221
Dunne, Mrs (Jack's cleaning lady), 351
Dunsany, Lord (satirical Irish writer), 274, 310
Dust Play, 180
Dusty Rose, A, 278–80, **279**; shown to Beckett, 278
Duthuit, Georges (French painter), visits Jack's Paris show, 345

Eads (schoolfriend), 21
Earp, T.W. (English art critic), 248
Eason, Hertha, 331; Jack speaks of Lily's death, 338
Echo's Bones (book of poems by Beckett), given to Jack, 247
Edwards, Hilton (actor-manager of Gate Theatre), 264
Edwards, Lionel (equestrian artist), 298
Edwards, Oliver (Sligo friend), 286
Eliot, T.S., 200, 207, 244; MacGreevy writes book on, 245–6, 280
Elliott, Robert (English art critic), 158, 389n.23
Ellis, Edwin J, 6–7, 8, 90
Elsinore, Rosses Point house, 6, 16
Elton and Edwards, comic banjo-players, 163
Elton, Oliver (English scholar), 60, 384n.17
Emigrant, The, 80, 85, 152
Emigrant, An, 120
Emmet, Robert, 78, 79, 144, 169
Empty Creels, 180, 196
Endgame (play by Beckett), 354
English Illustrated Magazine, 41
Ensor, James (Belgian painter), 221, 239, 248
Ernst, Max, 274
Everyman (periodical), article on Jack, 211
Evening Herald (Dublin evening paper), Jack reads regularly, 348
Evening Mail (Dublin evening paper) Jack reads regularly, 348
Evening Standard, 227
Evictions, The, 146

Express, The (Dublin newspaper), 85, 278

Faber (publishers), refuse *The Charmed Life*, 276; publish JBY Letters, edited by Hone, 320
Fair at Ballinasloe, The, 145
Fair Exchange, A ('nautical-farcical comedy' seen by Jack), 163
Fair of Carricknagat, The, 128
Falloon, Patrick (businessman), 318
Falstaff, 47
Family Herald, The, 159
Fancy, The (writings by John Hamilton Reynolds, illustrated by Jack), 161–2
Farmer, The (painting for *Irishmen All*), sold, 185
Farrar, Mrs (early patron), 37
Farrell, Patric (director of Museum of Irish Art, in New York), 253, 254
Faustmann, Herbert (East End promoter), 122
Fay, William (Abbey actor), 123; as 'Tramp' in *The Pot of Broth*, 126, 150, 156
Fearon, Professor (Dublin University), 268
Feeney, Frank (employee of Pollexfens), 286
Ferargil Galleries (New York), 253
Ferryman of Dinish Island, The 140, 141, 152
Fianna Fail (Irish political party led by Eamon de Valera), 205, 253, 284, 318–19, 320
Figgis, Darrell (writer and actor), 174, 211
Figgis, R.R., 'Bobs' (collector), 269, 270, 301, 341
Fingall, Lady (wife of Viceroy), 89
Finnegans Wake (by James Joyce), 236
Fitzgerald, Charles (Amercan artist, friend of JBY), 171
Fitzgerald, Charles Edward (surgeon oculist in ordinary to Queen in Ireland, friend of JBY), 51, 383n.39
Fitzgerald, Geraldine (Abbey actress), in *Harlequin's Positions*, 289
Fitzroy Road house (birthplace of Jack) 5, **5**
Flag of Distress, 39
Flapper Meeting, The, **185**
Folded Heart, The, 356
Foley, John Henry, 6, 379n.13
Ford, Cecil (Irish theatre director), directs *Harlequin's Positions*, 289
Formes (French avant garde literary magazine), 236
Fortune and her Wheel, 120
Foster, Captain (Tom Casement's assistant), 222
Four-oared Currach, A, 146
Freeman's Journal, 227, 231
Friends of the National Collections of Ireland, 251; bequests from Lolly, 296
From the Metal Bridge, 206
From Portacloy to Rathlin O'Beirne, 305
Fry, Roger (English art critic and painter), 207; described by Jack as 'old Gamp', 353
Fugue of Cinderellas, A (book by Bryan Guinness), praised by Jack, 354
Funeral of Harry Boland, The, 194, **194**, 219
Furlong, George, becomes director of National Gallery, 268, 290
Furniss, Harry (humorous illustrator), 36, 381n.17, 64
Furse, Charles, 104

Gael, The (Irish cultural publication), 128
Gaelic League, 123, 143
Galerie Beaux-Arts, Paris show there, 345
Galloping Horses
Gandon, James (architect of major eighteenth-century Dublin buildings), 206
Ganger, The, 153, 177
Ganly, Andrew (dentist, married to Dermod O'Brien's daughter, Brigid), 353
Ganly, Brigid (painter, daughter of Dermod O'Brien), 271, 316; speaks at P.E.N. Club dinner, representing her father, 326, 329; visit, 348
Gaffer, The, **84**, 153

Gas Company Theatre (in Dun Laoghaire), puts on *Godot*, 353
Gate Theatre, 318, 338, *Waiting for Godot* performed, 353
Gamesome Princes and the Pursuing Policeman, The, or *Wonderful Travellers*, 94
Geoghegan, Jack, early buyer of works, 145
German Who Played 'O'Donnell Aboo' in the Rosses, The, 80
Gertler, Mark (English painter), 291
Gieves Art Gallery (exhibits Jack's paintings, 1924), 226–7
Giacommetti, Alberto (Surrealist sculptor), 274
Gibbon, William Monk (Irish poet), 287, 325–6
Gillards (local Devon children), 73
Giorgione da Castelfranco, 223
Girls and Boys, 257
Glacken, John Sloan (American artist friend of JBY), 171
Gladstone, William Ewart, 1, 31
Glasgow Herald, 98, 130
Glass of Port, A, 229
Gleeson, Evelyn (Dun Emer Industries), 118, 118, 387n.4, 158;
    incompatibility with the sisters, 166–8; her character, 167, 212
Gleizes, Albert, 269, 291
Glen Cree Reformatory, 149
Glenavy, Beatrice (artist), involved in Loughrea work, 123, 222, 246, 287
Glory, 311, 313, 346
Glow Worm, The, 71
G'Morrow, Strawberry, given to Starkey by Jack, 326
Goddards (family friends), 55
Gogarty, Oliver St John (Dublin physician and writer), 204, 246
Going to the Races, 79
Going to Wolfe Tone's Grave, 304
Goldsmith, Oliver, 78
Gonne, Iseult, WBY proposes to, 201
Gonne, Maud, calls at Bedford Park, 48, 60, 82, 85, 182; WBY's final
    marriage offer rejected, 201
Goodman, Theodore (Dublin art critic), 321
Gore-Booth, Constance, 107
Gorman, Agnes (née Pollexfen, mother's younger sister), 170
Gorman, Robert (married to Agnes), 170; dies, 187, 391n.7
Gough, Captain, purchases *The Old Ass*, 208
Goya, Francesco, 161, 181, 248–9
Graham, R.B. Cunningham, 48, 383n.25
Grant Richards (London publisher), 145
Graphic, The (see *Daily Graphic, The*)
Gray, David (U.S. Minister in Ireland), 310
Great Cockney Tragedy, The, **58**, 58, 59
Great Southern Hotel, Sligo, 286
Great Tent has Collapsed, The, 332
Greater Official, The (in *Irishmen All*), 179, 198
Green, David H. (Harvard Synge scholar), visits Jack, 296
Green Sheaf, The (Pamela Colman Smith publication), 105, 130, 131
Greene, Graham, 274
Gregory, Lady Augusta, 36, 75, **75**, 384n.12; declines invitation to Coole,
    77, 80, 81, 82, 83, 85–6; invites Jack to meet Mark Twain, 89, 93;
    involved in *A Broadsheet*, 102, 106, 107–8, 118, 120, 122; supports
    Synge and Jack over *The Aran Islands*, 145, 150, 156, 157–8; and Dun
    Emer, 167; and Wilfrid Scawen Blunt, 16, 171, 182; on Jack's illness,
    190, 204, 206; on Civil War politics and Jack, 219; gives Jack book
    on Ensor, 221, 235; begins to fail, 238–9, 241; her death, 252; her
    views on *The Old Sea Road*, 266, 288, 293
Gregory, Robert, 36, 88, 155, 157; at Slade School, 158, 208
Grief, 311, **347**
Griffin (art school friend), 46
Griffith, Arthur, leader of Sinn Fein, 184; becomes president in 1921, 212
Gris, Juan, 291
Gros, Antoine Jean (French painter of battle scenes), 194
Grosvenor Gallery, 41
Guardian, The (Southport newspaper), 329
Guernica (by Picasso), 192
Guggenheim, Peggy (friend of Beckett), 247

Guilbert, Yvette, 163
Guildhall Exhibition (London, of Irish Art), 81, 130, 158, 159
Guiney, Louise Imogen (American poet), 65
Guinness, Bryan (Lord Moyne), 240, 269, 302, 354
Guinness, Elizabeth (Bryan's second wife), 354
Guthrie, Tyrone (Irish theatre director), 288, 396n.48, 310
Gwynn, Stephen (Dublin writer), Jack's strictures on his immorality, 263

Haftmann, Werner (art critic), 220
Haggard, H. Rider, 39
Hales, Sean, Pro-Treaty military leader, 218
Hall, Harry Reginald Holland (archaeologist), 40, 381n.32, 88
Hall, Patrick (Irish artist), 341
Hall, Sydney Prior (artist), 40, 381n.32
Hamilton, Eva, 158
Hamlet, 176
Hanlon, Father Jack (painter), 269
Hannay, James Owen (author of *Irishmen All*), 171, 178–80, 390n.43; on
    JBY's poverty, 182, 190
Happy as Larry (play by Donagh MacDonagh), 330
Hardy, Thomas, 39
Harlequin's Positions (play by Jack), Abbey accepts it, 288–9; production,
    with Anne's designs, 318
Harper's Weekly, 171, 343
Harris, Harry, theatrical entertainer, 163
Harte, Bret, 39, 128, 153, 284
Harty, Hamilton (composer), 253
Harvey, Arnold (friend of Jack), 88, 150, 154–6, **155**; Jack and Cottie visit
    in 1908; late visitor, 348; takes part in funeral, 355
Hasenclever, 220
Haverty, Joseph Patrick (Irish nineteenth-century painter), 251
Haverty, Thomas, 251 (founder of picture-purchase trust), 251
Haverty, Trust, 251; buys *The Liffey Swim*, 251; buys *While Grass Grows*,
    269
Healy, James A. (New York stockbroker), acts for Jack, 253
Healy, Maurice (artist), 123
Heather Field, The (play by Edward Martyn), 85
Hegarty, J.Y., 144
Heinemann (London publishers), Jack leaves them, 259; publishers of *The
    Amaranthers*, but *The Charmed Life* refused, 276
Helen Hackett Galleries (New York), 1930 exhibition, 253
Hempel (German ambassador during Second World War), 294, 300
Henri, Robert (American artist), 171, 181, 391n.49
Henry, Augustine (botanist and supporter of Dun Emer Industries), 118,
    387n.5; friendship with Cottie, 118, 154; fond of Lolly, 166; urges
    generosity in break-up of Dun Emer, 166–7
Henry, Grace (Irish painter), 220
Henry, Elsie, 243
Henry, Paul (Irish landscape artist), founding of Society of Dublin Painters,
    219
Here Comes the Chestnut Mare, 305
Here She Comes!, 180
Heron, Hilary (Irish sculptress), 318
Higgins, F.R. (Irish poet, Abbey Theatre director), 288–9
High Water – Spring Tide, 311
H.M.S. Childers, escort for Macha from France to Galway, 337
Hodgkins, Roseanna (family servant), 49, 383n.27, 51, 64
Holloway, Joseph (Dublin architect), 204, 263, 265
Hood, Thomas, 133, 162
Hooker's Owner, The, 146
Hooley (Jack's dog), 64; favourite subject, 71–3
Hooley, Ernest Terah, 64, 384n.30
Hone, Evie, 269, 291, 296
Hone, Joseph (Irish biographer of Yeats, Moore), 222; edits *J.B. Yeats:
    Letters, etc.*, 320; and writing *Life* of WBY, 320, 345
Hone, Nathaniel, 117, 387n.1; shares show in 1901 with John Butler Yeats,
    118, 196, 223, 293

Horizon (London literary magazine, edited by Cyril Connolly), Clark's article on Jack, 302

Horniman, Annie Elizabeth Frederika, patron of Irish theatre, attends Jack's 1905 show, 145

Horse without a Rider, 346

Hoult, Norah (English writer), admires *Sailing, Sailing Swiftly*, 262

Hour Glass, The (play by WBY), 176

Housman, Laurence, 104

Howe, Julia Ward (American hymn-writer), 169

Huckleberry Finn, 39, 89

Humanity's Alibi, 123

Humbert, General, 78

Hundred Jugs, The (by Nicholson), 303

Hurley Player, The, 234

Huxley, Julian (English, scientist), 310

Hyde, Douglas, 80, 385n.19, 81, 82, 83, 89, 106, 107; at Killeeneen *feis*, 120–1; at Jack's 1905 show, 145, 156; published by Jack, 169, 212; offers sympathies on Lolly's death, 295

Hyde-Lees, George (WBY's wife), their marriage, 201

IBM, art exhibition, San Francisco, 1939, 290

Illustrated London News, The (uses Jack drawings), 60

Illustrated Sunday Herald, 227

Inchcape Bell, The, 91

In Galway Town, 227

In Memory of Boucicault and Bianconi, 269

In Sand (Jack's play), the last to be put on in his lifetime, at Peacock Theatre, 340

In Tir na n-Og, 278

Inside the Whiskey Tent, 79

Institute of Contemporary Art, Boston, Jack's exhibition there, 343

International Exhibition of Modern Art (Armory Show), 181

International Fair, Ballsbridge (1903), 122

Ireland's Own (periodical), Jack's views on style, 211

Iremonger, Val (Irish poet and diplomat), 337

Irish Agricultural Organisation Society, 123, 143

Irish Citizen Army, 184

Irish Coast Life Saving Service, 222

Irish Exhibition of Living Art, 219; Jack's support for, 314, 339, 339

Irish Fairy Tales, 58, 59

Irish Homestead, The, 125, 126; illustrates Hannay in, 179

Irish Independent, 52, 83, 160

Irish International Exhibition (1907), 158

Irish Literary Theatre, 82, 85

Irish News, The, 227

Irish Race Congress (Paris, 1922), Jack's lecture there, 211, 220

Irish Statesman, 222

Irish Tatler and Sketch, The (weekly social magazine), 251

Irish Times, The, 158, 159, 205, 248, 303, 308, 325, 326; Jack writes Dermod O'Brien tribute for, 328; subscribes to, 348

Irish Times Pictorial, The, 348

Irish Transport and General Workers' Union, 184

Irish Volunteers, 184

Irishmen All (book by George A. Birmingham, illustrated by Jack), 171, 178–80, 185, 196

Iron-Roofed Cottage, Kerry, 186

Irving, Henry (actor), 47

Island Funeral, The, 208, 313

Island Horseman, The, 146

It Must have been an Allegory, 128

Italian Painters of the Renaissance (by Berenson), read by Jack, 348

It's the largest fi-irm in Ireland, 80

Jack B. Yeats: An Appreciation and an Interpretation (by Thomas MacGreevy), 205–6; published by Waddington, 326; Beckett reviews for *The Irish Times*, 326–7

Jack B. Yeats: Pictorial and Dramatic Artist (by Marriott), 175

Jack Yeats National Loan Exhibition, 320–2, **322**, 323–6, 328, 334

Jackson, Arthur (married to Jack's aunt Alice), 170–1, 186; death of, 283

J.B. Yeats: Letters to his Son W.B. Yeats and Others 1869–1922, edited by Joseph Hone, 320

Jackson, F. Hamilton, 41

Jackson, Robert Wyse, 299; memories of Jack as University Club member, 330

Jackson, Sir John (Hallsands speculator), 114

James Dance, or, the Fortunate Ship Boy, 96

James Flaunty, or, The Terror of the Western Seas, 93, 96, 103

Jammet, Louis (restaurateur), 341

Jammet's Restaurant, 318, 341

Jazz Babies, 305

Jellett, Mainie (artist), 182; exhibits with Dublin Painters, 220, 239; MacGreevy defends, 222, 224, 269, 291, 293, 308; praises *Now*, 314–15, 351

Jellett, William Morgan (politician, father of the artist), 182

Jerome, Jerome K. (author), 59, 384n.13

Jewell, Edward Alden (*New York Times* art critic), favourable review, 253–4

John, Augustus, 107, 227

Johnny Patterson Singing 'Brigid Donoghue', 80

Johnston, Denis (Irish playwright), 222

Jonathan Cape (English publisher), 280

Jones, Edward Burne, 41

Jones, Henry Arthur (playwright), 93

Jordan, Mrs, of Belmullet, drawn by Jack, 144

Jowitt, Martha (governess), 18, 40

Joyce, Giorgio (James's son), 246

Joyce, James, 120, 200, **236**; Jack's view of, 235–6; pictures purchased, 236, 241, 244, 246, 247, 262, 266, 311, 354

Joyce, Lucia (James's daughter), relationship with Beckett, 247–8

Joyce, Nora (wife to James), 245

Judy (published Jack's drawings), 60

Jugend, Die (journal from which Jugendstil took its name), 221

Jugendstil (German art nouveau movement), 220

Jury's Hotel, Dublin, 326

Kafka, Franz (Czech writer of Austrian birth), 354

Kaiser Wilhelm II (JBY on), 188

Kandinsky, Wassily (Russian painter), 181, Beckett compares Jack to, 327

Keane, Sir John, 310

Keating, Sean (Irish artist), 253, 290, 314

Keats, John (English poet), 292

Kelly, Tom, 145

Kelp-Making, 146

Keogh, William Nicholas (Irish judge), 205, 392n.13

Kernoff, Harry (Irish painter), 314

King Edward VII, 122

Kingsmill Moore (Irish lawyer, later judge), 308–9

Kinsella, Thomas (Irish poet), 356

Kipling, Rudyard, 109

Kirchner, Ernst Ludwig, 186

Kisling, Moise, 291

Klee, Paul (German-Swiss artist), Beckett compares Jack to, 327

Knewstub, Jack, London art dealer, 181

Kokoschka, Olda (painter's wife), 351

Kokoschka, Oskar (expressionist painter), meets Jack, visits Ireland, 220–1, 392–3n.12, 239; critics compare him with Jack, 248, 305, 343; renewed acquaintance, and visits Dublin with Olda, 350–1

Konody, Paul George (art critic), 68–9

Kuhn, Walt (American artist), 181, 391n.49

La La Noo (play by Jack), performed at Peacock Theatre, 310–11

Laffitte, Jean, pirate, 106

Lander, Major, early purchaser of work, 185

Lane, Hugh, 130, 155

Lane, John, publisher, 104

Larkin, James, Trade Union leader, 184

Last Poems (WBY's final volume during his lifetime), 285

Laughton, Charles (English-American actor), 288, 396–7n.48

Lavery, John, 158, 183; on board of National Gallery of Ireland, 296

Leaving the Raft 311

Le Brocquy, Louis (Irish painter), 310

Le Cid (play by Corneille), 248

Leger Galleries (London art gallery), 329

Légion d'Honneur (French order of merit), awarded to Jack, 341

Le Kid (play by Pelorson), 248, 394n.47

Lemass, Sean (politician who succeeded de Valera), 320

Le Nain, the brothers (three French 17th century painters), 282

Leech, William John, 158, 196

Leinster Hall (Molesworth Street, Dublin, used by Jack for exhibitions), 77, 83, 171, 390n.15

Lesser Official, The (in *Irishmen All*), 179, 196

'*Let Me See Wan Fight!*', 79

Let me Tear 'Un, 149

Lettres Nouvelles (French literary journal), essays in homage to Jack published, 346

Lever, Charles, 39

Levine, Nathan (Waddington's father-in-law), 315

Lewis, Cecil Day (English poet and critic), on Jack, 275

Lewis, Gifford (author of work on Yeats sisters), on Lolly's death, 295

Lhote, André (French painter, influential in Jellett's development), 291

Life in the West of Ireland (Jack's illustrated book), 145, 177–8

Liffey Swim, The, 227, **228**, 251, 275

Light on the Foam, The, 71

Lika Joko (humorous paper Jack worked for), 64

Lindsay, Sir Coutts, 41

Linton, Sir James Drogmole, 46, 382n.8

Little Fleet, The (Jack's book on model boats), 170, 175

Little Sister of the Gang, The, 321

Little Review, The, 245

Little Waves of Breffny, The, 269

Liverpool, The, (Pollexfen vessel), 334

'Lives', Jack's purpose in, **258**, 259–260, **261**

Lloyd George, David, 193

'Loan and Cross-Section Exhibition of Contemporary Paintings', 291

Lock to Lock Times (rowing periodical), 51, 59, 60

London Follies, The, attended by Jack, 163

London Society, 43

Longfellow, Henry Wadsworth, 112

Longford, John Manning (Jack) (gallery owner), 291, 397n.59, 315–16

Longford, Lord (Edward Pakenham, sixth earl, theatre impresario), 300, reads lesson at funeral, 355

Long Team, A, 80

Looking Back, 79

Looking Towards Fenit, bought by Dermod O'Brien, 186

Lord John Sanger's Circus, 77

Losing Crew Going Home, The, 80

Lough Gill, Kerry, 186

Love Songs of Connaught, The (Douglas Hyde), 106, 386n.18

Low Tide, admired by Beckett, 269

Low Water, Spring-tide, Clifden, 171

Lücken, 220

Lucy (Jack's pony), 37

Lyric Theatre, run by Austin Clarke, 330

Lyceum Theatre, 47

McArdle, Surgeon, 205

Macauley, Rose, affair with Father O'Donovan, 126

MacBride, Sean (Minister for External Affairs in Inter-Party Government), 337

McCarvill, Eileen (doctor and UCD professor), 351

McClure's Magazine (American magazine), 127

McColl, D.S. (English art critic), 236

McCormack, John (Irish tenor), 253

MacCormack, Mrs (Evelyn Gleeson's sister and partner), 166

McDermott, Kate (servant at Merville), 24

McDonagh, Deirdre (gallery owner), 291, 397n.60

MacDonagh, Donagh (poet and critic), writes on *Harlequin's Positions*, 290, 397n.54; poem as tribute to Jack, 329; Anne Yeats designs for his play, 330

McGonigal, Richard (collector of Jack Yeats), 341

'MacGowan', pseudonym used by Jack in *A Broadside*, 169

MacGowran, Jack, 21; produces *In Sand*, 340

MacGreevy, Thomas, 42, 52, 93, 172, 176, 193; views on *The Funeral of Harry Boland*, 194 and n; on *Communicating with Prisoners*, 195 and n.; his *Jack B. Yeats: An Appreciation and an Interpretation*, and the views on Jack's nationalism, 205–6, 219; central role in Jack's affairs, 222–5, 226; Joyce communicates with Jack through, 236, 238; sends *transition* to Jack, 244; dedicates poem, 'Dysart', to Jack, 245; his first book on Eliot, 245, 280; early efforts as a writer, 249; advised by Jack to apply for directorship of National Gallery, 268, 275; admires *The Amaranthers*, 275; proposes book on Jack, 280–2; Jack write about WBY's death, 286–7; on *Harlequin's Positions*, 290; identifies biblical origin for *Tinkers' Encampment: the Blood of Abel*, 294, 316; writes on 'Three Historical Paintings', 320; speaks at opening of National Loan Exhibition, 323, 324; his book on Jack published by Waddington, 326; Jack tells him of Cottie's ill-health, 331; interviews Jack on BBC, 334–5; 'Painsy' MacGreevy, 335; director, National Gallery of Ireland, 336; to helps with return of WBY's body to Ireland, 337–9, 342; writes about Jack for American touring show, 343; made joint executor of Jack's will, and bequeathed choice of a canvas, 350; summoned to Portobello, 355; pallbearer at funeral service, 355

McGuinness, Norah (American author), 256; theory on Jack's writing, 265–8; his nationalism, 265–6; on *The Charmed Life*, 278

McGuire, Edward, (business and artist), 296; on Waddington and Yeats, 314–15

McKelvey, Joe, (Irish anti-Treaty politician), 218

McKenna, Commander (of the Macha), 337

MacKenna, Stephen, 134–6, 388n.9, 145, 153

McKeown, General Sean ('The Blacksmith of Ballinalea'), 205

Maclagan, Eric (friend of WBY), 126

McLaughlin, C.F., 'The Gunman' (poet), 308

MacLiammoir, Mícheál (Dublin actor and playwright), 264, 265; present at Drumcliffe when WBY's body returns, 338

McMasters, Anew (Irish actor-manager), 264, 265

MacMillan, Propus, 310

McNamara, Francis (Irish writer), published by Jack, 170

MacNeice, Louis (Irish poet), visits Jack, **292**, 292; recalls Eárnan O'Malley, 323; present when WBY's body returns, 338

McNie, Isa (secretary of United Arts Club), 309

MacQuitty, Miranda (William's daughter), 333

MacQuitty, William, 318; his photographs in Jack's studio, 333, 399n.43

Macbeth, 47

Macbeth, William (Jack's New York agent), 128

Macha, Irish naval service vessel bringing WBY's body back, 337

Maffey, Sir John (British government representative in Ireland during Second World War), 299–300, 310

Maggie Man, The, 186, 196

Maggie (Yeats's servant in Greystones), 189

Magritte, René (Belgian Surrealist), 274

Mahaffy, John Pentland (Provost of Trinity College, Dublin), 89

Mahler, Alma (wife of composer), 220

Mail Car Driver, The, 145

Mainsail Haul, A (by Masefield), 108

Man from Aranmore, The, 153

Man of the West, The, 120

Man who told the Stories, p 146

Man who told the Tales, The, 128

Man with a Broken Head, A, 177

Manchester Courier, 55

Manchester Guardian, 60, 61, 131, 133–4, 144, 145, 146, 152, 162, 177, 208
Manchester Literary Club, 175
Manchester Quarterly, The, 175
Mancini, Antonio (Italian painter), 301
Mangan, James Clarence (Irish poet), 7, 169, 379n.19
Manning, Mary (novelist and playwright), 355
Manning, Mick (journalist), 85
Maria (family servant), 49
Market Day, Evening, 227
Market Day, Mayo, 227, 235
Markievicz, Constance, 160–1, 182
Markievicz, Count C., 159
Marquet, Pierre Albert (French painter), 291
Marriott, Ernest (author of first work on Jack), 175–6
Marsh, Clare (Irish landscape artist, founding member of Society of Dublin Painters), 85, 385n.10, 90, 219
Marshall, Norman (English theatre director), 310
Martyn, Edward, 82, 385n.3, 85; at Killeeneen *feis*, 121, 123, 204
Marx, Karl, read by Synge, 135
Masaryk, Jan (Czech government leader in exile), 319
Masefield, John Edward, 102; involved in *A Broadsheet*, 105–8; friendship with Jack, 108–15, 386n.24, 122, 130; Connemara expedition with Synge, 131, 133–5, 162; contributes to *A Broadside*, 169, 175, 225; views on *Sligo*, 244
Mask, The (Craig's theatre magazine), 176–7, 331
Mathews, Charles Elkin, 71, 96–7, 385n.46, 102–5, 127, 130; Synge sends *The Aran Islands* 145, 156; publishes *The Fancy*, 161–2; and Craig, 176, 220
Maunsel (Dublin publisher), 145, 177
May, Andie, Sligo shoemaker, 9
May, Frederick (Irish composer), 308
May, Phil (cartoonist), 43–4, 382n.51, 64, 65, 153
Mayo, Lady, 145
Mellowes, Liam (Irish anti-Treaty politician), 217, 218
Meredith, George, 187
Merry Wives of Windsor, The, 47
Merville (Pollexfen family home), 4, 13–14, 14, 380n.46, 15, 50
Meyer, Kuno, 102, 386n.5, 105
Michel George (French painter), 223
Middleton, Agnes (great-aunt), 13
Middleton Family (schoolfriend), 11, 21, 187
Middleton, John (great-uncle), 13
Middleton, Lucy, 21
Middleton, Mary (died from cholera), 13
Middleton, William (great-uncle), 10–12, 13, 14, 23; dies, 24
Middleton, William (great-grandfather), 11
Midland and Great Western Railway, The, 142
Mildmay, Colonel F.B., later Lord (M.P. for Hallsands), 114
Miles, J.C. (friend of Jack and Cottie), 64, 384n.30, 86; buys *The Publican*, 185
Millet, Jean François, 282
Mills Hall, Dublin (used by Jack for exhibitions), 182
'Mine Eyes have seen . . .' American hymn, published by Jack, 169
Miro, Joan (Surrealist painter), 274
Mitchell, Susan, 21, 380n.12, 119, 160, 174, 182, 204
Modern Aspects of Irish Art (lecture by Jack), 211
Modern Society, 159
Moir, 'Gunner' (boxer), 162
Montgomery, Niall (Irish architect and artist), 203, 205, **297**; does not understand Jack's writing, 241; regular visitor, 297–8, 338–9, 345, visitor at Portobello Nursing Home, 346, 348; with Jack night before his death, 355
Montgomery, Rose Mary, 297
Montgomery, Seamus (Niall's brother), dies young, 298
Monticelli, Adolphe (French painter), 301
Moody, T.W. (Dublin University historian), 330

Moon in the Yellow River, The (play by Denis Johnston), 222
Mooney, Ria (Abbey actress and theatre director), 289; directs *Harlequin's Positions*, 289, 290; Jack tells her of Cottie's death, 331–2; present at Drumcliffe when WBY's body returns, 338; directs *In Sand*, 340; frequent visits to Jack in Portobello, 355
Moore, George, 89, 93, 103, 104; contrasts Synge and Jack, 133–4, 145, 156; fails to buy from Jack, encounter with Lily, 158, 207, 268
Moore, Thomas, 78
Moore, Thomas Sturge, 108; does bookplate for WBY, 167
More Prick's than Kicks (book by Beckett), inscribed for Jack, 247
Morland, George, 161
Morning, acquired by Beckett, 268–9
Morning Long Ago, A, 311
Morris, Sir George and Lady, 89
Morris, May, employs Lily, 48–9, 51; Lily leaves her employment, 57, 118
Morris, William, 4, 41, 48, 383n.26, 118, 200, 220
Mortimer, Raymond (English critic), reviews Jack, 304
Moscow Arts Theatre, and Craig, 176
Mountjoy Prison, 205
Moynihan, Father Senan (Capuchin priest), **320**, 320; chairs committee for National Loan Exhibition, 320–1, 342
Mr Barnes of New York (play), 47
Muldoon (Irish official, on Congested Districts), 134
Muldoon (the jockey), 38, 79
Muldoon, 153
Munch, Edvard (Norwegian painter), 343
Municipal Gallery of Modern Art (Dublin), 207, 251, 323
Murnaghan, Judge, chairman of board of National Gallery of Ireland, 296
Murphy, Sean (Irish ambassador in Paris), 337
Murphy, William M., 13, 14, 37, 56; examples of effect on Jack of WBY comparisons, 307
Murphy (novel by Samuel Beckett), 277, 282, 283
Museum of Irish Art (New York), 253
Music in the Train, 255
My Beautiful, My Beautiful!, 311, 313, **347**
My Uncle Frank (memoir by Thomas Bodkin), 298–9, **299**
Myles na gCopaleen (pseudonym used by Brian O'Nolan, q.v.)
Mysterious Travellers, or, The Gruesom Princes, The, 96

Nation, The (Dublin weekly), 251
National College of Art, 323; Jack shows at Davis show, 328
National Gallery, 158, 222, 296, 311, 323
National Gallery of Ireland, and *The Liffey Swim*, 251–2, 290, 323
National Literary Society, 82, 123
National Sporting Club, 162
Napoleon III, Emperor, 34
Nazi Party, 249
Near a City Long Ago, 321
Nettleship, John Trivett, 6, 8, 17
Neuberg, Victor (critic of *Sligo*), 241
Neuberger, 220
New Age, The, 80
New Statesman, The (London weekly), reviews 1930 show, 248, 353
New York American, The, 106
New York Times, The, 253
Nicholson, William, 43, **301**; joint show with Jack, 301–4; words on painting, 303, 323
Nobel Prize for Literature, awarded to WBY, 217
Norton, William (Labour Party leader in inter-party government), outside church at Jack's funeral, 355
Not Pretty but Useful, 80
Now, 311, quintessential Jack, 313–14; considered for Tate Gallery, 328

O'Brien, Brendan (physician, son of Dermod), sings at United Arts Club, 308, 327, 331
O'Brien, Catherine (artist involved in Loughrea work), 123
O'Brien, Conor (architect and writer), 174

O'Brien, Dermod, 158, **296**; buys *A Country Jockey*, 185, 291, 296; speaks at United Arts Club dinner, 308; last illness, 326; death, 327–8

O'Brien, Kate (Irish writer), reviews *The Charmed Life*, 278

O'Brien, Kitty Wilmer (Irish landscape painter), 308, 327, 331

Occupation, An, 177; trustees of Haverty Trust, 251; brings Henry Tonks to Jack's 'At Home', 268

O'Casey, Sean (Irish playwright), meets Jack, 235, **235**

O'Connell Bridge, 228

O'Connell, Dan, local gamekeeper in Ballinfull, 163

O'Connor, Frank (Irish short-story writer), 330

O'Connor, Rory (Irish anti-Treaty politician), 218

O'Conor, Roderick, 231

'Odds and Ends' (Lily's scrapbook), 9, 379n28

O'Doherty, Brian, interview, and drawing of Jack, 349, 351–3

O'Donovan, Father Jeremiah (of Loughrea Cathedral), 123, 126

O'Duffy, Eimar (satirical writer), 274

O'Faolain, Sean (Irish writer, editor of *The Bell*), 309; Jack fellow-member of Russell Circle, 330

O'Grady, Standish, 83, 385n.4

O'Higgins, Brian (Abbey actor), 310

O'Higgins, F.R., 288

O'Kelly, Sean T., 212

Old Ass, The, 208

Old Sea Road, The (play), 254, 261, **266**; submitted to Abbey Theatre, but rejected, 266–7; Lady Gregory's views on, 266; Beckett on, 275; its influence on Beckett, 354

O'Leary, John, 48, 383n.23, 102, 119

Olympia (Earls Court), 32–4

Olympic Games, Paris, 1924, *The Liffey Swim* shown, 227

O'Malley, Earnán, 79, **324**, 384n.16; writes on *Bachelor's Walk: In Memory*, 191, 193; on 1920s change in style, 230; sees and wants to acquire *Death for Only One*, 280; writes on Jack in National Loan Exhibition catalogue, 323–4; present at Drumcliffe when WBY's body returns, 338

O'Malley, Power (Irish artist), 253

On the Spanish Main (by Masefield), 108

'Onct More's Circus' (miniature theatre entertainment), 95

O'Nolan, Brian (Irish comic writer, 'Myles na gCopaleen'), on Jack, 303–4, 397n.36, 315

Orpen, William, 41, 107, 117, 387n.2, 153; works on Lane commissions, 156, 158, 181, 183, 196, 206, 239, 246, 291, 293, 302

Orr, Alexander Barrington (uncle by marriage), 15, 50

Orr, Geraldine, 50

O'Sullivan, Miss (matron of Portobello Nursing Home), 331, 335

'O'Sullivan, Seamus' (poet, pseudonym used by J.S. Starkey), 158, 169, 174; founds *Dublin Magazine*, 225, 226; publishes review of *The Amaranthers*, 275

O'Sullivan, Sean (Irish artist), 330

Osborne, Walter, 155, 158, 196, 293

Outlook, 159

Paddock Life (racing paper), 51–2, 59–60

Page, Thomas Nelson, 102

Palme, Jack (boxer), 162

Panner•rammer•rammer• Of Edward VII's VISIT to the VERY POOR OR The King among the Pictures Dublin July 24th 1903. All Highly Coloured, 122

Park, Dr (TCD Librarian), visits Jack with Stephen Spender, 341

Parnell, Charles Stewart, 1 (Irish political leader) 31, 81, 136, 144

Pastimes of the Londoners, The, preparatory drawings, 89, 91

Peacock Theatre (small experimental theatre at Abbey), 289

People Walking Beside a River, 333

Pearse, Padraic (militant republican), 184

Pechstein, Max (German painter), 291

Pelorson, Georges (friend of Beckett), 247

P.E.N. Club, honours Jack with dinner, 326

Pennell, Joseph (American illustrator), 46, 382n.8

Perugino, Pietro, 282

Phibbs, Geoffrey (Irish poet), 247, 394n.43

Phillipson, Serge (art collector), 341; late visitor, 348

Picasso, Pablo, 224, 291

Pictorial World, 43

Pier, The, 146

Pike Theatre, Dublin, puts on *Godot*, 353

Pinero, Arthur Wing (playwright), 93

Piper, John (English artist and critic), 300; reviews Jack, 304–5

Pissarro, Camille, 40

Pissarro, Lucien (at Bedford Park), 40

Plaut, James S. (director of the Institute of Contemporary Art, Boston)

Playful Pilgrims, The, 94

Playboy of the Western World, The, 38; Jack's advice, 147; riots, 156, 183

Plays for miniature theatre, 91–9

'Pleiades, The', 41

Plunkett, George Noble, Count (founder of Academy of Christian Art), 220

Plunkett, Sir Horace, 83, 385n.4

Plunkett, Joseph (poet), 174

Political, 79

Political Meeting, A, 145

Pollexfen family, 1–2, 10, 379 80n.34; Pollexfen children's birth-dates, 11, 380n.37, 53, 65, 66, 187, 281

Pollexfen, Agnes, 21, 187

Pollexfen, Alfred (uncle), 186–7

Pollexfen, Alice, marries Arthur Jackson, 21; his death, 283

Pollexfen, Anthony, (great-grandfather)

Pollexfen, Arthur, 21, 37, 39

Pollexfen, Charles (uncle), 11

Pollexfen, Charles (great-grandfather's cousin and William Middleton's father-in-law), 10

Pollexfen, Elizabeth (grandmother), 11, **13**, 13–14, 24–28; artist herself, 28; sends geese for Christmas, 51

Pollexfen, Elizabeth (great-grandmother), 11

Pollexfen, Elizabeth (aunt, married name Orr), 15, 50

Pollexfen, Frederick, 24, 170

Pollexfen, George (uncle), 2, 12, 24, 28, 37, 49, 51, 55, 66, 143; possible financing of Dun Emer, 167; his death and will, 170, 186, 267

Pollexfen, Isabella (later Boyd), 8, 379n.21

Pollexfen, John, 39, 381n.24

Pollexfen, Robert, 21

Pollexfen, Ruth (daughter of Frederick), 119; on Jack's illness, 188, 263

Pollexfen, William (grandfather), 9, 28; helps JBY, 4; his character, physical appearance and other attributes, 8–11, 17; Freemason, Church of Ireland, 10, 379n.31; birth and Devon origins, 10, 379n.33; reading psalms, 10, 379n.29; courage, habits, reputation, 12–13, 15; takes to Jack, conflict with Willie, 14; life with Jack, 20–8; his politics, 31, 37; sends money to Yeatses, 51; and Jack's plays for miniature theatre, 97–8

Pollexfen, William I (uncle, died young) 11

Pollexfen, William II (uncle), 11, 28, 186

Pollock, B. (London dealer in miniature plays), 93, 385n.36, 254

Pony Cupid, A, 326

Porter, 146

Porter Boats, bought by Joyce, 236

Portobello Nursing Home, 318; Cottie goes there after heart attack, 331; after her death, more frequent visits by Jack, 332–3; his second home, 340, 345

Post Car, The, 168

Pot of Broth, The (play by WBY and Lady Gregory), 126

Pound, Ezra, 200, witnesses WBY's will, 284

Powell, Frederick York, 22, 60, 90, 101–2, 386n.1; involved in *A Broadsheet*, 105, 107, 123–4, 190; Powell, Mariella (FYP's daughter), 101, 103

Power, Arthur (Irish painter), 311, 325

Powerscourt, Lord, 89

Politician, The (in *Irishmen All*), 180

Prentice, Charles (publisher), 245

Proust (study by Beckett), given to Jack, 247
Proust, Marcel (French novelist), written about by Beckett, 245
Prudent (Beckett's would-be assassin), 283
Public Speaker, The, 196
Publican, The (in *Irishmen All*), 179; sold, 185
Punch, 22, 64; regular cartoons for, 168, 240; uses pseudonym, 'W. Bird', 240, 393–4n.6, 302
Purser, Dr Honor (physician attending Cottie), 331; visits to Jack, 355
Purser, John (author of work on Jack's writings), 242–3, 254, 395n.67, 256; theory about the writing, 265–8; on *The Charmed Life*, 278
Purser, Louis (Dublin University professor, friend of family), 47, 383n.18
Purser, Sarah, 32, 38, 40, 41–2, 51, 107–8; organises Hone-Yeats show in Dublin, 119, 120, 123, 127, 182; admiration for *Sligo*, 243–4, 268; her 'At Homes' known as 'Days of Wrath', 296, 310
Pursuing Policeman, The, 96
Putman, Jacques (French critic), 346
Pyle, Amy Patricia (Hilary's grandmother), visits Jack, 355
Pyle, Fitzroy (TCD professor, Hilary's father), 355
Pyle, Hilary, 39, 381n.26, 42, 89, 128, 161; on *The Circus Dwarf*, 182, 186; on *Bachelor's Walk: In Memory*, **192**, 190–3; on *Communicating with Prisoners*, 195, 269; on four 'Rose' paintings; and possible fifth, 278–80, 332, 355

Queen Victoria, her death, 101, 122
Quinn, John (American lawyer and patron), 119–22, **120** 387n.9; interest in Lady Gregory, 123; walking tour with Jack, 123; involved with brothers, 127; helps Jack in New York, 127–30; at 1905 exhibition, 145; Jack writes about Synge's death, 151, 152, 153, 161, 165; Jack's bookplate for, 167, 172, 173; responsible for Jack exhibiting at Armory Show, 181, 182; Lily writes to about Jack's illness, 189–90; responsible for JBY, 199, 207; JBY's death, 215, 217, 240, 245, 263

Race Card Seller, 171
Racine, 134
Raftery, Antoine (Irish blind poet of 18th century), 106, 120, 387n.14
Ragg, T. Murray (publisher at Routledge), 259–260; refuses 'Lives', 260; enthusiasm for Jack's writing, 275; book by MacGreevy discussed, 280–1; shares Jack's disappointment over *The Charmed Life*, 294; enthusiasm for *Ah Well*, 309, 310; their association ends, 316
Read, Herbert (art critic), describes Jack as 'surrealist', 273, 396n.1; reviews *Amaranthers*, 274–5; reviews joint show with Nicholson, 304–5; likes *Ah Well*, 309
Reality, bought by Niall Montgomery
Red Rover, The, 91
Redmond, John (leader of Irish Parliamentary Party), 184, 198–9
Reid, Eleanor (collector of Yeatsiana), 125, 181; Jack writes to her about *Waiting for Godot*, 354
Reid, Fred, Jack's influence on Beckett, 354
Reid, Nano (Irish painter), 300, 315
Rembrandt, Harmenz van Rijn, 248
Retrospective Exhibition, Dublin, 1945, 172
Returned American, The, 80
Reynolds, John (curator of Municipal Gallery), involved in row over *The Liffey Swim*, 252
Reynolds, John Hamilton (author of *The Fancy*), 162
Rhys, Ernest (author for whom Jack did illustrations), 58, 383n.9, 102; contributes to *A Broadside*, 169
Riders to the Sea (play by Synge), 199
Riopelle, Jean-Paul (Canadian painter), visits Jack's Paris show, 345
Riverside (Long Ago), The, 196, 231, **233**
Robert Emmet, 79
Roberts, George (Maunsel publisher), 145
Roberts, Lord, 122
Robinson, Lennox (Irish playwright), 235, **338**, 244, 247, 256; and rejection by Abbey Theatre of *The Old Sea Road*, 266, 288; present at Drumcliffe when WBY's body returns, 338; late visitor, 348
Roche (boxer beaten by Tommy Burns), 162–3

Rogue, The, 153
Rolling Donkey, The, 79, 130, 159
Ronsard, Pierre de, 224
Rooke, T.M. (at Bedford Park), 40
Room in Sligo, A, 305
Rose, A, 278–80, 279, 396n.22; shown to Beckett, 278
Rose in a Basin, 306
Rosenthal, Thomas, on *Bachelor's Walk: in Memory*, compares with *Guernica*, 191–3
Ross, Dr W.S. (Jack's Greystones doctor), 188
Rossetti, Dante Gabriel, 41
Rothenstein, John, 230–1; O'Malley brings him to visit Jack, 328; chooses to buy *Two Travellers* for Tate Gallery, 328
Rothenstein, William, 104, 107; Jack writes about his brother, 287–8
Rouault, Georges, 248; Sickert compares Jack with, 305; Beckett compares with Jack, 327
Rousseau, Henri Julien, 'Le Douanier', 282
Routledge (London publisher), Jack moves to, 259; publishing Beckett's *Murphy*, 282
Rowlandson, Thomas (artist and caricaturist) 268
Royal Academy of Arts, 41
Royal Dublin Society, Horse Show, 203
Royal Field Artillery, MacGreevy in, 222
Royal Hibernian Academy, rejects *The Circus Dwarf*, 181, 198; Jack an associate, 201; full member, 201, 205, 206, 219; *The Liffey Swim* shown, 1925, 227, 254; *Death for Only One* shown, 280; *Tinkers' Encampment: the Blood of Abel*, shown in 1941, 294, 296, 308; impact of *Now* when shown in 1942, 313–14; death of academy's president, Dermod O'Brien, 327
Royal Institute of Painters in Watercolours, 46
Royal Institution, 227
Royal Scottish Academy Galleries, 328, 330
Rubáiyát of Omar Khayyám, Cottie's illustrations, 101
Rubens, Peter Paul, 248
Ruskin, John, read by Synge, 136
Russell Circle (literary dining club), 330
Russell, George ('AE'), 83, **85**, 165, **253**, 293, 385n.7, 85; involved in *A Broadsheet*, 102, 105–7, 117; involved in Loughrea work, 123; his banner of St Patrick, 126; helps to sort out Dun Emer incompatibilities, 166–7, 173, 181, 228–9
Russell Hotel, Dublin, 330
Rutter, Frank (Art critic), 183
Rynne, Stephen (Irish art critic), 291, 321

Sadleir, John (politican and swindler), 205, 392n.13
Sailing, Sailing Swiftly (novel by Jack), 242, 249, 254, 255–7
St Columba's College, Rathfarnham, 319
St Louis Exhibition, 127–8
St Martin's-in-the-Fields, and memorial service for WBY, 286
St Patrick's Cathedral, and memorial service for WBY, 286; Jack visits frequently, 345
St Stephen's Church, Mount Street, Jack's funeral there, 355
St Stephens, 79 (check?)
Sala, George Augustus, 41
Salmon Leap, Leixlip, bought by Joyce, 236
'Sapper' (pseudonymous author of Bulldog Drummond stories), 265
Sarsfield, Patrick, 78
Sartre, Jean Paul (French existentialist writer and philosopher), 354
Scanlon (coachman at Merville), 25
Schneider, Pierre (French critic), 346
Scots Observer, The, 55
Scott, C.P. (editor of *Manchester Guardian*), commissions Synge and Jack, 134–5; his politics, 136, 146, 148, 162
Scott, Michael (architect), 318
Scourge of the Gulph, The, 96, 98
Secession, or *Sezession* (Austrian art nouveau movement), 220
Seurat, Georges (French painter), 231

Shannon, Charles (English painter), 253

Shaw, 'Aircraftsman' (T.E. Lawrence), attends Jack's 1929 exhibition, 237

Shaw, Captain, J.H. (bursar of Trinity College), 248

Shaw, George Bernard, 48, 383n.25, 163; attends Jack's 1929 show, 237; attacked by MacGreevy, 245; and the Troubetzkoi statue, 296, 331

'Shemus' (Dublin cartoonist), 205

Shepherd, Jack, highwayman, 105

Sheppard, Oliver (Irish sculptor), on board of National Gallery of Ireland, 296

Shouting, 311

Sickert, Walter, 104, 163; views on 1924 exhibition, 226–7, 239, 248, 268, 291, 304–5

Signac, Paul Signac (French painter), 291

Silencer, The (play by Jack), 310

Silent Traveller in Dublin, The (by Yee), read by Jack, 348

Simms, George Otto (Archbishop of Dublin), participates in Jack's funeral, 355

Simon the Cyrenian, 120, 161

Sinclair, Frances (née Beckett), known as 'Cissie', 246, 394n.40

Sinclair, William, 'The Boss', 246, visits Jack, 268

Singing 'My Dark Rosaleen', 210, 211, 226

Singing the Lament of the Irish Emigrant in a Liverpool Christy Minstrels, 128

Sinn Fein, 136, 156

Shelley, Percy Bysshe, admired by Synge, 136

Skeffington, Owen Sheehy (TCD lecturer), 320

Skelton, Robin (author), on Jack's plays, 265

Slade School of Art, 41, 158

Sleator, James (Irish painter), 338

Sleep (portrait of Victor Waddington), 318

Sligo (first novel), 240–2, 247, 254, 257; copy given to David Green, 297

Sligo Bay – Early Morning, 228

Sligo Champion, The, 79

Sligo Museum, 326, 332

Sligo Steam Navigation Company, 67

Smith, Leo (Dublin art dealer), 314–5, **317**, 321

Smuggler, The, 91

Snail's Castle (Jack's home in Devon, also known as Cashlauna Shelmiddy), 66

Skelt's *Juvenile Drama*, 91

Smith, Pamela Colman (working associate of Jack's), 95; involved in *A Broadsheet*, 102, 386n.11; difficult to work with, 103; involved in Loughrea work, 123, 127, 130; successfully designs for Synge's *The Well of the Saints*, 157

Smyllie, R.M. (editor of *The Irish Times*), 308

Society of Authors (London), Jack consults with, 282

Society of Independent Artists, 253

Society of Dublin Painters, founded, 219–20, 392n.9, 291

Society of Scottish Artists, 328, 330

Soldier of Fortune, A, 342

Solomons, Bethel (gynaecologist), 182

Solomons, Estella (Irish painter, wife to James Starkey), portrait of Jack, 225, 393n.29, 246

Soupault, Philippe (French Surrealist writer), 274

South Kensington School of Art, 34, 41

South London Palace, 163

Southport Visitor, reviewer uses phrase, '"Now" is the psychological moment', 329

Sparling, Herbert Halliday (May Morris's fiancé), 51

Speaker, 114

Spectator, The (London weekly), reviews 1930 show, 248; Read reviews *The Amaranthers* in, 275; Kate O'Brien reviews *The Charmed Life*, 278; Piper reviews Jack, 304

Spencer, Herbert, 14, 380n.47; read by Synge, 136

Spender, Stephen, 164; visits Jack in 1950, 341

Sphere, The, 348

Spiro, Mabel, becomes Victor Waddington's partner, 349; relationship with Jack, 349

Sporting Sketches (magazine Jack worked for), 64

Squireen, The, **85**

Squireen, The (oil painting, in *Irishmen All*), 179

SS Celtic, 130

SS Mesaba, 128

Stalin, Joseph, 249

Star Gazer, The, 130

Starkey, James Sullivan (poet, editor of *Dublin Magazine*, see under 'Seamas O'Sullivan'), 225, 393n.28; as president, hosts P.E.N. Club dinner for Jack, 326; present at Drumcliffe when WBY's body returns, 338

Starkie, Walter, 123

Steer, Philip Wilson (English painter), 291

Stephens, James, published by Jack, 169, 204; views on style change, 238, 274

Stephens, Mary (great-grandmother), 10

Stephenson, Patric (Irish artist), late visitor, 348

Sterne (English satirical writer), 274

Stevenson, Robert Louis, 15, 91, 98, 109, 262–1, 275

Still Alarm (play), 47

Stoker, Bram (writer), corresponds with JBY, 47

Stokes, Margaret (art historian), 89

Stories of Old Ireland and Myself, autobiography by William Orpen, 153

Storm, A, admired by Beckett, 269

Strand Races, The, 168

Strang, William (painter), 58

Strolling Donkey, The, bought by Lady Gregory, 85

Studio, The, 220

Sullivan, T.D. (Irish Parliamentary Party), 31

Summer Evening (in Ballycastle), A, 171

Summer Day, A, 180, 196

Sunday Independent, reviews Jack favourably, 345, 348

Sunday Times, The, 348

Surrealism, and Jack's art, 273–4

Swanzy, Mary, 158, 196

Sweeney, Jack (Harvard scholar), 298

Sweeney, James Johnson (art critic), 298

Symons, Arthur (author), 66, 384n.40, 159

Synge, John Millington, 38, 82, 85, 115, 120; and the Connemara expedition, 133–51; ill-health, 133; and *The Aran Islands*, 145; Jack's advice for *Playboy*, 147; ill-health, 147–51, 152, 153; Jack does sketches for production of *The Well of the Saints*, 157–8, 160, 161, 168, 177, 183, 199; on Jack's view of Synge and Joyce, 235, 262, 266, 275

Synnot, Pierce (friend of Betjeman), 300

T.C.D. A College Miscellany (Dublin University weekly), 248

Table Talk (society periodical), 68

Talbot Press (Dublin publishers), interested in book on Jack, 180

Tale of Piracy, A, 120

Tarpaulin Muster, A (by Masefield), 108

Tartar (Pollexfen vessel), 143, 286

Tate Gallery, 230; buys *Back from the Races*, 231–2; *Two Travellers* acquired by John Rothenstein, 328; exhibition there, 342, 350

Teeling, Bartholomew (United Irishman) 78–9

Temple, George (director of Guildhall Gallery), 130

Temple Newsam House, near Leeds, 1948 exhibition, 342

Terry, Ellen (actress), 47, 383n.14

That We May Never Meet Again, 346

Thatching, 146

Theatre Royal, Dublin, scene of third Burns fight, 162

'Theodore', 106–7

'There is a green hill far away', 335

There is No Night, 311

They Come, They Come!, 278

Thomson, Hugh (illustrator), 44, 382n.50

Three Card Man Meets his Match, 79

'Three Historical Paintings by Jack B. Yeats' (article by MacGreevy in Loan Exhibition catalogue), 320

Three Men in a Boat, 59
Three-Fingered Jack, the Terror of Jamaica, 91
Times Literary Supplement, review of *The Amaranthers*, 275; review of MacGreevy essay, 327
Timothy Coombewest, or, Esmeralda Grande, 93–4
Tinker, A, 153, 177
Tinkers – Early Morning, 208
Tinkers' Encampment; the Blood of Abel, 294, **295**; MacGreevy's explanation of, 294, **295**, 311
Titian (Tiziano Vecellio), 134, 282
Todhunter, John, 6–7
Toksvig, Signe (Dublin diarist), 254
Tom Sawyer, 39
To-morrow Never Comes (novel adapted for theatre), 265
Tone, Wolfe, 169, 263
Tonks, Henry (English painter), visits Jack, 268, 291
Torch Theatre (Dublin experimental theatre), 263
Tralee Bay looking South-East, 186
transition (literary magazine), 244
Treasure Island, 15
Treasure of the Garden, The, 12, 96
Tree, Herbert Beerbohm (actor), 47, 383n.16
Tristram Shandy (satirical novel by Sterne), 274
Troubetzkoi, Prince Paul (sculptor and musician), 296
Turf Cutter's Donkey, The (book by Patricia Lynch), illustrated by Jack, 263
Turf on the Canal, 255
Turner, Joseph Mallord William, 321
Twain, Mark, 42; Jack invited to meet, 89
Twenty-Five (play by Lady Gregory), 204
Twenty One Poems (by Tynan), published by Dun Emer, 167
Twisting of the Rope, The (play by Douglas Hyde), 107
Two Travellers, **312**, 313, 350
Tynan, Katherine, 31, 39, 45, 49, 50, 60; published by Dun Emer, 167, 182
Tyson's, men's outfitters, merchants with whom Jack dealt, 202

Ulster Volunteers, 184
Ulysses, 120, 245
United Arts Club, Jack joins in 1912, 174, 204, 206, 221, 251, 270, 274; and *The Amaranthers*, 275; vote of sympathy on WBY's death, 285–6; suicide of Tom Casement, 287, 308–9, 311, death of Dermod O'Brien, 327; becomes less congenial, 329
United Irishman (revolutionary magazine, edited by Arthur Griffith), Starkey writes for, 326
University Club (Dublin club for men), Jack becomes member, 329; takes Anne there, 340

Van Dongen, Kees (Dutch Post-Expressionist), 305
Van Velde, Bram (Dutch painter), 247; Beckett compares with Jack, 327; visits Paris show ten times, 345
Varley, Ida (daughter of Isabella, née Pollexfen), 58
Vegetarian, The (published his drawings), 39–40, 46, 51; publishes WBY's 'A Legend', 51, 53, 55, 59
Vegetarian Society, 40, 381n.31, 51
Vernon (schoolfriend), 21
Veseys, 47
Victoria, Queen, 32–4, 46
Village Shop in Kerry, A, 186
Vlaminck, Maurice de, 291
Vogue, 303
Vollard, Ambrose, French art dealer sells to Quinn, 181
Vynne, Miss (friend of Willie's), 57

Waddington Galleries, 313, 315, 330
Waddington, George (Victor's brother), 318, 341
Waddington, Leslie (Victor's son), 315
Waddington, Max (Victor's son), 315

Waddington, Theo (Victor's son), 315, 321
Waddington, Victor (art dealer), 269, 291, **314**; Jack's relationship with, 314–15; his origins, 315; promotion of Jack through Father Senan (*see* Moynihan), 320–1, 324; speaks at P.E.N. Club dinner 326; publishes MacGreevy essay on Yeats, 326, 332; Jack tells him, 'they should remember me as a painter', 340; entertains, 341; promotes Jack's international reputation, 342–5; 'the Yeats Man', 342; decides to move to London, 348–9; his financial losses, 349–50; pallbearer at funeral, 355
Waddington, Zelda (wife to Victor), 315; their separation, 349
Waiting for Godot (play by Beckett), successful performances, 353–4; Jack reads it, 353
Walker, F.S. (artist), 26, 380n.30, 40, 46, 380
Walker Art Gallery (for his London exhibitions), 77, 182
Wall, Mervyn (Irish novelist and playwright), 289, 355
Wallace (gardener), 73
Walpole's (of Wicklow street), merchants with whom Jack dealt, 202
Wanderings of Oisin, The, 45, 57
Waterford Municipal Art Gallery, receives *While Grass Grows* from Haverty Trust, 269
Watson, Mrs (family helper), 51
Watteau, Antoine (painter), 223, 231, 248–9
Wave, The, 219
Webb (channel swimmer), 10
Weekly Review, The, 55
Wellesley, Dorothy (English poet), involved in *A Broadside*, when restarted, 284
Wiener Werkstätte, 220
Well of the Saints, The (play by Synge), 157–8
Well's Central Hall (in Westmoreland Street, Dublin, used for exhibition by Jack), 120
West London School of Art, 34
Westerly Wind, A, 198, 208, **209**, 305
Westminster school of art, 34
Whackinist Grasshopper, The, 73
Whirly Horses, The, 95
Whistler, James McNeill, 104
Whitaker's Almanac, 348
White, Grove, 310
White, H.O. (Professor, Dublin University English Department), 248, 330, 355
White, James (formerly director, National Gallery of Ireland), 182, 325, 329
White, J.R. (leader of Irish Citizen's Army), 184
White, Polly (sister-in-law), 95; regular gifts sent by Jack, 351
White Stag Group (Dublin 1940s modernist painters), 330
White, Terence de Vere, 200, **270**; on 1920s change in style, 230; on general misunderstanding of Jack, 250–1; on Jack's marriage with Cottie, 262, 264–5, 332, 270, 302; splendid late tribute, 307; understanding of Cottie, 307–8, 316; late visits, 348; pallbearer at funeral, 355
Whitty, Margaret (Yeats's servant in Greystones), 172
Whoroscope (Beckett's early book of poems), 248
Wicklow, the Earl of (fellow-member of University Club), 329
Wight, Frederick S. (assistant to Plaut), 343
Wilde, Oscar, 104
Wilde, Sir William, treats Susan Yeats, 5
Wildenstein's (London art gallery), *Two Travellers* shown there, 328; 1946 show, 342, 345
Willie Reilly, 120
Wilson, George, 6
Wilson, Revd. J, rector of Drumcliffe, 338
Wind Among the Reeds, The, 103–4
Wise, Tucker, friend of Jack and Cottie, 173
'Wolfe T. MacGowan' (Jack's pseudonym), 225
Women's Printing Society, 119
Wonderland (in the East End of London), sporting arena, 162

Woods (schoolfriend), 21
Word Upon the Window Pane, The, 288

Yankee Table Cloth, The, later became *The American Table Cloth*, 80, 128
Yeats, Anne, 219, 284; designs sets for *Harlequin's Positions*, 289; her work
  for Irish Exhibition of Living Art, 314, 316; Jack's interest in her, 318;
  her visits to Jack more frequent after Cottie's death, 335; jokes at
  MacGreevy's expense, 335; growing friendship with, 337, 339–40;
  sends her money, 339; writes to her about health and the weather,
  340–1; Jack's main beneficiary, and made copyright owner, with her
  brother, 350; gifts by Jack in old age, 351; weekly visits at the end,
  354; summoned to Portobello, 355
Yeats, Benjamin (early ancestor), 15
Yeats, Cottie (Mary Cottenham, formerly White; Jack's wife), 51, **224**;
  meeting with Jack, 58–9; marriage, 62–3; as an artist, 63; her trust
  fund, 63; their life at Snail's Castle, 73–7; trip to Ireland (1898), 77,
  86, 90–1; illustrates *Rubáiyát of Omar Khayyám*, 101; friendship with
  Augustine Henry, 118; involved in Loughrea work, 123; happiness of
  marriage observed by Synge, 148; her love of Devon, 154; elegance
  noted, 182; her supposed indifference over Jack's illness, 189–90;
  Cottie and WBY's wife, 201, 212; Jack's portrait of, 225, 235;
  embarrassed about *Punch* cartoons, 240; her mother dies, 262; her
  gossiping, 263; secretiveness, 264–5; tea with Beckett's mother, 269;
  acts as hostess for Jack, 321; her joy at National Loan Exhibition,
  which coincided with their golden wedding anniversary, 323; death of
  Dermod O'Brien, 327–8; her own death, 331–2
Yeats, Elizabeth Corbet ('Lolly'); (sister), 15; born in London, 4; travel to
  Sligo, 7, 14, 18; receives Jack's Sligo letters, 21, 34, 36; closeness to
  Jack, 45; on Jack and Willie, 50; keeps family accounts, 55; views
  Willie as 'the poet', 57; visits to Jack and Cottie, 65, 90; return to
  Dublin, 118–121; involved in Loughrea work, 123–5; working in
  Dublin, 157; left money by Uncle George Pollexfen, 170, 174; JBY's
  death, 215, 216, Jack writes terminating Cuala arrangements, 234; her
  death, 295, 338
Yeats Family, birth dates, 379n.1; early history, 15–16, 380n.55; move to
  Dublin, 20, 157; family earnings, 55, 187; general view on WBY's
  marriage, 201
Yeats, George (née Hyde-Lees, wife of WBY), on her father-in-law's
  departure for the United States, 164, 212; enthusiasm for Jack, 237;
  with WBY at his death, 285; to Sligo, 286; concedes headship of
  family to Jack, 286; offers Cuala publication of *La La Noo*, 310; jokes
  about MacGreevy, 335; closer to Jack, 337–8
Yeats, Isaac Butt (uncle), 16, 86, 89, 118, 154, 388n.6, 199, 215
YEATS, JACK B. (1871–1957)
BIRTH & UPBRINGING: 1, 2; first trip to Sligo, 4–5; returns for longer
  visit, 7–8; love of, 8–9; Devon holiday, 'The Farm', 18, **18–19**; move
  to Sligo 'permanent', 20; his life there, 20–8; success at school, 21;
  amuses family, 22–4; his Christian faith, 31, 48
ART & ART EDUCATION: Early drawings, 18–20, 25; earliest, 26; in
  manuscript booklets, 26–8; prepares for art school, 32, 34; influences
  on, 42–4; debt to Randolph Caldecott, Phil May, Thomas Hood, 43–4;
  drawings of Buffalo Bill, 53; shortcomings as student, 61; his Walker
  Gallery show in 1898 reviewed, 79–80, 81; growing significance in
  Irish art, 117; comparison with Orpen, Hone, Russell, 117; early oil
  paintings, for *Irishmen All*, 180; paintings fail to sell, 186; his views on
  Bachelor's Walk: In Memory, 193; his views on *Communicating with
  Prisoners*, 195; and Modernism, 219–21; his portrait of Cottie, 225–6;
  change in style, 230–1; on his own technique, 237; falling output in
  1930s, 239; and modernism, 251; supposed antipathy to Gleizes,
  Cubism, Cézanne, 269–70; a Surrealist, 273–4; his output in later
  years, 311
EXHIBITIONS: Dublin venues, 390n.15; Clifford Gallery, Walker Gallery,
  Leinster Hall, Clarendon Hotel, Oxford, 102; 1903 show, 'Sketches of
  Life in the West of Ireland', reviewed by Starkey, 326; September, 1905,
  Dublin, 145; 1909, Dublin, 160–1; 1908–10, 171; contributes to group
  shows, 171; Armory Show in New York, 181–2; in London and Dublin,
  1914, 182; Post-war shows, 392n.24; Gieves Art Gallery, 1924

  exhibition, 226–7; his shows, 1924–9, 227; Alpine Gallery show, 1929,
  235, 236–7; 1930, 249; in New York, 1930–2, 253; bad experience
  there, 253; solo shows in London and New York, in 1930s, 291; group
  show, Dublin, 291; show at National Gallery, London, 300–6; seen as
  watershed, 307; National Loan Exhibition, 320–2, 323–6; United
  States, post war, 342–5; in Boston, 343, 400n.22; displeased with Plaut,
  343–4; exhibition in Paris, 345–6
FAMILY: Attitude to, 1; relationship with grandfather, 8–9, 13; view of
  father, 49–50; calls him 'the guvernor', 341; love of mother, 88–90;
  strife over father's interference, 126–7; Jack and his sisters, 166–7;
  death of Uncle George, 170; against his father's return from New
  York, 179; involved in Pollexfen legal affairs, 186–7; effects of Civil
  War, 218–9; little contact with WBY's family, 284; Anne and Michael
  hardly know him, 284; death of Lolly, 295; Jack Lolly's executor, 296;
  judgment of his father's painting, 341
FRIENDSHIPS: with John Masefield, 102–15, 122; with J.M.Synge, 133–
  51; with Joseph Holloway, 204; with Thomas MacGreevy, 205–6; his
  central importance, 222–5; with Samuel Beckett, 246–8, 269; Beckett
  and 'Rose' paintings, 278–9; MacGreevy and Beckett seem to wrestle
  over Jack, 282–3; depth of friendship with Beckett, 283–4; with Niall
  Montgomery, 297–8
LIFE & CHARACTER: his reserve, 24; influence of grandmother, 24; his
  taste in reading, 39; love of sport; becomes a volunteer, 46; early
  interest in theatre, 47; his seriousness, 50; closeness to Lily, 50; love of
  parties and dancing, 51; passion for horses, 52; part played in family
  earnings, 55; return visits to Sligo, 55; contributes financially to
  mother's medical care, 56; leaves home, 57; increases and changes in
  work, 59–60; earnings, 60; elegance of dress, 61–2; trip to Ireland,
  1898, 77; 1798 centenary, 77–8; comparison with Willie, 82–3; trip
  to Paris, 86; Norfolk Broads, 86; friendship with Frederick York
  Powell, 101–3; *A Broadsheet*, 102–8; Model Boats, with Masefield,
  108–15; the Hallsands controversy, 114–15; visit to New York, 117;
  on family's return to Dublin, 118–20; walking tour with John Quinn,
  123; touring in Ireland, 1903, 123–4; the Connemara tour with J.M.
  Synge, 133–51; *Manchester Guardian* articles, 133–45; collaborates in
  books with Synge, 145–6; works from photographs, 145–6; advises on
  Synge's *Playboy*, 147; Rhine trip, 148; changed in views on Ireland by
  working with Synge, 152–3; the sisters' move to Dublin, 157; Sligo
  visit with Cottie in 1908, 163–4; decision to move to Dublin, 164–5,
  166; problems with Dun Emer, need to help sisters, 166–8; his and
  Cottie's view, 167; move to Red Ford House, Greystones, November
  1910, 172; entertains Dun Emer staff there and in Churchtown, 174;
  his sense of humour, kindness, dress, 174–5; writes for Edward Gordon
  Craig on miniature theatre, 176–7; admiration for *Irishmen All*
  illustrations, 179; limited sales; adverse comparison with Orpen; 186,
  302; nervous breakdown, 186–91; Pollexfen legal problems probably
  contribute, 187; and First World War, 199; move to Donnybrook,
  199–200; attempts to revive Quinn's interest in his art, 200; Jack's
  Dublin life, 202; theatre-going, 204; his reliance on MacGreevy, 205–
  6; in Paris for Race Congress, 211–14; and the news Irish Free State,
  217–19; first meeting with Kokoschka, 220, 392–3n.12; his influence
  on Jack, 220–1; MacGreevy's importance to him, 222–5; Masefield
  writes about him, 226; character and development of his art in 1920s,
  227–31; de Vere White on, 230; argument with Tate Gallery over
  copyright, 231–4; and James Joyce, 235–6; final move, to Fitzwilliam
  Square, 239; and money, 239; WBY learns of work for *Punch*, 240;
  attitude to writing, 240–2; friendship with Beckett leads to closer ties
  with Dublin University, 248; Alpine show in 1930, best critical
  reception, but poor sales, 249; Haverty Trust and *The Liffey Swim*,
  251–2; proposals about Jack being Minister for the Arts, 252–3; his
  romanticism, lack of vulgarity, 263; walking habits, 264; his play, *The
  Old Sea Road*, rejected, 266–7; views on *Apparitions*, 267; friendship
  with Beckett, meets his mother, 269; verse epitaphs on friends and on
  himself, 270–1; Herbert Read on his 'surrealism', 273; dealings with
  Ragg at Routledge, 275–7; recommends Beckett and *Murphy* to Ragg
  at Routledge, 277; Beckett sees 'Rose' paintings, 278; his output in
  the 1920s and 1930s, 278; last meeting with WBY, 285; brother's

death, 285–6; WBY's death allows plays to be put on at Abbey Theatre, 288–9; critical of *The Word Upon the Window Pane*, 288; disappointing sales of *The Charmed Life, The Careless Flower* refused, 294; joint exhibition with William Nicholson, at National Gallery, 300–6; annoyed by Clark, 302; effect of regular comparisons with WBY, 307; publication of later novels, 309–11; late surge in painting, 311; National Loan Exhibition, his pleasure in, 320–2, 323–6; death of Dermod O'Brien, 327–8; death of Cottie, 331–2; makes his will, 350; will contains clear declaration against reproduction of his works, 350

MARRIAGE: First meeting with Cottie, 58; preparations, finds house, 62; marriage and honeymoon, 62–3; Hooley or Hooligan (Jack's dog), 64; purchase of Devon home and move from Chertsey, 66–7; working life in Devon, 71–3; trip to Italy, 75; happiness of observed by Synge, 148; Jack's dependence on Cottie, 154; their recreations, 154–6; White's view on sensuality in Jack, 262; success of their marriage, 264–5

Yeats, Jane Grace (sister, died in infancy), born in London, 4, 18

Yeats, Jervis (early ancestor), 15

Yeats, John (great-grandfather), 15, 286

Yeats, John Butler (father), 2, 7; proposal and marriage, birth of Jack, 2; views on father-in-law, 2; receives money from him, 4; financial affairs and failings, 2–4, 17; career as artist, 4, 15, 20, 380n.8; views on religion, art, politics, 6; born Tullylish 16; studies law, meets Susan, 16; on Jack's schooling, 20–21; on his drawing, 25–6; paints Jack on return to London, 29; criticism of Sarah Purser, 32; sells Thomastown property under Ashbourne Act, 32, 40; close to breakdown, 45; threatens to fight Willie, 45; craving for affection, relations with sons, 49; preference for Willie, 50; 'a lost cause', 55; views on Jack's marriage, 59; his hopes for his children, 61; struggles against debt, 75; advises on Coole and Lady Gregory, 77, 85–6; Enthusiasm for miniature theatre, 93; return to Dublin, 118; too much advice to Jack, 126–7; comment to Willie on Synge and Jack, 148; works for Hugh Lane, 155; continued troubles in Dublin, 157; departure for the United States, 164–5, 170; corresponds with Jack and Cottie, 171; pleased at Jack's move to Greystones, 173; admiration for *Life in the West of Ireland*, 178; possible return to Dublin, 179, 182; concern over Jack's breakdown, 188–90; cut off by First World War, 199; his death, 214–15; Letters of, 320

  Portraits by: (of Jack), 29, *Jack Yeats as Boy*, 30

Yeats, Matthew (uncle), 3

Yeats, Michael Butler, nephew, 205, 218, 284, 318, develops links with Fianna Fail, 318–19, 398n.32; Jack sees more of, 337

Yeats, Robert Corbet (brother), born in London, 4, 5; to Sligo, 7; 14; dies, 15

Yeats, Robert Corbet (uncle), 16

Yeats, Susan (née Pollexfen, mother), 2, 3, 4, 5; early marriage, unhappiness, 2, 4–7; love of Sligo, 4; return there, 7; her appearance, 5; at odds with husband on religion, art, politics, 6; only home Merville, 15;

breakdown in her health, 49; serious and chronic, 55–6; her death, 88–90, 170

Yeats, Susan Mary ('Lily'), (sister), 15; born in Sligo, 4; return there, 7; recollections of William Pollexfen, 9–10; of Uncle George and her grandmother, Elizabeth Pollexfen, 12–13, 14, 18, 18; on Jack in Sligo, 20, 22; on his drawing, 26, 28, 34, 36; her first wages, 45; her severity, 45; is unhappy with Morrises, 48–9; resigns job, letter to May Morris, breakdown, 57; visits to Jack and Cottie, 65; takes new job in France, 65; 82, 89, 90; return to Dublin, 118–21; involved in Loughrea work, 123–5; defends Jack from father's interference, 126–7; working in Dublin, 157; encounter with George Moore, 158; at 1909 exhibition, 160; controversy over Dun Emer, 166–8; controversy over Dun Emer, 166–8; left money by Uncle George Pollexfen, 170, 174; possible return to Dublin, 182; handling of Jack's breakdown, 186–90; JBY's death, 215, 216, 234; view of Cottie as 'unsafe' and prone to gossip, 263; at time of Lolly's death, 295, 307

Yeats, Thomas, 3, 5

Yeats, William Butler (brother), 14, 218, 288; born in Sandymount, 4; describes Sligo homecoming, 7; nostalgia about Sligo, 8; on his grandfather, 12; unhappiness at Merville, 14; and in London, 18; father's 'mind in fragments', 31, 36; writing stories, 37; interest in Jack's successes, 39; falls in love with Maud Gonne, 48; relationship with father, 49; contribution to family earnings, 55; groans when writing, 57; derisive towards cousin Ida, 58, 64; with Symons in Sligo, 66–7, 70; contrasted with Jack, 82; meets Mark Twain, 89; views on Jack's miniature theatre, 93; involved in *A Broadsheet*, 102, 108; and in family return to Dublin, 118; his involvement in Loughrea work, 123, 126; Lily's strictures on, 126–7; comments on *The Aran Islands*, 145, 148, 157; involvement in Dun Emer, 166–7; dominant influence on sisters, 167; left money by Uncle George Pollexfen, 170–1; sends Jack's *Life in the West of Ireland* to JBY in NY, 178; to pay for JBY's return to Dublin, 182; concern at Jack's breakdown, 188–9; marriage to George Hyde-Lees, 201; at Race Congress in Paris, 212; JBY's death, 215; separate life from Jack, 217, 219, 222; Jack writes to, on 'greatness', 234; knowledge of *Punch* cartoons, 240; admiration for *Sligo*, 243, 244, 252, 253, 263, 266; and rejection of *The Old Sea Road*, 266; refers to *The Charmed Life* as 'my brother's extreme book', 278; edits *A Broadside* when restarted in 1935, 284; last meeting with Jack, 285; his death, 285–6; effect of his blocking of Jack's plays, 288–9, 307; return of his body to Ireland, 337–9; ill. 339

Yeats, William Butler (grandfather), 15–16

Yeats, William Butler (uncle), 16

Yee, Chiang (Chinese author), read by Jack, 348

Yellow Book, The, 104

Young Ireland Movement, 329

Young Man's Troubles, A, 128

Zangwill, Israel (editor of *Ariel, or the London Puck*), 59, 383n.12